KINGMAKERS

KINGMAKERS

The Invention of the Modern Middle East

KARL E. MEYER
and
SHAREEN BLAIR BRYSAC

W. W. NORTON & COMPANY
New York   London

For information about permission to reproduce selections from this book,
write to Permissions, W. W. Norton & Company, Inc.,
500 Fifth Avenue, New York, NY 10110

For information about special discounts for bulk purchases, please contact
W. W. Norton Special Sales at specialsales@wwnorton.com or 800-233-4830

Manufacturing by RR Donnelley, Harrisonburg
Book design by Helene Berinsky
Production manager: Julia Druskin

Library of Congress Cataloging-in-Publication Data

Meyer, Karl Ernest.
Kingmakers : the invention of the modern Middle East / Karl E. Meyer
and Shareen Blair Brysac. — 1st ed.
p. cm.
Includes bibliographical references and index.
ISBN 978-0-393-06199-4 (hardcover)
1. Middle East—History—20th century. I. Brysac, Shareen Blair. II. Title.
DS62.8.M485 2008
956.04—dc22
2008007378

W. W. Norton & Company, Inc.
500 Fifth Avenue, New York, N.Y. 10110
www.wwnorton.com

W. W. Norton & Company Ltd.
Castle House, 75/76 Wells Street, London W1T 3QT

1 2 3 4 5 6 7 8 9 0

To our Oxford friends,
Gwyn Robyns, Isabelle Onians,
Godfrey and Hilary Hodgson,
and
Neville and Evelyn Maxwell

Contents

Abbreviations

BT, Baronet

CB, Companion of the Order of the Bath

CBE, Commander of the Order of the British Empire

CIE, Companion of the Order of the Indian Empire

CMG, Companion of the Order of St. Michael and St. George

CSI, Companion of the Order of the Star of India

DBE, Dame Commander of the Order of the British Empire

DSO, Companion of the Distinguished Service Order

GCB, Knight or Dame Grand Cross of the Order of the Bath

GCMG, Knight of Dame Grand Cross of the Order of St. Michael and
St. George

KCB, Knight Commander of the Order of the Bath

KCIE, Knight Commander of the Order of the Indian Empire

KCSI, Knight Commander of the Order of the Star of India

OBE, Order of the British Empire

OM, Order of Merit

MC, Military Cross

MP, Member of Parliament

PC, Privy Counsellor

RA, Royal Academy

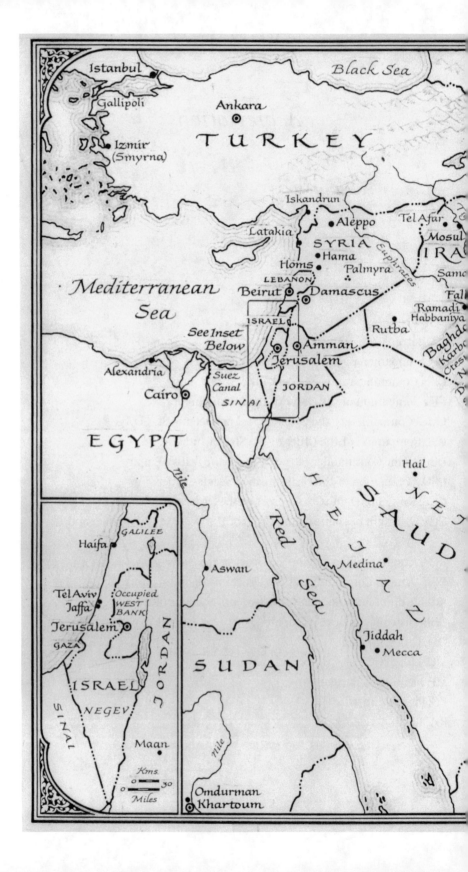

Authors' Note

As most of us realize by now, the Middle East is a region where the normal rules frequently vanish. This applies not just to spelling but to politics and religion, history and geography. Concerning the spelling of proper names (*Jiddah* or *Jidda? Faisal* or *Feisal?*), we echo T. E. Lawrence: "Arabic proper names can't be transliterated exactly into English. There are three 'scientific' systems for doing it. I despise 'em all, and spell anyhow, and variably, to show my feelings." Our rule has been to always respect the spelling in quoted texts, and in our own writing to favor the most familiar forms (*sheik* rather than *sheikh, Koran* not *Quran*), however inconsistent the system.

Another cross-grained difficulty concerns wars, coups, and treaties, secret or otherwise. Nothing Middle Eastern occurs without an informing context, internal and external. In writing about different people in successive chapters, we therefore repeat dates and descriptions of key figures. Readers can thus skip ahead and around, without losing their way in the labyrinth. As a further aid to a lay audience we append a chronology of benchmark dates and events. We also include an extensive bibliography to assist further reading on a subject that has stimulated a vast literature of specialized histories, tracts and polemics, biographies and memoirs, and even readable official documents. It is in this sea that we have gratefully fished, dipping where feasible into public archives and private papers to relate the region's modern history through the lives of key figures, seeking always the odd, illuminating specimens from the deep.

We have sought as best we can to recover, critically but empathetically, the mentality that propelled Europe's penetration of the Middle East and points south, since the "Scramble for Africa" stemmed directly from a struggle for mastery in what everyone once called the Near East or the Orient. Thus we revive the unjustly forgotten role of Flora Shaw, subsequently Lady Lugard, who as Colonial Editor of *The Times* named Nigeria and helped provoke the Jameson Raid, a failed attempt to force a regime change in Transvaal. She later married Lord Lugard of Abinger, the imperial administrator who shared her vision of an empire reaching, in Cecil Rhodes's phrase, from Cape to Cairo.

Lastly, it is helpful to remind readers that prior to 1914, a British pound was roughly equivalent to five U.S. dollars, a ratio that dropped by more than a fifth after the Great War. Still, this inadequately expresses sterling's once formidable buying power in an era when five pounds a week was deemed a living wage, and a book like this might have cost ten shillings, or but half a pound. Allowing for inflation, it is commonly reckoned that a thousand pounds in 1914 would be the equivalent of almost $100,000 in 2008.

KINGMAKERS

PROLOGUE

⌘

The Ever-Growing Egg

In these pages, our chief concern is with a region triply burdened, by geography, mineral riches, and its presumed sanctity. The Middle East, a name devised by Alfred Thayer Mahan, an American naval officer, forms the much-trampled passageway linking Asia and Europe to Africa. It comprises deserts and mountains rising from Arabia, flanked by Egypt and Iran and capped by Turkey. So great is its strategic importance that Napoleon and Hitler, along with Alexander and Caesar, all strove for its dominion. Its military significance doubled with the opening of the Suez Canal in 1869, and doubled again four decades later with the initial discovery of its underground ocean of oil. During World War II, State Department analysts concluded, half in dismay, that access to the Persian Gulf's petroleum had become essential to sustain America's expanding global role. "In all the surveys of the situation," recalled Herbert Feis, then the department's economic adviser, "the pencil came to an awed pause at one point and place—the Middle East."[1]

The awed pause was understandable. For centuries foreign efforts to court or conquer the Middle East have collided with the fervent claims of the devout. From this region arose three universal faiths, all steeped in messianic expectations proclaimed in three holy books, each an Authorized Version. Yet paradoxically, though each faith extols brotherhood and peace, compassion and humility, their mortal disciples through the ages

17

have engaged in reciprocal butchery. The very landscape of the Holy Land forms an outdoor museum of warfare. In June 1967, in the wake of what the winners called the Six Day War, one of the present authors during a single day passed in rapid succession biblical battlefields, Roman encampments, Crusader castles, Turkish parapets, British pillboxes, and the burnt-out trucks and tanks strewn from three Arab-Israeli wars. In his history of Jerusalem, the Israeli writer Amos Elon calculates that over four millennia the Holy City has known "twenty ruinous sieges, two intervals of total destruction, eighteen recent reconstructions, and at least eleven transitions from one religion to another." No less dismaying, assassins in this sanctified setting periodically slay peacemakers, notably in recent years Sweden's United Nations mediator Folke Bernadotte (1948), Jordan's King Abdullah (1951), and Israel's Prime Minister Yitzhak Rabin (1995). And in Cairo, Muslim zealots slew Egypt's Anwar Sadat (1981).[2]

Whether this lamentable reality serves a providential purpose is beyond our ken. Certainly the past century of Middle Eastern history bears a very human imprint. Our aim in these pages is to retell this history through the medium of individuals, British at the outset and American more recently. Their lives illustrate how the efforts to control progressed by incremental degrees deep into Africa, driven by fears for national security, rivalry with France and Germany, and the anxious quest for mineral riches. None in our gallery attained the summit of national power; all nevertheless were instrumental in building nations, defining borders, and selecting or helping to select local rulers. Some benefited in the private sector from their public service, but nearly all risked life and health to promote what they perceived as civilizing values. Nonetheless, after more than a century of Western assertiveness, peace remains elusive, sectarian passions are virulent, and with few exceptions the region's ordinary citizens have failed to profit from the petroleum windfall. Today, the kingdoms and republics nurtured by Anglo-Americans rest for the most part on sand, and the consent of the governed is (apart from Israel and Turkey) largely hypothetical.

In its totality, this melancholy record needs to be seen through the lens of irony and paradox. The one truly transcendent law in the Middle East is that of unintended consequences. This was assuredly true of William Ewart Gladstone, the great Liberal statesman who at first opposed British intervention, warning that entanglement would lead inexorably to the growth of an

African empire, from Cape to Cairo, as in an ever-growing egg. Gladstone then proved his point by ignoring his own warnings and thus establishing a cautionary template for the many incursions that followed.

Great Britain's first sustained intervention in the Islamic Middle East commenced in 1882, when Her Majesty's forces shelled, invaded, and occupied Egypt. In theory, Egypt was part of the Ottoman Empire under the nominal authority of the Turkish Sultan in Istanbul, some 768 miles distant. In reality, the Ottoman hold had long since loosened. In 1798, when the young Napoleon (he was twenty-nine) led a French army into Cairo, the Turks had to turn desperately to England (and Lord Nelson) to expel the invaders. France's brief occupation opened the way for an Albanian warlord, Mohammad Ali, who neither spoke nor learned Arabic, to found a dynasty that at first ruled and later reigned in Cairo until his great-great-grandson, the stout Farouk, was deposed in 1952.

For decades the wily Mohammad Ali defied the Turks. He opportunely played the British and French against each other, conquered the vast Sudan, and sent hundreds of Egyptians to Paris to study the agricultural and natural sciences, engineering, and medicine. Thus French culture permeated Cairo and helped germinate a state school system along Gallic lines. Ali's immediate heir, Abbas, leaned toward the British, who in 1851 completed the Alexandria-Cairo railway, the first to be built in Africa and Asia. The next Khedive (as the Ottomans called their viceroy), named Said, was an unabashed Francophile. He turned to European lenders to finance public works and welcomed foreigners, who began flocking to Egypt. Said awarded the concession for constructing the Suez Canal to a French engineer, Ferdinand de Lesseps, a boyhood chum. All this occurred independently of the Sublime Porte, as the Ottoman Sultanate was then grandly known.

These ingredients—Egypt's growing autonomy, the new canal, the leap in borrowing, the spread of European ideas, and growing concern in London and Paris for the safety of an expanding foreign colony—played a catalytic part in the very first Suez crisis. Its evolving themes would become a regional leitmotif: a colonels' revolt against a spendthrift autocrat, Khedive Tewfik, followed by popular rejoicing, promises of reform, and hopeful shouts of "Egypt for the Egyptians!" Then came panic among European bondholders, fears that Islamic extremists would massacre foreigners and seize the canal, and British exasperation over French waffling, thus precipitating a Downing Street decision to intervene unilaterally.

Victory was swift and overwhelming but there was no postconquest political plan. Britain's Liberal leaders promised to evacuate their troops the moment order was restored and a sensible, solvent regime was established in Cairo. Alas, that moment proved elusive. British forces and civilian advisers were to remain as Egypt's veiled masters for seventy-two years: this despite insistent cries of "Shame!" from the Empire's critics, the way led by the impassioned poet Wilfrid Scawen Blunt, the amorous husband of Byron's granddaughter.

Central to the drama was Gladstone, the wavering colossus of British Liberalism, a leader celebrated for his piety, erudition, and convoluted rhetoric. In 1882, his seventy-third year, he was known familiarly as the Grand Old Man, or GOM, although a disapproving Queen Victoria, then in her forty-fifth year as monarch, confided with a shudder that her First Minister was indubitably half-crazy. In the event, Gladstone paid dearly for his Egyptian intervention. It was among his few actions that elicited grudging royal approval, but otherwise it confused and divided his own party, and arguably cost him the legacy he most coveted: Irish Home Rule.

The Grand Old Man was well aware that his decision to intervene conflicted with his previous, oft-repeated parliamentary objections to martial bluster. He was not inflexibly opposed to using force, and was certainly less pacific than his more radical colleagues, John Bright and Richard Cobden. What troubled him was the reflexive impulse to add territory to an already bloated Empire, an impulse he discerned not just among his Conservative opponents but also on his side of the House of Commons among pugnacious Old Whigs and a new breed of Liberal Imperialists. Two years earlier, in 1880, Gladstone had waged and won what was perhaps the first democratic election in which human rights in faraway lands figured as a major issue. He had assailed the Turks for their "Bulgarian horrors," the attacks visited by Muslims against Christians in the Balkans, and he had upbraided his Tory counterpart, Benjamin Disraeli, for supporting wars that had devastated humble Muslim homes in Afghanistan and the tribal peoples of Zululand. Now Gladstone himself had seemingly succumbed to the imperial virus he had repeatedly deplored.

Worse: his targeted country was Egypt. Speaking for the Liberals, Gladstone had protested Disraeli's bold but popular 1875 coup in buying controlling shares in the Suez Canal Company. He purchased them from the father of Tewfik, the debt-ridden Khedive Ismail, known earlier as the "Magnificent" and later as the "Profligate." The canal, built in 1859–1869 with French and British financing, was administered after Disraeli's coup by a new British-led international consortium with its seat in London instead of Paris. The shift reflected the canal's strategic salience for the Victorian Empire. A decade after its opening, three-fourths of the traffic through Suez consisted of ships bound to or from India. It had become in the press cliché "the Imperial Lifeline," the vital artery that had pared the passage to India from months to weeks.

As Gladstone feared and predicted, owning the canal was the preamble to expansion. Soon enough, to protect their new lifeline the British installed a naval base in Aden at the entrance of the Red Sea, and looking south from Cairo, they were covetously eyeing Sudan. "[O]ur first bite in Egypt, be it by larceny or be it by emption," Gladstone cautioned in 1877, "will be the almost certain egg of a North African empire, that will grow and grow until another Victoria and another Albert, titles of the lake sources of the White Nile, come within our borders; and till we finally join hands across the equator with Natal and Cape Town, to say nothing of the Transvaal and the Orange River on the south, or of Abyssinia or Zanzibar to be swallowed by way of viaticum on our journey."[3]

His prescience was preternatural. Abyssinia aside, the Union Jack was to fly over each place on his list, either by way of conquest or viaticum (Gladstone's sarcastic term for "travel expenses"). How anomalous, therefore, that in 1882 it fell to the GOM himself to propel the awesome expansion that added eighteen major territories to the Empire in Victoria's reign, so that her realm eventually comprised nearly a fourth of the world's territories and peoples. As James Morris writes in *Pax Britannica: The Climax of an Empire* (1968), by the time of her Diamond Jubilee in 1897 every spasm of growth had found its facile pretext:

> "Adjusting the relations between the two countries" was a favorite euphemism for the process, and a whole vocabulary of evasive justification was devised to illustrate the strategies of Greater Britain, and define the blurred edges of Empire. Frontiers were habitually rectified. Spheres of influence

were established. Mutually friendly relations were arranged. River systems were opened to trade. Christian civilization was introduced to backward regions. One spoke vaguely of the confines of Egypt, the basin of the
Zambesi, the watershed of the Niger, and one could naturally not allow
the Sultanate of Witu to fall into the hands of a potentially hostile Power.
The imperial records were full of paramountcies, suzerainties, protectorates, leases, concessions, partitions, areas of interest, no-man's lands, and
related hinterlands—the last, an especially convenient conception, picked
up from the German within the past ten years.[4]

The first Suez crisis ignited in September 1881 when three rebellious colonels, suspecting they were marked for dismissal or worse, marched with
twenty-five hundred men and eighteen guns on the Cairo palace of the
young and unpopular Khedive Tewfik. The insurgents demanded the dissolution of Tewfik's cabinet and its replacement by nationalist reformers.
Leading the coup was Colonel Ahmed Arabi, then aged forty-one, a tall, well-
built son of a backwater village sheik. As a fledgling officer, Arabi resented
the favoritism shown non-Egyptians, notably Turks and Circassians, the
more so after he joined the Azhars, a reformist Islamic sect whose clerics
stressed the equality of all believers. "This threw him into the ranks of the
discontented and made him more than ever the advocate of the rights of his
own class," wrote his friend and foremost British champion, Wilfrid Blunt.
"He was eloquent and able to expound his views in the sort of language his
countrymen understood and appreciated, not very precise language perhaps, but illustrated with tropes and metaphors and texts from the Koran,
which his Azhar education supplied."[5]

The indecisive and rattled Tewfik gave way to the insurgents' demand to
appoint a new reform-minded cabinet, convene a constituent assembly, and
increase the army from twelve thousand to eighteen thousand men. Colonel Arabi became an overnight hero to ordinary Egyptians and his fellow
soldiers, and Cairo was gripped by popular euphoria. Hence the consternation among Europeans, who were doubly beneficiaries of a threatened status quo. Under long-standing privileges known as Capitulations, foreigners
were exempt from local laws, taxes, and tariffs. Additionally, owing to the
huge and ruinous debts incurred by successive Khedives, French and British
bondholders imposed a disciplinary system called Dual Control, whereby

Egyptian budgets were supervised and shaved by an English and a French controller, with major cuts inflicted on the military.

In theory, the Khedive, as the Ottoman Sultan's representative, was accountable to the Sublime Porte in Constantinople. But the Porte's authority had evaporated, and Egyptians increasingly viewed their Khedive as the puppet of European meddlers while soldiers clamored for their back pay. "By 1881," write the British historians Ronald Robinson and John Gallagher in a meticulous reconstruction, "the Khedivate was going the way of many Oriental regimes eroded by the penetration of European influences. The country was on the verge of anarchy. The symptoms were unmistakable: the restless peasantry, the discontented landlords, the immature liberal opposition, the broad movement against the foreigner, the collapse of traditional authority leading to a military *Putsch*."[6]

Such was the Egyptian setting as Britain's Liberal ministry—at the time also beset by a concurrent Irish crisis—tried to make sense of the turmoil in Cairo. The poet Blunt had emerged as a sympathetic interlocutor with the insurgents and helped render into English their manifesto, which was published in London by *The Times* on January 3, 1882. It insisted they sought a modernized and parliamentary Egypt, complete with a constitution, representative assembly, and free press. "The Egyptians have learned in the last few years what freedom means," the manifesto avowed, "and they are resolved to complete their national education ... The general end of the National Party is the intellectual and moral regeneration of the country by a better observance of the law, increased education and by political liberty."[7]

On its face, this was not a program to which a British Liberal might sensibly object. When Blunt met in London with Gladstone and other Liberal grandees, he mistook their nods of concurrence for heartfelt approval—a common error among the laity in dealing with political professionals. At first, Gladstone *was* sympathetic, even agreeably surprised by the professed goals of the Egyptian reformers. Yet as a fiscal conservative, he was adamant that the insurgents had to retain the system of Dual Control to protect bondholders—and also to deter the French from becoming dominant in Egypt. Early in the crisis, on September 12, 1881, he sketched his policy in a succinct minute to his Foreign Secretary, Lord Granville: "I sum up thus: 1. Steady concert with France. 2. Turkish General to go if need be. 3. Turkish troops in preference to any others. 4. No British or French forces, unless ships be needful for *bona fide* protection of subjects. 5. Apart from all this, I long for information on the merits of the quarrel."[8]

One reads Gladstone's minute with a twinge of empathy. He was truly sailing in uncharted waters. Not only was authoritative information about Islam lacking, but also the very vocabulary of the crisis was slippery. It was all very well to speak of "Egypt for the Egyptians," but who were the Egyptians? What of the minority Coptic Christians, who preserved the genes and language of the ancient pyramid builders—were they less Egyptian than their Arab conquerors? And what of long-established Greek, Jewish, and Armenian communities in polyglot Cairo and Alexandria? Would nationalists respect their rights? More generally, how deep was the chasm of mistrust dividing the Christian West from the Muslim world? Already in December 1881, the French were claiming that Colonel Arabi was probably plotting with the Ottoman Sultan to mobilize a pan-Islamic jihad to end French control of Tunis and Algeria. On the other hand, paradoxically, Gladstone himself looked for help from the Ottoman Turks, the very people the GOM had assailed in 1880 for their "abominable and bestial lusts," an empire guilty of such crimes that "Hell itself might almost blush."[9]

On one point, Gladstone was certain and settled: Britain had to act jointly with France. On this, he was in agreement with Lord Salisbury, the sagest of Tories on matters foreign. In September 1881, Salisbury offered this advice regarding Egypt: "You may renounce—or monopolize—or share. Renouncing would have been to place the French across our road to India. Monopolizing would have been very near the risk of war. So we resolved to share."[10] Yet France's policies were hostage to abrupt lunges in Third Republic politics. Initially the British dealt with Premier Léon Gambetta, an activist, go-for-it Radical Socialist who proposed an unequivocal declaration stating that the new Egyptian regime had to retain the intrusive Dual Control system, *pace* nationalist sentiment.

Reluctantly, uneasily, a majority of the Liberal Cabinet agreed to a Joint Note (thereafter capitalized), if only to placate the French, though this did not bind Britain to any course of action (a point not made fully clear to Gambetta). But within a month, for unrelated reasons, the French Premier's government fell, and his successor, in February 1882, was Charles de Freycinet, a nervous middle-roader, cautious as a bookkeeper, which he once was. Meanwhile the Joint Note not only proved a failure but also achieved the reverse of what was intended: it united diverse Egyptian army and nationalist factions in the indignant suspicion that the declaration was the prelude to military intervention. As a result, the volatile Colonel Arabi assumed a new post, as War Minister. Bondholders and shipping interests pressed Gladstone's cabinet ever more anxiously for a stronger response. So why not encourage the Turks to intervene in what was legally still part of their empire? Freycinet would have none of it.

By May 1882, as the crisis deepened, the British Cabinet also waffled. This inaction so vexed the hawkish Secretary for India, Lord Hartington (then a marquess and later the eighth Duke of Devonshire) that he protested sarcastically to the Foreign Secretary: "Has Araby Pasha given in, or has M. de Freycinet been persuaded to get out of bed? I wonder whether any human being (out of Downing St.) would believe that not a word has been said in the Cabinet about Egypt for a fortnight, and I suppose will not be for another week—if then." Yet Hartington's harshest barbs were directed at the French: "The French appear to be behaving worse than badly . . . Unless the French keep their word to us and are prepared to go in for Turkish intervention at once, we had much better cut ourselves loose from them. What is the use of such Allies? They have brought us into the frightful mess we are in, and I believe it would be easier to act with the Turks and with the whole of the remaining European Powers, than with them alone."[11]

Still, the Turks were no more willing to intervene, and when sounded, the Italians likewise counted themselves out. Given the gathering pressures on Britain to take the lead militarily, all that was needed was a martial buildup and a spark. The former materialized in the guise of a joint Franco-British naval flotilla, which was meant simply by intimidation to unseat Colonel Arabi and his cohorts, a course pressed by Britain's man on the spot, Sir Edward Baldwin Malet, then Consul-General in Cairo. But absent the threat of a Turkish landing, the naval show of force misfired; it radicalized rather than cowed the Egyptians. Then came the spark. On June 11–12, anti-European riots broke out in Alexandria, claiming anywhere from fifty to three hundred lives, and a mob mauled Charles Cookson, the city's British Consul. Within days, the insurgents began building shore batteries directed at Alexandria's anchorage. As the skittish French flotilla sailed away, the activists in Gladstone's Cabinet argued that unless Britain responded promptly, European lives and the Suez Canal would be forfeited.

All this occurred while the Grand Old Man contended with a nonstop parliamentary debate on Irish fiscal measures, and while his fractured Liberal ministry seemed on the verge of collapse. The haggard and badgered Gladstone confessed in his diary, "My brain is *very* weary." Faced with threats to resign, the Prime Minister acquiesced to an ultimatum ordering the demolition of the shore batteries (John Bright, who on this issue *did* resign from the Cabinet, privately called it "simply damnable—worse than anything ever perpetrated by Dizzie").[12] When Admiral Sir Beauchamp Seymour, the commander of the British squadron, demanded the surrender of the disputed forts, the Egyptians refused. On July 11, British warships bombarded Alexandria's waterfront for more than ten hours, leveling shorefront property and impelling Colonel Arabi to declare war against the infidel British.

Gladstone the Peacemaker suddenly found himself Gladstone the Warlord, and in a twist worthy of an Anthony Trollope novel, he relished his new role. A punitive army was mobilized in Cyprus under the command of Sir Garnet Wolseley, the imperial specialist in small wars, immortalized as "The Modern Major-General" in Gilbert and Sullivan's *Pirates of Penzance.* So gripping a national cause had the expedition become that Queen Victoria appeared to say good-bye to friends among the Horse Guards Brigade embarking for Egypt. Once ashore on September 10, Sir Garnet headed an army of fifteen thousand from England plus ten thousand more from India. It swiftly engaged an Egyptian force of twenty-five thousand at a village called Tel-el-Kebir, midway between Cairo and the canal. The battle proved "a neat, quick and resounding success," in the phrase of Gladstone's most recent biographer, the eminent Liberal Democrat, Roy Jenkins. The Egyptians were routed, with minimal casualties, and Colonel Arabi was banished to Ceylon, today's Sri Lanka. The expedition did not exceed the £2.3 million budget the frugal premier had set. A colleague of Gladstone's recalls dining with him at the Garrick Club, then going to Gilbert and Sullivan's *Patience* at the Savoy, where he was rousingly cheered: "I never remember seeing him in higher spirits," Sir Edward Hamilton wrote.[13] One imagines that as the Grand Old Man bowed to the crowds, a voice within murmured that Britain's civilizing mission had been vindicated. Experience teaches that no liquor is more intoxicating than military victory, followed by a shower of medals, promotions, satisfied winks from colleagues, and the hint of divine approbation.

Yet how should England, having invaded and occupied Egypt, govern it?

To this question, the great Liberal had what seemed a sensible and straight-forward response: help the Egyptians establish a stable and responsible political system, and then get out. Few realized they had stumbled into the proverbial quagmire. As British scholars Robinson and Gallagher write in their influential *Africa and the Victorians* (1961), the single-handed conquest of Egypt was plainly the outcome to which the British Liberals had intended above all to avert: "Not until a year later did the government discover that they had done something quite different from what they intended and had plunged into an ever-lengthening occupation and ever-increasing responsibility for administering and defending Egypt. Plainly, this outcome was shaped far more by circumstance than by policy. Gladstone and his colleagues had intended a supremacy of influence. They achieved instead a territorial occupation, financially insolvent, vulnerable to European hostility, unpopular among their own followers and in Egypt itself."[14]

It deserves stressing that Gladstone was formidable in mind, body, and spirit. Tall and fierce-eyed, he vented his surplus energy in downing trees at Hawarden, the Cheshire estate he inherited from his father, John Gladstone, who had amassed a fortune in the cotton, sugar, and tobacco trade. William followed in what became an accepted route for his caste, from Eton College to Oxford, though he reversed the usual ideological itinerary: starting as a conservative who defended slavery, and then moving steadily leftward.

He was an intellectual, literate in both classical and major European languages, and author of a learned, densely written three-volume analysis of the Homeric epics. He was a widely traveled believer in the Concert of Europe, the peacekeeping mechanism that evolved following Napoleon's defeat at Waterloo. In some respects resembling today's Security Council, with its permanent five members, the Concert was a limited forum in which neither European colonies nor the United States had a voice. It relied on persuasion and consensus to contain general European wars (which it did, for a century) and with less success sought to mediate conflicts among the Powers. By the standards of his time, Gladstone's vision was large, enlightened, generous, and rooted in his Christian beliefs.

When in 1868 Queen Victoria asked him to form his first ministry, the news arrived as he was felling a tree. His diary records his feelings: "The Almighty seems to sustain and spare me for some purpose of His own, deeply unworthy as I know myself to be. Glory be to His name."[15] As the years passed, his fervor waxed. He attended Anglican services once, twice, sometimes thrice a day. He courted ridicule with his celebrated habit of perambulating with his wife, Catherine, on the Haymarket, trolling for prostitutes whose salvation they sought. Yet a *Vanity Fair* cartoon by Ape in 1869 expressed a common judgment: "Were he a worse man, he would be a better statesman." As the accompanying text amplified, "The merits he possesses are so great that the only defects imputed to him are such that spring from their very excess."

True, the editor of Gladstone's diaries, H. C. G. Matthews, found that the Grand Old Man during his Suez crisis owned Egyptian bonds worth the equivalent of £2 million in the 1990s. "Yet I do not believe for a moment," writes biographer, Jenkins, "that his primary or even his significantly supporting motivation sprang from financial self-interest."[16] Not only was Gladstone among the most reluctant of the fourteen members of his Cabinet to accept the need for intervention, Jenkins notes, but he thereafter threw his weight against the influence of bondholders.

The great and decisive choices made by European and American leaders have been driven time and again by lofty motives; inadequate information; feckless forethought; the influence of ambitious, forward party subordinates; and religious sentiment. Still, their avowed moral purposes provided a lethal weapon to imperial critics. Wilfrid Scawen Blunt, for all his posturing, would have not only his revenge but also the last word, as we shall see. History never repeats, but attitudes and arguments, dilemmas and excuses, clichés and delusions recur with the inevitability of a sun setting on successive empires. What began in the Middle East with Gladstone and the shelling of Alexandria in the hot July of 1882 has yet to reach its finale.

ONE

⌗

The Proconsul

Evelyn Baring, first earl of Cromer (1841–1917), GCB, OM,
GCMG, KCSI, by John Singer Sargent, 1902

⌘

They that dig foundations deep,
Fit for realms to rise upon,
Little honour do they reap
Of their generation,
Any more than mountains gain
Stature till we reach the plain.
—Rudyard Kipling,
"The Pro-Consuls" (1905)

The office of Proconsul was devised in Roman times as a means of governing far-flung provinces, client states, and unruly tribes. Client states constituted a substantial part of imperial territory, notably in the Middle East. Close to Judea (a province) lay Nabatean Arabia, and farther east in Anatolia lay the supposedly Free League of Lycia and the client kingdoms of Cappadocia and Pontus. Writing in the first century AD, Pliny the Elder referred to this welter of seventeen territories as "tetrarchies with barbarous names." In captive states, the Proconsul spoke for Rome, his voice concealed behind an elaborate stage set of make-believe autonomy.

During the British Empire's noontide, Egypt was the classic client state. Though never formally part of the Empire, it remained effectively under British control from 1882 until 1954, when by mutual agreement royal military units finally withdrew. Yet to the end, Whitehall perpetuated the myth of Egyptian independence. When Prime Minister Anthony Eden visited Cairo in February 1955, he invited President Gamal Abdel Nasser to a meeting at the British Embassy. "Ah," President Nasser is supposed to have remarked, "At last I can see the place from which Egypt was ruled for so long." In Whitehall folklore, Eden is said to have replied, "Not ruled, Colonel Nasser, merely advised." And of Britannic advisers, none was more influential than Sir Evelyn Baring, the Proconsul's Proconsul, who holds pride of place in our gallery.

When Sir Evelyn, aged forty-two, stepped ashore at Alexandria in September 1883 as Queen Victoria's Egyptian Agent, Consul-General, and Plenipotentiary, he already knew his way around, having served, as Major Baring, on the debt commission created by foreign bankers to discipline a profligate Khedive. He was duly named one of two controllers-general of Egyptian finance, partnered with Ernst-Gabriel de Blignières, who represented French interests. Through an arrangement known as Dual Control, they had the "delicate task" of "guiding and invigorating" the bankrupt country "without appearing to govern."[1] It was an ill-kept secret. In theory, Egypt remained an integral part of the Ottoman Empire, and its Khedive was the Sultan's emissary. Yet before long, petitioners seated before official divans, sipping tea and smoking hookahs, correctly sensed that the real power in Cairo rested with a comparatively junior British Consul-General. Soon enough even the poorest peasant guessed as much, and in their eyes Baring became "Le Grand Ours" (The Great Bear). Dual Control evolved into Single Control, and so remained until Sir Evelyn Baring, better remembered as Lord Cromer, stepped down as Consul-General in 1907.

Cromer was perhaps the ablest and certainly the oddest of imperial proconsuls. His closest contemporary rival—Lord Curzon, Viceroy of India from 1898 to 1905—sought and received more public notice, but partly for that reason his tenure was briefer. For twenty-four years, Cromer was to all intents the Pasha* of Egypt, and in Kipling's phrase, he did indeed dig foundations deep. He not only rescued Egypt from insolvency but also foreshadowed Britain's moment of mastery in the Middle East, a region whose names and frontiers he and his disciples did much to determine. In his prime, Cromer was rated the fourth most powerful personage in the British Empire, preceded by Queen, Prime Minister, and Viceroy of India. His power, wrote his colleague Ronald Storrs, "amounted in Egypt, for foreigners as well as Egyptians, to that of 10 Downing Street multiplied by Buckingham Palace."[2]

His ascent was calibrated in *Burke's Peerage.* Knighted in 1883, becoming Baron Cromer in 1892 and Viscount Cromer in 1899, Baring was created the first Earl of Cromer in 1901. As related by his admiring contemporary, Sir Valentine Chirol, chief of the foreign department of *The Times*, "In the eyes of the Egyptians, he stood for a mysterious force, unseen by most of them but everywhere felt and on the whole beneficial, and as soon as they heard something had happened to him that gave him the title of Lord in his own country, they called him '*El Lord*' and nothing else."[3]

---

* Pasha is an Ottoman title bestowed on generals or high-ranking government officials. Abolished by Atatürk, it continued to be conferred in some Arab states including Jordan.

Still, El Lord's Egyptian system in the end proved, *pace* Kipling, more of a marsh than a mountain. The contrast was with British India, where Cromer apprenticed as a colonial administrator. Under the Raj (a word meaning "rule"), British authority was visible, formal, and final; even in the operatic princely states, where a bejeweled maharajah or nawab was "advised" by a British Resident (the title capitalized), subordination was not camouflaged. India's princely rulers by treaty openly acknowledged the Paramount Power (also capitalized) of the British Crown. When India attained independence in 1947, cultural impedimenta of the Raj survived, ranging from cricket and gentlemen's clubs, bagpipes and boarding schools, to edifices like the Viceroy's Lodge at Simla, the Government House in New Delhi, and even the Victoria Memorial (adorned with portraits of Her Majesty's ladies-in-waiting) in Marxist-governed Calcutta. The break was very different in Egypt. During a nationalist eruption in 1952, remembered as "Black Saturday," mobs in Cairo sacked the perceived symbols of humiliation, notably the twin imperial canteens, the Turf Club and Shepheard's Hotel. Whole blocks were set ablaze, and foreigners burnt alive. Subsequently rioters toppled the statue of France's Ferdinand de Lesseps, gesturing like a *maître de port* at the entrance of the canal built by unpaid native diggers. (Still, with pragmatic Egyptian fore-thought, the statue was stowed intact in a shed, for possible resurrection.)

In researching the origins of today's Middle East, one is struck by the fre-quently divergent approaches to imperial rule emanating from New Delhi and Cairo, with exasperated superiors in London becoming reluctant refer-ees. Their struggles recur as a leitmotif in the pages that follow.

With benefit of hindsight, Lord Cromer proved a difficult exemplar. In his person, he fused imperturbable authority with exceptional competence. He was a virtuoso at uses of power, and his technique improved until his less assured final years. Financial acumen flowed in his blood. As Evelyn Bar-ing, he was the grandson of an admiral, and son of a member of Parlia-ment who (more importantly) was a hereditary partner in Baring Brothers, a princely banking dynasty specializing in foreign loans. Following military service in Corfu (then a British protectorate) and Malta, he served as private secretary to Lord Northbrook, the Viceroy of India, and by useful chance his cousin; there he earned, and by many accounts deserved, an adhesive nickname, "Over-Baring."

John Singer Sargent's portrait in Britain's National Portrait Gallery conveys his essence. We see him suited in faultless dove-gray, sitting at ease in his study, his left hand casually brushing his thigh while his half-hidden right, we cannot fail to observe, closes in a fist. Cromer's arch-critic, the poet and anti-imperialist Wilfrid Scawen Blunt, noted as well "the bloated cheeks, dull eyes, ruby nose and gouty hand, half-torpid, having lunched heavily."[4] A less hostile and fairer view is ventured by James Morris, the prose muralist of *Pax Britannica*: "He was a man of profound and awful seriousness, the very antithesis of the light-hearted, volatile, affectionate and not very efficient Egyptians his duty it was to govern."[5]

On the whole, with reservations, El Lord delivered. He exercised the cold-shower rigor nowadays associated with the International Monetary Fund and World Bank, whose policies he anticipated. Cromer promoted frugal budgets, debt reduction, and free trade: lured experts on irrigation from India; and saw to it that chaotic courts were reformed. He gave priority to massive development schemes—for example, the first Aswan Dam, completed in 1902, which created a reservoir that made nearly a billion cubic meters of water available for irrigation in Upper Egypt. As Consul-General, he oversaw the strategy that ended a protracted Islamic rebellion in the Sudan, Africa's largest territory. Following the British-led victory at Omdurman in 1898, he came up with a suitably cryptic new status for the Sudan: it was designated an "Anglo-Egyptian Condominium." Conceiving himself a protector of Egypt's immemorial tillers, the fellahin, he reported with pride in 1891 that his policies had increased the annual value of Egypt's cotton by an average of £835,000, and that he had also sought tax relief for its impoverished growers. Early and laudably, Cromer pressed successfully for the abolition of the corvée, the long-standing and shaming system of forced labor used to create and maintain the Suez Canal (a reform fiercely resisted by agents of France's otherwise moralistic Third Republic).

What gave these attainments added luster were the peculiarities of Egypt's governance. Cromer received an informed testimonial from Alfred Milner, who drew on his personal experience in Cairo as a former Under Secretary of Finance to write *England in Egypt* (1892), a best-selling celebration of what was just becoming known as the New Imperialism. For a time in the 1890s, everybody British who mattered seemed to be a New Imperialist, a congregation that included Bertrand Russell, the budding iconoclast, and Beatrice Webb, the soon-to-be Fabian reformer. Lord Curzon expressed the prevalent euphoria when in 1894 he pronounced the British Empire as "under Providence, the greatest instrument for good the world has seen."[6] In the eyes of converts, the Empire stood for peace, free trade, and rule of law. In backward lands, it inculcated love of liberty and fair play; its commercial policies benefited rich and poor alike; and its opponents were either envious rivals like the German Kaiser, or "mad mullahs" promoting violence and religious hatred. New Imperialists like Colonial Secretary Joseph Chamberlain contended as well that Great Britain ought, if necessary, act unilaterally and proactively to advance the Empire's interests, since these coincided in any case with humankind's. And it was certainly true—although rarely acknowledged by beneficiaries of Pax Britannica, notably the United States—that by ensuring freedom of the seas at British expense, the Royal Navy was a force for stable and thriving global commerce.

Alfred Milner, himself a future Proconsul, was among the most eloquent of New Imperialists. With erudition honed at Oxford's Balliol College (where, like Curzon, he was a protégé of the school's renowned master, Benjamin Jowett), and a fluency learned during his years as a journalist for the lively *Pall Mall Gazette*, Milner cited Egypt as a paradoxical success story. He asked readers to remember that Egypt was not a colony or a dominion; it was a "veiled protectorate" (Milner's coinage). Egypt had been proverbially backward, and its docile inhabitants were incongruously wedded to an intolerant and fanatical religion. These inherently conservative people, he continued, had only recently encountered the disturbing winds of European innovation, and indeed their land was now overrun by foreigners whom Egyptian police could not arrest since Europeans were immunized by agreements with the Ottomans known as Capitulations exempting them from local laws. Nor could Egypt's nominal government legislate for its foreign residents without the consent of a dozen foreign powers, while its budgets were hostage to foreign bondholders. Even more strangely, Egypt's policies were (he wrote) "really inspired by the Envoy of a foreign state, who in theory is only one—and not even the *doyen*—of a large number of such Envoys, and the chief administrative power really wielded by a man, who in theory is a mere 'Adviser without executive functions.' "

Nonetheless, owing to British governing genius, Milner pursued, Egypt was no "Mikado"-like invention of comic opera, no nightmare of some constitutional theorist with a disordered brain, but prosaic, solid fact: "For in the Land of Paradox grapes do grow from thorns and figs from thistles."

(It helped that British troops were garrisoned throughout Egypt, and that British officers were installed in the Egyptian army under the command of a British general known as the Sirdar—all this stemming from the "temporary" occupation commencing in 1882 that was indefinitely extended.) *England in Egypt* passed through thirteen editions and became a New Imperialist manifesto, lauded by the young Winston Churchill as "a trumpet-call, which rallies the troops after the parapets are stormed, and summons them to complete the victory."[7]

Milner went on to become Britain's High Commissioner in Cape Town, a promoter of the Boer War, an architect of the postwar Union of South Africa, a Viscount and Proconsul whose celebrated "kindergarten" groomed a coming generation of imperial governors. Still, when *England in Egypt* was translated into Arabic, the effect was not what its author might have welcomed. The book confirmed, in authoritative detail, that Egypt's presumed leaders were puppets. According to Harvard's Roger Owen, Cromer's most recent biographer, popular passions that had been dormant since 1882 resurfaced as students rioted in Cairo, where a hostile mob even unhorsed the carriage of the despised chief puppet, the Khedive. (For his part, Cromer cited the agitation to appeal for more British troops.)

Among literate Egyptians, the stain on El Lord's reputation darkened and endured. As recently as 1998, according to Owen, a group of young Egyptians made their way to the small Norfolk town of Cromer, Evelyn Baring's birthplace. "Where is this Cromer buried?" they demanded from a local archivist, adding, "We would like to spit on his grave."[8]

On its face, such vehemence seems unwarranted, even puzzling. Whatever his deficiencies, the Earl of Cromer seems hardly an evil figure. If his post-retirement language was sometimes blunt, as in his references to "subject races," he used the prevailing vocabulary of his caste and nation. And it chanced that at this moment, we tend to forget, the label "Middle East" was devised by an American, given the benediction of *The Times* of London, and propelled by the propitious discovery of the region's oil riches. Pause for a moment to imagine the world as it seemed to Cromer and his British fellow subjects.

In 1901, the year of her death, Queen Victoria reigned over an empire that embraced roughly a fifth of the world's population and a fifth of its habitable territory; her scepter soon extended even to Antarctica. London was inarguably the world's greatest metropolis, its 4.5 million inhabitants outpacing runner-up New York's 3.4 million. The British Navy outclassed its closest rivals combined; the planet's leading manufacturer of weapons (Vickers) was British; and British steel and steam united the world's first global market, weaving together even the Empire's remotest outposts by undersea cables. Clocks and maps everywhere had as their common point of reference the Royal Observatory at Greenwich, the temporal navel of Planet Earth.

Still, of Britannic sinews, the most pervasive was least visible. As the nineteenth century ended, British exports declined and the trade deficit ballooned, but this was generously offset by income from foreigners—that is, from interest, rents, dividends, patent revenues, and financial services, all calculated in sterling, the universal gold-based currency. "London was the center of a financial empire, more international, more extensive in its variety, than even the political empire of which it was the capital," the American scholar Herbert Feis wrote in 1930. "... The names of foreign lands and ventures vibrated unceasingly in the shadowy dimness of the London Stock Exchange, and the financial journals gave a panorama of the world's strivings in factory, mine, and field."[9] As many as five hundred banks, brokers, and traders catered to needy foreign governments and entrepreneurs; in the front rank was Baring Brothers, flanked by Rothschilds, Brown Shipley, Glyn Mills, the Cassels, and other fonts of credit.

Founded in 1762, with ancestral roots in North Germany, Baring Brothers early on pioneered multinational lending through bills of exchanges. By 1818, the Duc de Richelieu (Louis XVIII's Prime Minister) marveled, "There are six great powers in Europe: England, France, Prussia, Austria, Russia and Baring Brothers."[10] The Sixth Great Power nourished the infant American republic, spectacularly in 1803, when it brokered the Louisiana Purchase: Napoleon's distress sale that doubled U.S. territory for only $15 million. When the Brothers guessed wrong, as they did in Argentina in 1890, global financial markets momentarily trembled. In their person, generations of Barings served the Crown as viceroys, finance ministers, ambassadors, proconsuls, and governors of the Bank of England, a procession continuing through London's Swinging Sixties.

Such was the world in which Evelyn Baring came of age, although during his Cairo years he pointedly never favored the family firm (favor was superfluous, skeptics noted, since on any major foreign loan, merchant bankers were sure to consult the Sixth Great Power). Cromer was fortunate in another sense. In Victorian times, British security concerns with Egypt centered on safeguarding the Suez Canal, "the Imperial Lifeline," and on keeping Tsarist Russia from threatening India by occupying Islamic lands, "the Great Game." By 1900, however, the strategic calculus had changed in what diplomats called "the Eastern Question." A new player, Kaiser Wilhelm, courted the Ottoman Sultan, volunteering himself as protector of the Muslims and as promoter of a German Berlin-to-Baghdad railway. Simultaneously, British naval reformers zealously promoted a transition from coal to oil for fueling warships, and worried admirals warned that Britain was too addicted to imported crude, chiefly from the United States.

The term "Middle East" appeared first in a September 1902 article titled "The Persian Gulf and International Relations" in a British monthly, *The National Review*. The author was an American, Captain Alfred Thayer Mahan, USN, whose *Influence of Sea Power upon History, 1660 to 1783* (1890) gained him a fan club that included emperors and admirals across the globe. When Mahan visited England, he was greeted virtually as a head of state; a leading article in *The Times* likened him to Copernicus. With an eye to this audience, his 1902 essay argued that British naval bases were needed around the Persian Gulf to protect the Suez Canal, to check Russia's southward expansion, and to counter Kaiser Wilhelm's schemes. This passage followed: "The Middle East, if I may adopt a term which I have not seen, will some day need its Malta, as well as its Gibraltar; it does not follow that either will be in the Gulf. Naval force has the quality of mobility which carries with it the privilege of temporary absences; but it needs to find on every scene of operation established bases of refit, of supply, and in case of disaster, security. The British Navy should have the facility to concentrate in force, if occasion arise, about Aden, India, and the Gulf."[11]

Mahan's article caught the eye of Sir Valentine Chirol, *The Times*'s foreign editor, who had toured the Persian Gulf earlier that same year. There he heard "less of Russia and more of Germany as the Power whose growing influence threatened to displace our own." To Chirol, it was obvious that the Berlin-to-Baghdad railway and its planned extension to the Persian Gulf were part of the kaiser's plan to use Turkey as "a bridgehead to German world dominion." Chirol had discussed his anxieties with Viceroy Curzon, who confided that he shared his concern and in fact planned to tour the Gulf and visit its emirates, with the particular goal of winning over the influential Sheik of Kuwait. (Chirol subsequently took part in Curzon's 1903 tour, both as a journalistic tout and as an official guest.)

Prompted by Mahan's essay, Chirol published twenty successive articles in *The Times* under the generic title "The Middle Eastern Question," which he later reshaped into a 1903 book, *The Middle East Question, or Some Political Problems of Indian Defence.* What had been commonly called the Near East, Turkish Asia, or simply the Orient acquired a new name. In today's parlance, Project Middle East, in its initial public offering, was an Anglo-American enterprise, centered on the Persian Gulf, meant to shut Russia out, keep Germany down, and implant a network of British bases in close alliance with traditional local rulers. Add "oil" to the equation, and a century of history was presaged by the phrase.

In confronting complex challenges, with one exception Lord Cromer evinced an assured smoothness of touch. The exception was Islam, a faith many Europeans saw as the source of much in the Middle East that was anachronistic, mysterious, and threatening. Indeed, the Prophet's religion was an old and mortal adversary. In England, generations of youngsters witnessed mummer plays depicting Mohammed as the blasphemous foe of the intrepid Saint George. This enmity was understandable, writes the British scholar Karen Armstrong, "because until the rise of the Soviet Union in our own century, no polity or ideology posed such a continuous challenge to the West."[12] From Islam's early conquests in Europe, through eight Western Crusades in the Holy Land, and during the rise of the Ottomans, Islam remained *the* enemy. "From the fury of the Muhammedan, spare us O Lord!" was a prayer heard for a millennium in European churches.

For Evelyn Baring, this was living history. While he attended the Royal Military Academy at Woolwich, the Great Mutiny raged in India, and among the fiercest rebels were Muslims striving to restore the Mughal Empire. While serving in Calcutta, then the seat of the Raj, Evelyn Baring needed no reminder that Victoria reigned over more Muslims than did any other sovereign. He learned as well that in the Islamic world even remote tremors resurfaced as local news in Delhi or Bombay.

Hence his concern in 1883 on becoming Consul-General in Cairo about the spreading Islamic insurgency in the Sudan. Its leader, the humbly born son of a carpenter, Muhammad Ahmad, had proclaimed himself the Mahdi, or the Awaited One, and his fame had spread like brushfire through the Sudan, officially an Egyptian province covering roughly a million square miles and home to nine million mostly Muslim inhabitants. The rebels slew or expelled Egyptian soldiers sent to arrest the Mahdi, and Cairo's writ barely extended beyond Khartoum. Eloquent and learned, pleasing in feature, and firm but civil in manner, the Awaited One imposed an exacting moral code on his followers. "Let us show penitence before God," he beseeched in 1882, "and abandon all bad and forbidden habits, such as degrading acts of the flesh, the use of wine and tobacco, lying, bearing false witness, disobedience to parents, brigandage, the non-restitution of goods to others, the clapping of hands, dancing, improper signs with the eyes, tears and lamentations at the bed of the dead, slanderous language, calumny; and the company of strange women. Clothe your women in a decent way, and let them be careful not to speak to unknown persons. All those who do not pay attention to these principles disobey God and His Prophet, and they shall be punished according to the law."[13]

Vigilant morality police punished miscreants, who risked execution, loss of limb, or flogging. Awe reinforced fear as the Mahdi's followers, armed initially with swords, spears, and sticks, routed the Egyptians he derided as blasphemous "Turks." Propitiously, a great comet rose in the eastern sky in 1882, which the Sudanese called "the Star of the Guided One." A lethargic Cairo government finally roused itself and dispatched southward a hastily mobilized army under the command of a retired British Indian army officer, General William Hicks. To Cairo's horrified astonishment, Hicks and most of his force were slaughtered at Shaykan, thirty miles south of the provincial capital, El Obeid. The Mahdi's sharpshooters had feigned retreat, luring inward Hicks's army of 7,000 infantry, 1,000 cavalry, and 5,000 camels, together with its precious cannons and a horde of camp followers.

An account of the final fatal day was subsequently found in a battered diary kept by one of the British officers: "The General [Hicks] orders the band to play, hoping the music may liven us a little; but the band stops for the bullets are flying from all directions; and camels, mules and men keep dropping down; we are all cramped up together, so the bullets fail to strike. We are faint and weary, and have no idea what to do . . . It is Sunday and my dear brother's birthday. Would God I could sit down and talk to him for an hour! The bullets are falling thicker."[14] In mid-sentence, the diary ends.

It happened that an adventurous correspondent for *The Times*, Dublin-born Frank Power, accompanied Hicks's army, and after developing dysentery, he had been sent back for treatment at Khartoum. From there, Power pieced together firsthand reports of the massacre. His telegraphed dispatches appeared, by ill chance for a flustered Liberal government, just as Prime Minister Gladstone's Cabinet was voting to reduce troop levels in Egypt. "It is time to put an end to this perverse pursuit of a doctrinaire's will-o'-the-wisp [i.e., ending the occupation of Egypt]," declaimed *The Times*, by then the imperial superego. "The responsibilities of our position in Egypt are now fully understood by the country and Ministers cannot afford to make any mistakes about them."[15]

The Hicks disaster precipitated the Gordon affair, a quintessential Victorian melodrama that ended with the death of its hero. It followed a familiar cycle: First a cry to "do something" swelled in Parliament, propelled by the press and echoed in pulpits and public meetings. Rattled Cabinet ministers deliberated, counsels were divided, the premier in charge retreated into a fog of euphemisms. Absent a decision, a fact-finding mission was authorized to test the wind and buy time as plausible alibis were stockpiled ("Who could have foreseen?" "Orders were disobeyed," "Intelligence was faulty," "Our allies let us down," "The weather was bad," "The messenger garbled our instructions," or the all-purpose formulation, "Mistakes were made").

What triggered the furor was an interview in *The Pall Mall Gazette* on January 9, 1884. Bold, brassy, and evangelical, the *Gazette*'s editors learned that Charles George Gordon, an almost mythic Christian soldier of fortune, had arrived in Britain en route to the Congo Free State on a mission for King Leopold of the Belgians. General Gordon was among the Empire's most famous warriors, though he had never held a significant command in the British military. He made his name commanding foreign mercenaries in China, suppressing a bloody rebellion, inspired by a self-proclaimed Christian messiah, and in the Sudan, where he had battled slave traders. Gordon was met at his sister Augusta's home in Southampton by the paper's indefatigable editor, W. T. Stead, who then accompanied him by rail to London, taking detailed notes (Stead was among the first to grasp the circulation potential of verbatim interviews). The questions Stead put to Gordon were simple. Some six thousand Egyptian troops had retreated to Khartoum following the defeat of Hicks's punitive force, and were now encircled by the Mahdi's warriors. Should these troops and imperiled civilians be evacuated at the risk of ceding the Sudan to the rebels? Or should an expeditionary army be sent to save the garrison and crush the rebellion?

Gordon could scarcely have spoken more plainly. Retreat was not an option, since it would cost far more to regain Britain's hold on Egypt proper "if you abandon your hold on the Eastern Soudan to the Mahdi or to the Turks." Gordon then offered a variation of the domino theory invoked by supporters of America's Vietnam War:

> The danger is not that the Mahdi will march northward through Wadi Halfa; on the contrary, it is very improbable that he will ever go north. The danger is of altogether a different nature. It arises from the influence which the spectacle of a conquering Mahommedan Power, established close to our frontiers, will exercise upon the population which you govern. In all the cities of Egypt it will be felt that what the Mahdi has done they may do; and, as he has driven out the intruder and the infidel, they may do the same.
>
> Nor is it only England that has to face this danger. The success of the Mahdi has already excited dangerous fermentation in Arabia and Syria. Placards have been posted in Damascus calling upon the population to rise up and drive out the Turks. If the whole of the Eastern Soudan is surrendered to the Mahdi, the Arab tribes on both sides of the Red Sea will take fire . . . for it is quite possible that if nothing is done the whole of the Eastern Question may be reopened by the triumph of the Mahdi. I see it is proposed to fortify Wadi Halfa, and prepare there to resist the Mahdi's attack. You might as well fortify against a fever. Contagion of that kind cannot be kept out by fortifications and garrisons. But it is real and that it does exist will be denied by no one cognizant with Egypt and the East. In self-defence, the policy of evacuation cannot possibly be justified.[16]

The interview inspired a salvo of speeches, editorials, sermons, and rallies exhorting the government to send Gordon to the Sudan, a province he knew firsthand, having earlier served there as the Khedive's Governor-General. As Stead expressed it, "We cannot send a regiment to Khartoum, but we can send a man who has proved himself more valuable in similar situations than an entire army." On January 18, Gordon was summoned to the War Office to confer with the Secretary of War and other senior ministers. There he agreed "to consider and report on the best mode of effecting the evacuation of the Sudan"—in short, to study the feasibility of the very policy he had just sternly condemned.[17] Prime Minister Gladstone, then at Hawarden, telegraphed his acquiescence, while stressing that Gordon should simply report, nothing more. One surmises that Gladstone, who had never met Gordon, thought he was prudently buying time at a moment when his Cabinet was divided and Liberals were preoccupied by a major electoral reform proposal. As for Gordon, one guesses that he accurately assumed that once on his own, he could do as he wished. He left this candid self-assessment in his journal, written eight months later in besieged Khartoum: "I own to having been very insubordinate to Her Majesty's Government and its officials. But it is in my nature and I cannot help it. I fear I have not even tried to play battledore and shuttlecock with them. I know if *I* was the chief, I would never employ myself, for I am incorrigible."[18]

For his part, Gladstone, though famous for his manly felling of trees at Hawarden, was thin-skinned to a fault. Nettled by an outcry among Liberals who feared that Gordon might plunge Britain into a morass, the Prime Minister in response chose to inflate the Mahdi's rebellion into a veritable clash of civilizations. The British task in Egypt, he informed Parliament on February 12, 1884, was "one which we are executing not alone, on our own behalf, but on behalf, I may say, of civilised mankind. We undertook it with the approval of the Powers of Europe—the highest and most authentic organ of modern Christian civilisation, but having undertaken it at their invitation, or with their concurrence, we must fulfill it as we received it from them."[19] Faced with valid questions about a risky policy, the Grand Old Man habitually lofted oratorical rockets into the unassailable empyrean: in his own way, Gladstone too was incorrigible.

Like Saint Sebastian, Gordon became an emblematic martyr of his time and place, and like the saint he was immortalized in a painting that depicted an awed heathen aiming a missile at his proudly upright body. (The 1893 painting, *Death of General Charles Gordon* by G. W. Joy, hangs in the Leeds City Art Gallery; it inspired a 1966 cinematic epic, *Khartoum*, starring Charlton Heston as Gordon and, strangely, Sir Laurence Olivier as the Mahdi.) In the consensual Victorian version, Gordon was a Christian gladiator innocent of political cunning who found guidance in the Bible he consulted daily.

John H. Waller, an American who served in Cairo with the Office of Strategic Services (OSS) during World War II, was struck by how much Gordon and the Mahdi had in common: "Both worshipped with a burning zeal the God of the Old Testament; both possessed charismatic military leadership qualities; both hated tyranny, and neither feared death."[20] Still, mixed in Gordon's character was a hard seam of vanity and calculation, and Waller (who in 1976 became Inspector General of the Central Intelligence Agency) might have added in *Gordon of Khartoum* (1988) that a mountain of bodies resulted from this collision of absolutists.

Caught in the middle was the notably secular-minded Sir Evelyn Baring, who knew all about Gordon, having followed him by a decade as a cadet at Woolwich. Like his fellow cadets, Baring was aware of Gordon's intrepidity as a sapper (or combat engineer) during the siege of Sebastopol in the Crimean War, and like most Britons he knew of his feats in China. There, commissioned by civic leaders of Shanghai, Gordon turned a mercenary force into the memorably named Ever-Victorious Army, which quelled the Taiping uprising (1854–64) led by a Chinese schoolmaster who claimed to be the younger brother of Jesus Christ. "Chinese" Gordon was celebrated as well for his charitable work as a base commander in Gravesend, where he housed and clothed the young and poor in his official residence ("God Bless the Kernel!" was chalked on the city's pavements). Evangelists knew him as a Christian soldier, though one doubts they were aware of his peculiar biblical theories (he located the Garden of Eden in Mauritius, his evidence being the vulval shape of a fruit unique to the island). And antislavery activists applauded his campaigns against Muslim slavers while serving as Governor of Equatoria, a trackless subdivision of the Sudan, and then as Governor of the entire Sudan, following his appointment in 1877 by the Khedive.

But Sir Evelyn also knew Gordon as an impulsive mystic who had undergone a spiritual crisis in Palestine in 1882 ("I am trying the experiment of giving up all hindrances to the holy life," he wrote to his sister Augusta).[21] Hence Baring initially cautioned against sending Gordon to Khartoum, then turned with the tide because (as he later explained) so many Britons he respected seemed to feel otherwise. Among Gordon's supporters was Lord Granville, the Foreign Secretary, who confided frankly in a private letter to Sir Evelyn, "He may possibly be of great use, and the appointment will be popular with many classes in the country."[22] When Gordon paused in Cairo for forty-eight hours en route to Khartoum, Sir Evelyn took part in his meetings with local notables, including Zubair Pasha, a past king-pin in the Sudanese slave trade whom the general had once chased across Darfur, then a crossroads for the traffic. Baring was thus present when Gordon, overwhelmed by a "mystic feeling," decided the ex-slaver was the ideal candidate to pacify the Sudan. Sir Evelyn deflected this impromptu proposal and helped persuade the Khedive to name Gordon, once again, as Governor-General of the Sudan. He did this, Baring advised London, believing it was vital to send "an English officer" with real leverage to Khartoum. As he put it to Lord Granville, "Gen. Gordon would be the best man if he will pledge himself to carry out the policy of withdrawal from Sudan as soon as possible, consistently with saving life. He must fully understand that he must take instructions from the British Representative in Egypt [i.e., Baring] and report to him."[23] (Years later, Baring confessed that approving Gordon's appointment was perhaps his gravest mistake, and in his massive two-volume *Modern Egypt* [1908] he retouched his own role by omitting the word "English" from the just-quoted recommendation he sent to London.)

On January 26, 1884, the general departed for Khartoum, accompanied by a cavalry officer, Colonel J. D. H. Stewart of the 12th Hussars, and by Frank Power of *The Times*. To Khartoum's besieged inhabitants, Gordon telegraphed this message: "Do not be panic-stricken. You are men, not women; I am coming."[24] On February 18, having turned the bend where the Blue and White Nile rivers converge, Gordon disembarked from the steamer *Tewfikieh* to an ecstatic welcome. "I come without soldiers but with God on my side to redress the evils of the Sudan," he declared. "I will not fight with any weapons but justice."[25] Power cabled *The Times*: "The Government books, recording from time immemorial the outstanding debts of an overtaxed people, were publicly burned in front of the Palace. The *kourbushes*, whips and other instruments used for administering the bastinado in Government House, were all placed on the burning pile."[26]

The euphoria was understandable. Here was the Khedive's official representative who seemed to promise that he would ease the Sudan's colonial bondage, write off debts, and even permit the resumption of the slave trade, unlawful since 1877. If the British abandoned the Sudan, Gordon reasoned, the slave traffic would in any case resume, presenting no obstacle to the former slaver Zubair Pasha, Gordon's unexpected nominee for Governor-General. This apparent crypto-realism dismayed Gordon's humanitarian supporters. Unfazed, the general gloated that he had converted *The Times* and Baring to his changed views on permitting the slave trade, and later, in August 1884, on learning that a force was being mobilized for his rescue, he gleefully marveled that he had forced Gladstone to send an expeditionary army into the Sudan. Gordon's other turnabouts were as abrupt. At one point he surmised that he could defeat the Mahdi in battle; at another he guessed that he could outwit or disarm him. To test the latter strategy, he sent the Mahdi a red robe of honor, a fez, and a letter offering him the sultanship of Kordofan, his home province. To which the Mahdi replied, "Know that I am the Expected Mahdi, the Successor of the Apostle of Allah. Thus I have no need of the sultanate, nor of the kingdom of Kordofan or elsewhere, nor of the wealth of the world and its vanity. I am the slave of Allah ... As for the gift which you sent Us, may Allah reward you for your goodwill and guide you to the right ... It is returned to you herewith with the clothing We wish for Ourself and Our Companions who desire the world to come."[27] (The Mahdi sent Gordon a jalaba, a patchy shirt-like garment worn by the Dervishes.)

In Cairo, Sir Evelyn Baring came to dread the daily influx of meandering, sometimes incoherent telegrams from Khartoum. Gordon himself mused that he must be *"perfect poison"* to word-weighing officials, adding in his journal, "I wonder what the telegrams about Sudan have cost Her Majesty's Government?" Once in the Sudan, as Lytton Strachey remarked astringently in *Eminent Victorians* (1918), "He was among his people—his own people, and it was to them only he was responsible—to them, and to God. Was he to let them fall without a blow into the clutches of a sanguinary impostor? Never! He was there to prevent that. The distant government might mutter something about 'evacuation'; his thoughts were elsewhere. He poured them into his telegrams, and Sir Evelyn Baring sat aghast. The man who left London a month before to 'report on the best means of effecting the evacuation of the Sudan' was now openly talking of 'smashing up the Mahdi' with the aid of British and Indian troops."[28]

Still, these anomalies signified little to a British public transfixed by a lone hero beset by fanatic Dervish warriors while a Liberal Cabinet, split between hawks like Lord Hartington, the Secretary of War, and doves like Lord Granville, the Foreign Secretary, dithered endlessly. By August 1884, pressed by Hartington, Gladstone finally agreed to earmark £300,000 for a rescue mission. Sir Garnet Wolseley, the imperial expert in short-order operations, mobilized an expeditionary army in Cairo, but practical difficulties delayed its departure until October, when his force of ten thousand began its sixteen-hundred-mile trek to Khartoum. By then, the insurgents had severed telegraph lines, and Colonel Stewart and *The Times*'s Frank Power had left Khartoum carrying messages, only to be slain by a Mahdist pretending to be their ally. Gordon began preparing for the final battle. In January 1885, England's nightmare scenario materialized as the Dervishes with their curved swords swept through the city. In the received account, Gordon was slain on the palace steps by four giant spear-wielding assailants, one of whom shouted, "O cursed one, your time has come!" Gordon's head was carried in triumph to the Mahdi and propped on a forked branch as a target for derision and food for kites. ("At last," Strachey sarcastically remarks, "the two fanatics had indeed met face to face.")[29]

On January 24, 1885, an advance British force of several hundred had embarked from a nearby upriver village on two steamers for the final dash to Khartoum. Delayed by the Nile's treacherous sixth cataract, the vessels reached Khartoum on January 26, only to discover that Khartoum had already fallen. Colonel Sir Charles Wilson, the intelligence officer in command, was greeted from the riverside with shouts of jubilation and "Death to the English!" A barrage of bullets and shells fired from shore batteries began "tapping like hail against the ships' sides, whilst the shells went screaming overhead." Khartoum had very clearly capitulated; Gordon's Egyptian flag was no longer visible through halos of smoke. Wilson felt he had no choice but to retreat down river at full speed.

"Too late!" was the caption of a *Punch* cartoon on February 5, showing a stricken Britannia bowed in grief as the Mahdi's hordes sacked Khartoum. "Too late!" said the chorus in Parliament and the press, their laments rendered into verse by Lord Tennyson, the Poet Laureate: "By those for whom he lived he died. His land / Awoke too late, and crowned dead brows with praise." In music halls, "G.O.M." was reversed to read "M.O.G.," Murderer of Gordon, in a jeering limerick:

> *The M.O.G. when his life ebbs out*
> *Will ride in a fiery chariot*
> *And sit in state*
> *On a red-hot plate*
> *Between Pilate and Judas Iscariot*

The other casualty in Khartoum's fall was Gladstone's second Liberal administration. Now seventy-five, the Grand Old Man insisted, sometimes to catcalls, that General Gordon was insubordinate. The Prime Minister sourly resisted even a word of praise for the fallen soldier in his first statement to the House of Commons. On receiving a message from Queen Victoria commenting that an earlier action might have saved Gordon, her First Minister rejoined that he was "under the impression that Lord Wolseley's force might have been sufficiently advanced to save Khartoum had not a large portion of it been delayed by a circuitous route along the river, upon the express application of General Gordon."[30] Gladstone seemed unable to fathom that Gordon had become in the popular mind a devout martyr who died bravely while on an impossible mission for an ingrate government. The divided and demoralized Liberals floundered, and in June their impenitent leader submitted his resignation.

As with later domino theories, the dire consequences that Gordon prophesied failed to occur. Six months after the fall of Khartoum, the Mahdi died of natural causes, and leadership of the insurgency passed to his designated successor, Abdullah ibn Mohammad, known as the Khalifa. For more than a decade, Dervish warriors repelled Anglo-Egyptian punitive forays, but the insurgents proved unable to extend their victories northward into Egypt, nor did their jihad catch fire elsewhere in the Islamic world. Sir Evelyn Baring was content to watch and wait, and though bred as a Liberal he forged a productive alliance with an equally taciturn Lord Salisbury, the last peer to serve as a British Prime Minister. Together they agreed on a "two flag" solution for the Sudan, whereby Egypt would formally become a partner—albeit silent and junior—with Britain in governing the vast province. And together they agreed to retake Khartoum through a massive assault led by a rising star, Major Herbert Kitchener, a methodical engineer whose gaze, mustache, and ramrod posture dissolved all doubts.

Having fought in Lord Wolseley's futile relief force, Kitchener knew the terrain. He had also mapped the Holy Land for the Palestine Exploration Fund, spoke Arabic, and yearned to avenge Gordon, "the noblest man who ever lived." By 1898, in his role as Egypt's Sirdar or Commander in Chief, Kitchener had mobilized 25,800 men, of whom a third were British, the rest Egyptian and Sudanese. Salisbury provided a government loan to Egypt, later converted into a grant, of £900,000, to which he then added an extra £750,000 to underwrite a camel corps, horses, paddle steamers, cannons, and (crucially) the recently invented Maxim-Nordenfeldt machine guns. In the subsequent battle at Omdurman, the Mahdist redoubt facing Khartoum, some fifty thousand Dervish warriors were decimated by Kitchener's Army of the Nile, half as large. The Khalifa erred fatally in ordering a daylight frontal attack against British infantry squares backed by howitzers and Maxims. Between ten and twenty thousand Sudanese fighters perished (estimates varied widely), while Anglo-Egyptian losses were but forty-eight. Recording the action was Second Lieutenant Winston Churchill, doubling as a war correspondent for *The Daily Telegraph*, who joined the 21st Lancers in one of the British Empire's last great cavalry charges.

In a macabre finale, which Queen Victoria deplored as "medieval," the Mahdi's bones were exhumed and his skull seized as a souvenir. ("The bones of the Mahdi have been chucked into the river," a disapproving Captain Sparks commented, "which I think rather bad form.")[31] Kitchener considered using the unusually large skull as an inkwell or drinking cup, but after hearing objections he suggested sending it to the College of Surgeons. On learning of this proposal, as Philip Ziegler recounts in *Omdurman* (1974), the Queen made plain her displeasure and Lord Salisbury telegraphed Cromer that such nonsense must stop. "I am very sorry Her Majesty should consider that the Mahdi's remains were unjustifiably mistreated," a flustered Kitchener cabled the Consul-General. "I will have the skull buried as the Queen wishes."[32]

In a final gesture to make clear whose Creator was paramount, the Sirdar arranged a victory service in the ruined choir of Gordon's palace at Khartoum. Four chaplains—Anglican, Presbyterian, Methodist, and Roman Catholic—joined in an ecumenical rite that culminated in "Abide with Me," believed to be General Gordon's favorite hymn.

Still, in retrospect, Omdurman proved an equivocal victory. The Mahdist state had indeed been crushed, and Gordon avenged. In Strachey's oft-quoted epitaph, it had ended "in a glorious slaughter of twenty-thousand Arabs, a vast addition to the British Empire, and a step in the peerage for Sir Evelyn Baring."[33] Yet the scale of the slaughter horrified even unsentimental Britons while the Maxim's lethal demonstration encouraged false expectations of further easy victories in Africa. A year later, most Britons expected their imperial army would make short shrift of Boer farmers, compounding the shock when renowned regiments fell back in disorder. Not least, the hecatomb at Omdurman widened the gulf between Islamic and Christian worlds. From pub to club, European superiority in all things was taken for granted; Egyptians dwindled into "Gypos" or "WOGs" (Worthy Oriental Gentlemen). Wilfrid Scawen Blunt was among the few voices of repute to ask why people elsewhere should not be permitted their own religious wars, or their own regicides, as the British had perpetrated in Cromwell's time. Was the Mahdi and his theocratic state truly so contemptible? What real British interest was served in forcibly demonstrating the European ability to humiliate non-European peoples? *Circa* 1900, questions like these were rarely addressed, save by infidels like Mark Twain, who was only a humorist (and an American).

It did not help that in Egypt, as elsewhere in the Islamic East, Europeans lived in their separate neighborhoods, segregated from the majority population, in an earlier version of what Americans today know as the Green Zone in Baghdad. Nowhere was the barrier more tangible than in Lord Cromer's Cairo. This came about despite repeated official declarations that no such partition was desired. "We do not want Egypt, or want it for ourselves," insisted Lord Palmerston, an earlier Liberal Prime Minister who was rarely shy about pressing British interests, "any more than any rational man with an estate in the north of England and a residence in the south would have wished to have possessed the inns on the road. All he could want would have been that the inns should be well-kept, always accessible, and furnishing him, when he came, with mutton-chops and post-horses."[34]

Yet once the British settled in as an occupying power, the well-kept inn grew into the Empire's premier stopover spa, a transformation epitomized by the Consul-General's domiciles. The Barings (Evelyn had married Ethel Errington, the daughter of a landed squire, Sir Rowland Errington, in 1876) initially occupied the Consul's existing mansion, later reborn as Cairo's Turf Club. Deeming the quarters inadequate, Baring immediately drafted plans for a more imposing residence and chancery. Known to Europeans as "the Agency," and subsequently to Egyptians as "Bayt-el Lurd" (the Lord's House), Cromer's citadel was wedged between riverfront palaces, a few hundred yards from the British barracks at Qasr al-Nil in the fashionable district called Garden City. Its grounds were later expanded to include formal gardens, a closely clipped lawn (where Cromer's successor, Lord Kitchener, kept a decorative stork), a swimming pool, a riverbank dock, and (during the Second World War) the obligatory bomb shelter.

There was much work to be done. The administration of Egypt was archaic. As the great eleventh edition of the *Encyclopaedia Britannica* (1910) explained, "The constitution was stillborn, and Sir Evelyn Baring arrived to find, not indeed a clean slate, but a worn-out papyrus, disfigured by the efforts of centuries to describe in hieroglyphs a method of rule for a docile people."[35] To build support for reform, Sir Evelyn and Lady Ethel hosted a busy social round. Their calendar included dances, amateur theatricals, "at homes," and dinners—the latter elaborate affairs in which turbaned Indian servants served reindeers' tongues and peach bitters, along with the chef's famous prawn curry. Egyptians rarely appeared at these events, and when *en famille*, Baring never tired of discussing Greek and Roman literature, or French novels (which he disliked). Not that Egypt was forgotten. The writer and diplomat Maurice Baring recalled his uncle's regaling guests with abuse about himself in the local press. Sir Evelyn quoted with delight an Egyptian journalist who described him as "combining the oiliness of a Chadband [an obsequious Dickens character] with the malignity of a fiend."[36]

While the Consul-General shunned notoriety, "he appreciated the importance of focusing the attention of the Egyptian public upon the reality of British power," writes his authorized biographer, the Marquess of Zetland. "He drove through the streets of Cairo, an imposing and remarked upon figure, preceded, in accordance with the custom of those days, by running *syces* [grooms] with white wands and flying sleeves. He played tennis, when time allowed, for exercise and recreation; during the periodic crises through which the affairs of Egypt passed, he made time for a leisurely set—not for recreation, but for the purpose of demonstrating his unconcern. 'During the worst of the crisis,' he wrote in February 1893, 'I played lawn tennis every day. It gave confidence to the English and annoyed the French and others extremely—in fact I did it partly on purpose to annoy them.'"[37]

When calling on the Khedive, the Consul-General wore a gray frock coat and a proconsular white plumed hat. His carriage was flanked by the scarlet jackets of his cavalry escort—usually the 21st Lancers—for, as the then-U.S. Consul-General observed, "No picture of Cairo that does not include the soldier can be considered complete, for the military aspect is in almost aggressive evidence . . . By company and regiment, soldiers are so frequently marched through the streets that the visitor might believe Cairo to be a vast military camp."[38]

In fact, Cairo was more than that. It was justly called "Paris on the Nile" soon after Khedive Ismail replaced its medieval center with wide boulevards that echoed the bold redesign of Paris by Baron Georges-Eugène Haussmann between 1850 and 1870. In Cromer's time, Cairo became the most populous metropolis in Africa. Its 374,000 inhabitants included Muslims, Copts, Druzes, Jews, Greeks, and Armenians, as well as a large population of "Franks," as the Arabs called the Europeans, implying a degree of disdain. Unlike contemporary Baghdad and Damascus, Cairo with its healthful winter climate and its trove of accessible antiquities was an alluring destination for Britons. Thus the European community in Egypt swelled from 10,000 in 1838 to 90,000 in 1881. The influx was abetted by the Capitulations. (The system, loathed by Egyptians, endured until its complete abolition in 1937.)

For the average Western visitor, Cairo might seem an opera set with a city attached. Besides the emblematic pyramids, scores of minarets and mosques brocaded the skyline, and steps away from the European center was an Oriental city as picturesque as a David Robert lithograph. Or in Mark Twain's graphic account in *Innocents Abroad*: "stately camels and dromedaries, swarthy Egyptians, and likewise Turks and black Ethiopians, turbaned, sashed, and blazing in a rich variety of flashy colors, are what one sees on every hand crowding the narrow streets and honeycombed bazaars."[39] By contrast, the city's newer, foreign quarters were fashionably Gallic, abounding in mansard roofs designed by École des Beaux-Arts graduates during the bubble years of the Suez Canal Company. In 1869, Khedive Ismail celebrated the canal's opening by dedicating an opera house, commissioning Verdi's *Aida*, and hosting a regal fifth of the *Almanach de Gotha*, including the French Empress Eugénie, Emperor Franz Josef of Austria, and the Prince and Princess of Wales. The Galerie Commerciale, a passageway linking two modern streets, was lined with tiny shops displaying European luxuries. A visitor to the Ismailia quarter in 1908 remarked that there was nothing Egyptian to be seen "except it be a Sudanese porter seated on a bench outside a sumptuous mansion, half hidden by palms and tropical shrubs."[40]

French predominated as the lingua franca among Cairo's political, business, and press elite. Yet by the 1880s, three-fourths of the ships traversing Suez were British, nearly all of them headed to or from India. English slang was heard everywhere on the tennis courts at the Sporting Club, and more loudly among the officers crowding the celebrated Long Bar in Samuel Shep-heard's Hotel. As one nineteenth-century traveler, William Fullerton, wrote, "With the polo, the balls, the racing and the riding, Cairo begins to impress itself upon you as an English town in which any quantity of Oriental sights are kept for the aesthetic satisfaction of the inhabitants, much as the pro-prietor of a country place keeps a game preserve or deer park for his amuse-ment."[41] Even the donkeys and camels carrying tourists to the pyramids at Giza were named after British Derby winners or American presidents.

That Egypt was also the intellectual capital of the Muslim Middle East was hardly apparent to the visitors who arrived aboard Thomas Cook's steamships, and who normally traveled first class from Alexandria by rail, constructed by the legendary Robert Stephenson. The chasm between Cai-ro's disparate worlds was implicit in Evelyn Baring's table talk. Though fluent in French, Italian, and modern Greek, and enjoying a working knowl-edge of classical Greek and Latin, Cromer did not learn Arabic instead con-versing in basic Turkish with the local elite. Small wonder that for many Egyptians the European quarter was an alien cyst, inassimilable and humil-iating. Nor was it a surprise, when the Consul-General retired in 1907, that his welcome at home was notably more laudatory than the frosty departure ceremonies in Egypt. The European colony turned out in force for his fare-well address; only three unsmiling Egyptians were visible; the rest boycotted the event. As his devoted aide Ronald Storrs remarked of the departure of Lord Cromer ("the greatest foreign benefactor that any Oriental nation has known"), his carriage passed "through streets lined by armed troops with ball cartridge, amid a silence chillier than ice."[42]

The chill was attributable in part to indignation stirred by El Lord's increas-ingly autocratic manner during his final years, illustrated by his insistence on posting yet more British "advisers" with native ministers; his bullying of Abbas II, a Khedive more assertive than his pliant predecessor; and his neglect of education (which Alfred Milner shrugged off in a chapter titled "Odds and Ends"). More immediately, Cromer's departure was clouded by the "Dinshawai Affair," which developed a year before his retirement. For-gotten abroad, its details remain familiar to every Egyptian schoolboy. Four villagers were hanged, and eight severely flogged, for taking part in a scuffle with five British officers who were engaged in a pigeon and quail shoot, their

leader memorably named Major Pine-Coffin. Unfortunately, a British officer died in disputed and murky circumstances, but indisputably the hunt-
ers should have been aware that breeding pigeons was a popular pastime in
Dinshawai, a tiny Delta village. The death sentences were pronounced by a
special tribunal consisting of two Britons and two Egyptians, under the presidency of a Coptic notable, Boutros Ghali (who was later assassinated by an
irate nationalist, and whose descendant would become Secretary-General
of the United Nations). With an assist from the pen of Wilfrid Scawen Blunt
(Dinshawai was no "exceptional error of judgment but part of a system
which [flouted] every principle of civilised law"), the affair became the talk
of political Britain, inspiring angry questions in the House of Commons.[43]
That the executions mocked Cromer's assertion of Britain's civilizing mission was vociferously argued by his critics. In a squib titled "The Denshawai Horror," Bernard Shaw asked his readers to imagine the reaction in an
English village "if a party of Chinese officers appeared and began shooting
the ducks, the geese, the hens and the turkeys and carried them off, asserting that they were wild birds as everybody in China knew, and that the pretended indignation of the farmers was a cloak for hatred of the Chinese,
and perhaps but a plot to overthrow the religion of Confucius and establish
the Church of England in its place."[44]

Stung by raillery, a defensive Earl of Cromer sought to explain imperial
rule and its heavy burdens to his unthinking critics. The title of his 1908
article in *The Edinburgh Review* telescoped his theme: "The Government of
Subject Races." Less prejudicially, in a prescient passage from an address
published in 1910 as *Ancient and Modern Imperialism*, he acknowledged an
abiding paradox. The Englishman as imperialist, he observed, "is always
striving to attain two ideals which are apt to be mutually destructive—the
ideal of good government, which connotes the continuance of his supremacy, and the ideal of self-government, which connotes the whole or partial
abdication of his supreme position."[45]

Could these goals be reconciled? Would "subject races" like the Egyptians ever acquire the vocation of self-government? By their very nature, he
feared, they were incapable of rational thought. As amplified in his monumental *Modern Egypt*, their want of accuracy easily degenerated into deception, a telltale characteristic of the Oriental mind: "The European is a close
reasoner; his statements of fact are devoid of any ambiguity; he is a natural
logician, albeit he may not have studied logic; he is by nature skeptical and

requires proof before he can accept the truth of any proposition; his trained intelligence works like a piece of mechanism. The mind of the Oriental, on the other hand, like his picturesque streets, is eminently wanting in symmetry. His reasoning is of the most slipshod description . . . Endeavor to elicit a plain statement of facts from any ordinary Egyptian, and his explanation will generally be lengthy, and wanting in lucidity. He will probably contradict himself a half-dozen times before he has finished his story."[46]

Yet paradoxically, while Cromer voiced grave doubts concerning the ordinary Egyptian's intellectual capacity, it cannot be said he exerted himself to improve Egyptian schools. As Peter Mansfield points out in *The British in Egypt* (1973), during his first decade as Consul-General, the education budget was lower than it had been under Khedive Ismail: "In all Cromer's years in Egypt, the amount spent on education did not exceed one percent of gross revenues." Nevertheless, following his retirement Cromer complained that "[t]he mass of the Egyptian population is still sunk in the deepest ignorance, and this ignorance must necessarily continue until a new generation has grown up."[47] Why then the downgrading of education? A credible explanation offered by his sympathetic biographer, Roger Owen, is that like other servants of the Raj, Cromer was convinced "that the education of more than a small Indian elite was leading to the production of a surplus of over-educated, unemployed agitators."[48]

In truth, whatever else Egypt lacked after Cromer, it was not impassioned agitators. The system El Lord personified embittered and estranged the very Egyptians closest to their British "advisers." As the post-Cromer decades proceeded, the question of Egypt's status became murkier. His immediate successor, Sir Eldon Gorst, sincerely wished to give Egyptians a greater say in their own affairs, a policy congenial to the Liberal Party, now back in power under Prime Minister Herbert Asquith. The problem, he found, was that given a morsel of power, Egyptian nationalists clamored for an entire meal, while those who cooperated with the British were castigated as turncoats. His consul-generalship reached its nadir in 1910 with the assassination of Boutros Ghali, whom Gorst had sponsored as Prime Minister. The assassin, Ibrahim al-Wardani, denounced the Coptic aristocrat as a traitor for agreeing in 1899 to share Egypt's sovereignty over the Sudan, for allegedly groveling to the Suez Canal Company, and for presiding at the unsavory Denshawai tribunal. Students swarmed Cairo streets crying, "*Wardani, Wardani, Illi 'atal as Nusran!*" (Wardani, Wardani, Slayer of the Nazarene).

The well-meaning Gorst's essential outlook was implicit in a single sentence in his memoirs in which he said of his own post, "Throughout the British Empire there is no place in which the occupant enjoys greater freedom of action than that of the British agent and consul-general of Egypt"—forgetting that Egypt was never part of the Empire.[49]

The anomaly of Egypt's status became a major embarrassment during World War I when Turkey—Cairo's official suzerain—allied itself with Germany and declared war on Britain. By this time, Gorst had been succeeded as Consul-General by Kitchener, who though shedding his uniform for a gray frock coat was nevertheless known to all as Field Marshal Kitchener, the first Earl of Khartoum. His three-year tenure was notable mostly for his regal authority, and for his dramatic exit in 1914 to become supreme commander of the British war effort. With his concurrence, Egypt ceased to be an Ottoman province and was designated a British protectorate. The Khedive became a Sultan, and the Consul-General was transmuted into a High Commissioner. Yet as the war evolved (following America's entry in 1917) into a campaign for democracy and self-determination, Egyptians not unreasonably assumed the pledge applied to them. It was not to be. Egyptian leaders who in 1919 tried repeatedly to communicate with Woodrow Wilson found, repeatedly, that their telegrams were blocked by official orders; nor were they allowed to present their grievances at the Paris Peace Conference, where the victors were dividing up the Middle East. Riots erupted in Cairo, martial law was imposed, and a harried British Government, led by the Liberal David Lloyd George, fell back on a time-tested device: a fact-finding mission. And who should head it? None other than Lord Alfred Milner, noted author of *England in Egypt* who, following his arduous service in the War Cabinet, was no longer an unqualified New Imperialist. He now expressed sympathy for Egyptian complaints as he and his colleagues traveled to Cairo and listened to nationalists, and the mission's final report confessed to uncomfortable truths: "We have never honestly faced the Egyptian problem, and our neglect to do so is in a measure responsible for the present situation. It appears to be frequently assumed in current talk and writing in this country that Egypt is part of the British Empire. This is not and never has been the case" (although the report also admitted that in practice Britain "controlled the internal and external affairs of Egypt").[50]

So what might be done? Milner and his associates proposed a new agreement recognizing Egypt as an independent monarchy, but including clauses that protected the imperial connection, the most important giving Britain the right to retain military bases and defend Egypt's territorial integrity—in short, Egypt was to be a semi-protectorate. This compromise was assailed by Egyptian nationalists as insufficient, and by British hardliners as a surrender (Lord Cromer, Milner's patron, did not take part in the debate, having died in 1917). Whatever its faults, the report prepared the way for a 1922 declaration affirming that Egypt was no longer a protectorate, but a sovereign state. The Sultan was to be called a King, and the British High Commissioner metamorphosed into an Ambassador. When King Fuad died in 1936, his young, more assertive heir, King Farouk, pressed successfully for a formal Anglo-Egyptian treaty to address persisting grievances. In a victory for Egypt, the treaty finally abolished the Capitulations. Yet as before, Britain reserved the unrestricted right to reoccupy Egypt, and to use its ports, airfields, and roads in the event of war. "If the 1922 declaration gave Egypt semi-independence, the 1936 treaty went half the rest of the way" in the nuanced judgment of Peter Mansfield in *The British in Egypt*.[51] This moiety of a moiety sufficed to make Egypt a veiled ally during World War II.

Like Alexander and Caesar, or like Napoleon and Nelson, both Churchill and Hitler understood that dominion of Egypt was critical to mastery of the nearby Sinai and its approaches to Asia and to inner Africa as well. They knew that Egypt's shadows reached from Suez to the sands of Libya, from the Red Sea to the Nile Delta, from Alexandria to Khartoum. Although Egypt was ostensibly neutral during the Second World War (at least until 1945, when it declared war in order formally to join the victorious United Nations), its possession was a prize of prizes. Egypt's centrality has been vividly evoked by Jan Morris, who in the 1950s as James Morris was *The Times*'s Cairo correspondent, quartered in a Nile houseboat known for decades thereafter to every dragoman. Cairo, Morris writes in *Farewell the Trumpets* (1978), was for the British in the 1940s the military capital of the British Empire, "the last assembly-point of the imperial power, the last place where, in a setting properly exotic, the imperial legions mingled in their staggering variety. Every kind of imperial uniform was to be spotted in Cairo during the first years of the war. There were kilts and turbans and tarbooshes, slouch hats and jodhpurs. There were Kenyan pioneers and Indian muleteers, and Australian tank crews, and English gunners, and New Zealand fighter pilots and South African engineers . . . Cairo had been a pseudo-imperial city for sixty years, and although since 1936 Egypt had been nominally independent, and was officially neutral in the war, the whole capital was now, in effect a British military base."[52] In wartime Cairo, this doggerel sounded in bars and barracks:

> *We never went west of Gezira,*
> *We never went North of the Nile,*
> *We never went past the Pyramids*
> *Out of sight of the Sphinx's smile,*
> *We fought the war in Shepheard's and the Continental bar,*
> *We reserved our punch for the Turf Club lunch*
> *And they gave us the Africa Star.*[53]

Such was the *mise en scène* in 1941 when Sir Miles Lampson, the British Ambassador, had to deal with an act of spirited rebellion by King Farouk, whom the envoy habitually referred to as "that boy" (he was twenty-two). Farouk declined to appoint a new Egyptian ministry that Lampson had proposed. Backed by an impatient Prime Minister Churchill, then desperate for a victory in North Africa, Lampson then gave the King a choice between abdication or submission. By chance, Walter Monckton, the lawyer who had drafted the abdication instrument for Edward VIII, happened to be in Cairo. Lampson prevailed on Monckton to compose a similar instrument, duly transcribed on embassy stationery from which the lettered heading had been visibly snipped.

Paper in hand, Lampson arrived in his outsize Rolls-Royce at the King's palace accompanied by his uniformed retinue, to be kept waiting by Farouk for five minutes, the king's customary display of independence. It was a memorable moment for Lampson, a mountain of a man, six foot five inches tall, built like a wrestler, indefatigable as a hunter, dancer, rider, even aviator. He lived in the same residence as Lord Cromer and other puissant predecessors, and now Sir Miles was about to display his authority in its most ungloved form. ("It doesn't often come one's way," he wrote in his diary, "to be pushing a monarch off his Throne.")[54] Lampson began by reading an indictment accusing the King of assisting the Nazis (who at this moment seemed to be winning), and in any case through his wanton and reckless behavior being "no longer fit to occupy the Throne."[55] Then, with the chug of arriving armored cars audible in the palace yard, he handed Farouk the abdication instrument, which read, "We, King Farouk of Egypt, mindful as ever of the interests of our country, hereby renounce and abandon for ourselves and the heirs of our body the throne of the Kingdom of Egypt and all Sovereign rights, privileges and powers over the said Kingdom and the subjects thereof, and we release our said subjects from the allegiance to our person."[56]

After complaining about the untidiness of the document, Farouk raised his pen to sign it. He paused, visibly shaken, and asked if he might have one more chance. Thus the drama ended, with the King having saved his throne by approving a British-nominated ministry, thus forfeiting permanently the respect of his people. After passing through the tanks and soldiers armed with tommy guns, an exultant Lampson returned to his embassy. "So much," he reported to London, "for the events of the evening, which I confess I could not have enjoyed more." "I congratulate you warmly," replied Foreign Secretary Anthony Eden. "Result justifies your firmness and our confidence."[57] For his part, Farouk dwindled into a playboy remembered for his girth, for his collection of pornography, and for remarking that in time only five kings would survive, those of hearts, diamonds, clubs, spades, and Great Britain. The reckoning came in 1952, when Farouk was deposed in a colonels' revolt led by officers to whom his spineless surrender a decade earlier persisted as a shaming memory.

TWO

The Empire's Power Couple

*Frederick John Dealtry Lord Lugard of Abinger (1858–1945),
PC, GCMG, CB, DSO, and Flora Louise Shaw, Lady Lugard, DBE (1852–1929)*

⌗

Burke said there were Three Estates in Parliament; but in the Reporters'
Gallery yonder, there sat a Fourth Estate more important far than they
all. It is not a figure of speech, or a witty saying; it is a literal fact—
very momentous to us in these times.

–Thomas Carlyle, from his lecture
"The Hero as a Man of Letters," May 19, 1840

A nd in the beginning of the Victorian era, there was the written word, and it flowed mightily in the United Kingdom, from the tip of Cornwall to the isles of Scotland. This is not a figure of speech or a witty saying but a literal truth. No people have excelled the British in their devotion to newsprint. A succession of events—repeal of the Stamp Act (derided as a "tax on knowledge"), the advent of telegraphy and railroads, the invention of the rotary press, and most of all near-universal literacy proved a godsend to Victorian scribblers and their employers. The devotion has persisted. A century after Carlyle's lecture, surveys showed that 90 percent of the adult British population regularly read at least one national paper—an appetite twice that of the Americans and three times that of the French. Writing in 1957, when thirty million newspapers piled on newsstands or doorsteps every workday (and another few million on Sunday), the Fleet Street veteran Francis Williams was able to claim, "No other product of modern civilisation has achieved so complete a saturation of its potential market."[1]

The unparalleled expansion of the Victorian Empire hinged critically on Britain's precocious information revolution. *The Times* set the pace. In 1837, to speed news from the Continent, it organized a pigeon post from Paris to an awaiting ship at Boulogne (the birds needed four hours, compared with a courier's fourteen). At that time it took nearly four months to obtain reports from Calcutta, the capital of the Raj, a schedule *The Times* was able to shrink to seven weeks by using an overland shortcut from Suez to Sinai. Enter telegraphy, a development as momentous for the Fourth Estate as Johannes Gutenberg's movable type. In 1844, *The Times* astonished its readers by reporting within four hours the birth at Windsor of Victoria's second son, using the new signal system on the Great Western Railway. In 1851, the year of the Great Exhibition, an underwater cable traversed the English Channel, and thereafter telegraphic tendrils threaded steadily overland to Russia and India, under the seas to Singapore, China, and Japan, across the Atlantic to North and South America, and finally to the very heart of Africa. The Empire's wired congregation attained its ritual consecration on June 22, 1897, Victoria's Diamond Jubilee. Seated in the telegraph room of Buckingham Palace, the Queen in a matter of seconds transmitted her message to every corner of her vast realm: "From my heart I thank my people. May God bless them." *The Times* hailed what it called a pan-Britannic festival. "History may be searched," marveled its leading article, "and searched in vain, to discover so wonderful an exhibition of allegiance and brotherhood amongst so many myriads of men."[2]

Yet *The Times*'s influence owed little to technology or catchy graphics. It eschewed flashy headlines; indeed in the 1930s its subeditors held a dullest-headline competition (the winner: "Small Earthquake in Chile; Not Many Dead"). Until the 1960s, its front page consisted of the detritus of daily life— birth, marriage, and death notices; coded and gnomic personal messages; and classifieds. What *The Times* offered in abundance was Authority, or its simulacrum. Its news and judgments were unsigned, and seemed to emanate from somewhere in the sky. Its correspondents were treated abroad as quasi-royal and were given privileged access to the governing elite. By cultivating well-placed sources, Henri Georges Stefan Adolphe Opper de Blowitz, the paper's Paris correspondent for twenty-eight years, penetrated a wall of secrecy at the 1878 Congress of Berlin. There the Great Powers assembled to discuss in confidence the vexatious and immemorial Eastern Question, yet Blowitz reported daily on what happened behind closed doors, crowning his feat by cabling the unpublished final text of the Berlin Treaty, a *Times* exclusive (Blowitz later claimed he and an unnamed insider swapped top hats at a fashionable restaurant; tucked within his informant's were the daily tidings). In the early months of the Civil War, Abraham Lincoln welcomed the legendary war correspondent William Howard Russell by calling *The Times* "one of the greatest powers of the world." In fact, he added, laying it on a bit heavily, "I don't know of anything that has more power, except perhaps the Mississippi."[3]

Hence our interest in the unjustly forgotten Flora Shaw, who as *The Times*'s Colonial Editor and Our Own Correspondent covering Africa from Cairo to the Cape figuratively and literally left her mark on the British Empire. During her hegiras she impressed and befriended Lord Cromer, Viscount Milner, Cecil Rhodes, George Goldie, and Lord Lugard, the Proconsul whom she later married. When Lord Curzon heard of her engagement to Lugard, he jotted a congratulatory note to him asking, "Not *the* Miss Shaw?" adding, "If she be another may she be equally brilliant and not less charming."[4] She was indeed *the* Miss Shaw, said to be the brightest woman in the British Empire, who rose higher in the Fourth Estate than any female contemporary. She was the first to put in print the name "Nigeria," where her husband would become that country's founding High Commissioner. Her book, *A Tropical Dependency*, marked the initial attempt in Britain to record African history before the arrival of Europeans. Although written by a Dame of the British Empire (an honor bestowed for her refugee work during the First World War) and despite her palpable paternalism, her history inspired future liberators like Nnamdi Azikiwe, the first president of Nigeria, and Kwame Nkrumah, the first president of Ghana.

Still, the signature event in Miss Shaw's career was her pivotal involvement in the notorious 1895 invasion of the Transvaal led by the buccaneering Leander Starr Jameson, known to history as the "Jameson Raid." For all its Mount Sinai air, *The Times* could barter its favors for the mundane promise of a world exclusive at the expense of hated rivals. Colonial Editor Shaw admired, and was admired by, Joseph Chamberlain, the dynamic Colonial Secretary. She and *The Times* unquestionably became accessories to a covert scheme promoted tacitly or actively by Chamberlain to force a regime change in the Boer Republic of Transvaal. The scheme failed ignobly, and Britain's official cover story was implausibly flimsy, anticipating the more calamitous Suez debacle in 1956. However, *the* Miss Shaw acquitted herself with greater honor than her superiors. It was her lot in life, indeed, to fashion suitable pedestals for imperial busts. And as Gladstone foresaw in the 1880s, Britain's southward thrust in Africa was the inescapable and logical extension of imperial entanglement in Egypt and India; securing the passage eastward required a British presence from Cape to Cairo.

Born into the Victorian world in 1852, Flora Shaw reached her journalistic apogee during the Queen's final decade, which witnessed the rapid expansion of the Empire; her influence persisted into the Edwardian era when she became Lady Lugard. She died in 1929, during England's second Georgian age, which marked the onset of the imperial recessional that Kipling foresaw. In India, Mahatma Gandhi, once a stretcher-bearer in the Boer War (which the Raid helped provoke), began mobilizing a campaign for complete independence. In Ireland, where Shaw's paternal grandfather maintained an estate outside Dublin, a nationalist uprising forced the British to accept the island's division into a Free State in the South, which was predominantly Roman Catholic, and a stubbornly Protestant enclave in the North. All this came as no surprise to a perceptive journalist who had traveled through-out the Empire, sending home reports for the major papers of the day from Egypt, Morocco, South Africa, Australia, Canada, California, the Klondike, and West Africa. Shaw was decidedly more influential than the famous Vic-torian "lady travelers"—Mary Kingsley, Isabella Bird, Jane Digby—favored by biographers, but perhaps because she always traveled on business and not for the sake of adventure, she is rarely included in their company. Yet during her peak years as a journalist, she elicited the age's surest sign of frenzied renown: she was caricatured in *Punch*.

Her family was upper-middle class. Her grandfather, Sir Frederick Shaw, was a member of Parliament representing the Anglo-Irish Protestant gentry and a leading Conservative under Sir Robert Peel. Her father, George Shaw, retired from the Royal Military College at Woolwich as a major general. Her forebears on her mother's side were Catholic and French. After bear-ing fourteen children, her mother, Marie, became ill, and Flora would nurse her until her death. Shaw herself was self-educated, an insatiable reader in the Woolwich library. To illustrate the power of books on her youthful mind, she recalled climbing an apple tree with a new book, Carlyle's *French Revo-lution*: "I went up the tree a Royalist and a Tory," and she added, "I came down the tree a passionate Democrat."[5]

Despite a fine profile, dark auburn hair, crystal blue eyes, and a slim fig-ure, Shaw was unmarried for forty-nine years, a state that in mid-Victorian England could have relegated her to a life as a governess or companion had it not been for her remarkable mentors, among them John Ruskin and George Meredith. She met Ruskin in 1869, at the crest of his fame, when he lectured at Woolwich, shortly before his epochal Oxford inaugural lecture, as Slade Professor of Art, which he delivered on February 8, 1870. In this address, which galvanized a generation, Ruskin summoned the youth of England to "make your country again a royal throne of kings, a sceptred isle, for all the world a source of light, a centre for peace; mistress of Learning and of the Arts ... This is what England must do or perish. She must found Colonies as fast and as far as she is able, formed of her most energetic and worthiest men; seizing every piece she can get her foot on and teaching these her colonists that their chief virtue is to be fidelity to their country, and that their first aim is to be to advance the power of England by land and sea."[6]

Ruskin had an eye for comely minors, and the seventeen-year-old Flora Shaw was no exception. He encouraged her earliest attempts at writing—three successful children's books, which were followed by a novel written for grownups, *Colonel Cheswick's Campaign*. Her writings had already gained her financial independence when George Meredith introduced her to W. T. Stead as "the finest flower of modern womanhood" with "the reasoning capacity of a man."[7] Stead, editor of *The Pall Mall Gazette* (whom we have already met in the General Gordon affair) was the son of a Congregationalist minister—W. T. would go down on the *Titanic* calmly reading his Bible in the first-class smoking lounge. The *Gazette*, with its illustrations, banner headlines, and readable style, furthered Stead's crusades to promote "the Imperialism of responsibility as opposed to Jingoism."[8]

Stead's competitive enthusiasm for a scoop was coupled with his intense loyalty to his protégés, among them the imperial apologist, Alfred Milner, the future High Commissioner for South Africa, and Flora Shaw. By the 1880s, the celebrated feats of the globe-circling American reporter Nellie Bly had begun to open the way for women in journalism, although many males still greeted their few female colleagues with derision. Stead was an exception. Writing in the magazine *Young Woman*, Stead sternly declared that any woman who comes into journalism and expects indulgence because of her sex sullies "the reputation and worth of women in journalism." A female reporter, he said, must become quickly accustomed to foul language, scathing editorial scoldings, demeaning assignments, and unchaperoned nights. "You have a right to ask that your sex should not be regarded as a disqualification," he opined, "but it is monstrous to erect that accident of your personality into a right to have opportunities denied to your brother."[9]

Flora Shaw seized the challenge. Wintering in Gibraltar in 1886–87 with family friends, the Younghusbands, she interviewed Zubair Pasha, the notorious slaver and former Sudanese Provincial Governor, whom General Gordon had first persecuted and then forgave. The British had recently deported him to Gibraltar after a Cairo police pickpocket found "incriminating letters" between the Pasha and the Mahdi and his followers.[10] Making her way to his "isolated cottage" over a period of weeks, Flora questioned

Zubair, who was suffering from a toothache, on the subject of slavery. "A Lady's Interview with the Captive Chief" appeared in *The Pall Mall Gazette* on June 28, 1887. Pressed with her direct questions, the Pasha denied ever being a slave trader. After publication, Zubair sailed back to Cairo and credited Shaw with his release. The page-one story in the *Gazette* established her reputation.

While in Egypt during the winter of 1888–89, Flora Shaw left her card with Sir Evelyn Baring, who fluently expounded the social benefits of imperialism. The Consul-General also briefed her for what became her debut in *The Times*, an article explaining Egyptian financial reform. (The paper's proprietor, Arthur Walter, exclaimed on reading her article, "[W]hoever wrote it [is] the sort of fellow we ought to get on *The Times*.")[11] When in 1890 she was duly hired by Moberly Bell, whom she had met in Egypt when he was Special Correspondent of *The Times*, Baring sent him this note: "I believe Miss Shaw is on your staff now. She would do well, probably better than any man—but I don't know if this would suit you."[12] Bell, who now presided as assistant manager in Printing House Square, the paper's London citadel, concurred with Baring. "If you were a man," he remarked on asking her to write a fortnightly column as a freelancer, "you would be Colonial Editor of *The Times* tomorrow."

Flora eschewed the usual female ghettos—the society column and arts reviews—her purview would be foreign affairs and the intricacies of international finance. The flamboyant Stead had thought her writing too severe: "Flora did not want to bring a lump to the throat."[13] More importantly, her expansionist stance was in line with the imperialist thrust of *The Times*, and she became a fixture at the Colonial Office. Writing years later to her husband, Shaw summed up her role as wandering "in the company of lions: I never thought of my work exactly as journalism, but rather as active politics without the fame. And that pleased me. Fame somehow doesn't interest me. I have never cared for it. I daresay that is only the bent of a woman's mind. We are brought up that way—rather to shun than to court public notice."[14]

To ensure that she would be taken seriously, she always wore black (until her retirement and marriage, when she abruptly switched to white). The fact that Shaw's writings were signed "By Our Correspondent" concealed her gender. Margery Perham, the biographer of Flora's husband, Lord Lugard, wrote, "[S]he never played the woman as a short cut to her professional objectives. Even so, her beauty, and especially the warm temperament that found its outlet in her expressive eyes and shone through the reserve and dignity of her manner, seemed to add a glow even to her purely intellectual activities. Public men, however cautious, found it surprisingly easy to give away official information to such an interviewer."[15] Her contemporary, the author and explorer Mary Kingsley, less charitably remarked that her rival was "a fine, handsome, bright, upstanding young woman, as clever as they make them, capable of any immense amount of work, as hard as nails and talking like a Times leader all the time. She is imbued with the modern form of public imperialism. It is her religion."[16]

The great British editors of Flora Shaw's era—Stead, Bell, and *The Manchester Guardian*'s C. P. Scott—tolerated a more generous mix of fact and opinion than is generally common in news reports today. Although its circulation in the 1890s only averaged around thirty-five thousand, *The Times*'s influence was pervasive. In the era of New Imperialism, in its dispatches as well as commentary, it championed expansion, especially in Africa, entente with France, the maintenance of British naval supremacy, closer relations with Russia, and containment of Germany. Tellingly, Kaiser Wilhelm II believed Moberly Bell to be his most dangerous British adversary.

Shaw urged Bell to cover the colonies and together they guided the paper in a less parochial direction. During her tenure in the 1890s, *The Times* became *the* house organ of New Imperialism. Her "Letters from South Africa," later published as a book, resulted in her becoming a full-time member of its staff traveling to Australia and North America. In 1892, Shaw embarked on her maiden voyage to southern Africa. Her first stop en route was the Cape Colony, founded by the Dutch East India Company in 1652. The peace treaty in 1815 that concluded the Napoleonic wars awarded the colony to Britain, and within decades there was a Parliament and a Prime Minister. In 1892, the office was held by diamond and gold entrepreneur Cecil Rhodes, who invited the journalist to the opening of Parliament. Soon she became a welcome visitor to Government House. "The absolute reliance of everyone on Mr. Rhodes is wonderful," she wrote.[17]

Traveling to Kimberley by train, Shaw toured De Beers' deep-level diamond mine with a candle in hand and judged it "a monastery of labour." She found Johannesburg, the commercial capital of the Boer Republic of

Transvaal "hideous and detestable, luxury without order; sensual enjoyment without art; riches without refinement; display without dignity." It
was a town with "no politics, much too busy with material problems."[18]
She wrote that the Republic "teems with wealth. Gold, silver, copper, coal,
iron lie in the ground on every side, and in order to get them out railways
must be built, waterworks constructed, timber planted, roads made."[19] She
interviewed Transvaal's President Paul Kruger in his residence in Pretoria
at 6:30 a.m. (He evidently assumed she was a man in disguise.) Summing
up her visit she wrote that in South Africa, "the steam engine has become a
more effective instrument of empire than the cannon."[20]

Indeed the competition for railway lines was to that time what the
scramble for air routes became decades later. Rhodes dreamed of a Cape-
to-Cairo railroad as a "Red Line" north to south through the continent (red
being the map color for Britain's possessions). Natural and political obstacles thwarted this scheme. In the same spirit, Kaiser Wilhelm II promoted a
Berlin-to-Baghdad line, also never completed, and Russia spent millions on
laying rails through the steppes and Siberia. And before World War I, Europeans had partitioned rail routes in the Ottoman Empire on lines that presaged the postwar creation of new Middle Eastern states.

In 1893, Shaw became the Colonial Editor of *The Times* with an annual
salary of £800, more than any other female journalist, and with the title
came the power to appoint all colonial correspondents. Two years later, she
was ensnared in an imperial misadventure, the Jameson Raid, that Winston
Churchill believed, writing years later, marked the beginning "of these violent times" that culminated in the Great War.

Unanswered questions still remain about the Jameson Raid, the abortive sor-
tie by an assortment of freebooters bankrolled by Rhodes, intended to overthrow the government of the Transvaal Republic. Yet it is now possible, by
drawing on diverse sources, to put jagged pieces together, revealing a coherent design. The episode is replete with the stuff of drama—fateful decisions
based on faulty intelligence, celebrated conspirators at the highest level, willing scapegoats, blackmailing lawyers, and finally a dramatic parliamentary
inquiry that imperiled careers and ruined reputations. As Margery Perham,
an old African hand and an admirer of Flora Shaw's, phrased it, "[T]he Raid
was a military fiasco but a political earthquake." Central to the debacle were

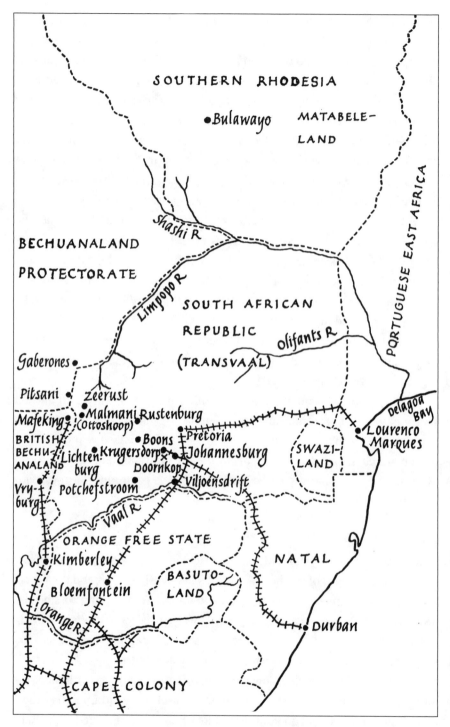

The Transvaal and its neighbors at the time of the Jameson Raid (1895)

Miss Shaw, Moberly Bell, and *The Times*'s South Africa correspondent, Francis Younghusband, a nephew of Shaw's past traveling companions.

The raid had as its prelude the subjugation of the African kingdoms in what became Rhodesia (today's Zimbabwe). Armed with a private militia authorized by a Royal Charter, supplied with Maxim machine guns, and led by Jameson, Rhodes's British South Africa Company seized the fertile highlands of Mashonaland and Matabeleland with what the biographers of Rhodes called "a rush of cynicism and conspiracy."[21] Jameson stayed on as Rhodes's envoy in Salisbury, the new capital whose name honored Victoria's incumbent Prime Minister. Having demonstrated what a mercenary force could accomplish in southern Africa, it seemed plausible that Jameson's men might reach for a still greater prize by changing regimes in the mineral-rich Transvaal.

The basic facts can be succinctly stated. After gold was discovered on the Witwatersrand, a ridge of land near Johannesburg, in 1886, thousands of mainly British and often rowdy foreigners, the Uitlanders (Afrikaans for foreigners), flooded into the Transvaal. Once settled in shantytowns, the Uitlanders chafed under the rule of the Boer government headed by President Kruger in Pretoria. By 1895, it was believed (or hoped by Rhodes and his supporters) that the foreigners, mobilized by a group known as the Reform Movement, were on the verge of rebellion. The putative spark was expected to be a Boer refusal to grant Uitlanders citizenship and voting rights.

The plan, prepared in Cape Town, financed by Rhodes, and encouraged (it now appears certain) by Colonial Secretary Joseph Chamberlain, was to oust the Boer government and establish a regime more congenial to foreigners, mine owners, and Britain. Upon news of an Uitlander uprising, Jameson—stationed at Pitsani, in neighboring Bechuanaland—was to lead his troopers into the Transvaal, while the Uitlanders seized the Pretoria arsenal. The British High Commissioner in South Africa, Sir Hercules Robinson, would then restore order and negotiate a settlement in Pretoria favorable to Rhodes and the British.

December 1895. Dr. Jameson, a slight, pixyish man with enormous brown eyes, is waiting impatiently in his white tent on a kopje overlooking the magnificent open veldt in Pitsani, three miles from the Transvaal. On Sunday, December 29, the bugle sounds, and 400 troopers sporting "smasher hats" give three cheers for the Queen and charge forward, led by "Dr. Jim," fawn-coated and mounted on a black stallion. Three miles into the Transvaal they are joined by another 120 members of the Bechuanaland Police. The men in charge of the horses (whose rumps are branded with "C.C." for Rhodes's Chartered Company) bring the number of raiders to around 600 men—far short of the 7,500 men Jameson had anticipated. But the raiders failed to cut all the telegraph lines, and news of the incursion has already reached Pretoria. Two Boer messengers appear. Jameson is ordered by the British High Commissioner to turn back. He refuses.

In addition to rifles, the raiders are armed with a twelve-pounder field piece and six Maxim machine guns. Jameson's men include veterans of the Chartered Company's recent wars in Rhodesia, where they fought Africans armed with spears. They assume their skirmish with Boer farmers will be a cakewalk. "I shall get through as easily as a knife cuts butter," Jameson boasts. To doubters, he adds, "You people do not know what the Maxim gun means. I have seen it at work."[22] But hubris mixed with alcohol—brandy for the men, champagne for the officers—will prove toxic. After four days of marching over unfamiliar terrain, under harassing fire by Boer guerrillas, the raiders are totally surrounded at Doornkop, two hours' ride from the mines of Johannesburg. Expert Boer marksmen using only old rifles and elephant guns rake the raiders from high ground. Jameson's Maxims jam, and after a short skirmish, the conspirators hoist a borrowed white apron of surrender. Sixty-five men have been killed or wounded. "Old Jameson has upset my applecart," Rhodes disingenuously lamented when he realized that the raid had been premature. "Twenty years we have been friends, and now he goes in and ruins me."[23]

The fervent anti-imperialist Wilfrid Scawen Blunt noted in his diary for January 5, "There is excellent news. Those blackguards of the Chartered Company in South Africa, under Doctor Jameson, have made a filibustering raid on the Transvaal and have been annihilated by the Boers, Jameson a prisoner. I devoutly hope he may be hanged."[24]

Kaiser Wilhelm sent a telegram congratulating President Kruger, who for his part famously remarked, "When I want to kill a tortoise, I wait until he sticks his head out."[25] On hearing that the Boer leader might visit London, Lord Salisbury, the Prime Minister, remarked that he hoped he would drown in turtle soup. *The Times* commissioned a multistanzaed ballad, "Jameson's Raid," from the new Poet Laureate, Alfred Austin. Deemed "spirited doggerel" by Blunt,[26] its most famous stanzas run:

Wrong! Is it wrong? Well, may be;
But I'm going just the same,
Do they think me a Burgher's baby,
To be scared by a scolding name?
They may argue and prate and order;
Go tell them to save their breath;
Then over the Transvaal border,
And gallop for life or death!

Let lawyers and statesmen addle
Their pates over points of law;
If sound be our sword, and saddle,
And gun-gear, who cares one straw?
When men of our own blood pray us
To ride to their kinfolk's aid,
Not Heaven itself shall stay us,
From the rescue they call the raid.

The humor magazine *Punch* struck back with the "The Laureate's First Ride":

Song, is it song? Well—blow it!
But I'll sing it, boys, all the same
Because I'm the Laureate Poet,
That's the worst of having a name![27]

After rounding up the raiders, the Boers shrewdly turn them over to the British for trial. Though no one from the Johannesburg Reform Committee, whose relief force was supposed to meet Jameson, appears, a judge in Cape Town convicts the raid's four leaders, including Rhodes's older brother, Frank, of treason. Their death sentences are commuted when Cecil Rhodes and his supporters pay hefty fines. After returning to England, Jameson and five raiders are tried "at bar," a procedure reserved for important cases. Dr. Jim receives a fifteen-month prison term but his health deteriorates and he is freed after only four months. Returning to Africa, despite his woeful record as an administrator in Salisbury, he becomes Prime Minister of the Cape Colony in 1904, a Privy Councilor in 1907, a baronet in 1911, and president of Rhodes's British South Africa Company in 1913. Four years later, he was buried next to Rhodes (d. 1902) in the Matobo Hills of Rhodesia, now Zimbabwe.

In January, Rhodes is forced to resign as Prime Minister of the Cape Colony, and he rushes to England to save BSAC's charter. Chamberlain agrees to let Rhodes keep his charter provided the "missing telegrams" that would reveal the Colonial Secretary's complicity in the raid are never produced. Unfortunately for the conspirators, the Boers had captured a black tin box hidden among champagne bottles containing incriminating telegrams between Rhodes and the Johannesburg committee, a letter purporting to be a plea for help from Johannesburgers, along with a diary and a codebook. In April, the Boers began publishing their cache. A hearing by a select committee of Parliament convened to determine who knew what, and when they knew it. But the inquiry failed to uncover the real roles of Rhodes, Colonial Secretary Chamberlain, and their go-between, Flora Shaw.

A fellow imperialist, Alfred Milner, once shrewdly surmised, "Men are ruled by their foibles and Rhodes's foible is size."[28] A large man with a massive head and classical features, Rhodes was endowed with a prodigious appetite for food, drink, and tobacco. He disdained conventional dark suits, maintaining he could "legislate as well in Oxford tweeds." A self-made man who fulfilled his dream of attending Oxford (his career there was undistinguished, although at the end of his life he was granted an honorary doctorate), Rhodes imbibed the expansionist creed espoused by the Slade Professor of Fine Art at Oxford, John Ruskin. Rhodes was possessed of a "big idea," versions of which exist in his "Confession of Faith," written in 1877 while he was at Oxford, and the eight successive wills he drafted: a "United States of Africa" under the Union Jack, stitched together by his railroad, which would run the length of Africa, from Cape to Cairo. "Africa is still lying ready for us," he writes. "It is our duty to take it. It is our duty to seize every opportunity of acquiring more territory and we should keep this one idea steadily before our eyes that more territory simply means more of the Anglo-Saxon race more of the best the most human, most honourable race the world possesses."[29] He further espoused a reunion with the United States, "making the Anglo-Saxon race but one Empire." This would mean "the end of all wars," for Rhodes believed that the British were "the finest race in the world" and the more of the world they inhabited "the better it is for the human race."[30] Rhodes proposed the formation of a secret society, which sounded like a latter-day CIA recruitment operation, that was to have "members placed at our universities and our schools [to] watch the English youth passing through their hands."[31] A band of brothers, dedicated millionaires who could unite all English-speaking peoples, would enforce world peace by "gradually absorbing the wealth of the world."[32] The Rhodes Scholarships to Oxford, initially awarded to the white sons of Britain's Empire and the "Anglo-Saxon" Americans and Germans, were the tangible outcome of these ideas.

Preparing for the raid, Rhodes informed a delegation of Uitlanders from Johannesburg that after ending Boer abuses, his goal was free trade with the other African states, leading to a customs union, an amalgamation of railroads, and finally a South African federation.[33] Rhodes assigned bargain shares of his companies to politicians and salted his boards with dukes and marquesses. One noteworthy appointment to the board of De Beers (the diamond-mining cartel Rhodes founded) was Sir Hercules Robinson, a shareholder in Rhodes's Chartered Company. Robinson's reappointment as Governor of the Cape Colony and as its High Commissioner (he had held these offices from 1881 to 1889) considerably strengthened Rhodes's hand. Faced with growing criticism of the displacement of indigenous Africans from areas he wished to control, Rhodes also became adept at massaging the press.

The collusion between Rhodes and the press—Stead, Bell, and most importantly, Flora Shaw—began in 1889 when he visited London to gain support for a government charter for his British South Africa Company. This was the enterprise that would amalgamate mineral as well as land rights in Matabeleland, the future Rhodesia. Yet Rhodes failed to find the anticipated gold in Matabeleland, and the costs of deep mines on the Witwatersrand were rising steadily, owing partly to higher taxes. If he were to maximize profit from his gold mines, Rhodes felt he must strike soon against the Transvaal Republic. A trust deed was in negotiation that would give his British South Africa Company virtually unlimited power to acquire, through conquest or by grant, control over much of central and southern Africa. Rhodes could then build railroads, levy taxes, coin money, fly his own flag (the Union Jack with a lion poised in the middle and the letters *BSAC*), and recruit his own police force. Rhodes defined his brand of robust imperialism as "philanthropy plus five per cent." As Whitehall's aim was to prevent the

Boers, Germans, French, Belgians, and Portuguese from claiming further territory in Africa, a royal chartered company offered the prospect of a bigger empire on the cheap—it would be Rhodes and his backers, not British taxpayers, who would pay.

Visiting the offices of *The Pall Mall Gazette*, the "Colossus" met Stead and his then colleague, Flora Shaw. After a three-hour encounter, Stead wrote excitedly to his wife: "Mr. Rhodes is my man!" Rhodes was full of "gorgeous" ideas of "federation, expansion and consolidation of Empire." To sweeten the arrangement, Rhodes gave Stead £2,000 to settle a libel judgment and promised an additional £20,000 immediately with the expectation of more later to promote their mutual ideas through the *Gazette* and other publications.[34]

Shaw was no less captivated. Rhodes was "a man of evident power," "self contained and practical." When she asked him why he was willing to spend such enormous sums on an imperial project whose returns were at best in the future, he replied, "Some men collect butterflies. I do this. It interests me."[35] They continued to meet through the summer, and despite his habit of walking "like a caged lion all the time through two rooms, answering my questions at times from the depths of the second room in which I was not," they became lifelong friends.[36]

In 1895, when he reappeared in London, Rhodes was the most powerful man in Africa: Prime Minister of the Cape Colony and a Privy Councilor to the Queen, and through BSAC he controlled vast territories—Rhodesia, Botswana, Malawi, and Zambia. He was also rich beyond avarice. The larger part of his income flowed from gold mines, but he also controlled through De Beers 90 percent of the world's diamond production. Jameson, his doctor, business associate, and administrator of Rhodesia, accompanied him. Once again Rhodes courted Flora Shaw, who by now was Colonial Editor of *The Times*. Her unsigned articles and editorials supported Rhodes and his expanding empire and echoed the grievances of the Uitlanders. Throughout his visit, they continued to see each other. Rhodes spoke candidly with Shaw, often using her as a sounding board, but according to Shaw, her relationship to Rhodes was strictly professional. Writing to her future husband, Captain Lugard, she emphasized that "Mr. Rhodes and I are not friends in an ordinary personal sense. I have studied him simply as an element in the public life of the day and as a result I catalogue him with all his defects among the best."[37] For his part, Rhodes instructed the secretary of the British South Africa Company, Dr. Rutherfoord Harris, on his missions to London to "cultivate Miss Shaw." He was so confident of Shaw that he asked Harris to hand over to her the secret code and bestowed on her a code name: "Telemones."

In the same letter to Lugard, who disapproved of Rhodes's tactics, Shaw underscored her friend's idealism and devotion to the imperial cause: "I have met now most of the English public men of my day and the impression conveyed to me by Mr. Rhodes is of an unselfishness of aim greater and more complete than I have ever recognized before. He appears to me to seek nothing for himself. He cares neither for money, nor place, nor power, except in so far as they are a necessity for the accomplishment of the national ideal for which he lives."[38]

In 1895, the Conservative leader Lord Salisbury formed a new government in which he was both Prime Minister and Foreign Secretary. He appointed Joseph Chamberlain as Colonial Secretary, and his own son-in-law, Lord Selborne, became Chamberlain's deputy. A welcome visitor at the Colonial Office at 12 Downing Street was the peripatetic Miss Shaw. Expansion was à la mode. The stage was now set for "a more imaginative Imperialist policy."[39]

Joseph Chamberlain was, as the young Winston Churchill noted, "incomparably the most live, sparkling, insurgent, compulsive figure in British affairs."[40] A monocle and a buttonhole orchid were his trademarks. In domestic matters he was a political radical but in foreign affairs "Pushful Joe" was the New Imperialist incarnate. With his clear, resonant voice, he was an outstanding public speaker who filled halls. But in spite of being a charter member of the industrial middle class in Birmingham, Chamberlain was initially hostile to Rhodes and known to be impatient with South African affairs. Shaw would persuade Chamberlain to promote Rhodes's agenda, writing that the new Colonial secretary "was intelligent enough and industrious enough" to become "a convert to the sound methods of a liberal colonial administration, to which he will add an ardour for unity at present totally wanting in the central administration."[41] Chamberlain soon assured her he wanted to work with a "strong man" if possible.

It seems certain that in August 1895 Chamberlain was aware through discussions he had with Rhodes's confidential agent, Harris, of the general outline of the proposed raid. After the Jameson debacle, Harris testified before the Committee of Enquiry that in his initial meeting with Chamberlain he had "referred to the unrest at Johannesburg and added a guarded allusion to the desirability of there being a police force near the border."[42] Referring to their meeting, Chamberlain claimed to have responded, "I don't want to hear any confidential information; I am here in an official capacity. I can only hear information of which I can make official use."[43]

In September, Harris disclosed the plan to Shaw. Replying to her queries, he confirmed that trouble in Johannesburg must break out and that police in neighboring Bechuanaland must be ready to help, adding, "It's all right, Chamberlain knows all about it."[44] He then headed to Scotland's grouse moors. On Nvember 4, he cabled Rhodes: "I have already sent Flora to convince J. Chamberlain support 'Times' newspaper and if you can telegraph course you wish 'Times' to adopt now with regard to Transvaal Flora will act."[45]

In November, Chamberlain ceded a strategic strip in the Bechuanaland Protectorate adjoining the Transvaal to Rhodes's Chartered Company. Protectorate police were released so that they could join Jameson. In exchange for these concessions from Chamberlain, Rhodes forfeited his £200,000 subsidy on a section of the Cape railway that would connect northward to Rhodesia, and absorb the £40,000 a year Her Majesty's Government paid for the Bechuanaland Border Police. To preserve appearances, on November 7, Harris sent Rhodes a telegram (one of those withheld from the investigating committee) in part reading, "Secretary of the Colonies says you must allow decent interval and delay fireworks for a fortnight."[46]

Historians now agree that by giving his tacit assent to these concessions, Chamberlain was complicit in the raid, though most assume that he never anticipated that Jameson would act without an Uitlander rising to justify it. Chamberlain's motive in ceding the strip to Rhodes was to avoid the appearance of a raid launched from British territory.

Enter Francis (later Sir Francis) Younghusband, the future leader of the eponymous expedition to Tibet in 1903–4 whose eight companies of Sikh Pioneers, backed up by a battery of Maxims, massacred at high altitudes a scraggly band of warrior monks armed with ancient matchlocks and magical amulets. But Lhasa was yet to come, and Captain Younghusband was now on leave from his duties on India's North-West Frontier. He was already known to *The Times*, having reported for them on the siege of Chitral, another imperial skirmish in a lofty kingdom at the far edge of India's frontier. On his way home on leave, this muscular imperialist and sometime mystic traveled to South Africa, where he met Rhodes. When he arrived back in London in November, Younghusband was summoned to dine with Shaw and Bell on November 15. Shortly afterward, equipped with the secret telegraph code Harris had given to Shaw, he sailed for Cape Town as *The Times*'s Special Correspondent. There he conveyed a message from Moberly Bell to Rhodes stating "that we hope the *New Company* will not *commence business* on a Saturday. P.S. Because of the Sunday papers."[47] (*The Times* did not publish on Sunday.) In *The Jameson Raid*, the South African historian Jean van der Poel plausibly observes that Bell "takes it for granted that Rhodes is in entire control of the so-called 'revolution' and can turn it on when he likes" and that he was "so well instructed in the plot that he knew that the 'genuine' rising had been fixed, provisionally, for 28 December—a Saturday."[48] Moving on to Johannesburg, Younghusband was the guest of Rhodes's brother Frank; there he expanded his brief, becoming the interlocutor between Cape Town and the raiders.

On December 10, Flora Shaw cabled Rhodes: "Can you advise when you will commence the plan, we wish to send at the earliest opportunity sealed instructions to representatives of the London *Times* European capitals; it is most important using their influence in your favor."[49] The following day Rhodes responded, informing her that the New Year would be the time. On December 12, Shaw reassured Rhodes that "Chamberlain sound in case of interference European Powers [in this case Germany] but have special reason to believe wishes you must do it immediately."[50] Four days later, *The Times* published a column and a half of Uitlander grievances and warned, "The time is past, even in South Africa, when a helot system of administration, organized for the exclusive advantage of a privileged minority, can long resist the force of enlightened public opinion." On December 18, Chamberlain fired off a "hurry up" message, remarking of the planned coup: "It seems to me that either it should come at once or be postponed for a year or two at least. Can we ensure this?"[51]

Initially, Younghusband, "the gentleman" or "the messenger" as he was dubbed in the special inquiry, sympathized with the conspirators. But by December 22, when he returned to Cape Town from the Transvaal, he was having second thoughts "about the rights of the thing." He had written to his father that "what is going to take place is a revolution against the Boers . . . But they must not quaver about it, and turn the whole thing into not only a fiasco but a disaster."[52] The Uitlander leaders in Johannesburg had indeed begun to waver, and they wanted Younghusband to sound out Rhodes about postponing "the polo tournament" until the New Year.[53]

Thirty years later, Younghusband recalled his conversation with the Cape Prime Minister amid the blooming hydrangeas at Rhodes's residence, Groote Schuur: "I told him the Johannesburgers were not for it and wanted Jameson stopped. He said, 'What! Do you mean to say that there is not a man in Johannesburg who will get up and lead a revolution and not mind if he's shot?' 'Apparently there isn't,' I said. 'Would you do it yourself?' he asked. 'Certainly not,' I replied. 'I don't want to lead revolutions in Johannesburg.' He gave his customary grunt as if he thought the whole crowd, including myself, were a whitelivered lot."[54]

A sullen Rhodes promised to wire Jameson "to keep quiet."[55] In fact, despite his assurances to Younghusband, Rhodes cabled a message on December 23 saying that the rising would take place on the following Saturday at midnight. He finished by expressing his concern that the Boers were aware of the preparations.

Meanwhile in campgrounds at Pitsani, telegrams to Jameson from Cape Town and Johannesburg piled up. On December 1, this missive came from Frank Rhodes: "Tell Dr. Jameson the polo tournament here postponed for one week or it would clash with race week." More optimistically, on December 23 word came from Rhodes: "Company will be floated next Saturday 28th." And then on December 26, a telegram from his brother, Sam Jameson, in Johannesburg: "Absolutely necessary to postpone flotation." And a further message from Harris calling off the rising: "You must not move till you hear from us again. Too awful. Very sorry." Dr. Jim, however, determined to act on his own. He informed Harris that if the Uitlanders were not prepared to move, "we will make our own flotation."[56] If successful, he would be forgiven and become a hero as well.

On December 26, Chamberlain informed Salisbury that "a rising in Johannesburg is imminent & will probably take place in the course of the next few days."[57] But three days later, the rising had failed to rise. Alerting Salisbury, he dispatched a cable to High Commissioner Sir Hercules Robinson, instructing him to warn Rhodes that without an Uitlander rebellion, an incursion into the Transvaal would jeopardize his charter. At Printing House Square, the presses were on the ready, and accounts of unrest in Transvaal filled the news columns. Then on Monday, December 30, *The Times* received this alarming cable: "Jameson has disregarded instructions and crossed the border with 400 men." Shaw rushed the message to the Colonial Office, but Chamberlain was on holiday at his Venetian palazzo, Highbury, in the Birmingham suburbs. According to his biographer, Peter Marsh, Chamberlain clenched his fists declaring, "If this succeeds it will ruin me."[58] The Colonial Secretary knew that without the pretext of an uprising, all the elaborate fictions would be seen as just that.

Shaw also received a telegram from Harris on December 31 with a copy of a letter containing an appeal from the Reform Committee in Johannesburg to Jameson outlining Uitlander grievances and calling on him to help save "thousands of unarmed men, women and children of our race" who would be "at the mercy of the well-armed Boers." The purposely undated letter had been signed by five members of the Reform Committee and reluctantly given to Jameson to produce in the event of an uprising. Jameson wanted the letter, he claimed, so that he would not trespass into Transvaal "like a brigand."[59] He needed something to show to his men and also to justify his action to the BSAC's shareholders. Jameson dated the letter December 28 and read it aloud to his troops. Rhodes forwarded it to Shaw (it was among the documents retrieved from the tin box by the Boers) and then telegraphed his permission to publish the letter. *The Times* did so on New Year's Day. No other paper received it; no other paper published it. It was an exclusive that remained an exclusive.

When it appeared that Jameson had ignored repeated warnings and that a fiasco loomed, Chamberlain opportunely repudiated the raid in a telegram to Robinson: "If the Govt. of the S.A.R. had been overthrown, or there had been anarchy at Jo'burg there might have been some shadow of an excuse for this unprecedented act." Instead, Jameson had committed "an act of war, or rather of filibustering."[60] Salisbury commented, "If filibustering fails, it is always disreputable.[61]*

Despite the panic in the Colonial Office, Shaw remained calm. According to Moberly Bell, "Chamberlain was at first furious, inclined to throw over Rhodes, Jameson, South Africa, the Charter and the whole bag of tricks, but that invaluable Miss Shaw of ours has acted with great diplomacy, and receiving the most amusingly dictatorial telegrams from Rhodes, 'Tell Chamberlain he must at once do so-and-so.' 'Tell Chamberlain to stop send-

---

* Long before the U.S. Senate allowed unlimited debate, the term *filibuster* referred to leading an insurrection in a foreign country.

ing foolish telegrams to the High Commissioner,' and so forth, and spending her days at the Colonial Office, has succeeded in keeping as watertight as possible the situation gravely compromised by Jameson."[62]

Writing some years later, Shaw commented, "I had an opportunity during the Jameson crisis of comparing from the inside the panic of the C.O. and the panic of *The Times* and it was six of one and half a dozen of the other."[63]

Younghusband arrived in Doornkop just in time to see Jameson arrested. He visited the "utterly broken and crushed" raider in his cell, who lamented that "all the officers at the time were labouring under a sense of having been deserted by the Johannesburgers."[64] The correspondent confided to his diary, "The Boers showed up at the very best during the week, and the Johannesburgers [the Uitlanders] at their very worst. The Boers won playing at the game they had played at all their lives. The Johannesburgers at one of which they had no experience. Besides which the Johannesburgers must not be taken as typical Englishmen. Jews, Germans and Americans probably preponderate, the Englishmen there are not of the best class."[65]

Rhodes embarked for London on February 3 to save his charter and stave off a parliamentary inquiry. Rhodes's confidant, Harris, and his solicitor, Bourchier Hawksley, met him at Plymouth. Their plan was to produce telegrams implicating the Colonial Office, and in the event of an inquiry they threatened to assert that the conspirators "had acted upon messages from London which committed the Colonial Secretary to the full knowledge and approval of the plot."[66] Chamberlain countered by warning Rhodes that if the telegrams were disclosed, it would mean the end of BSAC. No telegrams were produced; the charter survived.

The official inquiry by a select committee of Parliament opened in February 1897. Four telegrams between Rhodes and Harris mentioning Flora Shaw's name were placed in evidence. Both Shaw and Rhodes testified before the bipartisan committee, one of its ten members being the outspoken Liberal anti-imperialist, Henry Labouchère, who was expected to press aggressively for the truth. Chamberlain himself was the tenth member. Rhodes was allowed to evade the direct questions and no additional "missing telegrams" materialized, nor did he mention his close connection with *The Times*. According to Flora Shaw, "He displayed in the circumstances, characteristic qualities of pluck and candour. He made no concealment of his own share in the catastrophe; he took full responsibility for what had been done in his name by subordinates, and he accepted all the consequences which ensued."[67] Rhodes's self-described role was to play "the sacrificial lamb to save Chamberlain" and England.[68] His charter and investments survived, but Afrikaaners would never again trust the British.

Wearing black silk and pearls, and accompanied by her sister Lulu, Shaw testified twice, in May and July. The Grand Commission Room overflowed with journalists. A friend at the Colonial Office, Sir Herbert Stephen, remarked in a note to her on "the mild astonishment of the ingenuous reporters at discovering you were not a frump."[69] Even though her superior—Managing Director Bell—drafted key telegrams, she was the designated scapegoat, as detailed in a letter from the editor, George E. Buckle: "With regard to the Paper and your cables; the way I think the matter should be put is: that you sent them on your own responsibility and at your own expense, that you had no instructions to do anything of the kind, the action of The Times being limited to sending correspondents to report events; that they were sent without the knowledge or concurrence of the Editor . . . that the Editor only discovered what you had done in April . . . and that he expressed his strong disapproval of what you had done."[70]

According to her biographers, Dorothy Helly and Helen Callaway, Shaw preserved the note with an attached comment: "The spirit of disloyalty and official timidity embodied in this letter sent to me and received on the eve of an examination in which it was well known at the office that I intended to assume responsibility for acts which were not mine has given me one of the sorriest and most cynical lessons of my life."[71]

Despite the potentially incriminating telegrams, Shaw was cool, dignified, and well prepared. She evaded questions yet appeared forthcoming. "I feel there has been so much of what I may call mystery-mongering about all the business," she testified, that the evil of withholding was greater than that of disclosing everything. Like Chamberlain, she was aware of a possible uprising—a "plan," but not a "raid," no, that was impossible. Her position, as summed up in a letter she wrote in August to Bell, was that "[a] plan which could commend itself to a serious consideration of two governments and to the Directorate of a paper like The Times was not a harum-scarum expedition like Dr. Jameson's. Nor was it a plan of which there is reason to be ashamed."[72]

When Miss Shaw was pressed, Younghusband dwindled into an anonymous "messenger," and Bell was not involved. As to whether she had inspired a leading article (i.e., editorial) censuring Chamberlain and repudiating Jameson, Shaw informed her interrogators that her communications with her editors were confidential. She had "acted in her own right" in sending compromising telegrams without informing her editor. In Chamberlain's judgment, "in lucidity and frankness & general manner the Lady witness beat all the men."[73] He later elaborated that a more difficult witness to bully would be hard to find: "When asked a question, she went off at a tangent, and made a clever speech on things in general."[74] Or in the judgment of *The Times*'s official history, "by her powerful mind and compelling personality" Flora Shaw "directly influenced policies and statesmen" while protecting the paper's reputation.

The inquiry exonerated *The Times*—a fairer measure of its power than of the facts—but according to Shaw's biographer, Enid Moberly Bell (daughter of Shaw's editor), Buckle's letter "rankled and cast a shadow, never wholly lifted, on her work at Printing House Square."[75] For his part the "messenger" regretted his role as go-between, which is rarely mentioned in most accounts. Younghusband destroyed compromising papers and tore from his diary pages about Rhodes and Jameson. As he wrote to his future wife, Nellie Douglas, "I never saw more clearly in my life the evil of going crooked."[76] Flora Shaw, he added, had also been deceived by Rhodes and Harris: "They had led her to believe the situation in S.A. to be perfectly different to what it really was and made her think the 'women and children' letter from Johannesburg leaders calling Jameson bona fide and spontaneous whereas it was Jameson himself who concocted it."[77]

A differing judgment was expressed by Rudyard Kipling. Jameson's stoicism inspired "If," his single most quoted poem with its familiar lines:

> If you can keep your head when all about you
>   Are losing theirs and blaming it on you,
> If you can trust yourself when all men doubt you,
>   But make allowance for their doubting too;
> If you can wait and not be tired by waiting,
>   Or being lied about, don't deal in lies,
> Or being hated, don't give way to hating,
>   And yet don't look too good, nor talk too wise:
>
> If you can dream—and not make dreams your master;
>   If you can think—and not make thoughts your aim;

If you can meet with Triumph and Disaster
   And treat those two imposters just the same;
If you can bear to hear the truth you've spoken
   Twisted by knaves to make a trap for fools,
Or watch the things you gave your life to, broken,
   And stoop and build 'em up with worn-out tools:
   . . .
Yours is the Earth and everything that's in it,
   And—which is more—you'll be a Man, my son!

The Jameson Raid cast a long shadow. Field Marshal Jan Smuts, a future Prime Minister of South Africa, considered it "the real declaration of war in the great Anglo-Boer conflict" (1899–1902) with its grimmer horrors.[78] Because the raid deepened hostility between Britain and Germany (the Kaiser had championed the Boers), Kipling deemed it "the first battle in the war of '14–18."[79] In his preface to *The World Crisis*, Winston Churchill recalled a conversation he had while a young officer with Sir William Harcourt, a member of the Committee of Enquiry. When Churchill asked, "What will happen now?" the venerable statesman responded, "My dear Winston, the experiences of a long life have convinced me that nothing ever happens." Churchill disagreed: "Since that moment, as it seems to me, nothing has ever ceased happening. I date the beginning of these violent times in our country from the Jameson Raid."[80]

Wilfrid Scawen Blunt, the invaluable diarist and inveterate scourge, records a meeting with George Wyndham, a member of Parliament who had been "seeing much of Jameson." He told Blunt "confidentially" that Flora Shaw was "really the prime mover in the whole thing" and she "took the lead in all their meetings."[81] Blunt then added, "The English papers are sickening about the Transvaal, a mixture of swagger and poltroonery. One would have thought that the less said about Jameson's ignominious defeat by the Boers the better, but our blessed public must need make a hero of him, a man who fought for thirty-six hours, and had only fifteen men killed and then surrendered, not a pretense of its being in any better cause than money making and land-grabbing. The '*Times*' puts a poem in praise of him by the new Poet Laureate. So low are we sunk."[82]

As to Miss Shaw, she traveled to the Klondike to witness its gold rush, and to South Africa as an observer during the Boer War. In 1900, having written more than six hundred articles, editorials, and columns for *The Times*, she retired from daily journalism. She was now famous, "a very clever middle-aged woman" according to Blunt, but an unmarried one.[83]

Rhodes had been the first of her larger-than-life African friends. The second was Sir George Taubman Goldie, founder of the chartered Royal Niger Company whose private empire comprised three hundred thousand mostly unexplored square miles before it was subsumed by the British Government. The new Niger Coast protectorate, which at the time did not include the Lagos Colony and Southern Nigeria, was called Nigeria, a name devised by Shaw, who pressed successfully for its adoption in *The Times*.[84] (Nigeria narrowly escaped becoming, in a Rhodesian flourish, Goldesia, but Sir George tastefully declined the honor.) Shaw interviewed the womanizing empire builder, who shared her love for Africa, and fell in love with him. She expected to marry Sir George after his wife, Mathilda, died in 1898, but no proposal followed. Possibly on the rebound, Miss Shaw accepted a proposal from Sir Frederick Lugard, Goldie's friend and sometime employee. "You once said you would win my love," she wrote to him, "I, too, hope to win yours. We cannot force it. Let us not try on either side, but let us be content to marry as friends."[85]

Frederick Lugard, later Lord Lugard of Abinger, would be the third New Imperialist to gain the esteem of the Colonial Editor. Flora Shaw met him in 1893, when he appeared at Printing House Square in hopes of coaxing a favorable review for his semi-autobiographical book, *The Rise of Our East African Empire*. Shaw called it "a most important contribution that has yet been made to the history of East Africa." When he thanked her, she directly replied, "I am nearly always at home late in the afternoon."[86] In their discussions, Frederick found Flora's enthusiasm for Rhodes and Jameson excessive, remarking in his diary, "A woman's emotions always will dominate her intellect . . . I think a man shows more control. However stirred his emotions are he can—if he is a man—project himself outside of them to some extent and 'see things as others see them' and act logically—at least more than a woman does."[87]

Slight, with a sallow complexion and in poor health resulting from war wounds and bouts of malaria, Lugard possessed blazing eyes and the long mustache Kitchener had recently made famous. Morose and an obsessive workaholic—twelve-hour sessions were his norm—he might not have seemed an ideal husband for the sociable Shaw. But they were bound by a shared obsession with Empire and Africa.

A graduate of the Royal Military College Sandhurst, Lugard joined the Indian Army, served in the Second Afghan War (1879–80), and acquired a passion for tiger hunting and pig sticking. His acquaintance with Africa began with his service in the expedition to relieve Khartoum. On his next foray, against Arab slave traders in Nyasaland, he was severely wounded. In 1888, the British East Africa Company, founded by the Scottish shipowner Sir William Mackinnon, hired Lugard to establish its claim. He crossed the Nile to Uganda, where in 1890 he raised the Union Jack adorned with the East Africa Company's crown and golden sun. He crushed a rising by Muslim chieftains, and then brokered a peace between Protestant and Catholic missionaries.

Lugard became adept at the martial semiotics of imperialism. He insisted on pitching his white tents on the highest ground when treating with local chiefs—the more bits of flying bunting, dress uniforms, plumed hats, ceremonial swords, seventeen-gun salutes, and trumpet fanfares, the better. Aged thirty-five when he met Flora, and a convert to the New Imperialism, Lugard had few qualms about seizing territory. While in England in 1892, he launched a campaign to persuade Prime Minister Gladstone's new Liberal administration on the need to annex Uganda. He spoke tirelessly before geographical societies, at churches, and at town meetings, arguing as he did in *The Times* that Britain had a vital interest in "securing at all costs" a country that had experienced a "Christian revolution" and thus could contain the spread of Islam. But the decisive concern was strategic. A decade earlier, the Liberals had reluctantly occupied Egypt to protect routes to India, and as Gladstone had predicted, British power was projected from the Cape northward and westward to safeguard Egypt and sea lanes to India. Now Uganda, at Egypt's doorstep, became the next essential link in the great chain of empire.

The Times supported Lugard's two-year whirlwind campaign for annexing Uganda, with palpable results. On assuming office in 1892, the Liberals had little enthusiasm for imperial expansion, but two years later the mood had notably changed, thanks partly to Flora Shaw. Just before Parliament scheduled a major debate on Africa, Lugard stayed at Highbury to coach Chamberlain. The Colonial Secretary's opening statement on June 1, 1894, was "purely the result of our conversation," Lugard confided in a euphoric letter to his brother Ned. He was "excessively" pleased:

> Contrast the intimate knowledge shewn by the whole House on the question—on technical subjects such as the commercial treaties,—the tenure of the Sultanate, —the Slavery question,—the "Legal status."—the naval suppression, etc. etc., with the crass ignorance of 2 years ago. Even local names of places and peoples are quoted familiarly in the speeches. Contrast this with the debate of March 1892 before I came home, and you'll be struck with the difference. Contrast the extraordinary interest in Uganda, etc. with the ignorance about the place in 1890 before I went there, and you'll see that my ceaseless efforts there and in England have produced a wonderful result. I doubt if there would have been so full a House, so many speakers (and many more crowded out for lack of opportunity to speak), so well-informed, etc. on any possession of the British Empire, as there was about this little country in the centre of Africa.[88]

He went on, adding, "Miss Shaw, the specialist of *The Times*, told me that the conversion of Chamberlain was indeed notable, that in 1890 he had twice taken her to dinner, and he was quite half-hearted about Africa, now he is the leading enthusiast and goes further than anyone else in the House."[89] "Oh boy, this is a success I'm proud of," he wrote two months later to Ned: "A gigantic majority for the Unionists, & out of it all Mr. Chamberlain emerged as one of the strongest and most influential men in the country. Now you may know that I have had a great deal to do with him, & perhaps I am not wrong in saying that the very prominent part he has taken in African questions, the intimate knowledge he has shewn regarding them is due in a very large measure to myself."[90] (Lugard was again Chamberlain's houseguest during the 1895 election and his letter had been written in the expectation that he would be named governor of Uganda but to his chagrin, the post went instead to a rival, Sir Harry Johnston.)

But why the euphoria? What accounts for the Liberal turnabout, the spirited Commons debate, Chamberlain's conversion to New Imperialism? Here it is worth digressing to recall that in mid-Victorian times, Africa, explorers, and Christianity were to the British what space, astronauts, and moon rockets were to Americans during the Cold War. Books by Stanley, Burton, and Livingstone, heavy as bricks, were a feature of middle-class libraries; lectures at the Royal Geographical Society were political and social events; and a manic grandiosity tinged with religion was everywhere evident. Before his heroic demise in East Africa in 1872, David Livingstone called on Europeans to extirpate the slave trade and sow the three "C's" in a still-dark continent—Commerce, Christianity, and Civilization. "I beg to direct your attention to Africa," implored Livingstone at Cambridge University in 1857, "I know that in a few years I shall be cut off in that country [Africa], which is now open. Do not let it be shut again!"[91]

So intense was the competitive European rush to keep the doors open that Germany's Chancellor Bismarck in 1884 convened a conference in Berlin to establish rules for "the Scramble for Africa" (a phrase hatched in *The Times*). Doubtless the quest for profit greased the way, but more important was the quest for glory and its dubious twin brother, vainglory. Mix well with strategic arguments about Suez and India, and the brew proved lethal.

Shaw continued to support Lugard's African ventures. *The Times* in 1897 carried her five articles on West Africa, which introduced the name "Nigeria" and summarized the case against French probes on the Niger River. When Chamberlain chose Lugard to head a West African expeditionary force, termed by the French press "a veritable steeplechase," the incursion succeeded. And when Lugard exceeded his orders, she did her best "to keep the peace" between him and Chamberlain.[92] As she told Lugard, "I look upon it as part of my personal work to endeavour to bring all the influences which I believe to be working for the good in Africa into harmony with each other."[93]

Having served as a hired hand for four chartered companies, Lugard had emerged as one of the leading players in what his biographer, Margery Perham, was moved to describe as "the constructive processes of civilisation" through which "tattered, moustachioed and bearded white men, supremely convinced of racial superiority and of the national and humanitarian mission of their own nations, had walked their hundreds of miles in the bush under rain and sun, swum their rivers, shot their game, planted their flags and sweated or died of malaria in their little tents."[94]

On January 1, 1900, he assumed office as High Commissioner of Northern Nigeria, beginning a new career as imperial administrator and fluent theorist of what he called "Indirect Rule" (Lugard always capitalized the phrase). The strategy was an old one, dating to the Roman and Mongol empires, employed by the Chinese, elaborated in India by the Moguls, and taken up by the British Raj—implemented successfully by the two Law-rence brothers, John and Henry, who governed the Punjab—but its applica-tion to Africa was new. In Northern Nigeria, the emirs and chiefs continued to rule, but it was the British who governed through them. "A great chief," explained Claude Macdonald, a Governor of Lagos, "is a very valuable pos-session; his authority is an instrument of the greatest public utility, which it is most desirable to retain in full."[95] Or more broadly, in Lugard's words, the whole purpose of the British Empire was "to maintain traditional ruler-ships as a fortress of societal security in a changing world."[96] Guided less by race than class, "tropical" and "Oriental" colonies reflected British social hierarchies. At the top were the Britons, then came the Fulani emirs, fol-lowed by the Muslim Hausa, then the rest of the "bush" tribes. And in this enterprise, David Cannadine maintains in *Ornamentalism*, "the colour of a person's skin was less important than their position in the local social hier-archy."[97] Thus British rule signified a continuation, rather than a break, with the past, as Lugard made plain in an address to local sultans and their chiefs after he subdued Sokoto in 1902: "The Fulani in old times, under Dan Fodio, conquered this country. They took the right to rule over it, to levy taxes, to depose kings and to create kings. They in turn have by defeat lost their rule, which has come into the hands of the British. All these things, which I have said the Fulani by conquest took the right to do now pass to the British. Every sultan and emir, and the principal officers of State, will be appointed by the High Commissioner throughout all the country."[98]

As High Commissioner of Northern Nigeria, the largest of the Brit-ish Crown Colonies, Lugard was able to govern a huge territory—some 350,000 square miles—on a frugal budget, installing a British Resident, "the thin white line," at each of the Muslim courts, augmented by sub-sidies to the emirs and chiefs and by the occasional punitive expedition. The essence of Lugard's Indirect Rule was "authority combined with self-effacement." One of his Nigerian deputies, Hugh Clifford, summarized the credo: "The Political Officer should be the Whisper behind the Throne, but never for an instant the Throne itself."[99] Yet Indirect Rule involved two intractable contradictions. Though New Imperialism was justified as an agent of modernization, the British perpetuated existing hierarchies resis-tant to fundamental change. Moreover, since sultans and emirs owed their office to foreigners and infidels, they forfeited their legitimacy, too often becoming demoralized or dissolute. Nonetheless, notwithstanding the system's deficiencies, the British applied the same kingmaking formula to the Middle East, with results evident even today.

In 1901, Frederick proposed to Flora. After initially declining his offer, she relented, and the couple made their plans while he was *en poste* as High Commissioner of Northern Nigeria. The wedding took place in 1902 in Madeira amid the blooming jacaranda, roses, and bougainvillea. The bride was forty-nine; the groom, forty-four.

Although Lugard had a reputation for a spartan disregard for comfort and convenience and claimed to be uninterested in material things, in Nigeria he evinced a sybaritic side. Two years before his marriage, a ferry inched up the Niger laden with furniture, which included (in Sir Frederick's inventory) "enormous cases of writing tables, folding tables, sofas, armchairs, Almiras [cabinets], wardrobes, marble wash-stands, chests of drawers, settees, & chairs of rosewood, ice machines, huge sets of china (120 dinner plates of glass and electro-plate), carpets, utensils, every mortal thing."[100] Added to this were Flora's forty-six trunks and cases of necessities. Government House at Jebba had to be enlarged to accommodate the chintzes and the wicker the Lugards deemed necessary for a proconsular role.

Domestic comforts aside, the cosmopolitan Shaw faced a monotonous life in backwater Nigeria, as expressed in a letter to her niece:

> The days as they pass at present are absolutely without incident. I wake, between four and five. Early tea is brought at six. I send round to Fred's room to let him know that it has come. He comes in very sleepy to have a cup and then goes away to his office where piles of papers await him . . . At six Fred stops work. The sun then is just on the edge of setting and we go for a tearing walk in the dark which gives us exercise and brings us in streaming with perspiration to an extent which makes all my clothes seem exactly as [if] they had been dropped in the washtub . . . After dinner there is an hour on the verandah and between ten and eleven we usually separate for the night.[101]

Despite to all appearances being a woman who could go anywhere and "write three columns of good copy for a newspaper on the back of a portmanteau in a desert," Flora by her own admission was not really interested in exploring local life.[102] Lugard was often away and she became lonely and depressed. Both the climate and the virulent insects were trying. Increasingly idle, she fell ill, and the doctors ordered her home. She returned to the couple's country residence, Little Parkhurst, in the Surrey woods near Abinger, where the Lugards' public rooms were as African as Government House was British. She converted the large wooden doors, part of the audience hall at Kano, mementos of Lugard's northern conquests, into screens, and the main sitting room boasted spears, shields, big-game trophies, and the royal drum of Buganda (which summoned guests to dinner). "Yes, they were lovely things that you brought me last time from Canary," she wrote Frederick, "but I shall like the heads and skins which you have shot yourself the better. Already you know how I like the feeling that the hall is almost entirely furnished by the trophies of your 'bow and spear.'"[103]

Unable temperamentally to delegate—he even oversaw the purchase of toilet paper—Lugard left little to the imagination of subordinates. "I love this turgid life of command," he wrote Flora, "when I can feel that the sole responsibility rests on me for everything."[104] He expected his Residents to be administrators as well as diplomats. Lacking assistants or even typewriters, they nonetheless made up to thirty sets of records to be filed or forwarded, covering everything from taxes to caravans, as detailed in his celebrated "Political Memoranda" published in 1906. The "Chief's" micromanagement of protocol included the stipulation that a first-class tribal chief was to be offered a carpet in lieu of a rug, and that the Resident was to rise rather than remaining seated when received or dismissing a chief. Nevertheless, all powers—to tax, control the police and army, legislate, deal with foreigners, or depose the ruler's subordinates—were to remain with the Resident, though the Emir's "prestige" was to be preserved.[105]

To a reader nowadays, the Lugards' daily correspondence—filled with administrative details from him, and encouragement and ideas from her—makes depressing reading: so much work for so much posthumous indifference, or disdain. Although devoted to "the work," they found their long separation difficult. As a remedy, they devised a plan for "continuous administration," referred to entre deux as "the scheme," which would allow Lugard, always averse to vacations or delegating authority, to govern for six months from the Colonial Office on Downing Street and for six months from Government House in Nigeria. Not Africa but Whitehall, Westminster, Fleet Street, and Mayfair became the battleground. As Perham writes, "He gave general directions and supplied memoranda; she set to work to convert all the people who mattered and indeed, in her enthusiasm, many who might not have been thought to matter very much."[106] Chamberlain was plied with rare orchids gathered by Lugard, but by this time he had resigned from the Cabinet in 1903 following his advocacy of imperial trade preferences. Flora succeeded in persuading the new Colonial Secretary, the handsome and athletic Alfred Lyttelton, to come as a weekend guest to Abinger. But the couple's efforts came to nothing when "the scheme" was derailed by the 1906 election that replaced Arthur Balfour's Conservatives with Sir Henry Campbell-Bannerman's Liberals. On becoming Secretary of State for the colonies, Lord Elgin declined to ratify the unwritten arrangement the Lugards had reached with Lyttelton.

Loath to give up, Flora turned to *The Times*. A long leading article approving "the scheme" betrayed her hand. She lectured on Nigeria at the Royal Colonial Institute and the Society of Arts, provoking a rare reproving remark from Lugard: "Could she not have left me my one territory?"[107] Her book, *A Tropical Dependency*, dedicated to "my husband," appeared in 1906, with specially bound copies dispatched to King Edward VII, Balfour, Milner, and Lyttelton. In its pages, with Ruskinian tones, she remarks that British empire-builders were "chiefly composed of that type of young Englishmen who, whether as soldiers or civilians, have it in their minds to serve their country to the best of their ability in some adventurous capacity . . . Their experience in Africa was mostly *nil*, but they had the training of the public school, the army, and the university, which fits men equally for the assumption of responsibility and for loyal subordination to authority." They represented "the very best stuff of which the English nation is made."[108]

In spite of her campaign, the scheme had fallen victim not only to a change in government but also to resistance by Lugard's colleagues at the Colonial Office, who abhorred the idea of a "man on the spot" mixing with policy makers at home. Flora had laid siege to one of them, Winston Churchill, the new Under Secretary of State for colonies. She reported to Lugard on her interview with the thirty-one-year-old "ignorant boy."[109] "He could see no reason why the Colonial Office should become a Pantheon for Pro-Consuls."[110]

There was more to the story. The year before the 1906 election, Churchill had switched from the Conservatives to the Liberals, whose victory was partly owed to an unpopular Boer War that ended in a virtual draw. On assuming his new office, young Winston immediately confronted the moral quandaries of imperial police work. An uprising had broken out in Sokoto in Northern Nigeria, where a self-styled Mahdi named Mallam fomented a revolt in which two British Residents, a white officer, and seventy mounted police were butchered with hoes, axes, and spears. Lugard proposed striking back with Maxims. But Churchill balked at "the extermination of an almost unarmed rabble," complaining to colleagues that Lugard imagined himself a tsar, with Nigeria as his "sultry Russia." Churchill appended this minute to the order barring a punitive expedition: "The chronic bloodshed which stains the West African seasons is odious and disquieting. Moreover the whole enterprise is liable to be misrepresented by persons unacquainted with imperial terminology as the murdering of natives and stealing of their lands."[111]

A bristling Lugard returned on leave to England in the summer of 1906 and resigned in September. "The strenuous conditions were breaking down his health and as the Govt. had broken faith with him he felt no honourable obligations to continue," Shaw wrote.[112] After an interlude in Hong Kong as Governor, with Flora at his side, the Colonial Office lured Lugard back to establish a union of north and south Nigeria, a fitting coda to his career. During his second Nigerian tour, from 1912 through 1918, this time as Governor-General of an amalgamated Nigeria, he encountered the slippery challenge of applying Indirect Rule in territories in the south and west where there was no traditional hierarchy with an Emir at its apex. Despite numerous riots, he persisted in his strategy. With what result?

Writing in *The Dual Mandate in British Tropical Africa*, published in 1922, four years after his retirement, Lugard claims that his system of Indirect Rule was "the most comprehensive, coherent, and renowned system of administration in British imperial history."[113] He argued that the mandates were reciprocal, "that Europe is in Africa for the mutual benefit of her own industrial classes and of the native races in their progress to a higher plane."[114] The tropics were "the heritage of mankind." European skills would be exchanged for native resources. Lugard envisioned colonies run by idealized colonial servants from "the right class from our public schools and universities" "with an almost passionate conception of fair play, of protection of the weak, and of playing the game."[115] But critics countered that his system stifled indigenous institutions by favoring Muslim emirs, whose bodyguards donned medieval chain mail, at the expense of missionary-educated Nigerians. Worse, according to Lord Hailey, the authoritative chronicler of British Africa, what was intended to be a temporary policy hardened into a "political doctrine" and then into a "religious dogma.' "[116]

Moreover, in the critical reckoning, by favoring the Muslim emirs in the north, Lugard instituted a fault line that has persisted to the present day, a division exacerbated by the discovery of oil in the Christian south. Much in the mode of British Indian officialdom, Lugard characterized educated Africans in Lagos as "baboos," the derogative term for the Western-educated Bengalis, and discouraged Nigerians from teaching about the Stuarts deposed in England's Civil War for fear that this might "foster disrespect for authority."[117] His successors followed in his steps by also promoting the Muslim Fulani and Hausa ahead of the "coast African," breeding hostilities contributing to the civil discord that has plagued Nigeria since it attained independence in 1960. More importantly, as we shall see in future chapters, his recipe for Indirect Rule articulated for acolytes in his Political Memoranda, was the template for future imperial adventures in the Middle East, expressed in what one wit described as a "rent a sheik, buy an emir" strategy.

Lugard retired in 1918 but continued to serve on high-level committees and boards, and on the Permanent Mandates Commission of the League of Nations. Incapable as her husband of remaining idle, Flora continued to entertain and to write the occasional article. Never indifferent to the glittering prizes, Lugard harvested an array of honorary degrees and medals; in 1928, he was raised to the peerage as Baron Lugard of Abinger. As usual, Lady Lugard had the final word. Caressing his birthday present of fine linen handkerchiefs embroidered with a coronet, she murmured, "This is the kind of present I like, one which has taken a life-time to win."[118] Following a long illness, Lady Lugard died at Little Parkhurst on January 25, 1929. She was seventy-six. For the remaining sixteen years of her husband's life her room was kept exactly as she had left it. His memorial plaque at the Abinger church reads, "All I did was to try and lay my bricks straight."

THREE

⌗

"Dr. Weizmann, It's a Boy!"

Sir Mark Sykes (1879–1919), BT, MP

⌘

Bring me my spear! O clouds, unfold!
Bring me my chariot of fire!

I will not cease from mental fight:
Nor shall my sword sleep in my hand,
Till we have built Jerusalem
In England's green and pleasant land.

—William Blake,
"Milton" (1808)

With Sir Mark Sykes, a sixth baronet, traveler, nation-maker, caricaturist, and knight-errant, we leave the world of Kipling and enter
that of Trollope—not the Anthony Trollope of the clerical Barchester novels
but the Anthony Trollope of the admirable parliamentary sextet, with its cast
of highborn eccentrics and lowborn adventurers, imperious hostesses and
improvident Irish MPs. Typically a Trollope tale centers on a landed squire of
independent means, outgoing and warm-hearted, possessing a solid backbone
but perhaps a wayward eye, the child of idle and ill-matched parents who (as
the reader learns) harbor a dark family secret. In the final chapter, the threads
pull together, and the hero attains a prize worthy of his grasp, as did Mark
Sykes, the unlikely and commonly forgotten godparent of modern Israel.

Few Yorkshire squires were richer (or idler) than Mark's father, Sir Tatton
Sykes of Sledmere, proprietor of thirty-four thousand acres and husband
to Christina Jessica (Jessie) Cavendish-Bentinck, a daughter of a prominent Tory MP and a granddaughter of the fourth Duke of Portland. The
fifth baronet's wedding in Westminster Abbey was the talk of the London
season, owing partly to the groom's lavish bridal gifts (including a splendid tiara and a suite of diamonds) and partly because Jessica was eighteen,
Tatton forty-eight. Mark's biographer Roger Adelson reports that an illustrated novel found in Sledmere's library shows an old man dozing in a chair
with Jessie's penciled caption, "Honeymoon 1874." Yet it was not just the
disparity in ages that shadowed their marriage. The *Dictionary of National
Biography* tactfully observes that Sir Tatton "followed the traditional sporting pursuits of his caste, and was addicted to foreign travel." Jessica's inter-

ests were broader. She had studied art in Paris, doted on Ruskin (whom she visited in Venice), and like Lady Carbury in *The Way We Live Now*, subsequently turned to authorship, in her case composing well-received novels. She was square-jawed, gregarious, profligate, and rebellious; he was trimly built, penurious, immaculately groomed, and a conservative creature of iron habits.

In 1879, the couple's only child was born, known to the world as Mark but in the chapel registry as Tatton Benvenuto Mark Sykes (the "Benvenuto" being Jessie's italianate addendum and "Tatton" being both his paternal and an old Yorkshire name). When Mark was three, a providential act intruded. His parents shared a serious interest in religion and an enthusiasm for the Gothic Revival, so much so that Sir Tatton helped finance the restoration of fifteen Anglican churches. Theirs was also a time of spiritual ferment, exemplified by the unsettling Oxford Movement that divided congregations, Oxbridge high tables and the House of Commons (Gladstone viewed John Henry Newman's conversion to Catholicism as a "catastrophe"). Lady Sykes followed the path to Rome then led by Cardinals Newman and Alfred Henry Manning (with whom she corresponded while traveling in Italy with her husband). Cardinal Manning received Jessica into the Catholic faith, alongside her three-year-old son. Sir Tatton declined to share, but did not oppose, her decision. He agreed that she could direct Mark's religious upbringing. Yet the road had forked, and friends wondered how long, and to what lengths, the testy fifth baronet would oblige a strong-willed spouse, especially as she began leading a separate life as a Mayfair hostess and sought, vainly, to conceal her ballooning gambling debts.

What postponed the reckoning was the couple's addiction to travel, usually to far-flung destinations in Old and New Worlds. They moved in grand style, their party at points including son, cook, companion, and tutor. By the time Mark was eleven, he had explored the Via Dolorosa in Jerusalem, witnessed bullfights in Mexico, and filled his closet with exotic headgear acquired in Ottoman bazaars. More unusually, accompanied by his father, he also viewed deranged inmates in a Damascus asylum ("I shall never forget the scene of misery and horror") and sipped tea with Druze sheiks in their Lebanese redoubt ("their hospitality and dignity filled me with reverence"). His itinerary extended to India, where he met the Viceroy, and to Egypt, where at Aswan he gazed at the Dervish frontier—and where, in

Cairo, Lady Sykes became the lover of a young diplomat, John Eldon Gorst (who later succeeded Lord Cromer as Egypt's Proconsul and whose daughter, Edith Violet, would become Mark's wife).[1]

Back home, Jessica enrolled Mark in Beaumont College, known as "the Catholic Eton," located like its more celebrated sibling in Windsor. There the new boy periodically took his leave for months of travel with his parents, returning with turbans and tomahawks for use in war games in which he would mime an Arab warlord or a Red Indian. He impressed classmates with his high spirits, irreverence, and careless dress. Already he displayed a talent for caricature, filling his copybooks with playful sketches still preserved in the Sledmere family archive.

In 1895, ostensibly to prepare her fifteen-year-old boy for university, Lady Sykes placed him in a Jesuit school at Monte Carlo, where he shared an apartment in town with his mother, three pet terriers, and a tutor named Egerton Beck. Jessica lingered on, losing steadily at the gaming tables but also befriending the Prince and Princess of Monaco. Years later, his tutor remembered Mark's absorbing what was worth absorbing at Monte Carlo: "He was interested in his dogs and in mankind, and the absurdities of the toy State amused him, such as the miniature army, the blank wall used as an official gazette, and the culminating fact that Prince and Bishop, Church and State in Monaco were run by the Casino." Introduced by Monaco's ruling dynasty, the Grimaldis, Mark conversed in the palace gardens with the Duc de Richelieu (brother to the Princess of Monaco) and in his mother's company visited France's dethroned Empress Eugénie at Cap Martin. Yet as Mark remarked, what truly interested him was the casino where "I knew everything about the tables and knew most of the croupiers."[2]

Plainly Mark's was not the usual childhood. Other British boys might be fascinated by castles, armor, and chivalry, but on the great lawn at Sledmere the young heir erected a model fortress, ten-foot square, complete with bastions, lunettes, redans, and cannons, based on the designs of the French military engineer Sébastien Vauban. His percussive reenactment of a seventeenth-century siege chewed up the lawn, as did the costumed battles he staged with local youths cast as Roundheads or Cavaliers. Other youngsters might dream of things past, but Mark could peruse family manuscripts dating to Tudor times. Other young gentlemen might be curious about the veiled world of Victorian sexuality, but in Sledmere's eclectic library Mark could study Richard Burton's notes and the "Terminal Essay" attached to his translation of *The Arabian Nights*, detailing erotic practices in what everybody called the Orient.[3]

Yet abrupt and enigmatic incidents occurred. In 1896, Mark was transferred from Monte Carlo to another Catholic school, the Institute de St. Louis in Brussels. Since the school prohibited pets, he left his pack of fox terriers at Sledmere. Returning home at Easter (as recounted recently by his grandson Christopher Simon Sykes), he expected a loud welcome from his terriers, now numbering eight, but instead there was chilly silence, and family servants avoided his eyes. Then, as instructed by Sir Tatton, a groom led him down a long carriage drive: "There, beneath a tall beech tree by an iron gate, he met with a dreadful sight; the bodies of his beloved dogs, suspended from a branch, hanged to death on the orders of his father."[4]

An increasingly volcanic Sir Tatton, it would appear, exasperated by his wife's debts and widely gossiped infidelities, had struck back at her through her son, and then through the press. On advice of lawyers, he published this notice in *The Times*: "I, Sir Tatton Sykes, Baronet of Sledmere, in the County of York, and No. 46 Grosvenor Street, in the County of London, hereby give notice that I will NOT be RESPONSIBLE for any DEBTS or ENGAGEMENTS which my wife, Lady Jessica Christina Sykes, may contract, whether purporting to be on my behalf or by my authority or otherwise. Dated the 5th of December, 1896." This waiver of responsibility was enforceable under a law recently approved by Parliament, and Sir Tatton became the first husband to employ this shaming weapon.[5] Still, friends wondered if there was something else, some other offstage crisis, that might account for the squire's rage. It appeared there was, though its unlikely nature remained secret for nearly a century.

In June 1976, Christopher Hugh Sykes, the second of Mark's three sons (and uncle to Christopher Simon Sykes), received an astonishing letter from a stranger named Veronica Roberts. "My father, who is now very ill," her letter began, "is the son of your father and Alice Carter, and was born in 1895, when they were both pretty young." Purportedly Mark Sykes, then fifteen, had fallen in love with a village schoolteacher whose father had worked as a groom at Sledmere. The smitten heir and his betrothed eloped to London, where they were tracked by Lady Sykes. She pleaded with the couple to reconsider, and offered to care generously for Alice Carter, immediately finding her shelter in a friend's household. Mark was dispatched to Monte Carlo, accompanied by mother and watchful tutor. Several months later Alice divulged her pregnancy, so it was said, and Jessica promised to care for mother and child if the secret of its birth was kept from her son. The promise was honored, and by all accounts Mark was never informed of his presumed fatherhood, nor were his six children.[6]

Having long endured her husband's wrath, Lady Sykes delayed as long as possible informing Sir Tatton of the impending birth, and on finally hearing the news he reportedly vowed to disinherit his disgraced heir. He relented only to vent his rage on Mark's fox terriers, or so it now appears. Mark's natural son, named George, was born prematurely, and Jessica seemingly succeeded in suppressing the official record of his birth. The child was then adopted by Alice's cousin, Mary Page, and her husband, Frederick Lott. With grandmotherly help, George attended a state boarding school in Kent and then qualified for a commission in the Royal Navy when World War I broke out. He enlisted immediately as a private in a Royal West Kent regiment and by an extraordinary coincidence was bound in early 1915 for Gallipoli aboard the same troop ship on which his father was a serving army officer.

Why didn't George write a note to Lieutenant Colonel Mark Sykes (as he now was), whose identity his mother had secretly confided to him? When asked by his daughter Veronica, he reportedly replied, "You don't understand. You don't go writing notes to officers if you are a ranker. I'd have been in dreadful hot water. It just wasn't possible. Anyway it wouldn't have been the best time, would it, going up to him in front of all the other officers and saying, 'I'm your long lost son!' " It chanced that George fell ill and was sent to a hospital in Jerusalem and thus averted lethal gunfire on Gallipoli's shores. He never saw Mark again. At war's end, he married and fathered six children, the oldest being Veronica. George kept his secret until 1969, when Veronica's son was constructing a family tree and sought his grandfather's help. Yet father and daughter decided against contacting the Sykes family, fearing the story would be dismissed as the concoction of fortune-hunters.

In 1975, owing to George's failing health and prompted by the appearance of Roger Adelson's biography of Mark Sykes, Veronica decided to break her silence. She wrote to Christopher rather than his older brother, Sir Richard Sykes, assuming that Sledmere's incumbent squire was likely to suspect mercenary motives. An author of repute, Christopher Hugh Sykes was known for his authorized life of Evelyn Waugh, and had written an incisive and affectionate tribute to his father, focusing on Mark's conversion to Zionism. His first concern was to corroborate Veronica's account. Yes, it developed that in 1895 there was a barely remembered groom at Sledmere named Carter, whose daughter Alice did in fact teach at a village school. Christopher turned to his older sister, Freya, to contact their putative relations. She reported that her presumed half-brother George was "altogether delightful," adding that she told him that the Sykes family was oblivious of his existence. Still, until his death in 1978, Sir Richard Sykes "steadfastly refused to believe that the story was true," writes *his* third son, Christopher Simon Sykes, also an author of repute, known for his books and photographs on British country life.

Christopher Simon found the story sufficiently credible to include it as an epilogue titled "My Unexpected Uncle" in his account of Sledmere and its owners, *The Big House* (2004), along with a rare photograph of Alice Carter and her pupils at the village school. Our own foraging suggests that the story is consistent with the amply attested character of Sir Mark Sykes (as he became on succeeding to the baronetcy in 1913).

One cannot sensibly explain Mark Sykes's influence on Middle East policy without parsing his personal chemistry: his risk-taking spontaneity, buoyant knight-errantry, and radiant charm. Too, there was his fluency—he could spin a cocoon around a moonbeam—and the credible awareness that he had neither political nor monetary stake in the grandiose policies he advocated. Add absence of malice, zealotry, or pomposity, and Sir Mark was to all intents the cheerful Galahad even adversaries wished they might become. Roger Adelson justly subtitled his 1975 biography "Portrait of an Amateur," explaining that Sykes used this once-honorable term to describe himself as someone possessing a flexible and independent mind, and as a person impatient with self-serving experts or political persiflage.

"Though surrounded by every luxury and every temptation to lead an idle, pleasant country life," Winston Churchill wrote in a tribute four years after Sir Mark's death, "his fancy turned to the desert rather than to the moors, to travel rather than to sport, to some piece of Imperial service single-handed in the unknown East rather than to the enjoyment of the home duties of a country gentleman." As if saluting a kindred spirit, Churchill thus expands in prefacing a 1923 biography of Sykes by the Anglo-Catholic author Shane Leslie:

> He was a unique product. His parents gave him the advantage of a public school education in sparing and sporadic installments, with the result that his originality was never cramped, and he afterwards enjoyed a University career without becoming a slave to the conventions which it not infrequently implants in susceptible youths . . . The art of conversation he had inherited from his brilliant mother; the art of drawing he was wont to practice to the delight of his friends. He wielded an able and a facile pen. The art of public speech was his, and by the combination of his matter and his manner he could hold the ear of the House of Commons when he spoke on such different subjects as the Near East, the Territorials, the Dramatic Censorship, and Ireland.[7]

No less ingratiating is the portrait sketched by the urbane Sir Ronald Storrs, Cromer's Oriental Secretary, who saw him often in Cairo. Sykes could have successfully pursued a dozen careers, Sir Ronald writes, and as a speaker was among the few for whom the House of Commons always filled, adding, "As a caricaturist and political cartoonist he could have imposed his own terms on the evening Press . . . The same vein of artistry would transform him into a music-hall comedian, holding a chance gathering spellbound by swift and complete changes of character." Storrs remembered Sykes reciting a mock parliamentary debate into a Dictaphone, replicating accurately its stock jokes and varied accents. After meeting him in Jerusalem, where Storrs was soon to become a Governor, Sir Ronald jotted in his journal, "Mark with me again, giving as always a maximum of trouble and a maximum of delight."[8]

Compare with the more equivocal if acute likeness drawn by T. E. Lawrence, who came to know Sykes on the battlefield: "He would take an aspect of the truth, detach it from its circumstances, inflate it, twist and model it," Lawrence recalls in *The Seven Pillars of Wisdom*. ". . . He saw the odd in everything and missed the even. He would sketch out in a few dashes a new world, all out of scale, but vivid as a vision of some sides of the thing we hoped. His help did us good and harm." His passing at age thirty-nine during the Spanish flu epidemic (Lawrence writes) was for the Arab cause "a tragedy of tragedies"—as with hindsight, it also proved for Zionists, whose quest for a new national home Sir Mark crucially championed.[9]

From his first days at Cambridge University, Mark's unusual gifts were apparent to his tutors and to the Master of Jesus College (the school chosen, on impulse after a brief visit, by Lady Sykes). During his university years (1897–99), Mark impressed Cambridge's foremost Orientalist, Professor Edward Granville Browne, who approved his wish to explore Ottoman lands, for which his college provided time. By then his parents had irreparably quarreled, precipitating a public trial at which their son was compelled to testify as to whether his mother had forged letters of credit at Monte Carlo on Sir Tatton's bank account. Mark's anguished testimony was as evasive as the law permitted, but after hearing handwriting experts, the jury found against Lady Sykes. Small wonder their son all but fled to the Orient, equipped with introductions provided by Browne. (A scholar fluent in Persian, Arabic, and Turkish, Browne was also a forthright defender of the region's nationalists, an authority on its minorities, and author of an 1893 travel classic, *A Year Amongst the Persians.*)

Between parental lawsuits, Cambridge terms, and foreign travel, Mark found time to apply for a commission in the Yorkshire militia that his great-uncle Mark Masterman Sykes had founded. Upon the outbreak of the Boer War in 1899, he was called up, a "most infernal nuisance," as he confided to the comely Edith Violet Gorst, whom he was courting. Once in South Africa, Lieutenant Sykes and his troops in F Company of the Third Battalion of the Yorkshire Regiment were ordered to protect an upcountry bridge from Afrikaaner guerrillas. In two years Mark saw enough action to incur a head wound, contract malaria, and suffer an infection that left him partially deaf. He also witnessed war's savagery, acquired a lifelong allergy to orthodox military thinking, and (more surprisingly, given his subsequent history) blamed Jews, bankers, and imperialists for the war. He complained in letters home that it was "for these beasts"—that is, Jewish financiers and mine owners—that he regrettably was fighting, a prejudice commonly held by upper-class denizens of British gentlemen's clubs. And make no mistake: his sympathy might lie with underdogs, but Mark Sykes assumed without question that he belonged with the governing few (as did Churchill, a founder and fellow

member of The Other Club, a gathering of like-minded wellborn maver-
icks).[10] But after the Boer War, what career would Mark now choose?

Anthony Trollope spoke for his kind when he remarked in his 1883 autobiography, "I have always thought that to sit in the British Parliament should
be the highest object of ambition to every educated Englishman."[11] True to
his precept, Trollope stood for election in 1868, presenting himself as an
"advanced conservative Liberal" in Beverley, the county seat of East Riding
in Yorkshire, which returned two members to the Commons (the incumbent
Conservative in the second constituency was Christopher Sykes, Mark's uncle,
known as "Sykey," a loyal if abused intimate of Edward, Prince of Wales). To
the benefit of English letters, Trollope mercifully lost. He did not stand again.

Returning from the Boer War to a hero's welcome, Mark Sykes was readily drawn into the political scramble, and in 1907 was adopted by Conservative Unionists as their candidate in Sykey's old seat in East Riding. His
campaign, one might say, was distinctly Markist. He illustrated addresses
with impromptu cartoons and explained to prospective voters that unlike
Socialists, who were obsessed by the future, or unlike Liberals, with their
mania for the present, his Conservatism was rooted in the past that had
made Britain great. Symbols were crucial. Warning of their disappearance,
he quoted from Benjamin Disraeli's grim vision of an egalitarian society
in his novel, *Tancred*: "The crown a cypher, the church a sect, the nobility
drones, and the people drudges."[12] Like Trollope, Sykes lost.

Yet only for the moment. The young heir had by this time married the
personable Edith Gorst. He had written well-received and elegantly patronizing books about Ottoman lands. He had served, if briefly, as parliamentary secretary for Ireland and then as an honorary attaché to the British
Embassy in Constantinople. More relevant locally, as a member of the East
Riding County Council, he worked dutifully on subcommittees dealing with
public health and education. In the stormy year 1910, precipitated by the
Liberal government's radical budget that a defiant House of Lords rejected,
there were two national elections. Twice by very narrow margins East Riding rejected Mark Sykes. But by then he was a Yorkshire character, and
he was given a fourth shot, this time in the bustling maritime city of Hull,
where an ancestral Sykes had once been mayor. He prevailed, and until his

death Mark continued to represent Central Hull, becoming in 1911 the third member of his family in a half century to sit in the House of Commons.

What changed Mark's life, and by extension the history of the Middle East, was a lucky (for the assassin) pistol shot in Sarajevo. Before 1914, the new MP was known for his literate speeches on "the Eastern Question" and his reasoned case for Irish autonomy during the Home Rule crisis that preoccupied Parliament until that August, when the Liberal government entered the Great War. One of Prime Minister Herbert Asquith's first moves was to summon High Commissioner Horatio Herbert Kitchener from his duties in Egypt to serve as War Minister in Whitehall. In early 1915, while visiting the Western Front, Lord Kitchener came upon a familiar name among officers on the War Office staff. "Sykes," he said, "what are you doing in France? You must go to the East." "What am I to do there?" Captain Sykes asked. "Just go there and come back."[13]

It was a nod from an iconic warlord at the height of his glory. The first Earl of Khartoum had been Britannia's Commander in Chief in India, Egypt, and then South Africa; he had thrashed the Mahdist Dervishes at Omdurman, and had bloodlessly ousted the French from Fashoda, securing for Britain the sources of the Nile. No general was more familiar with the strategic topography of the Holy Land, which he had surveyed as a young officer in the Royal Engineers. His appointees and protégés manned strategic posts throughout the Islamic East. In Cairo, he had handpicked Sir Henry McMahon to succeed himself as High Commissioner. Kitchener's team also included the supple Sir Ronald Storrs in Egypt; the ambitious General Sir Francis Reginald Wingate, whom he chose as Sirdar of the Egyptian Army and then as Governor-General in the Sudan; and the canny Sir Gilbert Clayton, later the regional supremo of British military intelligence.

Yet of all his lieutenants, Sir Mark Sykes, MP, a self-styled amateur whom Kitchener barely knew and casually recruited, came closest to being the stage manager of the postwar Middle East, whose essential shape and character persist to the present. It is worth pausing to examine why, and how, this came about.

Despite his disclaimers, Sir Mark Sykes proved something more than an amateur in the black arts of bureaucratic intrigue. He managed at critical junctures to nudge superiors in his preferred direction, all the while keeping his balance on the Whitehall tightrope. Thanks to his insider status, he nurtured a network of confidants from the imperial Cabinet downward to the remotest British outposts in the Islamic East. Early on he grasped the cardinal importance of keeping a seat on interdepartmental agencies tasked with coordinating policy, most especially the Bunsen Committee. Chaired by Sir Maurice de Bunsen of the Foreign Office, the panel was formed to develop a consensual view concerning the Middle East among the Foreign, War, and India Offices, plus the Admiralty and Board of Trade, with input from the Committee of Imperial Defence and its recently appointed chief, Lord Hankey, and his very capable assistant, Sir Mark Sykes.

From this perch, Sykes tacked with shifting winds, which he gauged during periodic eastward travels, beginning with the grand tour ordained by Kitchener himself. Thereafter Sir Mark's networking skills gave him direct contact with every node of power. A specimen example: Lancelot Oliphant, a diplomatic colleague from his days in Turkey, introduced him to Colonel Oswald FitzGerald, longtime secretary and (so some averred) suspiciously close friend of the bachelor War Minister. Until the moment Kitchener dramatically vanished in 1916 aboard the HMS *Hampshire* when she was struck by a German mine, FitzGerald saw to it that Sykes's memoranda went directly to "K" himself. As Mark's biographer notes, the recommendations he prepared after his grand tour "probably had less influence on Kitchener than the good words FitzGerald put in for him."[14] Or in Sykes's own formulation, "I acted, FitzGerald spoke, he [Kitchener] inspired."[15]

In another respect, Sykes was no amateur. He grasped from the first the need to influence the flow of military intelligence, especially the secret reports pertaining to British operations in the Middle East. It was Sir Mark who proposed, nurtured, and monitored the Arab Bureau that materialized in Cairo in 1916. Its founding director was the Oxford scholar and archaeologist David G. Hogarth; its father figure was Colonel Clayton, the Director of Military Intelligence (DMI); and its media star was T. E. Lawrence (of Arabia). Nominally under the Foreign Office, the bureau quickly acquired an identity of its own, and was usually at odds with New Delhi (the Viceroy of India vehemently opposed its establishment) and often with its nominal overseers in Whitehall. Sykes himself edited its classified *Arab Bulletin*, and determined the need-to-know list for its accounts of the British-backed Arab Revolt, proclaimed in June 1916 by the Grand Sharif Hussein of Mecca—for which Sir Mark designed the Arab flag ("black fess for the Abbasid of

Baghdad, white for the Omayyads of Damascus, green for the Alids of Kerbala, and red chevron for Mudhar heredity").[16]

Finally, and not least, Sykes understood the need for suitably phrased agreements that would stand the test of multiple interpretations. His skills were called upon when Prime Minister Asquith and the Bunsen Committee pondered the postwar fate of the senescent Ottoman Empire. With Anglo-Indian armies advancing into Mesopotamia, Asquith was anxious to reassure a bleeding France that Britain was not stealing a march in the Middle East. Moreover, he also confided, if the British "were to leave the other nations to scramble for Turkey without taking anything for ourselves, we should not be doing our duty."[17] It was similarly important to placate Russia, now bogged down on the Eastern Front, her all-weather Black Sea ports blocked when Turkey entered the war and sealed the Bosphorus. Asquith and his Foreign Secretary, Sir Edward Grey, agreed that discussions were essential, first with the always difficult French. So why not designate a sympathetic Briton to sound out the two allies within carefully calibrated guidelines—someone like the popular Sir Mark Sykes, a Francophile and a Roman Catholic, but withal sensible and of sturdy English stock?

After a month's preliminaries, serious Anglo-French negotiations began in London in December 1915 upon Sykes's return from an extended tour of the Middle East. Speaking for the Quai d'Orsay was a seasoned twenty-year diplomat, François Georges-Picot (1870–1951), recently Consul-General in Beirut, scion of a colonialist family, and an outspoken expositor of France's *mission historique* in the Levant. He envisioned a French-dominated *Syrie intégrale* that embraced Damascus, Aleppo, and Beirut, along with Palestine's Holy Places, the ports of Alexandretta and Haifa, the Ottoman province of Mosul, and assorted lands extending southward from the Taurus Mountains to the borders of Egypt—a prospect viewed with utter horror by the British Arabists in Cairo. Working within Downing Street and Foreign Office directives, Sykes wrested a compromise. Agreement was reached on granting France direct administrative control in a Greater Lebanon and along the coastal areas of Syria, a so-called Blue Zone, while Britain would have parallel rights within southern Mesopotamia in a Red Zone, which leapfrogged from Baghdad to a tiny coastal enclave encompassing Haifa and Acre, along with rights to a railroad linking the three cities. Palestine and its Holy Places were to be internationally administered within a smaller Brown Zone, details to be resolved postwar.

In the extensive lands in between, the signatories agreed to "protect and recognize an independent Arab State or a Confederation of Arab States" under the suzerainty of an Arab chief, occupying a sizable territory that incorporated the historic inland cities of Damascus, Aleppo, Homs, and Hama (the celebrated quartet that, as Gibbon noted, the Crusaders never conquered) together with the province of Mosul. This hypothetical Arab State was to be further divided into spheres of indirect influence, within which Britain and France would each possess the exclusive right to "supply advisers or foreign functionaries at the request of the Arab State or Confederation of Arab States."[18]

Such was the essence of the notorious Sykes-Picot Agreement, whose principal negotiators proceeded in April 1916 to Petrograd, where Sir Mark checked in at the Astoria Hotel, purchased a sheepskin vest (as he reported to his wife, Edith), then met with His Majesty's Ambassador and braced for difficult talks with Russia's Foreign Minister, Sergei Sazanov. His apprehensions proved unwarranted. Russia had already been promised control of the Bosphorus Straits in a prior secret pact, and Sazanov raised only peripheral objections to the draft agreement. He did not oppose formation of an independent Arab state, nor the international governance of Palestine. What troubled him instead was the long reach of France's zone of "indirect influence" from Syria directly to the Persian frontier. In the end, as recounted by the British scholars Efraim and Inari Karsh in their careful reconstruction, a compromise was reached "giving Russia a 60,000-square-mile band of territory between the Black Sea and the Mosul area, including the provinces of Erzerum, Trebizond, Van, and Birlis in Ottoman Armenia, and substantial parts of northern Kurdistan."[19] A month later, Great Britain formally approved this modified agreement in an exchange of notes. Its provisions remained secret until the Bolsheviks, following their November 1917 triumph, opened tsarist archives and held up Sykes-Picot as a typically nefarious example of imperial hubris.

Seldom indeed has any diplomatic document been so widely reviled, not only in print but in films and plays such as David Lean's *Lawrence of Arabia* and Terence Rattigan's *Ross*. Still, seen with cooler eyes, it seems right to pose three questions: Was the agreement substantially at variance with prevailing Great Power morality? Were its provisions truly a shock to Arab chiefs who believed they had been promised an extensive independent state? And did the agreement conflict with undertakings privately made to the Arab Revolt's leader, Grand Sharif Hussein of Mecca, in his protracted correspondence in 1916–17 with Egypt's High Commissioner, Sir Henry McMahon? A reading of the full record suggests that on all three counts a reasonable answer is No.

To be sure, the Arabs whose lands were parceled out were not consulted about the agreement's projected political arrangements—nor were North Africans about France's earlier schemes for colonial rule, nor for that matter were Native Americans, Hawaiians, Mexicans, Filipinos, Haitians, Dominicans, Nicaraguans, Panamanians, or the newly sovereign Cubans consulted about Washington's equally intrusive maneuvers to shape all their constitutions. Subsequent research indicates, moreover, that Sykes-Picot's existence was known in substance to Grand Sharif Hussein and his sons, and that the charge of deception—ably and eloquently pressed by the Lebanese Christian George Antonius in *The Arab Awakening* (1938)—was overstated. No scholar has done more to unsettle two generations of judgment on these controversies than the late Professor Elie Kedourie, a London School of Economics troublemaker who chanced to have been born Jewish in Baghdad. His meticulous autopsy of the McMahon-Hussein correspondence, *In the Anglo-Arab Labyrinth*, published in 1976 and reissued posthumously in 2000, remains a revisionist landmark; it contends persuasively that the not-exceptionally-bright High Commissioner had indeed been evasive, sometimes confused and prone to employ fudge, but nowhere offered the categorical promises for expansive Arab nationhood claimed by the Grand Sharif and implied by T. E. Lawrence in *The Seven Pillars of Wisdom*.[20] In fact, although too seldom noted, Lawrence at different times expressed conflicting verdicts on Sykes-Picot.

Writing in November 1929 to the American William Yale (a Standard Oil representative who was present at the creation), T. E. Shaw, as Lawrence now signed himself, expressed amazement at Yale's belief that British officers in Syria tried to scuttle Sykes-Picot. Not at all, retorted Lawrence:

> The S-P treaty was the Arab sheet-anchor. The French saw that, and worked frantically for the alternative of the mandate. By a disgraceful bargain the British supported them to gain Mesopotamia. Under the S-P treaty the French got only the coast: and the Arabs (native administration) were to have Aleppo, Hama, Homs, Damascus & Trans-Jordan. By the mandate swindle, England and France got the lot. The S-P treaty was

absurd in its boundaries, but it did recognize the claims of the Syrians to self-government, and it was ten thousand times better than the eventual settlement.[21]*

In truth, everybody associated with British policy in the Middle East leaned one way or another at varying points during the long Great War, often depending on the day's telegrams, a newspaper report, or with whom and about what one was conversing. Sir Mark Sykes's own odyssey was striking for its wide arc, which carried him from conventional High Toryism to his personal brand of neo-Conservatism, leading him as if by destiny to Zion. One can map his journey.

In the gloomy final months of 1916, discontent pervaded the United Kingdom. From the workplace to the back benches of Parliament, unhappy Britons judged Prime Minister Herbert Asquith a tepid and unlucky warlord. When combat began in July 1914, people hoped or even expected that the fighting would end quickly, possibly by Christmas. Instead Asquith presided over an ongoing blood sacrifice in the Western trenches, and a sequence of defeats in the East—a debacle at Gallipoli, a failed attack on Baghdad, a humiliating surrender of starving Anglo-Indian troops at Kut. In an all-party revolt, Asquith was replaced in December by his restless, fertile, silver-tongued Welsh party rival, David Lloyd George, whose Nonconformist origins endowed him with a special concern for the biblical East. (When General Edmund Allenby began his drive on Jerusalem, Lloyd George sent him his own copy of *The Historical Geography of the Holy Land* by the Scottish scholar George Adam Smith; "the Bull" kept it in his saddlebags.) Lloyd George assembled a broad-based coalition that incorporated leaders of the rising Labour Party as well as such Tory luminaries as former Prime Minister Arthur Balfour, who now became Foreign Secretary, and Lord Curzon, the former Viceroy of India, newly named Lord President of the War Cabinet and soon to be chairman of the Middle East Committee.

The new administration's command center was the War Cabinet, whose five members (later expanded) met once or sometimes twice a day, chart-

---

* Lawrence refers here to the mandates awarded by the League of Nations for British and French rule in Iraq, Palestine, Syria, and Lebanon.

ing Britain's course until the Paris Peace Conference. Besides Lloyd George
and Curzon, its original members included another venerable lion, Viscount
Alfred Milner, a consummate imperial bureaucrat with a pipeline to *The
Times*, along with two comparative novices in global affairs, Andrew Bonar
Law, the Chancellor of the Exchequer, and Arthur Henderson, parliamentary chief of the Labourites. For guidance on foreign policy, its members
relied on two key assistants, Leopold Amery, whose brief included Europe
and the Far East, and his tireless friend and fellow Tory MP, Sir Mark Sykes.

    The advent of Lloyd George was "more than a change of government.
It was a revolution, British-style," writes one of the era's leading historians, Oxford's A. J. P. Taylor. The new Prime Minister (in Taylor's words,
"the nearest thing England has known to a Napoleon") was the first humbly born Briton to reach the top, and only the third (in Lloyd George's own
words) who "had not passed through the Staff College of the old Universities," the other two being Wellington and Disraeli. Although he did not lead
a party and had no real friends ("and didn't deserve any," injects Taylor),
Lloyd George recruited new men, created whole departments of state, and
experimented with new forms of parliamentary governance. Since his War
Cabinet lacked a staff, Lloyd George assembled a team of his own, White
House style, which he quartered in huts on the greens backing Downing
Street, known as "the Garden Suburb."[22]

    From the Garden Suburb, Sykes propagated his revised views about the
Middle East. Before the Great War, he had approved the long-standing British policy of seeking to defend intact and gently reform the creaking Ottoman Empire in Asia, seen strategically as a valuable buffer shielding the
Suez Canal and the paths to India. By 1913, when he elaborated his views
in Parliament, Turkey had already bungled two Balkan wars under an insolvent Sultan beset by erratic Young Turk reformers. After Sarajevo, Sir Mark
acceded to the different approach put forward by the Bunsen Committee. Its
members weighed three postwar options once Turkey entered the war: keep
the Ottoman Empire intact but submissive; annex it outright; or divide it
into semi-autonomous units. The committee favored the third option as the
most practical. By early 1915, Sir Mark veered toward dismemberment. As
he half-seriously admonished his friend Aubrey Herbert, formerly an attaché in Constantinople, "I perceive by your letter that you are pro-Turk still
... Your Policy is wrong. Turkey must cease to be. Smyrna shall be Greek,
Adalia [Antalya] Italian, Southern Taurus and North Syria French, Filis-

tin [Palestine] British, Mesopotamia British, and everything else Russian—including Constantinople . . . and I shall sing *Te Deum* in St. Sophia, *Nunc Dimittis* in the Mosque of Omar. We will sing it in Welsh, Polish, Keltic, and Armenian in honour of the gallant little nation."[23]

By 1917, Sykes all but disowned the secret pact that bore his name, presciently anticipating that its disclosure would provoke an unpleasant uproar. In Paris, he vainly sought to persuade Picot that annexation was a relic of imperialism past, and that France should moderate her claims in the Levant. He expressed dismay when the Allies secretly offered Italy, a late-coming co-belligerent, her own slices of postwar Anatolia. When Major General Stanley Maude and his Anglo-Indian army avenged prior defeats by capturing Baghdad in March, Sykes persuaded the War Cabinet to reject a low-key proclamation in favor of his own resonant draft affirming that the British came as liberators, not conquerors. Sir Mark did what he could to succor the Arab Revolt led by King Hussein of the Hejaz (as the Grand Sharif was now styled), with whom he and Picot met in May. Sir Mark even suggested a new protocol, at which Picot balked, envisioning thrones for King Hussein's sons in Syria and Iraq, "provided always that such an arrangement is fully in accord with the desires of the population of the respective areas," thus anticipating Churchill's regal dispensation for Iraq and Jordan.[24] In short, the main elements of the eventual postwar settlement had already germinated in Sykes's mind, with an exception he was about to resolve: Palestine.

Seismic events elsewhere contributed to the wholesale rethinking of long-standing British policy, especially of its rhetorical presentation. In Russia, military disasters and industrial strikes led to the once-unthinkable abdication of the Tsar and the emergence, in March 1917, of a revolutionary, pro-democratic Provisional Government. A month later, the United States and its high-minded Chief Executive entered the war against Germany (but not, as is commonly forgotten, against the Ottoman Empire; America formally remained an Associated Power, not an Ally). For ordinary Britons, 1917 was the war's bleakest year, a time of shortages, rationing, and queues (a foreign word for what quickly became a British institution, as did reduced hours for public houses, a wartime step meant to promote sobriety). All of the above widened the clamor for trade union rights, votes for women, pacifism, teetotalism, welfare benefits, Irish home rule, and self-determination (a radical new phrase introduced by Woodrow Wilson).

As "The War to End Wars" entered its climactic phase, visions of a braver, brighter, redemptive new world order—democratic, perhaps Socialist, hopefully pacific—gripped not just Great Britain but many of the Empire's colonial subjects. In May, Arthur Henderson, the leader of the Labour Party, proposed to speak out for a compromise peace at a Socialist conference in Stockholm. This was too much for his War Cabinet colleagues, and Lloyd George ruled that Henderson could speak for himself but not for His Majesty's Government. In Parliament, the Prime Minister's decision was fluently defended by Sir Mark Sykes. Yes of course Britons were fighting for the Empire, "but I do not speak in the Imperialistic sense when I use the word 'Empire.' We are fighting for those free people of European stock, our colonies beyond the sea who live in democratic communities, and we are fighting that we may carry democracy, civilisation, and progress into Asia in the years to come."[25]

"Hear, hear!" burst out Lloyd George from the front benches. It had become a Great War for Civilization, not for sordid spoils. Such was the moment, and such the mood, as Sykes galvanized support for the Zionist cause, his progress abetted by the steady advance of British arms toward Jerusalem and its Holy Places.

No one can pinpoint just when Sir Mark became a Zionist, his son Christopher Sykes has written, "but there is no doubt as to who first taught him Zionist principles."[26] His mentor was Dr. Moses Gaster, a Romanian-born émigré who resettled in London, where he became the Haham, or Chief Rabbi, of the Sephardic Community. On this, we have Sir Mark's own testimony, voiced at a Zionist rally in the London Opera House on December 2, 1917: "I should like to say, before I say another word, that the reason I am interested in this Movement is that I met one some two years ago who is now upon this platform, and who opened my eyes to what the Movement meant . . . I mean Dr. Gaster." At three propitious meetings in May 1916 with the Chief Rabbi, Sir Mark had discussed not only the origins of modern political Zionism—a movement figuratively reborn in an 1896 book, *The Jewish State*, written in white heat in Paris during the Dreyfus Affair by the Viennese journalist and playwright Theodor Herzl—but also the arcane politics of Diaspora communities in Russia, Germany, France, and especially neutral America.[27]

Thanks to his seat on the Bunsen Committee, Sykes was by then familiar with memoranda submitted early in the war by Sir Herbert Samuel, then Postmaster General and, as of 1916, the Home Secretary in Asquith's Liberal government. In his own words, Samuel was "the first member of the Jewish community to sit in a British Cabinet" (adding that Disraeli in his boyhood had left the Jewish community, and never rejoined). In two memoranda, Sir Herbert vigorously advocated the postwar establishment of a British protectorate in Palestine, a status preferable in his view to continued Ottoman rule, annexation by France, or international control. Such a protectorate, he contended, would be welcomed by world Jewry in the belief that Britain would encourage Jewish settlement and improvement of Palestine, laying the groundwork for a future "National Home" for the Jewish people—a phrase just coming into currency.[28]

For the moment, Samuel acknowledged, the time was not ripe for the creation of a sovereign Jewish state, the goal fixed in 1897 in Basel at the first Zionist Congress. Yet the auguries were auspicious. There was, to begin with, a well-established British tradition of Christian Zionism. Its roots can be traced to the 1830s, when Egypt's Governor, Mohammed Ali, rebelled against his nominal Ottoman rulers and dispatched an army to Syria, the Turkish province in which the Holy Places were located. To gain foreign favor, especially in England, Mohammed Ali encouraged Europeans to open consulates in Jerusalem and engage without harassment in missionary work. The British established a consulate in 1836, its implicit task being to protect Protestant institutions in the Holy City; the French assumed a similar role for Roman Catholics, as did the Russians for the Orthodox. This arrangement persisted after the Ottoman Sultan expelled the Egyptians and restored Turkish rule in Syria. A Protestant Episcopal See was founded in Jerusalem in 1841, and the equivalent of an Anglican cathedral, Christ Church, was consecrated in 1849. By then the British popularized the term *Palestine* to designate the Holy Land, the term stemming from the Greek *Philistia* or "Land of the Philistines," and adapted by Rome to refer to southern Syria, but otherwise unfamiliar to Turks and Arabs.

It is hard to overstate the enthusiasm prompted by the Victorian rediscovery of Palestine, especially among devout Protestants. Travel books, geographical treatises, and illustrated tea-table folios proliferated. The

Scottish-born David Roberts, R.A., explored the Holy Land between 1842 and 1849, producing tinted lithographs that filled large-format volumes. No less intrepid was the photographer Francis Frith, who in 1856 sailed eastward, where he hauled a wheeled darkroom across deserts to capture the Holy Land on camera for the first time. In her novel *Daniel Deronda* (1876), George Eliot, a quintessential "Gentile Zionist," sent Daniel to the Promised Land to reconnect with his heritage and establish an ideal Jewish Commonwealth. Americans followed close behind. The Protestant divine Edward Robinson began combing the region in 1838 to identify scores of Scriptural sites, as set forth in his three-volume *Biblical Researches in Palestine*, long a fixture in parsonage libraries. And in 1867, Mark Twain boarded the *Quaker City* to join the "Great Pleasure Excursion to Europe and the Holy Land," a voyage that incubated *Innocents Abroad*, the book that established him as a national sage.

Conveniently, theology converged with military necessity. Following the 1869 opening of the Suez Canal, and the British purchase six years later of the controlling shares in the canal company, safeguarding the "imperial lifeline" became an overriding security concern. This added a new dimension to spiritual interest in the Holy Land. When the Palestine Exploration Fund was founded to encourage scientific investigation of the "Archaeology, Geography, Geology and Natural History of Palestine," its birth in 1865 was hailed not just by the Church of England and the Royal Geographical Society, but also by Lord Russell, the Foreign Secretary. The fund soon collaborated with the Royal Engineers in mapping western Palestine, under the direction of a keen-eyed Indian Army officer. In 1877, Lieutenant Kitchener reported that his team had recorded every single river, road, and ruin in its assigned area.

Yet some prominent Christian Zionists had little use for nearby Jews. This was true of Lord Ashley, the soon-to-be seventh Earl of Shaftesbury, a leading member of the London Society for Promoting Christianity Among the Jews. As detailed by the British legal scholar Leonard Stein, at the very time Lord Ashley pleaded for the restoration of the Jews to Palestine, he viewed their wish to be eligible to sit in Parliament as "an insult to Christianity."[29] In fact, for "Restorationists" like Shaftesbury, the ingathering of Israel's tribes, and their collective turn to Christianity, was an essential prologue to the Second Coming, as it remains more recently for some American evangelists whenever war explodes in the Holy Land.

Thus for whatever reason—romantic or militarist, apocalyptic or secular, philo-Semitism or its obverse—the Zionist project found influential British well-wishers, so much so that early in the new century, a Conservative government seriously weighed opening the Egyptian Sinai and/or British-ruled Cyprus to Jewish settlement. Colonial Secretary Joseph Chamberlain, backed by a sympathetic Prime Minister, Arthur Balfour, put forth in 1903 an even bolder proposition: Why not colonize Uganda? The proposal was formally and astonishingly presented to Theodor Herzl, a private citizen speaking for a dispersed people. The "Uganda scheme" split the Zionist movement, and when Herzl died the following year, the proposal died with him. Yet the Zionist dream had found its way into the complex mind of Balfour, an otherwise worldly philosopher who had succeeded his uncle Lord Salisbury as Prime Minister and leader of the Tory Party. In 1905, while campaigning in Manchester, home for some fifteen thousand Jews, many of them refugees from Russia's Pale of Settlement, Balfour paused to meet a newly arrived young Zionist, Chaim Weizmann, to ask why his movement had spurned Uganda, acclaimed by imperialists as "the pearl of Africa." Dr. Weizmann recorded what followed: "I began to sweat blood to make my meaning clear through my English. At the very end I made an effort. I had an idea. I said: 'Mr. Balfour, if you were offered Paris instead of London would you take it? Would you take Paris instead of London?' He looked surprised. He: 'But London is our own!' I said: 'Jerusalem was our own when London was a marsh.' He said: 'That's true!' I did not see him again until 1916."[30]

Thus Balfour took seriously Herbert Samuel's proposal for imposing a postwar protectorate on Palestine. The real obstacle at that moment was the dismissive snort emanating from 10 Downing Street. In one heartfelt passage, Prime Minister Asquith confided to his journal, "I think I have already referred to Herbert Samuel's dithyrambic memorandum, urging that in carving up the Turks' Asiatic dominions we should take Palestine, into which the scattered Jews would in time swarm back from all quarters of the globe, and in due course obtain Home Rule. Curiously enough, the only other partisan of this proposal is Lloyd George, who I need not say, does not care a damn for the Jews or their past or their future, but thinks it will be an outrage to let the Holy Places pass into the possession or the protection of 'agnostic, atheistic France.' "[31] Yet Asquith's views ceased to matter following his abrupt displacement in December 1916 by David Lloyd George. The Zionist cause was no longer lost. Members of the War Cabinet and their advisers were all sympathetic, and the pro-Zionist Balfour was now reborn as Foreign Secretary in Lloyd George's coalition government.

The elements were thus in place, awaiting a catalytic spark, fittingly supplied by a bearded chemist from Manchester.

When he first met Mark Sykes in 1916, Chaim Weizmann was forty-two and had taught chemistry for three years at the University of Manchester. Born in the Russian village of Motol, he had earned his doctorate in Switzerland before migrating to Britain, where his terse English and mesmeric demeanor caught attention from the outset. "Weizmann was not only a dexterous and resourceful advocate—flexible, sure-footed, highly sensitive to atmosphere, and with an unerring instinct for timing," writes Leonard Stein in *The Balfour Declaration*, "he possessed in high degree the power to kindle the imagination and to impart to others some of his own mystical faith in the destiny of his people and the significance of their survival. Among the principle architects of the Declaration, two at least—Balfour and Mark Sykes—were highly sensitive to the Jewish mystique." Another fledgling diplomat who worked with Sykes was the future author Harold Nicolson, who remarked of Weizmann, "I sometimes wonder whether his fellow Jews realize how deeply he impressed us Gentiles by his heroic, his Maccabean quality."[32]

To his natural gifts, chance added a bonus. He had lived for two decades in Manchester, where radical idealism found its journalistic expression in the righteous but readable columns of *The Manchester Guardian* (as it was until its name was cropped in 1959). At a charity party in the autumn of 1914, Dr. Weizmann met C. P. Scott, the paper's formidable editor, and the enchantment was mutual. A few weeks later, writing to Scott, the émigré scientist with uncanny intuition outlined what was to come:

> Don't you think the chance for the Jewish people is within the limits of discussion at least? I realize of course, that we cannot "claim" anything, we are much too atomised for it, but we can reasonably say, that should Palestine fall within the British sphere of influence and should Britain encourage a Jewish settlement there, as a British dependency, we could have in 25–30 years about a million of Jews there, perhaps more; they would develop the country, bring back civilisation to it, and form a very

effective guard of the Suez canal—and perhaps against an aggression from Constantinople. I need not dwell upon all the possibilities. I have only put down the minimum. Palestine can easily become an Asiatic Belgium in the hands of the Jews.[33]

Not only did Scott from that moment embrace the Zionist cause, he also opened the corridors of power to its ablest prophet. On December 3, 1914, having already arrived on the night train from Manchester to London, the editor met Dr. Weizmann at Euston Station and with a flourish announced, "We're going to have breakfast at nine o'clock with Mr. Lloyd George!"[34] The meeting exceeded Weizmann's expectations, as did his initial encounter with Sir Herbert Samuel, whom he erroneously assumed to be too Anglicized to be a serious Zionist. And then the fortunes of war augmented the chemist's influence. A month after his breakfast with Weizmann, Lloyd George was named chairman of the government's Munitions Committee, which metamorphosed into a new Ministry of Munitions under the Welshman's excitable (and productive) direction. And lo, in his Manchester laboratories Dr. Weizmann struck upon a practical method for producing acetone, a key to the manufacture of cordite, a smokeless powder used lethally by British artillery. Years later, Lloyd George suggested that the Balfour Declaration was in essence a payoff for Dr. Weizmann's wartime services, although as a Low Churchman bred in chapel, Lloyd George otherwise liked to boast that he better remembered the kings of Israel than those of England, and had a better grasp of biblical geography than that of France.

Inarguably, worldly considerations helped clear the path that led to Cabinet approval of the Balfour Declaration. In Whitehall during the Great War, an abiding British concern was the real or surmised influence of American Jewry on the Wilson White House. Particular notice was taken of the President's friendship with Louis Brandeis, a committed Zionist and the first Jewish nominee to the U.S. Supreme Court. British policy makers were worried as well by antiwar sentiments spreading through Russia's alienated and sizable Jewish minority. Moreover, not a few Christian Zionists shared with anti-Semites a cabalistic presumption that Zionists could somehow conjure the support of their influential brethren in high finance, the arts, and journalism—a presumption that Dr. Weizmann and his allies did not endorse but certainly did not discourage. In reality, as the lawyer and historian David Fromkin has shrewdly noted, out of an estimated three million Jews living in the United States in 1914, a mere twelve thousand belonged to an amateurishly led Zionist Federation, which claimed but five hundred members in New York. Its annual budget prior to 1914 never exceeded $5,200, and the largest single gift it received totaled $200. It was not a powerful Zionist movement that brought about the Balfour Declaration, but the exact reverse.[35]

All this hung in the air as Sir Mark Sykes met Chaim Weizmann for the first time in January 1916 and asked him to prepare a memorandum defining Zionist goals. He did. It read as follows: "Palestine to be recognized as the Jewish National Home, with liberty of immigration to Jews of all countries, who are to enjoy full national rights; a charter to be granted to a Jewish Company; local government to be accorded to the Jewish populace; and the Hebrew language to be officially recognized."[36]

This text circulated over a two-year period through numerous meetings between senior Whitehall officials and British or non-British Zionists, among Jewish agricultural colonists from Palestine, and with café intellectuals from Eastern Europe, plus French and Russian diplomats with specific concerns about the post-Ottoman Middle East. As successive drafts made their way through Whitehall, their language prompted an impassioned dissent from Edwin Samuel Montagu, the second practicing Jew (after Herbert Samuel) to assume high office in a British Government (as Minister of Munitions succeeding Lloyd George, then as Secretary of State for India). Writing in August 1916 to a Foreign Office colleague, he said that the essential issue was whether Jews were members of a religion or a race: "For myself I have long made the choice. I view with horror the aspirations for national entity. Did I accept it, as a patriotic Englishman, I should resign . . . Nobody is entitled to occupy the position I do unless he is free and determined to consider, and consider only, the interests of the British Empire."[37]

Within Whitehall, Montagu was a minority voice. Nation-building and the redressing of historic wrongs were in the air, so much that by 1917 Mark Sykes was searching for language to reconcile the aspirations of Jews, Arabs, and Armenians. At a London rally in December, he envisioned a Zionist Palestine as bringing "the spirituality of Asia to Europe and the vitality of Europe to Asia," yet he also urged Zionists to think "of your fellows in adversity, the Armenians and the Arabs." Five days later, in Manchester, he indirectly responded to Montagu: "No British Jew will be less British because he can look to the cradle of his race with pride." He then reminded a Zionist audience that some eight million Arabs were favored by abundant manpower, virgin soil, petroleum, and brains: "What was that going to produce by 1950? The Mesopotamian canal system would be reconstructed. Syria must become the granary of Europe. Baghdad, Damascus and Aleppo would be each as big as Manchester. Therefore, I warn Jews to look through Arab glasses."[38]

For his part, Lord Balfour in May 1917 journeyed to America to discuss, among other things, policies in the Middle East. Shortly after arriving in Washington he was introduced to Justice Brandeis at a White House luncheon. "You are one of the Americans I wanted to meet," said the Foreign Secretary. In their ensuing discussions, Brandeis made plain his support for an exclusively British administration of Palestine, and discouraged any hopes for American participation. By the time Balfour returned to London, the prevailing views within Lloyd George's coalition substantially confirmed the intuitive assessment of the emeritus imperial statesman Lord Cromer, who remarked of Zionism in *The Spectator*: "Before long politicians will be unable to brush it aside as the fantastic dream of a few idealists."[39]

The stream of memoranda and innumerable discussions that occupied Mark Sykes in 1917 can be compressed. In July he collaborated on a draft declaration that was transmitted to the Foreign Secretary from the titular head of the British Zionist Federation, Lord Lionel Walter Rothschild. It read, "His Majesty's Government accepts the principle that Palestine should be reconstituted as the national home of the Jewish people. His Majesty's Government will use their best endeavours to secure the achievement of this object and will be ready to consider any suggestions on the subject which the Zionist Organization may desire to lay before them." The War Cabinet then debated and amended the draft: "the national home" first became "a home for the Jewish people" and finally "a national home for the Jewish people."

As the arguments advanced, so did British arms in the Middle East. General Sir Edmund Allenby, a seasoned cavalry officer, assumed command in June 1917 of an Egyptian Expeditionary Force, now revitalized and expanded at the express order of Lloyd George. In October, the eighty-eight-thousand-strong force invaded Palestine, plowing through Turkish defenses in an offensive intended to capture Jerusalem by Christmas, thus restoring

Christian dominion of the Holy City while also—a seasonal ribbon on the Yule tree—shutting out the French. Allenby delivered: Jerusalem fell on December 8, and after its British conqueror solemnly entered the Jaffa Gate on foot, he made clear to François Georges-Picot personally what nation was in charge.

In London, meanwhile, the Cabinet negotiations over the Zionist resolution had concluded. A new crisis added urgency to the declaration. Russia's Provisional Government was tottering, and its overthrow would likely mean that Russia would leave the war. Why not encourage Russian Jews to use their influence against peace talks?

The decision lay with a War Cabinet whose members by upbringing and belief were predisposed to Zionism. Of the nine persons who at different points served in the all-powerful War Cabinet, all but Lord Curzon were raised in a Low Church, evangelical, or nonconforming Protestant tradition. An especially ardent pro-Zionist was the sole non-Briton, Jan Christian Smuts, once a Boer general, later a British field marshal and member of the South African Parliament. "I need not remind you," he informed a Jewish audience in 1919, "that the white people of South Africa and especially the older Dutch population, have been brought up almost entirely on the Jewish tradition."[40]

Other Nonconformists included Sir Edward Carson, "the king of Ulster," who spoke for most unyielding Protestants in Northern Ireland, while the Cabinet's two Labourites, Arthur Henderson and George Barnes, were likewise Low Churchmen. So were its three Tories, Andrew Bonar Law, Lord Milner (raised as a Lutheran), and Austen Chamberlain (a Unitarian). The sole born-and-bred Anglican, Lord Curzon, was also the most ambivalent about Zionism, fearing an Arab backlash and urging a narrow, prudent interpretation of the Balfour Declaration's porous language. That Zionism's most effective lobbyist from within, Sir Mark Sykes, was a Roman Catholic added an unusual ecumenical touch to an unprecedented Christian gesture of reparations to a persecuted people.[41]

The epochal declaration came before the War Cabinet on the last day of October. Lord Balfour summarized the arguments for and against, specifically addressing Curzon's objections to the vague term "national home," maintaining that it did not mean the establishment of an independent Jewish state (although on different occasions he implied that it did). It signified instead, he said, that the Jews had to work out their own salvation and create "a real center of national culture and focus of national life" in Palestine.

And so it came to pass that His Majesty's Government that day approved the sending of this letter to the titular president of the British Zionist Federation. "Dear Lord Rothschild," it began, "I have much pleasure in conveying to you, on behalf of His Majesty's Government, the following declaration of sympathy with Jewish Zionist aspirations which had been submitted to, and approved by, the Cabinet."

In its final form, the declaration distilled two millennia of blood and tears into seventy-five words: "His Majesty's Government views with favour the establishment in Palestine of a national home for the Jewish people, and will use their best endeavours to facilitate the achievement of this object, it being clearly understood that nothing shall be done which may prejudice the civil and religious rights of existing non-Jewish communities in Palestine, or the rights and political status enjoyed by Jews in any other country." It concluded, if anticlimactically, "I should be grateful if you would bring this declaration to the knowledge of the Zionist Federation. Yours, Arthur James Balfour."[42]

As Sir Mark Sykes, after leaving the War Cabinet room, exclaimed for the ages on a sheet of paper that he handed to an anxious visitor in the waiting room, "Dr. Weizmann, it's a boy!"[43]

Initially, what was promptly called the Balfour Declaration did not cause a stir, at least among Christians. On November 9, 1917, the day the declaration became public, the bigger news was a coup d'etat in Petrograd led by V. I. Lenin, whose Bolsheviks vowed to give Russians peace, land, and bread—thus negating one of the tactical justifications for the declaration. Headlines in the British press—"Palestine for the Jews" (*The Times*) and "A State for the Jews" (*Daily Express*)—conveyed the common belief that a "national home" was tantamount to a Jewish state, although British officials in the Middle East defensively insisted to worried Arabs that no such status was envisioned. An astute American, William Yale, a Standard Oil executive then reporting to the State Department from Jerusalem, immediately sensed trouble. Yale contrasted the jubilation among Jews with the tepid disavowals offered by local British officials, one of whom confessed, "Officially I can say not a state, but unofficially I simply don't know."[44]

Nor was it clear that even the War Cabinet knew what the declaration portended, as was evident in tortuous statements its members made to the press and Parliament. Still, on one point there was agreement among Whitehall insiders—the idea of a British blessing for a "national home" may have originated with Dr. Weizmann, but it was Mark Sykes who gave the idea legs. An insider judgment was expressed by William Ormsby-Gore, an officer in the Arab Bureau in 1916–17 who then joined Sykes and Leopold Amery as a Third Assistant Secretary to the War Cabinet. "Mark Sykes was the chief motive force behind the British Government's Near Eastern policy in the war," Ormsby-Gore wrote in 1923. "He inspired both the Arab and Jewish policies, and was chiefly responsible for their adoption by Ministers at home. He was an invaluable champion of any cause, and he embraced the cause of the non-Turkish peoples whose land had been subject to Turkish misrule with all the generosity and enthusiasm for which he was so remarkable." Ormsby-Gore elaborated: "He never failed to see the big issues, and consequently perhaps was impatient of details. His ideas were rough hewn like his drawings, and his methods direct and at times boisterous. Consequently he was better in London than in the East, where, in the Arab world especially, every issue and every move is complicated by personal or parochial cross currents which tried the patience and ingenuity of every British officer who was trying to help on the spot . . . He was particularly resentful of racial prejudices and animosities, between Jew and Arab, on the grounds that both had everything to gain from co-operation and accommodation . . . But Mark always underestimated the particularism of the Arabs."[45]

Unspoken by Ormsby-Gore was the less estimable side of Mark Sykes's genius. Just as a youth he fought mock battles on the great lawn of Sledmere, just as he found it amusing that the make-believe kingdom of Monaco was defended by a toy army and financed by a casino, so to the adult Sykes, politics was a pageant, and wars akin to a medieval joust. He was insulated by his station not only from the quotidian irritations of ordinary life but also from taking full responsibility for an impulsive liaison that resulted (so it is plausibly surmised) in the birth of a son whose inconvenient existence was kept from him. It does not diminish his real gifts and chivalric altruism to add that like all mortals he was fallible.

Still, Ormsby-Gore's judgment overall was confirmed by contemporaries and is seconded by historians. Tracing the origins of the British mandate in Palestine, the Great War historian Barbara Tuchman calls Sir Mark "the one man who came the closest to holding all the threads in his hand at any one time."[46] In his autobiography, Chaim Weizmann singled out Sykes. "It seemed to me," he wrote, referring to events in 1917, "that the only man by whom the British Government could be adequately represented, who thoroughly understood the Near East, and who enjoyed the full confidence of the Arabs, Jews and Armenians, was Sir Mark Sykes, the man who had had this particular question in his hands for three years."[47]

Hence the near-universally expressed sorrow when Mark Sykes died on February 16, 1919, a few months before his fortieth birthday. Exhausted from his Eastern travels, he had arrived at the Paris Peace Conference. He had joined a friend on February 10 to attend a production of Massenet's *Thaïs*, set in fourth-century Egypt. He fell ill that night, a presumed victim of the Spanish flu epidemic, the deadliest of the century, which claimed twenty to forty million lives. His wife was also stricken but survived him. The news of his death elicited stunned and heartfelt tributes from friends and colleagues, and from the peoples whose causes he embraced: Jews, Arabs, and Armenians. His body was borne with military honors to Sledmere, where he had been designing a war memorial for friends and Yorkshire soldiers who had already fallen. One brass panel had been left unfilled, and on it was etched Sir Mark's likeness, wearing medieval armor, sword, and shield, with the Holy City in the background. "Had he lived," wrote his colleague Ormsby-Gore, "the history of the Near East since the war would have been different."[48]

But would it? Or had it all inevitably gone sour?

Nine decades later, in July 2006, as Hezbollah loosed showers of rockets from Lebanon and Israel massively retaliated, *Washington Post* columnist Richard Cohen expressed unorthodox misgivings that provoked a blizzard of impassioned emails. "The greatest mistake Israel could make at the moment," he wrote, "is to forget that Israel itself is a mistake." As he elaborated, "It is an honest mistake, a well-intentioned mistake, a mistake for which no one is culpable, but the idea of creating a nation of European Jews in an area of Arab Muslims (and some Christians) has produced a century of warfare and terrorism of the sort we are seeing now. Israel fights Hezbollah in the north and Hamas in the south, but the most formidable enemy is history itself."[49]

Richard Cohen's contention deserves more than an angry dismissal by friends of Israel. His is scarcely a new contention. That the Balfour Declaration would foment discord was foreseen by Americans like Colonel Edward House, at the time Woodrow Wilson's closest adviser, and as we have noted, by prominent British Jews like Edwin Montagu. Writing retrospectively about Britain's passing moment in the Middle East, the Oxford scholar Elizabeth Monroe remarks of the declaration, "Measured by British interests alone, it was one of the greatest mistakes in our imperial history."[50] This is (and was) not just a British view. In 1947, Loy Henderson, the director of the State Department's Office of Near Eastern Affairs, advised President Truman that the creation of a Jewish state was opposed by practically every member of the Foreign Service concerned with the Middle East. Almost the entire pantheon of the capital's Wise Men—George Marshall, Dean Acheson, George Kennan, Charles Bohlen, James Forrestal, and Robert Lovett—opposed recognizing an independent Israel, which they viewed (writes Robert D. Kaplan in *The Arabists*) "as an oil-poor impediment to good relations with the oil-rich and strategically located Arabs at a time when the United States was embarking on a worldwide struggle with the Soviet Union."[51]

Other Americans were no less wary about the Zionist experiment, an example being the liberal-minded foreign correspondent Vincent Sheean. In his widely read autobiography, *Personal History* (1935), he recalls arriving in Palestine as a pro-Zionist pilgrim, only to become one of the movement's critics. He was present during five bloody days of Arab-Jewish rioting that spread from Jerusalem's Wailing Wall to Hebron and beyond, the official toll being 120 Jews and 87 Arabs killed, and 198 Jews and 185 Arabs wounded. His reports on the melee appeared in *The New York World*, and in testifying before a British commission of inquiry, Sheean reiterated his belief that a deliberate, organized insult to Muslim Holy Places had needlessly provoked the slaughter. Elsewhere he had written about wars arising from historical necessity, "[b]ut here, in this miserable little country, no bigger in relation to the world than the tip of your finger, I could see no historical necessity whatever. The country was tiny and was already inhabited; why couldn't the Zionists leave it alone? It could never hold enough Jews to make even a beginning towards the solution of the Jewish problem, it would always be a prey to such ghastly horrors as those I saw every day and every night: religion, the eternal intransigence of religion, ensured that the problem would never be solved. The Holy Land seemed as near an approximation of hell on earth as I had ever seen."[52]

Yet one can view the same facts from a different perspective. For many Jews, what happened after the Balfour Declaration offered a foretaste of the dangers of relying on the goodwill of Christian Zionists. No British politician seemed more committed to that cause than David Lloyd George, yet not only did the Welsh Liberal lose interest (in his voluminous postwar memoirs, he devoted a single sentence to the declaration), but also he became, if briefly, a tout for Adolf Hitler. In 1936, he visited the Führer at Berchtesgaden and praised him as "the greatest living German." (His "rapturous accounts of his conversations make odd reading today," wrote a onetime disciple, Winston Churchill, in 1948.) Lloyd George informed readers of *The Daily Express* that Hitler was "a born leader. A magnetic, dynamic personality with a single-minded purpose," to raise living standards in a Germany that no longer desired "to invade any other land." A year later, when the character of the Nazi regime was clear to all but the purblind, Lloyd George confided to a friend that he only wished "we had a man of his [Hitler's] supreme quality at the head of affairs in our country today."[53]

(In contrast, Lord Balfour did not prove to be a fair-weather Zionist. Before his death in 1930, he remarked to his niece and biographer, Blanche Dugdale, "that on the whole he felt that what he had been able to do for Jews had been the thing he looked back upon as most worth doing.")[54]

As the mandate years advanced, the Zionists who settled in Palestine could grasp the cold truth of Lord Palmerston's maxim that England had no permanent allies, only permanent interests. In 1939, Neville Chamberlain's Conservative government approved a White Paper that effectively closed the gates of Palestine to Jews fleeing Nazi Germany. At that time, the American historian David S. Wyman writes in *The Abandonment of the Jews* (1984), Palestine "constituted the only society on earth willing to take in masses of Jewish refugees." The White Paper limited Jewish immigration to seventy-five thousand spread over three years, a trickle that would limit Jews to being a third of Palestine's population, ensuring an Arab majority.[55] During its New Deal years, the United States proved no more liberal about admitting Jewish refugees. And for all of Franklin Roosevelt's espousal of "Four Freedoms," when in 1945 he met aboard the USS *Quincy* with King Ibn Saud, he dropped mention of Jewish refugees after the Arabian monarch suggested that they should settle in Germany or in Poland (which had much available housing since the Nazis killed so many Jews). FDR could scarcely have been more placatory. He promised the Saudi ruler that he "would do nothing to

assist the Jews against the Arabs and make no move hostile to the Arab people." He went on to remark that Americans were misinformed about the Jewish question. In reporting to Congress after his return, the President said he
had "learned more about the Jewish problem in five minutes" with King Saud
"than I could have learned by the exchange of a dozen letters."[56] With full
allowance for FDR's age and declining health, it was not a proud moment.

Indeed, during the decades following the Balfour Declaration, Jews
everywhere learned the perils of entrusting their survival to the kindness
of Gentile strangers. Writing in *Personal History*, Vincent Sheean had complained that his Jewish friends seemed often to be obsessed by a "pogrom
complex," a remark that made odd reading a decade later. In the aftermath
of the Second World War, thousands of Jewish refugees in squalid camps
who had been denied legal emigration to Palestine, in desperation fled there
illegally. Weakened by the cold winter of 1947, unable to keep the peace
in Palestine, Great Britain formally ended its mandate, precipitating the
armed uprising that led on May 14, 1948, to the proclamation of Israel's
independent statehood. Chaim Wiezmann became the new country's first
president, serving until his death in 1952. In a violent century awash in a
blood-dimmed tide, a national home had become a lifeboat. In making its
existence possible, Sir Mark Sykes earned and deserved the chivalric armor
gracing his bronze memorial in Yorkshire.

A final thought: It is certainly true that Israel's 1948 war for independence uprooted hundreds of thousands of Palestinians whose plight thereafter has been a bitter reproach to Israel. Yet it is also a sad fact that almost
all the world's nations have been born in sin, and not one—certainly not
the United States, Great Britain, France, Germany, Russia, China, India,
Australia, Canada, Turkey or any African country—has been innocent of
dispossession. It is another of the world's lamentable truths: nationhood is
rooted in rites of violence we all prefer to forget.

FOUR

The Acolyte

Sir Arnold Talbot Wilson (1884–1940), KCIE, CSI, CMG, DSO, MP

⌗

The victories of our youth we count for gain
Only because they steeled our heart to pain,
And hold no longer even Clifton great
Save as she schooled our wills to serve the State.
—Sir Henry Newbolt, Head of School,
Clifton College, 1886

If ever a divinity shaped a beginning, it did so in the case of Sir Arnold Talbot Wilson, the forgotten territorial begetter of today's Iraq. A dark-eyed six-footer with a commanding gait and gaze, he subscribed early and clung late to the Imperial Idea in all its grandeur and folly. Writing shortly before his death in 1940, Wilson restated his creed as if it were his epitaph: "Before the Great War my generation served men who believed in the righteousness of the vocation to which they had been called, and we shared their belief. They were the priests, and we were the acolytes of a cult—Pax Britannica—for which we worked happily and, if needs be, died gladly. Curzon, at his best, was our spokesman, and Kipling, at his noblest, our inspiration . . . We read our Bibles, many of us, lived full lives, and loved and laughed much, but knew as we did so [that] by our fruits we should be judged in the days to come."[1]

A. T. seemed unerringly cast as a Britannic acolyte. That his father, an Anglican clergyman, taught sciences for twenty years at Rugby to the likes of Tom Brown and his scapegrace classmate Harry Flashman had a seemly symmetry. But that the Rev. James Wilson, after being ordained a canon, then became headmaster at Clifton College seems almost preternatural. Clifton occupies a special niche in the peculiar universe of British boarding schools. Situated on a hill above Bristol, it groomed thousands of the Empire's soldiers and administrators, reputedly graduating more World War I generals (including Commander in Chief Douglas Haig) and more Great Game heroes (among them Sir Francis Younghusband, the invader of Tibet) than any other school. To visit the college's vaulted chapel is to find the ethos of Kipling and Curzon transmuted into memorials for Old Cliftonians who fought and died for Crown and Empire. Their bard was Sir Henry Newbolt, also a Cliftonian, whose paean to cricket, "Vitaï Lampada," with its exhortation, "Play up! Play up! And play the game!" was hardwired into every schoolboy.

Young Arnold excelled at rugby, and in his climactic Sixth Form he earned Clifton's coveted rugby cap. He read classics, pored over military history (Mahan was a favorite), and studied French during continental holidays, evincing a discipline that impressed even an exacting father. In 1902, the retired headmaster's son followed a familiar path from Clifton to Sandhurst, the Royal Military College. There he placed first in his class, winning the King's Medal and the Sword for General Proficiency. Posted to India, Wilson served in the 32nd Sikh Pioneers, acquired a competence in polo, excelled at Asian languages, and within two years was promoted to the elite Political Department, recruited half from the Indian Civil Service, half from the army. In 1908, the twenty-three-year-old subaltern was dispatched as a Political Agent to South-West Persia.

It was an auspicious posting at a critical time. Arnold Wilson's attainments exert a particular interest since his life exemplifies the influence of a midlevel official with an ideological agenda on his presumed superiors, much as a strong undercurrent bends the course of a becalmed frigate. Wilson was scarcely alone in shaping Britain's moment of dominion in the Middle East, but on one urgent matter—his vision of a viable entity called Iraq—he left his mark, for better and worse, on the world's map.

Lieutenant A. T. Wilson's timing was exemplary. He arrived in Persia just as the Royal Navy began fueling warships with oil rather than coal, at a palpable gain in manpower and efficiency. Yet, as the Admiralty's worried Sea Lords learned, an otherwise resource-rich Empire was petroleum poor. With covert Admiralty assistance, a London-based syndicate began searching diligently early in the new century for the oil long believed to abound in Persia. As the quest proceeded, Russia and Britain struck a pragmatic bargain meant to end their geopolitical rivalry in Asia, enabling each to better contend with their new challengers, Japan and Germany. A major provision in the 1907 Anglo-Russian Convention carved Persia into so-called Zones of Influence, with Russia awarding itself the bigger northern area, embracing Tehran, while Britain claimed the southeast, the southwest in between being designated a neutral zone. This happened as the Persians were preoccupied with their own drama, precipitated by a bloodless revolt in 1906 against an aging Shah, who grudgingly authorized the election of an unprecedented National Assembly, or Majlis. Its deputies drafted a constitution, another first, which the old Qajar monarch signed before his death. Russia and its royalist Persian allies then prevailed on the old Shah's pliant successor to dissolve the Assembly, which had afforded a provocative example for the Tsar's neighboring subjects. A civil war ensued, pitting Persian royalists against reformers and tribal chiefs. Invoking the just-signed convention, and with British acquiescence, Russia militarily intervened in Tehran, stifling Persia's promising Constitutional Revolution (more details follow in chapter 9).

Such was the setting when Arnold Wilson and his cavalry escort pitched tents in 1908 near Masjid-i-Suleiman on a plateau in the Zagros Mountains. Here a near-bankrupt British syndicate had agreed to a positively final test-drill for petroleum. Rigs bloomed under the vigilant supervision of a fifty-year-old engineer, George Reynolds, known for aggressively challenging all obstacles, human or otherwise. Wilson formed an instant friendship with the taciturn Reynolds, who was (Wilson wrote home) "dignified in negotiations, quick in action and completely single-minded in his determination to find oil." Despite a sometime sarcastic veneer, Reynolds (A. T. judged) was "solid British oak."[2]

The solid oak's perseverance paid off on May 25, 1908, when a gusher spouted upward of fifty feet, dousing the rejoicing drilling team. Thus Persia triggered the Middle East's oil boom, and Wilson was fortunate to be present at the creation. The young officer instantly ordered his Bengal Lancers to surround the oil field as if it were British territory (though the field was actually within Persia's supposedly neutral zone). Wilson then wired this coded message to his superiors: "See Psalm 104 verse 15 third sentence" ("That he may bring oil out of the earth to make him a cheerful countenance").[3] By this time, the novice Political Officer, who frequently dressed like a native, had grown a beard, learned to prepare the indigenous cuisine, and befriended local sheiks, many of them Arabs who enjoyed virtual autonomy from distant Tehran. His dedication was awesome, his energy inexhaustible. "I must soak myself in the life of this place," he wrote home, "—[its] geology, natural history, botany, zoology, dialects, ethnology, archaeology—until it becomes part of my life."[4] During five-plus years in Persia, he explored the Zagros Mountains ("hitherto unvisited by any European, unmapped and rather inaccessible")[5] and surveyed some three thousand square miles on foot and horseback. He collected snakes for the Bombay Museum, shipped a cache of ancient coins to the Calcutta Museum, learned

to live frugally in caves to escape the summer heat (110 degrees Fahren-
heit), and reveled romantically in the wild beauty of the Zagros, as in this
snapshot, graphic if conventional, from his journal:

> The dawn comes slowly, and the clear-cut outlines of bare hills of liter-
> ally every colour are revealed against an upper background of grey . . .
> The golden disc of the sun comes over the shoulder of the hill and the
> camp begins to stir as the hoar frost vanishes from the surface of my
> tent. The hills and plains are carpeted with flowers; in the valley here
> and there are great beds of narcissus; my men, like Persians, bend low
> to their stirrups to smell them as they ride slowly through, putting up
> a wild pig or two. I can remember no time when my mind and eyes and
> ears enjoyed during all my waking hours such a feast of beautiful and
> interesting things. As Henry Newbolt writes, "Oh mother earth, by the
> great sun above thee, I love thee, O I love thee."[6]

So fluent did Wilson become in dialects that once in 1911, on being taken
prisoner by hostile tribesmen greedy for ransom, he talked his way to freedom: "I declined to take them seriously and turned the conversation to
lighter topics, mindful of Robert Walpole's saying that 'he always talked
bawdy after dinner, so that everybody could join in.' "[7] The tribal head-
men freed their engaging captive. Two years later, departing on leave for
England, Wilson with characteristic brio signed on as a coal stoker to save
money and build his muscles during the voyage home. When he reached
Marseilles, he bought a bicycle, which he rode the remaining nine hundred
miles to his family residence. He spent his savings on a natty bespoke suit.
Small wonder that, from the first, Wilson caught the eye of Sir Percy Cox
(1864–1937), the Raj's principal Political Officer in the Persian Gulf, who
will stalk through many of these pages with feline discretion.

To understand Cox, one must also understand the very oddity of the British position in the Persian Gulf. In theory, Persia was an independent sovereign power, and its monarch the suzerain of its Gulf ports; moreover
Arab emirates like Kuwait and Muscat were supposedly vassals of the fad-
ing Ottoman Empire. In reality, beginning in the eighteenth century, rulers of British India treated the Gulf as a proprietary lake and came to view

its emirates as semidetached annexes. The key to British influence was sea power, used beneficially by warships and merchantmen to clear the Gulf of piracy and to suppress the maritime slave trade, and employed strategically to open adjacent areas to commerce and to prevent hostile rivals from threatening India. In exerting its pressure, the Raj replicated its indirect rule in India whereby a Resident would "advise" a nominally self-governing princely state. As early as 1789, the East India Company began posting Residents in the Persian port of Bushire (today's Büshehr, the locus of Iran's major nuclear facility). As British trade and influence grew, so did the power of the Raj's senior Resident in Bushire, his title always capitalized. From Bushire, other Residents and Political Officers spread through the Gulf to "advise" sheiks, sultans, and emirs. This cumulative presence assured British India a plenary role in shaping imperial policy in the Islamic Middle East.

Hence the importance of Sir Percy Zachariah Cox, born middle class in 1864, schooled at Harrow and Sandhurst, and recognizable by his broken nose, à la Wellington (in Cox's case the result of a sports injury). A crack rifle shot, and as much at home on a camel as a horse, he was admired for his insatiable curiosity and linguistic skills. Cox followed the accepted route from Sandhurst to India, where to escape an unpromising posting he volunteered in 1893 to serve as Resident in chaotic British Somaliland on the Horn of Africa. There, faced with a tribal rebellion, Captain Cox took command of "52 trained Indian and Somali camelry and 1,500 irregulars whom Cox's diary shows to have been as absurdly unreliable as Falstaff's braves" (as evocatively phrased in his original entry in the *Dictionary of National Biography*). In six weeks of unauthorized warfare, he defeated the rebels with an imperturbability that impressed Lord Curzon, then Viceroy of India. Curzon offered Cox the delicate post of Political Agent and Consul in Muscat (to use the prescribed capital letters), whose Sultan Faisal had a decade earlier signed a secret agreement with British India. It was frayed by his favors to France, without the Raj's permission. Cox managed to restore cordial relations thanks to his knowledge of Arabic, his patient courtesy, and his Wellingtonian aura. Subsequently the Viceroy paid a state visit to Muscat (with Cox present), and with Britannic pomp Curzon invested Faisal with a GCIE (Grand Cross of the Order of the Indian Empire).

The episode foreshadowed Cox's modus operandi. He was a skilled listener, given to silent nods and complicit smiles. He knew just how far to stretch his brief. Arnold Wilson conveyed the flavor in recording this characteristic dialogue ("Your Excellency" being Cox):

> "Your Excellency's letter reached me at the Well of Ain Faris."
> "Your grandfather cleaned it and deepened it, did he not?"
> "Yes, Excellency."
> "I could not come sooner because I had Ibn Jasim with me."
> "Zubaid Ibn Jasim—who represents you at . . . ?"
> "Yes, that's the man. His brother was killed in a raid last month by the Ajman."
> "So you had to come by another road?"
> "Yes. I see you understand my difficulty . . ."[8]

In 1904, Major Cox (as he now was) became Acting Chief Political Officer and Resident in Bushire, where he arrived shortly before Persia's turbulent Constitutional Revolution. During his eventful tour, he showed a sure instinct for spotting future leaders. He was among the first presciently to size up Abdul Aziz Ibn Saud, an Arab warlord who had just regained his ancestral throne at Nejd. Cox saw to it that a promising "political" auspiciously named William Henry Shakespear, aged twenty-five, was transferred from a backwater Persian port to the Residency in Kuwait. This served as Shakespear's base for exploring the unmapped heart of Arabia, and for befriending Ibn Saud, who was to found and give his name to Saudi Arabia.

Cox from the first also knew he had a comer in A. T. Wilson, whom he had preceded at Sandhurst. He applauded the subaltern's initiative in encircling Persia's oil field with Bengal Lancers. Their subsequent meeting is graphically limned in Wilson's preface to a biography of Cox:

> In May 1909 Cox came up in the R.I.M.S. *Lawrence* to negotiate the agreement with the Shaikh of Mohammerah on behalf of the Anglo-Persian Oil Company, as it had now become. I was summoned from Masjid-i-Sulaiman to assist him and spent a full week as his Cipher Clerk and Secretary-Typist. I was, of course, closely examined by him on every phase of the Company's activities, so far as known to me, and upon what I had seen and done in Arabistan and the Bakhtiari country. He had traveled much in unknown parts of Arabia himself and had done some surveying, so he could criticize with knowledge and speak

with authority. He knew much of birds and was a close observer of wild animal and plant life. His Arabic was excellent: his bearing dignified.

He exercised from the outset great influence on the Shaikh of Mohammerah, but was careful not to press him unduly. His patience was unbounded, his temper unaffected by the great heat. It was my first experience of this kind of negotiation, and of the manner in which high British officials did business. Cox was content to sit like the Sheikh on cushions on the floor . . . He attached great importance to devising a form of words which should not give rise to disputes, and invariably drafted a clause in Persian or Arabic and discussed it in that form. Only when it had been agreed to in the vernacular did he essay a translation into English.[9]

In this vignette, one glimpses the methods by which the emissaries of England—an offshore nation little bigger than Massachusetts—acquired such preponderant authority in the Middle East. Still, the sheik's subsequent fate, described in chapter 9, suggests why England's handshakes were soon coldly reciprocated. On completing his Persian tour, Arnold Wilson joined the International Boundary Commission charged in 1913 with demarcating the exiguous frontiers between Persia and Turkey. With his usual enterprise, Wilson drew boundaries that also managed to protect British oil interests in Persia. Then, on June 28, 1914, a pistol shot in Sarajevo shattered Europe's long deceptive afternoon of peace.

With the outbreak of the Great War in July 1914, and after Britain joined the fighting, India provided a seemingly bottomless reserve of power. Lord Salisbury, Queen Victoria's last Prime Minister, once candidly remarked that India was "an English barrack in the Oriental Seas from which we may draw any number of troops without paying for them."[10] This was true. British India not only furnished boots on the ground for the Allies—as many as 1.2 million troops from 1914 to 1918, half of them serving in the Middle East, and most of the rest in France's trenches—but also paid the "ordinary charges" for those sent overseas, to which India added an outright gift of £100 million to the Allied cause. By war's end, more than 250,000 Anglo-Indian troops were still on active service in the Mesopotamian Command, including detachments fighting Bolsheviks in Persia and the Caucasus.

Given this contribution, India's British rulers understandably assumed they deserved at least an equal seat at the high table in framing Middle East strategy. When Ottoman Turkey in November 1914 entered the war on Germany's side, the Raj seized the initiative. Within hours of Britain's formal declaration, in an operation planned well before the event, Anglo-Indian forces embarked for the Persian Gulf, where they captured Bahrain and then Fao, at the mouth of Shatt al-Arab, the estuarial frontier dividing Persia and Mesopotamia. The army's initial orders, flagged as urgent, were to protect from possible Turkish attacks the tankers, pipelines, refineries, and oil fields of the Anglo-Persian Oil Company (APOC). So essential had Persian oil become for the Royal Navy that Parliament had just voted in June 1914 to authorize the government's purchase of majority shares in the oil company.

By November 24, three Indian brigades seized Basra, near the mouth of Shatt al-Arab, the port closest to APOC's vulnerable pipelines and refineries. The invaders then occupied Qurna at the head of the delta, ensuring British mastery of the Persian Gulf and its oil. Thereafter until war's end, the "Mespot" theater consisted of two acts, military and civil. The actors in each veered from excessive optimism to deepening gloom, usually followed by crisis and renewal, complicated by a struggle among officials in New Delhi, their counterparts in London, and the agents of the soon-to-be-established Arab Bureau in Cairo. Each center had its priorities and dogmas, each featured strong personalities, each contributed to the final conflation—a Middle East that was neither truly free nor truly an imperial responsibility. After the end of "the Bastard War," as its embittered veterans eventually called it, Allied policies in former Ottoman lands engendered what one may justly term "a Bastard Peace."

Militarily, all seemed to go well initially for the Anglo-Indian Expeditionary Army. Turkish counterattacks were handily repelled, so handily that the invaders swept up the Tigris for 75 miles and occupied Amara, the next important city. Buoyed by victory, the army pressed upriver another 150 miles to Kut, and from there to Nasiriyeh, where the Tigris meets the Euphrates. "The Turks were outgeneralled and outfought in a brilliant engagement in which the 117th Mahrattas particularly distinguished themselves," writes Philip Mason, a former servant of the Raj, in his military history, *A Matter of Honour* (1974). "Now we had the three angles of the triangle and it was time to stop." On November 2, 1915, Prime Minister Asquith proudly informed the House of Commons, "I do not think that in the whole course of the war there has been a series of operations more carefully contrived, more brilliantly conducted, and with a better prospect of final success." But Mason adds, "Those last three ominous words meant Baghdad."[11]

For Asquith, taking Baghdad (as Cox and Wilson advocated) had symbolic as well as strategic importance. It was a city whose name was known to all who read *The Arabian Nights*, and taking it could divert attention from the failed Allied landing at Gallipoli, which was meant to knock Turkey from the war. Conceived by Winston Churchill, opposed but then accepted by First Sea Lord John Fisher ("When I finally decided to go in," the admiral later acknowledged, "I went the whole hog, *totus porcus*"), the plan excited euphoric expectations. The goal was to seize the Dardanelles with an amphibious assault on the beaches at Gallipoli, and to press on to the Turkish capital. The poet Rupert Brooke was among the British, Australian, New Zealander, and French troops mobilizing for the landing. "I had not imagined fate could be so kind," Brooke wrote, "Will Hero's Tower crumble under the 15-inch guns? Will the sea be polyphloisbic [*sic*] and wine-dark and unvintageable? Shall I loot mosaics from St. Sophia, and Turkish Delight? Shall we be a Turning Point in History? Oh God! I've never been so happy in my life!"[12] (Brooke in fact died before he reached Gallipoli on the Greek island of Skyros, and is buried there.)

Indeed after the initial naval barrage on March 18, 1915, it appeared for a glorious moment that the Allies could smash through the straits, capture Constantinople, and knock Turkey from the war, thereby opening the Dardanelles to Russian ships: a *coup de maître*. Ottoman Turkey, Europe's proverbial Sick Man, had performed poorly in every recent war. Yet everything went wrong following the actual landing on April 24: Turkish mines sank aging ships, an overcautious admiral failed to proceed to undefended Constantinople, Anzacs with bad maps in hand waded ashore at the wrong beach, essential reinforcements evaporated, messages went undelivered, and momentously, the Turkish defenders were led by a commander of genius, Mustafa Kemal, the future Atatürk.

Gallipoli claimed an appalling 250,000 Allied lives, while the victorious Turks suffered an equally horrific toll. The debacle blotted Churchill's reputation and established Mustafa Kemal's. In London, a month after the final evacuation from Gallipoli, a flustered Asquith approved an advance on Baghdad even though Major General Charles V. F. Townshend's army was undermanned and its supply lines stretched thin. In September 1915, an Anglo-Indian force of twenty thousand proceeded upriver to within sixteen miles of Baghdad. At Ctesiphon, the Turks struck back lethally, their spirit and numbers fortified by reinforcements from Gallipoli.

On December 3, 1915, General Townshend "retired" (the official euphemism) downstream to Kut, an Arab town of some six thousand souls. His now-reduced force, with its thirty-nine guns, dug in for an epic siege. Six weeks later, the general reported to Basra that he had sufficient rations for twenty-two days although "by eating up the horses we can last out much longer." He waited in vain for a relief expedition. In April 1916, having held out for 147 days, Townshend surrendered. The Turks took as prisoners 277 British officers, 204 Indian officers, 9,580 mostly Indian enlisted men, and 3,248 noncombatants. The officers for the most part fared well; Townshend himself was treated as a privileged guest in a pleasant villa (later tenanted by Trotsky) on one of the Princes Islands near Constantinople. Most of the nearly thirteen thousand POWs perished of disease and hunger—a decimation bitterly remembered by the Indian military. As General S. L. Menezes, India's former Vice Chief of Staff, caustically remarks in *Fidelity & Honour* (1993), Townshend's dog Spot fared better than the British and Indian prisoners who died, "for he was transported to Britain, rejoining his master when the latter was repatriated."[13]

In mid–1916, British forces regrouped for an avenging assault on Baghdad. General Sir Frederick Stanley Maude (Eton, Sandhurst, Coldstream Guards) was given command of the Mesopotamian Army. A veteran of the Sudan and the Boer War, known for his meticulous planning, Maude took four months to prepare an offensive that commenced systematically in December. His fighters secured control of key rivers, recaptured Kut, and on March 11, 1917, stormed victoriously into Baghdad. Still undecided was how this famous city—and indeed, most of Mesopotamia—would now be governed.

From the Viceroy downward, New Delhi's rulers shared a common perception of the Middle East, a perception rooted in long experience in governing what everybody Western called "the Orient." Their premise was that Britons possessed an unusual aptitude for colonial rule, as demonstrated by the fact that India, for all its polyglot millions and religious diversity, was governed with perfunctory difficulty by a mere few thousand British officials. A related premise (shared improbably by Karl Marx and Friedrich Engels) was that Asia lagged behind the West owing to the anachronistic weight of what Marx called "Oriental despotism." Thus imperialism itself was a form of liberation, a favor to subject races, a shortcut from superstition to enlightenment, a path to the manifold blessings of progress. Should the infirm Ottoman Empire crumble, "Turkish Arabia" (the pre–World War I term for Mesopotamia) might make a logical and useful addition to the British Empire as a colony or a protectorate. And for the moment, who better to manage the civil affairs in occupied Turkish Arabia than Sir Percy Cox, along with his talented protégé, Arnold T. Wilson?

As Chief Political Officer in newly conquered Basra, Cox from the first sounded the avuncular New Delhi mode in his initial proclamation: "The British Government has now occupied Basra but, though a state of war with the Ottoman Empire still prevails, yet we have no enmity or ill-will against the population, to whom we hope to be good friends and protectors. No remnant of Turkish administration remains in this region. In place thereof the British flag has been established under which you will enjoy the benefits of liberty and justice both in regard to your religious and secular affairs."[14] Thus the Indian rupee immediately became occupation currency. Ottoman postage stamps were overprinted with Indian inscriptions. British Indian legal codes were applied and adjudicated by Indian judges. Even the municipal councils that the Turks had recently formed were replaced by Indian political officers.

Cox's decisions were vigorously implemented by his deputy, Arnold Wilson, whose own vision was set forth in a message to New Delhi: "I should like to see it announced that Mesopotamia was to be annexed to India as a colony for India and Indians, that the government of India would administer it, and gradually bring under cultivation its vast unpopulated desert plains, peopling them with martial races from the Punjab."[15] On being seconded as a political officer to a front-line column then advancing to Amara, Wilson amplified in a letter home:

> I see no need for alarm about military operations at the head of the Gulf;
> we are very cautious really and we have 100 years of solid work behind
> us . . . The Arab population here is quiescent, and those who are against
> us higher up country have had such a lesson in the last few days that I

do not think we shall have any more trouble with them; they have constantly before their eyes a great Arab population living peaceably under our rule [i.e., in Egypt] . . . As to our action in coming here being highhanded, quite so. But that does not necessarily make it inexpedient. We must go on expanding, slowly maybe, but expanding nevertheless till Providence decrees we have reached the limit.[16]

Wilson's enthusiasm may well have influenced the Viceroy of India, Sir Charles Hardinge, who confidently assured King George V in October 1915 that "[m]y little show in Mesopotamia is still going strong and I hope that Baghdad will soon be comprised within the British Empire."[17] Meantime, Cox assembled a talented and versatile administrative team with the tireless assistance of A. T. Wilson. All but one of Cox's nineteen "Politicals" were familiar with the terrain and spoke local languages; many would become influential actors in the Middle East theater.

Cox and Wilson spoke for New Delhi. As the war progressed, different views came to predominate in London and Cairo. Stated simply, for Prime Minister Asquith and his successor, David Lloyd George, the overriding priority in Europe was to assist, encourage, and placate embattled France and Russia. To that end, London entered into secret negotiations in 1916 concerning the peacetime division of a dismembered Ottoman Empire. Britain promised Russia the straits and Constantinople, while France was promised Syria and Lebanon, details to be resolved after the war. In Cairo meanwhile, British officials promoted an Arab Revolt proclaimed by Hussein, the Grand Sharif of Mecca. London swayed between Delhi and Cairo. As Hubert Young, a Middle East expert at the Foreign Office, summed it up in 1920, "Our policy in the Middle East during the last three or four years has been very largely influenced—I will not say controlled—by two strong personalities. On the Syrian side we have had Colonel Lawrence, encouraging Arab aspirations . . . On the Mesopotamian side we have had Sir Arnold Wilson checking the same aspirations and making no effort to disguise his reasons for doing so."[18] Over time, Lawrence won and composed a prose masterpiece, *The Seven Pillars of Wisdom*, to celebrate his feats; it was in a sense Oxford versus Clifton. Oxford prevailed.

Still, an American observer speculated early on that the Empire figuratively had no clothes. The observer was William Yale, an oil company executive who became a shrewd reporter to the State Department during World War I. In a confidential report to the Secretary of State dated November 12,

1917, Yale had this to say about British policy in Syria: "The part played by the British has the tendency to make people believe that they are playing a very deep game, with a very definite aim, which will be revealed at the right moment. However the truth seems to be that Downing Street has no definite policy . . . and [has] given their agents no clear program to work out."[19]

The confusion deepened in March 1917 when Anglo-Indian forces captured Baghdad: a triumph greeted with huzzahs in London since it helped atone for the humiliation at Kut. Yet what should be done and said concerning His Majesty's new subjects? Baghdad's conqueror, Major General Maude, reflecting Sir Percy Cox's counsel, cautioned that "local conditions do not permit of employing in responsible positions any but British officers competent to deal with military authorities and with people of the country. Before any truly Arab façade can be applied to the edifice it seems essential that foundations of law and order should be well and truly laid."[20]

Maude's prescription was challenged at the Foreign Office by Sir Mark Sykes, now an influential voice on matters Middle Eastern. Sykes had already warned the War Cabinet that "if you work from India you have all the old traditions of black and white, and you cannot run the Arabs on black and white lines."[21] Thus when Maude and Cox submitted for approval a draft proclamation calling on Baghdadis to cooperate with the new Anglo-Indian administrators, their draft was rejected. In its place arrived a rhetorical fusillade prepared by the more liberal-minded Sykes, and endorsed by Lloyd George's ministers, proclaiming that "[o]ur armies have come into your cities and lands not as conquerors or enemies, but as liberators" (phrases echoed in a similar proclamation when Baghdad fell to U.S. forces on April 9, 2003). The London-anointed declaration expressed the hope that the Arab race would once more rise to greatness and invited "your nobles, and elders and representatives" to share in the government.[22] To speed the process, London simultaneously ordered the withdrawal of Anglo-Indian personnel from occupied Mesopotamia.

Pace the Baghdad proclamation, the British were in reality uncertain as to how much power they were willing to accord Mesopotamia's diverse peoples. When it appeared that there were few qualified indigenous replacements for Anglo-Indian administrators, London decided to retain Indian incumbents "temporarily." As the American scholar David Fromkin remarks in *A Peace to End All Peace* (1989), General Maude was placed in the false position of preaching self-rule while discouraging its practice: "The compromise formula at which the British had arrived might have been expressly designed to arouse dissatisfaction and unrest. Having volunteered what sounded like a pledge of independence to an area that had not asked for it, the military and civil authorities of the occupying power then proceeded to withhold it."[23]

Trying to wrest a consensus from these mixed signals was Sir Percy Cox, newly empowered as Civil Commissioner of Mesopotamia, now headquartered in Baghdad rather than Basra. Joining him as his principal assistant was Wilson, by now an imposing figure. He had by then seen combat as an intelligence scout, and his deeds at Nasiriyeh gained him a Distinguished Service Order. When he held forth in the regimental mess, erect in his high-collared uniform with its special white epaulet designating a "Political," fellow officers listened attentively to his views, uttered with crisp certainty and displaying a fondness for classical apothegms. Soon he had his own protégés, dubbed "Wilson's Young Men," and was sought out by influential visitors to Basra, among them Ronald Storrs, the suavely polyglot soon-to-be Military Governor of Jerusalem. Storrs was impressed: "Wilson, the Political Officer, the Elect of Cox, good-looking, able, intelligent, and intensely ambitious." He had lost two brothers in the war, and "has had the good fortune to serve and to preserve an excellent Chief for eleven years."[24]

When Cox was summoned to Persia in 1918 to negotiate a complicated treaty, Wilson became Acting Civil Commissioner of Mesopotamia, having attained the rank of lieutenant colonel. "I can scarcely realize that I am at present responsible to Government for the administration and political relations of the whole vast area," the marveling colonel, now all of thirty-four, reported to his parents in early 1918. "I have next to no staff yet; they cannot be collected haphazard; I struggle like a conjuror to keep all the balls in the air and not let any drop . . . I flew to Ramadi this morning—eighty miles there and back, left at 6:30, arrived at 7:40, had breakfast, did my work, and was back at 10. I have hopes that the Government will send out a Commission, for which I am collecting materials already. I shall doubtless appear and have my say, and when I have done that and peace is declared I shall be ready to lay down my pen and take leave."[25]

By this time, Wilson's judgments had hardened irreversibly. He believed that Mesopotamia belonged to its conquerors as an imperial protectorate under direct British rule. Its territory, he argued, should comprise the Otto-

man provinces of Baghdad, Basra, and Mosul. The latter had been promised
to France and was believed to possess oil, meaning that its incorporation
into "Iraq" (an Arabic term just coming into use) could provide needed
revenues for the new protectorate. In September 1918, acting on his own
authority, A. T. abolished the separate status of Basra, doing so with no
objections from a preoccupied Whitehall. As the war neared its end, Wilson ordered the occupation of Mosul in its entirety, since "whatever form
of government might ultimately be set up in Mesopotamia, it was vital to
its effective continuance that it should cover the three vilayets [provinces]
of Basra, Baghdad, and Mosul."[26] Even after the November 11 armistice,
Anglo-Indian forces continued to expel Turks from Mosul.

Three days before the cease-fire, to the surprise of all concerned in the
Middle East, Britain and France agreed on a declaration offering peoples
"long oppressed by the Turks" a free choice of future governments. Referring expressly to Syria and Iraq, the joint declaration asserted that far from
wishing to impose any particular institution, the two Allies had "no other
care" but to support the governments that long-oppressed peoples "shall
have adopted of their free will."[27] The declaration echoed the Fourteen
Points proclaimed by Woodrow Wilson in January 1918, nine months after
America entered the war. Point twelve avowed that all "nationalities" under
Turkish rule were owed "an absolutely unmolested opportunity of autonomous development," which Arabs not unreasonably construed as self-
determination, a phrase introduced by the Socialist Second International
federation and warmly endorsed by V. I. Lenin as well as President Wilson.

One might deride the Fourteen Points (France's Georges Clemenceau
complained that God was content with ten), but with a peace conference
looming and with Woodrow Wilson about to make his triumphant entry
into Allied capitals, it was impossible to ignore them, or him. More than
anything else, the subsequent failure of Britain and France to honor these
wartime promises left peoples "long oppressed by the Turks" with an enduring sense of betrayal. But this lay in the future, and Colonel Wilson, who
believed Arabs incapable of self-government, was baffled and dismayed by
the Anglo-French declaration. As he protested to Sir Arthur Hirtzel, the Permanent Under Secretary of the India Office in Whitehall, "The Declaration
involves us here on the spot in diplomatic insincerities which we have hitherto successfully avoided and places a potent weapon in the hands of those
least fitted to control a nation's destinies . . . The average Arab, as opposed to

a handful of amateur politicians in Baghdad, sees the future as one of fair dealing and material and moral progress under the aegis of Great Britain ... Our best course is to declare Mesopotamia a British Protectorate under which all races and classes will be given forthwith the maximum degree of liberty and self-rule compatible with good and safe government."[28]

Or, as he elaborated a month later, an Iraqi protectorate also made strategic sense since Baghdad was bound to become the fulcrum of its region. By occupying Iraq, he reasoned, "we drove a wedge into the Moslem world, thereby preventing the possibility of a combination of Moslems against us in the Middle East. I submit it should be our policy to keep Mesopotamia as a wedge of British-controlled territory, that it should not be assimilated to the rest of the Arab world, but remain isolated as far as it may be and a model to the rest."[29] (As we shall see, T. E. Lawrence, from an opposing vantage, from time to time offered a similar argument.)

There was thus no consensus about the future Middle East among or within the victorious governments whose leaders gathered at the Paris Peace Conference from January to June 1919. During those long months, the Big Three—Prime Minister Lloyd George, President Wilson, and Premier Clemenceau—conferred at times daily to weigh peace terms, address the discontents of stateless peoples, and divide the spoils of three defunct empires. Regrettably, as described afresh in *Paris 1919* by Margaret MacMillan (herself a great-granddaughter of Lloyd George), these potentates often forgot what they had promised or to whom. On perusing the decisions that concluded "the War to End War," a disenchanted Briton (Archibald Wavell, who had fought in Palestine) feared its sequel would be "a Peace to End Peace."

From the Middle East came a caravan of supplicants. In the case of Iraq and Syria, three influential Britons were on hand to proffer advice: Colonel Wilson; his Oriental Secretary, the distinguished Arabist Gertrude Bell; and Colonel T. E. Lawrence, fomenter of the Arab Revolt. In the barter that ensued, the tireless and insistent A. T. Wilson won support for his three-province Iraq. Whitehall had favored a separate state for Kurdistan; Lawrence proposed separate emirates for Basra and Baghdad; the Emir Faisal (Hussein's son) pressed for a federation of Syria and Iraq, and the French wanted to attach Mosul (and its oil) to Syria. Colonel Wilson gained Lloyd George's crucial agreement, sealed in a brief conversation with Clemenceau

("You shall have Mosul," the aging Tiger, was said to have remarked), final boundaries to be determined at a later date. "If there is one man who can be called the architect of the present Iraqi state," justly writes A. T.'s biographer, John Marlowe, "the man is Arnold Wilson."[30]

Regarding Iraq's future status, Arnold Wilson proved less persuasive. A British protectorate was ruled out. Times had changed. President Wilson had popularized the term *mandate* to signify a transitional phase in which "backward peoples" would for a period be subject to "outside political control" until they were deemed fit to govern themselves—the phrases used by the concept's American deviser, George Lewis Beer, a historian critical of what he called "the Old Colonial System." As a member of Wilson's team of advisers (called "the Inquiry"), Beer had Iraq very much in mind as the regional keystone of a mandate system meant to reconcile Wilsonian idealism with Great Power realism. Or, in the blunt judgment of the British Liberal scholar, H. A. L. Fisher, "the crudity of conquest was draped in the veil of morality" (a phrase left intact in successive editions of his influential *History of Europe*).[31]

The mandatory administrators of non-Europeans—in the Middle East, in Germany's former colonies in Africa, and in the South Pacific—were in theory accountable to a still-embryonic League of Nations. Americans were particularly concerned with the status of former Ottoman lands, where Protestant missionaries had decades earlier established colleges, churches, and hospitals. Partly for that reason, the United States did not declare war on Turkey, only on the Central Powers, and thus America was formally an Associated Power rather than an Ally. More broadly, what might be called veiled imperialism suited the mood of the moment. Shortly before his premature death in February 1919, Sir Mark Sykes in a memorandum to the Foreign Office took account of the changing European ethos once America entered the war and the Russian (Bolshevik) Revolution had occurred. "[I]mperialism, annexation, military triumph, White man's burden have been expunged from the popular political vocabulary," he cautioned. "Consequently Protectorates, spheres of influence, annexations, bases, etc. have to be consigned to the Diplomatic lumber-room."[32]

While this may have been true in oratory, in practice the victorious British and French were in no way persuaded that their newly won territories could, or should, be free. In Iraq's case, Britain sought to combine the mandate principle with the practice of indirect rule long employed in India's princely states (and Nigeria)—that is, an Arab would outwardly govern but only with the "advice" of a British High Commissioner. "What we want," the India Office's Hirtzel candidly informed A. T. Wilson, "is some administration with Arab institutions which we can safely leave while pulling the strings ourselves, something that won't cost very much, which Labour can swallow consistent with its principles, but under which our economic and political institutions will be secure."[33]

As the Paris Peace Conference ended, only the contours of a new Middle East had been agreed on. Having initially promoted independent states for the Armenians and Kurds, Americans nervously began to pull back from any serious political engagement in the region. The notion of a Jewish "National Home" in Palestine, as promised in the Balfour Declaration, was still so nebulous that even Emir Faisal, nudged by Lawrence, gave the idea qualified approval. Wartime territorial promises made to tsarist Russia were deemed null and void following the Bolshevik Revolution, yet pursuant to their wartime agreement, Britain and France readied for their respective mandatory authority in Syria and Lebanon, and Iraq and Palestine. T. E. Lawrence turned homeward from Paris to campaign for Arab rights, while a dejected Colonel Wilson resumed his duties in Baghdad. In a letter to her friend Aubrey Herbert, a fellow "Easterner" and MP, Gertrude Bell lamented, "O my dear they are making such a horrible muddle of the Near East. I confidently anticipate that it will be much worse than it was before the war—except Mesopotamia, which we may manage to hold up out of the general chaos."[34]

In the event, Miss Bell was mistaken about Iraq. Not long after the Peace Conference's ceremonial finale at Versailles, British press accounts began depicting an occupied country simmering with unrest. "I imagine that the view held by many English people about Mesopotamia," a correspondent of The Times reported in September 1919, "is that the local inhabitants will welcome us because we have saved them from the Turks, and that the country only needs developing to repay a large expenditure of English lives and English money. Neither of these ideals will bear much examination . . . From the political point of view, we are asking the Arab to exchange his pride and independence for a little Western civilisation, the profits of which must be largely absorbed by the expenses of administration." (The anonymous correspondent was probably Perceval Landon, who in 1903–4 accompanied the Younghusband invasion of Tibet for The Times.)[35]

In April 1920, a conference summoned by the French and British at the resort of San Remo on the Italian Riviera provided the spark. Absent even token consultation with the peoples involved, the San Remo conferees announced on May 5 that formerly Turkish Arabia from the Mediterranean to Persia would come under British and French mandatory rule. Ottoman Syria was to be divided into an enlarged Lebanon and a diminished Syria, both under mandate to France. Palestine was to be severed from Syria and placed under British mandatory authority, an added proviso being that the Balfour Declaration's promise of a "National Home" for world Jewry would also be honored. Iraq too, in an expanded version that included (also at Syria's expense, thanks to A. T. Wilson) potentially oil-rich Mosul, would be subject to British tutelage. In *The Washington Post*'s headline summary, the conference perpetrated "The Carving of Turkey."[36]

The carving heralded the birth of a new sentiment in the Arab world, according to the Lebanese Christian author George Antonius in his influential *The Arab Awakening* (1938), namely, "that of contempt for the Powers of the West. It was not only the denial of the two cherished goals of independence and unity that provoked the revulsion of feeling, but also, and more profoundly, the breach of faith . . . In the eyes of the Arabs, the San Remo decisions were nothing short of a betrayal, and the fact that they violated a compact sealed in blood made the betrayal more hateful and despicable."[37]

Antonius's version of Britain's broken promises has long been disputed, but indisputably the San Remo decisions, promulgated virtually as a ukase, provoked outrage among newborn Iraq's political elite. Baghdad's notables reminded the British that in their English dictionaries *to mandate* signified "to command, enjoin or order," scarcely a democratic concept. Moreover, the May announcement followed ever-louder grumbling about the energetic collection of ever-higher taxes, imposed to help defray occupation costs, and the requisitioning of houses for British personnel: the perennial fuel of occupation discontent. However, Iraqis also nurtured specific grievances. In the south, Shiite clerics inveighed against submitting to infidel rule, recalling that whatever their faults, at least the Turks were Muslim brothers. In the north, Kurds protested paying tribute to an uncaring Baghdad; they worried about who would control their potential oil fields, and many clamored for the independence they believed Woodrow Wilson had promised. Across the Islamic spectrum, Sunni and Shia Muslims rankled at what they perceived as English partiality to Armenian, Greek, and Assyrian Christians, some of whom had fled Turkey's sectarian pogroms.

External factors compounded unrest. Emir Faisal had assumed, as explained in November 1919 by his chief adjutant, Nuri al-Said, that his kingdom would comprise "the liberated Provinces of Syria and Mesopotamia" to form "one great group of federal states on the same lines as the U.S.A." When Whitehall urged a response to Nuri Pasha, who had defected from the Ottoman army to fight with Faisal, Colonel Wilson responded that it was unworthy to address "small fry." This did not satisfy the Foreign Office, especially its newly appointed expert on Iraq, Major Hubert Young, who had served in Mesopotamia. He prepared a memorandum noting that of 233 British officers in the Iraqi civil administration, only 4 were older than forty-five. This inspired an unusual telegram from Lord Curzon, now Britain's postwar Foreign Secretary, to Sir Percy Cox, still on protracted assignment in Tehran. "Present situation in Mesopotamia is causing us considerable anxiety," the aging Curzon cabled. "The existing military administration which has been necessitated by the circumstances of the war is rigid, costly, and hampering the development of civil administration . . . It is for the most part in the hands of young officers who are necessarily lacking in experience. The system of civil government now being set up appears neither to fulfill joint declaration of November 1918 nor to satisfy local aspirations . . . It is a system of British government advised by Arabs (and this only to a small extent) rather than that of an Arab government with British advisers . . . The French are insisting on the absolute parallelism of Mesopotamia and Syria, and ask why we should do in Mesopotamia what we protest against their doing in Syria."[38]

Curzon concluded by noting that everybody agreed on the desirability of Cox's prompt return to Baghdad, though this was not feasible until he completed treaty negotiations underway with Persia. Short of that, however, what did Sir Percy think? In responding, Cox tactfully defended his protégé, Colonel Wilson, restated his reservations about the Franco-British declaration, and minimized the dangers of Iraqi discontent. Cox's optimism, it soon developed, was misplaced.

What really precipitated the insurgency that swept down the Euphrates in the spring of 1920? In a characteristic telegram sent on August 10, Acting Civil Commissioner Wilson defensively listed more than a dozen reasons why his administration had lost "the popularity it once enjoyed," beginning with his discovery that Iraq's tribal sheiks "did not possess the influence that they were supposed to have over tribesmen."[39] Fortunately, and by chance, a qualified American witness was present in Baghdad at the height of the Iraqi insurgency and remained there until its suppression that fall. He was Cornelius Van H. Engert (1887–1985), a European raised in California and educated at Harvard. As a fledgling Foreign Service Officer, he was posted to Ottoman Turkey at the outbreak of the Great War, and there he mastered Turkish, served as an interpreter, and not least, provided detailed accounts of the mass slaughter of Ottoman Armenians in 1915–19, commonly deemed the first genocide of the twentieth century. In 1920, Engert was en route to a new diplomatic post in Persia when he became marooned in Baghdad as the Iraqi insurgents rose up against the British, or more specifically against Acting Civil Commissioner Wilson. The Engert papers, accessible at Georgetown University in Washington, comprise a little-known, rarely consulted, and invaluable archive on Middle East history. Here is his summary report on the Iraqi insurgency, as cabled on October 7, 1920, to Secretary of State Robert Lansing:

Since the boundary between Syria and Mesopotamia was not fixed by the armistice, trouble soon arose between the advance posts of the British along the upper Euphrates and the Arabs controlled from Aleppo and Damascus. The British withdrew from Deres Zor [Dair al-Zur] on December 25 in order to avoid trouble and they further withdrew from the village of Abu Kemal in February of this year. Small raids were made on the Bagdad-Mosul railroad beginning in March and on May 24 a train was burned. At Tell Afar on June 4, British officers and staff were killed and two armored automobiles were ambushed and the occupants killed. The unrest spread rapidly amongst other tribes and although Tell Afar was reoccupied by the British, raids continued on Christian villages east of the Tigris. At the same time in Baghdad, an attempt was made to release by force a native employee who had been arrested for seditious speech and streets were then patrolled by armored cars. An unsuccessful attempt was made on June 16 to derail a train near Hilla and it was evident that trouble threatened in a new direction when placards were discovered inciting the murder of British officers. Open revolt was advocated in tribal gatherings and the British therefore bombed some of the insurgent villages and arrested ringleaders.[40]

Engert provided Lansing with a battle-by-battle account of rebel attacks and British counterstrikes, and of guerrilla assaults on the entire railway system (which prevented his traveling to Persia). He detailed the difficulties facing an undermanned British occupation force, its numbers recently reduced to save costs, and its command assigned to an ailing and superannuated General Aylmer Haldane, who knew nothing of Iraq and who left on holiday leave at precisely the wrong moment. According to Engert, and contrary to other accounts, the true size of the British garrison in August 1920 was 5,000 British and 30,000 Indian combatants, meaning that the 90,000 mentioned in British articles critical of Wilson was inflated because the figure "included native labor battalions." By summer, as the insurgency peaked—according to Wilson, but corroborated by Engert—the troop ration stood at 47,000 combatants, of whom "only 4,200 British and 30,000 Indians were available for duty in Mesopotamia, the balance being in Persia, sick, or in transit." The Acting Civil Commissioner estimated the garrison's annual cost at £35.5 million, a substantial outlay for a United Kingdom burdened by unpaid U.S. war debts, an uprising in Ireland, anticolonial riots from Cairo to Amritsar, turbulence in Persia, and an undeclared war against Bolshevik Russia.[41]

In Iraq, so Engert related, the embattled British faced "several hundred thousand well-mounted, mobile Arabs who had never been disarmed and were widely scattered." The insurgents obtained money and arms from Mustafa Kemal's nationalist Turkey, he reported, and from the monarchist agents of Emir Faisal, whom the French had dethroned in Syria. Rebel cadres were frequently led by former Turkish army officers, Engert attested, cheered on by the Islamic clergy. Bolshevik Russia likewise hailed the uprising and even acclaimed as a "liberation hero" the insurgent son of a Shiite religious chief in Karbala.

An American might feel a premonitory twinge in reading these accounts of the insurgency. The rising had its violent eruption in Tel Afar, the same village near the Syrian frontier cited in 2006 by President George W. Bush as an example of successful pacification (the following day, however, sectarian Muslim militias slaughtered the town's indigenous Christians). In 1920, British forces fought house to house in now equally familiar Iraqi cities—Najaf, Karbala, Fallujah, Samarra—as the civilian toll peaked in July and August. "Many casualties have been caused by unusually hot summer," Engert recounted. "Abnormally low rivers make navigation difficult. One year's military equipment was burned in Bagdad supply depot early in August. Aeroplanes can work only a few hours in the early morning on account of hot weather. As military measures, bombing of villages is futile and involves wanton destruction and cruelty."[42]

Futile or cruel, cost-saving air power appealed to British strategists, notably Winston Churchill, as the preferred weapon for quelling insurgents, as detailed in chapters 5 and 8. Besides reliance on cost-efficient warplanes, Churchill also brought about a marked change in political strategy. The shift was foreshadowed by Prime Minister Lloyd George during a House of Commons debate in March 1920 initiated by his predecessor and Liberal Party rival, Herbert H. Asquith, who with the support of Sir Charles Townshend (the same general who surrendered at Kut, now reborn as an MP) urged restricting British rule in Iraq to "the zone of Basra." Lloyd George found it surprising that anybody would propose abandoning oil-rich Mosul, the "more promising part of Mesopotamia." He then elaborated:

What would happen if we withdrew? . . . After the enormous expenditure which we have incurred in freeing this country from the withering despotism of the Turk, to hand it back to anarchy and confusion, and to take no responsibility for its development would be an act of folly and quite indefensible. If you take away the only central government that they [the Arabs] have, you must put another in its place. They have been consulted about their wishes in this respect and, I think, almost without exception, they are anxious that the British Government should stay there . . . It is not proposed that we should govern the country as if it were a part of the British Empire, making its laws. That is not our point of view. Our point of view is that they should govern themselves and that we should be responsible as the mandatory for advising, for counselling, for assisting, but that the government must be Arab.[43]

It was obvious that London's view of Iraq's future was different from that seen in Baghdad, and plainly Acting Civil Commissioner Wilson was out of step, and likely to be out of a job. What proved the decisive shove was administered by Colonel T. E. Lawrence.

⌘

The talk of London's West End in 1919 was an illustrated travelogue narrated by an unknown American journalist, still in his twenties, named Lowell Thomas. The year before as a reporter in search of a story, Thomas had struck the media equivalent of gold in the Middle East. His slide show entitled "With Allenby in Palestine and Lawrence in Arabia" opened at Covent Garden with a sixty-piece orchestral overture miming the Islamic call to prayer. Out of the darkness came the sibilant voice of Lowell Thomas: "What you are about to see, the journey you are about to make—all this was intended for presentation in America. Until your impresario, Percy Burton, arrived in New York and insisted I come to London, I never even dreamed you British might be interested in hearing the story of your own Near Eastern campaign and the story of your own heroes through the nose of a Yankee. But here I am, and now come with me to the land of mystery, history and romance."[44]

Thomas's presentation was scheduled to run for two weeks after its August debut. Yet so ravenous were British audiences for a redeeming heroic epilogue to a grisly war that he performed before full houses twice a day for five months, moving his show from Covent Garden to the still more copious Royal Albert Hall, then to Queen's Hall. All told, Thomas took his illustrated lecture on a four-year world tour attended by four million people at four thousand performances. Thanks in good part to his overnight celebrity, Lawrence was taken up by an influential circle that included Bernard Shaw and his wife, Charlotte; by the military theorist Basil Liddell Hart; and by the soon-to-be Colonial Secretary, Winston Churchill. Lawrence's views were solicited on all things Middle Eastern. To the public, he was (as Lowell Thomas phrased it) "the Uncrowned King of the Arabs" who with his "faultless classic Arabic" led an army of two hundred thousand, becoming "the world's champion train-wrecker," thereby achieving "what no sultan and no calif had been able to do in five hundred years."[45] Hence the attention when Lawrence, recently of Arabia, after meditating on the Iraqi insurgency, offered his views in a letter to *The Times* in July 1920 that the editors titled "Arab Rights—Our Policy in Mesopotamia."

Small wonder there was an uprising, Lawrence wrote, since "[t]he Government we have set up is English in fashion and is conducted in the English language. It has 450 British executive officers running it and not a single Mesopotamian. In Turkish days 70 per cent of the executive civil service was local. Our 80,000 troops there are occupied in police duties, not in guarding the frontiers. They are holding down the people." Lawrence proposed radically reducing the alien staff and withdrawing all Anglo-Indian troops within twelve months. "I believe the Arabs in these conditions would prove as loyal as anyone in the Empire," he concluded, "and would not cost us a cent . . . Of course there is oil in Mesopotamia but we are no nearer that while the Middle East remains at war and, I think, if it is necessary for us, it could be made the subject of a bargain."[46] In what became a refrain, he said he hoped Iraq would become Britain's first brown dominion, not its last brown colony.

Lawrence followed with signed articles in *The Observer*, the Labourite *Daily Herald*, and *The Sunday Times*, the latter, published on August 22, being the most categorical. It began, "The people of England have been led into a trap in Mesopotamia, from which it will be hard to escape with dignity and honour. They have been tricked into it by a steady withholding of information. The Baghdad communiqués are belated, insincere, incomplete. Things are far worse than we have been told, our administration far more bloody and inefficient than the public knows . . . The sins of commission are those of the British civil authorities in Mesopotamia (especially of the Colonels) who were given a free hand by London. They are controlled by no Department of State but from the empty space which divides the Foreign Office from the India Office." And the result? He offered a flood of numbers: "This year we are spending 92,000 men and £50 million . . . Our Government is worse than the old Turkish system. They kept 14,000 local conscripts embodied and killed a yearly average of 200 Arabs in maintaining peace. We have 90,000 men with aeroplanes, armoured cars, gunboats and armoured trains. We have killed about 10,000 Arabs in the rising this summer. Cromer controlled Egypt's 6 million people with 5,000 British troops. Colonel Wilson fails to control Mesopotamia's 3 million people with 50,000 troops."[47]*

Not by accident, much the same case was pressed in Whitehall by then War Minister Winston Churchill. He first met Lawrence at the Paris Peace Conference, but their encounter was not a success. Churchill had deplored T. E.'s refusal to accept honors from King George V because of his belief that

---

* The reader will note a considerable variance in all these statistics, depending on which official is making what argument.

Britain failed to fulfill its wartime promises to Arabs. Yet the more Churchill learned of Lawrence, the more Churchill was impressed. He believed, as did Lawrence in 1920, that a "most dangerous rebellion in Iraq," requiring forty thousand troops at a cost of £30 million a year, "could not go on." If not actually inspired officially, Lawrence's press campaign fortified an emerging political consensus on the need to change course. In Baghdad, Acting Civil Commissioner Wilson sensed the shift and tardily tried to tack by reversing his prior views and proposing to the Foreign Office that Emir Faisal, Lawrence's ally, having been dethroned by the French in Syria, should be offered the crown of Iraq.

It made no difference. Churchill and Curzon agreed that Wilson had to be replaced as soon as possible by Sir Percy Cox, whose tasks in Tehran were now completed. On October 12, bearing the grander title of High Commissioner, Sir Percy arrived in Iraq, to the applause of Baghdad's notables and to the relief of his superiors in London. Within months, having shifted to a new post as Colonial Secretary, Churchill persuaded Lawrence to serve officially as an adviser in establishing a new political order in the Middle East.

While preparing to depart, Colonel Wilson confided to his parents that he found it difficult to understand how people like Lawrence "can bring themselves to dogmatize with such confidence about Mesopotamia when they have never been there. Lawrence spent a week here during the war. During that week he never spoke to a single inhabitant of the country, and yet he has written with the same easy confidence of Mesopotamia as of Syria, and with equal inaccuracy."[48] Moreover, "If I am as bad as I am painted by *The Times*, Colonel Lawrence and Co., I should still be no worse than the best politician, so I do not think there is any need to worry." One feels a certain sympathy for this dedicated, stiff-necked imperial dinosaur. At least Wilson did not deceive himself about the essential fragility of the country he had striven to invent.

As he wrote to a military ally, Lieutenant General Sir George MacMunn, "In a month's time I shall have handed over to Cox . . . It has been a hard and heart-breaking job. Some of my best officers killed, anarchy in all directions, and no sort of understanding or sympathy in London where the dismal politicians seem to overwhelm everything else . . . What we are up against is anarchy plus fanaticism. There is little or no nationalism. Town after town has been looted, the Jews murdered, women raped . . . H.M.G. have put new wine into old bottles, and the bottles have burst." As to General Haldane, his military partner during the uprising, he was "sick, depressed and irritable; his constant vacillations have reduced his Generals to despair. He is too old and tired for the job." Short of soldiers, warplanes "have been the saving of us. Without them I really think we should have been out of Baghdad by now."[49]

In his final weeks, Wilson talked at length with Engert, to the extent of providing him with an advance text of his September 20 farewell speech (a copy is tucked in the Engert papers). There he expressed his loathing for "Nationalism," a European concept embraced by peoples who "had their part in Empires in which the common interests rather than the differences of the component parts were emphasized, but they did not see it." They preferred something smaller, and it was to protect the right of small nations that the Allies fought. No idea appealed more widely to the diverse races of the British Empire. "Critics of Nationalism as a constructive policy were silenced," Wilson declared, "doubters were perforce dumb. Nationalism held the field and every official utterance of the Allies, and of the Allied Nations' chosen leaders, emphasized this as the basis for future policy." Yet it was all nebulous, and when Britain conquered Mesopotamia, everything was placed on hold pending the Paris Peace Conference. Months passed. "On our borders there was war . . . The temporary military administration and continuance of war conditions in the large towns became extremely irksome to certain classes, but we could do little to guide the growth of public opinion. Our orders were clear: we were not to build [our forces] but we could and did foresee the delay meant trouble. Demobilization however went on until May last, and we only had 5,000 British and 30,000 Indian combatants."[50]

This forgotten history has a melancholy familiarity. In Iraq in 1920, British occupation forces were undermanned for budgetary reasons; the preexisting Turkish forces were demobilized too precipitately; Iraq's frontiers with Syria and Turkey were porous; radical ideologies—religious, nationalist, Bolshevik—flew like sparks in a hay rack; the newly conquered Iraqis were rashly promised freedom but without a plan; reliance on airpower sowed bitterness across a fragmented nation's ethnic spectrum; and the whole rickety structure caught fire. Still, it can be said in extenuation that in the Middle East the British were plunging into uncharted terrain, that they groped with novel Iraqi expectations regarding self-determination. Britain was bled and bankrupt by war, its treasury depleted, not least by the need to repay war debts to a pressing United States ("They hired our money," as President Calvin Coolidge coldly put it). No comparable extenuation can be advanced for subsequent invasions and occupations.

As we detail in the next chapter, in 1921 Churchill improvised an interim solution for the Middle East at a conference in Cairo. It was attended by Arnold Wilson as a civilian observer in his new post as managing director in the Persian Gulf operations of APOC. His acceptance of this job, with its palpable conflict of interest, provoked a sharp editorial in *The Times* ("We regard with some dislike the tendency of the great oil organisations to absorb the services of prominent servants of the State") and prompted a brief exchange in the House of Commons. Wilson was unapologetic. He defended himself in an address to the Central Asian Society, saying, "I should not trouble you with this statement were it not for the fact that the propriety of the action I have taken has been raised in Parliament . . . It is not the prospect of earning higher pay but the prospect of responsible constructive work in a region to which I have devoted the best years of my life that attracts."[51] This was largely true. Yet when Engert in 1920 sought permission for two Standard Oil of California geologists to prospect for Iraqi oil, Wilson blocked their entry, explaining ambiguously in a telegram, "Use of petroleum as main source of revenue in order to reduce share of British taxpayers burden for Mesopotamian expenses is the principal object in view."[52] (Then why not welcome the Americans?)

On returning to Britain and resigning from government service, Arnold Wilson was rewarded with a knighthood and married a thirty-year-old war widow, Rose Carver. He published voluminous accounts of his wartime service and his equally compendious history of the Persian Gulf; in 1933 he was elected a Conservative Member of Parliament from a rural English constituency. He saw himself as a radical on matters domestic, and an imperialist on matters foreign, yet he was credulous about Mussolini and Hitler and supported their appeasement, very typically citing Luke 14:28 ("For which of you, intending to build a tower, sittith not down first, and counteth the cost, whether he have sufficient to finish it?") to support a settlement with Germany. Nevertheless, to his eternal credit, when war broke out in September 1939, Wilson informed his constituents in Hitchin, "I do not wish to live behind the rampart of the bodies of a million corpses." Two weeks later he enlisted as an RAF tail gunner. He flew bombing missions over Rotterdam, Namur, and Aachen. On May 31, 1940, his Wellington was felled at Eringhem, near Dunkirk, where his remains were buried. The wooden cross above his grave bears the inscription "So he passed over, and all the trumpets sounded for him on the other side." "Sir Gunner," as his messmates called him, was an acolyte who had taken Holy Orders, and the faults were in his faith, not his character.

FIVE

"Dreadfully Occupied in Making Kings and Governments"

Gertrude Margaret Lowthian Bell (1868–1926), CBE

⌘

From Trebizond to Tripoli
She rolls the Pashas flat
And tells them what to think of this
And what to think of that.

—Anonymous

Everyone who was anyone in the Middle East kingmaking business gathered at Cairo's Semiramis hotel for the two-week conference that began on Saturday, March 12, 1921. T. E. Lawrence described their quarters situated picturesquely near the Nile as "marble and bronze, very expensive and luxurious." The "horrible place" made him "a Bolshevik." But, as he reported to his brother, "[e]verybody Middle East is here."[1]

Overhead, Bristol fighters and Handley Page bombers circled as thousands of spectators gathered at Station Square. But when the train arrived a half hour late, the carefully vetted notables were disappointed: the Colonial Secretary, Winston Churchill, had gotten off at a suburban station and motored "unseen and undisturbed" to the Semiramis, avoiding the "disorderly rabble" that had gathered outside Shepheard's Hotel crying, "Down with Churchill."[2]

Arriving the next day, Gertrude Bell informed her stepmother that Lawrence had met them (her father, Hugh, accompanied her) at the station—"I was glad to see him. We retired at once to my bedroom and had an hour's talk after which I had a long talk with Clementine [Churchill] while Sir P. [Percy Cox] was closeted with Mr Churchill. The latter I haven't seen yet, for he was dining out. I had Gen. Clayton to dinner and a good talk, with an amusing evening afterwards. Sir John Maxwell is here as a tourist and introduced himself to me. And AT [Wilson] is here! not at the Conference but as managing director of the Anglo Persian Oil Co. We had a cordial meeting but I've not seen him to talk to and don't much want to . . . I think this is going to be a nice Conference—it's immensely interesting."[3]

Bell was the only woman *invited* to the conference; the rest of the ladies who appeared at the obligatory photo opportunity perched atop camels were wives. Bell, who knew more than most of the delegates about the complexities of the Middle East, was for policy makers a necessary annoyance. Her 149-page report, *Review of the Civil Administration of Mesopotamia*, had been presented recently to both houses of Parliament, causing a "fandango" in the press. She had been sent some press clippings where the line taken seemed to be "that it's most remarkable that a dog should be able to stand up on its hind legs at all—ie a female write a white paper . . . By the way, Mother need not think it was AT [Wilson] who asked me to write it—it was the India Office, and I insisted, very much against his will, on doing it my own way, which though it mayn't be a good way was at least better than his. At any rate, it's done, for good or bad and I'm thankful I'm not in England to be exasperated by reporters."[4] As a rule, Gertrude avoided the press, condemning "the whole advertisement business" and maintaining that she threw all letters asking for interviews or photographs "straight into the wastepaper basket."[5] With her enthusiasms, her crushes, her air of "posh jubilance," and her imperviousness to criticism, Bell dominated many a discussion.[6]

The British economy had collapsed, and the British taxpayer had had to bear the costs of invading Russia; occupying Constantinople, Palestine, and Egypt; keeping open the routes to India; and nearer home, policing Ireland. Even *The Times*, in better times the house organ of imperialism, reviewing the events of 1921, urged, "We must evacuate Mesopotamia while we can, and now is the moment," in a series of articles that recommended, "So long as we stay there will ever be a fresh reason for staying, and a fresh reason for spending. Let us arise and go."[7]

The Empire was overstretched. There was little enthusiasm for further imperial adventures. But if Mesopotamia weren't to be abandoned, there was a need for some kind of military force even though Churchill had confessed that the army was "extremely weak and maintained with great difficulty and expense and we have not secured a single friend among the local powers."[8]

The British dreams of keeping both Cairo and Delhi as part of its empire had given way as Middle East policy became consolidated in a subdepartment of the Colonial Office. The new Colonial Secretary, Winston Churchill, was to take on "the odium of the Mesopotamian entanglement."[9] The Foreign Secretary, Lord Curzon, thought it a risky business because, in his words, Winston was "very imperfectly acquainted with the views or interests of the states of the Middle East."[10] Churchill believed, along with Whitehall, that the cost of maintaining Mesopotamia was too excessive. "Apart from its importance as a link in the aerial route to India and the air defense of the Middle East, and apart from the military significance of the oil deposits," Churchill had written when submitting his Army Estimates for 1920, "the General Staff are not pressing for the retention of Mesopotamia, or any part of it, on strategic grounds of Imperial security."[11] Commenting further to Lloyd George, he felt it "gratuitous" to squander slender military resources and pour "armies and treasure into these thankless deserts."[12]

In Cairo, Churchill was to be assisted by T. E. Lawrence. Among the topics for discussion were the future of the new entities of Palestine and Transjordan; how to protect British oil interests in Persia; how to cobble the three Ottoman provinces of Mesopotamia—Basra, Baghdad, and Mosul—together on the cheap, utilizing airpower instead of ground forces; and how to maneuver a malleable monarch onto the throne of Iraq, against the wishes of an intransient indigenous population.[13]

The Cairo Conference would mark the apogee of the formulation of postwar British Middle Eastern policy. The "forty thieves," as Churchill dubbed the delegates, were split between two committees: one political, with the Colonial Secretary presiding, and one military. From the outset, it appeared to the politicos that Lawrence had trumped the lame-duck Colonel A. T. Wilson, and that the notion of Arab "self-government" had triumphed over outright annexation. The "unanimous conclusion" at Cairo would be to offer the Iraqi throne to Emir Faisal, who promised "the best and cheapest solution."[14] Writing to Lloyd George, Churchill reminded the Prime Minister why the other candidates were impossible. If chosen, "Ibn Saud would plunge the whole country into religious pandemonium. Saiyid [Talib, son of the Governor of Basra], who is acutely intriguing for the job, is a man of bad character and untrustworthy. Naqib [the hereditary Governor of Baghdad, Abd al-Rahman al-Gaylani] is tottering on the brink of [the] grave. That [the] Shereefian system [offering Faisal the throne of Iraq] offers far better prospects than these, we have no doubt whatsoever. It is, in fact, [the] only workable policy."[15]

In exchange for giving up his claim to Iraq, Faisal's older brother, Abdullah, plump, affable, and so Westernized that a copy of the Paris daily *Figaro* arrived on his doorstep most weekdays, was being auditioned by the British for the crown in neighboring Transjordan. (Lawrence doomed Abdullah's Iraq ambitions, informing the conferees that the Emir was "lazy and by no means dominating.")[16] Cox also preferred Faisal for Iraq as his wartime exploits put him in the "best position for raising an army quickly."[17] Ibn Saud, by far the strongest ruler in the area, would be bought off by "a douceur" of £100,000 a year, paid monthly, to ensure the tranquillity of his central Arabian homeland, the Nejd. A matching sum was to be paid to Faisal's father, Grand Sharif Hussein, to protect the Muslim holy sites of Mecca and Medina. Now they must certainly see, as Churchill put it, that they "get the 'turtle' and not the 'mock turtle.'"[18]

There was still the problem of "gilding the Faisal pill" since French and British solidarity had disintegrated with the peace—the resurrection of Faisal, so recently expelled from Syrian soil, would not be greeted with *hourras* at the Quai d'Orsay.[19] A few months before, the French chargé warned that Faisal's enthronement would be seen as "*un acte peu amical vis à vis de la France*" and French newspapers were sniping at "*l'élégant émir de Berkeley square.*"[20] (Lawrence had recently chaperoned Faisal in London at the invitation of the British Government. He had a meeting with George V and three with Foreign Secretary Curzon at which the latter raved to Churchill that the Emir "behaved like a real gentleman & with a fine sense of honour & loyalty.")[21]

How could the French object if the Faisal initiative appeared to come spontaneously from the Iraqis? Surely the British would "not feel justified in vetoing his candidature." Churchill asked whether Cox and Bell could deliver an electoral vote in favor of Faisal: "Can you make sure he is chosen locally?" It would be up to Cox, now returned as High Commissioner, and Bell, his Oriental Secretary, to implement this strategy, of which she had so recently disapproved, having written in her *Review of the Civil Administration of Mesopotamia*, "The rank and file of the tribesmen, the shepherds, marsh dwellers, rice, barley and date cultivators of the Euphrates and Tigris, whose experience of statecraft was confined to speculations as to the performances of their next door neighbours, could hardly be asked who should next be the ruler of the country, and by what constitution. They would in any case have done no more but re-echo by command the formula prescribed by their immediate chiefs, and it was just as profitable besides being more expeditious to refer those questions to their chiefs only."[22] Nevertheless, Cox and Bell were left to hold a plebiscite and stage-manage Faisal's triumphal entry into Iraq.[23]

During one meeting, Bell provided some needed levity. As relayed by a participant, Sir Hubert Young, formerly of the Arab Bureau and now the new secretary in the Middle East department, Colonial Office, "A serious discussion was on when Lawrence made some *enfant terrible* remark that no one seemed able to deal with. Then Gertrude turned on him and said, 'You little IMP!' It was the only time that I ever saw Lawrence taken aback. He turned red to the ears and said nothing."[24]

Before the Military Committee, Air Marshal Sir Hugh Trenchard outlined his proposals for the control of Mesopotamia: eight Royal Air Force squadrons, including two bombing units, would be backed up by three British armored car companies. (On August 29, Churchill, who had once described the use of gas by Germans at Ypres as "this hellish poison," now wrote in an infamous letter to his chief air officer, Trenchard, advocating proceeding "with the experimental work on gas bombs, especially mustard gas, which would inflict punishment on recalcitrant natives without inflicting grave injury upon them."[25] (Bombs would become one of the most controversial components of the occupation after the British fired tear gas at Kurdish insurgents.)

Above all, airplanes were a more discreet method of intimidation than ground forces, as one RAF officer explained: "One objective must be selected—preferably the most inaccessible village of the most prominent tribe which it is desired to punish . . . The attack with bombs and machine-guns must be relentless and unremitting and carried on continuously by day and night, on houses, inhabitants, crops, and cattle. No news travels like bad news. The news would travel like wildfire." Brutality would prove efficacious "if the lesson is properly learnt."[26] The goal was to bring down the staggering costs of garrisoning the country by employing local Arab forces and reducing the British forces from nearly ninety thousand troops to fifteen thousand.

The Political Committee also discussed the possibility of a separate Kurdistan, which would act as a "buffer state" between Turkey and Iraq. Churchill did express some concerns—rightly so—as to how the Kurds would fare under a Hashemite* ruler backed by an Arab army, but the com-

---

* In Arabic, the term *Hashemite* literally signifies a person belonging to the "clan of Hashem" within the larger Quraish tribe. But to Arabs, it also signifies the dynasty that by virtue of its members' descent from the prophet Mohammed through his daughter, Fatima, had by tradition served as Sharifs, or guardians, of Mecca until 1924, when they were expelled from their ancestral home, the Hejaz, by Abdul Aziz Ibn Saud. The Grand Sharif Hussein had five sons: Ali, who briefly succeeded his father in the Hejaz; Abdullah, who became the Emir of Jordan, then its king; Faisal, who was King of Syria before the French deposed him and the British installed him in Iraq; Prince Zeid, who joined Faisal in Iraq; and Hassan, who died at an early age.

mittee unfortunately decided that in order to make Iraq viable it needed to be composed of all three provinces.

One Sunday, the group adjourned for a visit to the pyramids of Giza, commemorating the occasion for posterity in a series of photographs. The local newspapers reported that Churchill tumbled from his mount, prompting his wife to remark, "How easily the mighty have fallen!" But when he was offered a horse by the Egyptians, he refused. "I started on a camel and I shall finish on a camel," he snapped. A more accommodating beast was found, and the Colonial Secretary gamely rode the camel back to Mena House with Lawrence while Bell and the others preferred to return by car.[27] (Churchill was indifferent to the fact that many Egyptians loathed him— many carriages carried notices that read "à bas"—preferring to concentrate during his off-hours on painting the pyramids in his camp chair while being guarded by an armored car.)[28]

After the conference concluded, Churchill sent a cable informing Prime Minister Lloyd George, "Prospects Mesopotamia promising." He felt able to assure the House of Commons that his basic goals had been attained: occupation forces in Iraq would be substantially reduced, strategic air routes had been secured, and costs to taxpayers would fall by £5 million in the first year, £12 million in the second. "The ungrateful volcano," as Churchill called it, might yet become a model of constitutional Arab rule and a friendly ally. Describing the proffered mandate as "all this obsolescent rigmarole," he accepted it pragmatically.

A relieved T. E. Lawrence offered this judgment in 1922 to his early biographer, Robert Graves: "I take to myself credit for some of Mr. Churchill's pacification of the Middle East, for while he was carrying it out he had the help of such knowledge and energy as I possess. His was the imagination and courage to take a fresh departure and enough skill and knowledge of political procedure to put his political revolution into operation . . . Of course Irak was the main point, since there could not be more than one centre of Arab national feeling; or rather need not be; and it is fit that it should be in the British and not the French area."[29]

"It has been wonderful," Bell confided to a friend. "Mr Churchill was admirable, most ready to meet everyone half way and masterly alike in guiding a big meeting and in conducting the small political committees into which we broke up. Not the least favorable circumstance," she claimed, "was that Sir Percy and I, coming out with a definite programme, found when we came to open our packets that it coincided exactly with that which the S[ecretary] of S[tate] had brought with him. The general line adopted is, I am convinced, the only right one, the only line which gives real hope of success."[30]

Gertrude Margaret Lowthian Bell, CBE, was a distinctive hybrid, partly new woman, partly proper Victorian. She might have easily emanated from a play by George Bernard Shaw, or from a middle-period novel by Henry James. With her "Paris frock and Mayfair manners," Miss Bell strode with masculine self-assurance into the tents of tribal sheiks.[31] Nicknames are subsurface signatures, like watermarks. Wilson's was the clipped and no-nonsense "A. T.," while Sir Percy became "Kokus," the local pronunciation of "Cox." Writing home from Baghdad in 1917, Gertrude took amused note of these sobriquets: "The word Kokus is rapidly passing into the Arabic language, not as a name but as a title. You are a Kokus, just as once upon a time you were a Chosroes or a Pharaoh. I'm currently described as Kokusah, i.e., a female Chosroes. Isn't it delicious!"[32] (Later, her authority established as "al-Khatun," an important lady, she became one of the few representatives of His Majesty's Government remembered by the Arabs with anything resembling affection.)

Kokusah was born in 1868, the green-eyed, ginger-haired daughter of a wealthy and cultivated ironmaster, Sir Hugh Bell, and his wife, Margaret, who died when Gertrude was three. As incisively rendered by James Morris, the Bells of County Durham typified their Liberal caste and kind: "They lived lavishly, they read widely, they became baronets and Fellows of the Royal Society, they had their homes built by Philip Webb and their drawing-rooms decorated by William Morris."[33] Young Gertrude's intellectual promise was evident from childhood. At twenty, Miss Bell became the first woman at Oxford to qualify for a coveted brilliant First (class) degree in Modern History, telling her examiner, S. R. Gardiner, the great authority on the early Stuarts, that she differed "from his estimate of Charles I."[34] (Degrees, however, were not conferred upon women at Oxford until 1920.)

With focused intrepidity, she next undertook an exhausting grand tour, her itinerary ranging from the cultural and natural wonders of continental Europe (where she scaled the Matterhorn from the Italian side) to the dusty byways of the Ottoman Middle East. In Egypt, she left her card with Lord

Cromer. It was the beginning of her lifelong friendships with powerful and influential lords—Cromer, Curzon, and Robert Cecil. She would share their antisuffrage views and would dedicate one of her books, *Amurath to Amurath*, to Lord Cromer. An excerpt from her diary (June 2, 1898) gives an idea of a thirty-year-old dynamo in action:

> Up at 5 off to the Pyramids. Heaps of camels, Arabs, donkeys fellaheen coming over the bridge. Women in black robes and long black veil, exquisite carriage, generally with things on their heads. Through Ghizeh gardens, then along an avenue at the end of which the Pyramids. Standing sentinel on the edge of the desert which rises up above the valley in rocks and sand hills. At the foot a house built by Ismael for the P[rince] of Wales. Got out and walked to the Sphinx followed by white robed, black cloaked Arabs tall and beautiful, and camels. Sphinx's little round head sticking up over the sand, blank face looking out all over the plain to the opposite desert, sun full in face of her. All round the rocky sand hills like ruins of Titanic battlements. Wide open eyes that look and look and look and hypnotise you. Went down into the Temple of the Sphinx; then on camels to the 3rd Pyramid into which we were pushed and tugged and so home. Our own dragoman was called Hassan. Stopped at the Ghizeh Museum a most fascinating place. Mummies frightfully interesting, some women wreathed in flowers, one old priestess lying on her side just as she died. Statues of the builder of the 2nd Pyramid extraordinarily fine and two great statues of gods. Greek and Roman mummies with pictures on the mummy cases. Back to the hotel where I dropped M. [Maurice] and went on to the Citadel; mosque of Hassan first and opposite to it the unfinished mosque begun by Ismael's mother where he is buried; fine view from the Citadel, aqueduct, our Pyramids and Saqqarah Pyramids far away, the Dashur Pyramid out of sight in the haze of dust; old Cairo, mosque of Umr, and many domes and minarets. Home by an exquisite inlaid little mosque in the Shara'i Darondieh. Lunch, slept . . .

It was not in Egypt but in London that Bell met another lifelong friend, Lady Anne Blunt, the wife of Wilfrid Scawen Blunt. An inveterate traveler and horsewoman herself, Lady Anne wrote admiringly of her younger colleague. In spite of their thirty-year age difference, Blunt confided in her diary that

Bell was "naturally energetic and fond of talking and very physically vigorous ... besides Oriental knowledge, she cares for general reading, pictures, society, hunting, is a skilled mountaineer, has made adventurous expeditions."[35]

In 1905, Gertrude found herself in Beirut "deep in the gossip of the East."[36] She then ventured through the Syrian desert to the area of the mountain Druze, a trip she summarized in *The Desert and the Sown*, meanwhile queering the pitch for another putative traveler, Mark Sykes. When he was unable to get the necessary *laissez passé* from the Turks because of Bell's indiscretions, he wrote to his wife, "10,000 of my worst bad words on the head of that damned fool." (She had let slip to a local ruler, the Kaimakan of Salk, that Sir Mark's brother-in-law was the Prime Minister of Egypt when in fact Sir John Eldon Gorst was merely the financial adviser to the Khedive.) He described her to Edith as a "bitch" and an "infernal liar," the "terror of the desert" and a "silly chattering windbag of conceited, gushing, flat-chested, man-woman, globe-trotting, rump-waggling, blithering ass!"[37] In turn, Bell accused Sykes of inflating the cost of travel by overpaying for horses, mules, donkeys, and dragomen.

Bell attributed her ability to survive alone, albeit with the means to hire twenty camels, teams of muleteers, and dragomen to transport tents, linen, fine china, and silver cutlery along with the more practical theodolite and guns, to "the fact of my being English."[38] The stock of the British had "gone up in the world since five years ago." She attributed this to her friends Lords Cromer and Curzon: "I think it is due to the success of our government in Egypt to a great extent that counts with the learned who see their brothers in Cairo able to write and study as they please. The defeat of Russia [in the 1904–5 Russo-Japanese War] stands for a great deal, and my impression is that the vigorous policy of Lord Curzon in the Persian Gulf and on the Indian frontier stands for a great deal more. No one who does not know the East can realize how closely it all hangs together. It's scarcely an exaggeration to say that if the English mission had been turned back from the gates of Kabul the English tourist would be frowned upon in the streets of Damascus."[39]

Having polished her surveying skills at London's Royal Geographical Society, on subsequent trips to the Near East, Bell mapped uncharted wastes. A portrait of the intrepid traveler was left by Sir William Wilcocks, who was engaged in his great survey of Mesopotamia when he met her: "Coming towards me was a party of camel riders. They were clearly all Arabs except one, who seemed to be a woman. As they came nearer I was hailed in

English. It was Gertrude Bell, just arrived at the end of her 500 mile journey from Damascus. I was not expecting her, and could hardly believe my eyes when I saw a well-dressed Englishwoman, looking spick and span in spite of her weeks of desert travel. I never forgot that first striking impression."[40]

After another five-hour desert ride on the same trip, Bell descended on the Hittite site of Carchemish, where she encountered two young archaeologists, Campbell Thompson and T. E. Lawrence. Although engaged in sifting sand, the duo was also keeping an eye on the Germans who were building a section of the Berlin-to-Baghdad railway nearby. They showed her their finds while she cast a disapproving eye over their excavations, declaring their methods "prehistoric." Having come straight from the more thoroughly exhumed German sites, she proceeded to instruct them in the modern techniques of digging. The men determined to "squash her with a display of erudition."

According to Lawrence, "she was taken (in 5 minutes) over Byzantine, Crusader, Roman, Hittite, & French architecture (my part) and over Greek folk-lore, Assyrian architecture, & Mesopotamian Ethnology (by Thompson); prehistoric pottery & telephoto lenses, Bronze Age metal technique, Meredith, Anatole France and the Octobrists (by me); the Young Turk movement, the construct state in Arabic, the price of riding camels, Assyrian burial-customs, and German methods of excavation with the Baghdad railway (by Thompson)." This was merely the "hors d'oeuvre." They settled down to tea and Bell was left "limp but impressed." Lawrence described her as "pleasant," "about 36 [she was 43] not beautiful (except with a veil on, perhaps)."[41] Of Lawrence, Bell remarked that he was "going to make a traveller."[42] "Dear Boy" and "Gertie" would remain close for the rest of their lives.

Her unhappy forays into male attachment, the most serious one with a married man, Major Charles Hotham Montagu "Dick" Doughty-Wylie, who was to die at Gallipoli and be decorated posthumously with a Victoria Cross, left her free to concentrate on travel. In 1913–14, she probed deep into the Arabian Desert on her famous trip to Hail, meeting up with Ibn Rashid, the Emir of the central Arabian province of Jabal Shammar. These journeys would win her the gold medal from the Geographical Society in 1914. (She was also one of the first women elected as a Fellow in 1913.)

Nevertheless, she suffered bouts of depression brought on by "a profound doubt as to whether the adventure is after all worth the candle. Not because of the danger—I don't mind that; but I am beginning to wonder what profit I shall get out of it all. A compass traverse over country which was more or less known, a few names added to the map—names of stony mountains and barren plains and of a couple of deep desert wells (for we have been watering at another today)—and probably that is all . . . I almost wish that something would happen—something exciting, a raid, or a battle! . . . There is such a long way between me and letters, or between me and anything and I don't feel at all like the daughter of kings, which I am supposed here to be. It's a bore being a woman when you are in Arabia."[43] The archaeologist David Hogarth, a longtime friend and admirer of Miss Bell's, paid tribute posthumously to this pioneering journey where besides accumulating masses of information on the tribes, she "put on the map a line of wells, before unplaced or unknown but also cast much new light on the history of the Syrian desert frontiers."[44]

With her firsthand knowledge of local sheiks, tribes, and mapping skills, Bell was now poised, when World War I broke out, and after a hesitant Ottoman Turkey unwisely chose to side with the Central Powers, to be of service to her country in the Middle East. In November 1915, she traveled to Egypt to join the Arab Bureau being formed in Cairo. Under the supervision of General Gilbert Clayton, the bureau's mission was to gather intelligence, make maps, generate propaganda, and promote an Arab uprising against the Turks. Its director, Hogarth, recruited other seasoned excavators, many of them from Oxford, including Leonard Woolley, who later unearthed Ur in Mesopotamia, and T. E. Lawrence. She set to work compiling a handbook on north Arabia's Bedouin tribes and their complex lineage. ("I love doing it-you can't think what fun it is," she reported to her father, ". . . I'm getting to feel quite at home as a Staff Officer!")[45]

Over dinner at the elegant Savoy Hotel, where the bureau had its three-room office, complete with whirling ceiling fans and staff officers sporting desert boots and swagger sticks, Bell found herself chain smoking and agreeing with her colleagues on what would come to be known as the Cairo consensus. In broad terms, Cairo believed that France's postwar ambitions in Syria were insufferable and to be strongly resisted, and that the likeliest candidate to lead a British-backed Arab revolt was Hussein, the Grand Sharif of Mecca and King of the Hejaz, and not his blood rival, Abdul Aziz Ibn Saud, the warrior ruler of eastern Arabia, the husband of sixty-five wives, and champion of the otherwise puritanical Wahhabi doctrine.

Meeting Ibn Saud a year later, Bell remained intrigued by the strong man of Arabia, calling him "a remarkable person—one of the most striking personalities I've encountered." Splendid to look at—he stood six foot three—he displayed, she enthused, "an immense amount of dignity and self possession."[46] For his part, Ibn Saud, if we are to believe H. S. J. Philby, enthralled Saudi audiences with his high-pitched imitation of Bell: "Abdul Aziz! Abdul Aziz! Look at this and what do you think of that?"[47]

Although she continued to be in the thrall of her Savoy colleagues, her stint in Cairo was brief. After a mere two months, she was aboard the troop transport SS *Euripides* journeying to India at the invitation of the Viceroy, Lord Hardinge, already a family friend, although her visit was most likely suggested by Valentine Chirol, *The Times* correspondent. Relations between Cairo and Delhi had deteriorated to the extent, wrote Bell, that "[t]here is no kind of touch between us except rather bad tempered telegrams!" Her mission was to "establish more direct and friendly relations, so that each side might cease to regard the other as composed mostly of knaves."[48]

Bell spent her time in India perusing intelligence files, helping to compile the *Gazetteer of Arabia*, and trying to figure out how India, whose political caste feared a home-grown Muslim insurrection, and Cairo, whose cognoscenti were betting on an Arab revolt led by the Hashemites, could best cooperate "so that the same ground should not be covered twice . . . It seems obviously reasonable that we should not work in watertight compartments but it's not an idea which dominates official dealings, though I find everyone curiously ready to accept it when once it's mooted."[49] But throughout the period of the Arab Revolt, the Government of India's men would express doubts about the wisdom of Cairo's Arabophiliacs.

The great battle being waged at Kut between the Turks and the Anglo-Indian army was much in the air when Gertrude Bell visited Delhi, where she discussed the Mesopotamia campaign with senior British officials, from the Viceroy on down. In the early spring of 1916, Lord Hardinge dispatched Bell to Basra, still without a salary but with a positive recommendation to Sir Percy Cox, now serving as Chief Political Officer: "She is a remarkably clever woman with the brains of a man."[50] The generals of the Indian Expeditionary Force moved her to a pleasant veranda with a cool room behind it, where she helped draw maps and recommended guides to aid the army now struggling toward Baghdad. She needed all her contacts to win over the local tribes and their sheiks in order to obtain their help in defeating the

Turks, and make converts she did. One sheik spoke to his followers, "Now we all know that Allah has made all women inferior to men. If the women of the Angiliz are like her, the men must be like lions, in strength and valour. We had better make peace with them."[51]

Sir Percy's political staff treated Bell with the utmost suspicion. They ignored her at the officers' mess, called her conceited, lectured her on the Official Secrets Act, and censored her letters, but she persevered, and the Foreign Office commended her after complaining that no important information had reached either Cairo or London before her arrival.

Bell was sympathetic to the military, who were faced with severe food shortages and unaccustomed heat. On April 29, the day of General Townshend's surrender at Kut, where the British garrison of 13,309—most of them Indian—would be led into captivity, she confided in a letter home:

> I don't hold a brief for the Govt. of India but it is only fair to remember that K. [Lord Kitchener, the British Commander in Chief] drained India white of troops and of all military requirements, including hospitals and doctors, at the beginning of the war, that the campaign was forced on them *from* England, and that when it developed into a very serious matter—far too big a matter for India to handle if she had command of all her resources—neither troops, nor artillery, nor hospital units, nor flying corps, nor anything were sent back in time to be of use. And what was perhaps still more serious was that all their best generals had gone to France or Gallipoli many of them never to return . . .
>
> Politically, too, we rushed into the business with our usual disregard for a comprehensive political scheme. We treated Mesop[otamia] as if it were an isolated unit instead of which it is part of Arabia, its politics indissolubly connected with the great and far-reaching Arab question . . . The coordinating of Arabian politics and the creation of an Arabian policy should have been done at home—it could only have been done successfully at home. There was no one to do it, no one who had ever thought of it, and it was left to our people in Egypt to thrash out, in the face of strenuous opposition from India and London, some sort of wide scheme, which will, I am persuaded, ultimately form the basis of our relations with the Arabs. Well, that is enough of politics. But when people talk of our muddling through it throws me into a passion. Muddle

through! Why yes so we do—wading through blood and tears that need never have been shed.[52]

These were Gertrude Bell's thoughts when she crossed paths with Captain (later Colonel) Arnold T. Wilson, who was seconded to the expeditionary army's headquarters at Basra to serve as deputy to his old chief, Civil Commissioner Sir Percy Cox. When it became clear that Cox's diplomatic skill was also required in London and Tehran, involving protracted absences, Wilson became Mesopotamia's chief administrator.

"I'm not sure you realize who he is," Gertrude Bell reported in a letter home describing Captain Arnold Wilson, "a most remarkable creature, 34, brilliant abilities, a combined mental and physical power which is extremely rare." True, she elaborated in another letter, Wilson at first dismissed her as a "born intriguer," but they had ended "by becoming firm friends and I have the greatest respect for his amazing intelligence. I think I've helped to educate him a little also, but he educates himself and some day will be a very big man. He is getting so much more tolerant and patient, such a statesman. I love working with him."[53]

Her affection was but intermittently requited. As Bell's sympathetic friend Harry St. John ("Jack") Philby, the father of the infamous Kim, noted, Wilson never took her into his confidence on policy issues: "These were bandied about between Whitehall and Simla [Delhi's summer quarters] and Basra in code telegrams and secret dispatches, to which she was denied access and for knowledge of whole contents she had to depend, *faute de mieux*, on the *obiter dicta* of the great man, flung casually across the tea-table of the political mess."[54]

Wilson, a bachelor, admitted, with a note of condescension, that she was useful in organizing parties. In truth, with her air of assumed entitlement—she knew she was conceited—Bell courted masculine dislike. Above all, she could be tactless. One example suffices. Commenting on her colleague Harold Dickson's English bride, Violet, she remarked, "It is *such* a pity that promising young Englishmen go and marry such fools of women."[55] (Bell was to become a leading member along with Lords Cromer and Curzon of the Anti-Suffrage League.) Even the admiring Cromer wrote in a letter to Curzon, "She has not got much judgment and has a tongue."[56]

By now she was al-Khatun, an important lady, and it became her practice to bypass chains of command and lobby directly with the superiors of
her superiors. Her influential relatives, her elite schooling and her extensive
travels gave al-Khatun access to a network of powerful insiders—her letters
are filled with the names Montagu, Hirtzel, Hardinge, Trevelyan, Stanley,
Russell, Lascelle, and Cavendish, even that of an American expatriot named
Henry James. And she was well embedded with the press—one of her best
friends, "Domnul," was the red-headed and bearded sybarite Valentine
Chirol, who had been the foreign editor of *The Times* before he joined His
Majesty's Foreign Ministry. Bell's weapons were not only vivacity and wit
but also her stock of knowledge about a region whose strategic importance
was now as obvious as the governing class's mystified ignorance about its
fractious tribes and quarreling creeds.

In spite of her difficulties with Wilson, Cox and officials in Cairo and Delhi
agreed that Bell would stay on for the time being with the title of Oriental Secretary* and a salary of three hundred rupees, making her the only female
political officer in the British forces. (Her salary was one-fifth of what Wilson and other senior political officers were making and less than half of what
people earned as postal clerks.)[57] "I couldn't possibly come away from here at
this moment," she wrote her father. She hoped to take "something like a decisive hand in the final dispositions . . . It's amazing. It's the making of a new
world."[58] During this time, she also contributed articles to Hogarth's *Arabian
Report* and *The Arab Bulletin*, still read as the best contemporary sources for the
desert war. But any hope Bell had of tilting Baghdad toward the Arab Bureau's
views was futile as both Cox and Wilson were firmly in Delhi's camp.

On March 11, 1917, Anglo-Indian forces captured Baghdad, a triumph
met with cheers and a shower of medals in London since it helped erad-
icate memories of the humiliation at Kut. Gertrude Bell, her hair, as she
remarked, now turned white, resettled in Baghdad. Here, in a low rambling
riverbank bungalow, hidden Arab-style behind a high wall on a narrow
street (called "Chastity Close" by her mimicking juniors), she gave her Sunday teas, which became known as "PSAs" (pleasant Sunday afternoons).
At the suggestion of Cox, on Tuesdays she also served tea from her perfectly
appointed table to the wives of Arab notables, most of whom were veiled. In

---

* As defined by Sir Ronald Storrs, himself an Oriental Secretary in Cairo, the person who holds this
key position "is the eyes, ears, interpretation and Intelligence (in the military sense) of his Chief, and
might become much more." (*Orientations*, p. 59)

her large garden, she cultivated roses and imposed imported English hor-
ticultural staples—daffodils, hollyhocks, and chrysanthemums—on Baghdad's arid landscape with the same fierceness she would apply as imperial
taskmaster to the "few really first class shaikhs who will assume responsibility and preserve order."[59]

In 1914, A. T. Wilson had written, "I should like to see it announced that
Mesopotamia was to be annexed to India as a colony for India and Indians"—its desert wastes peopled "with martial races from the Punjab."[60]
He believed that Iraq, as the British now began to call it, under direct rule,
would become "a shining jewel in the British crown."[61] The defense of its territory would require all of the former Ottoman *vilayets* of Baghdad, Basra,
and Mosul. True, the latter territory had been promised to France, but it
already looked as if the Mosul province might turn out to be oil rich (drilling began in 1927), and its revenues could be used to finance the emerging
country. Bell at the moment agreed with much of this, writing to Chirol,
"The stronger the hold we are able to keep here, the better the inhabitants
will be pleased . . . they can't conceive an independent Arab government."[62]
But the publication in November 1918 of the Anglo-French Declaration,
which spoke of a "complete and final liberation" of former parts of the Ottoman Empire including Syria and Mesopotamia, encouraged the belief that
local populations would have a voice in choosing their governments. Wilson, now Acting Civil Commissioner, was horrified, while Bell noted that
the declaration threw things into a "ferment."

Bell, writing to her father, opined, "It doesn't happen often that people
are told that their future as a State is in their hands and asked what they
would like." But on two points practically everyone agreed: "[T]hey want
us to control their affairs and they want Sir Percy as High Commissioner.
Beyond that all is divergence. Most of the town people want an Arab Amir
but they can't fix upon the individual. My belief is (but I don't yet know)
that the tribal people in the rural districts will not want any Amir so long
as they can have Sir Percy—he has an immense name among them—and
personally I think that would be best. It's an immense business setting up a
court and a power."[63]

It was not the urban Sunnis who posed the greatest problem but rather
the Shia—"the grimly devout citizens of the holy towns and more especially

the leaders of religious opinion, the mujtahids, who can loose and bind with a word by authority which rests on an intimate acquaintance with accumulated knowledge entirely irrelevant to human affairs and worthless in any branch of human activity."[64] Control of the Shia holy cities of Najaf and Karbala was a matter of urgency, but Bell had slight access to their leaders, the most prominent being the Grand Ayatollah Sayyid Ismail al-Sadr (an ancestor of the current American nemesis Sayyid Muqtada al-Sadr), as she had been "cut off from them because their tenets forbid them to look upon an unveiled woman and my tenets don't permit me to veil."[65] (It is not beyond imagining that the subsequent history of Iraq might have had a different outcome if Bell, whose influence on Sir Percy was to be considerable, had been able to establish the close working relationship with the Shia that she would continue to have with the Sunni notables.)

Meanwhile Bell spent her time riding through the countryside by horse or by car on visits to sheiks, and back in Baghdad, installing, as one newspaper would wryly note, a British government with Arab advisers instead of the promised Arab government with British advisers. (One story circulated in the local coffee shops: when told that a mullah had prophesied that the Mahdi was coming immediately, the second Arab replied grumpily, "What good will that be? Christ will come too and he'll be the adviser.") "It's an amusing game," Bell wrote, "when you know the country intimately, as I do, thank goodness, almost all of it. Was ever anything more fortunate than that I should have criss-crossed it in very nearly every direction?"[66]

She would remain intoxicated by her own powers—"I feel at times rather like the Creator about the middle of the week. He must have wondered what it was going to be like, as I do"—signing this letter home, "Your very affectionate High Commissioner, Gertrude."[67] But the goodwill she had expressed toward her chief began to deteriorate, as their views on Iraq's future diverged further when Wilson delegated her to represent British interests at the Paris Peace Conference. Once there she came under the influence of T. E. Lawrence and met with his protégé, Emir Faisal.

"I'm lunching tomorrow with Mr Balfour," she reported matter-of-factly to her family. "Ultimately I hope to catch L[loyd] George by the coat tails, and if I can manage to do so I believe I can enlist his sympathies. Meantime we've sent for Col. Wilson from Baghdad and Mr Hogarth from Cairo—the latter at my instigation—and when they come I propose to make a solid bloc of Near Eastern, including Mr Lawrence, and present a united opinion."[68]

Otherwise her constant companion was Colonel Lawrence, variously "Imp" or "Dear Boy" in their teasing encounters.

Lawrence was the cynosure at Paris's grander hotels, with his cerulean eyes and fair hair framed by a khaki uniform and Arab headdress. After yet another dinner, Lawrence "explained the situation as between Faisal and his Syrians on the one hand and France on the other and outlined the programme of a possible agreement . . . he did it quite admirably. His charm, simplicity and sincerity made a deep personal impression and convinced his listeners."[69] After another luncheon, this one with Lord Milner, who was advising Lloyd George, they tempted him into some indiscretions—"It's Mr Lawrence, I think, who induces a sort of cards on the table atmosphere."[70]

Lawrence introduced Bell to Faisal. Always susceptible to crushes, she was impressed by Faisal's hawk-like visage, intelligence, and sly humor, his simplicity and sincerity sometimes articulated in the pleasing French he acquired at school in Constantinople. But she was not the only person to succumb to his charms. An American observer suggested, with a heavy dose of Orientalism, that the Emir's "voice seemed to breathe the perfume of frankincense and to suggest the presence of richly coloured divans, green turbans and the glitter of gold and jewels."[71]

On her way back from Paris she visited Damascus, where she admitted that "the Arab Govt. is all round perceptibly worse than that of the Turks."[72] In her report titled *Syria in October 1919*, she reiterated that the local government under Faisal* left much to be desired, but if it failed it would be due to "British indifference and French ambition." She concluded that the British had no other choice than to support Arab self-government in Mesopotamia. (Wilson forwarded this with his own arch comments in a covering note: her assumptions that an Arab ruled state was a possibility in Mesopotamia and that it would be "practical and popular," he alleged, were "erroneous.")

After Faisal was deposed by the French in Syria, Gertrude Bell became his indispensable champion in Baghdad. Yet in a prescient earlier paper, she had written:

Political union is a conception unfamiliar to a society which is still highly coloured by its tribal origins and maintains in its midst so many strongly

---

* Faisal was King of Syria from March 1920 until he was defeated by the French in the battle of Maysalun (July 27, 1920). He envisioned a united Syria and Iraq under his rule.

disruptive elements of tribal organization . . . The sole individual who might be regarded as a possible figure-head is the King of the Hejaz [Faisal's father, Grand Sharif Hussein] but though he might become the representative of religious union among the Arabs, he would never have any real political significance. Mesopotamia being preponderantly Shi'ah, his name carries no weight there . . . His religious position is an asset; it is probably the only element of union which can be found. But it cannot be converted into political supremacy.[73]

But now her *volte-face* and support for the Hashemites would bring her directly into conflict with Wilson, who blamed Lawrence and Faisal for Iraq-Syria border problems, which by the beginning of 1920 were moving eastward. Iraqis in Damascus declared that Iraq should become a Hashemite kingdom under Faisal's brother Abdullah. But on one point she agreed with her chief: more troops were needed. A. T. could not expect to govern 150,000 square miles with seventy police officers, but withdrawal was the worst option. "If we leave this country to go to the dogs it will mean that we shall have to reconsider our whole position in Asia. If Mesopotamia goes Persia goes inevitably, and then India. And the place which we leave empty will be occupied by seven devils a good deal worse than any which existed before we came."[74]

The mandates for former Ottoman lands were parceled out at San Remo in April 1920: Arabia would remain independent; Syria would go to France; Mesopotamia and Palestine, to the British. Then Churchill's "ungrateful volcano," Iraq, erupted. Nationalists sought complete independence and in May, during the month of Ramadan, there were demonstrations in Baghdad against the mandate; clerics in both Sunni and Shia mosques preached jihad. During the summer as the revolt spread, Colonel Gerald Leachman, who, like Lawrence, was a near-mythical figure but was exceedingly unpopular among Iraqis for advocating "wholesale slaughter" of insurgents, was ambushed and killed near Fallujah. (Years later, Saddam Hussein received the Brno rifle used by Leachman's assassin, Sheik Dhari, as a birthday present. It was displayed as a highlight in the Triumph Leader Museum.)[75] In Najaf, Karbala, and Kadhimain, Shiite leaders, helped by Faisal's agents crossing over from Syria, pushed for unity of Sunni and Shia, inciting their followers against the British. Only Baghdad remained calm, partly owing to the efforts of Sayyid Talib, eldest son of the Sunni Naqib of Basra, who recently returned to Iraq after years of British-enforced exile in India. About the situation in the capital, a chastened Bell remarked, "[I]t's very significant that there should be so few 'wise' people in Baghdad—i.e. people who want a British mandate. No one knows exactly what they do want, least of all themselves, except that they don't want us."[76]

At one time, an increasingly despotic Wilson had been able to exert control by air. According to Middle East scholar Elizabeth Monroe, the Royal Air Force "carried the acting High-Commissioner to be dropped at one point, and a few bombs to be dropped at another."[77] Despite pressure from Wilson, General Sir Aylmer Haldane had unwisely decamped in June with his troops to summer quarters on the Persian frontier. Bell lunched with Sir Aylmer the day he left, chatting about common acquaintances in London over iced melon and mayonnaise. As he went away she said, "I suppose if you hear when you reach Karind that the tribes have taken Baghdad, you'll go on to Kermanshah?" He replied, "Oh I don't feel any responsibility for what happens while I'm away." An irate Bell complained to her father, "We are not accustomed to having military authorities who don't take as eager a share in the game as we do, and we feel this desertion at such a moment pretty keenly."[78]

Relations between Wilson and his deputy irretrievably soured when Bell shared a copy of the constitution drafted by one of the nationalists with an Arab friend. As she wrote her father, Wilson was furious: "He told me my indiscretions were intolerable, and that I should never see another paper in the office. I apologized for that particular indiscretion but he continued: 'You've done more harm than anyone here. If I hadn't been going away myself I should have asked for your dismissal months ago—you and your Amir!' "[79] Their disagreements now were about Gertrude's championing, since her meeting with Lawrence and Faisal in Paris, a Hashemite solution. Earlier in the year, they had quarreled over Bell's warning missives to Whitehall expressing her personal views.

One message to Edwin Montagu, Secretary of State for India, was self-described as "an immense letter about the sort of govt. we ought to set up here" and "a rough draft of a constitution."[80] (Montagu had chastised her, replying by private and personal telegram, "If you have views which you wish us to consider, I should be glad if you would either ask the Civil Commissioner to communicate them or apply for leave and come home and represent them."[81] She sent another missive to Sir Arthur Hirtzel, Deputy Under Secretary of State for India, noting the impending danger from Syria to the west and the Bolsheviks to the north. As she wrote her mother, "They must see, they must know at home. They can't be so blind as not to read such gigantic writing on the wall as the world at large is sitting before their eyes."[82]

She apologized but Wilson was "choked with anger."[83] He fired off a letter to Cox that suggested firing the mischief maker on the spot. "If you can find a job for Miss Bell at home I think that you will be well advised to do so. Her irresponsible activities are a source of considerable concern to me, and are not a little resented by political officers. She will have finished Blue Book [Bell's *Review of the Civil Administration of Mesopotamia*] by the end of the month after which there will really be nothing further to do."[84]

When A. T. received his knighthood that spring, she wrote, "I'm very very glad. He well deserves it and I'm so specially glad of the recognition of this work by H.M.G." She continued ruefully, "I confess I wish that in giving him a knighthood they could also endow him with the manners knights are traditionally credited with."[85] Meanwhile she continued to express her frank opinions, albeit indirectly in letters home, which she suggested might be shared with former Prime Minister Herbert Asquith and Chirol.

Churchill, undoubtedly egged on by Lawrence's articles in *The Times*, vented his own frustration at Wilson in an unsent letter to Lloyd George: "It is an extraordinary thing that the British civil administration should have succeeded in such a short time in alienating the whole country to such an extent that the Arabs have laid aside the blood feuds that they have nursed for centuries and that the Suni [sic] and Shiah [sic] tribes are working together. We have even been advised locally that the best way to get our supplies up the river would be to fly the Turkish flag, which would be respected by tribesmen."[86] Bell commented further: "I suppose we have underestimated the fact that this country is really an inchoate mass of tribes which can't as yet be reduced to any system. The Turks didn't govern and we have tried to govern . . . and failed."[87]

"Mess-pot's" insurgency lasted several months. It was finally quelled when Wilson forbade meetings in mosques and imposed a general curfew. The cost was ten thousand Arabs dead, an estimated nine thousand from RAF bombs, many on civilian targets; several hundred British and Indian casualties; and a bill of £50 million. "The wild drive of discontented nationalism from Syria and of discontented Islam from Turkey might have proved too much for us however farseeing we may have been," wrote Bell, "but that doesn't excuse us for having been so blind."[88]

The end of the revolt marked the end of Wilson and his attempt to Indianize Mesopotamia, together with the end of the military regime and the beginning of an Arab provisional government. Rather than suffer a demotion (Cox was returning from Tehran, where he had been Acting Minister, to take up the post of High Commissioner), Wilson resigned. Gertrude was not sorry to see him go, vowing, "I would rather see the future in the hands of men of less mental power and greater human understanding."[89]

On October 17, 1920, Sir Percy Cox was welcomed on the Baghdad railway platform by a seventeen-gun salute, a band playing "God Save the King," a cheering crowd, and his overjoyed and overtaxed Oriental Secretary in her new Paris frock. About Cox, Bell was an incurable romantic: "I thought as he stood there, in his white and gold lace, with his air of fine and simple dignity, that there had never been an arrival more momentous—never anyone on whom more conflicting emotions were centered, hopes and doubts and fears, but above all confidence in his personal integrity and wisdom. The low sun picked out his tall white figure from the surrounding khaki as if its eye, like the eyes of all the rest of us waiting there, was fixed on no one but he. When he came into the enclosure and Sir Edgar [Bonham-Carter, adviser to the Ministry of Justice] presented me, while I made my curtsey, it was all I could do not to cry."[90]

Sir Percy immediately delegated Bell and Jack Philby to create a council for the provisional government. Expectations in England ran high, from Bell's reading of the papers: "It would appear that Sir Percy has only to say 'Hey Presto' for an Arab Govt to leap onto the stage, like another Athene springing from the forehead of Zeus. You may say, if you like, that Sir Percy will play the role of Zeus but his Athene will find the stage encumbered by such trifles as the Shi'ah problem, the tribal problem and other matters, over which even a goddess might easily stumble. But if he's not a Zeus he is a very skilful physician and one in whom his patient has implicit confidence."[91]

Next came the difficult questions of dealing with the punishment of the tribal insurgents. The crux, as Gertrude expressed it, was, "How are you going to punish people for rebellion against the British Military Govt when that no longer exists? You can punish them for the damage they have done to their own country but even then you're not on very sure ground because most of the damage has been done by British troops. Therefore when military operations are over there's nothing left but a universal pardon, the only possible exceptions being persons who are known to have committed murder."[92]

Elections had been promised but not held. Instead Bell and Philby assembled a provisional government with a council made up of ministers, nearly all of them chosen, following Ottoman practice, from the minority Sunnis, by the British authorities, who then attached themselves to each ministry as advisers. When the Shias protested, Bell explained to her father that in reality they were not really Iraqis since their "leading people, the learned divines and their families are all Persian subjects."[93] The Naqib of Baghdad, and head of the Sunni community, became Prime Minister; Sayyid Talib, the son of the Naqib of Basra, who had the support of the Sunni tribes of the south, was appointed Minister of the Interior; and a prominent Baghdadi Jew, Sassoon Effendi, became Finance Minister.

Among the Arab nationalists who had liberated Damascus with Faisal and who would join him in Iraq were Jafar Pasha al-Askari, the new Minister of Defense, and his brother-in-law Nuri Pasha al-Said. Both would accompany Bell and Cox on their trip to the Cairo Conference a few months later, and both would later be killed in coups. Over the years, the amply proportioned, blue-eyed, gravelly voiced Nuri would become Iraq's Prime Minister, fourteen times, and Britain's closest ally in the Middle East.

Bell immediately recognized Nuri Pasha's usefulness: "The moment I saw him I realized that we had before us a strong and supple force which we must either use or engage in difficult combat."[94] Bell also records a conversation with Jafar Pasha describing how he found the extreme nationalists in Iraq as deaf to reason as they had recently been in Syria: "I say to them, you want complete independence? So do I. Do we not each and all of us dream of a beautiful maiden, her age 14, her hair touching her waist? She does not exist! So complete independence under existing conditions is impossible." Bell amplified that complete independence was what the British ultimately wished to give. " 'My lady' he replied, 'complete independence is never given; it is always taken . . .' "[95] Taken it was, as Bell wrote in the autumn of 1920: "No one, not even His Majesty's Government, would have thought of giving the Arabs such a free hand as we shall now give them—as a result of the rebellion."[96]

The year 1921 opened with Sir Percy and Bell debating whether Meso-potamia, in view of the lack of British support for a continued military occupation, would have to be abandoned. Churchill proposed withdraw-ing troops from Mosul, but this meant a possible takeover by the revital-ized Turkish army, now led by Mustafa Kemal (Atatürk). It was proposed that the British retreat to Basra, but Bell convinced Cox of "the impossibility of our remaining at Basrah with an autonomous Moslem state behind us clamouring for their one port."[97]

It was rumored that the Sunni provisional government led by the Naqib of Baghdad was considering a Turkish Prince as an Emir because, as Bell wrote, "[t]hey are afraid of being swamped by the Shi'ahs, against whom a Turk might be a better bulwark than a son of the Sharif." Meanwhile noth-ing was being done to conciliate the Shias. "They are now considering a number of administrative appointments for the provinces; almost all the names they put up are Sunnis, even for the wholly Shi'ah provinces on the Euphrates with the exception of Karbala and Najaf where even they haven't the face to propose Sunnis."[98]

Such was the situation when Bell returned from the Cairo Conference in a "fever pitch of excitement," primed to begin her new career as kingmaker.[99] But despite Churchill's energy and eloquence, notwithstanding the admi-rable hopes expressed by T. E. Lawrence and Gertrude Bell, and for all of Sir Percy Cox's evident popularity as Iraq's inaugural High Commissioner, the British failed. The fault lay not in the stars, but in the British assumption of gratitude on the part of a new, barely unified Iraqi nation. Coming back from the conference, Miss Bell admitted that the imposition of Faisal came not from strength but from weakness. "The tribes of the Euphrates," she wrote to the American diplomat Cornelius Engert, "discouraged by the fail-ure of the rising which they now regard as a relapse into madness, are also bewildered to find that the sharif's house which last year (so they were told) was anxious to turn us out, is now regarded by us as a suitable source from which an amir might spring."[100]

Bell was willing to overlook the part that Faisal (and his agents) had played in stirring up the recent revolutionary fever. In the same letter, she describes Faisal as "a man of high principles and high ideals."[101] She believed, as did Lawrence, that once Iraqi chiefs met this charismatic claimant to the new throne, they would be impressed. After all, Emir Faisal was a direct descendent of the Prophet, a leader of the Arab Revolt, and a son of the Grand Sharif of Mecca. It was the nearest the British could come to establishing a dynasty whose sons could be sent to Harrow and Sandhurst, like proper English royals (and like Sir Percy Cox).

Still, the Hashemites were Sunnis, the dominant branch of Islam. The underclass Shiites, who constituted a majority in Iraq, plausibly suspected that the British promoted Faisal to empower their favored minority. Moreover, besides the Naqib of Baghdad, who was deemed too elderly to rule, there was the nationalist Sunni contender for chief of state, Sayyid Talib. Talib was campaigning with the slogan "Iraq for Iraqis" and giving thousands of British pounds to potential backers. Described by Bell as "the cleverest and perhaps the greatest rogue unhung,"[102] he was regarded as an able if slippery character by his British adviser at the Iraqi Interior Ministry, Jack Philby. Judging Talib more harshly as an unscrupulous demagogue "capable of anything,"[103] Bell helped rid Sir Percy of the problematic candidate.

Talib gave a diplomatic dinner party in April to honor *The Daily Telegraph* correspondent Perceval Landon. Among the guests were the French and Persian consuls and an English businessman and chum of Bell's, Arthur Tod. Bell, Philby, and Cox were absent. In an after-dinner speech, Talib complained that there were persons in Cox's entourage (read Bell) who were exercising undue influence in favor of Faisal. He wanted to make it clear to everyone present that the people of Iraq were not in favor of a Hashemite king. He then made a blustering threat that if the British would not let the Iraqis choose their own form of government, he would raise thirty thousand rifles. His father, the Naqib of Basra, he said, "will appeal to Islam, to India, Egypt, Constantinople and Paris."[104]

Tod hastened to inform Bell, who reported next day to Sir Percy: "It was an incitement to rebellion as bad as anything which was said by the men who roused the country last year, and not far from a declaration of jihad. It's not beyond the possibility that Talib may prosecute the electoral campaign so hotly as to find himself landed in gaol."[105] Cox felt his position would be untenable if he overlooked such threats and, persuaded by Bell, decided to take drastic measures.

Lady Cox invited Talib to tea, Bell serving as his interpreter. On his way home, in a breach of both English and Arab rules of hospitality, he was arrested, shoved into the Commander in Chief's armored car, and deported by nightfall to British-ruled Ceylon, today's Sri Lanka, where his family soon followed. An American visitor to Baghdad, the novelist John Dos Passos, was told by a local sheik, "We were glad to help the English fight the Turks. But now it is different. The English are like the old man of the sea: at first they are very light, but they get heavier and heavier. And if an important man is opposed to them . . . Cokus invites him to tea . . . and tomorrow he wakes up on the way to Ceylon." All important Iraqis, he suggested, were "very much afraid to be invited to tea with Cokus."[106]

"The wiliest man in Arabia had walked into the simplest of traps," said an incredulous Philby, who was then delegated to meet Faisal in Basra and escort him to Baghdad.[107] Yet even though the Emir could claim descent from the Prophet, his reception was lukewarm in the Shiite holy cities of Karbala and Najaf. He had never been to Iraq, his Arabic accent was strange to Iraqi ears, and his knowledge of Iraq's complex tribal politics (on which the Oriental Secretary had briefed him) was still imperfect. Moreover, Faisal was distressed to hear en route from Philby that even though the Khatun wanted him, Cox was neutral and Philby himself favored a republic.

Philby was not forgiven this indiscretion; he was forced to resign. "It's a real tragedy, he's dismissed, but he has no one but himself to thank. Sir Percy has given him a very long rope," Bell noted. "It is difficult to tell what spirit of evil has taken hold of Mr. Philby but the net result is that he has been thoroughly disloyal to his Chief and disobedient to the orders of his Government. Sir Percy, who never hesitates in what he thinks to be his duty, has cut the knot in the only possible way. I am, nevertheless, very very sorry."[108]

With Talib gone, the way was cleared for a plebiscite in July, but it was decided the promised general election would require too much preparation time. Since ordinary Iraqis had no say in this process, it could hardly be described as democratic. The plebiscite posed a single question, as articulated by Bell and Cox: "Do you want Faisal as king?" Iraqis said they did, by a suspiciously overwhelming (96 percent) majority. The Kurds, who opposed Arab rule, and the Shias in southern Iraq did not vote. Dos Passos's sheik, when asked about the referendum, laughed, "Oh yes, they had given out papers in the bazaars, but they were already printed with the vote for the mandate, so that the ignorant should vote for the government without knowing it. But only the Jews [who looked to the British to protect them] had voted and a few ignorant people; what man who knew his letters and the law would demean himself by voting anyway?" Dos Passos commented, "Oh self-determination, where is thy sting?"[109]

Baghdad in 1921 was scarcely an imperial city. Not since the Abbasid Dynasty ended in 1258 AD had it served as a capital. There was only one main, muddy street, renamed for General Maude, the victor of Baghdad, after he died during the cholera epidemic of 1917. In a city of mud-brick houses there were no buildings suitable to serve as a palace, so Faisal was temporarily given quarters in the Citadel.[110] Gertrude Bell orchestrated Faisal's coronation in the courtyard of the Baghdad Serai on August 23 at 6:00 a.m. The King, dressed in a khaki uniform, advanced on a carpeted path to the dais and a wooden throne modeled on that at Westminster (but according to one account, hastily knocked together from Asahi Beer crates).[111] Seated with fifteen hundred other guests and wearing her CBE star and three war ribbons, Bell caught the King's eye and gave him a "tiny salute."[112] With the help of her father, she was busy inventing traditions: Bell designed a new flag, a heraldically accurate coat-of-arms, and a national anthem, although the band played "God Save the King" at the coronation. News accounts described her as "the uncrowned queen of Iraq." (Faisal also promised her an Arab regiment—al-Khatun's own—a pledge not fulfilled.) Still for a few years after this, Elizabeth Monroe wrote, "Gertrude retained her close relationship with Faisal, rode with him, furnished his houses, fixed protocol for the royal ladies, advised him on ladies-in-waiting for his queen, or on whom to see next. She valued his friendship so much that she felt profoundly disturbed when she reckoned that he was temporizing with factions, and behaving in a way she thought unworthy."[113]

To Bell's surprise and dismay, once enthroned, Faisal opposed ratifying a treaty establishing Britain as Iraq's mandatory master and entrenching British rights. For the new King, a foreigner with no real following in the country, quickly discovered that attacking the British was the theme most likely to unite his subjects in foot-stamping cheers. A frustrated Cox was now describing his protégé as "crooked and insincere."[114] In a tea-time interview with the King in June 1922, Bell deplored his support for the "most ignoble extremists," and candidly described to her parents his purported lack of character: "With the highest ideals, he will trip every moment over the meanest obstacle—he has hitched his wagon to the stars, but with such a long rope that it gets entangled in every thicket."[115] An unhappy Bell told the King, "I had formed a beautiful and gracious image and I saw it melting before my eyes. Before every noble outline had been obliterated, I preferred to go; in spite of my love for the Arab nation and my sense of responsibility for its future, I did not think I could bear to see the evaporation of the dream which had guided me."[116] She had played her last card.

It was a learning process for Gertrude Bell, who summed up the defects in British policy in a wise and prescient letter: "At the back of my mind there's the firm conviction that no people likes permanently to be governed by another. Now we're trying to foster nationalism, but I am always ready to admit that nationalism, which is not at the same time anti-foreign, is likely to be a plant of weak growth. Faisal walking hand in hand with us will not be so romantic a figure as Faisal heading a *jihad* might be! He won't head a *jihad*, that's not his line. Can we get enough of a breath of life into him, without that, to enable him to put real inspiration into the Arab State? . . . All depends on his personality and Sir Percy's discretion in keeping in the background."[117]

In August, on the first anniversary of Faisal's accession to the throne, with Iraqis still deeply split over the treaty, Cox and Bell, who had come to offer their congratulations, were subjected to a final indignity: an angry crowd and two nationalist leaders making anti-British speeches from the balcony of the royal palace and shouting to resounding applause, "Down with the mandate!" When Cox demanded their punishment, Faisal demurred, pleading appendicitis, and it was Cox himself who took control of the government and meted out the penalties: the principal agitators were arrested and the extremist newspapers were shut down. Finally, having obtained face-saving assurances that Britain favored Iraq's prompt accession as a sovereign member of the League of Nations, Faisal prevailed on his parliament to ratify the unpopular treaty. But the British held the trump cards: the High Commissioner would still exercise the right of veto; Britain would control Iraq's foreign affairs and financial and defense policies.

Churchill continued to view Faisal as a British vassal: "We cannot accept the position of Feisal having a free hand & sending in the bill to us," he had written to Cox in 1921, ". . . but while we have to pay the piper we must be effectively consulted as to the tune."[118] Two years later, Churchill could conclude that the Cairo gambit had paid off: "[O]ur difficulties and our expenses have diminished with every month that has passed. Our influence has grown, while our armies have departed."[119] Departing also was the all-important Sir Percy, who retired in 1923. He was succeeded as High Commissioner by his deputy, Henry Dobbs, formerly the Revenue Commissioner who had been seconded to Iraq from the fiscal department of the Indian Civil Service. Dobbs neither spoke Arabic nor did he consult with Bell, his Oriental Secretary. A man of great charm, Dobbs shared her aversion to A. T. Wilson, but in the face of growing domestic pressure for withdrawal, Dobbs was a realist: "My hope," he wrote, "is that . . . [Iraq] may be able to rub along in a corrupt, inefficient, oriental sort of way, something better than she was under Turkish rule . . . If this is the result, even though it be not a very splendid one, we shall have built better."[120]

> G is for Gertrude, of the Arabs she's Queen,
> And that's why they call her Om el Mumineen [Mother of the Faithful],
> If she gets to heaven (I'm sure I'll be there!)
> She'll ask even Allah "What's your tribe, and where?"[121]

She had a comfortable house adorned with chintzes, Persian carpets, Sumerian shards, servants, two tall, silken saluki dogs, a white pony, the occasional pet gazelle, and a life devoted to rounds of picnics, swims in the Tigris, gymkhanas, shooting parties, balls, teas, and bridge—all of which defined British expatriate life. But with less to do, Bell assumed a new role, as Honorary Director of Antiquities of the Baghdad Museum, housed within the royal palace, supervising digs and portioning out finds among Baghdad, London, and Philadelphia. While flattered by her title, she knew that her position was temporary: the Director should rightly be a trained museum official and know cuneiform.

She was weighed down by the death of her half brother Hugo in 1925, and by the disappointment of her last crush on a married colleague: Kinahan "Ken" Cornwallis, more than fifteen years her junior. Educated at Haileybury College, the preeminent training school for imperial civil servants, and University College, Oxford, where he was a famous quarter-miler, Cornwallis served first in the Sudan, thereafter in the army, the Foreign Office, and finally in Iraq. In 1914, he was seconded to the Arab Bureau and succeeded Hogarth as its Director.[122] His contemporary, Colonel Lawrence, described Lieutenant Colonel Cornwallis in *The Seven Pillars of Wisdom* as "a man rude to look upon, but apparently forged from one of those incredible metals with a melting point of thousands of degrees. So he could remain for months hotter than other men's white-heat, and yet look cold and hard."[123]

A trustworthy friend of Faisal, he was deputized by Lord Curzon to offer him the throne and accompanied the Emir on his journey from Jiddah to Iraq in June 1921. Cornwallis then spent fourteen years as a permanent adviser to the Ministry of Interior and as a personal adviser to Faisal, finally retiring as Ambassador in 1945. "Perhaps the king does hold my hand more, though he embraces Mr. Cornwallis oftener," Bell wrote, "we compare notes."[124] She described her frequent bridge and dinner-party companion and fellow kingmaker as a tower of strength and wisdom. By guiding Faisal, she believed, the two of them were guiding the destinies of the Arab world. She had hoped that Ken would marry her when his wife abruptly decamped for home and dissolved their marriage in 1925. This was not to be. Although their subsequent estrangement was due to her disappointed hopes, she eventually patched it up through their shared interest in a litter of dogs.

Increasingly, Bell felt lonely and depressed, her letters home alternating between sanguine hope and bitter despair. Faisal no longer consulted her. "Except for the museum, I am not enjoying life at all," she wrote to a friend. "One has the sharp sense of being near the end of things with no certainty as to what, if anything, one will do next. It is also very dull, but for the work ... it is a very lonely business living here now."[125] Increasingly, she was ill, and on her last visit home in 1925, her London doctors counseled her to avoid the taxing climate of Iraq. But returning to England seemed out of the question: "I don't care to be in London much ... I like Baghdad, and I like Iraq. It's the real East, and it's stirring; things are happening here, and the romance of it all touches me and absorbs me."[126]

On the evening of July 11, 1926, three days before her fifty-eighth birthday, leaving no note but known to be depressed, she swallowed a lethal dose of pills and died in her sleep. Her last message to Ken asked him to look after her dog "if anything happened to her."[127] (He didn't.) Bell was given the honor of a military funeral, and thousands of Arabs followed her coffin to the British cemetery in Baghdad, where it was held aloft by her British colleagues acting as pallbearers before it was lowered into her grave—now overshadowed by the bombed-out remains of the Ministry of Higher Education. A memorial service was held at St. Margaret's Church, Westminster (London).

Faisal paid his effusive posthumous tribute to his friend in an interview for *Everybody's Weekly*: "Gertrude Bell is a name that is written indelibly on Arab history—a name which is spoken with awe—like that of Napoleon, Nelson or Mussolini . . . One might say that she was the greatest woman of her time. Without question her claim to greatness is on a footing with women like Joan of Arc, Florence Nightingale, Edith Cavell, Madame Curie and others."[128] Expunged by the Baathists from Iraq's history in 1973, she has now been returned to the educational syllabus.[129] But it is perhaps the once-estranged Philby who offered the most eloquent tribute to Bell nearly twenty years after her death:

> In spite of all the changes that have taken place in the status and civilities of women during the present century it is difficult to think of any woman of our time, whose achievement can seriously be compared with the unique record of Gertrude Bell. It is perhaps the quality rather than the actual details of her work alone, as it were, among the great men of all the ages. And we can best appreciate the quality of her work if we realise that, in an age that discouraged the intrusion of women into the time-honoured sphere of man and in a part of the world where her sex was a constant obstacle to success, she not only succeeded in doing work of the kind usually reserved for men but did it with a distinction, which only the best of her male contemporaries ever approached. And for it she got none of the customary rewards of good service—no great offices of State, no emoluments worth speaking of and only one very minor decoration! Well she could do without such things, and her work was its own reward. After all she did create a kingdom, while her influence on British policy in the Middle East during the important years between 1916 and 1923 was very much greater than most people realise.[130]

During a five-day conference in 1922 at Uqair in eastern Saudi Arabia, Sir Percy persuaded Arabia's future monarch, Ibn Saud, to recognize Iraq, and as advised as usual by Bell, determined Iraq's borders with Kuwait and the Nejd (later Saudi Arabia).* In spite of Ibn Saud's successes in driving his rivals from the Nejd, Cox treated him like a naughty schoolboy (accord-

---

* These controversial borders were disputed by Saddam Hussein in the 1990–91 Gulf War.

ing to the memoirs of Harold Dickson, the military attaché in Kuwait). Cox alone would decide the frontier. Taking out a map and a pencil, Cox drew the boundary between Iraq and the Nejd. The borders with Syria and Transjordan were defined similarly. The International Boundary Commission confirmed the border with Turkey in 1926: Iraq retained Mosul and its oil. (The Iraq Petroleum Company, owned by British, French, American, and Anglo-Dutch interests, held the concession.)

Seldom did these lines correspond to any political or geographical reality, nor did they reflect the wishes of the inhabitants. Nor was the government of Iraq popular or representative, composed as it was of a minority, the urbanized Sunni Arabs. That wise Baghdadi, historian Elie Kedourie, who considered the Hashemite solution a disaster, observed in an essay in *The Chatham House Version*: "When we consider the long experience of Britain in the government of eastern countries, and set beside it the miserable polity which she bestowed on the populations of Mesopotamia, we are seized with rueful wonder . . . We can never cease to marvel how, in the end, all this was discarded, and Mesopotamia, conquered by British arms, was buffeted to and fro between the fluent salesmanship of Lloyd George, the intermittent, orotund and futile declamations of Lord Curzon, the hysterical mendacity of Colonel Lawrence, the brittle cleverness and sentimental enthusiasm of Miss Bell, and the resigned acquiescence of Sir Percy Cox."[131]

Nor was there a peaceful end for their creation. In 1930, Nuri al-Said, now Iraq's Prime Minister, negotiated a treaty with the British providing for a "close alliance," which meant that the British would be consulted on matters of foreign policy and if war threatened they would take part in a common defense. Britain secured through the treaty not only air bases but also the exclusive right to supply weapons and train the Iraqi army, plus the exemption of British military personnel from Iraqi taxes and laws. In 1932, Iraq became the first Arab member of the League of Nations and was formally sovereign. But, upheld by British bayonets, Iraq was at best a pseudo-democracy.

Glubb Pasha (whom we shall meet), traveling through the Euphrates valley in 1927, met one of the Shiite tribal leaders who had shared in the revolt of 1920 that had enabled the followers of Faisal to attain power. Glubb observed that the Iraqis now had "a government, a constitution, a parliament, ministers and officials." What more could they want? The tribal leader replied bitterly, "Yes, but they speak with a foreign accent."[132] On its accession to the League of Nations, Iraq promised to protect its religious minorities. Yet after King Faisal's death in 1933, Iraqi troops were justly blamed for the slaughter of an ancient community of Assyrian Christians living in the province of Mosul.

Lord Lugard took part in a controversy spurred by the massacre that sadly illustrated the charmless vicissitudes of indirect rule. In 1931, as the British member of the Geneva-based Mandates Commission, Lugard decreed that the League could do nothing to punish Iraq when its army butchered this community of Christians. These pastoral peoples, some forty thousand in all, dwelled originally in the southeastern mountains of present-day Turkey, and were perceived during World War I as traitorous allies of Russian invaders. After Russia's military collapse in 1917, the Assyrians fled to British-occupied Iraq, where they were caught up in the chaotic 1920 uprising against foreign rule. Assyrian levies, or militias, fought alongside the British, inescapably breeding ill-will. On December 17, 1921, asked in Parliament about their fate, Lord Curzon as Foreign Secretary replied, "Insofar as they are now settled within the borders of British influence, they are assured of our friendly interest and protection."[133]

When the League of Nations in 1931 weighed ending Britain's mandate rule and admitting a formally independent Iraq, the Assyrians sought autonomous status. This was denied, and the best the Assyrians could obtain were Iraqi promises to the Mandates Commission that their community would not be molested. Wary leaders of this hardy pastoral people traveled to Syria to seek the right of resettlement from French authorities. Again, this was denied, and on returning "they got into a row with Iraqi border guards, and killed one," according to a credible American observer, William Yale. This precipitated an armed clash between Assyrian fighters, who had been trained by the British, and troops of the new Iraqi army. "Before the civilian government in Baghdad learned what happened," writes Yale, then a State Department adviser on Middle East affairs, "the Iraqi commander, General Bikr Sidky, who was reputed to be notoriously anti-Assyrian, permitted a massacre of 400 unarmed Assyrians, and invited Kurdish and Arab tribesmen to loot and pillage the Assyrian villages."[134]

So what would the Mandates Commission do to defend this vulnerable and stigmatized minority? In an angry letter to Lugard, A. T. Wilson, the wartime acting Civil Commissioner of Mesopotamia, protested that British authorities now wished only to be rid of the responsibilities for Iraq, "and if the position of the Minorities will suffer thereby, so much the worse for the Minorities. It is a cynical attitude and one which is bound to lead to grave difficulties in the future, culminating I fear, in the case of the Christians, in their virtual extermination."[135] A similar, more nuanced protest arose from the legendary Oxford classical scholar and spiritual godfather of the League, Gilbert Murray. He warned that Iraq needed twenty-five years at least for its different races ("Kurdish, Assyrian, Chaldean, Jewish, Yezidi and the rest") to become "accustomed to cooperation with the Arab tribes in making a united kingdom"—and that achieving this was the "chief object" of the mandate.

Lugard would have none of it. Once the British had approved a treaty that recognized Iraq's independence, "the internal affairs of Iraq will no longer be our special concern." This in effect was the epitaph for minority communities whose members took the risk of collaborating with the colonial administrator under Lugard's principles of Indirect Rule.[136]

Faisal's son and successor, King Ghazi, died in 1939 in a mysterious car accident (some say on the orders of British-backed Prime Minister Nuri al-Said). The government proved equally fragile: between Faisal's accession to the throne in 1921 and the murder of his grandson in 1958, fifty-seven ministries took office. Most revealing is the memoir of a Royal Air Force intelligence officer, Alan MacDonald, describing his two years in Iraq before it became nominally sovereign in 1932. MacDonald spoke Arabic and was stationed in the predominantly Shiite south. He recalled his encounters with Iraqis in *Euphrates Exile* (1936), written with a forthright and pungent style reminiscent of George Orwell.

"Here in Iraq," he writes, "we cannot breathe the words, we cannot accept the horrid fact, that we are unpopular, positively disliked, even hated. Our policy is framed on the assumption that our relationship with these people is warm and friendly." He found "there is much hatred at large here" but nevertheless "[i]t is maintained that such hatred is not personal, and that, in so far as political hatred exists, it is confined to the unimportant and frequently jobless section of the educated classes." This was partly true, he continues, but one had to remember that Iraqi officials know they could not dispense with English help, and that differences in language and culture presented formidable obstacles to friendship with ordinary Iraqis.

"An immense political disharmony is the result. It feeds on all those depressing superstitions from the past which hamper our effectiveness in the East . . . Old acceptances of Empire, colour prejudices, an overweening complacency in our own abilities. Is one surprised that such self-satisfaction evokes resentment and anger? The Iraqis have not yet reached the stage where they can receive it with ridicule, the only weapon which can capably and effectively counter it."[137]

Gertrude Bell's reputation seemed assured at the time of her death. As a tribute in *The New York Times* put it, "Not since the days of Zenobia has a woman played so dominant a role in the destinies of the Middle East."[138] Her male colleagues, true enough, noted the fickleness of her views. (Lawrence wrote that she was driven by emotion "changing her directions each time as a weathercock.")[139] She variously favored Arab independence, direct rule by Britain, and finally a Hashemite kingdom for Iraq. But in the longer view, she seemed far more cautious than her colleagues, more beset by doubts as to the outcome of their decisions. She was perhaps too capable of seeing the many sides of an argument—that of the Foreign Office, the India Office, the Colonial Secretaries with whom she corresponded, and finally, that of the Iraqis.

Gertrude Bell's practice of seeking out ruling sheiks by riding into the countryside, visiting their harems, and hosting them at her much-maligned teas, gave her a degree of access not shared by her male colleagues. Belatedly she has received both accolades and blame for the major work of her life: the creation of the Hashemite dynasty of Iraq. But it endured nearly four decades before succumbing to revolution and bloodshed. Her hopes were grievously mocked by the rise of Saddam Hussein, and in the knife's final twist, by the trashing and sacking in 2003 of the Baghdad Museum that she founded, even as newly arrived and triumphant Americans passively looked on.

Yet the larger responsibility for the earlier Iraqi tragedy lay with the British High Commissioners who came and went, and with their Whitehall superiors. They promised to support a democratic outcome in Iraq, and then imposed treaties that embedded indirect British rule, sowing the scorn and resentment that eroded fatally the legitimacy of a foreign-implanted monarchy. Sunni, Shia, and Kurds would remain unreconciled. Certainly no one could fault Gertrude Bell's generous intentions, or her hard-won expertise concerning the complexities of Iraqi politics. But no ship can sail for long with a faulty keel, and for all her successes, Gertrude Bell helped drown Iraq in a bitter sea filled with what Virgil called the "tears of things."

SIX

The Frenzy of Renown

Thomas Edward Lawrence (Lawrence of Arabia) (1888–1935)

⌘

All men dream, but not equally.
Those who dream by night
In the dusty recesses of their minds,
Wake in the day
To find that it was vanity:

But the dreamers of the day
Are dangerous men—
For they may act on their dreams
With open eyes, to make them possible.
This I did.

—Thomas Edward Lawrence,
The Seven Pillars of Wisdom (1926)

⌘

Here were the Arabs believing me.
Allenby and Clayton trusting me,
My bodyguard dying for me;
And I began to wonder if all established reputations
Were founded, like mine,
On fraud.

—Lawrence's reflections on turning thirty,
in *The Seven Pillars of Wisdom*

One name is universally remembered among the millions who fought in the First World War, a four-year conflict that embroiled eight empires plus the United States and inflicted an estimated 32,780,948 casualties.[1] The war's thousands of generals, brigadiers, admirals, and commanders—enough to capsize a dreadnought—are commonly forgotten, along with nearly all their political chieftains. But not Lawrence of Arabia. Thanks to his genius and against all odds, the war's most widely known combatant proved to be an undersize British intelligence officer of ambiguous sexuality who turned an obscure insurgency into a timeless work of art. There is an implicit parallel within Lawrence's own literary interests.

From his Oxford years, he was enamored of Homer, and in 1932 he published a fluent translation of the *Odyssey* (the twenty-eighth in English, by
his count). And in the poet's earlier *Iliad*, lest it be forgotten, the blind bard
centers his epic retelling of the Trojan War on Achilles, a junior warlord
who gained immortal fame by avenging a fallen comrade.[2]

Lawrence was the Achilles of the Great War, the supporting actor who
steals the show. His dominance is readily confirmed. As of November 2006,
his name was mentioned some 1,920,000 times on the World Wide Web, his
nearest British military rivals being Generals Kitchener (339,000 results),
Allenby (41,900), and Haig (33,600). Like medieval relics, anything Lawrence's hand once touched has acquired a sacred (and salable) aura. In
September 2006, the brass compass that reputedly steered Lawrence and
his camel through the deserts during the Arab Revolt fetched £264,000 at
Christie's. (The buyer was anonymous; the presale estimate had been only
£16,000; and doubts immediately surfaced concerning the relic's authenticity.) Countless enthusiasts make the pilgrimage from his birthplace in
Wales via Oxford to his Dorset cottage and his final resting place in a nearby
church in Moreton. In Jordan, travel agents feature "Lawrence tours" to
Petra and Wadi Rum. Even T. E.'s flimsiest ephemera take on weight. Visitors to the venerable Baron Hotel in Aleppo can peruse Lawrence's rever-
ently framed bill (unpaid) for six bottles of champagne. Visiting elsewhere
in Syria, the authors spotted a costly, hard-to-find reprint of *Crusader Castles*, Lawrence's Oxford thesis (which helped earn him a coveted first-class
degree in history) in a travelers' caravanserai abutting ancient Palmyra.[3]

In print, what collectors call "Lawrence material" is a cult phenomenon.
The initial Subscribers' or Cranwell edition, of *The Seven Pillars of Wisdom*
was published in 1926 in a limited edition of two hundred copies or so, and
sold for thirty guineas. Within months, a single copy was offered for sale
at £570. Nowadays the appearance of a Cranwell edition in a sale room is
trumpeted as if it were a Shakespeare First Folio. Translated into dozens of
languages, *Seven Pillars*—scarcely the most accessible of modern classics—
is inching toward two million copies in global sales.

As of 1984, a census listed thirty full-length biographies of Lawrence in
English; since then, by our reckoning, the figure has doubled, not including
works on his life by Turks, Argentines, Arabs, Italians, French, Germans,
and Spaniards. Indeed, one may now consult five major bibliographies of
works by and about T. E. Lawrence, of which the most recent, compiled by

Whittier College librarian and cross-country coach Philip O'Brien, consumes 894 pages.[4] Yet he was scarcely known during the Great War, and he was discovered, serendipitously, by a callow American journalist.

What follows is a selective tour through this immense literature in an effort to address afresh three questions: Is his fame in any rational measure commensurate with his achievements? How did the Lawrence legend acquire such epic proportions? And in any case, can one explain his ongoing allure in an age that devalues heroics?

Tellingly, "Lawrence of Arabia" was first conjured on film. In our imagination, we can re-create the initial frame. It is early 1918 as Lowell Thomas, twenty-something, Colorado-bred and Princeton-groomed, arrives in London in quest of uplifting propaganda for the Allied cause. He seeks advice at the Foreign Office from its wartime information director, the novelist John Buchan. Thomas learns that Prime Minister David Lloyd George is fed up with the deadlock on the Western Front and has sent Sir Edmund Allenby, a combative cavalry general then serving in France, to shake up "the Palestine show." Buchan suggests (as Thomas later writes), "That might be just my pigeon. Perhaps I could be given a lift in that quarter, if I cared to take it on."[5]

Flash forward to the Middle East, where young Lowell arrives and is joined by an American cameraman, Harry Chase. "Hardly had I reached Cairo before I was regaled with wild rumors about the Arab revolt against the Turk," so Thomas reminisces. "Yet it was remarkable that the name of Lawrence was known only to a bare handful of British officers, some of whom dismissed him with a shrug or openly denigrated his ideas, his tactics, his impatience with the hallowed routine of professional soldierdom." As he penetrates the Sinai into Palestine, the American hears more and more about the idiosyncratic warrior, and their first encounter, in Jerusalem, is no disappointment. Thomas sees a slim, short man arrayed ("the only word for it") in a magnificent white robe, girt with a belt holding a curved gold dagger normally worn by descendants of the Prophet. Thomas stares at the cold and lofty personage to whom he is introduced by Sir Ronald Storrs, the newly installed Governor of the Holy City. Beneath the white headdress, bound by a golden cord or agal, the American then perceives Lawrence's flashing blue eyes and Norman-English features. "[H]e seemed indeed the reincarnation of a Crusader in the train of Richard—or, had he been endowed with a mighty frame, the Cœur de Lion himself."

It is a first meeting as artfully retold as that of another journalist, Henry Morton Stanley, on his encountering Dr. Livingstone in the wilds of Ujiji. Spellbound and star-struck, Lowell Thomas accompanies Lawrence on his first steps toward Damascus, while Harry Chase's camera promiscuously captures a willing subject "in his most glittering raiment." Yet after the war, in narrating the long-running illustrated travelogue that launched and named "Lawrence of Arabia," Thomas stressed his discovery's self-effacing modesty. Only after Lawrence's motorcycle swerved fatally on a Dorset road in 1935 did his original publicist correct himself. "Now that he is gone," acknowledged Lowell Thomas in a collective memorial volume, "no such rot is necessary." Not only did "el Aurans" pose willingly in Arab regalia, but later in London on at least five occasions he furtively attended Thomas's hagiographic travelogue: "I never told anybody where he was and said nothing about his visits. Since I was, in all bona fides, drawing a picture of him as the most modest man who ever lived, I wanted to avoid complicated explanations [i.e., that he coveted fame but resented its intrusive price]." Thomas's considered judgment is shrewd, worthy of his Anglo-Norman hero, ending with a phrase that is by now hackneyed:

> Personally I feel I made a great mistake in my relations with Lawrence. He would protest that he wanted to be left alone by the world. He would laughingly insist that he never wanted a word said about him. But at heart, he loved it all. The mistake I made was eventually to take him at his word. After giving a number of years to spreading the story of his achievements, I left him severely alone. So he probably acquired the impression that I had lost interest in him . . . There is an old Turkish saying which admirably illustrates the character of T. E., and which, being interpreted, signifies: "He had a genius for backing into the limelight."[6]

All saints, George Orwell remarked of Gandhi, should be judged guilty until proven innocent. Inevitably, Lawrence became an irresistible target for demolition, a process initiated in Britain by the novelist Richard Aldington, whose *Biographical Enquiry* in 1955 exhumed various incidents in which T. E. clearly or seemingly claimed the impossible. Aldington for the first time made public what had been concealed by his family and friends: that Lawrence was the illegitimate son of an Anglo-Irish baronet named Chapman who had run off with the family nanny, abandoning a wife and four daughters, resettling first in Wales, then in Oxford, where "Ned" and his four brothers were reared. (Sir Thomas Chapman had legally changed his name, and as a youth Ned learned the truth of his parentage, with its chivalric as well as shaming overtones.)

When the London *Sunday Times* documented Lawrence's bizarre sadomasochism a decade later, the cracks in the pedestal widened. By 1977, the late Oxford historian Hugh Trevor-Roper (a reliable barometer of the academic zeitgeist) dismissed Lawrence as one of the century's least attractive "charlatans and frauds." To Trevor-Roper, writing in *The New York Times*, "the incredible thing is that it worked"—that is, otherwise sensible people took seriously "a giant humbug" whose war record, he averred, was as dubious as his literary aspirations.[7]

Yet in popular imagination, despite Aldington's debunking, the tide again turned in Lawrence's favor. The director David Lean shrewdly played to T. E.'s complexity in his Oscar-winning 1962 epic, *Lawrence of Arabia*, indelibly starring Peter O'Toole. And beginning with the Six Day War and through every succeeding explosion in the Middle East, soldiers and civilians alike rediscovered the Arab Revolt. In the spring of 2005, a highlight of the London season was an elaborate exhibition, "Lawrence of Arabia: The Life, The Legend," at the Imperial War Museum, accompanied by a lavish pictorial biography of the same title assembled by the BBC producer Malcolm Brown. (Among the show's curiosities was a bronze wreath once laid by Kaiser Wilhelm II on the tomb of Saladin in Damascus, seized in 1918 by Lawrence, who sent it to the War Museum with this penciled note: "Removed by me as Saladin no longer required it.") Visitors paid a £7 admission fee, and devotees paid £35 to attend a one-day symposium on Lawrence. Completing the apotheosis was an announcement that the BBC planned yet one more major documentary on Colonel Lawrence, while a flurry of news stories on both sides of the Atlantic reported that coalition troops in Iraq were reading, and pondering, his reflections on insurgency and on partnering with Arabs.[8]

This renewed interest was understandable. As a strategist, Lawrence was unorthodox, but scarcely a sham. He had no more illustrious defender than Britain's ranking military analyst, Sir Basil H. Liddell Hart (1895–1970).

Having fought on the Western Front, Liddell Hart came to loathe the stagnant bloodletting in the trenches. Postwar, while a military correspondent of *The Daily Telegraph*, he recalled the feats of "great captains" like Genghis Khan, whose mounted archers relied on surprise and mobility to overwhelm numerically superior foes. Liddell Hart became an early advocate of mechanized warfare, whose theories were applied, all too successfully, by Wehrmacht General Heinz Guderian. After studying the Arab Revolt, Liddell Hart concluded that it "inverted the conventional military doctrine in such a way as to convert Arab weaknesses into strength and Turkish strength into a weakness." No belligerent state could wage land war without relying on rails for supplies, he reasoned, and he predicted that what the Arabs did yesterday, aircraft, tanks, and mobile guerrillas would likely do tomorrow.[9]

It chanced that Liddell Hart was military editor of the *Encyclopaedia Britannica*, and in 1927 he urged Lawrence to write the entry on guerrilla warfare. Replying from India, where he was then posted as an RAF aircraftman under the name of Shaw, Lawrence suggested that Liddell Hart could splice together relevant passages from *Seven Pillars* and a 1920 article on the Arab Revolt in the *Army Quarterly*. Liddell Hart did so, and the fourteenth edition of the *Britannica* (1929) carried an unusual firsthand analysis of irregular warfare over the initials "T. E. L." Read today, it has an obvious resonance with America's travails in Iraq.

The insurrection began (Lawrence relates) in June 1916 with an attack by inexperienced tribesman on the Turkish garrison at the holy city of Medina, which failed, and the Turks were able to reinforce the garrison by rail from Syria. Then the Arab warriors managed to overwhelm Mecca, some 250 miles away. Part of the Turkish force tardily advanced to retake Mecca. In such circumstances, Lawrence writes, "the soldiers of all countries looked only to the regulars to win the war. Military opinion was obsessed by the dictum of [French Marshal Ferdinand] Foch that the ethic of modern war is to seek for the enemy's army, his centre of power, and destroy it in battle. Irregulars would not attack positions and so they were regarded as incapable of forcing a decision." However it occurred to the author (his *Britannica* article continues) that the virtue of irregulars lay in depth, not in face, and that it had been the threat of attack on the Turkish northern flank that made the enemy hesitate for so long. "The actual Turkish flank ran from the front line to Medina, a distance of some 50 miles, but, if the Arab forces moved northward towards the Hejaz railway behind Medina, it might stretch the threat (and accordingly, the enemy's flank) as far, potentially, as Damascus . . . The eccentric movement worked like a charm."[10]

Half the Turkish force remained in Medina and held the city until the armistice, while the remainder was deployed along railway tracks to fend off Arab guerrillas. "For the rest of the war the Turks stood on the defensive and the Arab tribesmen won advantage over advantage till, when peace came, they had taken 35,000 prisoners, killed and wounded and worn out about as many, and occupied 100,000 square miles of the enemy's territory at little loss to themselves."[11]

In fact, algebra favored the irregulars. Lawrence calculated the contested area comprised perhaps 140,000 square miles. Doubtless the Turks could defend all that territory with a trench across the bottom should the Arabs attack as an army with banners flying. "[B]ut suppose they [the insurgents] were an influence, a thing invulnerable, intangible, without front or back, drifting about like a gas? Armies were like plants, immobile as a whole, firm-rooted, nourished through long stems to the head. The Arabs might be a vapour, blowing where they listed. It seemed a regular soldier might be helpless without a target. He would own the ground he sat on, and what he could poke his rifle at." Lawrence calculated that it would take 600,000 Turks to cope effectively with the combined hostility of the local Arabs—but the Turks had only 100,000 men available. (Iraq's area, by way of comparison, is reckoned at 169,249 square miles.)[12]

Regarding the legal status of guerrillas, it is worth adding, the *Britannica* article was preceded by a succinct paragraph by Sir Thomas Barclay of the International Law Association. He summarized the rules as agreed upon at Brussels and The Hague, in 1899 and 1907, respectively. They stipulated that irregulars deserve recognition as lawful combatants if they are under a leader, wear a distinctive badge, carry arms openly, and conform to the laws of war. In the case of invasion, those who spontaneously take up arms too "shall be regarded as belligerent troops if they carry arms openly and respect the laws and customs of war, although they may not have had time to become organized."[13]

Yet the ledger needs to be balanced. Lawrence's strategy is a formula for denying victory, a variation of the adage that guerrillas win if they do not lose, and armies lose if they do not win. In fact, it needed General Allenby's massive conventional force in 1917–18 to rout Ottoman forces and take Jerusalem and Damascus, with irregulars playing a supporting role. Lawrence was not a professional soldier and served as a liaison intelligence officer with the Arabs, not as commander or master strategist. British army officers who teamed with defecting Ottoman regulars resented Lawrence's being accorded excessive credit for sabotaging Turkish supply lines. Turkish loyalists faulted his apparent indifference to civilian casualties, inflicted by blocking food and medical shipments to Medina. As to Liddell Hart, one suspects that his devotion to mobility formed the prism through which he viewed the Arab Revolt, and he saw what he wished to see (and until his death in 1970, defended Lawrence against all critics).

Where Lawrence (of Arabia) is most vulnerable as a strategist lies in the spongier domain of postwar goals. He sometimes spoke of Arab guerrillas as nascent freedom-fighters, led by enlightened princes who sought to recover Arabia's ancient glory in friendly partnership with the British. This was the psychological dimension that he emphasized in *Seven Pillars*, remarking of his guerrillas, "Their mind was strange and dark, full of depressions and exaltations, lacking in rule, but with more ardour and more fertile in belief than any other in the world. They were a people of starts, for whom the abstract was the strongest motive, the process of infinite courage and variety, and the end nothing."[14] Beyond dividing a future Arab kingdom among Hussein's sons, there is little hint in Lawrence's writings as to how a future Arab realm might look, where its frontiers should lie, and what should happen to its sizable minorities, religious, tribal, and ethnic. Lawrence's politics, like his guerrillas, were for the most part a vapor.

To this was added a conflicting measure of hardboiled pragmatism. Along with most British officers in the theater, he steadfastly opposed French colonial designs on Syria and Lebanon. Yet he knew that the later notorious 1916 Sykes-Picot Agreement had already parceled Ottoman lands among Britain, France, and Russia, staking the Gallic tricolor in the Levant. In *Seven Pillars*, he confides that he had "early betrayed the treaty's existence" to Prince Faisal, the revolt's military commander, and urged him "to help the British so much that after peace they would not be able, for shame, to shoot him down in its fulfillment" (which in fact the British did).[15] Elsewhere, privately addressing his superiors, he writes with condescending scorn about the Arabs, as in a 1916 staff paper advising, *"If properly handled they would remain in a state of political mosaic, a tissue of small jealous principalities incapable of cohesion"* (Lawrence's italics).[16]

Taken together, he left a bewildering paper trail. Lawrence could be an orthodox upholder of British imperial interests or, conversely, a champion of oppressed peoples, depending on date, whim, or circumstances. The British psychologist Kathryn Tidrick expresses a common frustration in her 1992 study of British Arabists. "We are none of us blessed with the consistency of character we like to believe is normal," she writes. "But in Lawrence this tendency seems to have been exaggerated. He was more of a chameleon than most of us, partly out of curiosity about himself and his effect on people, and partly because he couldn't help it."[17] One wonders whether in his adult life the real Lawrence ever stood up.

Still, his chameleon persona notwithstanding, Lawrence left a substantial imprint on policy. To understand why, one must sketch the setting. When the Great War broke out in 1914, few in Britain's ruling elite possessed on-the-ground experience in the Ottoman Middle East. Their number included Sir Mark Sykes, an ingratiating member of Parliament; another clever MP, the Hon. Aubrey Herbert; Sir Ronald Storrs, the learned and witty Oriental Secretary in Cairo; Gertrude Bell, already a luminary in Arabic studies; and importantly, Lord Kitchener, the hero of Omdurman who left his post as British Proconsul in Egypt to head the War Office in London. These were the "Easterners," and their role was pivotal in reversing a century of British strategy toward the multiethnic Turkish Empire. It had been long-established imperial policy to uphold the integrity of Ottoman Asia for hardheaded reasons—to safeguard routes to India, brake Russia's eastward expansion, and promote commerce—even as the Turkish Empire became torpid and senile. But from the moment that Turkey unwisely abandoned neutrality to side with Germany in late 1914, the Easterners challenged this orthodoxy.

Even before Turkey formally entered the war, Sharif Hussein, the guardian of Mecca and ruler of Hejaz, had written in September 1914 to War Minister Kitchener proposing that the Arabs might usefully help the Allies. Kitchener's response in October, probably drafted by Storrs, could scarcely have been more welcoming: "Till now we have defended and befriended Islam in the person of the Turks: henceforth it shall be that of the noble Arab. It may be that an Arab of true race will assume the Caliphate at

Mecca or Medina, and so good may come, by the help of God, out of all the evil which is now occurring."[18] (The Ottoman Sultans had assumed the ultimate spiritual office of Caliph after their conquest of Arabia in the sixteenth century, and the Arabs had long sought the caliphate's return.)

Few possessed a surer instinct about these shifting eddies than Mark Sykes. Within days of Turkey's declaration, he confided to his well-connected friend, a son of the Earl of Carnarvon, Aubrey Herbert:

> Now the important people whom we should get on our side are the Beni Sadr—they are the desert Bedawin and hate the Turks in their souls. However they must come to us not we go to them. We should establish a base at Akaba and an intelligence officer there with large powers ... The intelligence officer should find out what their idea is—also whether the Beni-Sadr will make up with the Druses. Then premiums might be offered for camels, say an exorbitant price £50 or £60, then a price for telegraph insulators, 2 francs each, then a price for interruption of Hejaz railway line, and a good price for Turkish Mausers, and a good price for deserters from the Turkish Army—the Beni Sadr would run these thro'.[19]*

There was more to Sykes than the widely reviled agreement he negotiated with France's François Georges-Picot. He was also the friend of nationalist movements—Arab, Zionist, Armenian—and the instigator of the Cairo-based Arab Bureau, whose star agent was T. E. Lawrence. In his letter to Herbert, Sykes uncannily anticipated the course of the Arab Revolt (whose banner he also designed). In essence, he advocated generous support for a nationalist uprising, offering rebels cash incentives, sabotaging Turkish rail lines, seizing and then using as a base the port of Aqaba, all the while relying on British agents to bond with nomadic Bedouins, the noble Arabs of true race—almost all seven pillars, one might venture, of Lawrence's own plan, with equal inattention as to what might come next.

On the August day that Britain entered the Great War, Lawrence was in England to complete, along with the archaeologist Leonard Woolley, their joint

---

* His reference to the Beni-Sadr is geographically implausible; he probably meant the Beni Sakhr.

survey of the Sinai for the Palestine Exploration Fund. Lawrence by then
had spent four seasons with Woolley excavating a Hittite city on the banks
of the Euphrates (now in a zone on the Turkish-Syrian frontier) and knew
the lay of the region. Within weeks he was on duty at the geographical section of the War Office, and on October 26 was commissioned a second lieutenant. Three days later, as Turkey formally declared war, an Anglo-Indian
expeditionary force embarked for Mesopotamia. After occupying Basra, the
invaders began moving upriver toward Baghdad, the first offensive in what
its fighters promptly dubbed the "Mespot" theater.

By December, Lawrence was posted to Egypt, where he joined the new
Intelligence Division headed by the seasoned Colonel Gilbert Clayton; this
was the cocoon that later hatched the celebrated Arab Bureau. Lieutenant
Lawrence burst upon Cairo (writes the bureau's historian, Bruce Westrate)
with an enthusiasm beyond the expectation of his rank: "he reveled in the
role of pesky maverick—tweaking the staid, upturned nose of officialdom at
every opportunity."[20] He and his colleagues called themselves "Intrusives,"
the telegraphic code name for GHQ (General Headquarters) Intelligence,
and as Lawrence recalled, "[W]e meant to break into the accepted halls of
English policy, and build a new people in the East."[21] Other arrivals included
Leonard Woolley, Aubrey Herbert, and Philip Graves (a polyglot Middle East
correspondent of *The Times* of London). They were later visited by Gertrude
Bell, the sole female "Intrusive." Their lair was the Savoy Hotel, a blend of
Oriental and Occidental decor featuring acrobatic baboons in the veranda,
its bar a mosaic of khaki and epaulets.

During 1915 the Middle Eastern Front seemed electric with expectation. In April volunteers from Australia and New Zealand under British
command joined at sea with a French force to begin a ten-month assault
on Gallipoli, the abortive attempt to knock Turkey from the war. In Mesopotamia, an Anglo-Indian army poised for a full-throttle offensive under
Major General Sir Charles Townshend to take Baghdad. Looking on impatiently from his desk as a map analyst and interrogator of war prisoners
was Lieutenant Lawrence, his mood darkened by the slaughter in France,
where his older brother Frank and his younger brother Will were among
the fatalities. "It doesn't seem right, somehow," Thomas Edward wrote
homeward in November, "that I should go on living peacefully in Cairo."[22]
Yet the war's most curious and disputed exchange of letters was about to
pitch him into Arabia.

The initiative came from Hussein, the hereditary Grand Sharif of Mecca, who wrote to Sir Henry McMahon, the High Commissioner in Egypt, proposing "joint action" in return for British recognition of independence for "the entire Arab nation." His offer was taken up, elaborated, qualified, and ambiguously redefined in a covert correspondence that continued until March 1916, generating a controversy that persists regarding who promised what to whom. The exchange coincided with Sykes's secret negotiations, first with France, then with Russia, concerning the postwar division of Ottoman spoils. In spirit if not in literal content, the Sykes-Picot Agreement and the McMahon-Hussein correspondence plainly conflicted. Still, as the historian Elizabeth Monroe reminds us, the difference did not seem so great at that time, since "1916 was the last year of an old familiar world of intact empires, letters from Nickie to Georgie, secret agreements secretly arrived at, and treatment of whole populations as chattel. It was also the last year of freedom from criticism by anti-imperial allies."[23]

Such was the setting in January of 1916, when at Sykes's initiative and over the vehement objections of the Viceroy of India Lord Charles Hardinge, an interdepartmental panel in London approved the establishment in Cairo of an Arab Bureau. By that spring, the ebullience had diminished in Cairo. The Gallipoli campaign had collapsed, and Townshend's Anglo-Indian force, after nearly reaching the outskirts of Baghdad, was driven back to the dingy riverside town of Kut. In Kut, some thirteen thousand soldiers and civilian noncombatants lived on short rations amid grumbling Arabs, waiting vainly for the expected relief force.

In London, a restive coalition government faced with losses on all fronts sought in March to buy its way out of Kut. To that end, Lawrence was sent to Mesopotamia, his first field mission, ostensibly to advise on aerial surveillance but in fact to help ransom the trapped soldiers. Once in Basra, he joined Aubrey Herbert, who had been authorized by Whitehall to offer £1 million (later doubled) to Khalil Pasha, the Turkish commander, in return for lifting the siege. The Ottoman general haughtily brushed aside the ransom offer and would agree only to an exchange of wounded prisoners and to indulgent surrender terms for General Townshend (and his dog). After 147 days, as many as thirteen thousand mostly Indian soldiers and noncombatants were herded away as POWs; barely a quarter survived the war.[24]

For Lawrence, the mission was formative. It gave him a firsthand glimpse of the Turkish army and its commanders, as well as the Anglo-Indian expeditionary force (he was struck by what he perceived as Indian antipathy toward Arabs). In Basra, he met key British political actors, among them Sir Percy Cox, the ranking Political Officer in Mesopotamia. Yet more generally, his mission presaged the grosser side of British strategy, its reliance on gold as a bait and lever.

By that spring in 1916, Middle East policy makers in Whitehall and Cairo broadly agreed on what they perceived as the correct road forward. Albeit rough at its edges, a deal concerning the postwar division of the Ottoman Empire—Sykes-Picot—had been struck with France and Russia. Its contents were disclosed in substance if not detail to senior officials in Egypt. The fledgling Arab Bureau had acquired a staff and structure. And acting on the very guarded promises made by High Commissioner McMahon, Sharif Hussein proclaimed the start of the Arab Revolt in May 1916.

Spurred by Hussein's four sons—Faisal, Abdullah, Ali, and Zeid—thousands of Arab irregulars captured Mecca, Rabegh, Lith, Taif, and Yenbo, but the key city of Medina held firm and by autumn the revolt had stalled. The guerrillas had no chain of command, and to its British advisers they seemed little more than an undisciplined rabble. Cairo's intelligence chiefs feared the rising had fallen. But not Lawrence, who from the outset believed in the Arab national movement, as he recalled, "and was confident, before I ever came, that it was the idea to tear Turkey to pieces, but others in Egypt lacked faith, and had been taught nothing intelligent of the Arabs in the field."[25] In October, having learned that Ronald Storrs was going to Jiddah, and himself being owed ten days' leave, Lawrence (by his own account) received permission to tag along and, incidentally, appraise the revolt's leaders.

Once aboard the steamer *Laura* en route to Jiddah, Lawrence listened restlessly as Storrs (speaking in German, French, and Arabic) debated the merits of Debussy and Wagner with Aziz el Masri, a defecting Turkish officer who was now a general in the Sharifian Army (as its Cairo patrons now called it). In Jiddah, Lawrence met first with Emir Abdullah, who rode to the British Consulate on a white mare attended by a score of armed slaves. Lawrence was unimpressed. At thirty-five, Abdullah seemed too pudgy, too patently ambitious, "too balanced, too cool, too humorous to be a prophet." Still, Storrs, with the Emir's assent, persuaded a reluctant Sharif Hussein (via telephone to Mecca) to allow Lawrence to extend his journey. At

Rabegh, Lawrence took critical measure of Emir Ali, "a pleasant gentleman, conscientious, without great force of character, nervous, and rather tired." And next, Emir Zeid, only nineteen, shy and beardless, "even less than Abdulla the born leader of my quest."[26]

Finally, in Hamra, a nondescript village of a hundred dwellings, Lawrence was introduced to a white figure waiting tensely for him: "I felt at first glance that this was the man I had come to Arabia to seek—the leader who would bring the Arab Revolt to full glory. Feisal looked very tall and pillar-like, very slender, in his long white silk robes and his brown head-cloth bound with a brilliant scarlet and gold cord. His eyelids were dropped; and his black beard and colourless face were like a mask against the strange, still watchfulness of his body. His hands were crossed in front of him on his dagger." It helped that Faisal, thirty-three years old, had attended school in Constantinople, spoke European languages, and seemed free of religious zealotry. In him, Lawrence felt, was offered to British hands "which had only to be big enough to take it, a prophet," the leader who could give form to the Arab Revolt: "It was all and more than we had hoped for, much more than our halting course deserved. The aim of my trip was fulfilled."[27]

Over time, though, Lawrence would evince the same supreme self-confidence in the Arabic cause—and in his ability to influence Faisal—that later led him as a writer to compare himself with Tolstoy. Even more wonderfully, he somehow persuaded his less imaginative, more prosaic superiors to act on his intuition. In the ensuing two years, the British wagered literally billions of today's dollars on the risky prospects of a dynasty and a cause of whom and about which they knew comparatively little.

It is difficult to exaggerate the importance of "subsidies," the official euphemism for the bullion used to secure the loyalty of Grand Sharif Hussein, his sons, and their tribal followers. Drawing on long-classified British records for a history of the Arab Bureau, Bruce Westrate has detailed the payments, beginning with an initial installment of £20,000 to Hussein in December 1915, which swelled into a monthly subsidy of £125,000, with frequent bonuses from General Sir Francis Reginald Wingate, Sirdar of the Egyptian Army and Governor-General of the Sudan. (At one point Wingate provided £375,000 to cover Islamic pilgrimage expenses.) Nonetheless, the Grand

Sharif of Mecca complained that he still needed an additional £75,000 monthly, which was grudgingly granted since (in Westrate's words) "British officials were aware that much gold had simply vanished, leaving discontented tribesmen months in arrears."[28]

Simply transporting the bullion was a logistic feat. An Old Etonian named Wyndham Deedes, a veteran of the King's Own Rifles who later served in the Ottoman Gendarmerie, managed the mint. He spent his Saturdays (as David Fromkin found in researching *A Peace to End All Peace*) packing gold sovereigns into cartridge cases, then supervising their camouflage on camel saddlebags destined for Arabia. Lawrence proved a casual accountant. At one point, without authorization, he removed £25,000 in gold from Aqaba, which he then sent to the wrong Emir, who had already received an equal amount from Cairo. Small wonder that a Bedouin sheik, when asked a half century later if he knew Lawrence, replied smilingly, "He was the man with the gold."[29]

The image of Lawrence as paymaster conflicts with that of Lawrence the rhapsodist of the Bedouin's noble savagery. By near-universal testimony, he treated Arabs with respect and empathy, and earned their trust. Still, gold tarnished their relations, for which there is no better witness than the monarch Lawrence auditioned. "Bedouins can be roused to do anything for honour," cautioned King Faisal of Iraq, speaking in 1930 to Captain John Bagot Glubb (the future Glubb Pasha), "but once you give them money, the whole moral tone of your relations with them is lowered."[30] More generally, Lawrence perpetrated a mosaic of romantic illusions about the Arab movement he fostered and celebrated. In a revealing passage in *Seven Pillars*, he characterizes Mark Sykes as "an imaginative advocate of unconvincing world movements" and "a bundle of prejudices, intuitions, half-sciences" whose ideas were too mutable because he lacked the patience "to test materials before choosing his style of building." Yet if one adds a dram of genius, the mixture could well describe Lawrence.[31]

Take, for example, Lawrence's version in *Seven Pillars of Wisdom* of the October 1918 capture of Damascus, the martial finale of the Arab Revolt. The victory was made possible by Allenby's massive offensive, spearheaded by an ANZAC army commanded by Australia's General Sir Henry Chauvel and made easier by the abrupt evacuation of the city's Turkish officials, ignobly

ending four centuries of Ottoman rule. Yet in *Seven Pillars*, it is the sharifians who dominate the drama. Faisal is greeted with tumultuous cheers and,
along with Lawrence, is then supposedly shocked on being told that Britain
had promised Syria to the French under the Sykes-Picot pact, about which
both professed complete ignorance. As Lawrence himself candidly acknowledged, *Seven Pillars* was a "personal narrative pieced out of memory" years
after the events it recalled. Writing to his biographer Robert Graves, Lawrence admitted that "I was on thin ice when I wrote the Damascus chapter" which was "full of half-truth."[32] A specimen half-truth was Lawrence's
blaming marauding Algerians or crazed Druzes for the chaotic trashing of
the Turkish Military Hospital.

It chanced that an American was present: William Yale, an oil company
executive turned diplomat in the Middle East (a military theater in which
the United States was neutral since it had not declared war on Turkey). Yale
was appalled by what he viewed as the vengeful sacking of the hospital by
the Arabs. Interviewed in 1966 by Dr. John E. Mack, a Harvard psychiatrist
and Lawrence biographer, Yale recalled protesting to the British authorities
and being told "to mind his own business as he was not a soldier."[33]

There is ample evidence that Bedouins joined actively in the postconquest looting, that the sharifian irregulars did not liberate Damascus, that
Sykes-Picot was scarcely a secret—its full text had been made public a year
earlier by the Bolsheviks in Russia—and that the welcome for Faisal was
at best tepid. Two credible witnesses can be summoned. Alec Kirkbride was
an Arabic-speaking British army lieutenant who arrived in Damascus along
with Faisal's guerrillas. He was surprised by the apathetic welcome for the
Hashemite claimant. "There were no cheers or signs of joy, which one might
have expected from a population supposed to be in the process of liberation
. . . I was rather pained by the lack of popular enthusiasm."[34]

Kirkbride joined up with Lawrence, whose Arabic he found fluent if
heavily accented ("he betrayed his origin the moment he spoke"). In another
observation (interestingly at variance with Peter O'Toole's sanguinary por-
trayal of T. E.) he adds:

> His tastes were anything but bloodthirsty, and he appeared to be genu-
> inely shocked by the free use which I made of my revolver during the
> evening after we entered Damascus . . . We must have looked an ill-
> assorted couple, he short and in Arab robes with no arms but an orna-

mental dagger, and myself long and lanky in khaki, wearing a large Service revolver. When we found anyone butchering Turks he went up and asked them in a gentle voice to stop, while I stood by and brandished my firearm. Occasionally, someone turned nasty and I shot them at once before the trouble could spread. Lawrence got quite cross and said, "For God's sake stop being so bloody-minded!"[35]

The problem, Kirkbride continues, was that the fleeing Ottomans left a vacuum and there was a paucity of occupation troops: the Damascene police, he writes, had "ceased to function and there was a political objection to calling in the British forces, who were camped on the outskirts of the town, and so admitting that the new Arab administration was incapable of controlling its own people."[36]

A second witness is Bedreddin Shellah, the longtime doyen of the city's trading elite, who at age eighty-four was found and interviewed by the American writer Milton Viorst. "I was thirteen years old when Faisal's caravan arrived," he recalled.

> Most of our people were bewildered. Only a few were nationalists. Many of our young men were still fighting in the Ottoman army. The masses welcomed Faisal, but not out of patriotism. Most hoped the liberation would put an end to our wartime suffering. We had contradictory feelings about the Ottomans. Because they were Muslims like us, we had not considered them a colonial power, and we counted on them to protect us against czarist Russia and European secularism. But they governed badly. Most of our people were poor and only a handful were educated, nearly all in Islamic schools. It was a pity that, while Europe was having a golden age, life was so bleak in Syria . . . Most Syrians thought it was time for a new start. That's why there was jubilation.[37]

Shellah's version is corroborated by the late Albert Hourani, an eminent Oxford historian of Lebanese Christian descent whose father had known Lawrence. In Hourani's judgment, only three groups with very different interests actually backed the Arab Revolt: "First there was a small group of mainly Syrians with a few Iraqi, nationalists who were mostly Ottoman army officers or officials. Second, there was the Hashemite family, Sharif Hussein of Mecca, and his sons. And third, there was the British government."[38] Each had different agendas, each distrusted the other, none had a truly indigenous following, and throughout the war each (including the British) weighed a separate peace with the Ottomans. The remarkable fact is that with this skimpy kindling, Lawrence was able to ignite a bonfire— notwithstanding his fallible judgment about the Hashemites. Events demonstrated that Sharif Hussein was in no way the match of chief Arabian rival Abdul Aziz Ibn Abdul Rahman Saud, who unified and founded the kingdom that bears his family name (and who deposed Hussein from his ancestral home in the Hejaz). As events confirmed, the Arab Revolt did not spring from a broad-based national movement but proved (in the scornful later phrase of an Egyptian Foreign Minister) an alliance of tribes with flags (and even its flags were designed by foreigners).

Nevertheless, Lawrence's personal impact was not just remarkable but phenomenal. This surely goes some distance in explaining his persisting allure. "Nobody who ever met him," writes Hourani, "even those who met him before 1914, ever thought he was quite like ordinary men, and this is a fact one has to remember about him."[39] The Hon. Aubrey Herbert, a shrewd judge, after their first meeting in 1916, found him "an odd gnome, half-cad—with a touch of genius."[40]

His odd genius was demonstrated following Lawrence's supposed "retirement" from public life in 1922. By then he had helped orchestrate a guerrilla uprising, had honorably supported the Arabian Emir Faisal at the 1919 Paris Peace Conference, and as Winston Churchill's chosen adviser, had assisted crucially a year later in securing thrones for Hashemite claimants in Iraq and Transjordan. (He also tried, less successfully, to reconcile Arab leaders with the creation of a British-sponsored Zionist "National Home" in Palestine.) On returning to England, Lawrence had been elected a Fellow at Oxford's All Souls College and was writing what he hoped might be a masterwork comparable to *War and Peace*, *Moby-Dick*, and *The Brothers Karamazov*.

To this end, Lawrence met, befriended, or corresponded with Shaw, Hardy, Forster, and Kipling; prized distinctive voices, old and new, such as Charles Montagu Doughty, venerated author of *Arabia Deserta*, and the best-selling Bengal lancer, Francis Yeats-Brown; and cultivated budding talents like David Garnett and Robert Graves (his first British biographer).

He was conversant with modernists in all the arts. He underlined Eliot's "Waste Land," acquired Joyce's works, volume by volume, and under a pseudonym, writing in *The Spectator*, unreservedly praised the innovative novels of D. H. Lawrence. "Unquestionably," remark the American critics Stanley and Rodelle Weintraub, "he loved lingering over the discriminating choice of an adjective, and found joy in stylistic changes which would have tortured the patience of practiced writers."[41]

There followed a second act—indeed a third act—that no playwright could contrive. In January 1922 he wrote to Air Marshal Sir Hugh Trenchard, saying that he wished to join the Royal Air Force ("with the ranks, of course"). At thirty-three, Lawrence feared he might not pass "your medical" and sought Trenchard's influence with the recruiting office. His motive? Well, his substantially completed book on the Arab Revolt was "nearly good," and he sought fresh material in the RAF "and the best place to see a thing from is the ground. It wouldn't 'write' from the officer level." On August 30, Aircraftman T. E. Ross, as he now legally became, contentedly left the recruiting office in Covent Garden, having by prior agreement given his age as twenty-eight and his trade as "architect's clerk." Ross trained as an ordinary recruit at Uxbridge, then at the RAF School of Photography in Farnborough, and all the while kept corresponding with Bernard Shaw about the possible abridgement of his sprawling *Seven Pillars* to a mere 130,000 words. Inescapably, since his identity was known to other rankers and to his superiors, news leaked out. As *The Daily Express* headlined it: "UNCROWNED KING" AS PRIVATE SOLDIER/ LAWRENCE OF ARABIA / FAMOUS WAR HERO BECOMES A PRIVATE / SEEKING PEACE / OPPORTUNITY TO WRITE A BOOK.[42]

Sir Samuel Hoare, the Secretary of State for Air, was dismayed by the press disclosure, as were (so he later claimed) the RAF officers drilling their new recruit: "How, they not unnaturally asked, were they to deal on the barrack square with a private who was a Colonel and a D.S.O., and one of the most famous of war heroes?"[43] Private Ross was discharged. Undeterred, Lawrence persuaded the War Office to permit his enlistment in the Royal Tank Corps, again as a private. In March 1923, Lawrence reported for duty at Bovington Camp in Dorset to begin eighteen weeks' basic training as Tank Corps Private T. E. Shaw. (At the War Office, an officer told Lawrence he must choose a fresh name. "What's yours?" "No you don't." T. E. then opened a nearby Army List, and at random picked the first one-syllable name he came upon—Shaw—at least in his telling.)[44]

Private Shaw completed his first rough draft of *Seven Pillars*, acquired a small cottage at Clouds Hill (a mile from his camp), and in November submitted a massive (330,000-word) manuscript to Oxford University Press. When OUP's readers turned down *Seven Pillars*, fearing it was libelous, Lawrence/Shaw decided to publish his pristine text privately. He calculated optimistically that a limited edition of approximately two hundred copies at thirty guineas each would cover costs for the volume's fine paper and binding, and for its copious illustrations, including thirty portraits, mostly from life, by Eric Kennington (for which the artist toured the Middle East to eye his quarry).

As galley proofs sallied back and forth, so did the author, who having wearied of the Tank Corps won reluctant permission to rejoin the Royal Air Force—this time as "Shaw" rather than "Ross." In January 1927, Aircraftman T. E. Shaw was aboard a troopship bound for Karachi, having approved an abridgment of *Seven Pillars* that Jonathan Cape duly published as *Revolt in the Desert* by "T. E. Lawrence." Twenty extracts were serialized in *The Daily Telegraph*, and when ninety thousand copies of the book had been snapped up, Lawrence/Shaw ordered its withdrawal. "The goose has laid its clutch," he wrote to his dumbfounded agent, Raymond Savage. "My overdraft incurred for Seven Pillars is fairly paid off, and there is neither rhyme nor reason in continuing to make unwanted money at the expense of my comfort and sense of decency." The story becomes odder. The book's Foreword, initialed "T.E.L.," was in fact evidently written by none other than Bernard Shaw, and when Lawrence received bound copies in Karachi, he suggested adding this Author's Note, a placatory crumb tossed to higher-ups:

This text dates from 1919, when the fate of the Arabic-speaking provinces of the former Turkish Empire still hung in the balance, and its tone was affected by the political uncertainty in which the Arabs stood. But two years later Mr. Winston Churchill was entrusted by our harassed Cabinet with the settlement of the Middle East; and in a few weeks, at his conference in Cairo, he made straight all the tangle, finding solutions fulfilling (I think) our promises in letter and spirit, where humanly possible, without sacrificing any interest of our Empire, or any interest of the peoples concerned. So we are quit of the war-time Eastern adventure, with clean hands, after all.[45]

In Karachi, Lawrence worked on his *Odyssey* translation and completed the manuscript for *The Mint*, a memoir of barracks life in the RAF, replete with earthy language (published privately in 1936, and commercially, in revised form, in 1955). During these literary labors, with *Revolt in the Desert* still on bookstalls, a wholly unexpected controversy pitched him back into the headlines. In May 1928, he was transferred to an RAF advance post in Waziristan on India's fractious North-West Frontier. Along with twenty-odd other Anglo-Indian troops, he settled in the dusty and remote Miranshah Fort, only ten miles from Afghanistan. Bored and music-starved, writing homeward, T. E. lamented the lack of a record player. On August 16, a "red-letter day" since it was "the only fortieth birthday I shall have," he received a sumptuous gramophone, the gift of Charlotte Shaw, the playwright's wife. "I went through the Elgar Symphony today," he gratefully reported. ". . . As I listen to it I feel always on the exciting brink of understanding something very rare and great. Of course it slips away."[46]

The idyll ended in the fall of 1928. In Afghanistan, a tribal rebellion had broken out against Amanullah Khan, a modernizing monarch who outraged Islamic purists by promoting Western-style education and whose efforts to collect taxes angered local warlords. (Amanullah also irritated the British by recognizing and befriending the Soviet Union.) On September 26, the London *Evening News* trumpeted: LAWRENCE OF ARABIA'S SECRET MISSION / COUNTERING RED ACTIVITIES IN THE PUNJAB / POSES AS A SAINT / WARDING OFF THE EVIL EYE AND CURING ILLNESS. Under a Bombay dateline, the paper's correspondent alleged that Lawrence resided in a "queer house" in a remote street of Amritsar, pretending to be a Pir (a Muslim saint) with miraculous powers, his cover for foiling Soviet plots.[47]

This was followed by similarly improbable sightings in *The Times* and on January 9, 1929, in the left-leaning *Daily Herald*, which described T. E. as "the arch-spy of the world." The story was picked up and embroidered in major European papers, and more darkly by the Soviet press. On December 16, the long-since-defunct *Empire News* touched a Buchanesque nadir, asserting that Colonel Lawrence had visited Kabul during the third week of November to brief the King and Chief of Police, then departed: "Somewhere in the wild hills of Afghanistan up the rocky slopes by the cave-dwellers, perched high on the banks by a mountain stream, a gaunt holy man wearing the symbols of a pilgrim and a man of prayer proceeds along his lonely pilgrimage. He is Col. Lawrence, the most mysterious man in the Empire.

He is really the ultimate pro-Consul of Britain in the East. The battle is now joined between the Apostle of Hatred and the Apostle of Peace."[48] (The story was wholly fabricated, attributed to a nonexistent missionary, and was most likely concocted at El Vino's on Fleet Street. An immemorial rule of journalism is that spy stories are agreeably proof against libel or official denial.)

Yet in all this compost there was a small seed of truth. Afghanistan indeed awakened Lawrence's kingmaking instincts. Writing to Edward Marsh, Churchill's friend and adjutant, he questioned his chief's eagerness to "go for Russia" since Britain could only go through Turkey, Persia, Afghanistan, or China "and I fancy the Red Army is probably good enough to turn any one of those into a bit of herself." He continued: "The most dangerous point is Afghanistan. Do you know I nearly went there last week? The British Attaché in Kabul is entitled to an airman clerk, & the Depot would have put my name forward if I'd been a bit nippier on a typewriter." He reminded Marsh that he was an old hand at secret work "& Russia interests me greatly. The clash is bound to come, I think."[49] In any case, Amanullah abdicated in early 1929, was given asylum in India, resettled in Italy, and in 1950 died in Switzerland. (If Shaw had been a better typist, one wonders, would this history have been different?)

The reports of Lawrence's alleged covert role provoked questions in Parliament, followed by cloudy disavowals from the Air Ministry. After two years abroad, Private Shaw was smuggled home in February 1929, landing in Plymouth in circumstances that blended John Buchan and the Marx Brothers. Chief of the Air Staff Trenchard and the RAF arrival party pleaded for secrecy and discretion. "However," relates Jeremy Wilson, Lawrence's authorized biographer, "their attempts to keep Lawrence's whereabouts secret failed at almost every step. In order to avoid Plymouth railway station, they drove to Newton Abbot, but as soon as they boarded the London train they were recognized, and by the time it reached Paddington a crowd of journalists was waiting. Trenchard had asked Lawrence to 'Endeavour as much as possible to avoid being interviewed.' They therefore pushed through the pressmen with hardly a word. After this, there was a farcical chase in taxis which lasted nearly an hour." Having been bribed to do so, the cab driver crawled slowly to South Kensington, flanked by a shouting horde of pursuers. The only words they obtained from their reclusive prey was, "No, my name is Mr. Smith."[50]

Lawrence plausibly feared the uproar would end his RAF career, but it did not. Overseas postings were ruled out, but such was the power of his legend (and of his network of friends) that Aircraftman Shaw continued to be billeted in the United Kingdom until his retirement from the service in February 1935. And throughout his life in the ranks, Lawrence fussed over the birth and reception of *The Seven Pillars of Wisdom*, the book he hoped would attain "titanic" status.

Seldom has a masterwork survived a more difficult gestation. It was begun at the Paris Peace Conference in 1919, its early drafts were reputedly lost or stolen at a British railway station, more was added in Cairo at another conference, then worked on in Jiddah and Amman, retouched at Oxford's All Souls College, and polished and worried over during successive military postings across half the world. The text grew fresh rings like an olive tree. In final form, it managed to enthrall and mystify, enlighten and obfuscate. Its title derives from Proverbs 9:1: "Wisdom hath builded a house: she has hewn out her seven pillars," or as Lawrence's younger brother Arnold unhelpfully elaborated, "The title was originally applied by the author to a book of his about seven cities. He decided not to publish this early book because he considered it immature, but he transferred the title as a memento."[51]

More cryptic was his dedication "To S.A.," followed by four stanzas with Homeric echoes, these being the first two:

> *I loved you, so I drew these tides of men into my hands*
> *And wrote my will across the sky in stars*
> *To earn you Freedom, the seven pillared worthy house,*
> *That your eyes might be shining for me*
> *When we came.*
>
> *Death seemed my servant on the road, till we were near*
> *And saw you waiting:*
> *When you smiled, and in sorrowful envy he outran me*
> *And took you apart:*
> *Into his quietness.*

Not since Shakespeare dedicated his sonnets to "W.H." has so much ink been wasted on an ultimately insoluble literary riddle. One suspects that Lawrence/Ross/Shaw, whom his friend Gertrude Bell called "Imp," planted his riddles deliberately. He archly subtitled *Seven Pillars* "A Triumph." Yet a more universal triumph was to come.

The question of T. E. Lawrence's sexual orientation (in today's stilted parlance) remains unanswered. It is probably unanswerable. He had no known amorous liaisons with females, and furious arguments swirl about the extent of his possible homosexuality. Did he have Arab lovers? He certainly wrote sensuously about Bedouin youths, and disapproving compatriots insisted that his admiration exceeded the merely visual. Was he traumatically raped while imprisoned in Ottoman-ruled Dera on the orders of a Turkish bey who implausibly failed to realize his captive was a robed English spy? Lawrence asserts as much in *Seven Pillars* and elaborated his ordeal in a March 1924 letter to Charlotte Shaw.[52] Yet skeptics cite documents indicating that he was elsewhere in November 1917 on the days he claimed to have been whipped and sodomized by the Turks. (Decades later, the still-living Turkish bey disputed the entire tale when contacted by two revisionist biographers, the Jordanian journalist Suleiman Mousa and the British author Desmond Stewart.)

Yet another diligent effort to resolve these riddles was attempted inconclusively by the young British scholar James Barr in *Setting the Desert on Fire* (2008). The least likely tale was confided by the novelist Somerset Maugham to Richard Aldington, whose *Biographical Enquiry* depicted Lawrence as a liar and mountebank. Maugham informed Aldington that he had been told by Trenchard that Lawrence learned he faced arrest for soliciting servicemen, and that his lethal accident was a suicide to avert exposure. Problem one: Maugham was notoriously an adder-tongued gossip; two: no corroborative evidence has been found for a tale even Aldington was disinclined to publish; three: a motorbike crash in second gear seems an uncertain means of killing oneself. (Lawrence in fact lingered for six days in a coma, and just before his accident had sent a telegram agreeing to lunch with the writer Henry Williamson, a member of Sir Oswald Mosley's British Union of Fascists, who believed fervently that "Hitler and Lawrence must meet.")[53]

More substantial are reports that in 1922 he took part in flagellation parties hosted in the Chelsea area of London by a slithery German known to patrons and the Metropolitan Police as Bluebeard. A year later, as two scavenging London *Sunday Times* reporters confirmed in 1968, Lawrence arranged to be whipped on his backside by a young Scotsman named John Bruce (to whom the paper paid £2,500 for details), a rite that seemingly persisted for a decade. Still another biographer, the British historian Lawrence James, judiciously crystallizes the essential point: "While the mainsprings of Lawrence's peculiar sexuality must remain obscure, its manifestation during the 1920s and 1930s meant that he was living dangerously close to scandal"—an injudiciousness, to be sure, that helps explain his abiding appeal.[54]

What is beyond dispute is that from boyhood Lawrence was smitten with machines, as evidenced by his fidelity to his two-cylinder Brough motorbikes. He kept buying successive models, and dubbed each "Boanerges," a scriptural name (Mark 3:13) meaning "Sons of Thunder." With sad clairvoyance, he reported to their manufacturer, George Brough, a year before his accident, "My breaking the speedometer has had the curious effect of putting up my average six miles an hour! My last two long rides have been at 49 and 51 m.p.h. respectively. It looks as though I might yet break my neck on a B.S. [Brough Superior]."[55]

A Lawrence aficionado has aptly classified him as a "mechanical monk." In wartime Arabia, he blessed "St. Rolls" and "St. Royce." He joined the RAF, so he informed Robert Graves, "to serve a mechanical purpose, not as a leader but as a cog in a machine. The key word, I think, is machine. I have been mechanical since, and a good mechanic, for my self-training to become an artist has greatly widened my field of view." Entering the RAF, Lawrence explained, was "the nearest modern equivalent of going into a monastery in the Middle Ages." This was doubly true, since "[b]eing a mechanic cuts one off from all real communication with women . . . No woman, I believe, can understand a mechanic's happiness in serving his bits and pieces."[56]

His mechanical brides included seaplanes and tanks, speedboats and motorbikes, and from first to last, cameras. A Kodak was as ubiquitous as his sketchpad during his youthful bicycle trips to inspect medieval churches and forts in France, and likewise on his Levantine pilgrimage in quest of Crusader castles. During four archaeological seasons (1910–13) at the Hittite site of Carchemish in Syria, Lawrence served as expedition photographer. (At Carchemish, he also trained a teenage donkey-boy, Selim Ahmed, as his photographic assistant. Nicknamed "Dahoum" or "little dark one," Selim remains lead candidate to be the "S.A." of *Seven Pillars* fame.) It was here, too, that Lawrence, reputedly acting as an unofficial British agent, trained his Zeiss lens on the German teams constructing the strategic Berlin-to-Baghdad railroad. In 1914 he paired with Leonard Woolley to survey the Sinai for the Palestine Exploration Fund (and the War Office), and took the photos that illustrated their report on the Wilderness of Zin. When Turkey entered the Great War in late 1914, and the Middle East became a "show," Lawrence would be among the first to pioneer the use of aerial photography to pinpoint enemy targets.

As we have seen, his fame as "uncrowned king of Arabia" was incubated in Lowell Thomas's slide show. How fitting, therefore, that Lawrence was to be posthumously deified on film by Director David Lean. When we think today of Lawrence, we visualize Peter O'Toole, blond as the desert sand, the intrepid champion of the Arab underdog, the scourge of vile imperialists, the artist with a bleeding inner wound. It is worth examining how this great epic came about, and whether it captured the essence, if not the detail, of a life surpassing strange.

That Lawrence's *Revolt in the Desert* was a cinematic natural was clear from the day of its publication. In 1927, the author was approached by the Hollywood producer and director Rex Ingram, whose popular credits included a war movie, *The Four Horsemen of the Apocalypse* (1921) and two desert romances, *The Arab* (1924) and *The Garden of Allah* (1927). Lawrence politely resisted, saying that his literary trustees had already turned down a Hollywood offer of £6,000 "or something." He added, "Long may they keep turning it down. I'd hate to see myself parodied on the pitiful basis of my record of what the fellows with me did."[57] But his refusal was less than categorical, and other suitors soon followed.

The most ardent was Alexander Korda, Britain's reigning cinematic impresario, an unabashed imperialist despite (or in part owing to) his Hungarian birth. In 1934, Korda acquired movie rights for *Revolt in the Desert* from the Lawrence Trust, paying a reported £6,000, which the trustees earmarked for RAF widows and orphans. It is difficult to believe the trust acted without consulting Lawrence. So confident was Korda that he announced in May that Leslie Howard would play the lead, and that Lewis Milestone (*All Quiet on the Western Front*) would direct. Discussions began with Captain Basil H. Liddell Hart, military expert and Lawrence biographer, to serve as consultant. At this point Lawrence seemingly had second thoughts. In

January 1935, he sought out the mogul, who proved unexpectedly sensitive (as Lawrence related to Charlotte Shaw) "when I put to him the inconveniences his proposed film of *Revolt* would set in my path . . . and [he] ended the discussion by agreeing that it should not be attempted without my consent. He will not announce its abandonment because while he has it on his list other producers will avoid thought of it. But it will not be done."[58] Still, the option remained on the table.

After Lawrence's fatal accident in May 1935, a fresh rush of interest followed what was virtually a state funeral. Six pallbearers bore his remains to the village church in Moreton: Sir Ronald Storrs, Eric Kennington, Corporal Bradbury, Private Russell, Pat Knowles, and Stewart Newcombe. Among the distinguished mourners were Winston Churchill, Nancy Astor, Major General A. P. Wavell, Jonathan Cape, Augustus John, Mrs. Thomas Hardy, B. H. Liddell Hart, and Siegfried Sassoon. Lawrence, who while living had declined royal honors, in death received from King George V an encomium addressed to A. W. Lawrence: "Your brother's name will live in history and the King gratefully recognizes his distinguished services to his country." In London seven months later, a sculptured likeness of Lawrence was unveiled in the crypt of St. Paul's as part of a final memorial salute from the mighty.[59]

In truth, Lawrence's adieu was a dramatist's dream. He died in the bloom of his years, like John F. Kennedy or James Dean, and thus escaped the ruthless editing of age. A thirty-six-minute documentary by Ace Films drawing on wartime film footage was quickly produced, and the Lawrence Trust reauthorized Korda to bring the Arab Revolt to the screen. His subsequent four-year struggle to do so was virtually an epic in itself. Shooting on location in Palestine was ruled out by civil strife. The Foreign Office pressed for censorship rights. After obtaining a draft script, the Turkish Embassy protested to the British Government that "the Turks were represented as tyrants and oppressors of Arabs," casting unacceptable aspersions on "Turkish history and national character." Documents now declassified reveal high-level discussions about lubricating official influence by offering Korda a "K," or knighthood. This was opposed as insulting by the Foreign Office's Permanent Under Secretary, Sir Robert Vansittart (a distant blood relation of Lawrence's who had recently signed a contract to advise Korda on imperial subjects). A colleague (slyly, one guesses) suggested that Sir Robert could appropriately write to the producer stressing "how much we wish and need to keep the Turks sweet."[60]

The back and forth in Whitehall stretched on for months. The producer offered to tone down negative portrayals of Turks and Arabs, and provided a detailed scene-by-scene synopsis. Yet the British Board of Film Censors' chief script reader, a Colonel Hanna, declared emphatically that it would be "most impolitic" to upset the Arabs. Meantime, Korda asked his brother Zoltan (*The Four Feathers*) to direct the film, while the search continued for a suitable lead actor. Candidates included Laurence Olivier and Robert Donat, but Korda stuck to his earlier choice, Leslie Howard. In a 1937 film magazine article, "How I Shall Play Lawrence," the debonair Howard felt the central theme had to be the tragic defeat of Lawrence's ideals by an obdurate British bureaucracy. "In the final sequence," he wrote, "I hope to show him riding to his death along a country lane on his powerful motor cycle. Then a quick shot back to Palestine with its intrigues and insurrections—a tormented stretch of land which, if only Lawrence had had his way might now have been a peaceful and united country." (Korda's 1938 script and the Howard interview were published in a slim 1997 volume, *Filming T. E. Lawrence*, compiled by three British cultural historians.)[61]

If Sir Alexander Korda (he eventually did get his "K") is to be credited, Winston Churchill himself wielded the silver stake. "I wanted to make *Seven Pillars* before the war," the producer reminisced after the war with his nephew, the publisher Michael Korda. "I thought it would be ideal for Zoli [Zoltan]. It would make a wonderful movie, only one should call it *Lawrence of Arabia*. But Zoli didn't like the idea, partly because of Palestine, and Churchill was very worried because he felt it was very important to have the Turks as allies when the war came, so nothing ever came of it. Now I don't know, it's still difficult to do, and with the Israelis and the Arabs, I'm not sure it would work. It's a great film, but I don't have the desire to make it, so I suppose I shall have to sell it to somebody."[62] Which, auspiciously, he did.

The film rights to *Seven Pillars* passed first to J. Arthur Rank in the 1950s (dates and details murky), whose candidate for the lead role was Alec Guinness. However, the project perished when location filming ran afoul successively of a burst of nationalism in Jordan, the convulsive Suez Affair in Egypt, and the massacre of the Hashemite royal family in Iraq following a 1958 military coup. Enter Sam Spiegel, a Vienna-born Hollywood producer who undeterred and determined, acquired film rights from A. W. Lawrence, then teaching archaeology at Cambridge University. And like the quixotic British officer in David Lean's *Bridge on the River Kwai* (the Oscar-winning film Spiegel also produced), he persevered against all obstacles.

It helped that *Lawrence of Arabia* was an Anglo-American venture, jointly financed by Horizon Pictures of London and Columbia Pictures of Los Angeles. David Lean, a Briton, was co-producer as well as director, and its script was the shared work of an American, Michael Wilson, and a Briton, Robert Bolt. After winning an Oscar for the script of *A Place in the Sun* (1951), Wilson was blacklisted in Hollywood for being an "unfriendly witness" before the House Committee on Un-American Activities. He became a McCarthy-era exile whose contract stipulated that he had to provide Spiegel with a "satisfactory statement" concerning his political past. In the event, Lean was unhappy with Wilson's script, deeming it "too American," and he and Spiegel turned to Bolt, whose play about Sir Thomas More, *A Man for All Seasons*, was currently a critical and box office success. Bolt received sole writing credit for *Lawrence*, but a careful comparison of successive scripts shows that he followed Wilson's structure and adopted many of his ideas. (The British Screenwriters' Guild, to which Wilson appealed for recognition, found in his favor, but Bolt refused to share credit with the American.)[63]

Spiegel initially approached Marlon Brando, cresting from his triumph in *On the Waterfront* (another Spiegel production) to play the title role. But Brando had a less exacting offer to star in *Mutiny on the Bounty*, and he chose Tahiti. When their second candidate (Albert Finney) also declined, the producer and director gambled on a scarcely known stage actor, Peter O'Toole. The son of an Irish bookmaker, fitfully schooled, and a foot taller than Lawrence, O'Toole became a blond (permanently) and underwent nasal surgery for the role. He combined cocky panache with tormenting self-doubt in a performance based on his own reading of *Seven Pillars*. As he put it in a 1962 press interview, Lawrence "spent his life in a quest for the truth about himself, and when he finally found what it was, it was terrifying."[64]

The film took two years to complete, its budget swelling to $12 million-plus. Its makers claimed it required $80,000 a day on location to truck water to 15,000 personnel, 5,000 camels, and 500 horses. O'Toole appeared in almost every scene of the 227-minute film, dominating a strong all-male cast that included Alec Guinness, Claude Rains, Omar Sharif, José Ferrer, Jack Hawkins, Anthony Quinn, Donald Wolfit, and Arthur Kennedy. The troupe, or members of it, migrated to and from locations in Spain, Morocco, and

Jordan (where the film itself was initially banned by skittish royal authorities). Queen Elizabeth II attended the December 1962 premiere in London, and when it opened in New York a week later, tickets cost an unprecedented $4.80. In a commercial blitz, Columbia Pictures propagated "Lawrence mania," a phenomenon *Vogue* called "desert dazzle" that extended from Elizabeth Arden's "Sheik-look Crème Rouge" to "Little Lawrence's Beach 'n Bath Burnooses," marketed by Gibbs Underwear in New York.[65]

The initial critical reception was mixed. *Lawrence of Arabia* rejected the clichés of military epics; it depicted a troubled hero fomenting a nationalist revolt only to learn that his warriors were likely to be cheated of the liberation he had promised. Speaking for perplexed middlebrows, *The New York Times*'s Bosley Crowther found the film visually striking but "devoid of humanity," its script at once "lusterless and over-written." More perceptively, *The New Yorker*'s Pauline Kael judged the picture "one of the most literate and tasteful and exciting of expensive spectacles." Nevertheless, it was apparent to her that most people in the audience "hadn't the remotest idea of what the Arabs and the Turks were doing in the First World War, or which was which, or why the English cared." Can complicated historical events and a complex hero, she wondered, "really get across in a spectacle?"[66]

In any case, few films have reached a broader audience and sowed a more pervasive message. *Lawrence* swept the Academy Awards for 1962, earning ten nominations and winning seven Oscars (Best Picture, Direction, Cinematography, Art Direction, Music, Film Editing, and Sound). When the young Steven Spielberg saw *Lawrence* in Texas, he determined to become a director, one of many such epiphanies. The film has ever since been revived whenever the Middle East is aflame. Footage originally deleted to shorten the U.S. version has been restored. These revivals attest not just to the film's cinematic quality but also to its populist/imperial ambiguity. As Harvard anthropologist Steven C. Caton concluded in a detailed exegesis, *Lawrence of Arabia* is at once anticolonialist and unblushingly Orientalist. To Caton's postmodern eyes, its complexities of "discourse and representation" spring both from the movie's imperial condescension and from its "historical (post-Suez) and cultural (angry young men)" contextual origins.[67]

Whatever its ingredients, the mix proved durable. A 2004 poll of British filmmakers voted *Lawrence of Arabia* the best British film of all time (runners-up included Lean's prior *Brief Encounter* and *Great Expectations*). Two years later, in a survey by the British film journal *Premiere*, Peter

O'Toole's lead role was chosen as the greatest-ever movie performance. And in an oblique but choice accolade, agents for Jordan's royal palace bid £164,800 at Sotheby's in 2006 for the actual cotton flag said to have been flown over Aqaba, the Turkish seaside fort whose conquest was vividly reenacted in the film. Yet doubts persist. Was it all spin and scam? T. E. himself called the Arab insurgency a "sideshow of a sideshow." Is the entire legend of "the Uncrowned King of Arabia" itself a fabrication?

The case for the prosecution is by now familiar. Doubtless Lawrence's politics were vague, rooted in anachronistic ideals of chivalry, fertilized with a layer of imperial paternalism. He was a fabulist, charitably in the Homeric mode, less charitably a congenital fabricator of his own one-man show. He shamelessly pursued fame even as he denied its importance. And inarguably, there was a flip and frivolous self-indulgence in the games he played, about which he could be disarmingly candid. As he wrote to a correspondent in 1929, "I must put in a last word about my abnormality. Anyone who had gone up so fast as I went (remember that I was almost entirely self-made; my father had five sons and only £300 a year) and had seen so much of the inside of the top of the world might well lose his aspirations, and get weary of the ordinary motives of action, which had moved him till he reached the top. I wasn't a King or Prime Minister, but I made 'em, or played with them, and after that there wasn't much more in that direction I could do."[68]

Here arguably was the inner key. Lawrence took neither himself nor life that solemnly; he remained a schoolboy until his final crash. Some have made much of his illegitimate birth, first made known to the world by Aldington in 1955. Yet of the five Lawrence boys, all illegitimate, only Ned became Lawrence of Arabia. And yes, there was his yearning for recognition of his wellborn Anglo-Irish ancestry, as Dr. Hourani ably argues, but the same applies to his brethren, none of whom made kings and prime ministers.

Our own conclusion, put simply is that Lawrence appeals to the populist devil in all of us, the rule-breaker and challenger of orthodoxy who compels the world to accept his own impudent self-valuation. His prose could be florid, but rarely pompous. His classical scholarship and his standing as a writer added to his glamour as a man of action, especially to desk-bound intellectuals, investing him in the pantheon whose other tenants include

André Malraux, Gabriel D'Annunzio, and Ernst Jünger. To lesser mortals, his doing penance as a ranker was as appealing as his foreswearing conventional baubles of status. His political beliefs verged on the mushy and medieval, but they were not mean. He was visually a man for all mediums, and his mocking eye rendered his Arab vestments proof against laughter. Orwell remarked of Gandhi that for all his faults he bequeathed a clean smell, and so too with Thomas Edward Lawrence.

SEVEN

The Apostate

Harry St. John Bridger Philby (1885–1960), CIE

⌘

The mind is its own place, and in itself
Can make a Heaven of Hell, a Hell of Heaven.
What matter where, if I still be the same . . .?
Better to reign in Hell than serve in Heaven.

—Satan in Milton's
Paradise Lost (1667)

If December 7, 1941, is a day that lives in infamy for Americans, how might one describe a less famous date, May 29, 1933? The mating of a blind eagle and a deaf camel, yielding grotesque progeny? The onset of an economic windfall, and an insoluble strategic conundrum? Or was it, at bottom, a British apostate's consummate revenge? With hindsight, the date signified all of the above, and more. The place is Saudi Arabia, less a nation than a corral of tribes lashed together in 1925 by the kingdom's founder, Abdul Aziz Ibn Abdul Rahman Saud, known commonly as Ibn Saud. The venue is the shabby Kazam Palace (the King is cash poor) in Nazla, a suburb of Jiddah. The principal personages at a signing ceremony are Sheik Abdullah Suleiman, the wily royal treasurer, and an affable forty-year-old American lawyer, Lloyd Hamilton, who represents Standard Oil of California (Socal).

Also present are Najib Sallia, the interpreter, and Karl Twitchell, the American mining engineer who with fruitful foresight demarcated the boundaries in a contract that awards Socal exclusive rights for six decades to extract oil from eastern Saudi Arabia (including offshore waters and islands) for £35,000 down, payable in gold, and an additional £20,000 to follow in eighteen months. Of this sum, £10,000 is an outright grant, the balance an advance against anticipated royalties, fixed at four shillings per ton payable in gold. Such are the core elements in what the State Department subsequently calls "the greatest commercial prize in the history of the planet."[1]

Fountain pens are bestowed on the various officials attending the ceremony. A briefcase is presented to the interpreter. "No money or other presents of any kind entered into the business deal," Twitchell recalls, "with the following exception: a 'reward' was given to me by the Saudi Arabian Government, as they had promised," to which his employer had no objection.

(For its part, Socal offers him 10 percent of future royalties for his services, but Twitchell, a frugal Vermonter, chooses instead a one-time payment of $75,000: a titanic mischance in Big Oil history.) Then an unforeseen hitch develops. Ibn Saud is adamant that he will accept only gold, and Franklin Roosevelt's incoming administration in Washington, coping with massive bank failures, has just gone off the gold standard. Socal seeks permission for a waiver, but Dean Acheson, newly ensconced as Assistant Secretary of the Treasury, rules otherwise. The oil company turns urgently to the London office of Morgan Guaranty Trust to obtain 35,000 gold sovereigns from the Royal Mint. The sovereigns duly arrive in seven boxes on a P&O passenger liner, each coin stamped with the image of a male British monarch in deference to the presumed gender obsessions of Saudi Arabians.[2] All this is arranged with the aid of the preppie, easy-going Lloyd Hamilton, who turns up in Jiddah as if on a holiday with his wife, Airy, (and his fountain pens), and then vanishes from history.

With the stroke of those pens, America ended the British stranglehold on Middle East oil. Less evident at the time, the pact mired Washington irrevocably in a region whose sulfurous hatreds evoke John Milton's *Paradise Lost* more appositely than Tom Paine's *Rights of Man*. Fittingly, the deal's midwife was Harry St. John Bridger Philby, a fallen Britannic angel. It was Philby who tilted the playing field against a British consortium seeking Saudi drilling rights. He encouraged the consortium to escalate the bidding while he misleadingly assured the Foreign Office that "all my knowledge and efforts" would be unreservedly at the disposal of Sir Andrew Ryan, the British Minister in Jiddah. In fact, Philby was secretly receiving $1,000 monthly from the California company, which promised a generous bonus if its bid prevailed—an arrangement that became known only as an aside in Philby's posthumous account of the deal, published obscurely in 1964 by the Middle East Institute in Washington.[3]

For Philby, the retainer came at a critical time. He was then an unpaid adviser in the Saudi court, living frugally on a British Civil Service pension, plus earnings from his freelance writing and commissions from British companies doing business in Arabia—commissions contingent on the palace paying its bills, which it did, but often years later. Moreover, heaped on Philby's desk were reminders of the fees needed for three daughters at

English boarding schools and of the tuition owed for his son, Harold, a first-year student at his own alma mater, Trinity College, Cambridge. Nicknamed "Kim" after the child-spy in Kipling's 1901 novel, Harold was born in 1912 when his father was a rising star in the Indian Civil Service. So it transpired that the formative Cambridge years of the century's most famous Soviet mole were subsidized by Standard Oil of California, itself the spawn of the arch-capitalist John D. Rockefeller.[4]

Still, lucre alone did not motivate "Jack" Philby. Consider his account of meeting with Sir Andrew Ryan after the deal was done. Philby and his wife, Dora, were preparing to travel to Cairo, where he was to discuss becoming the Ford Motor Company's agent in Saudi Arabia (which he did). Philby described what followed: "We talked about everything under the Arabian sun, but it was only when I got up to take my leave that I said to him: 'I suppose you have heard that the Americans have got the concession.' He was thunderstruck, and his face darkened with anger and disappointment. He had made certain that his influence behind the scene, unobtrusive as it was, would have turned the scales in favor of the British competitor. But it was not to be: even he had not appreciated the fundamental issue at stake, the size of the initial loan, of which the Ibn Sa'ud's Government stood in urgent need."

"Our final leave taking was somewhat strained," Philby adds, in a rare instance of understatement, "though we had always maintained friendly relations, in spite of the wide gap between our political and other views and aspirations. He was indeed the 'Last of the Dragomans,' bred in the school of traditional western dominance in the eastern world while I was surely one of the first of the champions of eastern emancipation from all foreign controls."[5]

This was true. In 1925, he had resigned a choice berth in the imperial political service because he opposed his government's Middle East policies, and because (the grievances were linked) he felt his merits and advice were insufficiently appreciated. Philby moved to the Saudi port of Jiddah, his base for his new role as a senior adviser to Ibn Saud, whom he had met while serving as a British Political Agent in World War I. It was a bold decision, for-tuitously timed. Ibn Saud was still learning the ways of the European Great Powers, whose rulers for their part were even more ignorant of his new-born kingdom's importance. In the 1920s, Saudi Arabia was chiefly reliant for foreign exchange on the episodic flow of Islamic pilgrims to Mecca and

Medina, of which Ibn Saud was now guardian, having deposed Hussein and his son Ali, their last Hashemite Sharifs. Yet from these unpromising beginnings, Philby emerged as the Western kingmaker who left the deepest strategic imprint on the Middle East.

Combative, cantankerous, zealously self-centered, Jack Philby seemed to glare at the world through his owlish shrubbery. "He's got a mad streak in him," confided a high-ranking colleague, Sir Reader Bullard, also an unorthodox diplomat, in his case gifted with a sense of the absurd. "He has quarreled with three administrations—in India, in Iraq, and in Trans-Jordan—and I cannot think he was the only honest, right-thinking person concerned. However, that is his own firm belief, and with that conviction, his immense energy, and the real ability which runs parallel with his streak of madness, he may stir up a lot of trouble . . . Philby *simply* [Bullard's emphasis] must feel that he's a sort of Prometheus, defying the gods for the general good."[6]

Bullard's 1924 prognosis was prescient. To many colleagues, Philby was simply (in the High Tory phrase) a bounder, but the Promethean impulse was always there. To dismiss Jack as a rascal is rather like calling Hamlet ambivalent or Don Juan oversexed. In truth, Jack Philby was as opaquely complex as his upbringing. His father, Harry Montagu Philby, a younger son in a middling Norfolk family, was shipped off to Ceylon in the 1870s to restart life as a coffee planter. There, on a colonial island notable for its religious diversity—Buddhist, Hindu, Muslim, and Christian—Jack was born, in 1885. He was the second of the four sons of "Montie" and his wife, Queenie, the eldest daughter of Colonel John Duncan, commander of the Colombo garrison. Like his son, Montie was also a bounder: he drank, gambled, womanized, and was an insolvent planter; it was Queenie, known to her family as "May," who steadily directed family decisions, turning at critical junctures to her more prosperous relations to finance the boys' boarding-school fees in England.

From his early years at a pre-preparatory school, whose headmaster was J. V. Milne (father of the author A. A. Milne), young Philby dazzled his tutors. On Milne's recommendation, Jack at thirteen became a Queen's Scholar at Westminster School, situated (as he nostalgically remembered) "in the shadow of the Abbey and the Houses of Parliament, with the chimes of Big Ben spelling out the fleeting hours."[7] He harvested every available prize—on the cricket pitch, the soccer field, the chessboard, and the debating platform—and in his final year became the school's head boy. Philby was among the Queen's Scholars who in 1901 took part in Victoria's funeral service at the Abbey, and a year later, then as a King's Scholar, he helped guard the royal regalia at Edward VII's coronation. He defined himself as a Conservative and a Christian, and to nobody's surprise, in 1904 he won a classics scholarship to Trinity College (Cambridge), the school with which Westminster had founding links.

Like Westminster, Trinity was regal in its aura and origins. A visitor stepping through its Great Gate (built in 1528–35) into its Great Court (the largest of any Cambridge or Oxford college) inescapably senses the ghosts of Albion past. Isaac Newton's rooms facing the inner court remind visitors of Trinity's preeminence in the sciences, spanning from Francis Bacon to Niels Bohr. As of 2007, the college could count no less than thirty-one Nobel Laureates (more than France and Belgium combined) and five Field Medalists (the equivalent for mathematics). Everywhere there are busts of the mighty in church and state, amid reminders of Trinity's gifts to letters, from Andrew Marvell and Lord Tennyson to Vladimir Nabokov. Among the treasures in its splendid library, designed by Christopher Wren, is the first draft of Milton's *Paradise Lost*. Yet when Jack Philby went up to Trinity in Michaelmas term of 1904, this legacy was being fiercely reexamined in arguments about socialism, Freud, feminism, pacifism, atheism, and Darwin (whose relations and disciples were locally omnipresent).

Criticism and controversy formed the "salt and savour of Cambridge life in those days," Philby recalled, and Trinity was to Cambridge what that university was to the United Kingdom, an intellectual free-fire zone.[8] The university's foremost philosophers (Bertrand Russell, Alfred North Whitehead, and G. E. Moore) were Trinitarians, as were the cultural innovators who formed the inner Bloomsbury circle (Lytton Strachey, Clive Bell, and Leonard Woolf, all being recent graduates). Philby's own cohort included James Strachey, Lytton's brother and translator of Freud, and Jawaharlal Nehru, whom Jack supported for membership in the Magpie and Stump, the college debating society. Yet during most of his residence, Philby concealed his growing radicalism. Revealingly, he took up acting, and in 1907 participated in a student production of Marlowe's *Doctor Faustus* (with Rupert Brooke playing Mephistopheles). Jack's acting skills inspired a jingle still remembered by a classmate sixty-years on, as recorded by Philby's biographer, the Oxford scholar Elizabeth Monroe:

> *Oh! St. J.B. Philby*
> *Whatever can or will be*
> *Your fate now you have taken to the stage?*
> *You might have been, and still may be an*
> *Enthusiastic Fabian . . .*[9]

In fact, Philby had already become a closet Fabian (i.e., a Socialist) and a freethinker. In his final year, his anxious intellectual conflicts precipitated a moral crisis. He had been asked to prepare a paper for Trinity's Sunday Evening Essay Society, and chose as his theme "The Inconvenience of Convention." In his own words, "It was the swan-song of my championship of orthodoxy, and I realized as I wrote it that I no longer believed in the validity of my arguments. The world I had lived in so far was crumbling about my ears, but I stuck to my guns in defence of any untenable position. That was toward the end of my last year at Cambridge, and it was in a very different arena that I made my first appearance as a protagonist of Socialism, freethought, agnosticism and other anathemas of a dispensation that until then had seemed so secure and satisfactory."[10] The "very different arena" to which Jack referred was the Orient, as everybody called it, with its multiple tongues and faiths, to which Philby was drawn by a remarkable Cambridge don.

Edward Granville Browne is among the uncelebrated influences on his generation's thinking about the Orient. During his teaching years at Pembroke College, everybody in Cambridge knew him by sight. "Physically considered," wrote one of his students, Laurence Graffety-Smith, "he epitomized the processes of evolution: he was short and broad in the shoulder, with a stoop, and grotesquely long arms dangled in his shambling walk. [Yet] his finely chiseled face was a radiance of intellect and of love for his fellow man." His lectures, added Graffety-Smith, later a consular official in the Levant, were like "a pack of hounds in full cry." Or, remembered Reader Bullard, another future diplomat, "he was a meteor, not a locomotive" who lectured at torrential speed.[11] A linguist nonpareil, Browne mastered Turkish, Arabic, Persian, and Hindustani as well as the usual European tongues (and did so although warned, on securing his first-class degree, that there were hardly any teaching jobs in Oriental languages). He translated and celebrated Persian literature, and wrote a widely read classic, *A Year Amongst the Persians*, in which he lamented that England "offers less encouragement to her sons to engage in the study of Oriental languages than any other great European nation."[12]

In short, Browne was an Orientalist, an example of the academic species sternly censured by Edward Said of Columbia University in his influential indictment, *Orientalism* (1978). To Professor Said, by origin a Palestinian Christian, scholars like Browne forged the intellectual armature for the West's oppression of the East. Still, with its vigor and sweep, Said's polemic does less than justice to Browne, among others. In a solidly argued rebuttal appearing in 2006, *For Lust of Knowing*, the British author Robert Irwin points out that Browne was never an apologist for imperial hegemony but instead was the scourge of the Foreign Office. When Britain and Russia in 1907 carved Persia into spheres of influence, and then jointly stifled that country's Constitutional Revolution, it was "Johnnie" Browne who tirelessly led the campaign on behalf of Persian freedom. And Browne, the incendiary champion of indigenous rights, became in the words of Elizabeth Monroe, "probably the most popular man in Cambridge" (a distinction arguably ascribed in the 1990s to Professor Said on Morningside Heights).[13]

After passing the exacting examinations that launched him into the Indian Civil Service, or ICS, the Empire's governing caste, Philby fell under Browne's spell. Having never left England since he arrived from Ceylon in 1891, Philby stayed on at Trinity to tackle Hindustani and Persian. On impulse, Browne that year decided to offer elementary Arabic, which Philby later viewed as "perhaps the finger of Fate beckoning me on a path I scarcely dreamed to tread." In his autobiography, *Arabian Days*, he describes Browne as "certainly the most inspiring teacher that ever crossed my path, wayward in the extreme but so wildly enthusiastic—and so deeply learned—that one became infected with a passion to know the East and its people."[14] Certainly, too, Browne had little in common with Said's demeaning paradigm of dons in Oxbridge colleges propagating a hegemonic discourse of racist imperialism.

In December 1908, Jack Philby embarked for India, where he headed to Lahore, the Punjab's provincial capital, arriving in time for Christmas festivities in the expatriate mode. First came the Lahore Hunt Ball, with dancing until dawn, followed by cricket and polo matches, culminating in horse races ceremonially opened by Lieutenant Governor Sir Louis Dane, who arrived in a camel-drawn coach followed by a Rolls-Royce modeled like a swan, featuring turbaned Indian princes. Philby then settled at his new post at Jhelum, a way station on the Grand Trunk Road linking the Punjab with the North-West Frontier. There the young district officer became known for his shrewd decisions as a local judge, and for keeping the peace among Sikhs, Muslims, and Hindus. To all intents, he was launched on a conventional ICS career.

It was not to be. In Calcutta, still capital of the Raj, the reform-minded Lord Minto had recently succeeded the imperial-minded Lord Curzon as Viceroy, and the Indian Office in London was headed by Secretary of State John Morley, the venerable Liberal biographer of Gladstone. To the consternation of old-line British officials, Minto talked of adding an actual Indian to his Governing Council, and of scrapping the mandatory "official" (i.e., British) majority on provincial councils. The latter innovation was duly approved, and the celebrated Minto-Morley reforms were among the tentative early steps to Indian self-rule. Change was palpably in the air, but Philby was daringly ahead of the curve. "I was probably the first Socialist to enter the Indian Civil Service," he asserts in his memoirs, "and I suppose I scandalized most of my friends by proclaiming from the beginning my adhesion to the ideal of Indian independence."[15]

When he appeared at the cavalry mess or officers' club, he instantly raised eyebrows and was dubbed "a redhot radical." Yet Philby's first rebellion did not involve politics, but marriage. In 1909, at a Christmas dance in Rawalpindi, he met and was smitten by Dora Johnston, a handsome redhead and the daughter of a minor British official. "Miss Johnston is one of the belles of Pindi," Philby wrote to his mother, "a beautiful dancer, and I have been honoured with several dances at all the dances I have been able to attend." Yet Philby's mother did not think Dora grand enough for her gifted son, and in a rare quarrel opposed their subsequent betrothal. In 1910, Jack and Dora were wed in the Anglican cathedral at Murree, a hill town meant to be a pastiche of an English village (it still so strives, as the authors discovered while visiting Pakistan in 1989). Philby's best man was his mother's young relation, Lieutenant Bernard Montgomery of the Royal Warwickshire Regiment, the future Field Marshal who dueled with Rommel in Africa and with Patton in Europe.[16]

Lieutenant Governor Dane's vexation with Philby deepened when the novice district officer was accused of unwarrantedly boxing the ears of an allegedly disrespectful Indian teacher during a village fracas. Yet when Philby was penalized for violating a firm ICS policy, he not only challenged Dane's ruling but also appealed for its reversal to the Viceroy, a once-in-career privilege granted every civil service officer. The Viceroy lessened the punishment but upheld the censure. Philby was almost surely spared further discipline, owing to his prodigious language skills and the arrival of a new provincial chief, Sir Michael O'Dwyer. An Irishman bred in the never-apologize, never-explain code of Oxford's Balliol College, Sir Michael liked Jack and Dora, appreciated Philby's contrary spirit, and (one suspects with a wink) asked him to censor seditious writings in the Punjabi vernacular press. "I sit upon the slightest flicker of sedition," he reported to his mother, though "if I were a journalist I would be a most seditious one, and a thorn in the side of government." His duties widened in 1914 after the outbreak of World War I when Philby became the local partner of the London-based Special Branch in the surveillance of Sikh militants suspected of receiving help from Germany.[17]

Word of Philby's energy and his polyglot talents reached Sir Percy Cox, a superlative talent-spotter and the chief Political Officer at Basra, the base for Anglo-Indian forces now advancing into Mesopotamia. With O'Dywer's commendation, Philby joined the Political and Secret Department, commencing its second century as the Raj's vaunted spy service. "My chance at last!" Philby excitedly wrote to Dora. "Just the thing I have been clamouring for for ages."[18] It was indeed his chance, and he made the most of it. In November 1915, his jacket freshly adorned by a Political Officer's white tabs, Philby reported for duty in Basra. He quickly befriended Cox's talented disciple, Gertrude Bell, an Arabist as capable as Philby himself. Within months, he became part of a regional network of midlevel officials—Sir Mark Sykes, T. E. Lawrence, David Hogarth, and Colonel A. T. Wilson—whose approaches sharply differed but who shared the common goal of embedding Britain in the Middle East once the "Great War for Civilisation" was mercifully over.

Relations were cordial but formal between the thirty-year-old Philby and Miss Bell, then in her late forties. For Gertrude, it was not "Jack" or "St. John" but "My dear Mr. Philby," and on his part it was always "Miss Bell," even as they traveled together to confer with Arab chieftains in the south-

ern marshes and to survey the Shatt al-Arab, the tidal river separating Persia and Mesopotamia. Through 1916, British military setbacks culminated
in the surrender of a besieged Anglo-Indian army at Kut. In this dispiriting
year, Philby's thankless task was to haggle with local clans on the compensation fairly owed (in British eyes) for food seized by invading expeditionar-
ies. Thus he learned to plead and curse in Arabic, using either local dialects
or the formal Turkish-Arabic favored by sheiks. By March 1917, the military tide turned in Britain's favor. The advancing army led by Major General
Stanley Maude stormed into Baghdad, the capital of an occupied territory
beginning to be known as Iraq. Cox relocated in Baghdad as the theater's
Civil Commissioner, and Gertrude Bell joined him as his Oriental Secretary.
Both strove to reconcile the New Delhi view—that Iraq was a prospective
British protectorate to be colonized by emigrating Indians—and London's
promises of liberation, as formally proclaimed by General Maude.

In May 1917, Philby was seconded to Baghdad, where he was immediately welcomed by Gertrude Bell with these heartfelt words (so St. John
recalled): "I am glad you have come. It is absolute chaos here, Sir Percy
hopelessly overworked, and nobody in the office who knows the first thing
about anything; it's really awful and you must get things straight." (In his
memoirs, Philby adds, straining to appear modest, "Gertrude was always
inclined to the use of superlatives—there were no half-tones in her reper-
toire.")[19] A relieved and grateful Civil Commissioner Cox turned over his in-
box to Philby's preliminary sifting. Jack drafted suitable responses for Cox's
approval, meaning, as he remembered, that "I came in quite a short time
to have a complete grasp of and insight into all the affairs of the Political
Department" and thus could "give free play to my own ideas about the various problems involved in the drafts that I submitted to Cox's scrutiny."[20]

Because of his privileged access, Philby learned in August 1917 that
Colonel R. E. A. Hamilton, the Political Agent in Kuwait, was proposing a
special mission to Riyadh to explore collaboration with its rising Arab chieftain, Ibn Saud. Fortuitously, at this same moment Colonel Arnold Wilson
arrived in Baghdad, hoping for relief from his onerous administrative duties
in Basra. After seeing Cox, Wilson stopped in Philby's adjacent office. "I've
been having a talk with Cox," he began, "and he suggested my having a talk
with you. The present situation is quite impossible." "Why, what's wrong?"
Philby asked ("as innocently as possible"). "I can't get anything done with
all this arguing between here and Basra," went on Wilson. "Things want

shaking up here; besides Cox is overworked and tired; he needs somebody
to help him." At this point, Philby came to the point: "Look here, Wilson,
do you mean you want to take my place at this table?" "Yes," the colonel
replied, "I suppose that is what it amounts to." "In that case," said Philby,
"the thing can be arranged very easily—on one condition. You know about
this proposed mission to Ibn Sa'ud. Persuade Cox to send me on that, and
you can have my job when you like." "All right," Wilson countered, "I'll go
and see Cox at once."

Five minutes later, Colonel Wilson, soon-to-be Acting Civil Commissioner and the future territorial architect of Iraq, returned, saying simply,
"Cox agrees." Philby thus outflanked Colonel Hamilton, fourteen years his
senior, and became Cox's anointed emissary to Ibn Saud—and that, St.
John reminisced with satisfaction three decades later, was "how I came to
the threshold of my destiny."[21]

Here one needs to step backward. In 1917, three kingdoms vied for mastery in central Arabia. There was the Hejaz, ruled by Hussein, the Sharif of
Mecca, who the year before, with British backing, had proclaimed an Arab
Revolt against the Ottoman Empire. In Hail, a warlord named Ibn Rashid
remained loyal to the Turks and opposed both Hussein and the Rashidis'
hereditary enemy, the Emir Ibn Saud, ruler of the Nejd. In this competition,
Ibn Saud possessed a decisive if double-edged weapon: the Wahhabis, jihadi
warriors long renowned for their fury and fanaticism.

Ibn Saud's kingdom owed its origins to a celebrated Islamic reformer
named Muhammad Ibn Abd al-Wahhab, born in 1703, who reputedly memorized the Koran at the age of ten. With learning and passion,
al-Wahhab assailed the laxity of fellow Muslims, turning with particular
wrath on worshippers of idols and saints, which in his eyes most especially
included blasphemous Shiites. The preacher's most notable convert, in
1745, was Muhammad Ibn Saud, who founded the first Wahhabi kingdom
at Nejd, which under his son, Abdul Aziz Ibn Saud, grew impressively into a
formidable desert empire. Collaterally, Muslim pilgrims to the Holy Cities of
Mecca and Medina began to convert to the militant Wahhabi faith, carrying its messages to the far corners of the Islamic world, spanning eastward
from India's North-West Frontier to Dutch-ruled Sumatra, and southward
from Egypt's Sudan to Somalia in the Horn of Africa.

The early Western explorers of central Arabia in the ninetenth century were impressed by the devout simplicity of the Wahhabis yet troubled by their fanaticism. Music, dancing, poetry, religious shrines, and bodily ornaments were all prohibited since in their view none were sanctioned by the Prophet. Not all Bedouins agreed. During a century of incessant tribal warfare, the size of the Wahhabi kingdom fluctuated, and by 1900 its once-extensive realm had shrunk to its inner core as Mecca and Medina were lost. In this turbulent era, Islamic pilgrims and European travelers alike learned to keep a prudent distance from the glowering Wahhabs, identifiable by their unkempt beards, bare ankles, and menacing swords. The idiosyncratic William Gifford Palgrave—Oxford-schooled, a onetime Indian Army officer, and later a French Jesuit—warned in 1865 that the Wahhabis were "incapable of true internal progress, hostile to commerce, unfavourable to the arts, and even to agriculture, and to the highest degree intolerant and aggressive." The sect constituted, Palgrave feared, "a new wellhead to the bitter wars of Islam" that might seriously threaten the non-Islamic world.

His concerns were echoed by an otherwise conventional Colonel Lewis Pelly, the British Resident in the Persian Gulf in the 1860s who distrusted Palgrave, given his French and Jesuit associations. Still, after visiting the Nedj himself, Pelly warned that "while the Imam himself was a sensible and experienced man . . . he was surrounded by the most excitable, unscrupulous, dangerous and fanatical people that one could come across."[22] Or, in the words of another British observer who spoke with particular authority, the Wahhabi movement was wedded to "a great idea" that had to be sustained at white heat: "Like a forest fire, it would be unconquerable as long as there was fuel to feed it, and in this case the fuel was constant aggression and expansion at the expense of those who did not share the great idea."[23] So observed Jack Philby in 1930 (his dislike was reciprocated by the Wahhabis, who greeted him with frosty scorn whenever he arrived in Riyadh to attend Ibn Saud's court).

Yet these were the impassioned believers who enabled Ibn Saud to evict Ibn Rashid from Riyadh in 1902, and then following a prolonged civil war, theirs were the swords that took Mecca and Medina from Grand Sharif Hussein's son Ali in 1925. Ibn Saud thus forcibly assembled a second Wahhabi empire, upon which in 1932 he proudly bestowed his family name. His feat was the more impressive since he had no regular army but relied on Wahhabi tribal fighters known as the Ikhwan, or the Brotherhood, dwelling in scattered cantonments. Ferocious and unforgiving in battle, the Ikhwans took no prisoners, excelled at beheading and amputation, and celebrated their victories with rows of spiked heads. In the estimate of a hostile but informed critic, Palestinian writer Saïd K. Aburish, from 1916 to 1924 there were at least twenty-six Bedouin rebellions against Ibn Saud, and each ended with Ikhwan-led mass killings.[24]

Allowance should be made for prejudice and exaggeration, but indisputably the self-styled "Soldiers of God" murdered one of the first Americans, a Protestant missionary, to journey into central Arabia. He was the Rev. Henry Bilkert, and he was traveling with Charles R. Crane, the Chicago-bred philanthropist and advocate of Arab rights. During the cool season in 1929 they were proceeding by Chevrolet from Kuwait to Riyadh, where they hoped to meet Ibn Saud. Near the Hamsa Ridge, they were ambushed by Ikhwan warriors, identifiable by their white headdress with black tassels, their henna-dyed beards, and the dark paint around their eyes. Bilkert was shot dead; Crane was fortunate to escape without injury. While recovering, Crane received a contrite letter from Ibn Saud (at Philby's instigation, one suspects) expressing regret that "the friend of the Arabs should have been attacked in Arabian lands," and inviting the millionaire to visit Riyadh.[25]

The incident and its sequel (to be described later) illuminate the abiding perplexity confronting well-wishing Westerners struggling to understand Saudi Arabia. Who, or what, does one believe? The earnest official avowals of friendship? Or the palpable fact that the same government proffering these assurances lavishes its funds and favors on Islamic militants claiming divine sanction to slaughter, torture, and amputate infidels?

Such was the perplexity facing Great Britain concerning central Arabia in the years leading to World War I. An optimistic interpretation was advanced by Captain William Henry Shakespear, namesake and descendant of the Bard and the first British official to urge a military alliance with Ibn Saud. An Indian Army officer, Shakespear had been posted by Percy Cox as a Political Agent in Kuwait, with the additional mission of exploring the unmapped Empty Quarter of Arabia. In January 1914, Shakespear headed on camel to Riyadh for discussions with Ibn Saud, whom he had first met in Kuwait in 1910. After being greeted in Riyadh, once again capital of the Wahhabi kingdom, the captain was assured by its youthful ruler that he was keenly interested in an alliance with the British against Turkey. As Shakespear quoted him, "We Wahhabis hate the Turks only less than we hate the Persians for the infidel practices which they have imported into the true and pure faith revealed to us in the Koran." In fact, the captain concluded, "hatred of the Turk seems to be the one idea common to all the tribes" so that "a revolt is not only probable but would be welcomed by every tribe throughout the peninsula."[26]

With the outbreak of the Great War in August 1914, Shakespear's advocacy of Ibn Saud found greater support in New Delhi than in London, where the "Easterners" canvassing a possible Arab revolt favored Hussein, the Sharif of Mecca. In their view, Hussein and his sons, having lived in Constantinople, were more sophisticated than the rough-hewn Ibn Saud, and in any case, as descendants of the Prophet, the Hashemites would be more likely to rally Arab support. Yet Shakespear's assessment proved more prescient, and over time the House of Saud was destined to become the world's richest, largest, and most powerful royal brood.

In January 1915, Shakespear was shot fatally while directing Wahhabi fire during a battle between Ibn Saud and the pro-Turkish forces of Ibn Rashid of Hail. The captain was thirty-six, and before the fighting began had been twice urged, and he twice refused, to exchange his uniform for a less conspicuous Arab robe. Rashid's soldiers seized Shakespear's sun helmet, which the Turks then displayed in Medina as evidence that Ibn Saud had reprehensibly fought alongside an infidel. A more gracious memorial appeared on February 23, 1916, in the British journal *The World*: "He was one of those Englishmen Kipling delighted to picture. Nothing daunted him. He bore an English name not easy to add glory to, yet he succeeded."[27] Had Shakespear survived, Philby mused years later, the Arab Revolt may well have been guided by him instead of T. E. Lawrence: "As it was, the Government of India was so stirred up by his death that it decided to abandon the Arabian adventure, and it was Egypt that took up its running with such satisfactory and romantic results."[28]

In November 1917, Philby himself was aboard a camel heading to Riyadh. He benefited both from the goodwill nurtured by Shakespear and from the prior diplomacy of Cox and Bell, who together had met and befriended Ibn

Saud the year before in Kuwait. Thanks chiefly to Cox's influence, the British agreed to provide Ibn Saud with £5,000 (gold) monthly as part of a limited alliance. The sum was relatively modest, and it offended Ibn Saud's pride to learn that his rival Sharif Hussein was receiving forty times that figure: £200,000 (gold) monthly, as well as tons of weaponry. Yet he bore his inferior treatment with dignity. This was consistent with Gertrude Bell's incisive appraisal of Ibn Saud that she prepared for the Arab Bureau, which included this fine verbal portrait, with its sensuous shading:

> Ibn Saud is now barely forty, though he looks some years older. He is a man of splendid physique, standing well over six feet, and carrying himself with the air of one accustomed to command. Though he is more massively built than the typical nomad sheik, he has the characteristics of the well-bred Arab, the strongly marked aquiline profile, full-fleshed nostrils, prominent lips and long narrow chin, accentuated by a pointed beard. His hands are fine, with slender fingers . . . His deliberate movements, his slow, sweet smile, and the contemplative glance of his heavy-lidded eyes, though they add to his dignity and charm, do not accord with the western conception of a vigorous personality. Nevertheless, report credits him with powers of physical endurance rare even in hard-bitten Arabia . . . As a leader of irregular forces he is proved daring, and he combines with his qualities as a soldier that grasp of statecraft which is yet more highly prized by the tribesmen . . . Politician, ruler and raider, Ibn Saud illustrates a historic type. Such men as he are the exception in any community, but they are thrown up persistently in the Arab race.[29]

When he reached the outskirts of Riyadh, Philby met the officer he was displacing, Colonel Hamilton, and presented him with a letter from Cox establishing that Jack would be speaking for Baghdad. Hamilton did not protest, but he lingered politely for ten days of talks with Ibn Saud and supported Philby's endorsement of the Emir's ambitious shopping list: four field guns, 10,000 rifles with necessary ammunition, £20,000 down for supplies, and £50,000 monthly to pay ten thousand Ikhwan fighters for a three-month campaign against Ibn Rashid. Hamilton then departed for Kuwait, leaving his younger colleague to continue confidential discussions with the Wahhabi chief.

Philby left no detailed record of these talks, but Elizabeth Monroe carefully weighed the available clues and concluded that the main topics were Ibn Saud's attitude to Christianity and his longing to outdo the Sharif of Mecca. In Monroe's reconstruction, Ibn Saud maintained that "by his standards Christians were of a kindred faith because they were 'people of the Book,' " and insisted that "purity of faith was more important to him than all else." (Monroe adds that Ibn Saud was obviously not speaking for his Ikhwan fighters, to whom "all Christians were dogs, unfit to eat with or even speak to.")[30]

By the time they parted, Philby was convinced that Ibn Saud was destined to lead and unite central Arabia, and that Cairo had erred grievously in betting so heavily on Sharif Hussein. Ibn Saud half-jokingly told his new friend not to return unless the British provided all the aid he had requested. In his first dispatch to Cox, Philby said that if the promised arms and money were forthcoming, "the Wahhabi army would be ready to march against Hail by April, 1918."[31] He then departed without waiting for a response. Philby decided to take the long way to Egypt, crossing the Arabian Peninsula from sea to sea. This was an arduous transit completed previously by only one European, Captain Foster Sadlier, a British officer, in 1819. It was the first of Philby's feats of endurance that established him as his generation's boldest desert explorer, earning him the Founder's Medal of the Royal Geographical Society. (The RGS archives preserve Philby's well-thumbed, sweat-stained journals, with their exemplary accounts of flora and fauna as well as notes on distances, elevations, and landmarks.)

En route, Philby paused in the Hejaz, where he conferred civilly with Sharif Hussein, who kissed him on both cheeks and addressed him as "*Ibni*" (my son). Philby's sketch of Ibn Saud's principal adversary is laudatory: "Hussain, though small of stature and nearly seventy at this time, was erect in bearing and decisive in speech . . . Beautifully robed in rich garments in the Hijazi style with a turban swathed round his Meccan cap, he spoke an immaculate literary Arabic in sonorous periods that delighted me, seldom and only in moments of emotion lapsing in the vernacular of the town or desert."[32]

Proceeding to Cairo, Philby lingered pleasantly "in the flesh-pots of Egypt," where he met with Sir Reginald Wingate, successor to Sir Henry McMahon as High Commissioner, and with David Hogarth and his Arab Bureau minions (save for T. E. Lawrence, who was accompanying Arab armies then advancing toward Damascus). Jack managed a side trip to Jerusalem, just captured by British arms, where he stayed at the newly named Allenby Hotel and met with the newly ensconced Governor, Sir Ronald Storrs. He relished his luck. What could be more exhilarating than to gaze from the Mount of Olives, where one could see the Turkish tents in the Jordan Valley? The Ottoman Empire was crumbling, and the long European war seemed near its end as American doughboys began flooding to the Western Front. Hence the tepid interest in increasing aid to Ibn Saud to do battle with Ibn Rashid of Hail, a sideshow of a sideshow of a sideshow. It was now Philby's lot to return to Ibn Saud with this unwelcome news. As he writes in his memoirs:

> Ibn Sa'ud was delighted to see me back and deeply interested to hear the story of my experiences with King Hussain. He was glad to hear that the military authorities in Mesopotamia were prepared to supply him with 5,000 rifles and 100 boxes of ammunition, and that his subsidy of £5,000 (gold) a month had been duly secured. In his turn, he was able to point to the desert, where the royal camels were having their fill of pasture in preparation for the hard riding of the forthcoming campaign, and the encampment of part of the host that would accompany them. It certainly seemed a goodly army.[33]

The Emir wisely tacked with changing circumstances, and chose this occasion to permit Philby a glimpse of his unusual conjugal habits. "Well, that's enough for tonight," Ibn Saud remarked at around 1:00 a.m. "I must go to my new wife—you know, I was married this afternoon." Philby had indeed heard, and yet the next morning the desert warrior arose at 5:00 a.m. to depart at dawn, and never again slept with his bride. They were formally divorced, royal gifts were bestowed on his now ex-wife, and her tribe was purportedly gratified by his one-night stand. "I came to realize with more experience," Philby later observed, "that much of Ibn Sa'ud's fabled wiving had a political or diplomatic colour."[34]

Ibn Saud was said to have bedded more than three-score virgins, and is known to have fathered fifty-three acknowledged sons. No count exists of the many daughters the Emir's fertile seed also brought forth, nor of his issue from numerous concubines. It suffices that in three generations, the House of Saud expanded exponentially; its total complement of princes today approximates seven thousand, the precise figure being a state secret.

We may credibly imagine that Ibn Saud liked to tease Philby with the tempting erotic benefits (for a male) in converting to the True Faith, and we may further guess that Jack was listening.

After the War to End Wars officially recessed in November 1918, Philby returned to England for an extended home leave, having justly earned kudos for his desert exploits. In London, he was dutifully consulted in Whitehall, especially concerning the developing armed conflict between Sharif Hussein and Ibn Saud. The war over, the British nevertheless continued to pay agreed subsidies to both Arab chieftains and claimed neutrality in their civil war. In reality, thanks in part to the fluency and celebrity of T. E. Lawrence, the Whitehall consensus favored the sharifians, despite the victories of Wahhabi irregulars over British-armed Hejazi regulars. Fearing a slaughter in Mecca and Medina ("butchery" was his term), Lord Curzon as Foreign Secretary urged Philby to undertake a peacemaking mission. Jack eagerly agreed, and en route to Arabia met Lawrence and then found (as he anticipated) that his services were not needed since Ibn Saud had prudently reined back his Ikhwan fighters, in part to avoid a confrontation with Britain.

In Iraq, meantime, an insurgency was sparked in the spring of 1920 at Tel Afar near Mosul, where a British garrison was massacred; the revolt swiftly spread down the Euphrates despite Acting Civil Commissioner A. T. Wilson's efforts to contain it. This coincided with, and was related to, France's deposing Faisal, the son of Sharif Hussein, as King of Syria. Philby's talents were again needed, and so was the calming presence of Sir Percy Cox (as he now was), who was asked to replace the floundering Wilson. Once in Baghdad, Cox asked Jack to serve as adviser to the Interior Ministry in the provisional government the British had cobbled together. Thus Philby became the friend and promoter of Interior Minister Sayyid Talib, son of the Naqib of Basra, a nationalist, and a Sunni whom Cox had banished to India in 1915, and who had returned (he hoped) to lead Iraq. Cox continued to view Talib as a demagogic troublemaker, Gertrude Bell despised him and was leaning to the sharifian solution, while A. T. Wilson believed Arab self-rule was essentially an oxymoron. In due course, as detailed elsewhere, Talib was forcibly abducted and exiled to Ceylon.

By this time, British policy, as agreed at the high-level Cairo Conference in March 1921, was to create a throne for Faisal in Iraq, and for his older brother Abdullah in newly established Transjordan. So it transpired that Cox asked Philby to escort Prince Faisal on his first tour of Iraq, in order to meet with his prospective new subjects. By his own account, St. John frankly told Hussein that he was not popular and would almost certainly lose in the honest Iraqi plebiscite that the British promised to conduct. Once back in Baghdad, Philby was summoned to Cox's office. "You don't seem to have gotten on very well with Faisal," Sir Percy began. "He has been complaining bitterly about your attitude on the journey up there. He declares that he won't stay unless he is assured of the active support of all British officials." Philby replied innocently that he was only adhering to Cox's policy, since the British had promised Iraqis a plebiscite, and everybody knew Faisal had little chance of winning, and indeed "I told him that quite frankly." Cox: "I know you did, but surely you understand now what the British Government want?" Yes, certainly Philby knew that, but he couldn't understand why the government "if it wants and intends Faisal to be King, doesn't appoint him in a straightforward manner instead of insisting on the farce of an election." The meeting concluded with Philby's resignation, Cox's polite expression of regret, and a friendly discussion of suitable successors.[35]

Less friendly was Dora Philby's reaction when her husband announced, during high tea in the family drawing room, "I've resigned!" When Gertrude Bell, who happened to be present, said, "Jack, I'm sorry to hear the news," Dora walked briskly past her to the door, exclaiming, "No, you're not!"[36] Dora was pregnant, upset about moving, and only partly mollified when Cox considerately allowed the couple to stay temporarily in their Baghdad bungalow. It did not help that Philby then informed her he was leaving her alone during his three months' holiday leave in Persia.

Philby returned from Tehran in October, a month before the birth of the couple's new daughter. Cox promptly showed him this telegram from the Colonial Office: "Lawrence temporarily Chief British Representative Trans-Jordan, wants to be relieved immediately and suggests Philby as successor. We agree. Please offer post to Philby, and if he accepts, he should proceed without delay by air to Amman for consultations with Lawrence and Abdullah. Thence he should visit High Commissioner in Jerusalem, and proceed thence as soon as possible to London, where Colonial Secretary [i.e., Churchill] will see him. Conformation of appointment will be conditional on agreement of all parties mentioned." "Well," inquired Cox, "what do you think?" "Of course I accept." Cox expressed relief, and told Philby to fly to Amman as soon as an aircraft was available, adding that Dora would be taken care of and that after her childbirth she could join him. Jack remarks in his memoirs, "My wife was astonished at this new development and perhaps a little aggrieved at being left in the lurch again so soon. But I really had no choice in the matter."[37] Such sentences suggest why the couple separated a few years later, and yet they never divorced. Until the end, Dora remained loyally supportive of her husband, doing so even as he took an Arab slave girl as a second wife. Despite his mother's disapproval of Dora, Jack Philby (or so it seems to the authors) was the spouse who married above his merits and station.

After becoming Chief British Representative to Emir Abdullah in October 1921, St. John and Dora settled uncomfortably in a four-room house without sanitation or a fireplace in an instant capital that was then little more than an overgrown caravan stop. Three phases can be distinguished in his relations with Abdullah: a brief honeymoon, a long truce, and finally cold war. From the beginning, there were problems. Abdullah viewed the adjacent areas of Syria, Palestine, Iraq, and Arabia as part of his patrimony, and cross-border raids were incessant, bloody, and reciprocal. Less lethal but touchy were the King's dealings with Sir Herbert Samuel, the High Commissioner in Palestine who ruled under an amorphous "mandate" to establish a "national home" for world Jewry, but without providing a genuine political role for the majority Arabs. Philby's relations with Samuel were cordial. But as months passed, he was annoyed to learn that Sir Herbert had dipped into his own budget to covertly pacify the improvident Abdullah, even as the King resisted Philby's pleas to curb his extravagance and honor his promises to establish a parliament.

The watershed year was 1924, when three events unsettled the Islamic Middle East. The first was Mustafa Kemal's decision in March to abolish the Caliphate, a hereditary title long held by the Ottoman Sultan, whom the newborn Turkish Republic's founder had deposed two years earlier. The Caliphate was a spiritual office with a complex history. In Islam's early centuries, disputes over succession to the office precipitated the fatal schism between Sunnis and Shiites. After the Turks conquered Arabia, the Ottoman Sultan acquired the office's title and prestige. Fortuitously in 1924, the British ended the wartime subsidies that helped keep the peace between Hussein and Ibn Saud. This gave the latter a free hand to make war on the former, who that same year—the third major development—had rashly named himself as Caliph, doing so at his son Abdullah's urgings during a state visit to Transjordan. Ibn Saud's zealous fighters now swept into the Hejaz to punish the presumptuous Caliph Hussein, whose forces scattered as their ruler fled, yielding his monarchical powers to his son Ali. The two Holy Cities fell with little resistance to Ibn Saud's Ikhwans, and Jiddah was then besieged by the lean, gnarled, one-eyed Wahhabi, who was to become the first monarch in more than a century to unify central Arabia.

Philby by that time was terminally weary of the torpid Abdullah; it was Ibn Saud's portrait that graced his desk. Buoyed by Ibn Saud's triumphs, Jack in April 1924 resigned from the Indian Civil Service to strike out on his own. We owe to the British author H. V. F. Winstone, a tireless excavator in intelligence archives, a piquant detail: An RAF censor had unsuspectingly intercepted Philby's covert correspondence with Ibn Saud at a time when the Chief British Representative was ostensibly the confidential adviser to Abdullah, whereupon (Winstone writes) Philby "turned his back on all the mandates and went to serve the only Arab leader he genuinely admired."[38] Philby's prior secret messages had been spotted by a clerk named Dillon, who recognized his Arabic handwriting and alerted Whitehall to Jack's dual loyalties.

Freed at last from bureaucratic bondage, Philby used the long terminal leave owed him to reconnect in 1924 with his English roots and resettle Dora and their children in London. There he hoped to turn his special knowledge to advantage as an author and possibly more lucratively as an agent for British investors. But he discovered little entrepreneurial interest. The prevailing Whitehall wisdom was expressed by David Hogarth, the wartime chief of the Arab Bureau, in a London lecture titled "Wahhabism and British Interests," delivered in January 1925 before a select audience. Yes of course, Hogarth allowed, Ibn Saud's military successes were noteworthy, and Arabia was indeed important as a strategic highway to India, but he asked, "What are our interests in Arabia?" and offered this answer: "It is best perhaps to say first what they are not. Unlike those that we claim in most other parts of the world, they do not arise, to any extent worth mentioning, from our need of products of the country or from concern about trade. Arabia neither sells nor buys nearly enough to weight the political scales. Nor, with all deference to certain enterprising firms and individuals who have gone on concession hunting since the War, do I foresee a day when this will cease to be true."[39] (Tellingly, in the transcribed discussion that followed, none of the eminent authorities present, including Sirs Percy Cox and Arnold Wilson, offered a contrary view.)

What did concern the British Government was the safety of Europeans trapped in Arabia, especially as Ibn Saud's forces besieged Jiddah. Some fifty thousand civilians were crowded into Arabia's second oldest city, a seaport favored by fair winds and a strategic gap in the coral reef sheltering its Red Sea harbor. Jiddah was crucially dependent on foreigners—on traders but even more on Muslim pilgrims averaging a hundred thousand annually, most of them speaking little Arabic, who on arrival sought guides known as sheiks to take them to Mecca. To the nearby Bedouins, however, Jiddah was known as Bilad al-Qanasil, or the "Town of the Consuls," which to the pious was synonymous with impiety. Hence the anxieties abroad when Ibn Saud's artillery began pounding the city's Ottoman walls and grazing Jiddah's picturesque Old City, with its narrow streets and overhanging balconies.

Although still formally a British civil servant, Philby headed to Jiddah to volunteer his services as peacemaker, to the acute displeasure of the Foreign Office. Reader Bullard, the British Consul in Jiddah, was instructed to make plain to all that Philby had no official standing and that if he evinced "any disposition to disobey orders of H.M.G.," he risked dismissal and loss of his pension.[40] Philby prudently avoided frontal combat with Whitehall, discreetly cultivated his ties with Ibn Saud, and left the impression that he was somehow still an agent of influence with His Majesty's Government. When Ali, Hussein's oldest son, surrendered, and Philby was told that it was safe for him to enter Jiddah, he did so, encountering the hostile glares of the victorious Ikhwan militants.

A new Dutch Consul, Daniel van der Meulen, arrived just as the Ikhwans had taken over. His consular post was especially significant since (as he liked to remind those locally in power) Queen Wilhelmina of the Netherlands reigned over the world's second most populous Muslim community in the Dutch East Indies (the most populous being in India). Van der Meulen learned to live amicably in Jiddah's two worlds, one Arab Muslim, the other Western Christian, now united by a common antipathy. Puritanism became the order of the day, rigorously enforced by religious police. Smoking was forbidden, along with music of every kind, although Westerners were permitted gramophone records so long as their notes did not aurally contaminate the cramped streets. All Muslims were ordered to grow beards, and foreigners who resisted became uncomfortably conspicuous and were scorned as Nasrani (Christians, or "Followers of the Nazarene"). Militarily, the Ikhwans remained a solid and menacing force. In the Dutchman's reckoning, they were spread through two hundred settlements and could quickly put twenty-five thousand soldiers in the field. Following their triumphs in Hejaz, they began ominously pressing to expand the Wahhabi kingdom even farther, since "[t]heirs was a divine mission and Allah's will and His way lay clear before them."[41]

Van der Meulen took heart after a cordial first meeting with Ibn Saud. When he asked about the exclusion of Christians from Mecca and Medina, the King replied, "Real Christians were allowed by the Prophet to be in Mecca." So did that mean his Dutch visitor could go? He had a right to go, Ibn Saud said, "[b]ut I am not going to give you my permission. If your colleagues heard you had gone, they would insist on being given equal rights, and I would never want to have them in Mecca. Besides, my beduin followers are unlearned fanatics. You would get into trouble with them and before I could help you, you might be killed." In his memoirs, van der Meulen adds that no Muslim, and certainly no Muslim leader, had ever before spoken to him like that.[42] The Dutch diplomat liked and befriended Philby, who informed all who would listen that he rejoiced in "my king's" accession to the throne of Hejaz.

Writing home in a letter headed, only half-seriously, "An Epistle to the Philibians," Jack reported that when the news of the coronation in Mecca reached Jiddah, "the Wahhabi flagstaffs were all gay with bunting while the salute of 101 guns (just a little ragged it was) proclaimed to the world that Jack was right again. But of course, he always is!"[43] Yet materially, the years 1925–30 proved lean for Jack: his various commercial ventures had ripened but had not yet borne fruit; he augmented his meager income by sending rare Arabian stamps to Dora, now settled permanently in London, for resale on the philatelic exchange. The need, he felt, was to become even closer to Ibn Saud, whose name he celebrated profusely in books and articles. The next step beckoned. Van der Meulen, who prided himself on living amicably on the line dividing the Muslim and Christian worlds, reports that in the late 1920s Philby proposed that together they should finally step across the line: "Let us become Muslims. You too want to see more of the other side. We shall not lose anything and may gain by it."[44] As a practicing Christian, van der Meulen politely declined, but Philby, who had long since defined himself as a freethinker, now looked to Mecca. "If only I was or would become a Mussulman," he wrote to Dora, "I believe I would get these concessions for the asking."

In 1928, he informed Ibn Saud that he wished to convert, but the King was then placating his restless Ikhwan warriors, and it would have been awkward to welcome Philby into the True Faith. Two years later, by which time Ibn Saud had prevailed in a bloody showdown with his Ikhwan jihadists, Jack sent a second letter seeking the King's permission. Ibn Saud replied by telephone (an innovation Philby had helped introduce) from the resort town of Taif, saying Philby must go to Mecca "for a ceremony." Philby hastily packed and traveled to just outside the Holy City, where he was met by two of the King's ministers and donned the ihram, a towel-like gown prescribed for pilgrims. In Mecca, the penitent Philby performed the Tawaf, the sevenfold circuit of the Kaba, kissed the sacred black stone set in the ancient wall, recited the ordained sets of prayers, prostrated himself at Abraham's Station, sipped from the Holy Well of Zamzam, ran the ritual course known as the Sai, and at sunrise uttered the sacred oath, "I testify there is no god but God, and that Mohammed is His Servant and Prophet," finally casting seven stones at Satan. Philby professed a sense of ecstasy, but characteristically confessed, "I must surely be the first Muslim to have performed the *Tawaf* before ever saying a single prayer." Summoned to a royal assemblage, Philby received from Ibn Saud his new Islamic name, Hajj Abdullah, "The Slave of God."[45] To his British critics, Philby's conversion was a final act of apostasy, yet of a puzzling sort. As a fellow diplomat and Arabist, Sir James Craig, a onetime Ambassador to Saudi Arabia, said of Jack, "[H]e was exasperatingly contrary, consistent only in his inconsistency . . . a champion of the Arabs who advocated Jewish immigration into Palestine, a British patriot who was interned during the war as a danger to his country, a rebel against the Establishment who loved the Athenaeum, *The Times*, the cricket scores and the Honours List. He treated his wife both shabbily and generously and didn't notice the difference. He was selfish, irritable, a stranger to humility, a difficult subordinate, an impossible colleague."[46] Still, it was this bounder who also (Craig acknowledged) was his era's greatest desert explorer and who (as Craig did not add) did more than any other Briton to turn the Middle East upside down.

As for Muslims, many of those who knew Philby questioned the sincerity of their new Islamic brother. Emir Abdullah spoke for them when he said tartly, upon hearing the news from Mecca about his erstwhile Chief British Representative, "Islam has gained little, Christianity has lost even less."[47]

From his turn to Mecca until his death in Lebanon on September 30, 1960, Jack Philby led a double life of incongruous and bizarre complexity. He virtually commuted between Great Britain and Saudi Arabia (as it officially became known in 1932). Beit Baghdadi, his home in Jiddah, bestowed by the King, was once the residence of the city's Turkish Governor: a full-busted palace which he shared with a troop of baboons, kept to scare away importuning pilgrims. Slave girls were likewise offered by the King to Hajj Abdullah for his diversion, and eventually in 1945, Ibn Saud presented him with a slim and lovely consort named Rozy, a sixteen-year-old described as an "eight-cylinder girl" by the envious driver who delivered her as a surprise gift. Probably of Persian origin, and possibly fathered by the King, Rozy bore Philby two sons. Ibn Saud was delighted, and provided the sixty-something father with a palatial mansion in Riyadh. Also thanks to the King's patronage, Philby was able to make two safe, extended forays into Arabia's Empty Quarter, confirming his standing as an explorer.

That reputation, augmented by his voluminous writings, stood him well in London. There Hajj Abdullah metamorphosed into Harry St. John Bridger Philby, Gent., a tweedy fixture at the Athenaeum, a club renowned for its literary and scientific membership, to which he had been elected on the fast track as a "candidate of distinction." In its richly upholstered lounge, Philby, a pipe perched in his jaws, perused *The Times* ("I always keep the Parliamentary page for binding") and chatted with friends about the wonderful progress of his son Kim, who had followed him to Westminster and Trinity and who seemed poised for an influential post in the government (an ambition, as the world was to learn, that Kim realized).[48]

What made Philby's double life possible was his pivotal role in mating corporate America with the Wahhabi kingdom. The match was neither easy nor obvious. After World War I, the British were adamant about preserving their dominion over the petroleum resources in the Middle East, a commodity essential to the Royal Navy and that the Empire then lacked.

This they did by outright ownership of the Anglo-Persian Oil Company, by political dominion of the Arab Middle East, by "British preference" hiring clauses in contracts, and by collusion with French and Dutch companies to limit competition from outsiders (i.e., Americans). In 1919, a British oil magnate named E. Mackay Edgar was able to boast that his country's position was "impregnable." All known or likely oil fields outside the United States, he declared, "are in British hands, or under British management or control, or financed by British capital."[49] This, to phrase it mildly, was irksome to American producers and their political allies; pressure from Washington was unremitting for an "Open Door," which more than one Briton complained was "a mysterious portal, with a habit of swinging shut, just as the Americans had got inside."[50] Not until 1928 were the first U.S. companies allowed to operate in the Middle East, and then only as junior partners in the British-dominated multinational Iraq Petroleum Company, in which all partners needed the agreement of all the others in seeking concessions within a "Red Line" drawn around the former Ottoman Empire. A hole was drilled in the Red Line when an outsider (Standard Oil of California) paid $50,000 to obtain a concession held by an insider (Gulf Oil) in Bahrain, which Gulf had acquired before becoming a partner in the cartel. Even so, the British insisted that the island's ruler could consent only if the subsidiary company was firmly under British management, and a way around this was found by assigning the Bahrain Petroleum Company Ltd. under Canadian law. In 1932, oil was struck on Bahrain, a matter of covetous interest to rulers of the great desert kingdom some twenty-five miles away.

"Oh, Philby," Ibn Saud had sighed only a year before, "if anyone would offer me a million pounds, I would give him all the concessions he wanted." His royal treasury was empty (indeed his available cash was stowed in a portable tin trunk carried by his treasurer); the Great Depression had already reduced the inflow of pilgrims, down to forty thousand from one hundred thousand annually; and funds were urgently needed for improving basic services. Thus Philby (in his telling) found a ready ear when he reminded the King that his country was full of buried riches, and that he knew a man who could help: "He came here a few years ago, and you refused to meet him. He is at Cairo now, and if you fix your own time to be at Jidda, I will let him know by wire, and I guarantee he will come along."[51] The helper in question was Charles Crane, the American whose friend, Rev. Henry Birkert, was slain by Ikhwan fanatics in 1929. This time, there would be no such trouble. Indeed, Ibn Saud, having united his country and furious over just such incidents, finally turned forcibly against his sacred warriors, curbing their violence if not their zealotry.

Charles R. Crane is among the uncelebrated figures who stalk through history and befriend its makers, serving as a ubiquitous go-between, and yet elude the eye of posterity. After inheriting an Illinois plumbing fortune, Crane had devoted his life to world affairs, especially East-West relations, and to America's liberal politics. In 1909 he provided the seed money for Wisconsin's Senator Robert M. La Follette Sr. to launch *The Progressive*, a peppery journal still published in Madison. At the University of Chicago, Crane endowed a Slavonic foundation that hosted a 1902 lecture series by Thomas Masaryk, thereby initiating the American connection that proved so instrumental in the founding of the Czechoslovak Republic.

Crane toured China and Russia, becoming acquainted with revolutionaries of every stripe. After a 1917 trip to Petrograd with the journalist Lincoln Steffens, he alerted Woodrow Wilson to the Sykes-Picot Agreement carving up the Middle East before the Bolsheviks made its details public. At the Paris Peace Conference, Crane—who had generously contributed to President Wilson's 1916 re-election campaign—was named co-chairman with Dr. Henry King, president of Oberlin College, of a Middle East fact-finding commission, whose report found against the Zionists in Palestine and for Arab rights in Palestine, Syria, and Lebanon.

When Crane arrived at Jiddah in February 1931, he came as an avowed friend of the Arabs and as Ibn Saud's first American guest. (The State Department had no consulate in Saudi Arabia and no embassy until 1942.) At the welcoming feast, the master stroke was a Bedouin sword dance and the chanting of Koranic verses by a blind cantor; then came horse and camel races, during which Crane was presented with two Arabian thoroughbreds. Crane reciprocated with a box of dates that he had grown in California, and with the offer to underwrite a resource survey of the kingdom to be conducted by Karl Twitchell, a mining engineer then employed by the philanthropist on a water development project in Yemen.

In April, Twitchell completed a fifteen-hundred-mile trip across the peninsula to search the kingdom's sands for water, gold, and oil. He found little evidence of accessible fresh water and some commercially promising traces of gold, but in the eastern region of al-Hasa, he discovered domed geological structures that could mean petroleum. When Socal drillers struck oil in offshore Bahrain, Twitchell obtained Ibn Saud's approval to ask if the company might be interested in a Saudi concession. Its executives were interested, and in May 1933, as we have seen, the Saudi door opened, exclusively, to the United States.

Test drilling began in 1934, but initial results proved disappointing, and then output increased by degrees. Finally, on October 16, 1938, the Damman-7 well "blew," gushing in excess of 1,500 barrels a day, compared with the daily average U.S. output of around a hundred barrels. Ibn Saud soon received his first royalty check ($1.5 million), inspiring a different kind of Saudi pilgrimage, as described by Rachel Bronson, a resident scholar at the Council on Foreign Relations, in *Thicker Than Oil*. On May 1, 1939, the King, along with a retinue of more than two thousand people packed into five hundred automobiles, "journeyed out of the eastern oil fields and turned the spigot that began the flow of oil into the first tankers. On the return trip, the king, along with some of his brothers and older sons, sang Bedouin raiding songs from their youth."[52]

Faced with the awesome fecundity of Saudi oil, Socal sought partners essential to pumping, shipping, refining, and marketing its treasure. Its Saudi subsidiary, the California Arabian Standard Oil Company (Casoc) merged in 1936 with Texaco, thereby benefiting from that company's marketing network in a tightly controlled global market. Yet even more capital was required for a concession roughly as big as Texas, New Mexico, and Arizona combined. After the first royalty check, a grateful Ibn Saud increased the concession by 80,000 square miles, giving the company exclusive rights to oil over 440,000 square miles, or more than half the kingdom. In 1944, Casoc became the Arabian American Oil Company (Aramco), which two years later partnered with Standard Oil of New Jersey (Exxon) and Socony-Vacuum (Mobil), forming an oil conglomerate of imperial dimensions. Gross Saudi daily output soared from 21,000 barrels in 1944 to 548,000 barrels in 1950, and at the King's insistence, since he distrusted Europeans, ownership remained entirely American.

His trust was repaid during World War II. Saudi Arabia remained officially neutral but leaned pragmatically to Britain, since necessary food supplies came from India and Egypt. Once America entered the war, U.S. help followed. In 1944, the State Department found that Saudi Arabia's security was of vital concern to the United States, qualifying the kingdom for direct and indirect wartime aid, which by 1945 totaled nearly $100 million. Washington's evolving policy was clearly foreshadowed in a January 1945 memorandum prepared for Assistant Secretary of State Dean Acheson by Wallace Murray, State's director of Near Eastern and African Affairs. "If the Saudi Arabian economy should break down and political disintegration ensue," Murray warned, "there is a danger that either Great Britain or Soviet Russia would attempt to move into Saudi Arabia to preserve order and thus prevent the other from doing so. Such a development in a country strategically located and rich in oil as Saudi Arabia might well constitute a *causi belli* threatening the peace of the world." Hence the necessity to keep Saudi oil resources in American hands, and to develop a military relationship that ideally should provide for airbases and flight privileges for U.S. warplanes.[53]

This emerging consensus was ceremonially ratified in February 1945, when President Roosevelt paused while returning from the Yalta Conference to meet Ibn Saud aboard the USS *Quincy*. In the enthusiastic words of the State Department's William A. Eddy, who served as interpreter, the encounter was "a consummation devoutly to be wished" that heralded a moral and strategic alliance with a doctrinally anti-Communist people in an area rich in resources.[54] As a result of this calculating and synergetic alliance, the Wahhabi kingdom has spent more per capita on arms than any other country in the world, and most of its purchases have been from the United States, making it America's premier weapons customer. And yet despite its multitude of rockets and jet fighters, it proved helpless in 1989–90 when Saddam Hussein's legions, having annexed Kuwait, threatened Saudi Arabia. It took OPERATION DESERT STORM's half-million foreign troops to free Kuwait and protect Saudi Arabia and its vital oil fields.

At least as curious, America's oldest expatriate community in the Arab world has grown roots in a country antipathetic to the core political values the United States professes. The kingdom remains an absolute monarchy lacking a parliament, constitution, and elections; it shuns freedom of worship, speech, press, and assembly. Yet within this unpromising environment, amid the unrelieved emptiness of eastern Saudi Arabia, lies an exotic American transplant, three Aramco townships that had formed by 1950: Dharan (population 10,000), Abqaiq (circa 5,000), and Ras Tanura (circa 5,000). Roughly a third of the three towns' inhabitants were "Aramcons," American employees and their families. Each town consisted of an inner ring with grass lawns and split-level houses for senior U.S. personnel, a more modest "intermediate" area for skilled foreign workers, and an outlying shantytown for Saudi laborers "reminiscent of the Hoovervilles of the depression era," in the words of Columbia University's Solon T. Kimball, who studied the towns.[55] A half century later, these alien enclaves remain, somehow surviving regional wars, revolutions, terror attacks, Saudi succession crises, OPEC "oil shocks," and the phased nationalization of Aramco, carried out in collaboration with its American managers, many of whom remain as executives of a state-owned company.

Still, it cannot be said that proximity has bred respect, much less affection. For decades Aramcon morale has suffered from prohibitions of drinking, smoking, and gambling, and from draconian dress codes for women venturing beyond their Little America—where even Christmas wreaths and Santa Claus effigies have provoked the rage of religious police. And despite, or perhaps because of, this protracted American presence, together with resentment over Saudi dependence on a condescending superpower, antipathy has been warmly reciprocated. In 2007, the Gallup Center for Muslim Studies surveyed ten thousand Muslims in ten countries and discovered that Saudi Arabians expressed the greatest dislike of the United States, the proportion being a startling 79 percent, compared with 52 percent of those polled in officially anti-American Iran. "These figures suggest a paradox in the Muslim world," commented the British-born historian Niall Ferguson. "It's not America's enemies who hate the United States most; it's people in countries that are supposed to be America's friends, if not allies." Moreover, the most hostile Muslims tend to be the most affluent and better-educated respondents, the Gallup surveyors found.[56]

This might not have surprised Jack Philby, who lived long enough to rue the results of the economic windfall that transformed Saudi society. He deplored the multiplying motorcars on Saudi highways, even though for years he had been the Ford Motor Company's principal agent. In articles and books he spoke out against the extravagance and corruption of Riyadh's royal family, so affronting King Saud, the eldest of Ibn Saud's sons, who succeeded to the throne in 1953, that Philby was forced into exile and resettled in Beirut. But then Philby was never inclined to self-censorship. During the 1930s he had sought vainly and quixotically to reconcile Arab states with Zionism, to the irritation of his patron, Ibn Saud. He was at various times a

General Charles Gordon faces the Mahdi's warriors, as depicted in a celebrated painting by George William Joy, although the true circumstances of his death can only be surmised.

Leeds City Art Gallery U.K./Bridgeman Art Library

Leander Starr Jameson as portrayed by Spy in Vanity Fair: "A raider, a freebooter a filibuster . . . Recent events have made him the most popular man in the Empire."

The Muslim Emirs of Northern Nigeria visit Lord Lugard (center) in England.

King Faisal (left) and his brother Emir Abdullah in Jerusalem shortly before Faisal's death. The white-turbaned Grand Mufti is in the middle.

The victorious General Edmund Allenby enters Jerusalem on foot through the Jaffa Gate, December 1917.

T. E. Lawrence entering Damascus in a Rolls-Royce, October 1918, the climactic episode of the Arab Revolt.

A recreational break at the Cairo Conference, March 1921. Gertrude Bell sits between Winston Churchill (left) and T. E. Lawrence (right).

Ibn Saud meets Sir Percy Cox and Gertrude Bell at Basra, 1916.

The future King Faisal of Saudi Arabia (lower left) visits Kim Philby (next to Faisal) at a boarding school in England. Jack Philby is second from the right in the top row; Dora, his wife, stands in front of him.

The future Reza Shah of Iran and his son and successor, Mohammed Reza. Ashraf, Mohammed's twin sister, stands at the right.

The Arab Legion under Glubb Pasha, the Middle East's crack fighting force.

Anglo-Indian riflemen take over the British-owned Abadan oil refinery during World War II.

*Two styles of negotiation.
Top: Ibn Saud and Sir Percy
Cox, 1924. Bottom: President
Franklin Roosevelt and King
Ibn Saud confer aboard the USS
Quincy in February 1945.*

Demonstrators in support of
Iran's nationalist Prime Minister
Mossadeq in Tehran, 1953.

Deputy Secretary of Defense Paul
Wolfowitz visits the Iraqi prison of
Abu Ghraib, May 2004.

Library of Congress

Reute

Socialist, a pacifist, an appeaser, and a patriot. In 1940, when he planned a lecture trip to the United States, his views were so suspect that British police arrested him in Bombay and shipped him to England, where he was held in detention for "[a]ctivities prejudicial to the safety of the realm" until March 1941, when he was released and joined Dora via the Athenaeum. Philby's unfinished memoir was justly titled "Out of Step." After his death in Beirut in 1960, he was buried in a walled Muslim cemetery in the Basra quarter; his son Kim chose the inscription on his tombstone: "Greatest of Arabian Explorers." Three years later, facing exposure as a KGB mole, Kim Philby bolted from Beirut to Moscow, where he joined his old Cambridge classmates Guy Burgess and Donald Maclean.

There seemed a subliminal linkage between Jack Philby's apostasy and his son's perfidy, a theme explored at length by Anthony Cave Brown in his dual biography, *Treason in the Blood*. Both led schizophrenic lives, both were proficient in the dark arts of bureaucratic deviltry, both turned against the values that nurtured them. Yet there also seems a less obvious parallel. The elder Philby's double life can also be seen as a metaphor for America's partnership with Saudi Arabia, the world's only sovereign state bearing its modern founder's family name. This, too, was a schizophrenic misalliance. Seen at one level, the match assured the United States access to the cheap energy essential to an automotive culture. But doing so meant turning a blind eye to a fossilized political system in which some seven thousand Saudi princes consume as much as a fifth of the kingdom's vast oil revenues, and to a culture where women were vilified as "Communist whores" for daring in 1990 to assert their right to drive (still disallowed). The glaring inequities of Saudi life are so palpable that the kingdom's nervous leaders rely inordinately on Islam to quell dissent and legitimize their authority. This effort received an inadvertent and phenomenal assist from the United States following the Soviet Union's 1979 invasion of Afghanistan. In what seemed like a shrewd bargain, the Carter White House asked Saudi Arabia to match dollar for dollar America's covert assistance to the Afghan resistance. King Fahd eagerly concurred, since this was a way of simultaneously pleasing Washington, enhancing the kingdom's global influence, and buying peace at home. Books and pamphlets called on Saudi youths to wage holy war against Russian infidels, and by 1984, around sixteen thousand students were enrolled in Islamic studies. Between 1981 and 1986, U.S. and Saudi assistance to Afghan insurgents grew tenfold (in the estimate of Rachel Bronson from a combined $120 million to $1.2 billion, all the aid being funneled to radical Islamic fighters through Pakistan's military intelligence. This was the program that hatched Al-Qaeda and gave Osama Bin Laden his all-important base. When the Soviet Union dissolved in 1991, its demise sped by its defeat in Afghanistan, a fresh opportunity arose for spreading the message of militant Islam. The Saudi Ministry of Pilgrimage and Religious Trust reported in the early 1990s that it had earmarked $850 million to build mosques and send seventy-three hundred prayer leaders to promote its brand of Islam in the predominantly Muslim former Soviet republics in Central Asia. The fundamental point is soberly expressed by Ms. Bronson: "For years the royal family had manipulated Saudi domestic politics to manage Cold War challenges. To build domestic legitimacy and rebuff external aggression, Saudi leaders had catered to the most radical elements of the kingdom's religious establishment. It was not that Washington had ignored Saudi Arabia's proselytizing, but rather that Washington accepted and at times actively encouraged it to secure geostrategic ends. There was a long-term price to pay for such policies. On September 11, those costs came due."[57]

Fifteen of the nineteen terrorists who perpetrated the 2001 suicide attacks were Saudi citizens who had gained ready access to the United States under a fast-track visa policy long provided as a favor to the kingdom's subjects—a kind of diplomatic dowry in a surreal marriage. Yet September 11 provides the apt epitaph for the life and deeds of Harry St. John Bridger Philby and the kingdom he helped create. The 1933 oil deal resulted in a trillion dollars in revenues pouring into a once-impoverished desert kingdom, and yet what are its fruits? Only one Saudi Arabian is known to almost every adult on the planet, and regrettably he is neither a statesman, nor a scientist, nor a business tycoon, an author, or a scholar. He is a mass murderer, inadvertently nurtured by Saudi Arabia and its American benefactors.

⌘

EIGHT

"A Splendid Little Army"

*Lieutenant-General Sir John Bagot Glubb (Glubb Pasha) (1897–1986),
KCB, CMG, DSO, OBE, MC*

⌗

A Jewish State of Palestine
If you do it
You'll rue it
An Arab State of Palestine?
Hardly a proposition
When you consider the opposition
Federation?
What situation?
Follows separation[?]
A Divorce[,] of Course
Partition
To partite and be neighbourly
Is far less labourly
Than putting up with banditry
And blaming the mandatory

—John Glubb, Rhymes on the Report
    of the Anglo-American Commission (ca. 1946)

In 1921, three years after Arthur Balfour's Declaration, Palestine was festering. The British were trying to decide how to reunite the Jews and Arabs on land both held to be sacred. As the Cairo Conference ended, Winston Churchill and T. E. Lawrence summoned Abdullah, the older brother of Faisal, to Jerusalem. Determined to place Faisal on the throne of Iraq, Churchill, with Lawrence translating, offered the inconvenient Abdullah, who had been expecting that same kingdom, a consolation prize: an emirate if he promised not to attack the French in Syria. Later the Colonial Secretary bragged that he had "created [Trans-]Jordan with a stroke of the pen one Sunday afternoon."[1] With a British subsidy and a British Resident to advise him, Abdullah became the ruler of Transjordan, an area the size of Indiana, east of the River Jordan in what had been a backwater of southern Syria, on a six-month probationary basis. During his audition, Britain granted Abdullah a stipend of £5,000 per month. Eventually, Palestine would remain under direct British administration; Transjordan would become part of the area controlled by British mandate, but unlike its western neighbor it would not be subject to Zionist colonization as per the Balfour Declaration. Abdullah would become its symbolic head.

With its scruffy capital, Amman, and its hinterland of unyielding sand and rock, Transjordan was a poor prize compared to Syria, with its glittering trophy, Damascus, now mandated to the French, and Iraq, with its historic Abbasid capital, Baghdad, and its compensating natural resource—oil. Always impoverished, ever a spendthrift, Abdullah, nicknamed Ajlan, "the hurried one," would become hostage to his ambition—to become King of Greater Syria, an area he hoped would include Lebanon, Syria, Palestine, and Iraq or, barring that, King of Palestine, for which it soon appeared the British had other plans. As a contemporary aptly remarked, Abdullah was a falcon trapped in a canary's cage.

In 1919, on the eastern border of the Hejaz, Ibn Saud had obliterated a Hashemite army of five thousand commanded by Abdullah's brother Ali. Now Abdullah was besieged by Syrian revanchist refugees bent on continuing a small-scale war with the French, by undefined frontiers, and even by his father, who claimed Transjordan as part of the remaining Hejaz. Abdullah settled down in a modest palace in the Jordan Valley with two wives and an African concubine, squandering his allowance on ineffectual bribes.

That was not to say that he lacked admirers. Kitchener's Oriental Secretary, Ronald Storrs, who met the Emir during a prewar visit to Cairo, found him a beguiling combination of aesthete and soldier. Storrs was amazed by the range of Abdullah's learning, reporting that he had sat entranced for two hours as his caller intoned for him "brilliant episodes of the Seven Suspended odes of pre-Islamic Poetry, the Glories and the Lament of Antar ibn Shaddad," while imbibing quarts of Arabian coffee. He delicately segued by "a series of delicately inclined planes, from a warrior past" to "the defenceless Arab present." Abdullah then boldly inquired "whether Great Britain would present his father the Grand Sharif of Mecca with a dozen, or even a half-dozen machine guns." Queried as to their purpose, Abdullah replied frankly, "For defence," against attack from the Turks. Storrs reluctantly informed the Emir that the British could not supply arms to be used against a friendly power—it was early 1914—but they parted on the "best of terms."[2] Although Faisal had better relations with the other Arabs, Abdullah would remain the chief proponent of an alliance between the British and his father, Grand Sharif Hussein.

T. E. Lawrence, dispatched to Amman at the end of 1921 to advise the

Emir, found Abdullah, in the words of Elizabeth Monroe, "feeling his way, sometimes threatening to quit, sometimes flirting with the French, and sometimes contemplating coalescence with Hijaz in order ultimately to establish a kingdom comparable to Faisal's in Iraq."[3] Lawrence was his early champion, describing him to the Arab Bureau in 1916: "Aged 35, but looks younger. Short and thick built, apparently as strong as a horse, with merry dark brown eyes, a round smooth face, full but short lips, straight nose, brown beard . . . In manner affectedly open and very charming, not standing at all on ceremony, but jesting with the tribesmen like one of their own sheikhs. On serious occasions he judges his words carefully, and shows himself a keen dialectician."[4] Lawrence's early enthusiasm for the provisional Emir of Jordan as "a person who was not too powerful . . . but who relied upon His Majesty's Government for the retention of his office" gave way to disillusionment.[5] "Abdullah was a rotter, a complete rotter," Lawrence confided to Gertrude Bell in 1922.[6] Too indolent and too weak to govern, Abdullah, it appeared, needed yet another strong Englishman by his side. That Englishman, the Colonial Office's Middle East expert, Hubert Young, decided, was Harry St. John B. Philby.

We first met "Jack" Philby in Iraq, where he and Gertrude Bell traded their tales of the exasperating A. T. Wilson. Philby lasted until Sir Percy Cox fired him after his brusque treatment of Faisal when Philby accompanied the sovereign-designate on his Basra-to-Baghdad progress. Now he joyfully confided to his diary, "[W]e are to have another run for our money."[7] An able administrator, Philby became, in November 1921, Chief British Representative and enthusiastic promoter of Abdullah's cause: "[He] is an ideal constitutional monarch, taking no active part in the administration except when referred to for a decision or for advice either by the Local Government or by the people."[8]

Philby's first task was to rein in the Emir's fiscal excesses. "I frankly like Abdullah," the unrepentant Philby confided to Bell, "a vain but well-read man with excellent ideas, though lacking in initiative or vigour of action. Of course nobody here or in Syria wants him or any member of the Sharifian family, but what matter? He is here and is as good a figurehead as anyone else would be. So long as he is not a drain on the exiguous local revenues, he is acceptable, but his debts which amount to about £25,000 to date, are a problem the solution to which will not be without difficulty. Pa and Ma especially[,] occasionally send him substantial tips and once or twice he has intercepted the pay of the Maan garrison for the benefit of his own pocket. He also hinted some time ago to Faisal that, as he had usurped the throne which was his by right, he might at any rate share the spoils; Faisal replied that he wasn't getting as much as he had hoped and sent a cheque for £1000 as being all he could spare."[9]

Despite Philby's financial restraints, in 1924 the British Treasury refused to countenance further profligacy. In exchange for their subsidies, the Chief British Representative, later Resident, would assume control of Transjordan's exchequer and military affairs and become the de facto highest power in the land. Forcing Abdullah into an impossible bind, Philby encouraged the Jordanians to run "a fully fledged independent Arab show," convinced "that the Arabs will never succeed in setting up a Government unless they are allowed to learn wisdom from their mistakes."[10] Philby warded off attempts by the Palestinian authorities to poach on his preserve, and gave advice but did not fret when it was not followed. Yet ultimately the fractious Resident could not get along with Sir Herbert Samuel, the High Commissioner in Jerusalem, who held firm to his belief that Transjordan's affairs could not be separated from Palestine's, and as in Iraq, Philby disagreed with what he perceived as the British Government's drifting policy in the Middle East. He resigned from public service.

Abdullah was not saddened by the loss of his chess partner, who had kept a picture of the Emir's hated nemesis, Ibn Saud, on his desk. Philby was succeeded in 1924 by Henry Cox and in 1940 by Alec Kirkbride (later Sir), who had served as Assistant British Resident in 1927 and would become, in 1946, the first British Ambassador to Amman. Kirkbride, who had grown up in Egypt speaking fluent Arabic and who had fought with Faisal and Lawrence in the Arab Revolt, had been in 1920–21 president of the short-lived postwar interim government of Moab, headquartered fifty miles south of Amman in Kerak, in what was to become at Churchill's pen stroke "Transjordan." His younger brother Alan had been the president of the equally transitory (1920–21) government of Amman.

A few months before the Cairo Conference convened on March 12, 1921, Sheik Abdullah left the Hejaz by camel caravan, leading a small army. His brother Faisal had just been expelled from the throne of Syria by the French and it was rumored that Abdullah planned a preemptive strike toward

Damascus to expel the usurpers and restore the throne to the Hashemites. After boarding a train in Medina, he arrived by the Hejaz rail in Maan on November 21, 1920, with three hundred men and six machine guns, on a "tour of inspection."[11] As Maan was located in a Hejazi province ruled by his father, now King Hussein, the British could not yield to French pressure to expel him. In March, Abdullah left for Amman. In the absence of clear instructions from Samuels in Jerusalem, Alec Kirkbride decided to adopt a "hat-in-hand policy," advancing from Kerak to the railway station in Amman to intercept his unwelcome visitor: "Am I correct," asked Abdullah grandly, "in assuming that you are here to welcome me on the behalf of the Government of Great Britain?"

"Well, as a matter of fact," replied the imperturbable twenty-three-year-old, "I come with my colleagues here to meet Your Highness as the Council of the National Government of Moab. I expect that His Majesty's Government will send a representative, in due course, who is more senior than myself."

Abdullah, with his customary charm, replied, "I could not wish to be welcomed by anyone more acceptable than yourself, who fought recently in the army commanded by my brother Faisal. I trust that you will remain to give me your support and advice in the difficult days which are to come. By the way has the National Government of Moab ever been recognized internationally?" Kirkbride, expressing deep appreciation of the Sheik's kindness, replied, "As regards the local Government, I am not quite sure of its international status. I feel however, that the question is largely of an academic nature now that Your Highness is here."

Abdullah leaned forward and said, "Ah, I was sure that we understood each other!"[12]

If Abdullah's preemptive strike failed to gain him Damascus, his march on Amman meant that at the Cairo Conference, his hold on Transjordan was recognized as a fait accompli. Thus began Kirkbride's long and fruitful association with the Hashemite kingdom.

Now we are to meet John Bagot Glubb, known as Abu Hunaik (Father of the Little Jaw) to the Arabs, Jack to his friends, and Glubb Pasha to the rest of the interested public. Almost entirely forgotten today, Glubb deserves a chapter for six reasons. 1) There was no better representative of the professional soldier enamored of the Bedouin nomads than Glubb, who led and advised the Arab Legion, the best equipped, best trained, and most disciplined of the Arab armies and the backbone of the Jordanian monarchy for more than a quarter of a century. 2) He was an agent, during his early career in Iraq, of one of the most controversial policies of the mandate: terrorizing the tribes through airpower. 3) During 1941, a desperate time for the British in the Middle East, Glubb's legionnaires gave crucial support to the army in their battle to save Iraq. 4) The Pasha led the Legion in what was one of the few victories in the first Arab-Israeli war, the occupation of East Jerusalem. 5) He exemplified many of the paradoxes and dilemmas of indirect rule—his very presence and authority undermined the legitimacy of the Hashemites, and his loyalty to Jordan would always be suspect. 6) Finally, it was his abrupt dismissal, by Abdullah's grandson Hussein on March 1, 1956, that precipitated the Suez Crisis, which ended British hegemony in the eastern Mediterranean.

"I spent thirty-six years living among the Arabs," so Glubb begins the preface of his autobiography, *A Soldier with the Arabs* (1957). "During the first nineteen of these years, I lived entirely with them, rarely meeting Europeans and sometimes not speaking a word of English for weeks on end. I originally went to Iraq in 1920 as a regular officer of the British Army, seeking fresh fields of adventure and a wider knowledge of the many different forms of modern soldiering. But when I had spent five years among the Arabs, I decided to change the basis of my whole career: I made up my mind to resign my commission in the British Army and devote my life to the Arabs. My decision was largely emotional. I loved them."[13]

Glubb personified the class of English public school boys described by the imperial historian James Morris: "The Bedouin struck a responsive chord in them," Morris writes. "With his patrician style and his picturesque appearance, his great flocks of goats and camels, his taste for coffee and beautiful boys, his blend of arrogance and hospitality, his love of pedigree, his fighting ability and what would later be called his *machismo*, the Bedouin was every Englishman's idea of nature's gentleman. He seemed almost a kind of Englishman himself, translated into another idiom. It was upon this romantic fixation, this idealization of a type or a legend, that the British were precariously to build their new position in the Middle East."[14]

John Bagot Glubb was born into an Anglo-Irish military family in 1897. His father was a major general of the Royal Engineers, and John followed him into the sappers. After graduating from Cheltenham College and the

Royal Military Academy at Woolwich, he served in France during World War I. Wounded three times—once nearly fatally in the jaw—he received the Military Cross. He returned to the Western Front but would thenceforth be disfigured (hence his nickname "Father of the Little Jaw"). A small cherubic man with a high-pitched voice, a sandy moustache, a notable temper, and a craving for action, he found it difficult to resign himself to being turned into a peacetime soldier.

In 1920, he volunteered for service in Mesopotamia, then in the midst of a major rebellion.[15] But when Glubb reached Iraq in September, the tribal revolt had been largely suppressed by imperial troops at a cost of between £30 and £70 million (estimates vary).[16] By the time the British established firm control in February 1921, A. T. Wilson had been supplanted by Sir Percy Cox, and Gertrude Bell, his omnipresent Oriental Secretary, could still be found working and hosting picnics and lunches at "Chastity Close." (Glubb makes a cameo appearance in her letters as "Capt Glubb, a very clever little Intelligence Officer.")[17]

As the reader may remember, a fateful decision was taken at the Cairo Conference: to replace the British Army with the Royal Air Force in the Middle East. Fathered by Air Marshal Sir Hugh Trenchard and godfathered jointly by Lawrence and Churchill, who hoped to govern Mesopotamia "with hot air, aeroplanes and Arabs," this controversial system of air policing—already tested in Somalia and Afghanistan—would be employed across the Middle East until the 1950s.[18] "Control without occupation" was how Sir Samuel Hoare, Secretary of State for Air in the 1920s, defined it.[19] Deputized with carrying out the Colonial Office's mission of tranquilizing the insurgent tribes, Air Vice Marshal Sir John Salmond believed there were three possible coercive mechanisms—damage, morale, and interference—and the greater the interference, the greater the coercion. His view, expanded in a 1924 staff memorandum, reads like a latter-day tactical manual for the Sudanese air force in Darfur:

> A tribe that is out for trouble is well aware when the patience of Government has reached breaking point; and negotiations inevitably end in what is in effect an ultimatum of some form or other. Complete surprise is impossible and the real weight of air action lies in the daily interruption of normal life which it can inflict, if necessary for an indefinite period, while offering negligible chances of loot or of hitting back. It can

knock the roofs of huts about and prevent their repair, a considerable inconvenience in winter-time. It can seriously interfere with ploughing or harvesting—a vital matter; or burn up the stores of fuel laboriously piled up and garnered for the winter; by attack on livestock, which is the main form of capital and source [of] wealth to the less settled tribes, it can impose in effect a considerable fine, or seriously interfere with the actual food source of the tribe—and in the end the tribesman finds it is much the best to obey Government.[20]

When still a sapper, Glubb was put in charge of building huts and hangers for the RAF base at Hinaidi just outside Baghdad. By the time he became the RAF ground intelligence officer in charge of directing strikes in an area spanning some five hundred miles along the banks of the Euphrates, his Arabic was fluent, better (it was later said) than most Arabs. He saw almost continuous action. "The theory was," as Glubb writes in his memoir, *The Changing Scenes of Life* (1983), "that when tribal disorders broke out in any district—possibly hundreds of miles away—aircraft would take off from Hinaidi and bomb the offenders . . . and the disorders would be ended between breakfast and lunch." Practically, the monotonous dusty plain intersected by endless small canals and irrigation ditches made targets difficult for pilots to identify, and Glubb admitted that occasionally the "government's most loyal adherents" were mistakenly bombed.[21]

For years the Beni Huchaim tribes had camped along the Euphrates in southern Iraq in threatening proximity to the Baghdad-to-Basra railroad, where they were sources of never-ending trouble. They had been major combatants in the 1920 revolt—the British had been unable to attack them in their native habitat because of numerous physical obstacles, including but not limited to impromptu irrigation ditches, which made it impossible for pack animals or motor vehicles to pass. The Ottomans had imposed taxes on the tribes but had been less than diligent in collecting them. Now the Beni Huchaim refused to recognize King Faisal's government. As the tribes received no tangible returns for their taxes, as a colleague of Glubb's observed, "many of them feel that they are merely supplying pay for some tomato-eating *Effendis* in Baghdad."[22] Their taxes were in arrears, rifle fines went uncollected, and raiding and kidnapping had gone unpunished. At the behest of the Iraqi Minister of Interior, it was decided to teach two tribes of the confederation—the Barkat and the Sufran—a lesson.

Glubb's task was to pinpoint certain sheiks, to bomb particularly those "whose influence amongst the tribes rendered them particularly suitable for attack."[23] In the summer of 1923, traveling with only his servant and a guide, and with a cloak over his British officer's uniform, Captain Glubb rode into the village of the Sheik of Barkat. He was offered the sheik's hospitality, and subsequently visited all the villages of the two tribes. He reported that the Barkat and Sufran were "exceptionally poor" and had given up all farming after a far more powerful chieftain diverted their water into his canals. "It is a regrettable fact," Glubb noted, "that Government at the moment presents itself to their minds as a kind of absentee landlord which never concerns itself with them except periodically to demand revenues."[24] Glubb candidly writes that during two trips, while he was enjoying the tribes' hospitality, he was making maps to enable the RAF to bomb them. He felt obliged, he recalled, to warn them that he, himself, would lead the bombers if they proved recalcitrant.

In due course, the RAF showered leaflets on the Barkat and Sufran, which summoned the sheiks to the nearby town of Samawah on forty-eight hours' notice. There they were issued an ultimatum requiring them to give a monetary deposit to ensure that their tribes would pay their taxes and guarantee the safety of the collectors. This proved impossible. The sheiks insisted that long ago they had lost the ability to control their tribesmen. For what happened next, we turn to Glubb for his account: "When summoned, the shaikhs did not report, and I duly led the bombers, each of the pilots of which had a copy of my map. As soon as the tribes heard the sound of the aircraft—knowing already from me what was going to happen—they all ran out of their villages and lay in the many irrigation ditches. Only one old woman was killed. As a result of the bombing, however, all the shaikhs of the Beni Huchaim confederation (not only the Barkat and Sufran) reported to the government, and the whole area was brought under control without bloodshed."[25]

However, Glubb's later recollections are sadly at odds with the official report detailing two days of continuous bombing by De Havilland planes, some at night in order to catch tribesmen returning to their villages after the daytime raids. (Glubb himself dropped a large bomb on target fourteen, leaning over the side from the observer's seat of the leading aircraft.) According to the official account, 144 died and untold numbers were wounded.[26] For further operational details and Baghdad's approving reaction, we turn to the omniscient Bell, writing to her father:

> We're doing extremely well. Our last success is some operations against persistently disobedient tribes near Samawah—I think I told you. There was nothing political in it—they just refused to obey any orders and waited in defiance to see what would happen. It happened and it was admirably organised. An Iraq battalion guarded the railway bridges and the aerodromes, the tribes were bombed, they came in to a man, and in the next two days the Police pulled down all their forts. Everyone has come in from far and near and yesterday Ken [Kinahan Cornwallis, Britain's military adviser to Faisal's government] and the Minister of Interior [Ali Jaudat] went down by air and held a huge majlis laying down all the things they were to do and telling them they were now forgiven ... Good, isn't it.[27]

"Aerial action is a legitimate means of quelling disturbances and of enforcing the maintenance of order but it should in no circumstances be employed in support of purely administrative measures such as the collection of revenue," Churchill cautioned Sir Percy Cox in June 1921, but aerial bombing for nonpayment of taxes became government policy.[28] Even as Faisal argued for a larger conscript army, the British preferred air policing, which was "extremely efficient" and "a merciful instrument of government."[29] Writing in a service journal in 1926, Glubb noted, "Aircraft do not, as a rule, inflict very heavy casualties. Their tremendous moral effect is largely due to the demoralization engendered in the tribesman by his feelings of helplessness and his inability to reply effectively to the attack."[30]

The RAF's demonstrations in Iraq, minimum force with maximum effect, harked back to the British practice in nineteenth-century India, when mutineers were strapped to canons and then blown apart, thus sending a message to spectators, a seldom discussed underside of indirect rule. As such, they were an early template for the Pentagon's twenty-first century's "shock and awe."

The symbolic message was first articulated by A. T. Wilson in 1920 and employed to good effect by his successors, Sir Percy Cox and Henry Dobbs, as recorded by Bell in 1924:

The most interesting thing which happened during this week was a performance by the R.A.F., a bombing demonstration. It was even more remarkable than the one we saw last year at the Air Force Show because it was much more real. They had made an imaginary village about a quarter of a mile from where we sat on the Diyala [(Sirwan)] dyke and the two first bombs, dropped from 3000 ft, went straight into the middle of it and set it alight. It was wonderful and horrible. They then dropped bombs all round it, as if to catch the fugitives and finally firebombs which even in the bright sunlight, made flares of bright flame in the desert. They burn through metal, and water won't extinguish them . . . I was tremendously impressed. It's an amazingly relentless and terrible thing, war from the air.[31]

As a tribesman confided to a colleague of Glubb's, "There are only two things to fear—Allah and the *hakumat al tayarrat* [government by aircraft]."[32] Even as the mandatory power argued that airpower was a legitimate and proper form of warfare, the slaughter of civilians inevitably provoked parliamentary questioning. The Labour MP George Lansbury characterized the Air Minister and his department "as the lineal descendants of the Huns," adding, "I know there is a sort of feeling that a coloured person is of less value than a white person, but I do not think so. I think you are baby killers, and inhuman baby killers, whether you kill a black baby or a white baby, I do not see any difference. I think that one is a crime and the other is a crime."[33]

The Secretary of State for the Colonies, Leopold Amery, toured Iraq in 1925 to assess indirect rule and air policing. He was impressed with the reduction of expenditure from £20 million in 1921–22 to less than £3.4 million, and argued that Iraq served as "a splendid training ground" for the RAF. He concluded, "With regard to military forces, the Royal Air Force . . . is the backbone of the whole organization. If the writ of King Faisal runs effectively throughout his kingdom it is entirely due to British airplanes . . . If the airplanes were removed tomorrow, the whole structure would inevitably fall to pieces. Any locally raised forces without assistance from the air could not maintain internal order nor resist external aggression. I do not think that there can be any doubt whatever on that point."[34]

Unsurprisingly, it was in Iraq that Squadron Leader Arthur Harris experimented with aerial raids on urban targets, which he later used against ill-defended German cities in the Second World War, winning him the sobriquet of "Bomber." As Harris half proudly wrote in 1924, "[T]hey [the Arabs and Kurds] now know what real bombing means, in casualties and damages; they know that within forty-five minutes a full-sized village can be practically wiped out, and a third of its inhabitants killed or injured."[35] William Yale, an American who witnessed much of this history, observed that in Iraq the British had in effect secured their "imperialist interests without the invidious burden of colonial rule."[36]

The political consequences of aerial warfare waged against a defenseless civilian population would haunt the British for the duration of the mandate, but airpower would remain the preferred instrument of punishment, a technological advantage that developed into a substitute for democratic administration. It became easier to bomb the Kurds than to govern them.

By the time Glubb resigned from the army in 1926 to join the British administration in Iraq, he had bonded with the local Bedouin in the southern desert, had traveled the five hundred miles from Iraq to Jordan on a camel with only his servant, Ali, and was a veteran of campaigns waged against the fundamentalist Wahhabi raiders (known as the Ikhwan or Brotherhood) whose sponsor, Ibn Saud, would continue to be the largest thorn in the Hashemite side.

Although Glubb argued for more ground troops, it was RAF bombs that finally brought the Ikhwan, albeit temporarily, to heel. Bell wrote, "The King . . . is very much delighted with the Akhwan business—and so am I. The next day, after they had fired on our aeroplanes we bombed their camp. They fled south 40 miles in the night and next morning our aeroplanes pursued them and bombed them again. They had made a wholly unprovoked attack, looted and killed our peaceful shepherds and carried off our flocks. I don't know when I've felt so proud of our power to strike back. The Akhwan with their horrible fanatical appeal to a mediaeval faith rouse in me the blackest hatred."[37]

In 1928, Glubb was appointed Administrative Inspector of the Southern Desert, and he attended a meeting at Jiddah where he met Ibn Saud for the first time, finding him "a tremendous personality" and noting that "[h]e would have ended up as prime Minister in any country in the world."[38] As Ibn Saud continued to consolidate power in the Arabian Peninsula, Saïd Aburish recounts in *The House of Saud*: "No fewer than 400,000 people were killed or wounded for the Ikhwan did not take prisoners, but mostly killed the vanquished."[39] Glubb had observed the massacres and frenzied flights. As the Hejaz was subdued, he witnessed one of its largest tribes, the Shammar, on its panicked march north toward Iraq.

When the great camel army of the Ikhwan advanced on Amman in 1928, only the combined British-supplied armored cars and machine guns and the RAF's bombers saved the capital. As a result, Glubb was invited to sign on with Jordan's Arab Legion as *feriq* (lieutenant general) to police the frontier and to end the intertribal quarreling. Anticipating that he had no future left as an English soldier in Iraq following the signing of the Anglo-Iraqi Treaty in 1930, he jumped at the offer.

The Arab Legion, with which Glubb will always be associated, was not his creation but that of another Englishman, Frederick Gerard Peake (1886–1970), better known as Peake Pasha. A Sandhurst graduate, Peake had served in the Sinai in 1918, commanding an Egyptian camel corps that had assisted Lawrence in his attacks on the Hejaz railroad. At the end of the war, Peake, now a lieutenant colonel, was seconded for duty in Transjordan as inspector of gendarmerie. In 1923, he reorganized and amalgamated it with the reserves and police and named it the Arab Legion. (The British declared that fifteen hundred men could scarcely be called an army.)[40] A stickler for etiquette and protocol, Peake always dressed for dinner even though he usually dined alone. No fan of the nomadic Bedouin, the Pasha drew his troops from the towns and villages of Transjordan and Palestine. In 1926, a rival imperial unit, the Transjordan Frontier Force, subsidized and officered by the British and under operational command of the RAF and the High Command for Palestine and Transjordan, was given the responsibility of protecting the country's borders. In 1929, 1936–39, 1945, and 1948, it was ordered into Palestine to suppress anti-Zionist violence. Emir Abdullah's Arab Legion, the Al-Jaish Al-Arabi, reduced in numbers, became an internal security force.

Glubb arrived in November 1930 to become second in command to Peake. One of his first acts was to have the Frontier Force withdraw from the desert. He replaced it with troops known as Al Badiya, or the Desert Patrol. Initially composed of twenty men in four Buick trucks and armed with World War I–issue Lewis and Vickers machine guns, the force was built with Bedouin recruits from desert tribes such as the Shammar, Beni Sakhr, and the Howeitat, whose sheik, Auda abu Taya, had been an ally of Lawrence and Faisal. Glubb molded them into elite units mounted on camels and assigned them to small regional forts linked by telegraphy. Previously, anti-Bedouin prejudice had been prevalent throughout the Middle East; when irritated, Lawrence had called them "unstable as water," and Jordanian officers looked with alarm on the promotion of their desert rivals. But it was with this small mobile force, dressed in their distinctive uniform—khaki robes over white cotton trousers bound with broad red sashes, bandoliers of bullets, silver daggers, and revolvers—that Glubb succeeded over time in suppressing raiding and fending off assaults by the Ikhwan. But the suppression of cattle-rustling had unintended consequences: the *ghazzu* had provided both sport and income for the Bedouin. When the raiding ended, Glubb wrote, "[We] discovered unexpectedly that raiding had not only been a pastime for the chivalry of Arabia but also a social-security system of which our ill-timed intervention had destroyed the balance."[41]

Glubb's men were devoted and loyal—some had followed him from Iraq. Alec Kirkbride would claim that the Pasha's ability "to attract and hold the affection of the Arabs" was because he was "half Irish and half Cornish" rather than the usual Englishman.[42] He was benevolent and paternalistic, giving rise to a custom he viewed with increasing alarm:

A serious and apparently increasing nuisance in the desert is the fashion spreading amongst bedouin fathers of dying and appointing me as guardian of the child ... The Arabs allege that a deathbed wish of this kind must be honoured and that there is no honourable means of escape. Naturally these thoughtful fathers always die in very reduced circumstances, if not over their ears in debt ... Were the matter limited to sheikhs, however, it would not be so bad, but in Transjordan every police post in the desert has two or three of my "wards" attached to it, where they are being taught to read and write. The parents, however, omit to leave them anything in trustee securities, and the cost of clothing and feeding them is a heavy monthly charge.[43]

Glubb was a devout Christian and his instincts were generous; he frequently paid school fees and hospital costs for dozens of his men from his modest salary.

Paternalistic but never condescending, Glubb was quick to defend his men against his English officers' prejudices, preferring officers with sensitivity to those with better military training. He is often pictured enjoying Arab hospitality, seated on the ground cross-legged in a goats' hair tent, wearing a *shamagh* (keffiyeh) and fingering worry beads. (He always wore a khaki drill uniform, never the silken flowing robes *à l'Arabe* as did Lawrence.) In later years when the Pasha appeared in uniform, he sported five rows of medal ribbons.

Glubb's monthly reports to Arab Legion Headquarters were forwarded to Jerusalem and thence to London. Wordy, frank, opinionated, they make fascinating reading. One of them, quoted by his biographer James Lunt, concerned the rumored discovery of oil in Saudi Arabia: "If this be true it may indeed mean a transformation in the future history of Arabia. Politically it might even enable the Sauds to hold on to the Hejaz, to the exclusion of the sheriffs."[44] If the Wahhabis acquired oil, Glubb presciently worried, it would radically change their nomadic life and have a huge impact on the rest of the Middle East.

Never had the British been as unpopular in the Middle East as they became after they crushed the 1936–39 Arab uprising in Palestine. They blew up homes and an entire quarter of Jaffa and imprisoned or executed rebels and exiled leaders. The revolt was ignited by a six-month general strike by the Palestinians involving work stoppages and boycotts of British and Zionist-owned businesses. It was fueled by the Third Reich's anti-Semitic edicts and acts, which led to a rapid increase in Jewish immigration to Palestine, and fanned by the anti-Zionist incitement of the Grand Mufti of Palestine, Hajj Amin al-Husayni, a relative of the future Palestinian leader Yasir Arafat. In an ill-conceived gesture, former Liberal MP, High Commissioner Sir Herbert Samuel had invented the title "Grand Mufti," elevating the bearer over more senior muftis, and appointed him head of Palestine's Muslim community. (Herbert, a Jew, made a point of appearing scrupulously fair to the Arabs, showing no favoritism to the Zionists.)

Although Transjordan remained relatively calm during the revolt, saboteurs attacked the country's communications installations, oil pipelines, and government offices. The British attempted to reverse their policy of admitting more Jews to Palestine and restricted immigration, a plan detailed in a 1939 White Paper approved by the House of Commons. Nevertheless, when war came, Abdullah was the only Middle Eastern potentate to offer help. Other Arab leaders hoped for Britain's defeat. But until a pro-Nazi coup took place in Iraq in early April 1941, instigated by four colonels (the "Golden Square") and supported by the Prime Minister, Rashid Ali al-Gailani, the Arab Legion's sole service consisted of guarding a British airfield in Palestine.

It was the darkest hour for an isolated Great Britain. After the fall of France and the British evacuation of Dunkirk in May–June 1940, military action shifted to the Middle East and the Balkans. In April 1941, a British Expeditionary Force, sent in a vain attempt to defend Greece, had been driven back to the sea. General Erwin Rommel's Afrika Korps had pushed Commander in Chief Middle East Archibald Wavell's forces back from Benghazi toward Egypt and the Suez Canal. Rommel's Panzers now besieged Tobruk, a Libyan harbor crucial to the British supply route, held by the Australians. After the French surrender in Europe, control of Syria and Lebanon passed to the puppet Vichy regime, and French soldiers, many from North Africa, became adversaries. Syrian and Lebanese airfields hosted Axis planes, and their railroads ferried munitions and supplies as far as Mosul. Axis agents based in Damascus operated freely in Jordan, alarming Abdullah. Hitler's strategic intentions were clearly spelled out in his May 23 directive: "I have decided to push the development of operations in the Middle East through the medium of going to the support of Iraq."[45]

In Iraq, King Faisal had been succeeded by his son Ghazi, who died in an automobile accident in 1939, leaving a shaky monarchy in the custody of a pro-British regent, Abdullilah (Abd al-Ilah, Abdel Illah), a nephew of Emir Abdullah and uncle of Faisal II. Tipped off about the impending colonels' coup, the pajama-clad Abdullilah was smuggled out of Baghdad on March 31 in the back seat of the American envoy's car to the RAF base at Habbaniya, then airlifted to Basra, where he boarded a British gunboat, HMS *Cockchafer*. He would await events in the relative safety of Amman with Iraq's pro-British former Prime Minister, Nuri al-Said, and the six-year-old Faisal.

On April 19, invoking British rights under a 1930 treaty—which granted Iraq formal sovereignty but left Britain with the right to military bases and access to Iraq's "railways, rivers, ports, aerodromes and means of communication"—a joint British and Indian division dispatched by General Claude Auchinleck, Commander in Chief, India, landed at Basra to establish a base and safeguard Persian oil.[46] In Baghdad, Rashid Ali repudiated the treaty after a second brigade of Indian troops landed at Basra, and on April 30, residents of the RAF base at Habbaniya awoke to find that the Iraqi Army, buoyed by recent German victories in North Africa and the Balkans and anticipating Axis air support, occupied the hills surrounding the base. Habbaniya's cantonment housed nine thousand civilians as well as twenty-two hundred soldiers and airmen within its seven-mile perimeter. In Baghdad, a cordon of Iraqi police encircled the British Embassy, by then overflowing with expatriate civilians and diplomats, among them the newly arrived Ambassador, the old Iraqi hand Sir Kinahan Cornwallis, and the travel writer Freya Stark.

The pro-Nazi Grand Mufti, who had fled Palestine and had been forced out of Lebanon, now found asylum in Baghdad. Voted funds by the Iraqi Parliament and with the backing of the Italian Legation, the mufti was the font of anti-British as well as anti-Zionist intrigue.[47] (Freya Stark, encountering him in Baghdad, described him as a "young-looking though white-haired, handsome man, wearing his turban like a halo, his eyes light blue and shining and a sort of radiance as of a just-fallen Lucifer about him.")[48] The propaganda war quickened when Germany's chief representative and zealous propagandist, Fritz Grobba, acquired a newspaper, il-Alem il Arabi, which published an Arabic translation of Mein Kampf in installments. Radio Berlin broadcast "evidence" that the British had poisoned Faisal I and then killed his son Ghazi.[49]

It was a precarious situation for the British. If Iraq were lost, Iran and Afghanistan might side with the Axis, and Britain could face a revolt in India; moreover, a vital air link between Egypt and India would be cut, and British oil supplies threatened. Both Wavell and Ambassador Cornwallis urged negotiating with Rashid Ali. Cornwallis even suggested de facto recognition of Iraq's new government, fearing that forceful action would be seen as an attack on Iraq's independence "and it is quite likely that he [Rashid Ali] could rouse such a fanatical and unreasoning people against us."[50] Wavell, faced with the deteriorating situation in North Africa, reminded Churchill of his warnings against involvement in Iraq, vowing "that no assistance could be given to Iraq from Palestine in present circumstances ... My forces are stretched to the limit everywhere, and I simply cannot afford to risk part of them on what cannot produce an effect."[51] Unpersuaded, Churchill rejoined, "It is essential to do all in our power to save Habbaniya and to control the pipeline to the Mediterranean."[52] A pessimistic Wavell still insisted that even if his overtaxed forces succeeded in relieving the base, they were not capable of entering Baghdad or holding Iraq.[53] In Wavell's view, an intervention would likely provoke an Arab uprising with terrible military consequences: "It would have repercussions in Palestine, Aden, Yemen, Egypt and Syria which might absorb [a] very large proportion of my force in maintaining internal order."[54]

Churchill, backed by the Indian government and Commander in Chief Auchinleck, prevailed. Wavell agreed to move one battalion from Palestine. Glubb was summoned to Jerusalem to meet the commanding officer in Palestine and Jordan, General Sir Henry Wilson, known as "Jumbo,"newly arrived from the catastrophic defeat in Greece. The Legion now numbered around sixteen hundred men and with British logistical support was the premier Arab fighting force. When the plans for "Habforce," the column that was to relieve Habbaniya, were discussed, Wilson asked Glubb, "Will the Arab Legion fight?" Glubb assured him, "The Arab Legion will fight anybody."[55] By contrast, the British-officered and British-paid Transjordan Frontier Force would mutiny; one squadron refused to cross the border and seven noncommissioned officers plotted to seize arms and fight the British, claiming "that there is no quarrel with the Iraqis and that the British made others fight for them."[56]

Habforce, some 6,000 troops, which included the now mechanized Household Cavalry, a battalion of the Essex Regiment, a battery of field artillery, and a company of trucks with supplies, assembled at H4, Iraq Petroleum's oil depot in the Jordanian desert, for what was believed locally to be a doomed operation: an advance on Baghdad to oust Rashid Ali. Three hundred and fifty men of the Arab Legion Mechanized Regiment, packed into open Ford trucks, their roofs fitted with World War I–issue Lewis guns, and into four home-made armored cars, drove along with the Habforce.

"Glubb's girls"—their long black ringlets and flowing robes prompted the British nickname—had rifles and daggers, but no artillery or mortars. (By an anomaly of the 1930 treaty, which required that the equipment for the Iraqi armed forces be the same as what the British had, the legionnaires with their outmoded weapons faced Iraqis armed with the latest Bren machine guns.)[57] Hampered by insufficient transport, Habforce requisitioned cars, trucks, and indignant civilian drivers from Palestine. When a vehicle broke down, Kirkbride reported, it was simply pushed off the road and abandoned. According to intelligence estimates, the Legion faced four divisions, or roughly sixty thousand Iraqis. One division was quartered north of the capital to defend the oil fields around Kirkuk; another formed a perimeter around the British Basra brigades; the last two guarded the Habbaniya airfield and Baghdad.[58]

Because of his mastery of Iraqi tribal politics, Glubb was to promote a revolt within Iraq with the Legion serving as his escort. He had long advocated an irregular force—small, highly motivated, and trained—that could be rapidly deployed for guerrilla operations; now he had the opportunity to prove his point. But not before Glubb had overcome the prejudices of the brigadier. "This man thinks he's the King of Saudi Arabia," J. J. ("Joe") Kingstone muttered to his intelligence officer and a Tory MP, Captain Somerset de Chair. "I am going to get him out of the way as soon as we leave here. The trouble is that I don't know whether he is senior to me or not."[59] When Glubb assured Kingstone that he wasn't even in the British Army but was a civilian, the two were able to collaborate closely (although Glubb suspected that the reason his legionnaires were sent ahead to reconnoiter was simply to get them out of the way).

The Arab legionnaires crossed the Iraqi border and reached the massive stone fort of Rutbah on May 5. Finding the fort too heavily defended, they withdrew just as an Iraqi mechanized force materialized. The Iraqis relieved the garrison, but the RAF successfully night-bombed the fort, impelling the Iraqis to abandon it, and Habforce occupied Rutbah on May 11. When the main British force arrived the next evening, it was agreed that one hundred legionnaires would be left behind as a garrison while the remaining 250 men would accompany a flying column called "Kingcol," after its commander. Together they would drive ahead to relieve Habbaniya.

On the morning of May 13, with the Arab Legion leading the way, the column left Rutbah for Habbaniya. But when the Legionnaires arrived within sight of Habbaniya Lake, no sign of the Kingcol could be found. Glubb found to his dismay that the army was mired in sand, because, as he feared, its officers had the "fatal inclination" to rely too literally on their compasses. It was left to the Arab legionnaires, some of them native Iraqis, to rescue the column. "The desert was their native heath," wrote de Chair of them in *The Golden Carpet*, "and they roamed about it, running in circles around us like destroyers guiding a convoy of big ships; often disappearing over our hard horizons, only to reappear unexpectedly from some other direction."[60] Glubb's men guided the troops through to Habbaniya only to find that the siege had already been lifted on May 6, when the Iraqi Army, panicked by artillery and RAF bombs and lacking the requested Axis air support, retired to Fallujah.

Although the Legion had sustained only two casualties (when its fighters were machine-gunned by four German Messerschmitts), reports reached British and American newspapers in mid-May that the man who had been called the "second Lawrence of Arabia" had been killed in action.[61] Later reports stated that he was wounded in clashes with the Iraqis. To Glubb's amusement, the reports turned out to be disinformation attributed to Rashid Ali.

While the main force remained at Habbaniya, the Arab Legion was deployed north of Baghdad along the route between the Tigris and Euphrates, as far north as Samara and as far south as Kadhimain, today a suburb of Baghdad. Glubb's men captured the railway station at Meshahida and cut the Baghdad-Mosul railway and telephone lines to prevent reinforcements and weapons from reaching the capital. The final advance on Baghdad began on May 27, with the Legion descending from the north and two British columns from the west and south. A day later, legionnaires captured the rebel governor of Baghdad, but lacking instructions, put him in a boat and floated him down the Tigris. On May 30, the mayor and rebel officers approached the British Embassy to request a truce. Fearing that the capital would be encircled, Rashid Ali and the German and Italian envoys, together with the Grand Mufti, fled to Iran. An armistice, drafted in part by Glubb, was signed. Clause 2 allowed that "the Iraq Army will be permitted to retain all its arms, equipment and munitions."[62]

When word reached Amman that the British had taken Baghdad, the Regent and Nuri al-Said, Iraq's perennial pro-British Prime Minister, returned. On June 1, as the triumphant Legion readied itself to decamp for Transjordan, Jews were celebrating the festival of Shavout. A mob attacked a group of them crossing Baghdad's Al Khurr Bridge. As in Damascus in 1918 and Baghdad in 2003, occupation troops failed to secure the city. Wavell, still in command, worried that an occupation army would seem to infringe on Iraqi independence. His officers feared fighting in narrow streets. Consequently the British remained on the right bank of the Tigris—where the British Embassy was located. In his account of the Iraqi campaign, *The Golden Carpet*, Habforce's Somerset de Chair claims that the instructions to remain outside Baghdad came from the Foreign Office: "From the hour of the Cease Fire their word had prevailed. Having fought our way, step by step, to the threshold of the city, we must now cool our heels outside. It would apparently be lowering to the dignity of our ally, the Regent, if he were seen to be supported on arrival by British bayonets."[63] Absent any government in Baghdad, rioters, many drawn from the Iraqi army and police, looted Jewish areas of the city and their shops on Rashid Street.

A curfew was finally imposed but the *farhud,* as the violence was called locally, had run unchecked for two days. The worst looting took place on the second day, when hordes of Bedouin streamed across the uncontrolled bridges from west Baghdad. Freya Stark commented that the British troops "were anxious not to enter the town unless invited, and the Iraqi forces of law were equally anxious to win their own fight unaided."[64] Thus the fiction that British troops had not defeated the Iraqi Army was maintained; the Regent would be "resuming his lawful authority which had been momentarily interrupted by a handful of conspirators now in flight."[65] Before the Regent finally imposed the curfew, some seven hundred Iraqis, most of them Jews but a sprinkling of Christians too, were killed and countless others injured.[66] One result of the *farhud* was to confirm in Iraqi minds that it had been conceived with diabolical intent by the unreliable and devious Britons; it seemed inconceivable that men with the experience of Wavell and Cornwallis would have allowed such an attack on the Jews. The *farhud* presaged the wholesale destruction after 1948 of the largest and oldest Jewish community in the Arab Middle East.

Though the Arab legionnaires met little resistance and sustained light casualties, in the judgment of their commander, "if they had not been there Baghdad would not have been taken."[67] Glubb usually claimed to eschew politics, but his views on the British-imposed monarchy in Iraq, expressed in a report he wrote to the Colonial Office, were unsparing:

> Thus, a small group of politicians were able to monopolise office for the better part of fifteen years. Every cabinet contained the same old crowd who just changed round their chairs at each change of government. In this process they all became very rich, and most of them became owners of great landed estates, at the expense of the fellaheen and the small farmer, who from being small independent landholders, became agricultural labourers of the big politicians. The latter had, meanwhile, borrowed the jargon of democracy from England and America, and they

also controlled the press and the radio. Thus, to the uninitiated observer, Iraq gave the impression of a model little democracy in action. In reality, a gang of political hacks were grinding out the same old tunes on the democratic barrel organ, while the men in the street, indifferent if not rather aggravated, by the discordant uproar, were occupied solely in making their livelihoods.[68]

Baghdad was the first major city to be captured by the British after the evacuation at Dunkirk, and Freya Stark celebrated the liberation of the embassy by buying three new hats. It seemed to Stark that the Iraq campaign "was a turning point in the Middle Eastern war."[69] Glubb reported the Legion's successes and its light casualties to a beaming Abdullah before crossing the Syrian desert to surround and occupy the fortress at the Roman ruin of Palmyra. In Damascus, the Vichyite government surrendered on July 11, and the pro-Gaullist Free French took control, once again dashing Abdullah's hopes for becoming King of Greater Syria.

In *The Golden Carpet*, de Chair called Glubb's contribution "decisive" and wrote that "the Glubb legend was more surely rooted in the hearts of the Bedouin than was Lawrence's . . . Lawrence was a name to conjure with in the Near East, but Abu Hunaik's [Father of the Little Jaw's] was accepted as of the Near East itself."[70] Britain's Iraqi victory in 1941 denied Hitler the eastern flank of the Middle East as well as access to Iraqi and Iranian oil. If the Germans "had secured their grip on Iraq," Glubb wrote, "it would only have been a question of time—and a short time at that—before they invaded Transjordan and Palestine, and advanced on Egypt from the east while Rommel attacked from the west. We had no idea then that a few weeks later Germany would attack Russia, and that streams of munitions and supplies would pour along the Haifa-Baghdad road and up the Persian Gulf to Basra to our hard-pressed [Soviet] ally."[71]

Reporting on the "Thirty Day War" to the House of Commons, in which the British deaths totaled only thirty-four (compared with the Mesopotamian campaign in World War I, which had taken three years and cost around one hundred thousand Anglo-Indian lives), Churchill made the most of the victory:

If anyone had predicted two months ago when Iraq was in revolt and our people were hanging on by their eyelids at Habbaniya and our ambassador was imprisoned in his Embassy at Baghdad, and when all Syria and Iraq began to be overrun by German tourists, and were in the hands of forces controlled indirectly but none the less powerfully by German authority—if anyone had predicted that we should already, by the middle of July [after Syria was taken] have cleaned up the whole of the Levant and have re-established our authority there for the time being, such a prophet would have been considered most imprudent.[72]

His faith in Wavell shaken, Churchill replaced him in June with Auchinleck. Rashid Ali sojourned in Saudi Arabia; the Grand Mufti continued his peregrinations, guesting in Berlin as an employee of the Foreign Ministry, where he recruited Arab volunteers for the Germans until the fall of the Third Reich. The four colonels who plotted the coup were executed when Nuri Pasha returned to power. Several hundred rebel officers were purged, among them Tulfah Khairallah who, after spending five years in prison, returned to Awja, a village near Tikrit. Khairallah became a schoolmaster and raised the ten-year-old son of his sister Sabha named Saddam Hussein. (Years later, Saddam, never sentimental, removed his uncle from his post as the "hugely corrupt" mayor of Baghdad.)[73]

As a reward for its wartime loyalty, Jordan received its formal independence in 1946, enshrined in a new treaty of alliance with the British, who received extensive military facilities and once again, squelched Abdullah's vision of a Greater Syria (if the Arabs were to be united, Winston Churchill preferred Ibn Saud). On May 24, the roads leading into Amman were jammed with camels, donkeys, and cars. Hundreds of sheep were slaughtered for the three-day festival. Rounds of celebratory gunfire competed with church bells and calls to prayer from Muslim minarets. Abdullah, dressed in Arab robes and headdress, crowned himself King Abdullah Ibn al-Hussein of the Hashemite Kingdom of Jordan.[74]

After the palace ceremony, Abdullah reviewed the Arab Legion—camel corps, cavalry, and a mechanized brigade with field artillery—to the accompaniment of pipes and brass. Standing at the King's side was Brigadier Glubb attired in summer uniform, spiked helmet, and dress sword. Later, he hosted an enormous feast for his sovereign and honored guests.

Few noticed that the hastily prepared coronation anthem heard amid the bagpipes sounded suspiciously like "God Save the King." Even as the mandate ended, the sons of the Hashemite rulers would continue to speak with Harrovian accents and receive their mandatory officer's training at the Royal Military Academy at Sandhurst. They would display a penchant for fast cars and airplanes, and would be more comfortable in Savile Row suits and military uniforms than in Arab robes. Now that Abdullah formally reigned, Sir Alec Kirkbride ruefully wrote, he "gradually assume[d] power to the extent which was hardly consistent with Transjordan's status of a constitutional monarchy."[75]

In the lopsided 1945 general election, and to widespread surprise, a Labour government led by Clement Attlee assumed power in postwar Britain. Its initial strategy for Palestine was to avoid partition by creating a binational state that would guarantee political and economic rights for a Jewish minority in an Arab country. This plan suited Abdullah, provided he was the King, but was unacceptable to the Zionists. Although committed to fulfilling the pledge, Foreign Secretary Ernest Bevin believed, along with many countrymen, including Glubb and Bell, that the Balfour Declaration was "the greatest mistake in imperial history."[76] Zionist acts of terrorism culminated in the July 22, 1946, bombing of the symbol of British rule, Jerusalem's King David Hotel. Carried out by the underground Irgun, it claimed ninety-one British, Arab, and Jewish lives. (Irgun's leader, Menachem Begin, would later boast to Golda Meir, "We created the method of the urban guerrilla.")[77]

Bevin was aware of the damaging perception of Britain's seeming to wage a war against Holocaust survivors by deploying a hundred thousand troops—one-tenth of the United Kingdom's entire armed forces—to defend an area no bigger than Wales. He also needed American loans and cooperation, but President Truman seemed to have been won over to the Zionist cause. Heading into an off-year election, he was known to be courting Jewish voters. (Worried about oil supplies, the State Department and its Director of Near Eastern and African Affairs, Loy Henderson, remained firmly in the Arab camp.) Shackled by a weakened postwar economy at home, contending with demands for Indian independence, and facing a Soviet threat in Greece and Turkey, Bevin yielded to Zionist and American pressure and referred the problem to the United Nations.

For his part, Abdullah sought to expand the size of his kingdom by annexing parts of Palestine adjacent to Jordan. The Zionists preferred an enlarged but friendly neighbor to an independent Arab Palestine with a hostile leader—perhaps even the Grand Mufti—at its head. Abdullah, backed by Glubb and Kirkbride, shared his views unofficially with the Jewish Agency, the body that had been conducting back-channel negotiations with Abdullah since the 1930s.[78]

On November 29, 1947, with the United States and USSR in uncommon agreement, the UN General Assembly voted to partition Palestine into Arab and Jewish sectors, with a greater Jerusalem area to be under international control. Among the thirteen countries that rejected the resolution were Egypt, Iraq, Lebanon, Saudi Arabia, Syria, and Yemen. The vote was denounced by both Arab and Irgun hardliners, each of whom opposed any compromise. In what would become an unhappy precedent, the UN failed to provide an international force to implement its resolution. For their part, the British failed to effect an orderly transfer of power. Instead they precipitately withdrew their troops from Palestine and left the Arabs and Jews to fight it out.

Immediately after the adoption of the UN resolution, a civil war broke out, escalating in the final months of the mandate. In December, the Grand Mufti, having returned from Germany to the Middle East, sent a commando brigade—the harbinger of the Arab Liberation Army—into Palestine with orders to seize control of the Jerusalem–Tel Aviv road, through which the Arabs hoped to invade Jewish territory. Massacres followed as Jewish convoys were attacked, but the plan failed, and the Zionists in turn seized a sizable chunk of Arab territory and were poised to seize the western sector of Jerusalem. Meanwhile, Menachem Begin's Irgun and the Lehi, led by Yitzhak Shamir and dubbed the "Stern Gang" by the British, launched a brutal campaign that included the hanging of kidnapped British soldiers and the massacre, on April 9–10, of some 245 Palestinians, mostly old men, women, and children, in the village of Deir Yassin.

In February 1948, a high-level Jordanian delegation met in London with Foreign Secretary Bevin to clarify treaty arrangements with Britain. Glubb, by now an advocate of partition, accompanied the delegation as its military adviser. Jordanian Prime Minister Tawfiq Abdul al-Huda requested a special meeting at the Foreign Office with the Foreign Secretary on February 7 at 11:30 a.m. from which even Jordan's Foreign Minister was excluded. With Glubb acting as an interpreter, Bevin approved the Zionist-Jordanian plan for the Legion to take over the West Bank to maintain law and order. In

Glubb's account, Bevin remarked, "It seems the obvious thing to do but do not go and invade the areas allotted to the Jews."[79]

On May 13, Secretary Azzam Pasha of the Arab League (an organization of Arab states formed in 1945) arrived in Amman to inform the Jordanians that it had decided to fight and that the Egyptians would invade Palestine, nullifying Abdullah's putative partition agreement with the Jewish state. That evening, in accordance with his orders, Glubb withdrew his soldiers from Jerusalem, provoking later Arab charges that he left the city "at the mercy of the Zionist gangs" and that "the Arab Legion was a British division stationed in the heart of the Arab world."[80] At midnight on May 14–15, King Abdullah drew his revolver and fired a "symbolic shot" into the air as a long column of legionnaires crossed the Allenby Bridge to occupy Palestine's West Bank. That same day, the British departed, and in Tel Aviv a provisional government led by David Ben-Gurion proclaimed Israel's statehood. Before the day ended, President Harry Truman extended de facto recognition to the new state, and within hours the Soviet Union followed suit. Five Arab armies now invaded newborn Israel, Egypt through Gaza, and the Iraqis through Judaea and Samaria (although, like the Jordanians, they scrupulously avoided crossing areas designated as Israeli by the UN). Token units of Syrians entered the Galilee (and the Lebanese moved their troops to their border). Only when it became clear that the Israelis were intent on occupying Jerusalem in violation of the UN's call for its international control did Glubb, on Abdullah's repeated orders and after falling on his knees to pray, reluctantly lead three hundred men into the Old City.

After a month of fierce fighting against the Israel Defense Forces, successor to the underground Haganah, the Egyptians seized the Negev and the Iraqis came within fifteen miles of Haifa and occupied a large part of the Galilee. After heavy alley-to-alley fighting, the Arab Legion captured East Jerusalem. Glubb now moved three regiments to Latrun to intercept the Tel Aviv–Jerusalem road, but he was scrupulous about not engaging the Israel Defense Forces in areas designated by the resolution. (For their part, the Israelis were less scrupulous about launching offensives into areas designated as Arab by the UN.) During the fighting, the British and Americans respected an international arms embargo on the area while Czechoslovakia airlifted weapons and munitions to the Israelis. It became increasingly clear that the outnumbered, disorganized, dispirited, and ill-equipped Arab armies were no match for the disciplined and motivated Israelis.

After months of intermittent fighting, in which the Legion proved that it was the most effective Arab army, the UN, in early 1949, brokered an armistice that enlarged Jordan, Egypt, and Israel, divided Jerusalem, and left more than seven hundred thousand Palestinians homeless. The Iraqis withdrew and the Jordanians faced the Israelis alone along a three-hundred-mile frontier. Given their opponent's overwhelming superiority, the Jordanians were forced to yield to Israeli demands for a narrow strip of land along the Mediterranean, opening Glubb and Abdullah to further criticism. Palestinians fled the cities of Jaffa and Haifa and more than five hundred of their villages were destroyed or ethnically purged, fueling an unyielding Arab outrage. Palestinians refer to their eviction from theses ancestral homes as al-Nakba (the Disaster).

Glubb was well aware he was caught between two masters, the Colonial Office and Abdullah. His pragmatism had served him well during the mandate, but now he became a lightning rod for anti-British anger. During the succeeding few years, he managed to preserve a fragile truce, battling both Israeli raiders and Arab infiltrators, but Abdullah failed to heed his warnings about incorporating the Palestinians of the West Bank into Jordan. Palestinian refugees now comprised 60 percent of Abdullah's subjects, as Glubb gloomily wrote a decade later: "[The] union of Trans-Jordan with Arab Palestine introduced into the country a new population—a population which had suffered an immense injustice as a result of Western policy. Gradually the Trans-Jordanians were partially submerged, and the rock of Jordan with its wise moderation and its broadminded comprehension of East and West, disintegrated in the flood of hate."[81]

In his final years, King Abdullah was a disappointed if not a broken ruler. He had failed to become King of Greater Syria or even Greater Palestine. He had not reconquered his father's patrimony, the Hejaz; his hopes of uniting Jordan with Iraq after Faisal's death were unfulfilled; and he was not able to broker a durable peace with Israel. Mistrusted by the Jews, he was hated by most Arabs: Palestinians led the list, but the Saudis, Egyptians, Syrians, and Lebanese were also his enemies. On July 21, 1951, the King left Amman to attend Friday prayers at Al-Aqsa Mosque on the Haram al-Sharif, which encloses the Dome of the Rock in Jerusalem. It was here that Muslims believed the prophet Mohammed ascended to Paradise, making this their third holiest site after Mecca and Medina. Abdullah's grandson Hussein accompanied him. Kirkbride begged the King to avoid Jerusalem but he refused, citing an old Arab proverb: "Until my day comes nobody can harm me: when the day comes nobody can guard me."[82] In Amman, the atmosphere was tense. Former Lebanese Prime Minister Riyad al-Sulh had been assassinated three days earlier by Syrian nationalists while he was en route from the Jordanian palace to the airport. Two days earlier Abdullah received an anonymous letter vowing that both he and Glubb would be murdered. Hearing of a possible infiltrator across Israel's nearby border, Glubb dispatched several hundred legionnaires to Jerusalem. On Friday, the Royal Hashemite Regiment cleared Abdullah's path from the hilltop grave of his father, Hussein, to the Great Mosque.

Just before noon, as the King's bodyguards stepped back to allow an old sheik at the mosque to kiss Abdullah's hand, an assassin leapt from behind its massive entry door. Abid Ukah, a twenty-one-year-old Palestinian tailor's apprentice with familial connections to the King's longtime rival, the Grand Mufti, shot Abdullah behind his right ear at close range. As the King's turban rolled across the marble floor, another bullet ricocheted off a medal on Prince Hussein's chest. Felled by a member of the guard, the assassin along with Abdullah died instantly. The Arab legionnaires, absent Glubb, panicked and fired indiscriminately. Twenty persons were killed, and as many as one hundred wounded.[83] The assassination, it transpired, had been plotted from Cairo by Abdullah al-Tall, an ex-legionnaire and former military governor of Jerusalem who had defected to Egypt after an abortive coup, and by his principal accomplice, a distant cousin of the Grand Mufti, Dr. Musa al-Husayni. A special court tried ten men: four were acquitted, and four were hastily hanged. Abdullah al-Tall and Musa al-Husayni were sentenced in absentia but could not be extradited from Egypt.[84]

"[T]he Arabs have lost a great champion," Winston Churchill remarked in tribute, "the Jews have lost a friend and one who might have reconciled difficulties, and . . . we have lost a faithful comrade and ally."[85] Abdullah's successor was his mentally ill son, the Emir Talal, who reigned just a year before abdicating. His grandson Hussein, only sixteen and still at Harrow, succeeded. Neither Kirkbride nor Glubb would enjoy with Hussein the close relations they had had with Abdullah. "The light went out of Kirk's life when the king died," Glubb reported, but his own "golden years" had also ended.[86]

⌘

In the 1950s, an expanded Arab Legion was reborn as the Jordanian Arab Army, numbering around twenty thousand men. By favoring the Bedouin over the educated and politicized city dwellers, the *hadari*, Glubb had hoped to immunize the Jordanian army from the governmental meddling and nepotism that had been the ruin of the Syrian and Iraqi armed forces. Now many new recruits were Palestinians who felt no particular loyalty to the King. The number of British officers was increased, despite the protests of Glubb. The British Treasury footed the bill in exchange for retaining airbases.

Glubb, as described by a British officer with the Arab Legion, was the consummate chameleon: "You never knew what was going on with Glubb . . . His mind had begun to work like an Arab's. He was all subtleties . . . He dealt as an Arab with the King's palace, as a beduin with the tribes, as a British officer with London. No one except Glubb knew everything that was going on."[87] Arabs suspected that in 1948 he had held the Legion back, and now they accused him of failing to adequately respond to Israeli raids on Jordanian frontier villages. In April 1948, a Syrian had placed a bomb outside his house, injuring his wife, Rosemary; hence the Pasha took to driving through Amman with a convoy of jeeps. Jews believed he was preparing a march on Tel Aviv; the Irgun threatened him with death.

Journalists found Glubb Pasha good copy, and his willingness to conduct briefings and give candid interviews very likely contributed to his downfall. He was touted by the press as "the uncrowned King of Jordan" and "the modern Lawrence," undoubtedly rankling the young monarch.[88] The army had become Jordan's principal industry, and King Hussein's own military accomplishments—an accelerated course at Sandhurst—were slight compared to Glubb's. An Israeli joke circulating at the time claimed that the first sounds out of baby Princess Alia's mouth were "Glubb, Glubb." In Hussein's own view, "so long as Glubb remained in command in Jordan, so long would every Jordanian Government consult him or the British Embassy before their own sovereign, when faced with some important political decision."[89]

Abdullah had provided Jordanians with an illusionary stability. Three years after his assassination, Glubb feared that Jordan would become "just one more unstable, passionate, blood-stained Arab country."[90] Hussein and Glubb disagreed about defending the West Bank: Glubb favored a military withdrawal until Britain could intervene in accordance with its treaty obligations; Hussein wouldn't hear of it. Glubb presented Hussein with a list of army officers, purportedly "subversives" who were unreliable and should be dismissed; Hussein refused. For his part, Hussein reputedly regarded Glubb as patronizing, old, and out of touch, and he was disappointed as well in the Pasha's inability to attract more British military equipment. In 1955, in an attempt to bolster its waning influence in the Middle East, Britain urged Jordan to join Turkey, Iraq, Pakistan, and Iran in the Baghdad Pact (also known as CENTO, the Central Treaty Organization), commonly perceived as an anti-Soviet, anti-Egyptian alliance. Abetted by the Saudis, who liberally sprinkled bribes among influential Jordanians, President Gamal Abdel Nasser of Egypt waged a campaign against the pact, accusing Iraq's Nuri al-Said of selling out to "imperialism and Zionism." Jordan and Syria declined to join.

On March 1, 1956, when Nasserism was at its peak and Radio Cairo regularly beamed attacks on Glubb, who was even accused of heading a British plot to control Jordan's armed forces, Hussein bowed to nationalist pressure and dismissed Glubb, along with several senior British and Jordanian officers, and seemed to be casting his lot with Nasser. As if to spite Glubb, the Legion's photogenic uniforms were changed. Swirling robes gave way to khaki drab. Checkered keffiyehs were replaced by field caps and berets. Horses and camels gave way to tanks and armored cars.

Fearing division in his army and a possible coup by Glubb's Bedouin supporters, Hussein gave him only a few hours to leave the country. With his family, one suitcase, and a hastily signed portrait of the King, Glubb rushed to the airport in the palace car. A special plane took him to Cyprus. Although deeply offended by the manner of his dismissal, Glubb behaved like the proverbial good soldier. In a brief statement to the press on his arrival in England, Glubb stressed the close ties that bound Jordan and Britain, declaring that the last thing he wanted was to cause any weakening of that friendship. "I'm neither shocked, dazed nor angry. I have spent more than thirty years of my life in the service of three generations of the Hashemite royal family. I have always been treated with the greatest kindness by the royal family and I've no complaints to make. I've had the honor to serve for twenty-six years as an officer in the Arab Legion. I have no hesitation in saying that it's a splendid little army. With all my heart I wish it every success in the future."[91]

Hearing the news, thousands of Palestinians danced in the streets. In

Amman, Britain's Ambassador Charles Duke accused Hussein of dismissing Glubb like a "pilfering house servant."[92] The rude treatment of Glubb caused a furor in Britain, where Prime Minister Anthony Eden responded with a flurry of telegrams to Amman, advising Hussein that "he could not fore-tell its final consequences upon the relations between our two countries." Suspecting Nasser's hand in the matter, Eden hoped that Jordan would reconsider, but basking in Arab acclaim, Hussein refused. Glubb urged cau-tion, and Kirkbride, now retired, was called to advise the British Cabinet. He counseled restraint, fearing that the young monarch might be toppled.

On July 26, 1956, during a dinner party at 10 Downing Street in honor of Iraq's King Faisal II and Prime Minister Nuri al-Said, Eden was informed that Nasser had nationalized the Suez Canal. Nuri, furious that the Iraqis had not been consulted by Nasser, expressed the hope that Britain would retaliate swiftly.[93] Smarting from successive blows from a man he consid-ered an upstart dictator, Eden joined with France in plotting to oust Nasser, with the subsequent help of the Israelis. The scheme failed, marking the end of Britain and France's hegemony in the Middle East.

When anti-Hashemite, pro-Nasser violence erupted in Mosul, Najaf, Kut, and Baghdad, Nuri instituted martial law, suspended Parliament, and threw hundreds of his opponents into jail. A bloody climax occurred on July 14, 1958, when troops loyal to Brigadier Abd al-Karim Qassem, armed with bazookas and antitank guns, surrounded the villa that served as the royal palace, and set fire to it. The royal family fled to the basement. Ordered out at gunpoint, the Regent, Faisal II, and other members of the family were machine-gunned to death. Fourteen-time Prime Minister Nuri Pasha crept out of his house disguised as a woman. Someone in the mob spotted his pajamas under his dress. He was stripped, killed, castrated, and dismem-bered, his legless trunk dragged through the streets behind a truck. Accord-ing to Baghdad reports, all members of Nuri's family, including his Egyptian wife and their two children, were also killed.

James Morris records the scene when the rabble converged on the once omnipotent British Embassy beside the river: "They pushed past its guards, trampled on its beloved lawns, looted its offices, killed the Comptroller of its lordly household, and destroyed the statue of General Maude, whose armies had driven the Turks from Baghdad forty odd years before. The British Ambassador took a room in a nearby hotel, and as his secretary arranged matters at the reception desk, a tradition petered limply out."[94]

In 1967, the Arabs suffered their own debacle when Israel defeated a collective attack by its Arab neighbors. Israel urged King Hussein to stay out of what became the June or Six-Day War. Instead the Jordanian army joined with the Syrian and Saudi Arabian armies under an overall Egyptian command; within thirty-six hours, Hussein lost everything that Glubb had won in 1948. The Israelis drove the Jordanians from East Jerusalem and the West Bank. Abdullah and his father, Hussein, had been evicted from the Hejaz; Faisal I had lost Syria and his grandson, Iraq. Now King Hussein had lost the West Bank of the Jordan.

Glubb arrived in Britain, aged fifty-nine, with only £5. Neither Jordan nor Britain awarded him a general's pension, although he received a knighthood from the Queen. He now had to provide for Rosemary and their four children. He became a devout, born-again Christian and turned to his pen and to lecturing, often in the United States, to support his family.[95] Glubb wrote twenty-two books, ranging from autobiographical to historical. His account of his Iraqi years, *War in the Desert* (1960), remains a military classic. The Pasha corresponded with his old colleague Jack Philby, who now gloated over Britain's foreign policy failures. "The line that divides me from you and your ilk," Philby wrote, "is your conviction that the best interests of these Arab countries can only be served in some form of subordination to British imperial policy sweetened by lavish British financial aid, whereas I am equally convinced that only in unity *inter se* can the Arab ever realize, their destiny . . . Perhaps you will not agree with me that your cause is lost beyond recall."[96]

On March 17, 1986, John Bagot Glubb died in his sleep, a month before his eighty-ninth birthday. At a memorial service in Westminster Abbey, King Hussein now saw virtues in the soldier he had peremptorily dismissed: "[H]e belonged to a unique generation of outstanding men who dedicated their entire lives to the establishment of a genuine understanding, deep friendship and mutual respect between the United Kingdom and the Hashemite Kingdom of Jordan . . . He was a down-to earth soldier, with a heart, a simple style of life and impeccable integrity, who performed quietly and unassumingly the duties entrusted to him by his second country, Jordan, at a crucial moment in its history and development."[97]

Glubb would surely have been pleased, taking sly note that Jordan's textbooks perpetuate the national myth that the Hashemites were not members of the Ottoman ruling elite but indigenous Bedouin sheiks, father figures for their country, their legitimacy garnered from their direct descent from the Prophet and their role in the Arab Revolt. Britain's role in their dynasty's ascension is all but forgotten. The Pasha's immense role in building and commanding the army, which in the 1948 war secured East Jerusalem and the West Bank, goes unacknowledged.[98] Glubb's memory persists among his ancient Bedouin soldiers, but among the politicians of Amman he is remembered only for his ouster. Glubb's enduring legacy was the relative stability of Jordan in the Islamic Middle East. He took control after Abdullah's assassination: there was no rioting or looting in Amman. Unlike their counterparts in most of the region—Syria, Egypt, Iraq—the Jordanian armed forces have proved a force for continuity especially during succession crises.

In 1999, while Hussein endured chemotherapy and bone marrow transplantation for lymphoma at the Mayo Clinic, his brother and Crown Prince designate, Hassan, prepared to assume the crown. It was even rumored that Hassan's Pakistani-born wife, Princess Sarvath, was redecorating the royal palace. An angry Hussein wrote a letter to his brother accusing him of disloyalty. He returned to Jordan to die but not before dismissing Hassan and designating a new successor, Abdullah II, his eldest son by an English wife. (His mother was the daughter of an English officer serving in the Jordanian army.)

The skirls of the funereal bagpipes had hardly died when Abdullah II, a major general, disregarded the official forty-day mourning period and sacked four senior generals to assert his control over the army, in which there appeared to be lingering support for Prince Hassan. King Hussein's dying wish had been that the next in line would be Prince Hamzah, his son by his American wife, Queen Noor. But in November 2004, Abdullah II suddenly stripped his stepbrother of the title. His own son Hussein by his Palestinian wife, Queen Rania, became Crown Prince. Nevertheless, of all the Middle Eastern kingdoms created or indirectly ruled by the British, only one dynasty remains enthroned nearly a century later. A country lacking resources or geographic advantage still stands (as of 2007) while its more-favored Arab neighbors have succumbed to either tyranny or chaos.

NINE

A Very British Coup

Brigadier-General Sir Percy Molesworth Sykes (1867–1945),
CMG, CIE, KCIE, CB

⊞

Three Percys have, for better or for worse,
Filled from Great Britain's coffers Persia's purse.
The first who propped her 'gainst external shocks
With British gold was Percy Cox.
Next, squandering gold as floods that burst their dykes
On Southern Persian Rifles—Percy Sykes.
Shrewd Cox! Brave Sykes! Their efforts still were vain,
Yet may the third redeem the other twain,
And luck attend Sir Percy of Loraine.
PERCII PERSORUM

—Written by Andrew Barstow on
Loraine's appointment as
Minister to Persia in 1921

Tehran, April 25, 1926. The Persian capital is bathed in sun and carpets—Kermans, Kashans, Kashmars—clustered edge to edge, covering balconies and windows. Red, white, and green bunting stretches across the streets, and hundreds of pictures of the new monarch, a former Persian Cossack colonel, hang from scaffolding. In his glass carriage drawn by six horses, Reza Khan Pahlavi makes his way through a triumphal arch and lines of soldiers to his coronation. Passing a low gray building, the Imperial Bank of Persia, he reaches the Gulistan Palace, its exterior covered in colored tiles. Waiting for him, in the arched and vaulted hall hung with banners that today serves as the throne room, is an Armenian priest smothered in purple velvet; a Turcoman wearing a tunic of rose-red silk, his head wrapped in a great lambs-wool busby; an assortment of Kurds in fringed silk turbans; Bakhtiari tribesmen sporting black felt hats; and bearded Shiite mullahs in long robes and gigantic turbans. Huddled in one corner, dimly lit by candles, are the relatives of Persia's recently deposed Qajar ruler. Standing on the right is the tall black-bearded Emir of Bokhara. The Bolsheviks have recently driven him from his Central Asian home. Another attendee is the elderly but stately black-clad Sheik of Mohammerah in Arab keffiyeh, a friend of the British whose tribal independence had been usurped by Reza.

He is now in exile in Tehran, remote from his imposing palace at Failiya surrounded by palm groves on the banks of the Karun River.

Lacking experience with coronations—the former ruling dynasty, the Qajars, had not followed any set tradition—the Persians had appealed for advice to Lady Loraine, the wife of the head of the British Legation,* Sir Percy Loraine, and Vita Sackville-West, wedded to Harold Nicolson, the newly appointed Counsellor. The two ladies pored over the descriptions of the Westminster Abbey coronation of George V, noting the symbols of power—thrones, swords, stones, crowns, rings, orbs, scepters—that they intended to emulate in the Persian ceremony. They scoured the jumble shops that were the Qajar jewel vaults; servants scurried about laying the treasures on a table covered in green baize. As Vita Sackville-West recalled:

> The linen bags vomited emeralds and pearls; the green baize vanished, the table became a sea of precious stones. The leather cases opened, displaying jewelled scimitars, daggers mounted with rubies, buckles carved from a single emerald, ropes of enormous pearls. Then from the inner room came the file of servants again, carrying uniforms sewn with diamonds; a cap with a tall aigrette, secured by a diamond larger than the Koh-i-Nur [Mountain of Light]; two crowns like great hieratic tiaras, barbaric diadems, composed of pearl of the finest orient . . . We plunged our hands up to the wrist in the heaps of uncut emeralds, and let the pearls run through our fingers. We forgot the Persia of to-day; we were swept back to Akbar and the spoils of India.[1]

Soon orders went out to shops throughout Europe. Vita was given authority to order china, glass, cutlery, and stationery from London's royal purveyors. She commissioned red liveries for the palace, modeled on those worn by the British Legation servants. The Foreign Office considered, but rejected, the idea of awarding Reza Shah a British decoration. Not wanting to begin his reign beholden to the British, he was deemed likely to decline it.[2] À propos of the coronation, Vita Sackville-West writes to Gertrude Bell "that she and Louise Loraine have been busy painting the throne room pink!"[3]

---

* The head of the British Legation was a Minister. During World War II, when the legation became an embassy, the Minister's rank was raised to Ambassador.

At half past two, the diplomats, in frock coats and gold lace, and military advisers take their places on a raised dais. The assembly waits silently for an hour; in deference to the mullahs, no music is played. At half past three, the shy six-year-old Crown Prince of Persia, Mohammed Reza, dressed as a miniature version of his father in military uniform and shiny patent leather boots, marches alone down the length of the room, salutes, and takes his place on the lowest step of a replica of the Peacock Throne—the original, brought as booty from the Mughals, has been destroyed, but the replacement is equally impressive. It is covered in gold, enamel and precious stones; tassels of rough emeralds hang from its arms. The generals and ministers, wearing light blue uniforms and cashmere robes of honor, enter the hall, then the Shah. The tallest person in the room, he is wearing a military uniform with newly minted medals, decorations, and a sash topped with a paisley-patterned blue velvet cloak encrusted with pearls. His French military cap is festooned with an aigrette held by a jewel known as the Ocean of Light (Daria-i-Nur), the largest unflawed diamond in the world. As he makes his way toward the throne, members of the foreign delegations bow and curtsey, the mullahs move forward, and the Crown Prince shyly hides under a corner of his father's cloak. The Minister of Court, Abdul Hosein Teimurtash, who has worked tirelessly to help Reza rise to power, hands the Shah the new crown, made by a local Russian jeweler, resplendent on a cushion. (Teimurtash will be rewarded for his loyalty by being murdered in his prison cell seven years later. Among his alleged crimes, which included the commonplace ones of corruption and bribery, is the accusation that he plotted to overthrow his master.) It had been the Qajar custom to be crowned by the senior member of the family, but the new Shah's origins are humble and there is no suitable relative among the Pahlavis, so the Shah removes his cap and crowns himself.

"The President of the Council invested him with the jewelled sceptre, the Minister of War, kneeling buckled on the diamond-encrusted sword of Nadir Shah," wrote Loraine's visiting mother-in-law, Mrs. Stuart-Wortley, in 1946. "So, crowned and sceptred and girt with the sword of the great conqueror, the Shah in Shah read his speech from the throne in a low voice, without a gesture, his manner totally devoid of anything theatrical, as if the moment were not the supreme one of his life . . . The ceremony being concluded the Shah rose, his pearl-embroidered cloak fell back showing the wonderful jewels with which his uniform was starred. The light caught the

Daria-I-Nour, his sword-hilt flashed, and with proud head held erect, this soldierly monarch left the hall."[4] Sir Percy thankfully observed that the ceremony was "economical, not unimpressive and short."[5]

Reza Shah would be the founder and penultimate member of the Pahlavi dynasty. History has credited a British general, Sir Edmund Ironside, with placing him on the throne, although a recently discovered diary by the general's number two man, Henry Smyth, has raised doubts. On the date of the coup, Ironside was on his way to the 1921 Cairo Conference, and both Whitehall and the British Legation seemed to have been in the dark about the coup.[6] But as with everything in the conspiracy-fixated East, the truth is not as important as what generations of Iranians have believed to be true. As an American political scientist, Richard Cottam, has observed, "[N]owhere in the world is British cleverness so wildly exaggerated as in Iran, and nowhere are the British more hated for it."[7]

For most of the twentieth century—that is, before the revolution of 1979—the story of Iran was the story of two Pahlavi Shahs and their attempts, often in the face of foreign interference and domestic religious opposition, to turn Iran into a progressive modern state before its oil ran out. Foreign interference before 1953 was British and Russian; afterward the Americans joined in. The original instrument of British control was the East India Company. Chartered by Queen Elizabeth I and granted the power to issue currency and raise armies, the company was quasi-sovereign until after the Indian Mutiny of 1857–59. From its base in Calcutta, through battles and bribes, by 1807 the company had subjugated most of India, ruling directly or via princely surrogates. At that moment, the twin threats to the Raj were France and Russia, then allied, and the logistics of a joint assault on India were actually examined by Napoleon and Tsar Alexander I: fifty thousand of the Grand Armée's French troops marching overland across Persia and Afghanistan would join forces with Alexander's Cossacks transversing the Indus into India. The alarmed British dispatched diplomatic missions to Tehran and Kabul. Then the alliance shattered. In 1812, the French led by Napoleon burned Moscow; the Russian Emperor Alexander I countered by marching down the Champs-Élysées in 1814. The British watched nervously as the distance between the Russian Empire and India—two thousand miles at the beginning of the nineteenth century—shrank so that by century's end, as the Russian Empire expanded eastward at the amazing average of fifty-five square miles per day, as little as twenty miles separated the two empires in Central Asia's Pamirs. Squeezed between these expanding powers was Persia, described by George Nathaniel Curzon, onetime Viceroy of India and subsequently Foreign Secretary, as one of "the pieces on a chessboard upon which is being played out a game for the domination of the world."[8]

A new Persian dynasty emerged in 1785, the Qajars, renowned for the shameful bribes they took and the vices they allegedly practiced. Descended from Turcoman chieftains in Central Asia, the Qajars sat uneasily on the Peacock Throne. British envoys, sensing the insecurity of the eight shahs, spread flattery with a trowel when bribes or bullying failed. Over the course of a century, Britain secured a privileged role in the Persian court, winning extraordinary concessions. Adding to this complexity was a peculiar arrangement whereby the British sent two sets of emissaries. The envoy at the Qajar court in Tehran represented London and was answerable to the Foreign Office. Meanwhile, Calcutta, beginning in the 1790s, posted a Resident, representing the Government of India, at Bushire (now Büshehr), an unprepossessing city on the southern Gulf coast. Thus began a rivalry that would mar the relations between the Foreign Office and a succession of governor-generals and viceroys. The Government of India preferred a highly decentralized Persian regime, so from the outset, successive Residents, including Major Sir Percy Cox (1904–13) and Lieutenant Colonel A. T. Wilson (Acting, 1912–13), cultivated ties with nearby sheikdoms. Curzon, visiting in 1889, spotted the Union Jack "fluttering from the summit of the Residency flagstaff" and wrote that it was "no vain symbol of British ascendancy." The British Resident "is to this hour the umpire to whom all parties appeal." Having at his command an effective naval force, imposed at will, "he may . . . be entitled the Uncrowned King of the Persian Gulf."[9]

Financiers, traders, speculators and adventurers flocked to Persia, most of them from Britain and Russia. Markets opened in the hinterland, consulates blossomed, and foreign shipping began competing for Persian markets. Baron Julius de Reuter, a naturalized Briton born in Germany and founder of the British press agency bearing the same name, brought off the most spectacular coup in 1872. In one stroke, he won the right to build railways, found a bank, and collect customs for twenty years. That was not all. He was granted exclusive rights for seventy years to mine minerals, operate tramways and water works, build irrigation canals, and fell timber, plus an option to found utilities, post offices, and other enterprises. Lord Curzon called it "the most complete and extraordinary surrender of the entire industrial resources of a kingdom into foreign hands that has probably ever been dreamed of, much less accomplished, in history."[10]

As Sir Denis Wright, formally the British envoy to Tehran, explains in *The English Amongst the Persians*, the Shah's interest was not only pecuniary: "He and his Prime Minister were worried by the Russian threat to Persian independence. They believed—or hoped—that by giving the British a large economic stake in the country they would become committed to defending that independence."[11] Within Persia, however, the Russians and the clergy helped provoke an outcry against foreigners. The Shah backed down and canceled the railway concession, but with the support of the British Foreign Office, Reuter was able to retain his banking and mining rights.

Hence the birth of the Imperial Bank of Persia, which in fact gained a reputation for honesty. But popular outrage over corrupt groveling to foreigners was reinforced in 1890 when the Shah awarded a fifty-year monopoly on the production, sale, and export of tobacco to a British army officer, Major Gerald Talbot, who paid the King of Kings £25,000 and his Prime Minister £15,000 for the privilege. So unsavory was the deal that diplomats feared a massacre of Europeans as massive protests followed an unusual call by Shiite clergy for total abstention from tobacco. Faced with a gathering boycott, the Shah voided the concession and paid a half million pounds— borrowed from the British Imperial Bank—in compensation to Talbot's Imperial Tobacco Corporation.

The Russians countered with their own bank, the state-subsidized Banque d'Escompte de Perse, useful for making "loans" to senior officials. They also obtained permission to build roads in their zone. And when Shah Naser al-Din visited his northern neighbor in 1879, he was so impressed by Alexander II's Cossacks that he founded his own imperial bodyguard, the Cossack Brigade. Although paid for by the Persians, it was officered by Russians and under orders of the Russian Minister of War. The Brigade would prove useful in quelling riots, but it nevertheless failed to prevent the assassination of Shah Naser al-Din in 1896 while he was on a visit to a religious shrine. We shall hear more of the Persian Cossack Brigade.

Persia at the turn of the last century was a land in chaos, a playground of Russian and British spies. It was deemed so dangerous that, much to the annoyance of the Persians, the British Consuls maintained, in addition to their Persian guards, an escort of *sepoys* and *sowars* in the uniform of the Queen's Own Corps of Guides, the Bengal Lancers, and other regiments while the Russian Cossacks chaperoned the Russians.

Meshed, the capital of the northern province of Khorasan, was of special importance in the Great Game waged between the lion and the bear. Meshed, a great pilgrimage center, became a listening post where Russians recruited agents and monitored the border with Afghanistan. And it was from Meshed that British intelligence dispatched agents into Central Asia, the better to monitor Russia's advance toward India.

When Curzon passed through Meshed on his grand tour of Persia in 1889, he was impressed by Russia's large residence and imposing guard: "A vigorous Russian representative in Meshed is a visible symbol of the real power whose movements and intentions form the subject of conversation in every Oriental bazaar, and whose ever-swelling shadow, witnessed with a sort of paralyzed quiescence by the native peoples, looms like a thundercloud over the land."[12] Curzon was likewise dismayed by the British Consulate, a structure that afforded "the scantiest possible evidence of the rank and importance of its inmate. It is little short of discreditable that the British Consul-General should be compelled to reside in such attenuated and miserable surroundings."[13] When the Foreign Office ignored his recommendations, Curzon wrote to *The Times* demanding that the consulate should have "quarters of sufficient splendour to impress the native mind with the prestige of a great and wealthy power."[14] A suitable two-story residence was built. Anglo-Indian in style with Corinthian columns and a veranda, it adorned an eight-acre compound that included houses, offices, and stables for the Consul's twenty-four-strong Indian cavalry escort and the twenty-two Turcoman *sowars* who ferried the mail between Meshed and Herat, thence through Afghanistan to India. The Government of India provided the cash, and that it was more lavishly housed and funded—their budget was nearly ten times that of the legation in Tehran—caused some consternation and jealousy at Whitehall.[15] The Meshed consulate reported to and was staffed by India, though Meshed did copy Tehran for forwarding to the Foreign Office on their official reports to Calcutta.

In an interesting twist, the Great Game would end in a draw following the

Anglo-Russian Convention of 1907. Ironically, this unblushing specimen of imperial presumption was the product of an ostensibly anti-imperial Liberal government. The general election of 1906 had resulted in a top-heavy Liberal majority in Parliament. Sir Edward Grey, the new Foreign Minister, was determined to settle matters with St. Petersburg. The venerable Liberal, Lord Morley, now Secretary of State for India, had long argued that the Russian menace was overblown and that conciliation was preferable to confrontation. Moreover, Kaiser Wilhelm's Germany with its fleet of dreadnoughts, not Russia, had emerged as Britain's chief European rival. London now approached St. Petersburg about reaching a comprehensive agreement on Afghanistan, Tibet, and Persia—areas that had provoked a century of Anglo-Russian rivalry. The British Ambassador, Sir Arthur Nicolson (later Lord Carnock and father of the author and diplomat Harold Nicolson), initiated negotiations with Alexander Izvolsky, the Russian Foreign Minister.

On August 31, the accord was signed. Without informing, much less consulting, its leaders, the two powers divided Persia into spheres of influence: a British zone in the southeast, a Russian sphere in the north, and a southwestern neutral zone (where Bushire was located), in which the Russians and the British undertook reciprocally not to seek exclusive concessions. Though the oil fields, which were in the neutral zone, were being explored, their richness was not yet known. Russia's sphere was by far the biggest and included the capital, Tehran, plus Tabriz and Isfahan, reflecting Russia's proximate and superior influence. His Majesty's Minister in Tehran, Sir Cecil Spring-Rice, expressed the prevailing government sentiment: "If Grey can get *real* agreement with Russia, it is well worth sacrificing Persia—though I doubt whether a great country can afford to be mean even in the smallest things."[16] Lord Curzon, no longer Viceroy of India but now an opposition leader in the House of Lords, assailed the treaty, maintaining that Britain had sacrificed the efforts of a century for "nothing or next to nothing in return."[17] Spring-Rice admitted that by surrendering so much to Russia, "[w]e are regarded as having betrayed the Persian people."[18] In St. Petersburg, by contrast, the Duma resounded with cries of "Bravo" when the agreement was unveiled.

The Persians were stunned. The news that their country had been surgically partitioned coincided with its Constitutional Revolution, whose main aim was to restore Persia's independence and self-respect. Assailed by charges of corruption and misrule, the enfeebled Qajar ruler, Mozaffer al-Din Shah, had acceded after a bloodless revolt in December 1905 to the election of a National Assembly, or Majlis, the first of its kind in Persia. The assembly expeditiously convened and drafted a new constitution with fifty-one articles, which the old Shah sullenly signed before his death. Russia rallied its Persian allies to undermine the parliament, which had brashly refused a new Russian loan and whose independence might serve as an unsettling example for the Tsar's nearby Muslim subjects. In his diplomatic history of Iran, Rouhollah Ramazani, himself a native of Tehran, writes that Russia's subsequent intervention "destroyed the foundations of the Constitutional government twice in about four years."[19]

A newly enthroned and stubbornly feudal Qajar ruler, Mohammed Ali Shah, commenced hostilities in 1908 by peremptorily jailing his Prime Minister. With a loan underwritten by the Russian bank and with his crown jewels as security, the Shah hired rioters to storm the Majlis. When the assembly successfully resisted, the Russian-officered Cossack Brigade moved rapidly to dissolve parliament and to impose martial law. The Cossacks shelled the parliament building, igniting a blaze that destroyed its records and killed eight Iranians. The Russian commander proclaimed himself military governor of Tehran. In London, Sir Edward Grey did little but wring his hands. "Prior to the 1907 convention," in Ramazani's rueful summary, "Great Britain acted as midwife of the new order, but despite Grey's good intentions, British performance generally favored Russia at the expense of Iran. Grey's policy toward Iran from beginning to end was nonintervention and friendship with Russia."[20] Nevertheless, Grey complained that "Persia tried my patience more than any other subject."[21]

And then, incredibly, a popular uprising united ethnic, religious, and Westernizing factions that agreed on little else, and the insurgents overwhelmed the Cossack gendarmes, forcing the despised Shah to abdicate. His twelve-year-old son, Ahmad, was proclaimed successor, and in 1910, a Hamadani landowner, Abul Ghassem Khan Nasser ul-Molk, who had been at Balliol with Curzon, Grey, and Cecil Spring-Rice, was named as Regent. Unimaginably, all this was chronicled by a free press that had sprung up during the First Majlis. Amid this tumult, the Persian Foreign Minister instructed his embassy in Washington to seek out a "disinterested American expert as Treasurer-General" to establish for a near-bankrupt Persia an honest system for collecting taxes. The choice fell on W. Morgan Shuster, a forty-three-year-old American lawyer already deservedly known for his service as customs collector in the new Republic of Cuba. From 1901 to 1906, Shuster had also reorganized tax collecting in the Philippines, with the full support of President Taft, formerly Governor-General in Manila. Shuster agreed to serve for three years in Persia. Accompanied by a quartet of assistants, he sailed from New York in April 1911 into Persia's sea of mirrors. He immediately encountered a chill (which Shuster heartily reciprocated) on the part of Tehran's European colony and had to quickly learn how to distinguish Persian friends from unctuous enemies. Then came the report that with Russian support, the ousted Shah was plotting to reclaim his throne. The finale occurred in November 1911 when Treasurer-General Shuster's special police brushed past a Cossack guard and seized the home of the ex-Shah's absent brother for nonpayment of back taxes. With British support, Russian authorities demanded Shuster's dismissal for trespassing on their spheres of influence. When the Majlis balked, Russian troops advanced on Tehran, killing anti-Russian liberals and clergy and shelling the defiant assembly. In Meshed, the Russians bombarded the holy shrine of Imam Reza, inciting riots by Shiite Muslims. Having landed troops in Persia's south ostensibly to protect their area of influence, the British looked on idly as the Russians occupied the north. On Christmas Day, Persia's constitutional government ousted Shuster, who on returning home wrote an impassioned account of his mission, *The Strangling of Persia*, which ended on this note:

> The Persian people, fighting for a chance to live and govern themselves instead of remaining the serfs of heartless and corrupt rulers, deserved better of fate than to be forced, as now, to sink back into an even worse serfdom, or to be hunted down and murdered as "revolutionary dregs" ... [W]ith the exception of corrupt grandees and dishonest public servants, all desired that we should succeed. Russia became aware of this feeling, and unwittingly *paid us the compliment of fearing that we would succeed in our task.* [Shuster's emphasis] That she never intended to allow; the rest of the controversy was detail.[22]

Such was the initial fruit of the 1907 convention. As a former British Ambassador in Tehran, Sir Denis Wright, subsequently observed, "The Persians, who had come increasingly to look upon Britain as their protector against Russia and the champion of liberal ideas, were shocked beyond measure by this alliance with the devil."[23] The Yale scholar Firuz Kazemzadeh, in his authoritative *Russia and Britain in Persia, 1864–1914*, writes, "[I]t was in September 1907 that the modern Persian image of Britain crystallized . . . Justifiably or not, most Persians would, from then on, be prepared to believe only the worst of England."[24] The reckoning lay a decade ahead, after the Great War.

Sir Edward Grey defended the Russians while Lord Curzon denounced them. It was, in fact, George Nathaniel Curzon, Marquess of Kedleston, who kept the Persian Gulf on Britain's imperial agenda, and keeping it there became his personal *idée fixe*. As a thirty-year-old member of Parliament, he first visited Persia on horseback in 1889. Curzon documented this six-month tour in the magisterial two-volume *Persia and the Persian Question*, published in 1892 while he was serving as Under Secretary for India. In 1903, accompanied by a Gulf armada composed of the steamship *Hardinge*, four cruisers, and some smaller boats, he embarked as Viceroy of India on another grander visit. He concluded a treaty with the dazzled Sheik of Kuwait, in which the latter agreed not to surrender his territory to a third party, and he obliged the Sultan of Muscat (where his protégé Percy Cox was stationed) to cancel a lease with the French establishing a coaling station. He fired off a dispatch to London in which he claimed "the Persian Gulf even at the risk of war, should be closed to all intruders."[25] It was Curzon who had memorably warned about Russia's ultimate ambition—the domination of Asia. "It is a proud and not ignoble aim, and it is worthy of the supreme and material efforts of a vigorous nation," he observed in a 1901 minute. Yet if Russia were entitled to her aims, "still more so is Britain entitled, nay compelled, to defend that which she has won, and to resist the minor encroachments which are only part of the larger plan." Piecemeal concessions were to be shunned since each morsel "but whets the appetite for more, and inflames the passion for a pan-Asiatic dominion." It was the integrity of Persia which "must be registered as a cardinal precept of our Imperial creed."[26]

What gave Persia higher priority for the British was a pervasive new ingredient in twentieth-century diplomacy: oil. Archaeological evidence indicates that oil had been known in Mesopotamia and Persia since antiquity. In nearby Baku on the Caspian, oil literally oozed from the ground, starting Russia on its path to becoming a world oil power. In 1892, a claim that there were oil deposits in southwest Persia appeared in an article in *Les Annales des Mines* written by a French archaeologist, Jacques de Morgan, who had noticed seepages during his travels in Persia. Morgan's findings were brought to the attention of Persia's Commissioner General, who approached Sir Henry Drummond Wolff, a Conservative member of Parliament, at the Paris Exposition of 1900. Wolff in turn introduced him to an entrepreneurial buccaneer, William Knox D'Arcy, a high-living millionaire who had amassed a fortune in Australia's gold rush. When reports of Persian oil surfaced, Russia vied with Britain for the concessions, but with diplomatic assists and well-placed bribes, D'Arcy's agents prevailed. For £20,000 in cash, plus shares worth the same amount, £650 annual rent, bribes to notables, and 16 percent of net profits, "the Concessionaire" wrested a warrant for sole rights in 1901 from the Shah of Persia. Written in French, the contract was valid for sixty years and covered three-fourths (480,000 square miles) of Persia, excluding the five northern provinces, which were omitted out of deference to Russia. "Such was the contract that turned out to be one of the more significant documents of the twentieth century," writes Professor Kazemzadeh. "Its subsequent fate, the vast industrial complex to which it gave rise, the passionate hatred it evoked, the conflicts it precipitated, could not have been guessed by its signers, who, in a city remote from the centers of world power, in almost total secrecy, acted out a drama the implications of which they were only half aware."[27]

Yet this generous concession nearly bankrupted D'Arcy, who spent upwards of £220,000—a royal ransom at the time—on bringing oil to the markets. What saved him was a partnership with Burmah Oil, headquartered in Glasgow, which took over D'Arcy's concession and injected further capital, and the British technician, George Reynolds. (The tale of the discovery at Masjid-i-Suleiman is told in chapter 4.) All rights were further transferred in 1909 to Anglo-Persian Oil Company (APOC) which evolved into Anglo-Iranian Oil Company (AIOC), eventually becoming today's British Petroleum (BP). APOC negotiated directly with the Bakhtiari khans who controlled the area where oil drilling was occurring; to protect their wells, 3 percent of their profits would be deducted from Tehran's share. (The Persian government refused to recognize this 1905 agreement.)[28]

In a master stroke the Raj's Political Resident at Bushire and de facto Proconsul of the Gulf, Major Percy Cox, assisted by his Political Officer, Arnold Wilson, negotiated an agreement in 1909 with Sheik Khazal of Mohammerah (present-day Khorramshahr). His lands known as Arabistan (Khuzistan) included the Shatt al-Arab, where the Tigris, Euphrates, and Karun rivers merged. At Abadan, an offshore island 138 miles from the oil fields, APOC would construct refineries. In return for annual leases granting six hundred acres, raised to twenty-four hundred in 1918 to provide a right of way for a pipeline, the sheik was to receive a loan of £10,000 and the assurances of British goodwill and protection: "His Majesty's Government will be prepared to afford you the support necessary for obtaining a satisfactory solution in the event of encroachment by the Persian government on your jurisdiction and recognised right on your property in Persia."[29]

To the annoyance of Tehran, in all their negotiations the British treated the Arab sheik and the Bakhtiari khans as if they were sovereign. After the deal was completed in 1910, Cox steamed up the Shatt al-Arab in his official launch, the 900-ton *Lawrence*, and bestowed on the sheik the insignia of Knight Commander of the Most Eminent Order of the Indian Empire (KCIE) at an impressive durbar. The British also granted him a twelve-gun salute. In return, the sheik provided a thousand laborers from the surrounding villages, and in violation of Persian sovereignty, a protective British umbrella instantly opened over the field as a thousand more laborers were imported from India. About the negotiations, Wilson confessed to his diary, "I have spent a fortnight upon Oil Company business, mediating between Englishmen who cannot always say what they mean and Persians who do not always mean what they say. The English idea of an agreement is a document in English which will stand attack by lawyers in a Court of Justice: the Persian idea is a declaration of general intentions on both sides, with a substantial sum in cash annually or in a lump sum."[30]

In what became a chronic grievance, APOC gave Britons and Indians the best jobs, relegating Persians to menial roles. Foreigners occupied the best houses, claimed membership in the exclusive Persian Club, and sent their children to schools in segregated cantonments. There were even fountains marked "Not for Iranians," feeding the cycle of enduring resentment that was to characterize subsequent relations.

The speed with which Britain committed itself to Persian oil owed much to D'Arcy's ongoing friendship with Britain's preeminent naval "oil maniac,"

Admiral Sir John Fisher. They first met in July 1903 at Marienbad, the gracious Bohemian spa to which "Jackie" Fisher commuted for rest and recreation and to indulge his lifelong passion, dancing. Fisher's overriding concern was to convert the British Navy from coal to oil. He liked D'Arcy, and on becoming First Sea Lord a year later, Fisher found essential backing to keep the Persian operation going. Then all these elements—oiling the naval fleet, Darcy's concession, and British strategy—converged in 1911 when Winston Churchill, still a budding Liberal MP, became First Lord of the Admiralty. He was Jackie Fisher's devoted fan, and he coaxed the old admiral—who had retired by then and was twice Churchill's thirty-seven years—into heading a Royal Commission on Fuel and Engines.

Looming on Britain's ocean-going horizon was Germany's emerging dreadnought fleet. Ships burning oil were faster, could travel further, and didn't require platoons of able-bodied stokers. Armed with this intelligence, Fisher and Churchill moved a balky service forward full throttle, and conversion became a fact. But to replace coal, which Britain had in quantity, with oil, which she and her colonies lacked, required fifty thousand tons of oil per year. On June 17, 1914, Churchill put before Parliament a bold matching proposal: for £2.2 million, the British Government could acquire 51 percent of the shares and two seats on the all-British board of D'Arcy's Anglo-Persian Oil Company. This could ensure the Royal Navy rock-bottom prices for APOC's petroleum for thirty years, which proved the case. (The exact prices were secret for decades.) On June 28, Parliament approved a bargain rivaled only by Disraeli's coup in acquiring majority shares in the Suez Canal Company. At the end of the war, Curzon remarked that the Allies "floated to victory on a wave of oil."[31]

On the outbreak of World War I, Persia immediately declared itself neutral, although its sympathies lay with a Germany at war with its old enemies, Britain and Russia. This did not deter both sides from violating Persian territory from the opening shot until long after the last. When World War I began, Russian forces occupied Tabriz, Meshed, and other northern cities. Garrisoned near Tehran was Russia's Fifth Column, the Persian Cossack Division, subsidized by the Tsar and commanded by Russian officers. Then as Turkey joined the Central Powers in November 1914, its regiments entered western Persia to block further Russian incursions. Adding to the confusion was a recently formed Persian gendarmerie whose Swedish officers were deemed pro-German.

Even before hostilities began, Britain dispatched a brigade of Indian cavalry to push up the Shatt al-Arab to protect the oil refineries. By mid–1915 there were about twenty-five hundred troops in Persia, but the British had been forced to withdraw consular guards from central Persia to provide troops to the Western Front and the Mesopotamia campaign. Then in 1916, Brigadier General Sir Percy Sykes, a polo-playing officer formerly of the Queen's Bays, who had been an explorer and Consul in Iran, raised a force of locals and incorporated the Shiraz Gendarmerie, exchanging their pro-German Swedish officers for British ones. Sykes's South Persia Rifles put down brigands, neutralized the Germans, and occupied southern Persia, eventually reaching Shiraz. After the Russian Revolution, even the Persian Cossacks commanded by a White Russian, Colonel Starosselsky, depended on Britain to pay expenses. By war's end, there was scarcely any food, as the 1917 crop had failed and Persian landowners, hoping to benefit financially from the shortage, hoarded grain. Making matters worse, the Russians had seized roofing, windows, and doorframes for firewood, rendering thousands of Persians homeless. Over a hundred thousand Persians died of starvation and cholera, and ten thousand villages were abandoned, impelling the British diplomat Harold Nicolson to lament, "Persia had been exposed to violations and suffering not endured by any other neutral country."[32]

So pervasive was privation and disorder that in 1918 British troops occupied tracts of Persian territory primarily to prevent a postrevolution Bolshevik advance. By war's end there were about fifty-five hundred men in the South Persia Rifles, and the British Government, overstretched in Mesopotamia, faced with Irish rebels and labor unrest at home, and undermanned in Egypt, insisted on retrenchment and demobilization. Nevertheless Lord Curzon, now serving as acting Foreign Secretary and fearful of a Bolshevik thrust toward India, maintained that the moment was ripe for placing British relations with Persia on a durable basis. In a memorandum to his Cabinet, he argued that it was impossible to allow Persia "to rot in picturesque decay . . . her geographical position, the magnitude of our interests in the country, and the future safety of our Eastern Empire render it impossible for us now—just as it would have been for us at any time during the past 50 years—to disinterest ourselves from what happens in Persia."[33]

Curzon himself drafted a new treaty whose first article reiterated "in the most categorical manner the undertakings which they have repeatedly given in the past to respect absolutely the independence and integrity of Persia." The Anglo-Persian Treaty (in what Sir Percy Cox defined as "direct help") authorized the posting of British experts to create a national army, build railroads, supply arms, reorganize the national finances, and revise tariffs—all to be financed by a £2 million loan to be repaid from revenues collected by British officials. It was a singularly ill-timed initiative. This well-meant but anachronistic scheme was seen by the Persians as evidence of Britain's desire to turn Persia into another client state like Egypt.

Asked how he expected to counter Persian opposition to his treaty, Curzon's quick answer was, "The case will be settled by cash."[34] After protracted negotiations by Sir Percy Cox, now Minister to Tehran, and with the lubricant of ready cash—reputed to be £131,000—secretly paid to the triumvirate running the government, a treaty was signed in August 1919. Curzon claimed victory prematurely. ("A great triumph and I have done it all alone.") When the bribes were exposed, the treaty was blocked by the Majlis, and three successive Persian prime ministers fell. (Curzon had failed to note a technicality: Article 24 of Persia's oft-violated Constitution required ratification of treaties by the Majlis, which had not met since 1915.)

Cox fortunately escaped to Mesopotamia, leaving his successor, Herman Norman, to bear Curzon's wrath. Norman cautioned: "We are replacing the hated Russians [and] His Majesty's Government must decide whether they will allow all the money sunk in Persia to be lost, our commerce destroyed ... our interests and position in the country ruined ... our policy represented by the Anglo-Persian Agreement to be scrapped, Mesopotamia rendered intolerable, our hold over India jeopardized."[35] Sir Denis Wright notes that Norman continued "to warn Curzon in a series of courageous reports that he was putting his money (almost literally) on the wrong Persian horses and that his proposed agreement was unlikely to succeed. This was not what Curzon wished to hear or was prepared to believe: in consequence Norman, whom events were to prove right, was recalled to London and was never again employed by the Foreign Office."[36]

The Bolshevik Revolution and the ensuing civil war between Red and White armies in the Caucasus and Central Asia spread chaos on Persia's northern border. A 1918 mission by Major General Lionel Dunsterville to Baku failed, forcing a British retreat. At dawn on May 18, 1920, the Reds captured a White Russian flotilla at Bandar Anzeli on the Caspian, which was nominally under British protection. A Persian Communist Party was subsequently founded in the province. It was apparent that the diminished British forces were unable to protect their ally. Yet the British Government ordered still another army, the North-West Persia Force (or NORPERFORCE), into Tehran and its environs in the autumn of 1920.

NORPERFORCE's colorful major general was Sir Edmund Ironside. Born in 1880, the son of the Scottish surgeon major of the Royal Horse Artillery, Edmund followed his father into the military. A gifted linguist, he learned Afrikaans in order to become an undercover agent in the Boer War. When he was mentioned in dispatches for his bravery in South Africa, the Ironside legend took root—he was alleged to have squeezed a Boer to death with his bare hands. As a spy disguised as a Boer transport driver, he next accompanied a German military expedition into South-West Africa (present-day Namibia), where its mission was to quash a native rebellion. This episode inspired the theory that Ironside was the real-life model for the Scottish superspy Richard Hannay in John Buchan's *The Thirty-Nine Steps* and *Greenmantle.* As a gunnery captain, he was among the first British officers to land in France in 1914. He ended his war a brigadier general, and after the armistice, he was sent as Commander in Chief of a goulash of British, French, and White Russian troops fighting the Bolsheviks in north Russia in 1918–19. Accompanied by an omnipresent bull terrier, accident prone ("every means of conveyance breaks down under him"),[37] and already known as a "master of retreats," Ironside supervised the troop withdrawal from the doomed enterprise. He was awarded a knighthood and a promotion to major general, the youngest in the British Army. He was then dispatched to Admiral Miklós Horthy's Hungary to manage yet another evacuation—that of an occupying Romanian force—while settling the boundaries between the two countries. Another massive withdrawal followed in Turkey, where he commanded an Anglo-Greek army that had attempted unsuccessfully to carve up the Ottoman Empire.

"He is a remarkable creature," Gertrude Bell wrote after she met the 275-pound officer in Iraq, "being in the first place one of the biggest men I've ever seen and in the second having a pretty sound knowledge of affairs from Arch-angel to the Black Sea. A major general at 37, a first class interpreter in 7 languages—all that's not nothing. But above all he's a man, a sex for which useful employment can be found in North Persia."[38] John C. Cairns in his frank *Dictionary of National Biography* entry thus describes Ironside:

> Healthy, solidly built, handsome into old age, keen, observant, and with something like a photographic memory, he was warm, sensitive, impet-uous, mercurial and blunt. He had virtually no appreciation of music or poetry, little of theatre, none of dance but wrote easily, indefatigably, better than he believed. Photography, architecture and practical handi-crafts delighted him. No stranger to the vulgar racial, cultural, and gen-der prejudices of class, nation, and time, he made harsh judgements even of friends and often shattering criticism of others—especially air marshals, time-serving soldiers, politicians, pacifist university dons, dip-lomats, shipboard companions, nearly all women in what he considered the male domain and most foreigners. Certain of British superiority, he professed special dislike of the Irish, Jews, Latins and "lesser races", that is most of mankind.[39]

In Persia, "Tiny" Ironside's orders were "to hold the fort until decision by the Cabinet to withdraw all the troops . . . not to get troops embroiled in the country [Persia] . . . to use his influence to subdue Starosselsky [the com-mander of the Persian Cossacks] . . . and other Persian forces [inimical to] the political authorities in London."[40] But Ironside would stretch his orders by trying his hand at kingmaking.

With the Bolsheviks ascending, the British retreating, and the Tehran government losing control of the country where Herman Norman now served as the luckless Minister carrying out Curzon's orders, Ironside, who disputed Whitehall's forward strategy—"India should be defended behind her own frontiers and not in advance of them"—also began to implement independently his own Persian policy.[41] He disapproved of the financial bur-dens—borne, in the most part, by the Government of India—incurred by Curzon's forward policy. Even if it were successful, the outcome would be an indefensible Persian frontier with Russia while India's own mountains made a Russian invasion unlikely. Ironside believed, and India concurred, that it was necessary only to defend south Persia, where British oil interests lay. Ironside's opinion, as he confided to his diary, was that "a military dicta-torship would solve our troubles and let us out of the country without any trouble at all."[42]

He began by weeding Russian officers from the Persian Cossack Divi-sion commanded by Colonel Starosselsky but now equipped from British stores and paid for with British cash. Then with the assistance of Lieuten-ant Colonel Henry Smyth, he engineered the White Russian commander's ouster. Minister Norman supported Starosselsky's dismissal. Ahmad Shah reluctantly agreed but was opposed by his Prime Minister, who resigned in protest. Still hoping for the ratification of the Anglo-Persian Treaty and viewing these events with distant dismay, Curzon warned Norman, "In deciding upon new policy . . . and in the selection of agents to work it, you will doubtless recognize that General Ironside and yourself have assumed no slight responsibility, which will require the justification of success."[43]

Meanwhile Ironside spotted Colonel Reza Khan, ramrod erect under a karakul hat, tough as leather boots, and (because he carried the regiment's Maxim gun) nicknamed "Machine Gun Reza." "There was no denying that he had a kingly presence," observed Vita Sackville-West, but this "alarming man" with a "huge nose, grizzled hair and a brutal jowl" looked what he was: "a Cossack trooper."[44] Ironside demurred. "A man and the straightest I have met yet," Ironside recorded in his diary, "the real life and soul of the show."[45] Ironside installed Reza Khan as Commander of the Qazvin Cossacks. Before leaving Persia for Cairo on February 12, Ironside, in a meeting with Smyth, now the de facto commander quartermaster and paymaster of the Qazvin Cossacks, and with Reza Khan, informed the Persian that Britain would not oppose his seizing power if he would agree not to depose Ahmad Shah. Reza Khan agreed.[46] On February 20–21, Reza Khan led an overnight march on Tehran at the head of a column of around six hundred Cossacks.* Tehran was undefended. The gendarmerie and police had been ordered to remain in their quarters, and in an almost bloodless coup, Reza Khan overthrew the cabinet.[47] At the time of the coup, Ironside had just survived a crash land-ing near Hamadan on the first leg of his journey to the Cairo Conference. The Princeton scholar Richard Ullman writes in his careful account of the events of 1920–21, "It is idle to speculate upon whether or not he would

---

* The figures on the number of Cossacks run from six hundred to three thousand. We have taken the lower figure supplied by Lieutenant General Morteza Yazdanpanah, who participated in the coup.

eventually have come to power had Ironside not singled him out; but it is clear that Ironside and his British colleagues were largely instrumental in placing Reza Khan in a position to bring about the *coup d'état* of 21 February 1921 which put effective power into his hands."[48] On February 23, Ironside, now in Baghdad, noted in his diary, "I fancy that all the people think I engineered the *coup d'état*. I suppose I did, strictly speaking."[49]

In April, NORPERFORCE withdrew, leaving behind small arms, ammunition, artillery, and animals—gifts for Reza's Cossacks. Although Ironside had warned the doubtful Norman before the coup, many British officials were taken by surprise. This turned to dismay when the newly ensconced Prime Minister, a newspaper editor named Seyyed Zia ed-Din Tabatabai, imprisoned their wealthy and powerful friends, most probably to squeeze their embezzled fortunes from them. But Seyyed Zia pursued reforms that required either of two abominations—foreign loans or higher taxes—and his alliance with Reza, now War Minister, brokered by Norman was short-lived. Reza, supported by the Shah and by the Soviet Minister, sacked him. From Baghdad, Gertrude Bell observed on May 29, "Our news this week is chiefly Persian. Seyyed Zia ed-Din's fall will throw Persia into the melting pot and I fear that the resulting liquid may be highly explosive. He was overturned by the O.C. Cossacks, a certain Riza Khan who is an ignorant soldier quite incapable of administration and anxious to establish a dictatorship. Once our troops were gone all the effective force in the country was in his hands."[50]

One of the new regime's first acts was to summon the Majlis, whose members rejected Curzon's treaty, doing so pointedly on the same day their country's envoys in Moscow signed a Russo-Persian Treaty. (The Bolsheviks, in a move calculated to win Persian approbation and undercut British expansion, had already voided the 1907 Anglo-Russian agreement and declared all tsarist claims null and void.) Curzon conceded the failure of his policy, although he preferred to lay the blame on others, maintaining that the withdrawal of British troops had "shattered the Persians'" belief in England's will and ability to protect Persia. "More serious," amplifies Harold Nicolson, "was his misconception of the attitude of the average Persian towards Russia and Great Britain. He did not realize that in 1919 it was Great Britain who was regarded as the oppressor and Russia as the potential friend."[51]

The Soviet invasion of Persia that Curzon and Norman feared never happened. On becoming Commander in Chief, Reza refused to retain any British officers, and as he also objected to British financial advisers, by September they too had been forced to withdraw. As the Oriental Secretary, George P. Churchill, ruefully minuted, "[T]he alleged hostility of the populace and the impression that the British are responsible for the coup d'état, lead to the belief that the present regime is not likely to be a success."[52] Thereafter, most Persians viewed the coup as proof of Britain's perfidy. Curzon's mishandling of the Anglo-Persian Treaty effectively ended for two decades British dominance in Persian affairs.

Curzon dispatched Sir Percy Loraine to Tehran, by this time deemed to be a graveyard of diplomatic ambitions, to replace Norman, who had been recalled and scapegoated for nonratification of the treaty. Groomed at Eton and New College, Oxford, Sir Percy was good at games—polo, poker, bridge, and backgammon. He was industrious, shrewd, remote, and given to wordy dispatches—his Foreign Office colleagues dubbed him "Ponderous Percy." From the start the new Minister admired Reza for his frankness, informing Curzon, "He gets straight to what he has to say, and does not waste time in exchanging the delicately phrased but perfectly futile compliments so dear to the Persian heart . . . an ignorant and uneducated man; nevertheless he betrays no awkwardness of manner, nor self-consciousness, he has considerable natural dignity, and neither his speech nor his features reveal any absence of self-control."[53]

Judging Reza Khan a likely winner, Loraine proposed to follow a novel hands-off policy. He received a reassuring letter from Gertrude Bell in Baghdad: "It looks as if the policy of sitting by in a detached manner was going to do more to forward our interests than any eager advocacy of them. I'm not sure that isn't true of the East in general. If we don't force ourselves upon them they are bound to turn to us."[54] To which Loraine sensibly replied, "All I feel really certain about is that I'm on the right line and the only one that may deliver the goods, if perhaps not exactly in the form and manner that Lord C[urzon] of K[edleston] might like or expect. The Persians have got to learn for themselves, and if you want them to do that it's no use fiddling with them and their affairs, still less intervening and pretending you don't. It is producing an effect and my camp, silent and cowardly as it is, is steadily growing."[55]

Still, despite his vow of noninterference, Loraine supported Reza in several important ways. He persuaded London to advance money for Reza's army, now numbering some eighteen thousand men; he endorsed a mission by the American A. C. Millspaugh to straighten out Persia's finances; and he sided with Reza against Britain's ally, Sheik Khazal.

Even by crude imperial standards, the tale of Great Britain's relations with Sheik Khazal of Mohammerah is discreditable. In 1921, Khazal, whose tribal lands included (besides the oil-refining area of Abadan) part of the area around Basra, put himself forward as a candidate for the Iraqi throne; then in 1922 he proposed partitioning Iran, nominating himself as the prospective ruler of southern Persia. Reza Khan, dedicated to a strong central government, parried by claiming that the sheik had failed to pay large sums in taxes to Tehran, while Khazal, in turn, claimed to have spent an equally large amount defending Persia's southern borders during the war. In 1923 His Excellency Sheik Sir Khazal Khan, KCIE, received Loraine in Mohammerah and spoke of Wilson and Cox and of his loyalty to Britain. (Khazal had proved to be a reliable friend, protecting British oil interests during the war, and in 1919 the British had given him a river steamer, four mountain guns, ceremonial saluting guns and three thousand late-issue rifles for his services.)[56] Loraine carried a letter from Reza Khan, in which he stated that he bore the sheik no ill will and counted on his cooperation. Loraine attempted to act as an intermediary, eliciting a humble apology from the sheik, and a promise (subsequently broken) from Reza Khan not to cross into the sheik's Khuzistan territory. But in the spring of 1924, Khazal invited the Bakhtiaris and Qashgais to join him in resisting the government. It remains unclear whether he expected British support, but Reza Khan countered by mobilizing a large army on the Khuzistan border.

It was left to Loraine to decide whether to honor Britain's pledges made by Percy Cox and Arnold Wilson (currently heading APOC's operations in the Persian Gulf) by sending troops from India to his aid or to allow Reza Khan to prevail. Principle yielded to expediency, and the British stood aside as Reza Khan advanced and the outnumbered Khazal submitted. He promised Reza Khan his allegiance and vowed to pay his back taxes. Nevertheless he was arrested and spirited away to Tehran. As the Foreign Office Permanent Under Secretary, Sir Eyre Crowe, had advised Loraine, Britain was "a State disarmed . . . with a public opinion opposed to all employment of force whatever—equally for a right as for a wrong cause."[57] For backing "the right man," Loraine was rewarded with a knighthood and one of the Empire's splendid prizes: he became High Commissioner to Egypt and the Sudan in 1929. But as Gertrude Bell admitted, Loraine "had been thoroughly bamboozled by Riza Khan about the Shaikh of Muhammarah and keeps writing enormous despatches to prove that he hasn't. He may have succeeded in convincing H.M.G. but not us."[58] The sheik remained under house arrest in Tehran until he died under suspicious circumstances, in 1936. (His heir, Abdullah, prudently fled to Iraq.) Bell remained critical of His Majesty's Government's role in the affair (even though it was Sir Percy Cox who had conducted the original negotiations): "It was a pity that we were in the habit of entering so lightheartedly into engagements which would be extremely difficult to fulfill if need were. We did, of course, let the Shaikh down, but could any Govt have gone to war with Persia ... on his account? H.M.G. were ready at a pinch to bring over a couple of battalions from India, at considerable expense, and at that moment we were involved in the crisis in Egypt and their one idea was to avoid further commitments."[59]

The subjugation of Khazal had been the final step in Reza Khan's unification of Iran, and now Loraine greenlighted Reza Khan's ascent to the throne. When he was told that Reza Khan wanted to get rid of the Qajars but feared London's disapproval, Loraine told the official, "I did not myself see what Reza Khan could hope for more than our loyal and friendly attitude of strict non-intervention."[60] When the Majlis deposed the absent Qajar Shah, and four months later Reza crowned himself Reza Shah Pahlavi Shahanshah of Persia, the Foreign Office observed, "[T]he revolution has passed off calmly."[61] Yet as the deposed monarch fell, the British lost their Capitulations, their twenty-three consular courts, *sowar* escorts, and military salutes, their Persian naval bases, and Bushire's sovereign residency.

Who was this Reza Khan who, with the backing of the British, had assumed the leading role on Persia's political stage? He was born in 1878 in the small northern village of Alasht, the son of a Persian father and a Turkish-speaking Caucasian mother. As a fifteen-year-old with little or no education, he enlisted as a stable hand in the Cossack Brigade, where, owing to his drive and natural ability, he had reached the rank of colonel by 1915. He earned a reputation of being a fireman—someone who was sent to quell disturbances or round up thieves. At the time of the coup, he was forty-three.

Before founding his own Pahlavi dynasty, Reza Khan had toyed with proclaiming a republic, following the example of Kemal Atatürk, the Turkish soldier-reformer he sought to emulate. The King of Kings claimed to be a reluctant monarch, only agreeing to ascend the throne at the urging of the *ulama* or mullahs, who thought conservative Persia would fare better with a shah than with a democracy. At the time, royal titles were very much in the desert air—hence King Faisal, King Ibn Saud, Emir Abdullah—so he chose the Peacock Throne. The choice measures the difference between President Atatürk and Reza Shah. Reza wanted it both ways: to preserve the feudal prerogatives of royalty while seeking the global prestige of being Persia's enlightened modernizer.

In the spirit of Atatürk, Reza Shah founded and energized a unifying national army. He consolidated the country and promoted railroads (Persia's first) from the Caspian to the Gulf. He established twenty-five hundred schools and numerous hospitals and powered cement and textile factories with new electric lines. Moreover, he sent Persians abroad to study, especially at German and French universities. He disarmed the tribes and undermined the *ulama*, clashing with Shiite mullahs over female dress codes—securing legislation that in 1936 officially barred women wearing chadors from hotels, restaurants, cinemas, buses, and taxis, a ruling that proved unpopular and was soon rescinded. He banished the untasseled fez and the *sardari*, men's traditional coat. He abolished titles such as those borne by government officials—The Helper of the Kingdom, The Defender of Sovereignty—and (as did Atatürk) he decreed that Persians, who had only borne first names followed by their father's first name, adopt a surname, often a place or trade name. He also sought glorifying links with Persia's pre-Islamic empires (his dynasty took its name Pahlavi from the language spoken by the Sassanians). And he insisted upon reviving the ancient name of Iran for his country, hence in 1935 APOC became the Anglo-Iranian Oil Company.

Reza Shah's whim was absolute, his memory extraordinary, his thirst to avenge proverbial, his skin gossamer. No elective constitutional system was allowed to grow roots under the Pahlavis, another break from Atatürk's example. To the untraveled Shah, the concept of a free press was unfathomable. When Reza discovered that Iranians were still using postage stamps bearing the portrait of the deposed Ahmad Shah, he sent his troops to seize the entire supply. For some weeks Iran remained stampless, and since the newly minted ones with Reza's portrait were slow in arriving from Holland, the old stamps had to be retrieved and circulated, albeit with the exiled Shah's effigy blacked out.

One of his most controversial reforms allowed landlords to confiscate land from their peasants, much of it reverting to the Crown. The Shah's own pathological appetite for land was so widely known that the French press mocked him in a cartoon which showed "*le chat de Perse*" devouring Iran. Even the British became disenchanted with their man. "The Shah has become most unpopular," wrote Godfrey Havard, the Oriental Secretary, in 1927. "[H]e is one thousand times worse than Ahmad Shah in his love of money and land and in the short two years that he has been proclaimed Shah, he has amassed a *huge, huge* fortune."[62]

On the matter of oil, Reza Shah's outrage was warranted by any reasonable standard. The still-extant D'Arcy concession had been modified in 1920 (but only modestly, as Persians bitterly remarked, since a British Treasury official, Sir Sydney Armitage-Smith, served as chief negotiator for Persia). When royalties from Anglo-Persian sharply declined during the Great Depression, a defiant Shah in November 1932 unilaterally canceled the company's concession. This followed years of inconclusive haggling over long-standing Persian grievances: that the company interpreted "net profits" to apply only to its operations in Persia, that it evaded Persian taxes, and that it wrongly withheld royalties as compensation for Persia's unavoidable failure to prevent wartime attacks on its pipelines. Moreover, Reza Shah was indignant over Britain's recognition of the new kingdom of Iraq, on Persia's western border, a country he viewed as an imperial concoction. All this was compounded by the oil company's quasi-governmental status. In the words of Daniel Yergin, "The management of Anglo-Persian could endlessly repeat that the company operated as a commercial entity, independent of the government, but no Persian would ever believe such an assertion."[63]

Finally, after mediation by the League of Nations, the two parties agreed in 1933 to a new contract that reduced Anglo-Persian's concession to 100,000 square miles and a new royalty fixed at four shillings per ton on sold or exported petroleum, thus ensuring Persia 20 percent of worldwide profits to shareholders in excess of £671,250. The new formula guaranteed Persia annual proceeds of at least £750,000. This seemed a victory for Persia since the company also promised to recalculate royalties from prior years and to speed "Persianization" of the work force. In reality, as oil prices and profits soared in the years ahead, the company's tax payments to Britain were roughly triple its royalties to Iran, and moreover, the Iranians were denied real access to company books, so that the Royal Navy's bargain-basement prices for its oil remained secret.

Little wonder, given his combative temper and suspicion of the British, that Reza Shah began looking to Germany as a potential counterweight to Britain and the Soviet Union. Early in the 1920s Germans had begun trickling into Tehran; friendship societies and student exchange programs had sprouted. This accelerated in the 1930s as Reza Shah sought a sharp decrease in trade with an ever-more domineering Soviet Union. In 1940–41, commerce with Germany peaked: nearly half of all imports came from the Third Reich, and 42 percent of all Iranian exports headed there. Whether Reza Shah was ideologically pro-Nazi is harder to ascertain. His son and successor, Mohammed Reza Pahlavi, insisted this was a falsehood, though his formulation is less than flattering: "My father mistrusted Hitler from the very beginning, if for no other reason than as an authoritarian ruler he was deeply suspicious of another who used such brutal methods . . . True, we employed a number of German technicians, but their employment had nothing to do with politics."[64]

Nevertheless, Reza Shah came to loathe and distrust Britain and Russia alike, and seemed to calculate that Hitler would prevail. Inarguably, he was thrown off balance by the Nazi-Soviet Pact of August 1939, and certainly he spoke from the heart in affirming Iran's wish to be neutral when war broke out the following month. Understandably, he was confused after the German invasion of the USSR in June 1941, when the Russians and Britons became allies. That summer they issued an ultimatum to "Persia" (Churchill instructed his officials always to use the old name because otherwise there was a tendency among the armed forces to confuse Iraq and Iran) demanding the expulsion of all German nationals. General Archibald Wavell followed up, writing on July 10, 1941, "If the present Government is not willing to facilitate this, it must be made to give way to one that will."[65] More importantly, the British believed that Iran was essential to the defense of India, and when the United States joined the war, Iran would become the route by which the Soviet Union received supplies. When Reza Shah demurred, British and Russian forces invaded on August 25, 1941. The British Navy bombarded Iran's southwestern ports, and 35,000 British troops poured into Iran's southern provinces. The Soviets crossed the Azerbaijan border with what was estimated to be 120,000 troops; their air force bombed Tabriz. Overwhelmed, the Iranian army collapsed within two days and sued for peace. The Shah abdicated, explaining to his son, "I cannot be the nominal head of an occupied land, to be dictated to by a minor English or Russian officer."[66]

The Majlis immediately proclaimed the twenty-one-year-old Mohammad Reza Pahlavi the new King of Kings as British and Soviet troops moved into Tehran. The ex-Shah was hustled with his family onto a British ship to Mauritius in the Indian Ocean, where he was politely briefed by two veterans of the Eurasian power game, Sir Clarmont Skrine, formerly Vice Consul at Kerman, and Sir Olaf Caroe, future Governor of British India's North-West Frontier. Reza Shah complained of the unhealthy climate of Mauritius and after some negotiations was taken to Johannesburg, South Africa, where he was kept under house arrest, dying there from a heart attack in 1944.

As for the kingmakers, Sir Percy Cox capped his career with an appointment as High Commissioner in Iraq. Awarded a GCMG in 1922, he chaired the Mount Everest Committee and became president of the Royal Geographical Society in 1933. A generation of children in Iraq was named "Kokus" in his memory. Curzon refused to see Herman Norman in London after the latter's recall following the treaty disaster. Norman declined to be posted as Minister in Santiago and retired in 1924. By war's end, Sir Percy Sykes, who had spoken out against the 1919 Treaty, had alienated Curzon, who saw to it that he never got another post. He further irritated Foreign Secretary Arthur Balfour through his self-promoting arrogance. Sykes was recalled to London and subsequently retired from the army. Writing, lecturing, and reviewing occupied his retirement years until his death in 1945; he had also served as honorary secretary of the Royal Central Asian Society.[67] Sir Percy Loraine traveled up the ambassadorial ranks, ending in Rome. But his diplomatic achievements were overshadowed (he had supported appeasement and failed to keep Italy out of the war), as he was the first to admit, by his success in breeding race horses, one of whom, Darius, placed third in the Derby. Loraine's heraldic banner as a Knight Grand Cross of the Order of St. Michael and St. George still hangs in Hexham Abbey, Northumberland. Swashbuckling Major General Sir Edmund Ironside, at the time of his departure, received from the Shah Persia's highest decoration, the Order of the Lion and the Sun. "Tiny" was recalled and made chief of the Imperial General Staff but proved difficult to handle. Prime Minister Neville Chamberlain sacked him in January 1940. In May–June of that bleak year, he supervised his final retreat, the evacuation of Dunkirk. Shortly afterward he received his Field Marshal's baton. His next assignment was commander of the Home Forces, but he quarreled with Churchill, who preferred to run his wars himself. The Field Marshal abruptly retired but was elevated to the peerage in 1941 as Baron Ironside. He died in 1959 and was buried with full military honors, including a nineteen-gun salute and a service in Westminster Abbey.

TEN

The Quiet American

Kermit (Kim) Roosevelt, Jr. (1916–2000)

⌘

They came among us, these aspiring American spy-masters, like
innocent girls from a finishing-school anxious to learn the seasoned
demi-mondaine ways of old practitioners—in this case, the legendary
British Secret Service.

—Malcolm Muggeridge,
Chronicles of a Wasted Time (1973)

⌘

I owe my throne to God, my people, my army—and to you.
—Mohammed Reza Shah to Kermit Roosevelt,
quoted in *Countercoup: The Struggle for*
the Control of Iran (1979)

"The morning was muggy, close to rain. My anticipation rode high but was accompanied by a nagging dread. On this day, June 25, 1953, our course of action in Iran would be decided. Would we follow the plan on which I had already agreed with the British, tentatively in my mind but decisively in theirs?" So began Kermit Roosevelt's 1979 book *Countercoup*, his account of "the struggle for control of Iran." The Central Intelligence Agency's chief of Near Eastern operations was on his way to a meeting in Secretary of State John Foster Dulles's office carrying a twenty-two-page plan for OPERATION AJAX whose goal was to overthrow the constitutional government in Tehran and replace its Prime Minister, Dr. Mohammed Mossadeq. John Foster Dulles, and his younger brother Allen W. Dulles, the Director of Central Intelligence, not only were fully cognizant of the Soviet threat to Iran but also happened to be partners in the law firm of Sullivan & Cromwell, which represented an A-list of multinational corporations including Anglo-Iranian Oil. Allen Dulles had spent his wartime years in Berne, Switzerland, where he earned his intelligence stripes serving with the Office of Strategic Services (OSS). After the war, he helped create the CIA in 1947, emulating the British tradition of recruiting the very best men from elite schools. Dulles, who had Kipling's *Kim* near his deathbed, was imbued with the belief that a few good men using hidden levers in the right place and time could move the world.

His star recruit, now heading toward Dulles's office, was thirty-seven-year-old Kermit "Kim" Roosevelt, grandson of Theodore Roosevelt, son of Belle Wyatt Willard (daughter of the U.S. Ambassador to Spain) and the senior Kermit, a noted explorer and soldier. Born in Buenos Aires, the younger Kermit was also a distant cousin of Franklin D. Roosevelt and had followed the rest of the Roosevelt males from Oyster Bay, Long Island, to the Massachusetts preparatory school Groton, and then to Harvard, where he graduated *cum laude*. In 1937, he married Mary "Polly" Gaddis, with whom he would have four children. While teaching at Harvard and at the California Institute of Technology, he pursued a Ph.D. in history with a dissertation entitled "Propaganda Techniques in the English Civil Wars," which reflected his lifelong interest in the manipulation of the media. Kermit also wrote an article on the kind of clandestine service organization the United States would need in the event of war. He sent a copy to his cousin, the columnist Joseph Alsop, who suggested he should forward it to the head of the OSS, Major General William "Wild Bill" Donovan.

After the war, Kim joined the CIA, already thickly populated with "gentlemen spies," where he soon headed the Near East and Africa division, based in Cairo. Another "Kim," H. A. R. Philby, described "the quiet American" as "a courteous, soft-spoken Easterner with impeccable social connections, well-educated rather than intellectual, pleasant and unassuming as host and guest . . . In fact the last person you would expect to be up to his neck in dirty tricks."[1] Yet, like Philby, Roosevelt and his deputies, Donald Wilber and Miles Copeland, became leading participants in Cold War espionage. According to Copeland, it was the Roosevelt penchant for adventure that motivated Kim's choice of career.

The other attendees at the critical full-dress meeting at the State Department, besides the Dulles brothers, were Loy Henderson, the U.S. Ambassador in Tehran; Charles Wilson, Secretary of Defense; General Walter Bedell "Beedle" Smith, the Under Secretary of State; Robert Bowie, director of the State Department Policy Planning Staff; Henry "Hank" Byroade, Assistant Secretary of State for the Near East, Africa, and South Asia; and Robert D. Murphy, Deputy Under Secretary for Political Affairs—a who's who of Potomac Cold Warriors.

Dulles and Roosevelt outlined the scenario for AJAX, which drew on a British draft, code-named OPERATION BOOT, as revised by Donald Wilber, an archaeologist, architectural historian, rug collector, and the agency's man in Tehran. The aim of the operation as detailed by Wilber in the official CIA account of the mission was "to cause the fall of the Mossadeq government;

to reestablish the prestige and power of the Shah; and to replace the Mossadeq government with one which would govern Iran according to constructive policies. Specifically, the aim was to bring to power a government which would reach an equitable oil settlement, enabling Iran to become economically sound and financially solvent, and which would vigorously prosecute the dangerously strong Communist party."[2]

At the end of the presentation, Dulles asked everyone for their views. Most supported the plan with varying degrees of enthusiasm. Only the State Department's Bowie and Byroade remained noncommittal. Ambassador Henderson, according to Roosevelt, was clearly unhappy. "I don't like this kind of business at all," he said. "You know that. But we are confronted by a desperate, a dangerous situation and a madman who would ally himself with the Russians. We have no choice but to proceed with this undertaking, May God grant us success."[3] If Roosevelt's memoir is to be credited, when AJAX was approved and the meeting adjourned, John Foster Dulles looked around the room and said, "That's that, then; let's get going."[4]

Ever since Morgan Shuster's attempt to eliminate blatant corruption in Persian tax collection ended in 1911, Americans had been popular in Iran. Older Persians recalled that Woodrow Wilson supported Persia's request (vetoed by the British as meddling) to address the Paris Peace Conference in the hopes of obtaining war reparations. And American advisers were present during the rise of Reza Shah: In 1922, the economist Arthur Millspaugh arrived with a few compatriots to attempt once again to instigate fiscal reform by introducing a number of taxes and canceling exemptions previously granted to Persian notables and their heirs. By prior agreement, Reza Khan, then Minister of War, received the lion's share of the revenue for his army. But after the American's successful three-year term (when a prominent British visitor was quoted as saying, "Millspaugh administers Persia in much the same way that Cromer administered Egypt"), his contract was canceled because the expected flood of American capital, the raison d'être for his employment, failed to materialize.[5]

The British were wary of American poaching in their pond. Lord Curzon's Anglo-Persian Treaty was greeted with dismay in Washington. Secretary of State Robert Lansing instructed his Ambassador in London, John Davis, to let Curzon know of American displeasure, but an uncomprehending Foreign Secretary lectured the messenger, the U.S. diplomat Cornelius Engert: "To anyone familiar with conditions in Persia and the character of her people it will seem quite natural that Persia should turn to us for guidance and support. We knew them probably better than anybody else, we had done more for them, and had spent more money in their country than anybody else. I therefore cannot understand why the U.S. or any other power, should suddenly object to our position in Persia. You seem to take it for granted that the Persians are clamoring for American help. You are quite mistaken: the Persians are only clamoring for American money, to be spent by themselves as they see fit!"[6]

Behind the friction between World War I partners was the suspicion that the Americans wanted in on Middle East oil concessions. Although Standard Oil had supplied one-fourth of Allied oil, by war's end America's known assets were rapidly bottoming out. The country's love affair with the automobile had taken hold, and it was apparent that the United States had to seek foreign wells. A prospective solution lay in Iraq and Persia. But Iraq's reserves were as yet unknown, and whatever concessions there were belonged to Turkish Petroleum, a byzantine consortium yet to be sorted out, although it looked to be firmly in the hands of the Anglo-Persian Oil Company. For a time it appeared that Standard Oil, with the backing of the Majlis, might win a fifty-year concession in northern Iran, but Britain invoked her exclusive rights to Persian oil. Then the British countered by offering Standard Oil of New Jersey a joint venture deal with APOC. As Curzon noted, "Better Americans than the Bolsheviks."[7] But on June 10, 1923, the Majlis passed a law granting the government the power to negotiate the northern concession with any "independent and responsible American company" provided that the company could come up with the entire $10 million loan.[8] A further clause barred the transfer of the concession to any non-US company, eliminating the possibility of an APOC–Standard Oil joint venture. Then another suitor appeared. Sinclair Oil gained the backing of the Majlis, and of Secretary of State Charles Evans Hughes, but failed to raise the essential money.

As the Second World War ended in August 1945, northern Iran stood on the periphery, out of Allied sight but very much on Joseph Stalin's mind. No thread of continuity was more durable in Soviet foreign policy than the *Bolshaya Igra*, the Great Game, and its leader's determination to repossess every sliver of territory once claimed by the Tsar. Stalin's revolutionary career had begun as a union organizer in Baku's oil fields. He knew the geography of Inner Asia and he understood the strategic importance of oil—Hitler's assault on the Russians failed in part because his Panzers could not reach the Caucasian oil fields. Stalin also believed that northern Iran properly belonged in Russia's sphere, as provided in the 1907 Anglo-Russian Convention.

Hence the crisis over Iran that heralded the Cold War. In their Tehran Declaration, Stalin, Churchill, and FDR, meeting in the capital in 1942, affirmed Iranian independence, sovereignty, and territorial integrity. At war's end, the USSR and the British duly agreed to withdraw all their forces by March 1, 1946. As the deadline neared, the Soviets began arming a separatist Azerbaijani movement in northern Iran, while their forces barred Iranian troops from entering the area. In Washington, Acting Secretary of State Dean Acheson understood that America had little military leverage but ample moral authority. Acheson chose to respond firmly while avoiding ultimatums and leaving the Soviets a graceful way out. He cabled Moscow, cautioning them against further troop movements toward northern Iran. He warned of serious international complications and urged the Soviets to work out a deal with the Iranians—the honorable exit. His tactics succeeded. After Iran's promise of a possible oil concession (which never materialized), and with a nudge from the United Nations, Soviet troops withdrew.

There were humanitarian and moral reasons for the American presence in Iran, but Secretary of State Cordell Hull had advised President Roosevelt that "from a more directly selfish point of view, it is to our interest that no great power be established on the Persian Gulf opposite the important American petroleum development in Saudi Arabia."[9] America's position was clarified vis-à-vis Britain by Roosevelt's reply to Churchill's direct query about the United States' interest in Iranian oil. "Please do accept my assurances that we are not making sheep's eyes at your oil fields in Iraq or Iran," Roosevelt promised the Prime Minister, though he acknowledged that the State Department was studying the question. Churchill thanked him and replied, "Let me reciprocate by giving you the fullest assurance that we have no thought of trying to horn in upon your interests or property in Saudi Arabia."[10]

In 1951, both houses of the Iranian parliament vented years of pent-up anger and voted to nationalize the Anglo-Iranian Oil Company. This followed a British refusal to modify the terms of the 1933 concession by bringing it more in line with the fifty-fifty agreement that Aramco had recently negotiated with the Saudis. Although the Labour government had recently nationalized British oil and coal industries, Prime Minister Clement Attlee anticipated that an AIOC agreement similar to the Aramco arrangement would prove as traumatic as the loss of empire for the British position in the Middle East. Articulated by Sir Donald Ferguson, Permanent Under Secretary at the Ministry of Fuel and Power, Britain's inflexible stand was that the oil in Iran rightly belonged to the British: "It was British enterprise, skill and effort which discovered oil under the soil of Persia, which has got the oil out, which has built the refinery, which has developed markets for Persian oil in 30 or 40 countries, with wharves, storage tanks and pumps, road and rail tanks and other distribution facilities, and also an immense fleet of tankers. This was done at a time when there was no easy outlet for Persian oil in competition with the vastly greater American oil industry. None of these things would or could have been done by the Persian government or the Persian people."[11]

When Iran demanded the right to inspect AIOC's books, to consider an increase in Iranian personnel, and to price oil within Iran at cost rather than at world levels, Assistant Secretary of State George McGee appealed to the company and the Foreign Office to grant these rather insubstantial requests, but by then the British offer was too little and too late. Events overtook the stalemate when Prime Minister Hadj Ali Razmara was assassinated on March 7 while attending the funeral of a mullah. Razmara had AIOC's fifty-fifty agreement in his pocket, according to the MI6 resident.[12] On March 15, 1951, the Majlis unanimously passed the bill nationalizing the oil industry. Acheson, by now Secretary of State Acheson, remarked of British recalcitrance, "Never had so few lost so much so stupidly and so fast."[13]

To wide applause, the Shah named nationalization's chief proponent, seventy-year-old Mohammad Mossadeq, as Prime Minister. Mossadeq was a wealthy Swiss-educated lawyer whose mother was a Qajar Princess. At only sixteen, he had been appointed to his first government post, as chief tax auditor for the province of Khorasan, where he experienced firsthand the endemic corruption that marked Persia's ruling elite. On his return to Tehran, the Shah granted him the title "Mossadeq" (signifying "one who has been tried, tested and found to be worthy"). Skinny as a stork with a beaked nose that proved a cartoonish delight, "Old Mossy" suffered from ulcers and was given to outbursts of tantrums, tears, and legendary fainting spells. In

1925, when the Majlis loudly objected to Reza Khan's proclaiming himself Shah, Mossadeq abandoned politics, retired to his farm, and then retreated to a self-imposed European exile. When he returned to Iran, he was imprisoned by Reza Shah, just before the British forced the King of Kings into exile and enthroned his young son.

Now Old Mossy led the National Front, a coalition of the secular, tribal, and religious disgruntled. His most important clerical ally was the fiery anti-British Ayatollah Abdul Qasim Kashani, a harbinger of the 1979 revolution's Ayatollah Khomeini. The aging lion's fiercest enemies were on the Left. Mobs organized by the Tudeh, the Iranian Communist Party, assailed him as a capitalist tool.

Meanwhile in Britain, the Labour government in the early 1950s began weighing armed intervention to save the oil fields. "If Persia were allowed to get away with it," warned Defense Minister Emmanuel Shinwell, "Egypt and other Middle Eastern countries would be encouraged to think they could try things on. The next thing might be an attempt to nationalize the Suez Canal."[14] The view from London, purveyed in an *Observer* profile, was that Mossadeq was "wholly impervious to common sense arguments of expediency," that he was "surrounded by crooks, adventurers and madmen" and was "truly a Frankenstein."[15] The Foreign Office's analysts went further, commenting that Mossadeq was "cunning," "slippery," "completely unscrupulous," "short with bandy legs," "looks like a cab horse," and "diffuses a slight reek of opium."[16]

The British closed down the Abadan refinery, their largest overseas asset, and in a familiar imperial ritual moved paratroopers to Cyprus and a cruiser to the Persian Gulf. For a moment, it seemed as if those who sought to settle the matter by force would prevail. But Washington was wholly out of step with this martial stance; its analysts stressed that Iran was the major supplier of oil to a still-recovering postwar Europe. At White House insistence, Downing Street agreed to a special mediating mission by the seasoned diplomat and soon-to-be Governor of New York, Averell Harriman. His Tehran mission failed. In a defining final flourish, AIOC's British employees, toting tennis rackets and golf clubs, gathered in front of Abadan's Gymkhana Club and prepared to embark for Basra. According to the company's official history, "The ship's band, 'correct' to the end, struck up the Persian national anthem and the launches began their shuttle service . . . The cruiser *Mauritius* steamed slowly up river with the band playing, the assembled company lining the rails and roaring in unison to the less printable version of 'Colonel Bogey.' Next day Ross and Mason [two senior officials] drove away. The greatest single overseas enterprise in British commerce had ground to a standstill."[17]

This was followed by the British imposition of economic sanctions on Iran, precipitating an oil boycott by all the major international petroleum companies. Whitehall next froze Iran's sterling assets and tried to coax Washington into moving directly against Mossadeq. President Truman and Secretary of State Acheson, who leaned toward Mossadeq's side and tried vainly to mediate when the Iranian leader visited Washington in October 1951, firmly resisted. The State Department's view was that Mossadeq was "supported by the majority of the population," and that he was "alert," "affable," "honest," and "well-informed."[18] *Time* magazine chose the Iranian as its "Man of the Year" for 1951, with a cover portrait identifying him as "The Dervish in [a] Pin-Striped Suit."[19]

Without a single tanker in its possession and without the expertise needed to run the refinery, Tehran reeled as work at Abadan ground to a halt. Talks with Mossadeq proved fruitless. The Iranians searched the home of the head of the oil company's Tehran office, where they exhumed documents, later published, proving that the oil company had interfered in all aspects of Iranian political life. Majlis deputies and former cabinet ministers who opposed AIOC had been forced from office; newspapers were bribed to publish articles defaming members of Mossadeq's party.[20] With ominous vehemence, a Tehran daily editorialized, "Now that the curtain is lifted and the real identity of traitors posing as newspaper men, Majlis deputies, governors and even prime ministers is laid bare, these men should be riddled with bullets and their carcasses thrown to the dogs."[21]

Iran took its case to the World Court, which ruled that it had no jurisdiction. Mossadeq then appeared at the United Nations, in vain. But the fault was not entirely Britain's. Like other populists, Mossadeq excelled at attack but drew back from articulating difficult truths to his own supporters. In retrospect, Acheson wrote, "This unique character truly sowed the wind and reaped the whirlwind."[22]

In London, as the space for accommodation narrowed, the Foreign Office cast about for a radical remedy. The first spark came with the publication of an unsigned article in *The Times* on March 22, 1951. Written by Ann Katherine Swynford Lambton, a Reader in Persian at the University of London's School of Oriental and African Studies who had seen wartime service in the Tehran embassy, the article deplored Iran's instability and "the stupidity, greed and lack of judgement of the ruling classes of Persia" that resulted in a corrupt and parasitic government. This led to a meeting with Lambton in Whitehall at which she suggested an uncompromising hard line toward Mossadeq, steady nerves, and changing Iran's government by "covert means." She added that Robin Zaehner, an opium-smoking, hard-drinking lecturer in Persian, and future Professor of Eastern Religions at All Souls College, Oxford, would be "the ideal man" to set the course.[23] The eccentric, squeaky voiced Zaehner was not an obvious choice as an intelligence operative but he had one exceptional qualification: he had operated covertly in Iran during the war.

Sent now to Tehran by the Foreign Office and not MI6, Zaehner quickly organized a network of Mossadeq haters and Anglophiles, a special prize being the three wealthy Rashidian brothers, Seyfollah, Asadollah, and Qodratollah. Importers of British goods and financiers of the National Will Party, they proved experts at organizing street mobs. The historian James A. Bill described the three MI6 assets: "Seyfollah, the eldest and a musician and philosopher, was the brains of the triumvirate and a superb conversationalist and host. He was a student of political history and liked to quote verbatim from Machiavelli. Asadollah was the organizer, political activist and confidante of Reza Shah's son, Mohammed Reza Shah, while Qodratollah was the business man and entrepreneur."[24] Although independently wealthy—they kept a family suite in London's Grosvenor Hotel—the brothers received a monthly subsidy of £10,000 (around $28,000) from their employers, which they used to bribe clerics, newspapermen, and deputies in the Majlis and for spreading anti-Mossadeq propaganda in the newspapers and bazaars. Helping out was AIOC's own intelligence service, the Central Information Bureau, which had extensive press contacts and links to the politically potent, oil-rich Bakhtiari tribe, now reeling from the cutoff of company subsidies.

Meantime, a new and distinguished MI6 station chief took over in Tehran. In wartime, C. M. "Monty" Woodhouse, having been made a colonel at age twenty-seven, headed the Allied Military Mission working with the guerrillas in German-occupied Greece. With a countess for a wife and a peer for a father, this understated, upper-class Englishman later represented Oxford as a Conservative Member of Parliament. In 1951–52, as new chief of the MI6 station in Tehran, Woodhouse was housed within the British Embassy's gigantic compound: a walled fifteen-acre, velvet-lawned cantonment. Assisting him was his Persian-speaking deputy, Norman Darbyshire, who had been stationed in Iran during World War II and who would draft the original plan for OPERATION BOOT.

Under the 1906 constitution, the Shah had the power to name and dismiss the Prime Minister. Now he clashed with Mossadeq over the latter's demand for wider powers, especially over the Ministry of War. In July 1952, the Shah forced his Prime Minister's resignation, but after three days of violent rioting, the flustered monarch, having underestimated Mossadeq's popularity, had to reappoint him and grant most of his demands. Then Mossadeq overreached. He extended martial law and instituted a curfew, suspended elections for the National Assembly, abolished the Senate, and dissolved the Supreme Court. In September, he rejected a formula for settling the oil dispute approved by Truman and Churchill, who had just returned triumphantly as Prime Minister to Downing Street. The crisis deepened as Mossadeq expelled the British diplomatic mission, thus defending his actions: "You do not know how crafty they are. You do not know how evil they are. You do not know how they sully everything they touch."[25] Given ten days to clear out, MI6 turned over its intelligence "assets," including the Rashidian brothers, to the Americans while closely tracking the crisis from Cyprus.

Following the November 1952 election of Dwight Eisenhower, Anglo-American differences regarding Iran ceased. Three weeks after his victory, the President-elect met with Churchill's Foreign Secretary, Anthony Eden, to discuss "the Persian Question." A week later, Kermit Roosevelt met with his MI6 counterparts in London. Woodhouse also traveled to Washington to approach the American "cousins" afresh. "When we knew what the [new team's] prejudices were," Woodhouse acknowledged, "we played all the more on those prejudices." A war was being fought with North Korea, Joseph McCarthy was grandstanding in the Senate, and the Rosenbergs had been tried, convicted, and sentenced to death for spying; therefore Woodhouse opted to stress "the Communist threat to Iran rather than the need to recover control of the oil industry." He argued "that even if a settlement of the oil dispute could be negotiated with Mossadeq, which was doubtful, he was still incapable of resisting a coup by the communist Tudeh Party if it were backed by Soviet support. Therefore he must be removed."[26] Otherwise, the Soviet Union would "take the country over as it had just taken over Czechoslovakia."[27] (Fortuitously, for the Americans and British, Stalin died in March 1953, throwing the Tudeh Party into disarray.)

The CIA agreed to study the proposed operation although the head of the Tehran station, Roger Goiran, resigned rather than put "US support behind Anglo-French Colonialism."[28] Woodhouse for his part heaped scorn on an unnamed senior State Department official who preferred diplomacy (the likely culprits were Assistant Secretary of State Henry Byroade and Ambassador Charles "Chip" Bohlen). The Americans proposed instead discrediting the anti-British Ayatollah Kashani and his left-wing friends, "so as to make it easier for Musaddiq to act effectively against the Tudeh party." Woodhouse contemptuously noted, "It was a piece of clever silliness characteristic of those Americans who still thought that Musaddiq could be retained and manipulated, and who dreaded the consequences of his downfall."[29]

Washington already had a large diplomatic (59) and military (123) presence in Iran, and the CIA's Donald Wilber had recruited a team of local agents to cultivate the press and recruit willing thugs. By mid-April, planning for AJAX (as the Americans re-christened OPERATION BOOT) was underway and a budget was approved. U.S. Ambassador Loy Henderson acted as a conduit between the British and the Shah. The State Department relayed his revealing assessment to the Foreign Office: the Shah was "harping on the theme that the British had thrown out the Qajar dynasty, had brought in his father and had thrown his father out. Now they could keep him in power or remove him in turn as they saw fit. If they desired that he should stay and that the crown should retain the powers given to it by the constitution he should be informed. If on the other hand they wished him to go, he should be told immediately so that he could leave quietly."[30]

As the clandestine momentum developed, Foreign Secretary Anthony Eden, who had read Arabic and Persian at Oxford and was thus the self-appointed Cabinet expert on all things Iranian, fell ill, and the more proactive Prime Minister Churchill temporarily assumed his duties. Churchill urged the Shah to dismiss Mossadeq, and even offered instructions on how to do it. His message, unearthed and published by British writer William Shawcross in *The Shah's Last Ride*, deserves full quotation: "I should be glad

if Mr. Henderson, U.S.A., would transmit to the Shah the following observation of a general character which I believe is correct and in accordance
with democratic principles. Begins. It is the duty of a constitutional monarch or President when faced with violent tyrannical action by individuals
or a minority party to take the necessary steps to secure the well-being of
the toiling masses and the continuity of an ordered state. Ends."[31]

The CIA's Roosevelt and Wilber now traveled to London with the coup
proposal they had drafted together in Cyprus. After meetings with MI6, a
reworked version emerged. The plans were next submitted to the Americans
at the famous June 25 meeting mentioned earlier. Churchill greenlighted
the operation on July 1, and President Eisenhower on July 11. (Woodhouse
notes that "Churchill enjoyed dramatic operations and had no high regard
for timid diplomatists.")[32] Wilber instigated what he described as "a war of
nerves," with the help of two Iranian assets, code-named Nerren and Cilley. A CIA courier arrived with a large number of anti-Mossadeq cartoons
and posters that enabled Wilber to launch a massive propaganda campaign
aimed at discrediting Mossadeq's government. Articles stressing the Communist threat were planted in the foreign and local press.[33] Intelligence networks were meshed, and agent provocateurs, specialists in inciting trouble
that could be blamed on the Communists, were hired. Weapons were distributed to the tribes. An armed gang kidnapped, tortured, and killed Tehran's
chief of police. The Grand Ayatollah conveniently issued fatwahs against
the Communists.

The operational pace had accelerated by the time Kim Roosevelt, his
nerves tingling and spirits soaring, made his way from Beirut to Damascus. Under the alias James F. Lochridge, he crossed Iran's borders carrying a
hundred thousand dollars' worth of small Iranian bills and arrived in Tehran on July 25 to direct the operation.

A successor to Mossadeq had already been auditioned by the Americans,
and found worthy. He was General Fazlollah Zahedi, a devoted royalist and
bon vivant who had served as Interior Minister in Mossadeq's first cabinet.
The choice annoyed the British. In 1942, in an operation code-named PONGO,
they had kidnapped Zahedi and exiled him to a Palestine internment camp
for plotting with the Nazis. PONGO was led by the legendary Fitzroy Maclean,
Churchill's "kilted Pimpernel" and reportedly an inspiration for the fictional

James Bond. (According to Maclean, his search of Zahedi's Isfahan bedroom turned up "a collection of automatic weapons of German manufacture, a good deal of silk underwear, some opium, an illustrated register of the prostitutes of Isfahan and a large number of letters and papers.")[34] Zahedi's troubles with the British now worked to Roosevelt's advantage as the Iranian public's perception of the general was that he was anti-Communist and would not be suspected of being pro-British. Zahedi's son, Ardeshir, who had attended college in Salt Lake City, would serve as liaison between his father and the Americans. (Ardeshir, who married the Shah's daughter before becoming the sometime consort of Elizabeth Taylor, was to become the Shah's free-spending Ambassador in Washington and London.)

Roosevelt's next step was to confer with the jittery Shah, whose hold on the throne was precarious—he had survived two assassination attempts and had yet to produce a male heir. Wilber advised his superiors that the Shah required special preparation: "By nature a creature of indecision, beset by formless doubts and fears, he must be induced to play his role, and this role must require a minimum of affirmative action and cover as brief a period as possible."[35] The Shah also displayed a "pathological fear of the 'hidden UK hand.' "[36] The plotters needed "Boy Scout," their nickname for the Shah, to sign two royal firmans or decrees: one firing the "Old Bugger," the other naming Zahedi as his successor. If necessary, Wilber assured Zahedi, the coup would be executed "without the Shah's active cooperation."[37]

The Shah's "forceful and scheming twin sister," Princess Ashraf, then gambling in France's casinos, was approached in an effort to stiffen the Shah.[38] Her lack of enthusiasm for the task was overcome when MI6's representative presented her with a mink coat and a large infusion of cash. She attempted to visit Tehran secretly on July 25 but left five days later under orders from Mossadeq, after a stormy meeting with her brother. MI6 also arranged to have the nightly broadcast of the BBC's Persian Service tweaked: it was to begin with "It is now *exactly* midnight" instead of "It is now midnight in London"—signaling to the Shah that he indeed had British backing. To prove he also had American support, Roosevelt arranged for Eisenhower to depart from an unrelated speech he was giving to a conference of governors in order to state that the situation in Iran was "very ominous to the United States" and that the Soviets "must be blocked and blocked now."[39]

Another timely interlocutor materialized: retired General H. Norman Schwarzkopf (father of the 1991 Gulf War commander), who had gained the Shah's confidence when he headed the U.S. Military Mission to the Imperial Iranian Gendarmerie. The general interrupted his world tour, dropping by the palace with a mission: to get the decrees. In a bizarre encounter, the paranoid Shah indicated that he thought the ballroom was bugged, and their conversation took place with both men sitting atop a small table in the center of the room. Schwarzkopf reported that the Shah had refused to sign the decrees and asked for more time. The general urged his friend Kim to stop dealing through intermediaries and to meet directly with "H.I.M.," which Roosevelt did on August 3. In the first of a series of secret meetings in which "relentless pressure was exerted in frustrating attempts to overcome an entrenched attitude of vacillation and indecision," the Shah protested that "he was not an adventurer and, hence, could not take the chances of one," leading Roosevelt to conclude that he was a "wimp."[40] Over the course of the meetings, Roosevelt detailed the plan, which included the prepared firmans and providing several thousand dollars for handouts to encourage pro-Shah demonstrations. The Shah finally agreed to sign the firmans. Roosevelt suggested that he fly to his Caspian retreat with his wife and wait. Roosevelt conveyed Eisenhower's final message: "I wish Your Imperial Majesty godspeed. If the Pahlavis and the Roosevelts working together cannot solve this little problem, then there is no hope anywhere. I have complete faith that you will get this done!"[41] Until the decrees arrived, Roosevelt bided his time swimming in a country villa, drinking vodkas with lime during games of backgammon, and repeatedly playing the operation's theme song, "Luck Be a Lady Tonight" (from *Guys and Dolls*) on his phonograph. Adding to the urgency of the moment, on August 12, the Soviets successfully tested their first hydrogen bomb.

Suspecting an Anglo-British plot, Mossadeq had held a successful referendum calling for the dissolution of the Majlis, thus preventing the CIA from obtaining a quasi-legal vote through bribes against him. The Shah, angry that Mossadeq had reduced him to a figurehead, signed the decrees, which were promulgated on August 13. On Sunday night, August 15, the coup began but faltered and nearly failed when it was compromised by a talkative army officer. The commander of the Imperial Guards delivered the royal decree to Mossadeq, but backed by heavily armored troops, the Prime Minister denounced the decree as a forgery. He had the messenger arrested and instigated a massive search with a 100,000-rial reward, the target being Zahedi. When a dawn broadcast on Tehran radio proclaimed the failure of the coup, the Shah, unsure of the army (Zahedi had no troops at his disposal) and without alerting Roosevelt's team, fled with his wife, Soraya, in a single-engine plane, first to Baghdad, where his embarrassed fellow monarch King Faisal II proved less than welcoming, then onward on a British Airways flight to Rome. (He checked into the Hotel Excelsior, where his fellow guest was Allen Dulles.) The Mossadeq press raged at the United States for its involvement in the coup attempt.

Cyprus groaned and Churchill wavered. In Washington, gloom pervaded the Quonset huts where the CIA was temporarily quartered. However, this proved to be Kermit Roosevelt's finest hour. What turned the tide wasn't luck but the agency's cash. Ignoring a cabled warning from the home office to get out of town, he left his embassy bunker and drove up to Shimran, the resort north of Tehran, where he consulted with the Ardeshir Zahedi. He arranged a meeting between Ardeshir and *The New York Times*'s Kennett Love and gave the reporter copies of the firmans. Roosevelt also sent a message to the Associated Press bureau asserting that Mossadeq had been replaced by Zahedi. Then working with Woodhouse's and Wilber's extensive contacts, Roosevelt dipped into the agency's slush fund (estimates varying from $50,000 to $100,000 or more), and with the embassy's copy machine printed and distributed thousands of copies of the decrees. (When his Iranian agents declined to help because they feared arrest, he first offered them money, and when they refused, he threatened to have them killed. They accepted the cash.)

The Prime Minister and his supporters were outorganized, outspent, and outfoxed. Nerren and Cilley hired a mob of provocateurs to join with a real Tudeh mob that had been tearing down statues of the Pahlavi shahs. On August 18, Ambassador Loy Henderson, who had been "exiled" to Switzerland and had returned to Tehran on a military plane the previous afternoon, met with Mossadeq. He began by casting doubt on the Prime Minister's legitimacy. When Mossadeq asserted that it was the parliament not the Shah that had the authority to elect premiers, Henderson threatened to evacuate all Americans unless Mossadeq controlled the mobs that were threatening them. Lulled by the Shah's departure and the arrests of some plotters, Mossadeq banned street demonstrations and asked his supporters to stay off the streets. Henderson now trapped him into calling in the police and royalist troops, many of whom were on the CIA payroll, while the Prime Minister's followers remained in their barracks.

On August 19, as the Iranian papers published the decrees, troops loyal to the Shah escorted the Rashidians' hired "black crowds": "[W]ith the army standing close guard around the uneasy capital, a grotesque procession made its way along the street leading to the heart of Tehran. There were tumblers turning handsprings, weight-lifters twirling iron bars and wrestlers flexing their biceps. As spectators grew in number, the bizarre assortment of performers began shouting pro-Shah slogans in unison. The crowd took up the chant and there, after one precarious moment, the balance of public psychology swung against Musaddiq."[42]

Armed with clubs, the hired thugs looted and burned the headquarters of Mossadeq's party and sacked opposition newspaper offices. A supporting cast plied the crowd with ten rial notes and plastered Mohammed Reza's picture, printed by CIA agents, on automobiles and city walls. By late afternoon, crowds shouting, "*Shah piruz ast!*" ("The Shah is victorious!") controlled police headquarters and the Ministries of Foreign Affairs, Press, and Propaganda. Especially important was the seizure of the radio station and central telegraph office, precipitating a stream of telegraphs to alert the nation to the uprising and persuade other garrisons to support the Shah.

As Ayatollah Kashani and other prominent members of the Shiite clerical establishment switched sides, Sherman tanks surrounded Mossadeq's fortress-like White House and after a climatic battle, left it in ruins with the loss of some two hundred lives. The Prime Minister fled over the roof, only to surrender the next day. General Zahedi emerged from hiding and proceeded by tank to Radio Tehran. There he addressed the nation, proclaiming himself the lawful Prime Minister. Crowds poured through the streets shouting, "*America Zindabad!*" ("Long Live America!"). In Rome, when the Shah heard the news from an excited Associated Press reporter, he blanched and declared, "I knew that they loved me."[43]

The Shah on his victorious return to Tehran thanked Roosevelt effusively with a vodka toast, saying, "I owe my throne to God, my people, my army— and to you!" Roosevelt quickly adds in his account, "He meant me *and* the two countries—Great Britain and the United States—I was representing. We were all heroes." As he escorted Kermit to his car, the Shah presented him with a gold cigarette case "as a souvenir of our recent adventure."[44] Roosevelt had spent less than three weeks in Iran; *The New York Times* estimated that after the battle, three hundred people lay dead and another hundred lay wounded.[45] The bribes worked; the "spontaneous uprising" succeeded.

Roosevelt was smuggled out of Tehran and picked up by a military air transport for a flight to London, where he met with his British counterparts. Winston Churchill, having suffered a debilitating stroke, was in bed when he received him at 10 Downing Street. At the Prime Minister's urging, Kim recounted his escapades, prompting the envious remark, "Young man if I had been but a few years younger, I would have loved nothing better than to have served under your command in this great venture!"[46] Sir Winston expressed the official Anglo-American consensus that AJAX was "the finest operation since the end of the war."[47] Reviewing the events in his diary, Eisenhower noted, "It seemed more like a dime novel than an historical fact."[48] Nevertheless, in a ceremony—for obvious reasons secret—the President awarded Kermit Roosevelt the National Security Medal. As for his role in the operation, Wilber peevishly wrote that Roosevelt marked the victory with a celebration that consisted of "a Dutch treat lunch at a Chinese restaurant on Connecticut Avenue, which did not serve liquor."[49]

Yet the British balked at dividing the spoils, and the fact that the Americans took full credit for the coup rankled. A year earlier, Foreign Secretary Eden had written, "I do not like the idea of bringing American companies in."[50] Notably, the first official U.S. visitor to Tehran after the coup was oil expert Herbert Hoover Jr., a close friend of Kermit Roosevelt's. The son of the former President, Hoover was now Secretary Dulles's special adviser and a conduit between the CIA and the oil companies. His mission was to negotiate, as per a prior understanding with Britain, a consortium agreement that would open Iran to American companies. Purportedly, the Shah told Hoover that the CIA help would be paid for in oil. After arduous negotiations, assisted by the Dulles brothers' law firm, a new agreement proved a benchmark in oil diplomacy. Chastened by Mexico's nationalization of oil and pressed by a Truman-initiated Justice Department antitrust suit against the international petroleum cartel, the big oil companies began showing a more prudent regard for local sensibilities. Under the arrangement, Iran would own all the country's oil resources, yet it would not interfere in the decisions of independent operating companies. The split was 40/40, with Anglo-Iranian, renamed British Petroleum, qualifying for 40 percent of the consortium and the Americans getting 40 percent (each of five major U.S. companies received 8 percent). The rest went to Royal Dutch/ Shell (14 percent) and a French company, Compagnie Française de Pétroles (6 percent). In oil historian Daniel Yergin's view, set forth in *The Prize*, there was a bigger bottom line: "With the establishment of the Iranian consortium, the United States was now *the* major player in the oil, and the volatile politics, of the Middle East."[51] As if to underscore its succession to Britain's role in Iran, Washington expeditiously advanced loans it had refused to give to Mossadeq: $60 million in 1954, $53 million in 1955, and $35 million in 1956.

As for Mossadeq, his supporters were jailed, his Foreign Minister executed, and the deposed firebrand tried for alleged political crimes. But Mossadeq turned tables by using his trial to make the best and most eloquent case for his doomed administration. He was found guilty, imprisoned for three years, and kept under house arrest at his ancestral estate, albeit with a pension arranged by Roosevelt, until his death in 1967. In *Daughter of Persia*, his cousin, Sattareh Farman-Farmaian, offers this tribute: "Mohammed Mossadegh . . . had represented a true mobilization of our national will. His twenty-eight months in office had been one of the few times Persians had ever cooperated and achieved something together. He had been obstinate, made many mistakes, and once even resorted to unconstitutional trickery. But he had not failed because of the way he looked, or because of his eccentricities and mannerisms. He had failed because he struggled too hard and too uncompromisingly against a superpower."[52]

Having recovered his throne, Mohammad Reza Shah seemed a different sovereign. His previous uncertainty gave way to certitude, his shyness to love of limelight, his deference to boldness. Unable to tolerate any threats to his power base, he soon exiled General Zahedi to an ambassadorial post in Geneva. He rejoiced when his third wife, Farah, produced the essential male heir, assuring the continuation of the Pahlavi dynasty. In 1967, on his forty-eighth birthday, dressed in the pearl-embroidered cloak his father had worn in the same palace where Reza Shah had placed the Pahlavi crown on his own head, his son crowned himself King of Kings in a fête featuring a 101-gun salute, a coronation hymn ("You Are the Shadow of God"), and a city-wide shower of 17,532 roses for each day of his life, scattered over the capital by the Royal Iranian Air Force. The self-proclaimed "Light of the Sun" broke with tradition by also crowning Empress Farah, who was dressed by Dior and wore a pink and white diamond tiara designed by Van Cleef and Arpels. He appeared more certain than ever that he was destiny's child, having survived assassination attempts, British guile, and Soviet efforts to dismember Iran.

The coronation was followed in October 1971 by an even more stupendous gala at Persepolis, the ancient seat where Darius and Xerxes once held court. The three-day celebration marked the 2,500th anniversary of the founding of the Persian Empire, at an estimated cost of more than $300 million in a country with a per capita income of $350. Taking note of conspicuous absences, *Newsweek* commented that "[y]ou just weren't important if you weren't invited; but you couldn't have been important if you actually showed up."[53]

Queen Elizabeth declined her invitation in light of a warning by the Foreign Office that she might "find herself among a crowd of B-list leaders" in an event that was "likely to be arduous, disorganized and possibly undignified and insecure."[54] But as the British wished to avoid an offense that placed British oil concessions at risk, Prince Philip and Princess Anne joined an international gallery: Yugoslavia's Marshal Tito, Romania's dictator Nicolae Ceausescu, Philippine President Ferdinand Marcos and his wife, Imelda, America's soon-to-be-disgraced Vice President, Spiro Agnew, and ten monarchs, including the soon-to-be-deposed Emperor Haile Selassie of Ethiopia. A-list notables who declined included President Nixon, West Germany's Chancellor Willy Brandt, and France's President Georges Pompidou, who chortled, "If I did go, they would probably make me headwaiter."[55]

Despite widespread drought and famine that year in Iran, notwithstanding student protests, international press criticism, and prudent misgivings expressed by Empress Farah about the foreign catering, the Iranian Air Force shuttled more than fifty yellow-and-blue air-conditioned tents designed by the Paris firm of Jansen (purveyors to the Kennedy White House), which were arranged in the shape of a star, their floors covered in priceless Persian carpets, their beds and marble baths sporting the finest Porthault linens and personalized Limoges china (presented as farewell lagniappes), to accommodate top-tier dignitaries. Lesser luminaries, among them oil tycoons and the CIA's Donald Wilber, sojourned at hotels and motels forty miles away in Shiraz, where even the Savak prison, operated by the Shah's notorious security and intelligence service, had been redone.

At a state dinner, five hundred guests washed down pounds of Imperial Caspian caviar with hundreds of bottles of vintage wine, including a 1945 Chateau Lafite-Rothschild, and gallons of French champagne in Baccarat crystal goblets. The 165 Maxim chefs and sous chefs dispatched from Paris prepared a lavish feast of quail eggs stuffed with caviar, crayfish mousse, roast lamb with truffles, and foie gras–stuffed peacock. For dessert, a port-glazed fig and raspberry delight was served. The evening ended with a *son et lumière* performance and fireworks that focused the guests' attention on Persepolis and featured actors representing the Persian Kings Cyrus, Darius, and Xerxes, all speaking in French. Security helicopters circled before the tomb of Cyrus the Great while the Shah, in a voice shaking with emotion, addressed the great Persian king: "To you Cyrus, Great King, King of Kings, from Myself, Shahanshah of Iran, and from my people, hail! . . . Cyrus we stand before your eternal dwelling place to speak these solemn words: Sleep on in peace, forever, for we are awake and we remain to watch over your glorious heritage."[56] (The Shah seemed to have forgotten that the ancient Persian capital had been reduced to ruins by Alexander the Great. Jason Burke, a journalist visiting in 2001, found an official sign outside the still-extant Shah's tent reading "Examine what your predecessors did and learn a lesson.")[57]

On the following day, 1,724 costumed soldiers paraded by the spectators, mimicking the procession of ancient races bearing gifts depicted in the relief on the staircase of Persepolis's Apadana. Present among the six hundred journalists was Lesley Blanch. In her ill-timed official biography (1978) of the Empress Farah, she described the pageant of Iran's armed might through the centuries:

> . . . the tight crimped beards of the Medes and the Persians, the small pointed beards of the Safavids, or the fierce moustachios of Qajar troops. Shields, lances, pennons, broadswords and daggers of earlier warriors, all were there. Beneath a scorching sun, but shielded by parasols provided for those in need, the guests, who were seated on a rostrum below the pillared ruins of Cyrus' might, watched this impressive procession. Achaemenian foot guards, Parthian warriors, the cavalry of Xerxes, litters, chariots, tanks, Bactrian camels, Fath Ali Shah's artillery, warriors from the Caspian or the Persian Gulf, the Air Force, the new Women's contingents of the armed forces . . . all were there at Persepolis, all attested to Iran's glories, past and present.[58]

Five years later, in a further bold and confusing gesture, reflecting the longevity of the monarchy, the Shah decreed that the traditional Islamic calendar was to be supplanted by the Pahlavi calendar. All documents—

newspapers, calendars—would be dated 2535, its first year marking the putative foundation of Persian kingship. The Islamic calendar year 1355 (1976) had been confusing enough for those Iranians engaged in business with the West. But this new Pahlavi calendar especially enraged the Shi-ite clergy, with whom the Shah had quarreled since 1963, the year that land reforms in his much-touted modernization program, the "White Revo-lution" had begun to take effect. Faced with clerical criticism at that time, the Shah angrily dismissed objections by "lice-ridden mullahs," whereupon Islamic anger swelled, notably in the religious center of Qum, where Ayatol-lah Ruhollah Khomeini first attracted attention with his wrathful attack on the Shah. Widespread riots followed the sermon and led to the Ayatollah's arrest, conviction, and imprisonment, until his release in 1964.

Soon after Khomeini's release, President Johnson held out to the Shah a tempting offer of U.S. military advisers and a credit line of $200 million for what was to become in later years a diet rich in Phantom jets, Chief-tain tanks, a miscellany of helicopters, torpedo ships, and cutting-edge mis-siles. The credit line included a proviso: Iran had to adopt a Status of Forces Agreement (SOFA), giving American personnel immunity from local laws. The SOFA measure was rubber-stamped by the Majlis, now a caricature of its former self, its two parties having earned the popular nickname "Yes" and "Yes, Sir." There followed another thunderclap from Qum:

Does the Iranian nation know what has happened in recent days in the Assembly? Does it know what crime has occurred surreptitiously . . . Does it know that the Assembly, at the initiative of the government, has signed a document for the enslavement of Iran? It has acknowledged Iran is a colony, it has given America a document attesting that a nation of Muslims is barbarous, it has struck out all our Islamic and national glories with a black line . . . If the Shah should run over an American dog, he would be called to account but if an American cook should run over the Shah, no one has any claims against him . . . I proclaim that this shameful vote of the Majlis is in contradiction to Islam and has no legality . . . If the foreigners wish to misuse this filthy vote, the nation's duty will be clearly specified.[59]

For this, Ayatollah Khomeini was banished, finding asylum first in Turkey, then in Iraq, and finally in France before his tumultuous return in February

1979. His jeremiad against SOFA crystallized outrage over America's indirect dominion and stoked the fires of retribution.

Having launched his White Revolution, which eliminated most of Iran's large landowners and drove the impoverished peasants into the cities, the Shah called his next Iranian project "the Great Civilization," a process whereby Iran would leapfrog into the modern era. The propellant would be oil, whose price soared dramatically as a result of the oil embargo that followed the Yom Kippur War in October 1973. The price of oil quadrupled within two months, meaning that Iran's yearly petroleum revenues of $5 billion could potentially rise to $20 billion. The Shah's appetite for military hardware, whetted by the Johnson administration, became voracious during the Nixon-Ford years, partly owing to the monarch's friendship with Secretary of State Henry Kissinger. (Iran's military became the world's fourth largest.) A grand strategic vision had mutual appeal: Let Iran assume guardianship of the Persian Gulf, thereby easing Washington's military burdens in the region, in return for American arms and training expertise. Despite the Pentagon's misgivings, the Shah was given unrestricted access to the most advanced U.S. arms, excluding nuclear weapons.

From 1972 to 1976, Iran spent $10 billion on American military hardware, making it Washington's leading foreign customer. When the Democrats took over the White House in 1977, the strategic partnership continued to prosper under Jimmy Carter. Not long after Carter's well-publicized New Year's toast to the Shah ("Iran, because of the great leadership of the Shah, is an island of stability in one of the more troubled areas of the world"), demonstrators in the streets of Iran defied the hated U.S.-organized Savak, the Shah's omnipresent secret police, and his huge military establishment. A thousand grievances—the inequities of a boom economy, the insolence of Westerners in their compounds, the affronts of immodest female fashions and infidel missionaries—welded a coalition of the dispossessed and disenchanted, of secular radicals and theocratic reformers. The bubble burst on January 16, 1979. The country was frozen by strikes, the armed forces mutinied, and the fifty-nine-year-old King of Kings boarded a blue-and-white Boeing 707 and, once again, fled his country. In his own self-serving memoir, he quotes a loyal general facing a firing squad as saying, "[The Americans] threw the Shah out of the country like a dead mouse."[60] On February 1, an Air France jet bearing Ayatollah Khomeini landed in Tehran.

The cancer-ridden Shah began his international peregrinations from Egypt to Morocco, the Bahamas, Mexico, the United States, Panama, and back to Egypt, where President Anwar Sadat, encouraged him to settle, a move that contributed to the assassination of the Egyptian leader. The second and last of the Pahlavi Shahs died on July 27, 1980, in Cairo, having spent his last days as a guest of Sadat.

In the immediate aftermath of AJAX, Kim remembered advising Secretary of State Dulles, "If we, the CIA, are ever going to try something like this again, we must be absolutely sure that people and army want what we want. If not, you had better give the job to the Marines." But according to Roosevelt, this was advice Dulles did not wish to hear, because within weeks Roosevelt was offered the chance to direct the CIA's Guatemalan coup of 1954. He declined to lead OPERATION PBSUCCESS, which overthrew the elected President of the small Central American republic.[61] But on a visit to London in 1956, MI6 approached Roosevelt in the hopes of persuading him to participate in OPERATION UNFASTEN, whose object was to assassinate General Gamal Abdel Nasser, but Roosevelt prudently desisted and the plan came to naught.

Roosevelt retired from the CIA in 1958, becoming vice president in charge of government relations in Gulf Oil's Washington office. Subsequently he worked as a highly paid lobbyist—he helped Northrup obtain more than $1 billion in Middle East business—traveling to Iran five or six times a year, staying with his clients, the Rashidians.[62] Other blue-ribbon patrons included the Shah and the Saudis. Nevertheless, despite his extensive research and experience, Roosevelt, as Sallie Pisani writes, "ignored political and religious movements in Iran's history," believing that the power of the mullahs "would fade away as modernization took place."[63] He edited the two-volume history of the OSS that appeared in 1976, and in 1979 he attempted to publish *Countercoup, the Struggle for the Control of Iran*, his account of his role in the 1953 coup. However, the first edition of seventy-five hundred copies had to be scrapped when British Petroleum, the successor to AIOC, threatened to sue. (Roosevelt had submitted the manuscript to the CIA for review and had made the changes the agency demanded. BP claimed the book was not only misleading but also "wrong, inaccurate and thought to be libelous.")[64] The book was finally published in 1980 after the

American hostages held by the Khomeini regime were released. Roosevelt died following a stroke in 2000.[65]

Wilber, who had been AJAX's principal planner, resented Roosevelt's failure to mention his own role in *Countercoup*. After the events of 1953 Wilber received a routine civil service promotion to GS–14, as he was to complain, "below average for a person of my experience and length of service."[66] Following his retirement from the CIA, he wrote his heavily agency-censored *Adventures in the Middle East*. He died in 1997, at age eighty-nine. Only in 2000 did the CIA finally release Wilber's 1954 clandestine history, "Overthrow of Premier Mossadeq of Iran, November 1952–August 1953."

Reflecting on the operation for a television documentary, the CIA's onetime Inspector General, John Waller, declared, "We considered ourselves the Paladins of the Cold War."[67] From the CIA's perspective, the coup had given Washington twenty-five more years of the pro-American Pahlavi dynasty and "enabled the international oil industry to export at favorable terms 24 billion barrels of oil."[68] But even the agency's official reprise of the events is cautionary. Its authors rightly expressed concern over the possibility of "blowback" against the United States from such operations.

The complete story of the 1953 coup will probably never be written, since many British and American files were destroyed, and many continue to be unavailable. (As late as the year 2000, about a thousand pages of documents remained in the agency's vaults.) What might the withheld files reveal? In the view of City University of New York's Professor Ervand Abrahamian, "[I]t is one thing to admit that the CIA distributed 'grey propaganda,' funded demonstrations, played 'dirty tricks,' and urged officers to carry out the coup. It is another thing to admit that the CIA worked through local Nazis, and had a direct role in kidnappings, assassinations, torture, and mass street killings."[69]

Although the coup succeeded because of active or passive Iranian support, nobody can credibly doubt that it was stage-managed by the British and Americans. The 1953 overthrow of Mossadeq proved to be Washington's most successful regime change in the Middle East. But the coup derailed Iran's fragile electoral system, and as the United States became embroiled in Iranian domestic politics, disenchantment with the Yankees was inescapable. After the Shah's flight and after the United States granted him asylum in 1979, militant Iranian students seized fifty-two American hostages in part to prevent a repetition of 1953. The hostage crisis by common account cost Jimmy Carter the 1980 presidential election. As the Yale scholar Abbas Amanat wrote in *The New York Times*, "Every schoolchild in Iran knows about the C.I.A.-sponsored coup that toppled Prime Minister Mohammed Mossadegh. Even an Iranian with little interest in his or her past is conscious of how Iran throughout the 19th and 20th centuries served as a playground for the Great Game . . . A quarter-century later, Americans were 'taken by surprise' when an Islamic revolution toppled the Shah and transformed a country that seemed so friendly to the United States. But if Americans suffered from historical amnesia, for many Iranians, among them Ayatollah Ruhollah Khomeini, the thread of memory led clearly from the Great Game to the Great Satan."[70]

ELEVEN

The Apprentice Sorcerer

Miles Axe Copeland, Jr. (1916–1991)

⌘

We were not a lot of evil geniuses plotting to brainwash the world ...
On the contrary, we were innocent kids with new toys—and a license
to steal.

> —Miles Copeland,
> *The Game Player* (1989)

⌘

Miles is the only man who used the Central Intelligence Agency
for cover.

> —Wilton Wynn,
> Middle East correspondent, *Time*

If you were lucky enough to visit Beirut before 1975, there was only one place to linger for a drink if you were a CIA case officer, an arms merchant, a femme fatale, or a foreign correspondent. The place was the St. George Hotel Bar at the heart of the Lebanese capital, which itself was the conspiratorial epicenter of the Middle East. Jean Bertolet, once the hotel's manager, fondly recalls his role in "a unique, once in a century happening. I felt as if my clients were running the Middle East, occasionally the world." From the 1950s onward, Beirut was the "Paris of the Orient"; it reigned for two decades as the financial capital of the Arab world, and only Cairo rivaled it as the intellectual capital. *Fortune* magazine in 1973 ranked the St. George among the world's top seven hotels for American executives, praising its "generously mixed drinks, and competent, unobtrusive service."[1]

Yet from our perspective, what matters was the hotel's centrality to coup plotting and regime changing. As a watering hole for inquisitive journalists and their (sometimes) reliable sources, the St. George for its time ranked with, or even ahead of, Shepheard's in Cairo, the Alcron in Prague, or the Athénée Palace in Bucharest. Built by a French company in the 1930s, its décor devised by the modernist Jean Royère, the five-story hotel reposed on a manmade V-shaped thumb projecting into the lovely Bay of Jounieh. Its tiers of balconies looked out on the bay's girdle of mountains, dotted with forests and villages and capped with snow. "On rare days in early spring, you could sit on the terrace for a noonday drink and watch people snow- and

water-skiing in a single line of vision," writes the hotel's most recent historian, the Palestinian writer Saïd Aburish. "At night the village lights rose
with the mountains until they became difficult to distinguish from the stars.
No other place in Beirut or, to my knowledge, in the world, could duplicate
its beauty of location."[2]

Let us eavesdrop on a typical day. An early regular, the co-chairman of
the bar's locally renowned Ten A.M. Club, is Sam Pope Brewer, chief Middle East correspondent of *The New York Times*. He chats briefly with Myrna
Bustani, part owner of the hotel and past member of the Lebanese parliament who hosts the St. George as if it were a national treasure. The morning shift in the hotel's oversize staff (around 285) has already scrubbed the
terrace's glass-topped tables, sponged the chairs, and swept the hotel's grill
and wood-paneled barroom. Brewer checks to see if he has any mail, the
hotel being a secure, much-used postal drop. He greets the bar manager, Ali
Bihar, and the chief bartender, Abu Khalil, who is dicing his home-grown
peppers for use in the hotel's popular Bloody Mary.

Then to work—which for Brewer signifies having a coffee and a croissant
or a pre-lunch Gibson (a chilled Martini with a pearl-sized onion) while gos-
siping with the incumbent station chief of the CIA. The agency is less than
a decade old, but Brewer is familiar with its ways. After schooling at Phillips
Exeter and Yale, he turned to journalism in the 1930s and first caught attention with his coverage of the Spanish Civil War for *The Chicago Tribune.* During World War II, he was recruited by the Office of Strategic Services (OSS),
the CIA's predecessor, and in the European theater he befriended Cyrus L.
Sulzberger, *The New York Times*'s foreign affairs columnist. Sy was impressed
by Sam—tall, thoughtful, bow-tied and soft-spoken—and at war's end he
opened the way for his employment at the *Times.* Still, Sulzberger was wary
of Brewer's intelligence connections. "I made him swear he had broken
all his ties," the columnist recalled. "That was a must." Yet another senior
Times correspondent, Harrison Salisbury, in reviewing his paper's complex
and difficult relations with the CIA, found "no evidence Sam did sever his
connections. In fact he probably maintained them until the end of his life."[3]
(Brewer died in New York at age sixty-six in 1976.)

Everyone at the St. George bar knew of Brewer's links to U.S. intelligence. When Wilbur Crane Eveland, while still a novice covert operator,
landed in Beirut in 1955, he immediately conferred at the St. George with
Brewer, sizing him up as an invaluable source and patient listener. Brewer

showed Eveland an internal foreign desk message reporting that Egypt had just signed an arms deal with Czechoslovakia, its first with a Soviet-bloc country. "Later that night," Eveland relates in his memoir, *Ropes of Sand* (1980), "another cable came in. Assistant Secretary of State George Allen was being sent by Secretary Dulles to Cairo for talks with Nasser. As if to convey the impression that the Egyptian-Czech arms deal didn't concern us, the trip was billed as a routine area visit by Allen to several countries to 'discuss current problems.' I'd had enough of that baloney for one night and left Sam to his work."[4] (Eveland details a half-dozen stories he provided to Brewer, and the *Times*.)

With an insider's intuition about fabricated cover stories, Sam cultivated everybody who mattered in the Middle East spy business. Among regulars at his table were Theodore Roosevelt's grandsons, Kermit and his cousin Archibald, the CIA's leading Arabists. A quotidian source was the Palestinian Abu Saïd Aburish, a stringer for *Time* and a trusted CIA "asset" (also, the father of the author Saïd Aburish, who reported for Radio Free Europe). Preeminent among Britons was H. A. R. (Kim) Philby, *The Economist*'s man in Beirut, who had recently resigned under murky circumstances from the British secret service. Philby impressed the Ten A.M. Club with his impeccable manners (when sober), his chronic stammer, and his opaque blue eyes. Sam and Kim had met during the civil war in Spain, where Brewer reported from the leftist Loyalist side while Philby, writing for *The Times* (of London), did so from the insurgent pro-fascist camp. In Beirut, their friendship rekindled, and when Sam left town on assignment, he asked Kim as a favor to look after his wife. On September 12, 1956, Philby and Eleanor Carolyn Kearns Brewer met (inevitably) at the St. George bar. When Sam returned, the three seemed inseparable—until a year later, when Eleanor sought and obtained a Mexican divorce as Kim stammered his intention to marry her ("You mean that you are asking my wife's hand in marriage?" Brewer reputedly asked).[5]

Yet there was a fourth man in the century's gaudiest spy scandal. He was Miles Copeland, the CIA's original political operative and its first agent to write indiscreetly and voluminously about his own role as a regime changer. He helped establish a distinctively American covert strategy by cultivating army officers rather than, in the British mode, kings, emirs, or tribal chiefs. He was sufficiently successful to become a byword in his craft and to elicit a singular testimonial from Kim Philby following the latter's mystifying disappearance from Beirut and his resurfacing in Moscow, where his Ameri-can bride Eleanor subsequently joined him. "I've known that intriguer for twenty years," Philby remarked in a live interview for Radio Moscow in the 1960s, "so I can say with authority that Miles Copeland's book, *The Game of Nations*, is itself a move in the CIA's monstrous game."[6]

And who was this egregious intriguer? Miles Copeland (born circa 1916) was the least wraith-like of U.S. intelligence agents. His brother operative, Wilbur Crane Eveland, recalled arriving at the Cairo airport in 1953 and being welcomed by a beaming extrovert, six feet tall with thick sandy hair, horn-rimmed glasses, and "eyes that danced with excitement."[7] Copeland's obituary in *The Times* of London (he died in Oxfordshire in 1991) described him as a "genial bear of a man" who "remained almost ostentatiously American" though he lived much of his life in England.[8] His devoted pro-tégé, Larry J. Korb, recalled meeting him while leaving the New York flat of arms dealer Adnan Khashoggi. "Hello, you're Larry Korb aren't you? I've heard of you," began Miles as the elevator descended. The novice agent indelibly remembered Copeland's seersucker suit and black-framed glasses that "looked just like my father's."[9] Yet though Copeland's figure is vivid, its outlines are fuzzy. For example, *The Times* of London's obituary gave Cope-land's age at death as seventy-seven, as did *The Washington Post*. However, *The New York Times* put his years at seventy-four, while the London-based *Guardian* reckoned he was seventy-six. Copeland's own memoir, *The Game Player* (1989), avoids telltale dates but establishes that he grew up in Bir-mingham, Alabama, where he graduated from the Erskine Ramsay Techni-cal High School in 1931, or possibly 1932, indicating that he was closer to seventy-seven at his death. Yet any of the above might be true.[10]

A similar uncertainty principle applies to most of his self-biography. Did he play the trumpet so well in high school that he was asked to per-form with the otherwise black group that evolved into Erskine Hawkins's Big Band in Tuskegee? Did he perform in Harlem's Cotton Club and then join Glenn Miller's still more celebrated orchestra, debuting as fourth trum-pet on the Roosevelt Hotel rooftop in New Orleans in September 1940? "As a jazz band musician," he writes, "I earned top dollar (for that era, I mean), and even the admiration of my colleagues. I enjoyed playing big-band jazz more than I've ever enjoyed any vocation or avocation, before or since."[11]

Exaggerated or not, Copeland's proficiency at jazz became established CIA folklore, and his actual (or putative) trumpet was exhibited as a cherished relic at the agency's fiftieth-anniversary fête in 1997.

In 1940, Copeland joined the National Guard, and like all recruits he took the Stanford-Binet intelligence test. He asserts in his autobiography that he scored 160, "the highest recorded in the whole US Army" or (as he elaborated) roughly the level estimated for Einstein, Goethe, and Jesus as somehow divined by psychologists at Stanford University.[12] True or not, Copeland indeed proved a genius at networking. Posted to the army's Corps of Intelligence Police (CIP) in Washington, he contacted "the finest man in the world," John Sparkman, his Alabama Congressman and later U.S. Senator. Sparkman opened the door to the Office of Strategic Services and its chief, General William J. Donovan. The two immediately struck it off, "the way people from opposite ends of the social scale like one another," so Copeland remembered. "In two minutes I was telling anecdotes about maneuvers in the Louisiana swamps . . . He laughed and laughed, and asked me if I had lunch. So there I was, minutes later, having sandwiches and beer at the desk of Wild Bill Donovan at a time when he was all but inaccessible to everyone in the outside world except President Roosevelt. I walked out of there with assurances that I'd be hearing from him."[13]

In fact, Copeland was not recruited into the glamorous OSS, which in the oft-repeated jibe of nonadmirers stood for "Oh So Social." He served instead in the more humdrum CIP, which in January 1942 was reborn as the Counter-Intelligence Corps (CIC), heavily staffed with linguists for interrogation and surveillance tasks. (Copeland's memoirs do not specify his rank, but most CIC agents were noncommissioned officers.) That same year he sailed to wartime London, where he billeted in fashionable Mayfair on South Audley Street. There he improved his French and socialized with British intelligence agents, among them Lorraine Adie, the daughter of a Harley Street neurosurgeon, herself a budding archaeologist, who was to be his lifetime spouse. Copeland apparently obtained top-secret "Bigot" clearance for access to detailed plans for OPERATION OVERLORD, and he purportedly took part in "game room" exercises at 20 Grosvenor Square, where General Eisenhower and his staff pondered their strategy for the Normandy landings.

In June 1944, in the wake of D-day, Copeland entered France along with other CIC agents, among them (as he liked to note) Henry Kissinger, J. D. Salinger, and William Saroyan. He was present before, during, or after the liberation of Paris (versions differ) and may have hoisted glasses with Ernest Hemingway, among others. But the CIC's overriding mission lay in Germany. While in London, Copeland first learned of OPERATION PAPERCLIP, a plan to scoop up German rocket scientists before advancing Soviet forces did the same. Besides corralling the makers of the V–1 and V–2 missiles, the CIC also sought out former Nazi officers such as General Reinhard Gehlen, who claimed to possess the Kremlin's secret files, as well as war criminals such as Klaus Barbie, "the Butcher of Lyons," who was put on the CIC payroll before being smuggled to South America on what agents called the "rat-line." Having visited Nazi death camps, and because many of his CIC colleagues were Jewish, Copeland admits to moral qualms over what was clearly a dirty business. Yet he also learned firsthand that covert rules were morally elastic, that pious official disclaimers were so much eyewash, and that viewed from the wings the contest for foreign mastery was, in truth, a game, which confirmed "the amorality of power politics," the subtitle of his first book.

There was no more avid game player than Wild Bill Donovan, who a year before VJ-day proposed endowing his OSS with permanent status. Donovan delighted in the operational feats of his agents, skills that would be needed, he counseled, because Moscow was already looming as Washington's postwar rival. But he ruffled with his evangelical fervor, and misread the popular mood. In September 1945, a month after Japan's surrender, President Truman formally disbanded the OSS. Yet Donovan successfully managed to find employment for hundreds of intelligence agents, including Copeland, in a new, blandly named Strategic Services Unit, or SSU. This was the embryo of the Central Intelligence Agency, whose birth Congress authorized in the 1947 National Security Act.

The legislation stipulated the CIA's five functions, four of which dealt with the gathering, analysis, and dissemination of intelligence related to national security. A vaguely phrased fifth authorized the agency to "perform such other functions and duties related to intelligence affecting the national security as the National Security Council shall from time to time direct." Since the new NSC was solely accountable to the President rather than to Congress, this opened a substantial loophole for covert operations against an expanding Soviet empire. (Subsequent legislation provided for limited congressional oversight of the CIA, but the agency's budget remains secret, and it was made a federal offense to identify a serving covert agent, as Americans were subsequently reminded in *United States of America v. I. Lewis Libby*, also known as "Scooter" Libby.)

The agency's birth coincided with the cold and epochal winter of 1946–47, when a straitened Great Britain informed the United States that it could no longer militarily assist a Greek government challenged by Communist guerrillas, or help Turkey defend its long frontiers with Soviet Russia. Washington responded in March 1947 with the Truman Doctrine, which provided for immediate armed aid to Greece and Turkey, and which pledged support for free people anywhere who resist "attempted subjugation by armed minorities or by outside pressure." All this electrified the air as the CIA's first two hundred employees, Miles Copeland included, reported for work in the makeshift huts on the Mall still surviving from wartime Washington.

Seemingly overnight, the payroll ballooned. In 1961 the agency moved to headquarters sufficient for fifteen thousand employees on a 125-acre site in Langley, Virginia. The campus atmosphere was enhanced at the entrance by a statue of Nathan Hale, the first American to be executed as a spy. It was a faithful copy of the original at Yale, which Hale attended (class of '73), commencing his college's long association with secret services. (In the 1980s, the statue was moved inward, reputedly because President Reagan's CIA chief, William J. Casey, felt the initial location sent the wrong message, since Hale, however gallant, failed in his mission.) The CIA's founders fixed the widest possible horizons for their offspring. In a speech at Yale in 1958, Allen Dulles, the fifth Director of Central Intelligence (DCI), declared that the National Security Act "has given Intelligence a more influential position in our government than Intelligence enjoys in any other government in the world."[14]

It was in this spirit that the agency's founders labored to invent traditions appropriate to America's first peacetime stand-alone espionage apparatus. Few agents proved more inventive than Miles Copeland, who likened his comrades-in-stealth to innocent kids given a new toy and a license to steal. In September 1947, Copeland was posted to Damascus, officially as a junior diplomat but in fact as the CIA's first operational chief in Syria. Like many musically talented persons blessed with good ears, he had an aptitude for languages, and within a year, assisted by his deputy, a native speaker, he was by his account sufficiently fluent to compile a colloquial Arabic dictionary. (The first of its kind, claimed Copeland, "making me, as my tutor said with pride, 'the Dante of the Arabic language.' ")[15]

Yet what policy or policies was the novice operator meant to promote? (Copeland was thirty-one, give or take a few years.) In reviewing the legation correspondence with Washington, Copeland concluded that the prevailing if unstated consensus held that the Arab states were in needless conflict with the United States, almost entirely due to "mischievous and misguided leadership—theirs, not ours." Indeed, given enlightened and effective leadership, the Arabs were America's natural allies. Copeland summarized what he felt official America believed:

> The Arabs had every reason to fear the Soviets, and nothing to fear from us, and it was against nature for them not to welcome our offers of protection. Our oil companies were going to make them rich. They would be the principal beneficiaries of an "amicable settlement of the Palestine question" such as only we could ensure. The refusal of their leaders to see it thus was regarded as ample reason and justification for us to overthrow them—or rather, to enable their own people to overthrow them. If national leadership anywhere in the world was such as to benefit from our interference in their affairs, we thought, it was Arab leadership.[16]

Copeland therefore assumed he had discretionary leeway to promote a change of regime in Syria, then governed by aging, tired, and uninspiring veterans of the nationalist struggle against France. He first recruited as a "special friend" one of the legation's local employees, Yussuf Dabbous, an effusive fixer who appeared to know everybody Syrian who mattered, and who possessed a figure and face shaped like an avocado. Copeland informed him that Washington had chosen Syria as a test case in promoting sensible government, preferably through free and fair elections. Hearing this, "Yussuf nodded solemnly, barely able to conceal his delight." Thus Syria in early 1949 became the first Middle East country to experience the newborn CIA's "skills at 'interfering in the internal affairs of sovereign nations.' " Copeland then candidly describes how to interfere, deniably.[17]

The new political operator began by asking his chauffeur to steal a Defense Ministry telephone directory. Presumably with Yussuf's help, he next persuaded the city's most notorious loan shark to identify insolvent officials. Two penurious candidates were approached; both agreed to steal documents for cash, although it transpired that one informant was already providing the same service for the local KGB agent. Meanwhile, Copeland secured Washington's approval for the transfer to Damascus of Stephen Meade, a seasoned military attaché then serving in Beirut. The colorful and ingratiating Meade struck up a friendship with Colonel Hosni Za'im, the Army Chief of Staff, and either promised or insinuated that if Za'im chose to seize power, the United States would promptly extend recognition.

Whatever assurances Meade might have offered, the colonel clearly understood that Washington had four topics of concern: Tapline, Turkey, Israel, and Communism. In 1947, the Trans-Arabian Pipeline Company (Tapline) had begun laying a pipeline meant to link Aramco's oil fields in Saudi Arabia with the Lebanese port of Sidon. But transit approval was stalled by politicians in Syria and Lebanon who denounced the plan as a giveaway to colonialism. Similarly, talks were deadlocked on the status of the key port of Alexandretta (present-day Iskandron), claimed by both Syria and Turkey in a potentially volatile dispute. Nor would Damascus take part in armistice talks with Israel after its armies were humiliatingly mauled in the 1948 Arab-Israeli war. Finally, as seen from Washington, Syria's incumbent rulers were either foolishly naïve or willfully complicit in their lenience concerning an ever-expanding domestic Communist Party.

The coup took place on March 30, 1949. As the purported but essential pretext, Colonel Za'im confronted his civilian chiefs with intentionally unattainable demands, whose rejection prompted a proclamation, composed by one of Copeland's Defense Ministry accomplices, which went like this: "Soldiers and patriots: A great moment has arrived in the proud history of our nation! A new era has begun! Corruption has ended. Puppets of imperialism and Communism have fallen. For the first time in centuries, we Syrians are a free people!" (In Copeland's recounting, the reference to Communism was added as a concession to Stephen Meade.) As this was proclaimed, rebel troops arrested Syria's President, Premier, local police chief, and key ministers and deputies. These ensuing events were reported play-by-play to desk officers in Washington, who assumed that Meade and Copeland engineered the whole thing, "an impression we saw no reason to correct since it was giving such pleasure to our admirers back home, and since neither of us was averse to the winning of a few brownie points in our respective 201 files."

The takeover was virtually bloodless. Writing forty years later, Copeland claimed that his and Meade's only substantive contribution was a promise of American recognition once Za'im was securely in power. Yet he then adds, "Steve did ride around the city with Hosni in the back seat of his limousine pointing out targets to be seized (the radio station, the main power generator, the central office of the telephone company, and all politicians who might be able to rally resistance), and Hosni politely pretended that he hadn't thought of these already. Also, I gave him a list of 'dos and don'ts' in the way of security procedures, and thanks to Agent A in the Defense Ministry, I was able to present certain information bearing on the plans that Hosni couldn't get from the ministry without arousing suspicion."[18]

Copeland's initial description of the putsch was more expansive. Before de facto U.S. recognition was extended, he writes in *The Game of Nations* (1969), Meade was constantly at President Za'im's elbow, "telling the new dictator who should be Ambassador at the Court of St. James's, which officers should be promoted into diplomatic positions, and what diet should be given to the deposed President." Yet once Washington extended its recognition, President Za'im seemed a new man. He informed his American mentors that henceforth they should address him as "*vous*" rather than the familiar "*tu*" (their common language being French). Still better, Za'im went on, they could call him "Excellency."[19]

In office, His Excellency did take steps long sought by Washington. Concerning the contentious matter of Israel, Syria finally joined armistice talks then underway with other Arab states in a makeshift hideaway on the Syrian frontier. There was indeed a crackdown on Syrian Communists. Za'im's administration ratified Tapline's route through Syria, sweetened by the pipeline consortium's offer of as much as $40 million in loans. Relations with Turkey over the vexed issue of Alexandretta improved when Za'im declared his willingness to join a pro-Western military bloc in return for military aid. Moreover, President Za'im, whose origins were Kurdish, enfranchised women, disapproved of traditional Arab headgear, and abolished such feudal titles as Bey and Pasha. Yet as a politician, in the judgment of Patrick Seale, Britain's leading historian of Syria, Za'im was less successful: "Concerned from the start with the illegitimacy of his regime, his desire was to become President and stand as an equal beside the kings and Heads of State with whom he now had to deal . . . Gradually he moved into the rarified air of personal authority and broke with the handful of activist officers with whom he had planned and carried out his putsch."[20]

A corroborative verdict is offered by Anthony Nutting, a British junior minister who resigned in protest over his own government's gross misjudgments during the 1956 Suez Crisis. "The CIA could hardly have chosen a man less likely to succeed," he related in 1972, than this stocky army colonel with a florid face and a boisterous manner, who was "by any standards a popinjay." Once in power, Colonel Za'im "adorned himself with resplendent uniforms and a marshal's baton costing over a thousand pounds and indulged in such fanciful notions as being able to turn the Arabs' 1948 defeat into victory by personal negotiations with [Israeli Prime Minister David] Ben Gurion . . . And when the twists and turns of his maneuverings had alienated all his earlier well-wishers [he] was overthrown by another coup, led by another colonel."[21]

It seems fair to say that the short-term benefits for Washington of this first CIA-promoted coup were obliterated by the long-term costs of triggering a sequence of coups that empowered the armed forces as political arbiters of key Middle Eastern states. More subtly damaging, the Syrian putsch propagated a culture of paranoia that imputed exaggerated omnipotence to U.S. intelligence agencies, whose agents were commonly assumed to be linked hip and cloak with Israel's Mossad. In any case, Syria was a questionable venue for an experiment in "political action," the CIA euphemism for covert intervention, in light of its peculiar and painful history.

Syria and Lebanon were promised to France in 1916 under an agreement reached secretly with Great Britain on sharing the prospective spoils of a defeated Ottoman Empire. But boundaries were not precisely demarcated. In the territorial swapping that followed World War I, the British prevailed on France to detach Palestine and oil-favored Mosul from Syria, annexing the latter to Iraq and dividing the former into the mandatory states of Palestine and Transjordan. There followed a further subtraction when the French, claiming rights dating to the Crusades, assumed a victor's rights in Syria and Lebanon. Their triumphant mood was voiced by General Henri Gouraud, later High Commissioner in the Levant, when he entered Damascus in July 1920. Pausing at the tomb of Saladin in the Grand Mosque, the general kicked it and exclaimed (as he thought) for the ages, "Awake Saladin! We have returned! My presence here consecrates the victory of the Cross over the Crescent!" The French then further recarved the Levant. The compact Ottoman entity known as Grand Liban, long the stronghold of Maronite Catholics, was expanded at Syria's expense to create Greater

Lebanon, at the cost of increasing its non-Christian population. In a final slice, the Allies ceded the coastal area north of Aleppo, including the site of ancient Antioch, to Turkey. By the time France formally withdrew from Syria in 1946, the newly independent state comprised roughly 115,000 square miles, compared with the more than 186,000 square miles of the former Ottoman province. To this day, Syrian tourist maps designate the lost lands as being within "temporary boundaries."

Nevertheless, in a self-delusory trance, the French deemed their occupation of the Levant a success, as measured by improved rail networks, modernized ports, newly built schools and factories, and other indices of presumed progress. Hence the shock in 1925 when a revolt surged through Syria and Lebanon, precipitating the French bombardment of Damascus (which together with Aleppo has long claimed to be the world's oldest continuously inhabited city). "When the smoke lifted," writes the Harvard historian Joyce Laverty Miller in a detailed analysis, "much of Damascus was in ruins; the reported loss of life and liberty appalled world opinion and galvanized Arab dissidents. A torrent of violent and emotional criticism was unleashed. In some quarters, it was even hinted that the League of Nations would remove [its] mandate from French control."[22] Instead, within months the disorganized insurgency faded, and the world's attention moved on.

According to Miller, the roots of the revolt lay in the imposition of an artificial nation-state on Syria's many subgroups, whose members had a long tradition of self-governance in local affairs under the Ottomans. In her words, "The early French administrators in Syria, in their efforts to develop and modernize a Syrian nation, were of necessity inflaming groups which had always mistrusted one another within the Ottoman Empire and had coexisted only because 'the nation,' the empire, was weak. In short, the revolution of 1925 was not the nationalist revolt of a united people against a French oppressor but a power struggle among and within divisive groups who could agree on only one thing: the French must go." Revealingly, the uprising had its origins in a Druze department of fifty thousand inhabitants, whose leaders were outraged by a French administrator's efforts to inculcate the blessings of modernity, including a museum that displayed pagan (and nude) classical statuary.[23]

Doubtless much has changed in Syria since the 1920s, but one is struck by the egregious self-confidence of Westerners, then and now, who presume to know what is best for a people whose language they cannot speak and whose customs they cannot fathom. By faith and ethnicity, Syrians are Sunnis, Shiites, Alewites, Druzes, Kurds, Turkmen, and Ismailis (the latter being the ancient patrons of the Assassins, a Syrian sect that flourished during the Crusades). Syrians are also Greek and Armenian Christians, Roman and Maronite Catholics, as well as Protestants of a dozen denominations— not to overlook an Aramaic-speaking sect in Maaloula, a hilltop town near Damascus, where monks recite the Lord's Prayer in what is reputedly the language of Jesus. Nor should one forget the Yezidis, a Kurdish sect whose adherents believe God has forgiven, and reinstated, Lucifer.[24]

This uncongealed diversity had to have been obvious to Miles Copeland, but its implications seemingly did not register. For instance, he names the key commanders whose backing made the 1949 coup possible. "For the benefit of future historians," he writes in his memoirs, "I think I should record that the four commanders were Adib Shishakli (a Circassian), Mohammad Nasser (an Alewite), Bahij Kallas (a blond-haired and blue-eyed Christian), and Showkat Shuqeir (a Lebanese Druze)."[25] (With an insider's relish, he adds that Colonel Shuqeir was second cousin to Selwa "Lucky" Roosevelt, wife of the CIA's Archibald Roosevelt, and in her own right a well-regarded reporter for the old *Washington Star*, and later chief of protocol for President Reagan.) Yet Copeland fails to note that not a single leader of the cabal belonged to Syria's Sunni Arab majority. In effect, the coup's American promoters expected, or hoped, that a portly Kurdish colonel with grandiose ambitions and limited abilities could impose an American-flavored policy with token regard for consent of the governed. Instead, there then ensued a dozen further coups and counter-coups, culminating in the current Ba'athist dictatorship.

President Za'im's rule lasted less than five months. He was ousted in August 1949 in a British-backed countercoup orchestrated by Colonel Shishakli on behalf of yet another brigade commander, Colonel Sami al-Hinnawi. Rebel soldiers seized and executed President Za'im, then buried him in a French cemetery. "We are doing you the favor of treating him as a French agent," Copeland was consolingly informed by Shishakli, who then proceeded to oust Hinnawi in the same year's third coup, this time on his own behalf and with CIA backing. President Shishakli, the ablest of the original cabal, survived until February 1954, when he was overthrown. By then the Syrian army and its allied security police had so permeated politics that they provided the repressive talons for an air force general named Assad, who in 1970 established his seemingly impregnable hereditary police state.

Hafez al-Assad was the grandson of a locally renowned village wrestler, and the son of a minor Ottoman notable who in 1927 changed his family name from Wahhish, or "savage," to Assad, or "lion." The Assads are Alewites, adherents of a dissident Islamic sect that emerged, along with the Shiites, Ismailis, and Druzes, a millennium ago during the turmoil following the death of Islam's third Caliph. As their name indicates, Alewites believe that Ali, the Prophet Mohammed's cousin and son-in-law, was robbed of his birthright as the Caliph's heir. The Alewites divided into four tribes that settled in Syria's coastal highlands, the region known today as Latakia, where they constitute about 12 percent of the country's 18 million inhabitants.

Although orthodox Sunnis shun the Alewites as heretics, Assad turned the sect's minority status to advantage by imposing a reciprocal live-and-let-live tolerance on Syria. His political instrument was the Ba'ath Party, established in 1941 by Michel Aflak, a Christian and a Sorbonne graduate (who also wore a fez). Secular, ostensibly socialist, and purportedly pan-Arabic, the Ba'athists under Assad created the illusion of popular consent and a wider unity when Iraq also became a Ba'ath republic under Saddam Hussein. In truth, power in both countries remained in the barracks (and in interrogation cells) under warlords who loathed each other. They had two policies in common: hostility to Israel and a shared distrust of successive Egyptian rulers, from Nasser to Mubarak, their fellow military dictators. Mix in opportunistic arms deals with the Soviet bloc, and flirtation with Washington on matters of common concern (oil and Iran), and you have the essential elements of most Middle East diplomacy during the Cold War.

Like Saddam Hussein, Hafez al-Assad preferred fear to affection. This was underscored by a bloodletting in the riverside town of Hama, known to travelers for its venerable and huge waterwheels. The British journalist Robert Fisk was present in 1982 when Syria's special forces, under the command of Hafez's brother Rifaat, put down an uprising by the fundamentalist Muslim Brotherhood. As Fisk recalls, "I stood by the River Orontes as Syrian battle-tanks shelled the ancient city; I saw the wounded, covered in blood, lying beside their armored vehicles, the starving civilians scavenging for old bread. Up to 20,000, it was said, died in the underground tunnels and detonated buildings. The real figure may have been nearer 10,000, but most of the city was destroyed."[26]

The massacre established what became known as "the Hama Rule." There were no further uprisings during Assad's thirty-year reign, which ended with his death by natural causes in 2000. (Assad was succeeded by his younger son Bashar, his older son Basil having died in a high-speed car accident in 1994. The Western-educated Bashar abandoned a medical practice in London to enter Syria's military academy, from which he emerged in record time with the highest possible grades and a colonel's stripes. The Syrian constitution was expeditiously amended to enable him to succeed legally to the presidency at age thirty-four, as he did.)

All this was in the future as Miles Copeland left Syria for a new life in Egypt. In 1953, he formally resigned from the CIA to join Booz, Allen & Hamilton, in his estimate "the world's most prestigious management consulting firm." During a long lunch in Washington with the firm's chief executive, he was offered a well-paid position in Cairo, an offer warmly seconded by Frank Wisner, the CIA's overseer of covert operations. By that time, everybody at Langley knew that the fast track to advancement led through Wisner's antiseptically named Office of Policy Coordination (OPC), "a tail wagging the whole CIA dog," in Copeland's phrase. (An OSS alumnus, Wisner backstopped successful coups in Iran and Guatemala, and at the height of the Cold War his office covertly assisted the Congress for Cultural Freedom and the London-based *Encounter* magazine. Admired for his ingenuity and energy, Wisner suffered from manic depression and in 1965 killed himself with one of his son's shotguns.)[27]

Once in Cairo, Copeland headed a team of thirty persons carrying out a management study of Egypt's sprawling national bank, Banque Misr. This complemented his off-the-book work for the CIA, then seeking new friends in the Society of Free Officers, a junta of reform-minded colonels who in July 1952 carried out a successful coup against the corpulent, unloved, and unremembered King Farouk. The more radical Free Officers favored creation of a republic, socialist and secular, but the movement's initial public face was that of the affable General Mohammed Naguib, an accommodating moderate whom the junta named Prime Minister and then President. Soon enough, however, all Cairo realized that the dominant figure in the Revolutionary Command Council was Colonel Gamal Abdel Nasser, son of an Alexandrian postal worker, then in his mid-thirties: tall, fit, and compellingly keen-eyed.

When Naguib urged prompt elections with full participation by the mildewed Wafd nationalists and the volatile Muslim Brotherhood, Nasser dissented. He shunned the religious and Marxist ideologues no less than the failed and corrupt Wafd; he urged banning them all. His was a vision of a proudly reborn Egypt, at the vibrant center of three intersecting circles—the Arab, Islamic, and African worlds—views he elaborated in his manifesto, *The Philosophy of a Revolution*. And he sought an Egypt strong enough to avenge its 1948 humiliation by Israel, which his fellow officers experienced firsthand.

Nasser faced down his rivals and turned to trade unions, students, peasants, and the press for support. He escaped near-assassination by a Muslim Brotherhood gunman; he resorted to repression and censorship to stifle dissent; and he rose rapidly: Interior Minister (1953), Deputy Prime Minister (1953), Prime Minister (1954), and finally President (1956).[28] Every step was tracked by the CIA's Middle East team, beginning in October 1952 when Kermit Roosevelt opened back-channel contacts with Nasser and his like-minded Free Officers, though for appearances sake, the stolid U.S. envoy in Cairo, Jefferson Caffrey, formally conferred with General Naguib. Among the CIA's key figures, until the Suez debacle in 1956, was Miles Copeland, who later said he had "probably seen more of Nasser than any other Westerner."[29]

How baffling it must have seemed to Colonel Nasser and his brother officers, many of them, like him, mostly self-educated, little traveled, and novices in great power diplomacy. Who truly spoke for the lords of the Potomac? Was it Caffrey at the front door, or Roosevelt at the back? What should one make of prominent members of Congress (and their wives) who combined shopping and tourism with their official visits? How seriously should one take effusive assurances of sympathy from important-sounding American journalists anxious for access? This much was widely apparent: a strategic reappraisal was underway in Washington concerning the Middle East, given its surge of nationalism and the waning powers of Great Britain.

A prevalent view, especially among Democrats, had been articulated in 1952 by Secretary of State Dean Acheson during a three-day meeting in Washington with Winston Churchill, then in his final years at Downing Street, and with his soon-to-be successor, Foreign Secretary Sir Anthony Eden. To Acheson, the Middle East "presented a picture that might have been drawn by Karl Marx," with its poverty-stricken proletar-

iat, lack of a real middle class, and a corrupt ruling elite catering to foreigners who sought to exploit priceless resources "whether oil or canal."
He asked, "Was there ever such an opportunity to invoke inherent xeno-
phobia to destroy the foreigner and substitute the Communist solution?
Anglo-American solidarity on a policy of sitting tight offered no solution,
but was like a couple locked in a warm embrace in a rowboat about to
go over Niagara Falls. It was high time to break the embrace and take to
the oars."[30] This elicited a chuckle from Churchill (Acheson later related),
who kept muttering, "Take to the oars!" Eden was more optimistic, but
Acheson was insistent. He writes in his memoirs, "I argued that the policy of sitting tight in solidarity offered little promise for British interests"
and considerable danger for Washington. "I pressed this point on Mr.
Eden with such asperity and impatience as to require subsequent amends,
which were good-naturedly accepted."[31]

The asperity was mutual. A common British apprehension was expressed
in a memorandum to Eden from Sir Roger Makins, his Ambassador in
Washington. The influence of Americans in the Middle East had "greatly
expanded since the end of the Second World War," Makins wrote, "and
they are now firmly established as the paramount foreign influence in Turkey and in Saudi Arabia. They are gaining a similar ascendance in Persia,
and it now seems that Pakistan may to some extent be drawn into their
orbit." He closed rhetorically, "Are the Americans consciously trying to
substitute their influence for ours in the Middle East?" and left little doubt
about his answer.[32]

Makins was writing in early 1954, the critical year when Prime Minister Nasser wrested, with American approval, the prize that had eluded a
succession of khedives, sultans, and kings (their titles kept changing, but
not their status as British vassals). In a landmark treaty, Nasser secured
the phased withdrawal of eighty thousand British troops still posted in the
Canal Zone and elsewhere in Egypt, ending a "temporary" occupation that
commenced in 1882. As a face-saving gesture, Nasser agreed to a "reacti-
vation" clause stipulating that in the event of an attack by the Soviet Union
or an unspecified "outside power," Britain and Egypt could renew their military alliance. It was a measure of long-suppressed Egyptian rage that even
this cosmetic concession was assailed by Muslim extremists as well as the

Marxist Left. For his part, Eden was heckled in Parliament by a vocal "Suez Group" of Tory dissidents for yielding anything to Egypt.

Langley's team in Cairo applauded the treaty, which complemented its determined courtship of Nasser, who for his part sought a firmer security relationship with Washington. He first proposed a $400 million arms deal, later reduced to $200 million. Eventually, the actual package dwindled to "just two or three million dollars worth of parade items" such as helmets, pistol holsters, and "shiny equipment that would dress up a parade" (Copeland's paraphrase). It was American unwillingness to provide Egypt with planes, tanks, and advanced weaponry that caused Nasser to turn to the Soviet Union. This unwillingness had hardened following the advent in 1953 of John Foster Dulles as Secretary of State. Foster (as friends called him) brought a seigniorial loftiness to his long-sought post. A formidable, lantern-jawed lawyer, he had negotiated the peace treaty with Japan, helped write Republican foreign policy platforms, and was a partner of a top-rank Wall Street law firm (Sullivan & Cromwell)—and for good measure his younger brother Allen had just been named Director of Central Intelligence.

Lacking in Secretary Dulles's impressive resumé was experience with, interest in, or sympathy for what everybody called the Third World. His focus was on the Cold War, and he had no use for neutralism, which he bluntly condemned as immoral. By 1955, two contrasting global outlooks crystallized in the formation of the Baghdad Pact and the meeting of Third World leaders at Bandung, Indonesia. The pact, formally called the Central Treaty Organization (CENTO), was expressly meant to prevent Soviet poaching in the Western-dominated Islamic East, its signatories being Britain, Turkey, Pakistan, Iran, and Iraq (then led by its ardently pro-British Prime Minister, Nuri al-Said). Dulles and Eden each visited Cairo in the vain hope of recruiting Egypt into the regional security alliance. As vainly, Nasser tried to explain that he regarded Israel as his most likely potential aggressor, not the Russians—and by the way, when would Washington finally approve its long-delayed weapons sale?

By 1955, Nasser's frustrations had peaked. Nothing galled him more than the imperious condescension of Eden, who that February in his sole visit to Egypt treated him (Nasser complained) like "a junior official who could not be expected to understand politics."[33] At one point during the winter Nasser was sharing a terrace table in Cairo with Miles Copeland when Israeli warplanes buzzed overhead with impunity. "I have to sit here and take this," he said to Copeland, "and your government won't give me arms."[34] Such was Nasser's mood as he embarked on his first major foreign trip in March 1955 to meet with leaders of thirty newly independent Asian and African states in Indonesia. There Nasser befriended and impressed the Bandung Big Three: his host, President Sukarno, India's Prime Minister Nehru, and China's Foreign Minister Chou En-lai. Was it possible, Nasser asked Chou, for China to sell Egypt the modern weapons it required? No, China needed all it could then buy from Russia, but Chou said he could put in a word with Moscow, and perhaps the Soviets might oblige. It was this conversation that led, step by incremental step, to the Suez Crisis of 1956, the era's most spectacular attempt at regime change whose outcome prompted Miles Copeland to warn Washington (in vain) about the limits of covert action.

The first fateful move occurred immediately after the Bandung conference. In April 1955, to the enormous relief of his Tory Party, a visibly weary Winston Churchill gave way at 10 Downing Street to his designated heir, Sir Anthony Eden. Certainly the best dressed and among the best looking of British premiers, Eden was a decorated hero in World War I, becoming at twenty the youngest major in the British Army. After the war, he received a first-class degree in Oriental languages at Christ Church, Oxford, and from time to time adorned his speeches in Parliament with his own translations of Persian poetry. He had resigned as Foreign Secretary in 1938 to protest what he perceived as truckling to dictators.

Concerning the Middle East, Eden was the proud begetter of the Baghdad Pact, and brushed away a top-secret Foreign Office scheme, the Alpha Project, calling for a comprehensive settlement of the Arab-Israeli dispute based on reciprocal concessions. (Interestingly, both Eisenhower and Dulles were less dismissive.)[35] Instead, he soon blamed Nasser for every British setback in the Middle East, his vehemence intensified by his dependence on a mind-altering narcotic, Drinamyl, a blend of amphetamines and barbiturates. This followed a botched gall bladder operation, as verified decades later by David Owen, a physician who also once served as Foreign Secretary. Neither the public nor Parliament were aware that Eden was verging on a nervous breakdown in the months leading to the Suez Crisis.[36]

And it was that crisis that brought down Eden, turned Nasser into an Arab demigod, and marked the end of British primacy in the Middle East.

James Morris, once a Cairo correspondent for *The Times* of London, expressed a widely shared judgment. "It was an operation clouded in secrecy, duplicity, and irrationality," he remarks in *Farewell the Trumpets: An Imperial Retreat* (1978). "It was almost a cruel parody of the British imperial style. Eden cast himself as an elegant younger Churchill, saving the world by his exertions. Nasser he portrayed as a Muslim Hitler—'I want him destroyed!' cried the Prime Minister to one of his Ministers . . . All was shameful and underhanded."[37] Most unforgivably, it failed.

Not long after returning from Bandung, Nasser was contacted by Daniel Solod, the Soviet envoy in Cairo. He confirmed that the Chinese had passed along Nasser's request, and that Moscow would be pleased to provide tanks and aircraft against deferred payment in the form of cotton and rice. He added, unexpectedly, that his government would also like to help finance major projects such as the Aswan High Dam, the centerpiece of Nasser's ambitious plan to generate power and irrigate the Nile Valley. "It was a remarkable offer by any standards," remarks Anthony Nutting, who as a British Minister took part in the events he describes. "During the Farouk era, Moscow had persistently opposed Egypt and the Arabs on the Palestine issue and had voted with America for the U.N. partition plan and the creation of a Jewish state."[38] What appears to have turned this policy around was the downfall of Farouk and the rise of the still-undefined but anti-imperial Free Officers. With Russia's offer in hand, Nasser now turned with ill-concealed relish to London and Washington, repeating his urgent request for arms. Dulles brushed him off, and Eden warned that if Egypt obtained weapons from Russia, it could expect no further aid from Great Britain.

That July, a perspiring Soviet visitor, Dmitri Shepilov, then editor of *Pravda* and shortly to be Vyacheslav Molotov's successor as Foreign Minister, turned up in Cairo, ostensibly to help celebrate the third anniversary of the Egyptian revolution. Within days, Shepilov drafted an agreement to provide MIG fighters, Stalin tanks, and Ilyushin bombers for $80 million, payable with cotton rather than cash. All weapons were of Soviet manufacture, but at Nasser's insistence the weapons were to be shipped through Czechoslovakia to play down the Russian connection. To no avail. Dulles instantly dispatched Assistant Secretary of State George Allen to Cairo to admonish Nasser in what was billed a "routine" visit.

Now both Dulles and Eden were furious with Nasser. Washington and London had previously agreed to help finance the Aswan High Dam ("our new pyramid," as Nasser remarked to Morris of *The Times*) once the World Bank had certified its feasibility. As Eden confided to Nutting, his aim was "to keep the Russian bear out of the Nile Valley." But following the arms deal, London and Washington posed new conditions: no Communist countries could bid competitively on construction contracts, Egypt was to accept no loans from any other country without World Bank clearance, and a third of Egypt's budget was to be earmarked for the dam. This prompted a special mission by Kermit Roosevelt, who assured Nasser that these were simply normal bank rules, and he grudgingly assented. Negotiations dragged on until May 26, 1956, the day Nasser announced that Egypt would recognize and establish full diplomatic relations with then-outcast Communist China.[39]

How dare he? A fuming Dulles informed Egypt's Ambassador in Washington that the loan approval hung by a thread. The flustered envoy flew to Cairo and Nasser all but shrugged, contending that Egypt could obtain the High Dam funds by nationalizing the Suez Canal Company, and in any case if the West withdrew its support, the Russians would step in. Yet once again, yielding to ardent appeals from his diplomats, Nasser relented and agreed to the remaining conditions, thus forcing his adversaries' hands. On July 19, 1956, an unappeased John Foster Dulles informed Nasser that the United States was withdrawing its offer of financial support for the High Dam, claiming the Egyptian economy was "too weak" to bear huge construction costs. Two days later, the British followed suit.

Strangely, few in Washington or London anticipated President Nasser's countermove. With its trademark omniscience, *Time* magazine published a cartoon showing a shrewd chess-playing Dulles checkmating an astonished Nasser. On July 19, the impenitent Nasser flung the chessboard over in an hour-long speech at Alexandria greeted with jubilant roars from a hundred thousand throats. Why shouldn't Egypt buy arms from Communists? "In Egypt they are Egyptian arms." He decried the onerous Anglo-American conditions for the World Bank loan as "imperialism without soldiers." In times past, he reminded Egyptians, "we were kept waiting in the office of the British High Commissioner and the British Ambassador, but now they take us into account."

Then to the astonished delight of his listeners, Nasser announced his decision to nationalize the Suez Canal Company. Since its opening, the canal had been operated by a French concessionaire, the Compagnie Universelle du Canal Maritime de Suez, in which the British Government held the controlling shares (45 percent). Nasser was canceling the concession, compensation would be provided, and toll revenues would finally belong to Egypt; no longer would the company be a state within a state: "We shall build the High Dam, and we shall gain our usurped rights!"[40]

By chance (or perhaps not by chance), Nasser's Suez speech occurred on the same day Sir Anthony Eden was hosting a Downing Street dinner party for Faisal II, the British-groomed King of Iraq, and Nuri al-Said, Britain's preferred Prime Minister in Baghdad. "Hit him," counseled Nuri, after a shaken Eden read out the news from Egypt, "Hit him hard, and hit him now!"[41] As the dinner party dissolved, its male guests still clad in knee breaches and white ties, consultations began with France's Prime Minister Guy Mollet, whose Socialist-led government was convinced that Nasser was covertly fueling a nationalist uprising in Algeria. Within hours, the British called up military reserves, froze Egyptian assets, and ordered the withdrawal of the canal's foreign pilots (a step springing from Eden's certainty that Egyptians lacked the skills to manage the waterway). Yet when Eden made urgent contact with Washington, he found his partner-in-toughness, Foster Dulles, was in a notably less martial mood.

During most of his presidency, Dwight Eisenhower did not often second-guess his Secretary of State, though the two Republicans were of very different temperaments. As a professional soldier, Eisenhower drew back from the use of force save as a last resort. If costs were modest and risks limited, covert operations could be justified, as in Iran and Guatemala, but the President shunned "brinkmanship" (a word Dulles popularized) that might escalate into a superpower collision. Moreover, he was heading into a second-term election and still convalescing from a heart ailment. Eisenhower made clear that he wanted a peaceful resolution of the canal crisis, and nothing else. The general's determination was evident in Dulles's call for forming a Suez Canal Users Association (SCUA) that could accept tolls pending a negotiated resolution of the conflict—a course pressed by Arab neighbors and the United Nations.

To Anthony Eden, it was Munich and appeasement all over again. SCUA was toothless and hopeless; action was essential. Without consulting his Cabinet, military commanders, the Foreign Office, or his ambassadors in

Cairo and at the United Nations, or the White House, Eden sounded out the French on a military intervention to unseat Nasser. How was it to be done? A seemingly ingenious scenario evolved. Why not secretly encourage the Israelis to charge across the Sinai into Suez, then jointly intervene to safe-guard the international waterway and "separate the combatants," in the process ridding the region of Egypt's stiff-necked troublemaker?

This was the "Israeli pretext" agreed to at a hastily convened confer-ence on October 22 in a secluded villa at Sèvres, just outside Paris. Speak-ing for Britain was Foreign Secretary Selwyn Lloyd; others present included France's Premier Mollet and Foreign Minister Christian Pineau, and a high-level Israeli delegation consisting of David Ben-Gurion, Moshe Dayan, and Shimon Peres. The Israelis had their reasons for taking part. Since August 1955, they had combated cross-border incursions by Egyptian-trained fedayeen guerrillas, an irregular force condoned if not aided by Cairo; in addition, yielding to Egyptian pressure, the canal company had closed the Suez to Israeli shipping. Notwithstanding their bitter differences on mat-ters past and present, the Sèvres conspirators approved General Dayan's plan for a Sinai offensive to commence October 29, eight days before the American election.

The operation proved a near-perfect debacle. Only the Israelis success-fully attained their military objective. The Egyptian army did not collapse, as Eden expected, but resisted a fumbled Anglo-French invasion long enough for the UN General Assembly to vote 65 to 5 for a resolution demanding an instant withdrawal of the invaders (only Australia and New Zealand dis-sented, along with the three perpetrators). Few world leaders were angrier than President Eisenhower, who was caught by surprise on the eve of his reelection. Just as unforgivably, the Suez invasion diverted attention from the simultaneous Soviet throttling of the Hungarian uprising, and neither he nor Foster Dulles were consulted or properly forewarned about a scheme reeking of anachronistic imperialism.

The canal itself was rendered useless when the Egyptians bombed and sank seventeen ships trapped in its waters, blocking "Britain's windpipe." Instead of diminishing Nasser, the Suez Crisis quadrupled his stature, while in England the aftershocks of failure brought down Eden. The value of the pound plunged. A fourth of Britain's imports and most of its oil passed through the Suez. When Washington warned that absent an immediate withdrawal, it would not defend a weakened British pound with loans essential to offset soaring oil prices, the game was up. Then in an inspired postscript, three UN second-level diplomats—Canada's Lester Pearson, America's Ralph Bunche, and Britain's Brian Urquhart—virtually overnight assembled a peacekeeping force, the first of its kind. Nasser was adamant that the United Nations Emergency Force (UNEF) needed uniforms visibly unlike those of the invaders. Urquhart came up with an improvised solution: In Europe there were ample stores of U.S. Army helmet liners, and these were then spray-painted UN blue. Thus the Blue Helmets (les Casques Bleus) became the sole affirmative and enduring memorial to Suez.[42]

Such was the context in which Kermit Roosevelt, Miles Copeland, and their partners on the CIA team vainly tried to divert what became a headlong march to folly. For the Americans, this was strange new terrain. In earlier years, U.S. covert agents viewed their British counterparts with something close to awe, but by the time of Nasser's Soviet-bloc arms deal in 1955, awe soured into disdain. That year, Chester L. Cooper, a young and eager CIA agent, was sent to London to collaborate on Middle East matters with Britain's Joint Intelligence Staff. On his first encounter, it seemed to Cooper that height was the primary qualification for his new colleagues: "I was passed from giraffe to giraffe. 'Cooper, y'know—new boy.' Each stooped and shook my hand briskly . . . I found myself sitting between two giants wearing identical black suits (Savile Row), identical blue striped ties (Eton), and identical spectacles (National Health)."

Cooper was so dismayed by what struck him as an air of frivolous amateurism, interspersed by chit-chat over cricket scores, that he felt it necessary to remind his colleagues that the new arms deal marked the first time the Soviets had sold weapons to a non-Communist regime. As an American, he was especially struck by the languid condescension with which the British tried to recruit signatories for Eden's pet project, the Baghdad Pact.[43]

Still, in this offstage rivalry, the Americans possessed an advantage their British cousins palpably resented—cash, bundles of it, in seemingly endless quantities. Yet the CIA itself misjudged the downside of this advantage, especially if employed (in today's vernacular) Tony Soprano style. During the stalled negotiations over arms aid, Copeland was told in 1953 by

Henry "Hank" Byroade, a soon-to-be Ambassador to Egypt, that $3 million from the President's household budget was available for presentation to Nasser as a "personal gift." Copeland, then nominally a private citizen, was recruited as the most suitable courier to deliver the cash to Hassan Touhami, a personal aide to Nasser. The dollars were stuffed in two suitcases, which Copeland accompanied from the U.S. Embassy to Touhami's home. Bemused armed guards stood by as Touhami carefully counted the notes, and determined that the actual amount was $2,999,990. "We won't fuss about the missing $10," he said before conveying the "personal gift" to his chief's residence. He later reported that Nasser accepted the "gift" with a mixture of annoyance and amusement, and at first wanted to return the money forthwith. Then he nodded in agreement when an aide suggested installing two statues in full view of the about-to-be-built Hilton Hotel, one figure with a large nose to which the other figure thumbed with four fingers extending skyward.

"Nasser thought the idea very good, but lacking in subtlety," Copeland writes in *The Game of Nations*. "Instead, he ordered 'something unidentifiable but very large, very conspicuous and very expensive—costing, oh, say, something in the neighborhood of three million dollars.' The result is the 'Tower of Cairo' which we American friends of Egypt see across the Nile every morning as we breakfast on our balconies of the Nile Hilton." Kermit Roosevelt, who first proposed the gift, learned in due course that Nasser's aides referred to the tower as *el wa'ef rusfel*—"roughly translatable as 'Roosevelt's erection.'"[44]

Copeland found the episode distasteful and clumsy, and was similarly critical of other aspects of U.S. policies in the Middle East. He learned early in Cairo that the best intelligence was useless if its ultimate consumer possessed a mind that "couldn't be opened with a crowbar," which he claimed was the case with John Foster Dulles.[45] The Secretary seemed unable to fathom (in Copeland's view) that it was futile to press another government to adopt policies likely to threaten its leader's survival, such as pressing Nasser to join an anti-Soviet security organization. Having helped Colonel Nasser gain power, the first priority was to keep him there: "he was no good to us out of power and no alternative was in sight." Copeland was as dubious about the prevailing Washington conviction that free elections were the preferred solution to another country's problems: "More often than not, a free election in a so-called 'developing' country will be won by one of two types: first, a politician or political group whose first priority in getting into power will be to ensure that there are no more free elections, or, second, a demagogue making promises he can't possibly keep and who, after victory, will make demands on us we can't possibly meet and then blame us for his failure."[46]

Drawing on his own experiences, Copeland offers his cautionary wisdom on remaking regimes: "If you must change either the character or the course of another government, you must do it by use of forces already existing *inside* the country. If no such active or dormant force exists, you must try another approach, or simply adjust to an imperfect world." He paraphrased a principle enunciated by a Chinese military strategist three thousand years ago: "You must never enter upon a fight unless you can see an acceptable chance of success at the end. In political action, the costs of failing to solve a problem are invariably greater than the costs of leaving it unsolved; and the costs of *conspicuously* failing to solve it can be positively suicidal."[47]

Finally, he warned against expecting praise or thanks from beneficiaries of U.S. aid: "We must recognize that *most* of our best work with a government we wish to remain in power must be secret, not because we need the secrecy but because our client needs it. No, Virginia, we are *not* popular in most parts of the world; leaders in countries which receive our largesse do *not* gain in the eyes of their peoples from advertising their friendship with us—although all too many of them from time to time win a few points by boasting about how they have made suckers of us. In all but a few instances where regional leaders have become known as pro-American they have lost prestige or their lives as a result."[48]

These axioms stand up more than fairly well in light of Washington's current frustrations in the Middle East. Yet Miles Copeland's own life and works also suggest the ultimately destructive, less visible costs of the intervention, covert or overt, that he pioneered.

His tasks in Cairo completed, Copeland resigned from Booz, Allen & Hamilton and in July 1957 moved to Beirut to begin a new career as a management consultant in partnership with a fellow CIA veteran, James Eichelberger. The firm's plush offices were strategically situated next to the suite occupied by Tapline, and Copeland & Eichelberger's initial clients included Gulf Oil, with assets of $3.5 billion, the fortunate owner of a half share of the fecund Kuwait Oil Company. But it was generally assumed that Miles Copeland's other client was the CIA, an assumption that did not injure the firm's commercial prospects.

This was an interesting moment in Lebanon. With Nasser's star ascendant, Washington was anxious about the survival of President Camille Chamoun, a Maronite Christian so pro-Western that he hazardously opposed President Nasser during the Suez debacle. In 1957, Chamoun welcomed the Eisenhower Doctrine and its offer of security assistance to Middle Eastern regimes that were threatened by either Nasser or the Soviets. In Lebanon's elections that year, Chamoun and his pro-Western allies were generously and secretly subsidized by the CIA. (Copeland insists the sums were modest "in the sense that they were about the same amounts that the British, French, Soviet and Egyptian embassies were contributing to their respective candidates.")[49] Then in the chaotic year of 1958, populist colonels seized power in Baghdad and their followers slaughtered the Iraqi royal family, and lynched the country's pro-British premier, Nuri al-Said. Fearing foreign attack, Chamoun appealed frantically to Washington for military aid. Eisenhower responded with OPERATION BLUE BAT, the first U.S. airborne and seaborne operation in peacetime. Within seventy-two hours on July 19, the Sixth Fleet landed eight thousand Marines and seven thousand troops on Lebanese beaches, where they were greeted by bikini-clad swimmers and friendly youngsters selling lemonade.[50] The intervention, in which British troops joined, was deceptively painless and preserved Chamoun's tenuous authority.

Yet everything about Lebanon was deceptive. Outwardly it seemed a thriving and Westernized country, the "Switzerland of the Middle East" in an oft-heard cliché. Beirut in the 1950s boasted more banks than New York City, more newspapers than London, and (in Miles Copeland's reckoning) more confidential newsletters than New York, London, and Paris put together. Of its multiples, however, religion was the most revealing: its constitution recognized eighteen faiths. Under the National Covenant negotiated in 1943, its highest offices were to follow a fixed formula: a Maronite President, a Sunni Prime Minister, and a Shiite Speaker in parliament with six Christian seats to every five held by Muslims, but real power lodged at the top. Yet the formula's viability was demographically doomed by France's demarcation in 1920 of a Greater Lebanon, which doubled the area of the former Ottoman province and increased by half its 1913 population of 414,800, thus adding around 200,000 predominantly Muslim inhabitants to the new republic. This enlargement was triumphantly proclaimed by General Henri Gouraud, the one-armed French hero of the Marne, who from "the foot of these majestic mountains" extolled Greater Lebanon as "an impregnable stronghold of its faith and freedom." (His declaration mentioned Phoenicia, Greece, Rome, and Lebanon's "ancient friendship with France," but not Islam.)[51]

In the critical judgment of Philip K. Hitti, a Lebanese-born Princeton historian writing in 1957, what Lebanon gained in area it lost in cohesion: "It lost its internal equilibrium, though geographically and economically it became more viable. The Christian overwhelming majority was seriously reduced."[52] By the 1950s, the demographic balance had tilted irreversibly toward Islam, owing to Christian emigration, a higher birth rate among Muslims, and a massive influx of Palestinian refugees. From that time onward, Lebanon's history became a kaleidoscope of revolts, coups, assassinations, several Israeli invasions and occupations, a Syrian invasion and near-permanent occupation, massacres, suicide bombings, and a generation-long civil war (ignited in 1975 by the killing of twenty-seven Palestinians in a bus driving through a Christian neighborhood)—all abetted by an indissoluble legacy of foreign-assisted militias.

Does serious blame attach to the United States, and most especially to the CIA, for this bloody morass? Certainly by any reasonable historic reckoning, American influence on Lebanon was initially benign. In 1834, the Protestant missionary Pliny Fisk arrived in Beirut with the region's first Arabic printing press, and he was followed in 1863 by the founders of the American University of Beirut, ever since a beacon of enlightenment. After World War I, the Lebanese cause had no firmer advocate than the philanthropist Charles R. Crane, who advised Woodrow Wilson on Middle East policy. Hence the added weight of the bluntly adverse judgment put forward by Crane's distant relative, Wilbur Crane Eveland, the CIA's principal liaison with, and covert underwriter of, President Camille Chamoun. "By using Lebanon as a base for the CIA's covert operations," he writes in *Ropes of Sand* (1980), "America undermined that country's stability and precipitated attempts by its Arab neighbors to bring down the Lebanese government. Although the might of U.S. military power saved Lebanon from possible fragmentation in 1958, the country never recovered completely and America was left with few friends in the Arab world."[53]

In short, save for Beirut's majestic mountain setting, nothing in the city was what it appeared to be, a common observation among visitors. The British aesthete Sacheverell Sitwell, writing in 1957, found that dress and physical features proved opaque: "The individual you feel certain is a Moslem turns out to be a Christian; but is he, then, Greek Orthodox or Maronite? Or Armenian? What language does one expect them to speak? One does not know." The city's geography was similarly bewildering, its streets and alleys "all running in the wrong direction." In fact Beirut's only "sited building," Sitwell discovered, was the St. George Hotel.[54] What more appropriate venue, therefore, than this maze of mirrors for Miles Copeland's emblematic encounters with the era's most celebrated double, or perhaps triple agent, Kim Philby?

We end where we began, at the St. George Hotel Bar, where in 1957 everybody was talking about the lavish receptions hosted by two American newcomers, Miles Copeland and his partner James Eichelberger. Years later, Copeland confirmed what his guests probably suspected, that his hospitality was underwritten by the CIA. He had been asked in particular by the agency's counterintelligence chief, James Jesus Angleton, to "keep an eye on" Kim Philby, who recently resigned from MI6 to begin a new career as a foreign correspondent in Beirut. Miles had met Kim in wartime London and their friendship thickened in Washington, where Philby, as intelligence coordinator, met regularly with Copeland and Angleton. At some point the saturnine counterspy began to suspect that Philby was a KGB agent and (according to Copeland) Angleton even told him so while dining at a Georgetown restaurant. Philby only laughed, and purportedly said, "You'll never get anyone to believe you."[55]

Soon after resettling in Beirut, the Copelands threw a dinner party for Sam Pope Brewer and his wife, Eleanor. As if on cue, Kim Philby turned up uninvited. Thereafter the three became regulars at Miles and Lorraine's buffet evenings, catering expenses borne by the CIA. "I earned what Jim paid me," Copeland later wrote. "For example, I arranged for a senior official in the Lebanese Sûreté, whom I cultivated for general intelligence purposes, to subject Philby to the occasional 'spot' surveillance, and to report back anything of interest." Philby expertly eluded his trackers and vanished into Beirut's labyrinthine Armenian quarter. Copeland then learned that Philby was involved in a clandestine affair with Eleanor Brewer, and decided "all that sneaking about was in aid of that."[56]

After the Brewers divorced and Eleanor married Kim, the Copelands and Philbys saw each other frequently, exchanged gossip, and took reciprocal care of their respective children during vacations. Lorraine Copeland, an archaeologist, liked and befriended Kim's father, the aging explorer Harry St. John Philby, who lived with Kim until his death in 1960 (his last words, locally oft-repeated, were, "God, I'm bored"). All seemed normal on January 23, 1963, when Glen Balfour-Paul, a Political Officer at the British Embassy, invited Kim and Eleanor to dine with him at home. Kim accepted "with pleasure," then telephoned his wife to say he would be stopping at the Central Telegraph Office to cable London and would be delayed. Philby was last seen at the St. George Hotel Bar, where he greeted a Palestinian colleague, downed several drinks alone, and vanished without notifying either his host or wife. That evening the Soviet steamer *Dolmatova* entered Beirut harbor, took Philby aboard, then headed for Odessa, as related years later by Kim's KGB chief, General Oleg Kalugin.[57]

What prompted Philby's flight? In the long-authorized version, the chiefs of British intelligence concluded after a diligent inquiry that Kim Philby was indeed the long-sought Third Man; that he had been recruited as a spy at Trinity College, Cambridge, along with his schoolmates Guy Burgess and Donald Maclean; and that in 1951 he alerted them that their treachery had been discovered, enabling them to escape to Moscow. To avoid a recurrence, the chiefs sent an emissary to Beirut with an offer they hoped he could not refuse: a promise of legal immunity if he confessed. Philby chose instead to bolt, surfacing in due course in Moscow, where he was later joined by his new American wife.

Yet this version was riddled with anomalies. The British seemed curiously uncurious about Philby's escape and the Soviet authorities were singularly unwelcoming to their prodigal comrade: his Moscow flat was bugged, he was followed always by minders, and he was allowed to give but one lecture during his quarter-century as a Soviet resident. Anthony Cave Brown, the British authority on espionage, discovered that both Angleton and the legendary "C" (Sir Stewart Menzies) somehow kept communicating by oblique means with the notorious apostate. These anomalies were succinctly examined by the industrious American writer Ron Rosenblum, who tracked down Graham Greene's annotated copy of Philby's archly written memoir, *My Silent War*. After examining it, Rosenblum concluded that it was a false trail leading nowhere. Britain's Phillip Knightley, author or co-author of two seminal books on Philby, whom he interviewed at length in Moscow, has now acknowledged second thoughts about the long-authorized British version. One hypothesis is that the British wanted Philby to flee because he became a useful scapegoat for Anglo-American intelligence failures, such as blaming him for the breach of security that led in 1950 to the slaughter by Albanians of seaborne anti-Communist guerrillas. Others surmise that the CIA and MI6 used Philby before and after his flight to convey far-fetched plans of a massive retaliatory strike should Moscow attack Western Europe—revisionist doubts elaborated in *Deceiving the Deceivers* by S. J. Hamrick, a former U.S. Foreign Service officer, as analyzed by Knightley in *The New York Review of Books*.[58]

All of which underscores a conundrum that Miles Copeland failed to address: that it is possible to say anything and everything about secret services because for those who yearn to believe, even the most outlandish claims are met with either silence or official denials that are ipso facto disbelieved. The ordinary litmus tests for historical veracity do not apply to covert agencies, since key archives are suppressed or released only in sanitized form. From this vantage, the world of espionage is (in Angleton's phrase) "a wilderness of mirrors." This has been an undoubted boon to novelists, dramatists, and filmmakers who endow spy agencies with superhuman prowess. There is no better example than Copeland's own life and deeds. A hard-digging scholar named Andrew Rathmell has mined all accessible documents in writing his 1995 treatise, *Secret War in the Middle East: The Covert Struggle for Syria, 1949–1961*. There he concludes that Copeland's claim that he and Stephen Meade masterminded the first Syrian coup "owed more to his well-known tendency to exaggerate his own role than to the facts." Rathmell adds that an unnamed former CIA director told him that "if you can sort out fact from fiction in *The Game of Nations* you are a clairvoyant."[59]

Put aside the quandary of accepting the word of the director of an agency that routinely suppresses revealing files, as Rathmell acknowledges, an agency whose censors in recent years remove without notice previously accessible documents, especially relating to the Islamic East. Rathmell misses the main point. Exaggerated or not, Copeland's account heralded an era when U.S. covert intervention was perceived as the norm, an era when covert armies emanating from somewhere in the sky undermined regimes and provided hostile politicians of every stripe with an easy target for discrediting rivals—easy because who could prove the nonexistence of a diabolic conspiracy? In this game of nations, everything is possible and nothing truly deniable. Call it the Copeland Conundrum.

TWELVE

The Man Who Knew Too Much

Paul Dundes Wolfowitz (b. 1943)

⌗

Man is neither angel nor brute, and the unfortunate thing is that he
who would act the angel acts the brute.

—Blaise Pascal, *Pensées* (1670)

As the bombs began falling on Baghdad in March 2003, most Americans living beyond the Washington Beltway surely knew little or nothing about Paul D. Wolfowitz, the Deputy Secretary of Defense. This is not surprising. He epitomized the bright, loyal, tireless, and usually anonymous Number Two who prepares and promotes the great decisions that the Number One then promulgates. Bob Woodward, commonly viewed as the court chronicler for the George W. Bush Administration, put the matter correctly in his insider account, *Plan of Attack* (2004): Wolfowitz was the "intellectual godfather and fiercest advocate for toppling Saddam Hussein."[1] When the post-toppling went badly, and as near-anarchy engulfed Iraq, Americans began to hear more about the earnest, soft-spoken Wolfowitz, especially following his own brush with death in Baghdad on October 16, 2003. Insurgents somehow discovered that he was staying overnight at the al-Rashid Hotel, at which they loosed a volley of rockets, piercing the supposedly impregnable Green Zone. Wolfowitz survived, but a U.S. Army officer did not, and seventeen other people were injured. Adding to the mayhem, terrorists struck the following day at the International Red Cross headquarters in Baghdad, killing more than a dozen and wounding hundreds.

This ongoing and brutal bloodletting was not what Paul Wolfowitz envisioned in a liberated Iraq. In testimony before Congress, press interviews, and closed-door advocacy within the Pentagon, he acknowledged that yes, there might be some postwar difficulties but that most Iraqis loathed their despotic ruler, that Iraq had become predominantly secular, that an acceptable if not perfect elected government in Baghdad would serve as a liberalizing beacon for Iraq's mostly despotic neighbors, and that such an outcome need not entail an onerous, protracted, and costly occupation—indeed, given its oil riches, Iraq itself could cover much of the costs. Above all, a defeated Iraq could be defanged, its sinister nuclear and chemical weapons programs terminated, eliminating the possibility that Saddam Hussein would provide weapons of mass destruction to Osama Bin Laden, with whom he was almost certainly linked.

Wolfowitz's contentions were echoed by a corps of colleagues, some of whom he had coaxed into government service, notably I. Lewis "Scooter" Libby Jr., the Vice President's Chief of Staff; others included longtime Cold War allies, among them the fluent, almost mesmeric Richard Perle, chairman of the Defense Policy Board; and trusted protégés like Douglas Feith, the Pentagon's Under Secretary for Policy, and Elliot Abrams, the Middle East hand at the National Security Council, along with friends and acolytes at major universities, research institutes, and the press—a formidable phalanx indeed. Its members were readily identified by their if-you-knew-what-we-knew air, acquired during their service in earlier Republican administrations whose wise and tough policies, in their view, humbled an Evil Empire without firing a shot.

Not only did this remarkable victory suggest that history was on America's side but, as Francis Fukuyama, their ideological ally at the State Department's Policy Planning Staff, wrote in 1992 in *The End of History and the Last Man*, history itself had all but ended, given the global triumph of free markets and democracy. This bold thesis recurred in a September 19, 2002, state paper, *The National Security Strategy for the United States of America*, its robust tone established in President Bush's prefatory statement: "The great struggles of the twentieth century between liberty and totalitarianism ended with a decisive victory for the forces of freedom—and a single, sustainable model for national success: freedom, democracy and free enterprise." Stated simply, planet earth had become *unipolar*, a term popularized by *Washington Post* columnist Charles Krauthammer in a much-discussed *Foreign Affairs* essay, which announced, "The center of world power is an unchallenged superpower, attended by its Western allies."[2]

And what of these attending allies? A common view among Americans loosely described as neoconservatives was graphically articulated by a talented intellectual duelist based in Brussels, Robert Kagan. In his 2003 manifesto, *Of Paradise and Power*, he contended that Europeans foolishly assumed that they had entered a posthistorical paradise of peace, in contrast with American policy makers who tough-mindedly knew they had to assert global power in a Hobbesian world: "That is why on major strategic and international questions today, Americans are from Mars and Europeans are from Venus."[3] Even liberal Democrats were captivated by this image of America's prowess. As phrased by Madeleine Albright, Bill Clinton's Secretary of State, the United States stood taller than other nations, and thus could see farther. And momentarily, in the wake of the traumatic 9/11 attacks on New York and Washington, it truly seemed that America loomed godlike in its efficient, calibrated military response. With lightning speed, a mobile force armed with smart bombs and ample cash plowed into Afghanistan, routed the Taliban regime that had sheltered Osama Bin Laden, and did so with broad global approbation. Military victory was followed by a justly applauded postwar settlement, brokered by the United Nations, that even the sullenly hostile Iranians were willing to support.

How distant that moment now seems! The red planet winked, and the same team that wrested a skillful victory in the treacherous passes of Afghanistan then stumbled into a lethal swamp. Why? Among many reasons, one stands out: the authors of the Iraqi war somehow ignored a salient precept in *The Leviathan* by Thomas Edward Hobbes (1588–1679), the political philosopher whose unsentimental realism supposedly guided them. Having observed human behavior in his own disordered century, Hobbes expressly cautioned (Part One, Chapter 8), "During the time men live without a common power to keep them in awe, they are in that condition which is called war; and such a war as is every man against every man." Having made no preparations for imposing a common power in postconquest Baghdad, Iraqi awe yielded to bewilderment, looting, and insurgency, which then spread everywhere (save the less turbulent Kurdish north, which for a decade enjoyed relative autonomy, protected by a U.S.-enforced no-fly zone). In little more than a year, much of Iraq plunged into wholesale chaos, deepened by suicide bombers and proliferating militias, triggering a massive refugee flight, its furies intensified by foreign fighters flocking through unguarded frontiers.

How did it happen? The war's architects had evidently conjured an unreal posthistorical vision of an Iraq gratefully embracing the triad deemed globally essential for national success: freedom, democracy, and free enterprise. Seen from its aftermath, it was not a failure of will but of imagination that turned OPERATION IRAQI FREEDOM on its head. Paul Wolfowitz, a man of unquestioned intelligence, was emblematic of this failure.

With a mind and imagination honed at the University of Chicago and by years of Pentagon service, Wolfowitz prided himself on gauging the imponderables of military strategy. Speaking at a West Point commencement months before the terror attacks on New York and Washington, he recalled Pearl Harbor and all the missed clues that signaled Japan's surprise attack: an object lesson, and not just for cadets. Civilians too needed to ward off complacency and "replace a poverty of expectations with an anticipation of the unfamiliar and unlikely."[4]

In the months leading to the invasion of Iraq, Wolfowitz shunned boilerplate clichés and offered thoughtful, sometimes startling responses to commonplace questions. For example, if Iraq were a democracy, wouldn't the Islamists win? "Look," he told one interviewer (as quoted by *The New Yorker*'s George Packer), "fifty percent of the Arab world are women. Most of those women do not want to live in a theocratic state. The other fifty percent are men, I know a lot of them. I don't think they want to live in a theocratic state."[5] He spoke with the furled brows of a good listener, his professorial demeanor enhanced by his years as dean of Johns Hopkins' School of Advanced International Studies in Washington. On his travels or while receiving visitors on his lofty post-Iraq perch as president of the World Bank, he invariably impressed with his authenticity. Lanky, jug-eared, tousle-haired, he seemed a man without vanity, capable of casually wetting a pocket comb with his saliva, or of shedding his shoes before visiting a Turkish mosque, thereby revealing a homely hole in his sock. His track record mattered. Until the Iraq war, he rarely stumbled. His career has been carefully retraced by the journalist James Mann in *Rise of the Vulcans* (2004), the name half-jocularly bestowed on a loose-knit group of Pentagon and National Security Council insiders. Besides Wolfowitz, the Vulcans included Richard Armitage, Dick Cheney, Colin Powell, Condoleezza Rice, and Donald Rumsfeld, their collective tenures spanning the Nixon, Ford, Reagan, and George H. W. Bush administrations.

In varying degrees and ways, the Vulcans believed that America's unmatched power ought to be used for worthy ends, the implicit corollary being that what was good for the United States was usually good for the world. True, there were differences within the group, especially concerning the first Gulf War. When Iraq seized and occupied Kuwait in August 1990, an intense debate ensued within the George H. W. Bush administration on how to respond. Recalling that American forces had never before intervened massively in the Middle East, Chairman Colin Powell of the Joint Chiefs of Staff favored containment, not assault. Secretary of Defense Dick Cheney and his Under Secretary for Policy, Paul Wolfowitz, disagreed. Together they worked over an alternate strategy drafted by Henry S. Rowen, the Assistant Secretary of Defense for Security Affairs, a scholar on leave from the Hoover Institute and subsequently president of the RAND Corporation. While on holiday, Rowen had come upon an account of the commonly forgotten, British-led ground and aerial assault on Baghdad in 1941, an engagement that reversed a pro-Nazi military coup in Iraq (as detailed in chapter 8). In a critical victory, given the Third Reich's lack of oil, Glubb Pasha's Arab legionnaires, along with British troops, charged northeast from Jordan across the desert toward Baghdad and combined with a second British force to retake Iraq, as urgently ordered by Churchill.

On returning to Washington, James Mann relates, "Rowen laid out his ideas to Wolfowitz and then to Cheney. 'Set up a team, and don't tell Powell or anybody else,' Cheney told him. Wolfowitz and Scooter Libby, his civilian aide for contingency planning, set up a secret group to explore Rowen's ideas."[6] Their offensive, dubbed OPERATION SCORPION, was rejected as unworkable by General H. Norman Schwarzkopf, who in his memoirs said he feared the three planners had succumbed to a common phenomenon at the Pentagon: "Put a civilian in charge of professional military men and before long he's no longer satisfied with setting policy but wants to outgeneral the generals."[7]

Nevertheless, the Cheney-Wolfowitz-Rowen scheme formed the embryo of OPERATION DESERT STORM, which commenced on January 17, 1991, and involved the massed infantry and air forces of eight countries, plus six U.S. Navy battle groups. Within a month, the coalition's ground, sea, and air assault freed Kuwait and shredded Saddam Hussein's scattering army. The enemy was humbled, Kuwait liberated, and the coalition still intact, Generals Powell and Schwarzkopf called for a cease-fire, which Cheney and the White House immediately approved. Wolfowitz was dismayed by its timing. By delaying the cease-fire agreement, and doing so without slaughtering fleeing Iraqis, he remarked later in the 1990s, "the United States might have bought time for opposition to Saddam Hussein to build and to act against him."[8] What dissenters viewed as a too hasty cease-fire was followed by General Schwarzkopf's allowing Iraqi helicopters to fly through coalition airspace, purportedly to airlift Iraqi officials from the battle zone.

This concession to Saddam was vainly contested by Wolfowitz and by the State Department's Middle East troubleshooter, Dennis Ross. Predictably, these Iraqi helicopter gunships slaughtered Kurdish and Shiite rebels who had taken to the field on the assumption that the American-led coalition would provide air cover.

Finally and more problematic, should the allied victors press on to Baghdad and oust its tyrant? Weighing the risks, President George H. W. Bush and his National Security Adviser, Brent Scowcroft, chose to hold back, in part for reasons set forth in their jointly written *A World Transformed* (1998):

> Trying to eliminate Saddam, extending the ground war into an occupation of Iraq, would have violated our guideline about not changing our objectives in midstream, engaging in "mission creep," and would have incurred incalculable human and political costs . . . We would have been forced to occupy Baghdad and, in effect, rule Iraq. The coalition would have instantly collapsed, the Arabs deserting it in anger and other allies pulling out as well . . . Going in and occupying Iraq, thus unilaterally extending the United Nations' mandate, would have destroyed the precedent of international response to aggression that we hoped to establish. Had we gone the invasion route, the United States could conceivably still be an occupying power in a bitterly hostile land. It would have been a dramatically different—and perhaps barren—outcome.[9]

Still, there was a further, more cynical explanation for this judicious restraint, as General Powell acknowledges cursorily in *his* memoirs: "Our practical intention was to leave Baghdad enough power to survive as a threat to an Iran that remained bitterly hostile to the United States."[10] This morally ambiguous concession to Realpolitik dismayed other Americans, not just Paul Wolfowitz, and during the 1990s he referred frequently to the missed opportunities in the first Gulf War. While an academic dean, he and his allies even persuaded President Clinton and Democrats in Congress that "regime change" in Baghdad was a valid U.S. foreign policy goal (as critics of the botched Iraq War were to be frequently reminded). Still, it was not the goal but the means employed that stirred the most dissent. To Zbigniew Brzezinski, Jimmy Carter's National Security Adviser, the 2003 Iraq War ranks as America's greatest foreign policy folly, a $300 billion geopolitical disaster in which "fighting rebellious Iraqis who oppose the U.S. occupation became the substantive definition of a war that was aimed vaguely at 'terror', a technique for killing but hardly an identifiable enemy."[11] By 2007, these dissents had become commonplace among foreign affairs professionals, a judgment echoed in polls recording a precipitous plunge in President Bush's approval ratings. How, then, did so brilliant an analyst as Paul Wolfowitz help steer the United States into this seemingly bottomless morass?

Four strands can be distinguished in the intellectual development of Paul Wolfowitz: his Polish-Jewish origins; the imprint of the University of Chicago and its free market in Great Ideas; the influence of two important women, his former wife of thirty years, the anthropologist Clare Selgin, and his more recent companion, the Arab feminist Shaha Ali Riza; and finally, his respect for and friendship with Iraqi exiles, notably Ahmad Chalabi.

Wolfowitz was born of an immigrant cohort whose character prompted an insightful essay in 1919 titled "The Intellectual Pre-Eminence of Jews in Modern Europe" by the early-day political sociologist Thorstein Veblen. His reflections were inspired by the Balfour Declaration, which the year before announced British approval of a Zionist plan to establish a home for the Jewish people in Palestine. As he weighed the various and passionate claimants for self-determination emboldened by America's entry into World War I, Veblen gave his highest marks to the Zionists, whom he praised for their "sobriety, good will and a poise of self-assurance."[12] Still, assuming the Zionist plan was good for the Jews, would its realization be good for Europe?

Few would dispute (Veblen wrote) that the Jews had contributed far more than their share to the intellectual progress of Europe. Why was this so? Himself the son of Norwegian immigrants, Veblen reasoned that Jews belonged to a hybrid minority whose offspring viewed the orthodox mores of their majority society through skeptical and creative bifocals. Thus in rising from a close-knit subculture, the gifted Jew becomes "a disturber of the intellectual peace," if at the price of losing "that peace of mind that is the birthright of the safe and sane quietest." Hence Zionism's gain could very probably be Europe's loss.[13] Similarly, the United States with its melting-pot culture benefited hugely from its many minorities whose brightest offspring encountered fewer obstacles than in Europe with its fossilized hierarchies. (The phrase *melting pot* was introduced by the British author and early-day Zionist Israel Zangwill, in his 1908 play so titled containing these lines:

"America is God's Crucible, the great Melting-Pot where all the races of Europe are melting and re-forming.")

Jacob Wolfowitz, Paul's father, was a lifelong Zionist, a distinguished mathematician, and a beneficiary of America's melting pot. Born in Poland, Jacob arrived in New York in 1920 at the age of ten along with his parents, Samuel and Helen. After attending local public schools, young Wolfowitz was able during the Great Depression to earn a bachelor's degree at the welcoming and intellectually challenging City College of New York. He then taught high school mathematics, earned a doctorate at New York University, and collaborated at Columbia University with Professor Abraham Wald on basic research on statistical theory. Wolfowitz's work gained him a professorship first at Cornell in 1951, then in 1970 at the University of Illinois, where he taught until his retirement. Regarded as a giant in his field, he wrote 114 papers and an important book, *Coding Theorems of Information Theory*, and spent a fruitful sabbatical year at a research institute in Israel, where his daughter Laura had settled and married an Israeli. Jacob Wolfowitz died in 1981.[14]

Paul and Laura Wolfowitz thus came of age in a household where Franklin Roosevelt was revered, where appeasement of Hitler was excoriated, and in which welfare measures and civil rights found warm approval. Decades later, Wolfowitz confided to journalist Christopher Hitchens that while young he had been a "bleeding heart" who joined with his sister in Martin Luther King Jr.'s March on Washington. Still, at college, there were competing influences. Athough admitted to Harvard as an undergraduate, Paul chose Cornell for filial and financial reasons (lower tuition for faculty children). He roomed at an elite student dormitory called Telluride. There he befriended the conservative political philosopher Allan Bloom, subsequently known for his best-selling *Closing of the American Mind* and as the inspiration for Saul Bellow's *Ravelstein*. "Bloom emboldened Wolfowitz to follow his childhood fascination with world affairs," according to *The New York Times*'s Bill Keller, in an early profile, "to the enormous dismay of his father, who regarded political science as roughly equivalent to astrology."[15]

So it happened in 1965 that Paul Wolfowitz headed to the University of Chicago, his graduate school status entitling him to a draft deferment during the Vietnam War. What were his views about that conflict? He told Keller in 2002 that it was a paradigm of good intentions gone wrong: "Wolfowitz was sympathetic to the war and only later came around to the view that it was 'a very costly overreach.' At the same time, he wonders if the American role in Vietnam might have given the anti-Communist forces in Asia time to gather strength. 'We know the costs of Vietnam,' he said. 'They were horrendous.' And then he adds a quintessentially Wolfowitz kicker: 'But we don't know what that part of the world would have looked like if [the war] hadn't been.' "[16] Nor, it might be added, do we know how Wolfowitz might have felt about Iraq had he experienced firsthand the tragic imponderables of actual battle. In any case, at the University of Chicago, a different kind of battlefield, he acquired the risk-taking certitude that became his most potent bureaucratic weapon.

On December 2, 1942, a team of scientists headed by the gifted immigrants Enrico Fermi (Italy) and Leo Szilard (Hungary) produced the world's first sustained man-made nuclear chain reaction, heralding the bigger bangs at Los Alamos and Hiroshima. This literally earth-shaking event occurred beneath the stands of Stagg Field at the University of Chicago, the institution that a year later acquired ownership of the venerable *Encyclopaedia Britannica*, first published in Edinburgh in 1768. Benefiting from the profits and prestige of the *Britannica*, the university then brought forth The Great Books, comprising fifty-four volumes packed with 25 million words and costing (in 1952 dollars) $249.50, obliterating its sole American rival, Harvard's canonical Five-Foot Shelf. Going further, the university's scholars determined that there were exactly one hundred and two Great Ideas, ranging from Angel to World, all dissected in *The Syntopicon*, "a uniform reference library in the realm of thought and opinion," according to its academic impresario, Dr. Mortimer J. Adler, a close associate of President Robert Maynard Hutchins (still the same intellectual dynamo at age fifty-two as he was on becoming dean of Yale Law School at age twenty-nine).[17]

This startling conjoining of nuclear physics, the Scottish Enlightenment, and aggressive pedagogy was typical of an American university which so valued cogitation that Hutchins (unthinkably) ended its participation in intercollegiate football (distracting and irrelevant) and welcomed precocious fifteen-year-olds as undergraduates. Among the outstanding youngsters drawn to Chicago was the Californian Susan Sontag (BA, '51), who entered at a mature sixteen and there met and married the sociologist Philip Rieff before commencing her own career as a disturber of the peace. By that time the phrase "Chicago school" had become a generic label for frontier trends in the hard sciences, social sciences (notably in economics, sociology, and politics), and all the liberal arts (including language and punctuation usage as decreed in an authoritative style book).

The university's determination to become "the Harvard of the Middle West" was evident from its founding in 1890 with funds provided by John D. Rockefeller (totaling $45 million by 1910). Its first president, William Rainey Harper, sought to blend the spirit of Oxbridge colleges with that of German graduate schools, and to do it with a splash. The results were reflected in the university's architecture (Gothic, artificially aged); its innovative four-quarter academic year, which included summer courses; its pioneering extension classes; and its emphasis on research and graduate studies. It sprouted upward seemingly overnight. As early as 1910, Chicago had enrolled more graduate students than any other U.S. university except Columbia, and its astronomers viewed the universe through the world's largest telescope, Yerkes. Visitors gaped at its men's dining room (a copy of Christ Church Hall, Oxford), its Law Building (inspired by the chapel of Kings College, Cambridge), and its unexpectedly rich collection of Middle Eastern antiquities at the Haskell Oriental Museum, (now the Oriental Institute), notably Iranian material from Persepolis and Egyptian treasures annotated by America's preeminent Orientalist, James Henry Breasted.

This assertive ambition reflected the university's urban setting. Rising seemingly out of nowhere, the Windy City remains at once bracing and overblown. America's first skyscrapers rose on the shores of Lake Michigan, as did the fine early work of Louis Sullivan and Frank Lloyd Wright. The city's Democratic political machine is to this day the oldest and hardiest in the nation. Its criminal gangs were world famous, yet Chicago also nurtured poets, satirists, novelists, little magazines, and exotic brands of political radicalism (it became home to the Wobblies, the anarcho-syndicalist Industrial Workers of the World). Here too flourished *The Chicago Tribune*, its logo blazoned for decades with the slogan "World's Greatest Newspaper," placed there by its Anglophobic proprietor, Colonel Robert McCormick, and retained until his embarrassed successors removed it in the 1990s. (In fairness, it should be noted that the *Tribune* pioneered the newspaper column, the op-ed page, and the comic strip.)

"There is in America an incredible city named Chicago," wrote a discerning British visitor, Rebecca West, in her 1926 preface to Carl Sandburg's *Selected Poems*, "a rain-colored city of topless marble towers that stand among waste-plots knee-high with tawny grasses beside a lake that has grey waves like the sea. It has a shopping and office district that for miles around is a darkness laid on the eyes, so high are the buildings, so cluttered up are the narrow streets with a gauntly striding elevator railway, and a stockyard district that for miles around is a stench in the nostrils."[18] It was here, during the hyperactive 1960s, that Paul Wolfowitz acquired his erudition, his certitude, and his affinity for big and sweeping ideas.

In the fall of 1965, at a faculty tea for incoming graduate students at the University of Chicago, Wolfowitz was asked by a political scientist named Albert Wohlstetter if he knew a "Jack Wolfowitz." "That's my father," said Paul, to which Wohlstetter replied, "I studied math with him at Columbia."[19] Out of this encounter, as related by James Mann, grew a mentor-disciple relationship of importance for U.S. foreign policy. A New Yorker who attended City College before studying math at Columbia, Wohlstetter early on became fascinated by the concept of "fallibilism" developed by the American philosopher Charles Sanders Peirce, the notion that the unexpected and uncertain should be of vital concern in any inquiry. During the 1950s, while working as a policy analyst at the RAND Corporation, Wohlstetter applied Peirce's concept to the Pentagon's nuclear strategy doctrines, and judged them grievously inadequate.

Specifically, the Strategic Air Command, or SAC, with its scattered U.S. and foreign air bases was too vulnerable to a surprise Soviet nuclear first-strike, a "lacuna of monumental proportions." Working with his RAND colleague Henry Rowen and with other analysts, Wohlstetter prepared a "murder board" detailing all that might go wrong, heralding the subsequent shift to hardened bases for Intercontinental Ballistic Missiles (ICBMs) and round-the-clock flights by SAC bombers, using a "fail-safe" system (Wohlstetter devised the term) to avoid triggering an accidental nuclear exchange.

Wohlstetter moved on to Chicago and for decades remained a commanding voice in an ongoing insider debate over Mutual Assured Destruction (MAD), the pros and cons of Strategic Arms Limitation Treaties (SALT), and the feasibility of banning Anti-Ballistic Missiles (ABMs) through mutual agreement. Wohlstetter was troubled by MAD's amorality, he opposed SALT as giving parity treatment to the Soviets and freezing America's innovative potential, and he favored moving full-speed forward on a U.S. missile defense program, views pressed vigorously by his disciples working with or for Senator Henry ("Scoop") Jackson, Democrat of Washington, the leading hawk in his party.[20]

High on Wohlstetter's list of worries was the likely proliferation of nuclear weaponry, especially in the Middle East. When the Johnson Administration began promoting desalination projects in the region, he agreed that the intent was laudable but the desalting plants could also yield plutonium, the essential ingredient for nuclear weapons. On returning in the late 1960s from a visit to Israel, whose leaders were considering a U.S. engineering company's plans for just such a plant, Wohlstetter handed a pile of documents to his graduate aide Paul Wolfowitz and asked if he could read Hebrew. The answer was yes, and Wolfowitz's researches yielded a doctoral dissertation contending that proliferation risks outweighed the likely benefits of desalting facilities. Moreover, should Israel develop nuclear weapons, their military value was questionable since any Israeli nuclear force would depend on relatively simple delivery systems, which would be vulnerable to conventional attack.

"An Israeli nuclear threat would weaken Israel's conventional military position," the dissertation warned, "by cutting her off from friendly countries in the West, and by encouraging, if not forcing, the Soviet Union to intervene actively in behalf of the Arabs . . . Israeli nuclear weapons would push the Arabs into a desperate attempt to acquire nuclear weapons, if not from the Soviet Union then at a later date from China or on their own."[21] For a graduate student, it was a shrewd and confident forecast (Israel has never acknowledged but is commonly assumed to possess a nuclear arsenal, generating demands for similar weaponry in Iran, Saudi Arabia, Egypt, and Saddam Hussein's Iraq).

But Wohlstetter's prime concern was with nuclear strategy, and his analysis technical. Among his colleagues at the University of Chicago were two German émigrés who offered students broader but contrasting views on democracy's prospects during the Cold War. Nowadays Leo Strauss (1899–1973) is better known as the putative mentor of neoconservatives, but in the 1960s, when he took a leading part in teach-ins opposing the Vietnam War, Hans Morgenthau (1904–1980) was the more celebrated. Both professors were born Jewish in Germany, where each attended university (Munich in Morgenthau's case, Marburg in Strauss's), and both fled Nazi-dominated Europe to restart their academic careers in America (initially at Brooklyn College and Kansas State in Morgenthau's case, at the New School for Social Research in Strauss's).

Their paths diverged sharply. Morgenthau saw national interest as the defining signpost in global conflicts, and believed strongly that a leader's virtue and motives were irrelevant. He noted that the disastrous British appeaser Neville Chamberlain had the best of intentions, while the implacable revolutionary Robespierre's very moral purity impelled him to consign the less pure to the guillotine. Morgenthau dismissed as blasphemous the notion that any nation was the agent of Providence. Concrete results, not universal principles, ought to be the test of a policy's morality. In his view, prudence—weighing the consequences of alternative actions—was the supreme virtue in politics. All this he elaborated in *Politics Among Nations: The Struggle for Power and Peace*, which for two decades was the dominant textbook in its field, passing through four editions after its debut in 1948.

The final chapter distills "four fundamental rules" that Morgenthau hoped would prevail in world politics: "Diplomacy must be divested of the crusading spirit; the objectives of foreign policy must be defined in terms of national interest; diplomacy must look at the political scene from the point of view of other nations; nations must be willing to compromise on all issues that are not vital to them."[22] Among writers frequently cited by Morgenthau were such ironists and relativists as Tocqueville, Max Weber, Reinhold Niebuhr, Raymond Aron, Joseph Schumpeter and Isaiah Berlin. He especially liked this passage by the nineteenth-century American sage William Graham Sumner:

> If you want a war, nourish a doctrine. Doctrines are the most frightful tyrants to which men are ever subject, because doctrines get inside of a man's own reason and betray him against himself . . . [A doctrine] is a metaphysical assertion. It is never true, because it is absolute, and the affairs of men are all conditional and relative . . . If you allow a political catchword to go on and grow, you will awaken some day to find it standing over you, the arbiter of your destiny, against which you are powerless, as men are powerless against delusions.[23]

How different was the Zeitgeist of Leo Strauss! The relativism that Morgenthau commended was to Strauss the wellspring of the ideological poisons that pervaded the modern world. His prose was frequently opaque, his arguments oblique, often consisting of meditations on Plato, Xenophon, Hobbes, and Locke meant to offer cautionary warnings to often feckless Americans. He dwelled gloomily on what he saw as the crisis of liberalism, "a crisis due to the fact that liberalism has abandoned its absolute basis and is trying to become entirely relativistic." And relativism readily degenerated into "the easy going belief that all points of view are equal (hence none really worth passionate argument, deep analysis or stalwart defense) and then into the strident belief that anyone who argues for the superiority of a distinctive moral insight, way of life, or human type is somehow elitist or antidemo-cratic—and hence immoral."[24]

Because he had witnessed firsthand the collapse of the Weimar Repub-lic, Strauss viewed America's effervescent political system with brooding apprehension. Yet this analogy was misleading, contends the British politi-cal theorist John Gray in *Black Mass: Apocalyptic Religion and the Death of Utopia* (2007): "Strauss's diagnosis of democracy is mostly a diagnosis of Weimar Germany, but mass unemployment, hyperinflation, war repara-tions and national humiliation destroyed any legitimacy the Weimar regime ever had."[25] Little of this applied to postwar America, whose strength and vitality Strauss and his disciples consistently underestimated (especially when Presidents were Democrats), just as they overestimated the power and threat of the Soviet Union.

Strauss's inborn gloom stemmed in part from the influence of two heavyweight German philosophers, Martin Heidegger, the formulator of existential angst, and Carl Schmitt, the iconoclastic arch-conservative. In the 1920s, young Leo studied with the former at Freiburg University, while the latter was instrumental in obtaining for Strauss the Rockefeller grant that enabled him to leave Nazi Germany for Paris in 1933. Yet lamentably, both thinkers made their peace with the Third Reich; what helped recon-cile them to Hitler was their disgust with what they saw as the nihilism of the Weimar years, just as many American conservatives were repelled by the radical excesses of the 1960s. In Strauss's view, the disorders of democ-racy confirmed the need, as in Plato's ideal Republic, for a master class able to see farther by rising above the herd. As he frankly phrased it in a 1959 commencement address in Rockefeller Chapel at the University of Chicago, "Liberal education is the necessary endeavor to found an aristocracy within democratic mass society," to which he added, "We must not expect that lib-eral education can ever become universal education. It will always remain the obligation and the privilege of a minority."[26]

As a corollary, Strauss believed that in politics, lying was not just a regrettable necessity but might be a virtuous and noble instrument of sound policy. "The idea's provenance could not be more elevated," comments the intellectual historian Earl Shorris in his 2007 taxonomy, *The Politics of Heaven*: "Plato himself advised his nobles, men with golden souls, to tell noble lies—political fables, much like the specter of Saddam Hussein with a nuclear bomb—to keep the other levels of humanity (silver, brass, iron) in their proper place, loyal to the state and willing to do its bidding. Strauss too advised the telling of noble lies in the service of the national interest, and he held Plato's view of aristocrats as persons so virtuous that such lies would be used only for the good, for keeping order in the state and in the world."[27]

Just how much influence Leo Strauss's disciples exercised on the George W. Bush administration is a matter of dispute. Paul Wolfowitz, who took two of Strauss's courses, has dismissed as an exaggeration claims that he is a Straussian. Yet his circle was crowded with Leo Strauss's disciples. From the 1960s onward, fearing the West was losing the Cold War, Wolfowitz and the Straussians opposed détente, Kissinger, and arms control, urging instead that the heroic projection of American power, unilaterally if need be, was imperative to turn the tide. In a characteristic manifesto, *The Present Danger: Do We Have the Will to Reverse the Decline of American Power?* the conservative polemicist Norman Podhoretz warned that American liberals were infected by a "culture of appeasement," and that a "collapse of American resolve" signaled the country's eventual political and economic subordination "to superior Soviet power." His somber meditation was published in 1980, just a decade before the collapse of the Soviet empire.[28]

Disciples of Strauss who shared this almost apocalyptic pessimism included Chicago's Professor Allan Bloom, who offered dramatic obituaries of American liberalism to packed classrooms; Harvard's Professor Harvey Mansfield and his pupil, William Kristol, subsequently the founding editor of *The Weekly Standard*; the arms control specialist Richard Perle, dubbed "the Prince of Darkness" and known for his adamant opposition to any concessions to the Soviets; the scholar-diplomat Francis Fukuyama, who would later celebrate the end of history; and Abram Shulsky, a devoted Straussian who in 2001 became director of the Pentagon's Office of Special Plans, created to supplement (or more accurately, correct) the CIA's uncongenial fuzziness about Saddam Hussein's ties to Osama Bin Laden.

Strauss's influence was celebrated in an essay Abram Shulsky coauthored with Gary Schmitt, titled "Leo Strauss and the World of Intelligence (By Which We Do Not Mean *Nous*)," the italicized word being the Greek philosophical term for a superior form of rationality. The authors praise Strauss's "gentleness, his ability to concentrate on detail; his consequent success in looking below the surface and his seeming unworldliness," adding that he "may even be said to resemble, however faintly, the George Smiley of John Le Carré's novels." By contrast, CIA analysts "were generally reluctant throughout the Cold War to believe they could be deceived about any critical questions by the Soviet Union or any other Communist states. History has shown this to be exceedingly naïve."[29]

Yet this is not the whole story. In 1976, expressly to address this alleged naïveté, George H. W. Bush, as Director of Central Intelligence, recruited an independent group of experts to offer a hawkish corrective. This was the agency's famous Team B, directed by the Harvard historian Richard Pipes, and its membership included Paul Wolfowitz, then teaching at Yale. ("He was probably the quietist member of the group," Pipes later recalled.) Team B's conclusions by common consent overstated the Kremlin's prowess; by contrast, if any Straussian foresaw the Soviet Union's looming collapse, it has escaped attention.[30]

Soft-spoken, quiet, and seldom strident, Wolfowitz impressed associates as the very embodiment of reason and not as a partisan ideologue. On ending his long association with the Democratic Party after joining the Reagan Administration in 1981, he described himself as a "Scoop Jackson Republican," referring to his old boss, the Democratic Senator from Washington. Wolfowitz did not oppose welfare state measures, or make lame excuses for America's less savory Cold War allies. In three posts at the State Department—Director of the Policy Planning Staff, Assistant Secretary for East Asia, and Ambassador to Indonesia—he acquitted himself creditably. While still a novice diplomat, Dennis Ross was invited to work for Wolfowitz on the department's planning staff after he had briskly faulted a Team B report. "What I always found in him that separates him from everybody else on that side of the political spectrum," Ross told Keller of *The New York Times*, "is not that he didn't have predispositions, but that he was much more open, much more intellectually open, to different kinds of interpretations."[31]

Nor did Wolfowitz relish the ceremonial rituals of diplomacy. Secretary of State George P. Shultz recalls in his memoirs an occasion during his first official trip to Japan when, after lunch with the upper echelons of the Foreign Ministry, he had to give a formal toast. "I saw Paul Wolfowitz, the new assistant secretary for Far East Affairs, with his chin on his chest. He was passed a note that read: 'Rule One for a new assistant secretary: *never* fall asleep during the secretary's toast.' " (Wolfowitz later asked a dining partner, a veteran of these rites, how he managed to stay awake. "I have been sitting on my fork," came the whispered reply.)[32] Otherwise and overall, Shultz was favorably impressed by Wolfowitz's handling of relations with China and of the department's policy during the transition from the Marcos dictatorship to a rebirth of Filipino democracy. So when Wolfowitz asked if he could go into the field as Ambassador to Indonesia, Shultz agreed.

It was an interesting choice. Few countries are at once as important and as generally ignored as Indonesia, the world's most populous Muslim nation, numbering 235 million inhabitants in 2007. As in Manila, a dictator then reigned in Jakarta: the aging President Suharto, an American ally who in 1975 forewarned a visiting President Ford and Secretary of State Kissinger that he planned to invade and annex East Timor, a Portuguese possession; he received an orange light and the invasion followed, precipitating a harsh and prolonged occupation. Still and more promisingly, as in Manila there was also a growing indigenous democratic opposition in Jakarta.

Moreover, Wolfowitz's wife, Clare, knew the territory and spoke the language. She had been an exchange student in Indonesia while in high school, and her Ph.D. dissertation in social anthropology centered on the country's ethnic mix. As *The New Yorker*'s Peter J. Boyer discovered, journalists who traveled with Wolfowitz noticed that Indonesia was a subject sure to brighten his mood. "I really didn't expect to fall in love with this place," he told Boyer, "but I did. I mean, I don't think I made the mistake of forgetting which country I represented, or overlooking their flaws, but there was so much that was just enormously appealing to me."[33]

With an enthusiasm still remembered in Jakarta, Ambassador Wolfowitz learned the language sufficiently to take questions at public meetings. He participated in academic seminars and took particular pride in winning third prize in a women's magazine cooking contest with a dish he called "Madame Mao's Chicken." He met, liked, and befriended an opposition leader,

Abdurrahaman Wahid, a devout, urbane, and tolerant Muslim who favored separation of mosque and state. "He's a remarkable human being," Wolfowitz said of Wahid, "I mean, there's the leader of the largest Muslim organization, and he's an apostle of tolerance. How can you not admire him?" And in his final ambassadorial audience with General Suharto, he infuriated the old autocrat by pressing for a democratic regime change. In due course Wahid's Muslim organization became a political party, and in Indonesia's first free election its leader was elected to the presidency.[34]

These experiences helped persuade Wolfowitz that a successful transition to democracy was feasible in Iraq, and that American policy could and should play a catalytic role. We have already noted his frustration during the first Gulf War when the George H. W. Bush Aministration (in his view) threw away a chance of unseating Saddam Hussein. From the moment Bill Clinton assumed office in 1993, Dean Wolfowitz of the Johns Hopkins School of Advanced International Studies renewed his campaign against the Iraqi despot. His efforts were crowned in 1998 when Congress adopted the Iraqi Liberation Act calling for Saddam's eviction and authorizing support for the Iraqi National Congress (INC), a London-based opposition group that over a six-year period gleaned upwards of $27 million in U.S. aid.

In these campaigns, Wolfowitz's indispensable ally was Ahmad Chalabi, the indefatigable exile who next to Saddam Hussein did more than any Iraqi to trigger the 2003 American invasion of his country. As *The New York Times*'s Dexter Filkins remarks in a fine fact-filled profile, "It was Chalabi after all—a foreigner, an Arab—who persuaded the most powerful men in the United States to make the liberation of Iraq not merely a priority but an obsession." Fluent in accented English, with a smile permanently fixed on an amiable balding visage, dressed always in a faultless bespoke suit, Chalabi is the scion of a notable Shiite dynasty: his grandfather had been a member of the Iraqi parliament in the 1920s and his father, a wealthy Baghdad grain exporter, headed the Iraqi Senate until a 1958 putsch felled the monarchy. Before the coup, the Chalabis owned close to two and a half million acres throughout Iraq, much of it north of Baghdad in Khadimiya, where there is still a town called Chalabi. (One of the Chalabis, Musa, was Gertrude Bell's Baghdad landlord.)

"The Chalabis were part of the small Shiite elite," writes Filkins, "most of the rest of the Shiite majority formed a vast underclass. The remnants of that Shiite elite now form a sizable slice of the political establishment of post-Saddam Iraq."[35] In the 1950s, Ahmad attended Baghdad College, a Jesuit high school in which his Shiite classmates included Ayad Allawi, a relative who was to become a postinvasion President, and Adil Abdul Mahdi, a future Vice President. When the old Iraqi order collapsed in 1958 and as radical Ba'athists reached for power, the wealthier Shiites fled, taking what they could.

Chalabi settled in America, studied mathematics at MIT, graduated cum laude, and went on to the University of Chicago, earning his Ph.D. with a dissertation on the Theory of Knots. In Beirut in 1971, Dr. Chalabi married Leila Osseiran, daughter of a prominent Lebanese nationalist. Presiding at the ceremony was the Iranian-born Ayatollah Musa al-Sadr, a cousin of Moktada al-Sadr, the militant Shiite cleric and future ally of Ahmad Chalabi—typifying the intricate mesh of family and clan relationships that insiders absorb as if by osmosis, and outsiders ignore at their peril. Chalabi chose a career in banking and became indelibly identified with a scandal in Jordan, where he stands accused of embezzling $300 million from the Petra Bank. He was found guilty of fraud and sentenced in absentia to twenty-two years in prison. (Chalabi has consistently denied wrong-doing, and has blamed Saddam Hussein for faking the incriminating evidence; in 2005, Jordanian authorities indicated a willingness to pardon him, but Chalabi demanded a public apology, which was refused.)

Chalabi was to spend forty-five years away from Iraq. Since his entry into exile politics as architect and guiding hand of the INC, Chalabi has made American friends and enemies in equally impassioned measure. He has been shunned by the State Department, and CIA officers continue to argue over his or their degree of blame for the "Bay of Goats" debacle, the botched 1995 uprising against Saddam. In Potomac power plays, his non-admirers have been more than offset by his close ties with senior civilians in George W. Bush's Pentagon and with Vice President Dick Cheney and his Chief of Staff, Scooter Libby. Yet how sound was the intelligence Chalabi's group supplied, and where do his deeper loyalties lie? According to a report by the Senate Intelligence Committee in 2006, the Iraqi defectors produced by the INC swayed key judgments in the National Intelligence Estimate that preceded the critical Senate vote in 2003 authorizing the use of force against Iraq. The committee finding was categorical, stating that the INC "attempted to influence United States policy on Iraq by providing false information through defectors directed at convincing the United States that Iraq possessed weapons of mass destruction and had links to terrorists."[36]

Just as damaging have been persistent allegations that Chalabi has conspired with Iran to ensure a Shiite-dominated regime in Baghdad, and has helped funnel Iranian aid to Iraqi insurgents. At one point, indeed, U.S. security forces raided his Baghdad offices, spurred by reports that he had given away to the Iranians the fact that occupation authorities were intercepting cross-border messages. To resolve doubts, Dexter Filkins of the *Times*'s Baghdad bureau sought and received Chalabi's permission to join him on a flying trip to Tehran in late 2005. Chalabi produced a visa for Filkins overnight: an unusual feat, since it was an Iranian national holiday. The pair then breezed through Iranian border controls and jumped into a waiting executive jet for the flight to the capital. There (with the American at hand) Chalabi met with President Mahmoud Ahmadinejad and Iran's national security adviser, Ali Larijani (who praised Chalabi as "a very wise man and a very useful person"). Was it therefore possible, Filkins wondered, that Chalabi, the American-adopted champion of democracy, was actually "a kind of double agent for one of America's principal adversaries"?[37]

The safe answer as of this writing is that no one can say for sure. Inarguably, Chalabi has impressed Americans, Iraqis, and Iranians with his irrepressible self-assurance, his extensive network of highly placed contacts, and his skill at turning with the political tide. In postconquest Iraq, he was soon serving as Deputy Prime Minister and Oil Minister, a considerable feat since his political base has been wafer thin. In Iraq's 2005 national elections, the INC won barely 30,000 votes out of 12 million cast, a miniscule fraction insufficient to elect a single deputy to the new Iraq parliament. This caused little surprise to veteran analysts, since a natural antipathy often exists between exiled opposition groups and the internal resistance to a foreign-imposed or an autocratic regime. Postliberation political prizes most often go to those who stayed at home and endured prison terms (viz, Mandela, Nehru, Havel, and Kenyatta) with some notable exceptions (viz, Willy Brandt and Charles de Gaulle).

Inarguably as well, Ahmad Chalabi in 2001 had no American ally more steadfast than George Bush's only recently sworn-in Deputy Secretary of Defense, Paul Wolfowitz.

⌘

Given Wolfowitz's own roots and experience, one can readily understand why he found Chalabi persuasive and congenial. Here was an immigrant with an aptitude for mathematics who had risen through elite universities to gain a Ph.D. at the University of Chicago. Chalabi was a dedicated secularist whose vision of a democratic, middle-class Iraq overlapped with Wolfowitz's own hopes. In a summer 1991 article in *Foreign Affairs*, Chalabi decried what he claimed was the Western stereotype of Iraq as "a country fraught with violence, unruly and hard to govern" that therefore required a strong, even brutal government. A gross caricature, he maintained, since before the 1958 coup, Iraq was already developing a constitutional system and Sunnis had finally begun to realize they had to share power with the Shiite majority. Once Saddam Hussein was overthrown, "the significance of categories—Shiite and Sunni, Arab and Kurd"—would diminish. Indeed, after decades of misrule and ideological politics, "the politics of community, with standards of accountability, is likely to enjoy tremendous appeal."[38]

In Wolfowitz's case, a new development in his private life may well have made Chalabi's optimism appear more plausible. After separating from his wife, he had begun seeing the intelligent and personable Shaha Ali Riza, a senior communications officer for the Middle East and North African regional office at the World Bank. Ms. Riza's biography seemed to touch every corner of the Muslim Middle East: her father was Libyan, her mother part Syrian, part Saudi; she was raised in Tunisia and Saudi Arabia, and earned a master's degree at St. Antony's College, Oxford, after studying at the London School of Economics, institutions long involved in Middle East studies. A British subject, and divorced from her Turkish husband, Bulent Ali Riza, she and her son had been living in Washington for more than a decade, where she worked for the National Endowment for Democracy before joining the World Bank in 1997. When the press learned of her relationship with Wolfowitz, she was demeaningly described as his "girlfriend." She was in her fifties, he in his sixties, but both duly became the quarry of the media—"the hounds of Gutenberg," as a *Time* magazine bureau chief once dubbed his colleagues—with their stakeouts and shouted questions.

A feminist, secularist, and democrat, Ms. Riza helped persuade Wolfowitz that Iraq was overdue for a chance to rejoin the modern world under a decent government. And at the outset of the Bush II administration, the auguries seemed favorable for a more assertive policy toward Baghdad. The new Secretary of Defense, Donald Rumsfeld, an aggressive offspring of Chicago's North Shore, was determined to demonstrate his belief that America's global strategy could be better advanced by a slimmer, mobile, yet effective armed force. First Afghanistan, and then Iraq, would be the proving grounds. (To this end, he showered subordinates with "snowflakes"—tersely written memoranda—and from time to time relished correcting his learned Deputy Secretary's spelling or grammar.) In the new Vice President's office there was Scooter Libby, once Wolfowitz's student at Yale, dubbed by some "Dick Cheney's Dick Cheney," having become the drafter of his chief's muscular declarations about sustaining American primacy. And thanks largely to Chalabi and Wolfowitz, federal money was now flowing to the INC, the presumed embryo of a free Iraq to come. The fuse was in place. What was needed was a spark.

"We were having a meeting in my office," recalled Wolfowitz in a taped May 2003 interview with Sam Tannenhaus for *Vanity Fair.* "Someone said a plane had hit the World Trade Center. Then we turned on the television and we started seeing the shots of the second plane hitting, and this is the way I remember it. It's a little fuzzy . . . There didn't seem much to do about it immediately, and we went on with whatever the meeting was. Then the whole building shook. I have to confess my first reaction was an earthquake. I didn't put the two things together. Rumsfeld did instantly."

At 9:43 a.m., a hijacked airliner, American Flight 77, slammed into the Pentagon, killing two hundred people; tens of thousands were evacuated. Leaking fuel fed a torrid and smoky blaze that spread through the building's wooden roof. Half the Pentagon was temporarily closed. In the urgent high-level meetings that followed in Washington and Camp David, details differ as to who said what and when. In Wolfowitz's recollection, two debates developed, the first about tactics and timing, in which President Bush came down squarely on striking Afghanistan first. On the wider question of strategy, recalls Wolfowitz, "it is at least clear with 20/20 hindsight that the President came down on the side of the larger goal"—that is, Iraq. From all accounts, it is clear that the most dogged, impassioned, and persuasive advocate of unseating Saddam Hussein was Paul Wolfowitz. And even before OPERATION IRAQI FREEDOM commenced, there were clues as to why so smart a man proved so wrong about the Iraq War and its sanguinary epilogue.[39]

All analogies are deceptive, a wise Washington observer once remarked, noting that the Fall of Man was instigated by a false analogy—the Serpent promised Eve that if she tasted the apple she would be "as a God." In the Philippines and Indonesia, two fragmented Third World nations, Wolfowitz witnessed a transition from autocracy to democracy—a messy transition to an imperfect new elective system, to be sure, but nevertheless successful. In interviews, he frequently cited the instance of Romania in the wake of the disorderly collapse of the Ceauşescu regime—when mob justice claimed the lives of the ruling party's longtime leader and his wife—remarking that if postinvasion Iraq looked anything like post-Communist Romania, he would count the project a success. Yet in all these cases, the transition was precipitated by *internal* events, not by a massive foreign intervention. Nor did the United States have a convincing *casus belli*. So flimsy was evidence for Saddam's alleged nuclear-chemical-biological weapons program that the Iraq War was deemed unwarranted or illegal by heads of government in neighboring Mexico and Canada, by the Vatican and Pope John Paul II, and by UN Secretary-General Kofi Annan, no less than the predictable nay-saying in France, Germany, Russia, and China. A common view is that Wolfowitz and his allies were merely gullible in crediting the self-interested claims of Iraqi exiles intent on embroiling a superpower on their side of a domestic conflict. Referring to Wolfowitz, the former chief weapons inspector in Iraq, David Kay put it bluntly: "He was a true believer. He thought he had the evidence. That came from defectors. They came from Chalabi."[40]

This seems too simple. Although the full record of what the authors of the Iraq War said to each other off the record is not yet available, it seems plausible that they believed that a quick victory would bury doubts concerning the preliminaries. As John Kennedy famously remarked after the 1961 Bay of Pigs fiasco, victory boasts a thousand fathers while defeat is an orphan. On its face, the notion of a quick victory was not fantasy. Only months before, Rumsfeld's New Model Army had swept into Kabul and easily ousted the Taliban regime. How such triumphs can affect an official's demeanor was described by Nicholas Lemann in *The New Yorker* in April 2002, when preparations for the assault on Iraq were underway. He met with Scooter Libby in the Executive Office Building. "He appears absolutely sure of himself," Lemann writes, "and whether by coincidence or as the result of the influence of his boss [Dick Cheney], speaks in a tough, confidential, gravely rumble. Like Condoleezza Rice and Bush himself, he gives the impression of having calmly accepted the idea that the project of war and reconstruction which the Administration has now taken on may be a little exhausting for those charged with carrying it out but is unquestionably right, the only prudent course."[41]

Everybody knows how this prudent course ended. Partly for budgetary reasons, the invading force was insufficient to keep order in liberated Baghdad. Matters were worsened by the abrupt dissolution of the Iraqi Army, flooding the country with jobless, demoralized, and armed warriors. Instant and massive "debaathification" loosed another torrent of unemployable, disgruntled bureaucrats. Something grandly called the Coalition Provisional Authority (CPA) was staffed with young American political appointees who shared a common ignorance of the language, history, and religions of Iraq. There was a widespread impression, fanned by his media fans (notably *The New York Times*'s Judith Miller, playing the role of Flora Shaw), that Ahmad Chalabi would step forward to become Iraq's savior, amid the acclaim of a long-oppressed people.

In Washington, sponsors of the war were plainly caught by surprise when their confident predictions of Iraqi gratitude were confounded by a developing insurgency. When Chalabi turned up in Baghdad in the wake of its proclaimed liberation, it appeared few Iraqis knew who he was, and the occupation authorities drew back from enthroning him. "It was a puppet show!" Chalabi later complained. "The worst of all worlds. We were in charge, and we had no power. We were blamed for everything the Americans did, but we couldn't change any of it." He hurtfully elaborated, "The real culprit in all this was Wolfowitz. They chickened out. The Pentagon guys chickened out."[42]

In truth, many highly intelligent senior Pentagon officials had come to believe in their own abstract construct of a fictional Iraq, misled by its facade of secular modernity and the upbeat assurances of its Westernized exiles. The Defense Department simply discarded a multivolume assessment of likely occupation hazards prepared by the State Department. When prior to the invasion, a delegation of archaeologists presented Secretary Rumsfeld with a list of high-value excavation sites and museums urgently in need of protection, its members were thanked and their list vanished. In the wake of Baghdad's fall, Barbara Bodine, a former Ambassador to Yemen who knew Iraq well, was invited to the Pentagon and found top officials uninterested in her views. As recounted by Larry Diamond, a Stanford University expert in democracy promotion, Paul Wolfowitz pressed his own radical views. "Why not redraw all the provincial and district boundaries?" he suggested. Bodine told him: "Look at the road network. This is the way the roads go. This is the pattern that has evolved over centuries. This is how the Iraqis see themselves." The boundaries were not redrawn.[43]

Ali A. Allawi, Iraq's first postwar Minister of Defense, fairly phrased an overall judgment in a volume titled *The Occupation of Iraq* (2007):

> The terrible social legacy of the previous two decades was hardly recognized by the American troops who entered Baghdad on 9 April 2003. Neither did returning Iraqis fully fathom the changes that had taken place in their country, and the fundamental change that the Iraqi psyche had undergone over the decades of dictatorship, war and sanctions. The naïve, ideological or self-serving analysis of Iraq, conducted from the vantage points of Washington or London, bore little resemblance to the facts on the ground. The CPA [Coalition Provisional Authority] was handed this legacy to manage.
>
> It was not only hampered by its own weaknesses and shortcomings but was also bewildered by the total strangeness of the Iraqi social, political, institutional, and economic landscape. The CPA was driving itself ever more into a physical and psychological ghetto, even before the external violence became unsupportable. The task of administering, let alone reforming, Iraq in the face of such hurdles, was well nigh impossible.[44]

Paul Wolfowitz never truly addressed the aftermath of the war he was instrumental in promoting. He made several flying visits to liberated Iraqi, and in interviews and at news conferences he offered vague and almost plaintive homilies. He insisted that he had never suggested the occupation would be a breeze; he acknowledged that very possibly the war's planners underestimated the havoc wrought by Saddam's tyranny on Iraqi society; that for its part, the press invariably focuses on the negatives and underplays real progress on building schools and hospitals; that concerning weapons of mass destruction, as he remarked in his *Vanity Fair* interview, the truth was that for bureaucratic reasons the threat of Iraq developing those weapons was the one issue that everyone could agree on.

At the Pentagon, Wolfowitz kept pressing occupation authorities for a quicker transfer of power to the Iraqis, to be followed by prompt elections.

When Iraq's fourteen-month American proconsul, Ambassador L. Paul "Jerry" Bremer III, visited the Pentagon in September 2003, he had a strained encounter with Wolfowitz. He records this exchange in *My Year in Iraq*:

> "[W]e've got to move quickly on the political front," [Wolfowitz] said. "What if we just expanded the GC [Governing Council] to a group of 100 or 200 to make them more representative, and *then* gave them sovereignty?"
>
> "I guess we could do that, at least in theory," I replied. "But it'd be enormously time-consuming . . . and a waste of the time we consumed." I reminded him that it had taken the U.S.-U.K. Governance Team, about fifty of them, working twenty hours a day for more than two months, to come up with the initial twenty-five Iraqis for the GC. "God knows how long it would take to expand them."
>
> "Well, why not let the GC expand itself, then?"
>
> "Paul, these guys have shown no capacity to broaden their representativeness, neither back in May, nor when they appointed the PrepCom, nor two weeks ago when they named the ministers."
>
> Wolfowitz did not seem persuaded and shifted the subject to the security situation. Couldn't we find ways to speed up the training of Iraqis so they could replace Americans?
>
> *Where have I heard that before?* [Bremer's italics][45]

These were difficult times for Wolfowitz. His aura of omniscience had vanished, so much so that he began to joke about it. On returning from Iraq on July 27, 2003, he said to an Associated Press reporter, "Sometimes it's nice to have a reputation for being almost godlike, but, frankly, I think it produces this phenomenon that if something isn't happening, it must be because the Americans don't want it to happen, and they begin to invent the most elaborate reasons to explain it. And the fact is—you know it—we often just make mistakes. We do stupid things." By then, his detractors were circulating his off-the-cuff blunders, such as his February 2003 observation that the difference between Iraq and Saudi Arabia was that Iraq had no holy cities. Oft quoted was Wolfowitz's March 27, 2003, testimony to a congressional panel that oil would pay for Iraq's reconstruction, claiming that Iraqi annual oil revenues of between $50 and $100 billion over two or three years meant that "[w]e are dealing with a country that can easily finance its own reconstruction and relatively soon."

Absent in his quoted remarks was either contrition or acknowledgment of a tragic error. As noted earlier, Wolfowitz himself warned West Point cadets in 2001 against the "poverty of expectations," an unwillingness to consider the unexpected in strategic calculation—or, as his mentor Albert Wohlstetter termed it, "fallibilism." By 2004, as the toll and costs of Iraq mounted, Wolfowitz became less and less visible in Washington; like Lewis Carroll's Cheshire cat he seemingly faded away until only his trademark pursed lips could be seen. A year later, with little fanfare, he resigned as Deputy Secretary of Defense to head the World Bank, the premiere global development agency whose president is by tradition an American choice. His nomination by George W. Bush was unanimously confirmed, if with misgivings, by the bank's European shareholders, but it was received with perplexity in Washington. Even before his confirmation, two British dailies (*The Times* and *The Daily Mail*) and *The Washington Post* reported on the relationship between Wolfowitz and Shaha Ali Riza, then still a senior communications officer at the World Bank. Yet World Bank rules barred the employment of couples if one spouse reported directly to the other.

True, Ms. Riza did not report directly to Wolfowitz, but the risks of embarrassment were obvious, especially since as president he planned to make a signature issue of combating corruption in countries receiving bank loans. A compromise was struck whereby Ms. Riza would be given a special post at the State Department, with the bank paying her salary, which it increased from $132,660 to $193,590, thus exceeding the compensation to Secretary of State Condoleezza Rice. An uproar ensued when *The Washington Post* disclosed this arrangement. Other reports, leaked by the bank's disgruntled career employees, claimed that Wolfowitz had given his former Pentagon aides choice posts at the bank, passing over the bank's internal hierarchy. All this was taken up by the European press as the World Bank's governors were convening for their annual spring meeting.

The dispute came to a head in June 2007, a terrible month for Paul Wolfowitz, Shaha Ali Riza, and much that they cared about. Every day brought awful tidings from Iraq. Its elected government seemed incapable of taking any important decisions. Following the bombing for the second time of the Shiite mosque in Samarra, U.S. authorities disclosed that they had begun arming Sunni militias to combat their erstwhile Al-Qaeda allies. The news broke as four Sunni sheiks were murdered in a Baghdad hotel as punishment for their collaboration with American forces in Anbar Province. For their part, so distrustful were occupation officials of Iraqis that a Kuwait contractor was building the new U.S. Embassy complex, comprising twenty-one buildings on 104 acres at a cost of $592 million. According to a June 7, 2007 *Wall Street Journal* account, the Americans feared the Iraqi workers might smuggle explosives to the work site, and thus closed their eyes when a Kuwaiti firm imported at subsistence wages laborers from Egypt, Pakistan, and Bangladesh, prompting a Justice Department inquiry into possible human trafficking. At that time, the unemployment rate in Baghdad was reckoned at 50 percent. In an especially bitter final blow, a federal jury found Scooter Libby guilty of perjury and obstruction of justice. (As Dick Cheney's Chief of Staff, he lied about his role in outing a covert CIA agent and faced thirty months in prison and a fine of $250,000; President Bush subsequently commuted his jail sentence.) Wolfowitz had written to the sentencing judge on Libby's behalf, recalling in a three-page, single-spaced letter how he had induced Libby to join the public service, and praised his efforts to protect reporters ensnared in preinvasion secrecy scandals. The judge released the letter, subjecting Wolfowitz to a barrage of mockery on the Internet.

By June's end, under duress, Paul Wolfowitz submitted his resignation to the World Bank. By 2008, after five grim years, the Iraq War still seemed to claim all that it touched, especially its architects. Sir Christopher Wren's epitaph in the crypt of St. Paul's Cathedral all too sadly sums up the career of the brilliant and broken chief promoter of a bad war: "If you seek his monument, just look around." (Or, as in the terser Latin, "*Si monumentum requiris, circumspice.*")

✜

Echoes in a Long Corridor

Sages through the ages have agreed on the futility of seeking to recapture, fully grasp, deal objectively with, or learn from things past. To the Hellenic philosophers in ancient Asia Minor, time was a river in whose waters one could never step twice. To Thomas Carlyle, history was little more than a distillation of rumors, while to the less famous but oft-cited British author L. P. Hartley, the past was a foreign country where they did things differently. To America's acerbic, nay-saying Ambrose Bierce, history was an account, mostly false, of unimportant events brought about by rulers, mostly knaves, and soldiers, mostly fools. Indeed one has to be jejune or an ideologue to believe the past predetermines the future, otherwise every stock trader would be rich. Nevertheless, common sense and simple prudence argue the value of looking backward for danger signs, much as a sailor approaching a new coastline would want to know the location of likely reefs and previous shipwrecks.

Concerning empires, past and present, a useful parallel image is of an imaginary corridor of power commencing in classical Rome and ending in present-day Washington, a corridor lined with well-marked alcoves. To be sure, many Americans would instantly object that the United States is not formally an empire. "Yet who can doubt that there is an American empire?" the late Arthur M. Schlesinger Jr. asked in *The Cycles of American History* (1986) "—an 'informal' empire, not colonial in polity, but still richly equipped with imperial paraphernalia: troops, ships, planes, bases, pro-

consuls, local collaborators, all spread wide around the luckless planet."[1]
Whether this expansionary drive has stemmed from economic, political, or
moral considerations is a matter of warm dispute, but undeniably, America is *perceived* as an imperial power in much of the world, among friends
no less than foes. The notion of American exceptionalism—the self-flatter-
ing image of a City on the Hill whose special quality has made the United
States freer, wiser, and purer than its sovereign sisters—is hardly shared
elsewhere. Yet a society's claim of special virtue is widely shared, and has a
venerable history, as one finds by pausing at the first alcove in our corridor,
marked "*Casus Belli*," signifying the legal justifications for a state of war.

Washington has always insisted officially that its wars, great or less
great, have been waged for a just cause. And if we are to believe the high
priests of ancient Rome, not once in a millennium did that city's legions
wage an aggressive war. The origins of this claim have been carefully traced
by an American classical scholar, Tenney Frank, in *Roman Imperialism*, first
published in 1914. As Professor Frank writes,

> From time immemorial a semipolitical priestly board existed whose
> province it was to supervise the rites peculiar to a declaration of war and
> the swearing of treaties, and which formed, as it were, a court of first
> instance in such questions of international dispute as the proper treat-
> ment of envoys and the execution of extradition. When any complaint
> arose that a neighboring tribe had committed an act of war, it was the
> duty of the board to investigate the matter for the Senate, and, if it found
> the complaint was just, to send a herald to the offending state with a
> demand for restitution. His formula read: "If I unjustly or impiously
> demand that the aforesaid offender be surrendered, then permit me not
> to return to my country."
>
> If restitution was not made, a respite of thirty days was given, after
> which the herald notified the offending states that force would be used,
> employing the following formula: "Hear me, Jupiter and Quirinus, and
> all other gods. I call you to witness that this nation is unjust and does
> not duly practice righteousness, and our elders may consider by what
> measures we may secure our due."[2]

Under the institution known as *fetial*, the sacred college sanctioned
only defensive wars and rejected as blasphemous the idea that any conflict

involving aggression or territorial ambitions could receive divine approbation. Then a way was found to make the college's task easier. As Roman
rule spread across the Mediterranean and into the far reaches of Europe,
the imperial government entered into scores of mutual defense treaties with
tributary states or tribes. Alleged violation of these treaties readily provided
a *casus belli* for the thirty-day ultimatums proclaimed by heralds. Thus the
Roman Empire formally fell with its martial virtue intact.

By the same token, the score or so "little wars" waged by the British in
the Victorian era were never acknowledged as aggressive—always there was
the mistreatment of an envoy, the breach of an agreement, or the nefarious dealing with a European rival. In America, generations of schoolchil-
dren have been bred on textbooks suggesting that not once—not in Mexico,
Hawaii, Cuba, Puerto Rico, the Philippines, Guam, Samoa, Haiti, Guatemala, Honduras, Panama, Nicaragua, El Salvador, the Dominican Republic, Chile, or Iran—did the United States promote violence or wage a war
of aggression. Indeed, even the evilest empires profess similar virtue: Hitler
concocted a Polish act of aggression to justify Germany's declaration of war
in 1939, and all of Stalin's wars were purportedly in defense of the Soviet
socialist motherland. And even when empires cease to exist, their political
heirs stubbornly resist acknowledging human rights abuses long past, as
is the case with Japan regarding war crimes in China and Korea, or with
Belgium regarding Emperor Leopold's offenses in the Congo, or with Turkey
regarding the massacre of Armenians under the Ottoman Empire.

Thus Americans can scarcely be surprised by the widespread skepticism
expressed about the *casus belli* variously invoked to justify the Iraq War, notably the development of weapons of mass destruction or Saddam's links to
terrorism or the need to promote Arab democracy. Cynical Middle Easterners
believe the war was really about oil; or implanting permanent military bases
in Iraq; or helping Israel and containing Syria or protecting the militarily
incompetent Saudi Arabians; or preventing Iran from dominating the Persian Gulf; or finally (in the war's initial stages), about waving a bloody flag to
embarrass and intimidate Democrats. How astonishing if an American President ever dared to emulate the Wizard of Oz and come clean about the evasive doubletalk and moral fallibility that characterize the lofty declarations
of Great Powers, even the world's sole superpower. And alas, how unlikely.

Another alcove bears the poster "Indirect Rule." Once again, this was an imperial technique that flourished under the Romans and which nowadays haunts American ventures in the Middle East. The Romans hit upon indirect rule—the installing of an indigenous candidate on a captive throne—as a practical means of lowering occupation costs and of outwardly respecting ethnic and religious differences, especially in the East. "The value of state and tribal clients in the system of imperial security was a commonplace of imperial statecraft," writes the American military expert Edward N. Luttwak in his 1976 analysis of the grand strategy of the Roman Empire. As he elaborates:

> Inherently dynamic and unstable, client states and client tribes required the constant management of specialized diplomacy. Roman control and surveillance had to be continuous. In the East, the dynasts who operated the client system were sufficiently aware of their own weakness (and of the inevitability of Roman retribution) to remain strictly loyal. Even so, internal dynastic rivalries and the complications of interdynastic family relations could threaten the stability of the whole system. Thus Herod's troubles with his sons—or his senile paranoia—upset the internal equilibrium of his own important client state. Worse, these factors had repercussions on Cappadocia, since Glaphyra, daughter of Archelaus, ruler of Cappadocia, was married to Alexander, one of Herod's executed sons.[3]

British officers who contended with the dysfunctional Hashemite dynasties during and after World War I would surely nod with sympathetic concurrence. Yet despite the difficulties, the pluses of indirect rule outweighed the minuses in the eyes of Britain's leaders, especially given the country's straitened state after the Great War. Lord Cromer's backstage government of Egypt seemed a relevant model for Iraq, Jordan, Palestine, and even fractious Persia. In Africa, Lord Lugard had in 1906 synthesized the canonical texts for Indirect Rule (which he capitalized). Later as Proconsul in Nigeria, he applied these principles to the recently conquered emirates in the Muslim north. The same principles were at a moment of choice endorsed by T. E. Lawrence, regarded as the foremost British champion of Arab rights. In a 1919 letter to a skeptical Lord Curzon, then Foreign Secretary, Lawrence said he hoped that the Arabs "should be our first brown dominion and not our last brown colony." Don't attempt to drive them, he counseled, because "you can lead them without force anywhere, if nominally arm in arm." In an article a year later for *The Observer* that dealt with the growing insurgency in Iraq (as the British psychologist Kathryn Tidrick relates in *Empire and the English Character*) Lawrence urged Britain to give Iraqis real responsibility and then "stand by and give advice." His model, he said, was Egypt under Lord Cromer: "Cromer dominated Egypt not because England gave him force, or because Egyptians love us, but because he was so good a man."[4]

Even if Lawrence were serious, not always a safe assumption, this seemed peculiar advice. It was not Lord Cromer's virtue that mattered to Egyptian politicians as much as the British financiers and the occupation army that backed him (see chapter 1). Besides, the indigenous ministers that Cromer "advised" risked derision and condemnation by the radical nationalists who called themselves Young Egypt. Among Cromer's protégés was Boutros Ghali, a forebear of the future UN Secretary-General. He was moderate, he was capable, and he was a Christian. Sadly, as the anti-imperialist poet Wilfrid Blunt was to write in his diary on February 22, 1910, "Boutros Pasha, the Coptic Prime Minister, has been assassinated at Cairo by one Ibrahim Wardani, a young Nationalist . . . He says he did it to rid Egypt of a minister who was betraying her, as he had already betrayed her on other occasions. It was the first instance of bloodshed by an Egyptian Nationalist."[5] In effect, the murder was a warning shot to Copts and all other minorities about the perils of working with infidel foreigners.

Indirect rule impacted not only politicians and minorities but also hereditary rulers. Around six hundred princely states existed in British India before independence, some as big as Belgium, others as small as London's Hyde Park. A Resident was posted to advise the various Hindu maharajahs or Muslim nawabs, but as the Oxford scholar Sidney Owen found in the 1850s, "the native Prince, being guaranteed in the possession of his dominion but deprived of so many attributes of sovereignty, sinks in his own esteem, and loses that stimulus to good government which is supplied by the fear of rebellion and deposition. He becomes a *soi fainéant*, a sensualist, an extortionist miser, or a careless and lax ruler."[6] This was the double underside of indirect rule. Its regal beneficiaries in yielding to a foreign embrace lose self-respect and turn into princes of pleasure, as happened with Egypt's King Farouk, or they take the contrary course by slapping back at their offstage patrons to demonstrate their manhood, as did Jordan's freshly enthroned

King Hussein when he fired Glubb Pasha, the British commander of the Arab Legion, giving him a day to leave. The gesture indeed helped Hussein avoid the fate of his grandfather Abdullah, who was assassinated by a Palestinian militant. But Glubb's dismissal outraged Anthony Eden, who in 1955 had finally succeeded Winston Churchill at 10 Downing Street and who was now eager to earn his own battle stripes. In Eden's eyes, the blame did not lay with Jordan's well-spoken, Sandhurst-schooled monarch, but with an insufferable Egyptian, Gamal Abdel Nasser. In Eden's view, Nasser by word and deed was sowing sedition throughout the Arab world and had to be stopped. Thus the way opened for the Suez debacle, the failed military intervention in 1956 that cost Eden his office, transformed Nasser into a demigod, and momentarily turned even the United States against its closest European ally.

One senses a cautionary symmetry in respect to indirect rule. It is telling that arguably the most volcanic eruptions against foreign dominion have taken place in Egypt, Iran, Iraq, and Cuba, although none of the four was formally a colony. In each country, radicals seized power by deposing regimes perceived as being the craven tools of alien wire-pullers. When John F. Kennedy in his 1960 television debate with Richard Nixon reminded his Republican rival that before the Cuban Revolution, everybody in Havana knew that the island's second most powerful personage was the U.S. Ambassador, his taunt expressed a reality that helped keep Fidel Castro in power for nearly half a century.

Moving along, we come to an alcove marked "Regime Change," a phrase heard in Washington during the 1990s and enshrined as official American usage by President George W. Bush. Yet by whatever name, the imperious practice of intervening either overtly or covertly to unseat a foreign troublemaker has a long and dubious history. In a familiar cycle, an externally managed regime change is at first followed by instant relief and cheering on the part of its wire-pullers, as alleged malefactors flee and fresh faces appear on television, their waists adorned with the sashes of power. Soon enough, however, there is pain and embarrassment as the new leaders excel at torture, extortion, and nepotism, yielding an enduring legacy of bitterness and cynicism, and in extreme cases opening the way for yet more radical regimes.

This pattern held during the Cold War, when Washington for strategic reasons promoted or assented to coups against inconvenient yet elected leaders in Syria (1949), Iran (1953), Guatemala (1954), Greece (1967), and Chile (1973). Other regime changes effected with varying degrees of American involvement took place in the former Belgian Congo, South Vietnam, the Dominican Republic, Indonesia, Grenada, Guyana, Haiti, Panama, Liberia, and Cyprus. It is hard to discern benign results in any of these regime changes. Yet this is not simply an American pattern. We owe to the experienced British perhaps the most misbegotten of regime changes, in Uganda, in an unintended long-term result of Lord Lugard's policies. The tale begins in a town called Jinja, the headquarters of a British colonial battalion called the King's African Rifles. The Polish foreign correspondent Ryszard Kapuściński sets the stage, writing in *The Shadow of the Sun* (2001):

> The model for this army was devised toward the end of the nineteenth century by General Lugard, one of the architects of the British Empire. It called for divisions of mercenaries recruited from tribes hostile toward the population on whose territory they were to be garrisoned: an occupying force holding the locals on a tight rein. Lugard's ideal soldiers were young, well-built men from the Nilotic (Sudanese) population, who distinguished themselves by their enthusiasm for warfare, their stamina, and their cruelty.[7]

These ideal fighters were known as Nubians, a word that over time in Uganda evoked a shudder. Years passed, and one day an English officer noticed a Nubian with a formidable physique and a winning smile who was hanging around the camp. He was Idi Amin, who promptly enlisted and soon distinguished himself with his toughness and bravery in bush wars. By the time Uganda won its independence in 1962, Amin was a major general and deputy commander of the army, as well as a prize-winning heavyweight boxer and a good rugby player, esteemed not just by his British advisers but by the Israelis with whom he had also trained. Uganda was then led by a populist and erratic president, Milton Apollo Obote, smart, conceited, and too sure of himself, especially when he flew in 1971 to Singapore to take part in a British Commonwealth conference. In his absence, Amin seized power in a coup that the British, impatient with the boastful Obote, either allowed to happen or covertly abetted. Once in power, Amin began by expelling Uganda's Asian minority and followed up by aligning himself with Arab radicals; he then instigated an ethnic bloodbath that claimed the lives of as many as two hundred thousand Ugandans (in the estimate of Amnesty International). Now styling himself the Conqueror of the British Empire, Amin repaid his Israeli mentors by toying cruelly with passengers aboard a hijacked El Al airliner that landed at Entebbe airport, prompting a commando rescue that coincided memorably in July 1976 with America's bicentennial fête.

President Amin was finally overthrown in 1979 and fled to Saudi Arabia, where he died in bed in 2003. Only in its extravagance and cruelty did the Amin saga differ from a score or more regime changes carried out by Third World officers trained by Europeans and Americans, often encouraged with promises of swift recognition if they eliminated a troublesome chief of state. As we shall see, there are still more radical examples of miscalculation in the name of regime change.

Let us proceed to the next alcove, labeled "Cross, Crescent, and Hammer," telegraphing the risks of treating absolutists, religious or ideological, as foreign policy partners. Nowhere have the vicissitudes of regime change proved more disastrous than in Afghanistan, invaded by the Soviet Union in 1979, becoming a battleground in a ten-year proxy war, next enduring a civil war with a dozen different foreign players that ended by empowering radical Islamists, leading to an American-led invasion in 2002 whose eventual outcome is still in doubt. As *The Washington Post*'s Steve Coll observes in *Ghost Wars* (2004), "Afghanistan after 1979 was a laboratory for political violence conceived abroad and imposed by force. The language and ideas that described Afghan parties, armies, and militias originated with theoreticians in universities and seminaries in Europe, the United States, Cairo, and Pakistan. Afghans fought as 'communists' or as 'freedom fighters.' They joined jihadist armies battling on behalf of an imagined global Islamic *umma*."[8]*

In this complex tangle, one strand can be readily detected: neither the Soviets nor the Americans truly took Islam seriously. Seeing Afghanistan through Marxist spectacles, Soviet party leaders assumed their narrowly based Kabul clients could somehow handily quell tribal irregulars and that the allure of modernization—tractors, television, schools, women's rights—

---

* The word *umma* refers to the Islamic community founded by the Prophet and ruled by his deputies.

would reshape a backward land. To the Americans, the all-important point was that Islamic fighters loathed Communism and killed Russians: the rest was detail. Thus in the wake of the December 1979 Soviet invasion meant to prop up a wobbly Communist regime, the Carter Administration struck a deal, few questions asked, with Pakistan's military dictator: America will covertly provide the guns, and your military intelligence service can distribute them. Saudi Arabia simultaneously agreed to match American aid, dollar for dollar, which it earmarked for its chosen Islamic militants.

Thus the war was in effect franchised to Pakistan and Saudi Arabia, both deemed strategic allies, and through them money and guns streamed to radical jihadists, funding the training camps that would nurture a global network of Islamic terrorists. During the Reagan years, America's covert help exponentially increased and included surface-to-air Stinger missiles, the weapon essential for felling helicopters. This was in good part due to the enthusiastic support of an earthy, whiskey-drinking Texas Congressman, Charlie Wilson, a Democrat who held a key seat on the powerful House Appropriations Committee. If Wilson cared a jot about Islam, it is not apparent in the pages of an admiring book, *Charlie Wilson's War*, by his friend, the late CBS producer George Crile. In his forays to the battle zone, Wilson managed but one single brief encounter with Gulbuddin Hekmatyar, who was the Afghan warlord most favored by the Pakistan military—but who also despised America and all its works (save weapons). When the journalist Robert Kaplan interviewed Afghan guerrillas, the moderates among them were baffled by this favoritism. In *Soldiers of God* (1990), Kaplan describes a meeting with the tough and sensible Afghan commander Abdul Haq: "Americans were of no help to him. Despite bankrolling [Pakistani President] Zia to the tune of hundreds of millions of dollars annually, the American intelligence community knuckled under to ISI [Pakistan's interservice intelligence agency], convincing themselves that Hekmatyar was not half as bad as everyone said he was."[9] (Abdul Haq was murdered, probably at Hekmatyar's orders, as U.S. forces entered Afghanistan in 2002.)

This utilitarian view of faith as weapon in Afghanistan has a venerable pedigree. In *Decline and Fall of the Roman Empire* (Volume I, Chapter Two) Edward Gibbon thus summed up the Roman outlook: "The various modes of worship which prevailed in the Roman world, were all considered by the people, as equally true, by the philosopher, as equally false, and by the magistrate, as equally useful." As in Rome, worldly politicians nowadays tend to treat the other-worldly as useful and pliable partners. Yet over and over again, this attitude has backfired, sometimes fatally. Democratic Israel remains hostage to tens of thousands of settlers who regard themselves as soldiers of God and who occupy as much as 40 percent of the contested West Bank. Israel's elective system maximizes their influence. From the early days of the Jewish state, secular parties in the Knesset have haggled for the support of the small religious parties, whose votes can be critical in a closely divided parliament.

The result is chronicled in *The Accidental Empire* (2006) by Gershom Gohenberg, an American-born writer living in Jerusalem. He details how Israel's long-ruling Labor Party, emboldened by victory in the Six-Day War, sought to create "facts on the ground" by seeding religious settlers in newly occupied territories. Many if not most settlers insist that God has given them clear title to their land, and that yielding as much as an inch would be sacrilege. When in 1995 Prime Minister Yitzhak Rabin, a Laborite, proposed trading land for peace, a demented Jewish fundamentalist killed him. After his death, settlements proliferated. Nobody cheered these devout pioneers more ardently than the secular-minded former general and Likud Party leader Ariel Sharon. Speaking on Israel Radio, Sharon urged settlers to "grab more hills, expand the territory. Everything that's grabbed will be in our hands. Everything we don't grab will be in theirs."[10] The grabbing escalated as mobile homes were parked in "outposts" in the occupied West Bank. However, when Sharon himself became Prime Minister and sought in 2005 to withdraw unilaterally from Gaza, the settlers he had extolled refused to budge, shouting that Sharon was a traitor. They had to be evicted by grim-faced Israeli soldiers. In the midst of this dispute, the highly stressed Sharon was felled by a stroke and sank into a protracted coma: an unexpected casualty in the ongoing conflict between the apocalyptic demands of faith and the worldly calculus of politics.

This conflict has spread to, and even infects, all great world religions. Often forgotten is the cautionary career of Solomon Bandaranaike, the founding Prime Minister of independent Ceylon (present-day Sri Lanka). He was a secularist who pragmatically bid for the votes of Ceylon's Buddhist majority; he discarded his Western suits, led the festivities marking the two thousandth anniversary of Buddha's ascent to Nirvana; and gave Sinhalese Buddhists a language advantage in obtaining choice civil service jobs. But in 1959, when he sought to conciliate the now-estranged Tamils, he was slain by a censorious Buddhist monk. It proved the seed of Sri Lanka's unending civil war.

In India, the secularist Prime Minister Indira Gandhi opportunely and unwisely promoted a young Sikh firebrand named Jamal Singh Bhindranwale in order to divide and punish the mainstream Sikh party in the Punjab, Akali Dal, which was giving her own Congress Party trouble. In 1983, Jamal's followers seized the Golden Temple in Amritsar. Hundreds were killed when the Indian army besieged the holiest of Sikh shrines, precipitating Mrs. Gandhi's assassination by her Sikh bodyguards, which in turn provoked an avenging Hindu pogrom against Sikhs.

One senses that behind these utilitarian miscalculations is a common human trait. Politicians by their nature tend reflexively to dissimulate. They may well also assume that priests, preachers, imams, rabbis, and monks mean only half of what they say. Nor do the hard-headed normally take seriously the secular equivalent of messianic religious faiths such as Communism and Nazism. (Herr Hitler could not really mean what he declared in *Mein Kampf*; once in office, he will behave more responsibly.) A fateful instance of such a miscalculation occurred in 1918 and was the work of the hard-faced realists on Imperial Germany's General Staff. For years Germans had been discreetly aiding exiled Russian Bolsheviks and their leader V. I. Lenin. Now the generals saw a chance to knock Russia out of the war and gain a favorable peace on the Eastern Front through a regime change in Petrograd, at the time the seat of provisional but unsteady democratic government. Since the Bolsheviks promised to sue for peace, Lenin and his lieutenants were allowed transit by train from neutral Switzerland via Germany to Petrograd—like a plague bacillus, as Winston Churchill lamented in *The World Crisis*. But who sanely believed the Bolsheviks meant what Lenin preached?

This is not unlike the dilemma Americans confront in deciding how or whether to engage the maddening Islamic Republic of Iran. Taking hostile ideologies seriously does not preclude seeking the sources of their popular appeal. It might be helpful to pause in the last of the alcoves in our corridor, with its placard marked "Empathy Is Power." Empathy and sympathy are not the same; one does not have to like or agree with or feel sorry for another person in striving to see how the world looks through his or her eyes. If you were an Iranian, what would you make of the United States? Yes, it is outwardly a free country, and Americans do elect their leaders. But who elects the spy agencies, the Pentagon, the multinational corporations, the masters of the media, the think tanks, and lobbies that—in the eyes of many Iranians—form an interlocking and impenetrable mosaic? Why, Iranians wonder, is it permissible for Israel to develop nuclear weapons but a crime punishable by sanctions for Iran to explore the peaceful development of nuclear power? After all, the nonproliferation treaty formally commits existing nuclear powers to the steady reduction and total elimination of their own stockpiles. But instead of honoring that promise (as seen from Tehran), Americans are developing a new generation of bunker-piercing weapons expressly intended for use against countries like Iran.

And why, many Iranians wonder, do Americans say Tehran is part of an Axis of Evil? Do they forget that Iranians helped defeat the Taliban regime in Afghanistan and establish the new regime in Kabul that Washington supports? As to charges that Iran is helping Iraqi insurgents, an Iranian might remark that we have our own separation of powers, and we read with interest that members of the U.S. Congress charge the Bush Administration of acting with lawless and reckless independence on such serious matters as condoning torture. Is it inconceivable that Iran, too, has its rogue elements? And that our President simply does not know what to say without himself seeming weak?

These are common views in Tehran; still, such questions are seldom addressed on America's Sunday talk shows or by political pundits. Yet empathy does not require special knowledge about distant lands. As earlier chapters amply suggest, British Arabists and Persian scholars, for all their expertise, created an unstable new order in the Middle East, still in semi-colonial bondage. Decency and common sense can percolate upward from ordinary witnesses to the region's travails. The authors were impressed by six U.S. Army sergeants who joined with an Army specialist in submitting by email a courageous essay titled "The War As We Saw It" to *The New York Times* and published on August 19, 2007.* In the twelve hundred words written as their tour in Iraq was almost over, they sought to distill their

---

* Army specialist Buddhika Jayamaha, Sergeants Wesley D. Smith, Jeremy Roebuck, Omar Mora, Edward Sandmeier, Yance T. Gray, and Jeremy A. Murphy. On Monday, September 10, 2007, Staff Sergeant Gray and Sergeant Mora were killed in Baghdad when the five-ton cargo truck in which they were riding overturned.

combat experience. "In the end," so they concluded, "we need to recognize that our presence may have released Iraqis from the grip of a tyrant, but that it has also robbed them of their self-respect. They will soon realize that the best way to regain dignity is to call us what we are—an army of occupation—and force our withdrawal."

The empathy implicit in these words is inspiriting. As our own researches suggested to us, the many real and would-be kingmakers erred not through malice or ignorance, but through excess of ambition. These proconsuls and paladins undertook—to state it simply—to do the impossible for the ungrateful.

Selective Chronology

1882 The British invade and occupy Egypt.

1883 Sir Evelyn Baring (Lord Cromer) becomes Queen Victoria's Consul-General to Egypt.

1885 General Gordon dies in Khartoum at the hand of the Mahdi.

1893 Flora Shaw becomes Colonial Editor of *The Times*.

1895–96 Leander Starr Jameson leads a raid on the Transvaal Republic (December–January).

1897 First Zionist Conference is held in Basel, Switzerland.

1898 Kitchener defeats the Mahdi's successor at Omdurman.

1899–1902 The Boer War pits Britain against the Afrikaaners.

1900 The British government terminates the Royal Niger Company charter and declares a protectorate; Frederick Lugard becomes High Commissioner of Northern Nigeria.

1902 Ibn Saud recaptures Riyadh from the Rashidi dynasty.

1906 In the "Dinshawai Affair," four Egyptians were hanged and eight flogged after a scuffle with five British officers in which one officer is killed; Constitutional Revolution in Persia establishes the National Assembly (the Majlis).

1907 The Anglo-Russian Convention divides Persia into spheres of influence.

1908 A. T. Wilson is present as the British strike oil in South-West Persia, the first in the Middle East.

1909 The Anglo-Persian Oil Company is formed; the British government buys a 51 percent stake in 1914.

1912 Lugard returns to Nigeria as Governor General.

1914 World War I breaks out (August); the Ottoman Empire enters as an ally of the Central Powers (November); the British occupy Basra, invade Mesopotamia; Egypt becomes a British protectorate; Britain and Russia occupy Persia.

1915 Dardanelles campaign at Gallipoli takes place (April 1915–January 1916); McMahon-Hussein correspondence begins in July; Cox signs a treaty with Ibn Saud.

1916 The Arab Bureau is founded in Cairo and recruits Gertrude Bell and T. E. Lawrence; the besieged British Army surrenders at Kut; Lawrence is sent to bribe Turks; Chaim Weizmann meets Mark Sykes; Sykes-Picot Agreement divides Ottoman lands between Britain, France, and Russia; Arab Revolt against Ottoman rule is proclaimed (June); Lloyd George replaces Asquith as British Prime Minister (December).

1917 The British enter Baghdad, vowing liberation (March); Percy Cox is named Civil Commissioner of Mesopotamia; United States declares war on Germany but not on the Ottoman Empire (April).

1918 Woodrow Wilson unveils his Fourteen Points (January); Tsar is deposed in Russia's February revolution; Faisal "captures" Damascus (October); the Ottomans surrender to Allies (October 30); World War I ends (November 11); Britain occupies Mesopotamia and A. T. Wilson replaces Cox as Acting Civil Commissioner; British Cabinet unveils the Balfour Declaration (November); Bolsheviks seize power in Petrograd (November) and divulge the text of Sykes-Picot Agreement.

1919 Britain signs a self-serving treaty with Persia, which is later rejected by Reza Khan; anti-British riots occur in Egypt; Amritsar massacre takes place in India; Paris Peace Conference is attended by Mark Sykes, T. E. Lawrence, Gertrude Bell, A. T. Wilson, Emir Faisal, and Nuri al-Said; Lowell Thomas's illustrated travelogue debuts in London.

1920 Faisal is crowned King of Syria (March), then deposed by the French (July); the San Remo Conference (April) confirms the postwar status of Iraq, Syria, Lebanon, and Palestine; the Treaty of Sèvres (August), concluded between Britain, France, and Italy (excluding the United States) and with Turkey, dismembers the Ottoman territory, but later is superseded by the Treaty of Lausanne (1923) following establishment of a Turkish Republic; insurgency breaks out in Iraq (March–August); Cox returns as High Commissioner for Mesopotamia, and Bell resumes post as his Oriental Secretary.

1921 Winston Churchill becomes Colonial Secretary and summons the Cairo Conference (March), which recommends Hashemite throne for Iraq and creates Transjordan; Faisal I is crowned in Iraq (August); coup led by Colonel Reza Khan seizes power in Tehran, with assistance of the British.

1922 Britain grants Egypt nominal independence but continues to occupy the Suez Canal; "Treaty of Alliance" is signed between Britain and Iraq.

1924 The Turkish Republic abolishes Caliphate; Hussein of the Hejaz proclaims himself Caliph; the British end wartime subsidies to Hussein and Ibn Saud, who captures Mecca and Medina and besieges Jiddah; H. St. J. B. Philby resigns from British political service and becomes adviser to Ibn Saud.

1925 Ibn Saud takes Jiddah and completes conquest of central Arabia; the Syrians revolt against French control, and Damascus is bombed; Reza Khan deposes Qajar Dynasty and proclaims himself Shah.

1927 The British strike oil in Kirkuk, Iraq.

1932 Saudi Arabia kingdom is founded and the reign of Ibn Saud formally begins; Standard Oil of California (Socal) discovers oil in Bahrain; Iraq becomes nominally independent.

1933 Socal, assisted by Philby, signs a concession contract with Ibn Saud, granting exclusive rights for sixty years to oil drilled in eastern Saudi Arabia.

1935 Reza Shah renames Persia as Iran.

1936 An Anglo-Egyptian treaty is signed, confirming British military rights.

1936–39 Arabs revolt against Zionist immigration to Palestine.

1938 Oil is discovered in Kuwait; major oil strike in Saudi Arabia.

1939 A British White Paper decrees severe limits on Jewish immigration to Palestine as the exodus swells from Nazi Germany, and the door is closed as Europeans and Americans follow suit; World War II begins (September).

1941 A coup by pro-German officers in Iraq is followed by British occupation; Syria is occupied by the British and Free French; Britain and the USSR occupy Iran and force Reza Shah into exile, replacing him with his son Mohammed Reza Shah.

1945 Ibn Saud meets with President Roosevelt (February); the Arab League is founded by Saudi Arabia, Egypt, Syria, Iraq, Lebanon, Transjordan, and Yemen; World War II ends (August).

1946 Transjordan becomes Jordan, notionally independent as the mandate ends; the French withdraw from Lebanon and Syria, and both gain independence; the Irgun, a militant Zionist group, bombs the King David Hotel in Jerusalem, killing ninety-one.

1947 The United Nations votes to partition Palestine into Arab and Jewish states.

1948 The State of Israel is proclaimed (May), and war breaks out with surrounding Arab nations.

1949 The CIA's Miles Copeland assists in Syria's first coup d'état, led by General Hosni al Za'im; in a third coup Colonel Shishakhli seizes power.

1950 Jordan annexes the West Bank.

1951 The British boycott Iranian oil following nationalization by Mossadeq of the Anglo-Iranian Oil Company assets; Jordan's King Abdullah is assassinated by a Palestinian.

1952 On "Black Saturday" (January 26), Egyptian mobs destroy the Turf Club and Shepheard's Hotel, ten foreigners are burned to death; a Free Officers' coup led by Gamal Abdel Nasser deposes King Farouk.

1953 Ibn Saud dies and his son Saud succeeds him; with British aid, CIA orchestrates overthrow of Iranian Prime Minister Mossadeq.

1954 Britain agrees to withdraw from the Suez Canal zone.

1955 Iraq, Turkey, Pakistan, and Iran sign the Baghdad Pact, later joined by Britain.

1956 During the Suez Crisis, Nasser nationalizes the Suez Canal (July); the British and French, in secret collusion with Israel, seek his overthrow at same time (October–November) as Soviet tanks crush a Hungarian revolt; President Eisenhower joins with the Soviets in forcing a cease-fire in the Suez war and withdrawal of foreign forces.

1957 The Eisenhower Doctrine confirms entry of the United States as a regional overlord in the Middle East, replacing Great Britain.

1958 Faisal II and Nuri al-Said are assassinated in Baghdad as a military coup ends the Hashemite era in Iraq; Egypt forms the United Arab Republic with Syria (which dissolves in 1961); the United States and Britain intervene in Lebanon on behalf of the besieged Maronite leadership.

1960 OPEC (Organization of the Petroleum Exporting Countries) is founded.

1964 King Saud is deposed by his brother, Crown Prince Faisal.

1967 The Six-Day War (June) ends in decisive victory by Israel following preemptive strikes against Egypt, Syria, and Jordan; Israel occupies the Golan Heights, West Bank, and Sinai Peninsula.

1970 During "Black September," the Palestine Liberation Organization is expelled from Jordan and establishes a new base in Beirut.

1973 During the October or Yom Kippur War, Egypt and Syria attack Israel; their early gains are reversed by Israeli counterattack; in wake of war, OPEC triples the price of crude, an "oil shock" championed by the Shah of Iran.

1975 Civil war begins in Lebanon; Saudi Arabia's King Faisal is killed by his nephew.

1979 Islamic militants occupy Mecca's Grand Mosque for ten days; the Iranian revolution led by Ayatollah Khomeini ousts Mohammed Reza Shah, and American hostages are taken in Tehran; the Camp David treaty is signed between Egypt and Israel; Saddam Hussein becomes President of Iraq; the Soviets invade Afghanistan (December).

1980–88 The Iran-Iraq War.

1981 President Anwar Sadat of Egypt is assassinated.

1978–1982 Israel invades Lebanon; Christian militias massacre Palestinians at Sabra and Shatila camps as Israeli forces stand by; the PLO is forced out of Lebanon.

1983 A suicide bomber kills 241 in attack on U.S. Marine barracks in Beirut; President Reagan withdraws American forces.

1990 Iraq invades Kuwait, initiating the first Gulf War.

1998 U.S. Congress approves Iraqi Liberation Act calling for eviction of Saddam Hussein and support for Iraqi National Congress.

2001 On September 11, Al-Qaeda attacks the World Trade Center and Pentagon; the United States mounts reprisals in Afghanistan.

2002 President Bush denounces Iraq, Iran, and North Korea as "Axis of Evil."

2003 The United States, supported by Great Britain, invades and occupies Iraq (March).

Acknowledgments

Speaking in 1898 at an Eton College reunion, Lord Curzon, the least falsely modest of Indian viceroys, candidly confessed, "The East is a university in which no scholar takes his degree." Although this is our third venture into the imperial past of the East, we remain undergraduates. Fortunately, the modern Middle East has inspired an exceptionally rich literature compiled by the region's kingmakers, their political friends and foes, generating a land-fill of histories, polemics, and learned monographs by scholars and firsthand observers. Our first debt therefore is to various libraries and archives, and to their electronic sentries, the indispensable Internet search engines.

In Great Britain, we were again well served by the manuscript division of the British Library, now in its immaculate new quarters; and by the Royal Geographical Society, which catered to our queries even on the chaotic day of the London bomb attacks on July 7, 2005. We also benefited from the accessible open shelves at the School of Oriental and African Studies (SOAS) and from the declassified documents at the Public Records Office. Thanks are owed to the picture archivists at the Imperial War Museum and at the National Portrait Gallery. In Oxford, we were courteously aided by Debbie Usher at St. Antony's Middle East Archives (where tea breaks devolve into seminars), by Marion Lowman at Rhodes House, and by the staff at the Bodleian Library. For online assistance, we add our thanks to Mark Jackson and J. G. Crow at the Gertrude Bell Archives in Newcastle, and to Helen E. Roberts at Hull University, for help with the Mark Sykes material.

In America, major academic libraries were the indispensable source for fugitive monographs and rare books, notably New York University's Bobst,

Columbia's Butler, and Princeton's Firestone libraries. The privately operated New York Society Library preserves long-out-of-print works on the Middle East; and as always our archive of last resort was the New York Public Library. In Washington, we again benefited at the National Archives from John Taylor's phenomenal memory, and from the efficient assistance of Nicholas Sheetz at the Georgetown University archives. At all other times, we relied on Connecticut's excellent public libraries, most especially in Westport, Fairfield, Weston, and the Pequot Library in Southport. As vital mechanically, John David of Fairfield kept our computers running.

Among the colleagues who agreed to read chapters and alert us to egregious blunders were James Barr, Alon Ben-Meir, Edward and Perdita Burlingame, Amos Elon, Dorothy Helly, Anthony Kirk-Greene, Roger Owen, Gwyn Robyns, Jinx Rodger, Jon Lellenberg, and Anthony Wynn. Needless to add, none are responsible for errors of fact or judgment that the authors may have perpetrated. This applies in particular to inconsistencies of spelling and nomenclature: a minefield through which there is no safe passage.

Throughout, we were privileged to take part in conferences and seminars on the Middle East, including key sessions of Nicholas Rizopoulos's Foreign Policy Roundtable, Gary Sick's Middle East seminars, Joanne Myers's Carnegie Council breakfasts, and Mustafa Tlili's programs on the Middle East, including a memorable conference on "Who Speaks for Islam?" held at the Alhambra Palace Hotel in Spain. We were likewise fortunate to attend lectures on the creation of today's Middle East by Rashid Khalidi and Amy Zalman, and on modern British history by Susan Pedersen. Earlier, in 1994–95, we received a crash course on the Middle East at the Wissenschaftskolleg zu Berlin from other fellows, notably Aziz Al-Azmeh, Karine Chemla, Mamadou Diawara, Florian Coulmas, Ramachandra Guha, Salma K. Jayyusi, Fatema Mernissi, Rushdi Said, and Anouar Abdel-Malek.

We owe special thanks to Linda Wrigley, managing editor, and Benjamin Pauker, her successor, at the quarterly *World Policy Journal*, for filling in whenever their editor (Meyer) was absent abroad on book-related foreign travel. Our travel companions in the Middle East, who bore good-naturedly with our specialized interests, included Emmett Wallace, Holly Brown, Marty Karnoff, Elaine Wyden, Anne Pollen, and Jeremy Barnett. For hospitality during these forays, we proffer thanks to John and Elizabeth Onians and to Martha and Bob Lewis. In Oxford, we obtained much-needed shelter from the Reuters Foundation thanks to the help of its then-director, Paddy

Coulter, and his deputy, Jennifer Darnley. As welcome were the annual October meetings at Wellfleet in Cape Cod hosted by Robert Jay Lifton and B. J. Lifton, where friends from near and far deliberate on the American predicament, especially in the Middle East. We were especially grateful to meet and befriend Roberto Toscano, the Italian ambassador to Iran, and his wife, Francesca.

Finally, our thanks to our agent, Tina Bennett, at Janklow & Nesbit; to our mapmakers, Anita Karl and James Kemp; to our editor at W. W. Norton, the judicious Starling Lawrence; to his indefatigable number-two, Molly May; to our copy editor, Mary Babcock, for her meticulous scrutiny—a standard by which we shall judge all others; and finally to production manager Julia Druskin and designer Helene Berinsky for bringing this work from its inception to delivery in spring 2008.

—Shareen Blair Brysac
Karl E. Meyer

Illustration Credits

Notes

Prologue: The Ever-Growing Egg

1 Quoted in Daniel Yergin, *The Prize*, 396.
2 Amos Elon, *Jerusalem: City of Mirrors*, 63–87.
3 Quoted in John Morley, *Life of Gladstone*, vol. III, 72.
4 James Morris, *Pax Britannica*, 45.
5 Wilfrid Scawen Blunt, *Secret History of the English Occupation of Egypt*, 100.
6 Ronald Robinson and John Gallagher with Alice Denny, *Africa and the Victorians; the Climax of Imperialism in the Dark Continent*, 87.
7 Blunt, *Secret History*, 133.
8 Robinson and Gallagher, *Africa and the Victorians*, 95.
9 Quoted in Roy Jenkins, *Gladstone*, 403.
10 Quoted in A. J. P. Taylor, *The Struggle for Mastery in Europe, 1848–1918*, 287.
11 Robinson and Gallagher, *Africa and the Victorians*, 105–06.
12 Jenkins, *Gladstone*, 504.
13 Ibid., 505.
14 Robinson and Gallagher, *Africa and the Victorians*, 159.
15 John Morley, *Life of Gladstone*, vol. II, 256.
16 Jenkins, *Gladstone*, 503–09.

Chapter One: The Proconsul

1 Roger Owen, *Lord Cromer: Victorian Imperialist, Edwardian Proconsul*, 125.
2 Ronald Storrs, *Orientations*, 45.
3 Valentine Chirol, *Fifty Years in a Changing World*, 56.
4 Owen, *Lord Cromer*, 321.
5 James Morris, *Pax Britannica*, 244
6 G.N. Curzon, *The Problems of the Far East*, dedication.
7 Alfred Milner, *England in Egypt*, 4–5.

 8 Owen, *Lord Cromer*, vii.
 9 Roger Adelson, *London and the Invention of the Middle East: Money, Power, and War*, 72.
10 Philip Ziegler, *The Sixth Great Power*, x.
11 Quoted in Adelson, *London and the Invention of the Middle East*, 23–24.
12 Karen Armstrong, *Muhammad: A Biography of the Prophet*, 10–11.
13 Alan Moorehead, *The White Nile*, 218.
14 John H. Waller, *Gordon of Khartoum*, 318.
15 *The History of the* Times, 20.
16 Christopher Silvester, ed., *The Norton Book of Interviews*, 64–66.
17 Waller, *Gordon of Khartoum*, 326.
18 Gordon, *General Gordon's Khartoum Journal*, Sept. 19, 1884, 54.
19 Philip Magnus, *Gladstone*, 294.
20 Waller, *Gordon of Khartoum*, 305.
21 Ibid., 294.
22 Ibid., 327.
23 Lytton Strachey, *Eminent Victorians*, 287–88.
24 Waller, *Gordon of Khartoum*, 342.
25 Ibid., 351.
26 Ibid.
27 Byron Farwell, *Prisoners of the Madhi*, 87.
28 Strachey, *Eminent Victorians*, 301.
29 Ibid., 347.
30 Roy Jenkins, *Gladstone*, 514.
31 Philip Ziegler, *Omdurman*, 220–22.
32 Ibid.
33 Strachey, *Eminent Victorians*, 350.
34 Peter Mansfield, *The British in Egypt*, 4.
35 *Encyclopedia Britannica*, 11th ed., vol. VII, 484.
36 Maurice Baring, *The Puppet Show of Memory*, 168.
37 Zetland, *Lord Cromer*, 191.
38 Thomas Skelton Harrison, *The Homely Diary of a Diplomat in the East, 1897–1899*, 230–31.
39 Mark Twain, *Innocents Abroad*, 615.
40 Max Rodenbeck, *Cairo: The City Victorious*, 137.
41 Ibid., 36.
42 Storrs, *Orientations*, 10.
43 Owen, *Lord Cromer*, 338.
44 Ibid., 339.
45 Cromer, *Ancient and Modern Imperialism*, 12.
46 Cromer, *Modern Egypt*, vol. II, 146–67; Edward Said invokes this passage virtually as state's evidence for his argument in *Orientalism*, 38.
47 Mansfield, *The British in Egypt*, 139–45.
48 Owen, *Lord Cromer*, 313–14.
49 Mansfield, *Orientations*, 180.
50 Ibid., 233–34.

51 Ibid., 265.
52 Morris, *Farewell the Trumpets*, 437–38.
53 Ibid., 438.
54 Ibid., 441–42.
55 Ibid., 441.
56 Ibid., 441.
57 Ibid., 442.

Chapter Two: The Empire's Power Couple

1   Francis Williams, *Dangerous Estate*, 1.
2   James Morris, *Pax Britannica*, 31.
3   Frank Giles, *A Prince of Journalists*, 56.
4   Curzon to Lugard, March 25, 1902, MSS Perham, Box 308/5. Rhodes House, Oxford.
5   Quoted in Elizabeth Harman Pakenham Longford, *Jameson's Raid*, 150.
6   The lecture was published in Ruskin's *Lectures on Art* and appears online at www.wwnorton.com/college/english/nael/20century/topic_1/jnruskin.htm (*The Norton Anthology of English Literature*, Norton Topics Online).
7   Quoted in Longford, 150.
8   Robert Rotberg and Miles Shore, *The Founder: Cecil Rhodes and the Pursuit of Power*, 281.
9   Stead, "Young Women in Journalism," quoted in Brooke Kroeger, *Nellie Bly*, 194.
10 Roger Owen, *Lord Cromer: Victorian Imperialist, Edwardian Proconsul*, 212.
11 Quoted in Joanna Trollope, *Britannia's Daughters: Women of the British Empire*, 137.
12 Baring to Bell, Cairo, Dec. 25, 1890, *The Times* Archives, Moberly Bell Correspondence.
13 Enid Hester Chataway Moberly Bell, *Flora Shaw*, 91–92.
14 Flora Shaw to Frederick Lugard, ca. Nov. 13, 1904, MSS Perham 309/1, Rhodes House, Oxford.
15 Margery Perham, *Lugard*, vol. 2, 59.
16 Kingsley to John Holt, Feb. 20, 1899, Holt MSS, quoted in Dorothy O. Helly and Helen Callaway, "Lugard, Dame Flora Louise, Lady Lugard (1852–1929)," in H. C. G. Matthew and Brian Harrison, eds., *The Oxford Dictionary of National Biography*.
17 Bell, *Flora Shaw*, 103.
18 Ibid., 108.
19 Ibid., 107.
20 *The Times*, Aug. 12, 1892, quoted in Dorothy O. Helly and Helen Callaway, "Journalism as Active Politics: Flora Shaw, *The Times* and South Africa," in Donal Lowry, ed., *The South African War Reappraised*, 53.
21 Rotberg and Shore, *The Founder*, 288.
22 Ibid., 535.
23 Ibid., 523.

24 Quoted in Longford, *Jameson's Raid*, 103.

25 Quoted in Rotberg and Shore, *The Founder*, 525.

26 Quoted in Longford, *Jameson's Raid*, 103.

27 Quoted in *The Jameson Raid: A Centennial Retrospective*, 36.

28 Quoted in Longford, *Jameson's Raid*, 25.

29 Quoted in Kathyrn Tidrick, *Empire and the English Character*, 50.

30 Shula Marks and Stanley Trapido, "Rhodes, Cecil John (1853–1902)," in *The Oxford Dictionary of National Biography*.

31 Quoted in Tidrick, *Empire and the English Character*, 215.

32 Quoted in Jean van der Poel, *The Jameson Raid*, 4.

33 *Select Committee on British South Africa*, vol. IX, iii.

34 Rotberg and Shore, *The Founder*, 282.

35 Bell, *Flora Shaw*, 80.

36 Ibid., 95.

37 Shaw to Frederick Lugard, Nov. 7, 1895, MSS Perham Box 308/3, Rhodes House, Oxford.

38 Shaw to Frederick Lugard, Nov. 7, 1895; quoted in Perham, vol. 1, 570.

39 *The History of the* Times, 162.

40 Winston Churchill, *Great Contemporaries*, 72.

41 Quoted in Bell, *Flora Shaw*, 174–75.

42 311 of 1897, Q, 6920, quoted in van der Poel, *The Jameson Raid*, 27.

43 Van der Poel, *The Jameson Raid*, 27.

44 *History of the* Times, 169, and J. L. Garvin, 82–83, quoted in van der Poel, *The Jameson Raid*, 30.

45 Minutes of Evidence, The Select Committee on British South Africa, vol. 311 of 1897, 311, Appendix 14, quoted in Helly and Callaway, "Journalism as Active Politics," in Lowry, ed., *The South African War Reappraised*, 54.

46 Quoted in van der Poel, *The Jameson Raid*, 49.

47 Quoted in Longford, *Jameson's Raid*, 208.

48 Van der Poel, *The Jameson Raid*, 53–54.

49 *History of the* Times, 598.

50 Shaw to Rhodes, Dec. 12, 1895, Jameson Raid File, *The Times* Archives, quoted in Helly and Calloway, "Journalism as Active Politics," in Lowry, ed., *The South African War Reappraised*, 55.

51 Chamberlain to Rochfort Maguire, quoted in Longford, *Jameson's Raid*, 212.

52 Younghusband to his father, Dec. 21, 1895, British Library, Mss. Eur F197, OIOC, British Library.

53 Van der Poel, *The Jameson Raid*, 65.

54 French, *Younghusband: The Last Great Imperial Adventurer*, 127.

55 Quoted in van der Poel, *The Jameson Raid*, 74.

56 *History of the* Times, 177.

57 Chamberlain to Salisbury, Dec. 26, 1895, Salisbury papers, quoted in Peter Marsh, *Joseph Chamberlain: Entrepreneur in Politics*, 382.

58 Marsh, *Joseph Chamberlain*, 383.

59 Quoted in van der Poel, *The Jameson Raid*, 60.

60 Chamberlain to Robinson, Dec. 31, 1895, printed as No. 11 in C. 7933,

"Correspondence re the Jameson Raid," British Parliamentary Papers LIX (1895–96). Quoted in *The Jameson Raid: A Centennial Retrospective*, 103.

61 Salisbury to Chamberlain, Dec. 31, 1895, in Ethel Drus, "A Report on the Papers of Joseph Chamberlain relating to the Jameson Raid and the Inquiry," *Bulletin of the Institute of Historical Research*, vol. XXV (1952), 37.

62 Enid Moberly Bell, *C. F. Moberly Bell* (London, 1927), 210–11, letter probably sent to Buckle according to Helly and Callaway, "Journalism as Active Politics," in Lowry, ed., *The South African War Reappraised*, 64, fn. 31.

63 Flora Shaw to Frederick Lugard, Nov. 8, 1918, quoted in ibid., 55.

64 Younghusband, *South Africa Today*, 95.

65 British Library, OIOC, MSS Eur 197/260, no date, but with a facing entry for Jan. 3, 1896.

66 van der Poel, *The Jameson Raid*, 156.

67 *Encyclopaedia Britannica* (11th ed.), entry on Rhodes written by Flora Shaw.

68 Quoted in Rotberg and Shore, *The Founder*, 548.

69 Quoted in Trollope, *Britannia's Daughters*, 139.

70 Buckle to Shaw, quoted in Bell, *Flora Shaw*, 187.

71 Quoted in Helly and Callaway, "Journalism as Active Politics," in Lowry, ed., *The South African War Reappraised*, 58.

72 Flora Shaw to Moberly Bell, Aug. 3, 1896, quoted in ibid., 57.

73 A. F. Wilson, Chamberlain's secretary to FS, May 26, 1895, quoted in ibid., 59

74 Perham, *Lugard*, vol. 2, 73–74.

75 Bell, *Flora Shaw*, 188.

76 British Library, OIOC MSS Eur 197/222 Francis Younghusband to Nellie Douglas, Pretoria, Jan. 4, 1896.

77 Francis Younghusband to Nellie Douglas, July 4, 1897, MSS 197/222, OIOC British Library.

78 Iain R. Smith, "A Century of Controversy over Origins," in Donal Lowry, ed., *The South African War Reappraised*, 32.

79 Quoted in Gilmour, *The Long Recessional: the Imperial Life of Rudyard Kipling*, 116.

80 Quoted in Longford, *Jameson's Raid*, 20.

81 Francis Younghusband to Nellie Douglas, July 4, 1897, MSS Eur 197/222, OIOC British Library.

82 W. S. Blunt, *My Diaries*, vol. 1, 264.

83 Ibid., 226.

84 *The Times*, Jan. 8, 1897.

85 Quoted in Trollope, *Britannia's Daughters*, 140.

86 Perham, *Lugard*, vol. 1, 443.

87 Lugard Diary, March 30, 1896, quoted in Perham, *Lugard*, vol. 1, 581.

88 Frederick Lugard to Edward Lugard, June 15, 1894, MSS British Empire, s. 57, Rhodes House, Oxford University.

89 Ibid.

90 Frederick Lugard to Edward Lugard, Aug. 19, 1895, MSS British Empire s. 57.

91 Thomas Pakenham, *The Scramble for Africa*, 1.

92 Perham, *Lugard*, vol. 1, 647.

93 Quoted in Perham, *Lugard*, vol. 2, 64.

94 Perham, *Lugard*, vol. 1, 630–31.

95 Quoted in David Cannadine, *Ornamentalism*, 61.

96 Ibid., 124.

97 Ibid.

98 Flora Shaw, *A Tropical Dependency*, 450.

99 Quoted in Tidrick, *Empire and the English Character*, 208.

100 Frederick Lugard to his brother Ned, Feb. 1, 1900, Lugard Papers, MSS British Empire, Rhodes House,

101 Flora Lugard to H. Brackenbury, Lokoja, July 28, 1902, MSS Perham, Box 308/5/41.

102 Unidentified newspaper clipping, MSS Perham, Box 308/1.

103 Flora Lugard to Frederick Lugard, Feb. 5, 1905, MSS Perham, Box 309/1.

104 Lugard to Flora, Jan. 2, 1906, quoted in Perham, *Lugard*, vol. 2, 248.

105 Lugard's Political Memoranda, quoted in Perham, ibid., 157.

106 Ibid., 226.

107 Ibid., 233.

108 Shaw, *A Tropical Dependency*, 424.

109 Flora to Frederick Lugard, March 20, 1906 and Nov. 1906, Perham Papers, Box 309, File 1.

110 Flora to Frederick Lugard, Nov. 1906, quoted in Perham, *Lugard*, vol. 2, 242.

111 Quoted in Pakenham, *The Scramble for Africa*, 652–53.

112 Notes on Lady Lugard's sketch for his life, Lugard Papers, Rhodes House.

113 Perham, *Lugard*, vol. 2, 138.

114 Sir Frederick Lugard, *The Dual Mandate in British Tropical Africa*, 617, quoted in Anthony Kirk-Greene, *Britain's Imperial Administrators, 1858–1966*, 49.

115 Lugard, *Dual Mandate*, 131, quoted in Kirk-Greene, *Britain's Imperial Administration*, 232, 290.

116 Anthony I. Nwabughogu, "The Role of Propaganda in the Development of Indirect Rule in Nigeria, 1890–1929," *The International Journal of African Historical Studies* 14, 1 (1981). Lord Hailey, "Some Problems Dealt with in an African Survey," *International Affairs*, March/April 1939, 202.

117 Quoted in Cannadine, *Ornamentalism*, 105l.

118 Bell, *Flora Shaw*, 300.

Chapter Three: "Dr. Weizmann, It's a Boy!"

1 All details from Roger Adelson, *Mark Sykes: Portrait of an Amateur*, 35–41.

2 All details from Shane Leslie, *Mark Sykes: His Life and Letters*, 20–65.

3 Ibid.

4 Christopher Simon Sykes, *The Big House*, 223.

5 Adelson, *Mark Sykes*, 49.

6 Sykes, *The Big House*, 377–86.

7 Leslie, *Mark Sykes*, v–vi.

8 Ronald Storrs, *Orientations*, 196, 323.

9 T. E. Lawrence, *Seven Pillars of Wisdom*, 58.

10 Adelson, *Mark Sykes*, 71–89.

11 Anthony Trollope, *An Autobiography*, 290.

12 Adelson, *Mark Sykes*, 126.

13 Barbara Wertheim Tuchman, *Bible and Sword: England and Palestine from the Bronze Age to Balfour*, 125–26.

14 Adelson, *Mark Sykes*, 179.

15 H. V. F. Winstone, *The Illicit Adventure: The Story of Political and Military Intelligence in the Middle East from 1898 to 1926*, 182.

16 Leslie, *Mark Sykes*, 280. See also Bruce Westrate, *The Arab Bureau: British Policy in the Middle East, 1916–1920*.

17 John Keay, *Sowing the Wind: The Seeds of Conflict in the Middle East*, 57.

18 Efraim Karsh and Inari Karsh, *Empires of the Sand: The Struggle for Mastery in the Middle East, 1789–1923*, 124–26; the full text of the agreement can be found in Adelson, *Mark Sykes*, 302–06. See also Leonard Stein, *The Balfour Declaration*, 240–69.

19 Karsh and Karsh, *Empires of the Sand*, 226.

20 See George Antonius, *The Arab Awakening*, and Elie Kedourie, *In the Anglo-Arab Labyrinth: The McMahon-Husayn Correspondence and Its Interpretations, 1914–1939*.

21 *The Letters of T. E. Lawrence*, ed. David Garnett, 670–71.

22 A. J. P. Taylor, *English History: 1914–1945*, 73 *et seq.* In the appendix, Taylor provides an invaluable guide to successive British cabinets, noting and dating all significant changes.

23 Spotted by David Fromkin in *A Peace to End All Peace*, 149, as quoted in full by Margaret FitzHerbert, *The Man Who Was Greenmantle: A Biography of Aubrey Herbert*, 147–48.

24 Adelson, *Mark Sykes*, 232.

25 Ibid., 238.

26 Christopher Sykes, *Two Studies in Virtue*, 176.

27 Stein, *The Balfour Declaration*, 286.

28 Ibid., 103–16.

29 Stein, *The Balfour Declaration*, 10–11.

30 Blanche Dugdale, *Arthur James Balfour*, 326.

31 Christopher Sykes, *Two Studies in Virtue*, 172.

32 Stein, *The Balfour Declaration*, 126, 129.

33 Daphna Baram, *Disenchantment: The Guardian and Israel*, 34. See also David Ayerst, *Guardian: Biography of a Newspaper*, 381–85.

34 Baram, *Disenchantment*, 33.

35 Fromkin, *A Peace to End All Peace*, 299.

36 Adelson, *Mark Sykes*, 220.

37 Christopher Sykes, *Two Studies in Virtue*, 213.

38 Leslie, *Mark Sykes*, 271–72.

39 Dugdale, *Arthur James Balfour*, vol. II, 168–70; see also Alpheus Thomas Mason, *Brandeis: A Free Man's Life*, 452–53.

40 Stein, *The Balfour Declaration*, 485.

41 See Jill Hamilton, *God, Guns and Israel*, for details on the War Cabinet's denominations.

42 The declaration appears in reproduction as the frontispiece of Stein's *The Balfour Declaration.*

43 Chaim Weizmann, *Trial and Error,* 108.

44 Elizabeth Monroe, *Britain's Moment in the Middle East, 1914–1956,* 43.

45 Leslie, *Mark Sykes,* 288–89.

46 Tuchman, *Bible and Sword,* 325.

47 Weizmann, *Trial and Error,* 195.

48 Leslie, *Mark Sykes,* 290.

49 Richard Cohen, "Hunker Down with History," *Washington Post National Weekly Edition,* July 24–30, 2006, 26.

50 Monroe, *Britain's Moment in the Middle East,* 43.

51 Robert D. Kaplan, *The Arabists: The Romance of an American Elite,* 85.

52 Vincent Sheean, *Personal History,* 367.

53 Quotations from Winston Churchill, *The Gathering Storm,* 250; Martin Gilbert and Richard Gott, *The Appeasers,* 34; a full report of Lloyd George's conversation with Hitler appears as an appendix in Martin Gilbert, *The Roots of Appeasement,* 197–211.

54 Dugdale, *Arthur James Balfour,* vol. II, 173.

55 David S. Wyman, *The Abandonment of the Jews: America and the Holocaust, 1941–1945,* 157.

56 See the official summary of the March 3, 1945 meeting in *Foreign Relations of the United States: 1945* (Washington: Government Printing Office), vol. VIII, 7–9. See also Robert Lacey, *The Kingdom,* 271–75.

Chapter Four: The Acolyte

1 Arnold Talbot Wilson, *SW. Persia: A Political Officer's Diary,* 3.

2 Ibid., 27.

3 John Marlowe, *Late Victorian: The Life of Sir Arnold Talbot Wilson,* 52.

4 Ibid., 38.

5 Ibid., 59.

6 Ibid., 47–48.

7 Wilson, *SW. Persia,* 190.

8 In Wilson's foreword to Philip Graves, *The Life of Sir Percy Cox,* 12.

9 Ibid., 92–93.

10 Quoted in Keith Jeffrey, "An English Barrack in the Oriental Seas," *Modern Asian Studies,* vol. 13, no. 3, 369–86.

11 Philip Mason, *A Matter of Honour,* 431.

12 Alan Moorehead, *Gallipoli,* 109.

13 S. L. Menezes, *Fidelity & Honour: The Indian Army from the Seventeenth to the Twenty-first Century,* 257.

14 Full text in Arnold Talbot Wilson, *Loyalties: Mesopotamia, 1914–1917,* 311.

15 Quoted in Edwin Black, *Banking on Baghdad,* 213.

16 Marlow, *Late Victorian*, 99.

17 Black, *Banking on Baghdad*, 174.

18 Quoted in Timothy Paris, "British Middle East Policy-Making after the First World War: The Lawrentian and Wilsonian Schools," *The Historical Journal*, vol. 41, no. 3 (1998), 794.

19 Papers of William Yale, GB 165–030, Box 1, Middle East Archive, St. Antony's College, Oxford.

20 David Fromkin, *A Peace to End All Peace*, 306–07.

21 Ibid., 305.

22 Full text in the appendix of Wilson, *Loyalties*.

23 Ibid., 307.

24 Ronald Storrs, *Orientations*, 211–14.

25 Marlowe, *Late Victorian*, 131.

26 Ibid., 132.

27 The text of the Anglo-French declaration is in George Antonius, *The Arab Awakening*, 435–36.

28 Marlowe, *Late Victorian*, 136–37.

29 Ibid., 146.

30 Ibid., 240.

31 See Toby Dodge, *Inventing Iraq*, 12–13.

32 Ibid.

33 Margaret MacMillan, *Paris 1919*, 398.

34 Ibid., 400.

35 Robert Fisk, *The Great War for Civilisation: The Conquest of the Middle East*, 144.

36 Black, *Banking on Baghdad*, 241.

37 Antonius, *The Arab Awakening*, 305.

38 Marlowe, *Late Victorian*, 158.

39 Arnold T. Wilson, *Mesopotamia, 1917–1920: A Clash of Loyalties*, 251–52.

40 Cornelius Van Engert Papers, Box 2, Folder 49, Georgetown University, Washington, D.C.

41 Wilson, *Mesopotamia*, 271.

42 Engert Papers, Box 2, Folder 49.

43 Wilson, *Mesopotamia*, 241.

44 Joel C. Hodson, *Lawrence of Arabia in American Culture*, 31.

45 Ibid., 52.

46 Stanley and Rodelle Weintraub, eds., *Evolution of a Revolt: Early Post-war Writings of T. E. Lawrence*, 78–80.

47 Ibid., 96–99.

48 Marlowe, 229–30.

49 Ibid., 130.

50 Wilson, *Mesopotamia*, 318–19.

51 Marlowe, *Late Victorian*, 243.

52 Engert Papers, Box 2, Folder 49.

Chapter Five:"Dreadfully Occupied in Making Kings and Governments"

Chapter title is quoted from a letter from Gertrude Bell to her stepmother, Florence Bell, Aug. 28, 1921. The Gertrude Bell Archive, University of Newcastle upon Tyne Library, online at www.gerty.ncl.ac.uk.

1   *The Letters of T. E. Lawrence*, ed. Malcolm Brown, 185.
2   *The Palestine Weekly*, quoted in Martin Gilbert, *Winston S. Churchill*, vol. IV, 544.
3   Gertrude Bell to Florence Bell, March 12, 1921 (www.gerty.ncl.ac.uk).
4   Gertrude Bell to her parents, Jan. 17, 1921 (www.gerty.ncl.ac.uk).
5   Gertrude Bell to Florence Bell, Sept. 6, 1917 (www.gerty.ncl.ac.uk).
6   David Hogarth, March 8, 1917, Hogarth Private Papers, St. Anthony's Middle East Archives, Oxford University.
7   *The Times*, Dec. 27, 28, 29, 1921, quoted in Aaron Klieman, *Foundations of British Policy in the Arab World: The Cairo Conference of 1921*, 240.
8   Churchill Cabinet Memorandum, Dec. 16, 1920 (Chartwell 16/53), quoted in Christopher Catherwood, *Churchill's Folly: How Winston Churchill Created Modern Iraq*, 93.
9   Elizabeth Monroe, review of Aaron Klieman, *Foundations of British Policy in the Arab World*, in *International Affairs*, vol. 47, no. 3, 610.
10 Ibid.
11 Quoted in Catherwood, *Churchill's Folly*, 74–75.
12 Quoted in ibid., 87.
13 Cairo Conference Folder 3 FO 371/6350—Cairo Conference no. 1, Mr. Churchill to Colonial Office, received March 15, 1921, copy in St. Antony's Middle East Archives, Oxford.
14 Ibid.
15 Quoted in Catherwood, *Churchill's Folly*, 152.
16 Quoted in ibid., 130.
17 Quoted in ibid., 129.
18 Churchill to Curzon, Jan. 12, 1921 (Chartwell 17/26), quoted in ibid., 97.
19 Ibid.
20 Klieman, *Foundations of British Policy in the Arab World*, 151.
21 Curzon to Churchill, Jan. 9, 1921 (Chartwell 17/2), quoted in Catherwood, *Churchill's Folly*, 96.
22 Gertrude Bell, *Review of the Civil Administration of Mesopotamia*.
23 Cairo Conference Folder 3 FO 371/6350—Mr. Churchill to Colonial Office, received March 15, 1921, copy in St. Antony's MEA.
24 Elizabeth Monroe, "Gertrude Bell (1868–1926)," *Bulletin (British Society for Middle Eastern Studies)*, vol. 7, no. 1 (1980), 5.
25 Churchill to Trenchard, Aug. 29, 1920 (Chartwell 16/52), quoted in Catherwood, *Churchill's Folly*, 85.
26 A. N. Wilson, *After the Victorians*, 219.
27 *Palestine Weekly*, quoted in Gilbert, *Winston S. Churchill*, 556.
28 Jesse Raven, quoted in Catherwood, *Churchill's Folly*, 128.

29 Robert Graves, *Lawrence and the Arabian Adventure*, 348.

30 Gertrude Bell to Frank Balfour, March 25, 1921 (www.gerty.ncl.ac.uk).

31 Marguerite Harrison, "Gertrude Bell: A Desert Power," *New York Times*, July 18, 1926.

32 Gertrude Bell to Hugh Bell, June 8, 1917 (www.gerty.ncl.ac.uk).

33 James Morris, introduction to *The Letters of Gertrude Bell*, vii.

34 Janet (Hogarth) Courtney, quoted in Elizabeth Monroe, "Gertrude Bell (1868–1926)," *Bulletin (British Society for Middle Eastern Studies)*, vol. 7, no. 1 (1980), 4.

35 Quoted in Winstone, *Gertrude Bell*, 147.

36 Gertrude Bell to Hugh Bell, Jan. 18, 1905, in *The Letters of Gertrude Bell*, Florence Bell, ed., 149.

37 Mark Sykes to Edith Sykes, quoted in Janet Wallach, *Desert Queen: The Extraordinary Life of Gertrude Bell*, 72–73.

38 Georgina Howell, in her 2006 biography of Bell, calculated her 1913 journey to Hail in the Arabian desert to have cost $59,477 adjusted for present-day money. *Daughter of the Desert*, 485.

39 Gertrude Bell to Florence Bell, March 3, 1905 (www.gerty.ncl.ac.uk).

40 Elizabeth Monroe, "Gertrude Bell (1868–1926)," *Bulletin (British Society for Middle Eastern Studies)*, vol. 7, no. 1 (1980), 3.

41 *The Letters of T. E. Lawrence*, ed. Malcolm Brown, 36.

42 Gertrude Bell, May 21, 1911 (www.gerty.ncl.ac.uk).

43 Gertrude Bell Diary, Feb. 16, 1914 (www.gerty.ncl.ac.uk).

44 Quoted in Susan Goodman, *Gertrude Bell*, 73. (See www.gerty.ncl.ac.uk).

45 Gertrude Bell to Hugh Bell, Jan. 3, 1916 (www.gerty.ncl.ac.uk).

46 Gertrude Bell to Hugh Bell, Dec. 1, 1916 (www.gerty.ncl.ac.uk).

47 Quoted in Howell, *Daughter of the Desert*, 289.

48 Gertrude Bell to Hugh Bell, Jan. 16, 1916 (www.gerty.ncl.ac.uk).

49 Gertrude Bell to Hugh Bell, Feb. 26, 1916 (www.gerty.ncl.ac.uk).

50 Quoted in Wallach, *Desert Queen*, 160.

51 Monroe, "Gertrude Bell (1868–1926)," 19.

52 Gertrude Bell to Florence Bell, April 29, 1916 (www.gerty.ncl.ac.uk).

53 Gertrude Bell, May 24, 1918 and April 24, 1918 (www.gerty.ncl.ac.uk).

54 H. St. J. B. Philby, *Arabian Days, an Autobiography*, 103.

55 Quoted in Wallach, *Desert Queen*, 291.

56 Quoted in Susan Goodman, *Gertrude Bell*, 52.

57 "Iraq: Civil Administration, 1919–1920," Philby Papers, Box 6, File 1, 20, St. Antony's Middle East Archives.

58 Gertrude Bell to Hugh Bell, May 18, 1917 (www.gerty.ncl.ac.uk).

59 Gertrude Bell to Hugh Bell, Feb. 8, 1918 (www.gerty.ncl.ac.uk).

60 A. T. Wilson, Nov. 1914, quoted in Wallach, *Desert Queen*, 159.

61 Quoted in Philby, *Arabian Days*, 188.

62 Gertrude Bell to Chirol, Feb. 22, 1918, quoted in Burgoyne, *Gertrude Bell, from Her Personal Papers*, vol. II, 78.

63 Gertrude Bell to Hugh Bell, Nov. 28, 1918 (www.gerty.ncl.ac.uk).

64 Gertrude Bell to Florence Bell, March 14, 1920 (www.gerty.ncl.ac.uk).

65 Ibid.

66 Gertrude Bell to Hugh Bell, Dec. 6, 1918 (www.gerty.ncl.ac.uk).

67 Gertrude Bell to Florence Bell, Dec. 5, 1918 (www.gerty.ncl.ac.uk).

68 Gertrude Bell to Hugh Bell, March 7, 1919 (www.gerty.ncl.ac.uk).

69 Gertrude Bell to Hugh Bell, March, 1919 (www.gerty.ncl.ac.uk).

70 Gertrude Bell to Hugh Bell, March 18, 1919 (www.gerty.ncl.ac.uk).

71 Quoted in Wallach, *Desert Queen*, 226.

72 Gertrude Bell, Oct. 12, 1919 (www.gerty.ncl.ac.uk).

73 Gertrude Bell, undated, Bell Archives, Miss. Collection, Robinson Library, Newcastle, quoted in Howell, *Daughter of the Desert*, 267.

74 Gertrude Bell to Florence Bell, April 10, 1920 (www.gerty.ncl.ac.uk).

75 Jon Lee Anderson, "Nervous Iraqis Remember Earlier Conflicts," *The New Yorker*, March 24, 2003.

76 Gertrude Bell to Hugh Bell, Aug. 30, 1920 (www.gerty.ncl.ac.uk).

77 Elizabeth Monroe, *Britain's Moment in the Middle East*, 60.

78 Gertrude Bell to Hugh Bell, June 7, 1920 (www.gerty.ncl.ac.uk).

79 Gertrude Bell to Hugh Bell, June 14, 1920 (www.gerty.ncl.ac.uk).

80 Gertrude Bell to Hugh Bell, Jan. 4, 1920 (www.gerty.ncl.ac.uk).

81 Montague to Bell, Aug. 6, 1920 in Burgoyne, *Gertrude Bell, from Her Personal Papers 1914–1926*, vol. II, 154.

82 Gertrude Bell to Florence Bell, Jan. 12, 1920 (www.gerty.ncl.ac.uk).

83 Gertrude Bell to Hugh Bell, June 14, 1920 (www.gerty.ncl.ac.uk).

84 Private and Personal for Sir Cox, July 14, 1920, in the Philby Papers, Box 17, File 2, St. Antony's College, Oxford, Middle East Collection.

85 Gertrude Bell to Florence Bell, May 23, 1920 (www.gerty.ncl.ac.uk).

86 Aug. 31, 1920 (Chartwell 16/48), quoted in Catherwood, *Churchill's Folly*, 88.

87 Gertrude Bell, Aug. 23, 1920 (www.gerty.ncl.ac.uk).

88 Gertrude Bell to Florence Bell, Sept. 5, 1920 (www.gerty.ncl.ac.uk).

89 Gertrude Bell to Hugh Bell, Sept. 27, 1920 (www.gerty.ncl.ac.uk).

90 Gertrude Bell to Hugh Bell, Oct. 17, 1920 (www.gerty.ncl.ac.uk).

91 Gertrude Bell to Hugh Bell, Sept. 17, 1920 (www.gerty.ncl.ac.uk).

92 Gertrude Bell to Hugh Bell, Oct. 17, 1920 (www.gerty.ncl.ac.uk).

93 Gertrude Bell to Hugh Bell, Nov. 7, 1920 (www.gerty.ncl.ac.uk).

94 Gertrude Bell to Hugh Bell, Feb. 24, 1921, in *The Letters of Gertrude Bell*, 476.

95 Gertrude Bell to Hugh Bell, Nov. 1, 1920 (www.gerty.ncl.ac.uk).

96 Gertrude Bell to Hugh Bell, Sept. 19, 1920, in Burgoyne, vol. II, 164.

97 Gertrude Bell to Hugh Bell, Jan. 10, 1921 (www.gerty.ncl.ac.uk).

98 Gertrude Bell to Hugh Bell, Jan. 22, 1921 (www.gerty.ncl.ac.uk).

99 Gertrude Bell to Frank Balfour, March 25, 1921.

100 Gertrude Bell to Cornelius Engert, March 3, 1921, quoted in E. Kedourie, *The Chatham House Version and Other Middle-Eastern Studies*, 262.

101 Ibid., 263.

102 Gertrude Bell to Florence Bell, Feb. 23, 1920 (www.gerty.ncl.ac.uk).

103 Gertrude Bell to Hugh Bell, April 17, 1921 (www.gerty.ncl.ac.uk).

104 Quoted in Wallach, *Desert Queen*, 304.

105 Quoted in ibid., 304.

106 John Dos Passos, *Orient Express*, 107.

107 Philby, *Arabian Days*, 199.

108 Gertrude Bell to Hugh Bell, July 7, 1921 (www.gerty.ncl.ac.uk).

109 Dos Passos, *Orient Express*, 109.

110 Gerald de Gaury, *Three Kings in Baghdad, 1921–1958*, 26–28.

111 Ibid., 29.

112 Gertrude Bell to Hugh Bell, Aug. 28, 1921 (www.gerty.ncl.ac.uk).

113 Elizabeth Monroe, "Gertrude Bell (1868–1926)," 20–21.

114 Quoted in Catherwood, *Churchill's Folly*, 197.

115 Gertrude Bell, June 4, 1922 (www.gerty.ncl.ac.uk).

116 Ibid.

117 Gertrude Bell to Hugh Bell, June 12, 1921 (www.gerty.ncl.ac.uk).

118 Churchill to Cox, Aug. 15, 1921, quoted in Catherwood, *Churchill's Folly*, 172.

119 Churchill, "Mesopotamia and the New Government," 696–97, quoted in Klieman, *Foundations of British Policy in the Arab World*, 238.

120 Quoted in Joel Rayburn, "How the British Quit Mesopotamia," *Foreign Affairs*, March/April 2006, 36.

121 Ditty composed by the American missionary John Van Ess, quoted in Winstone, *Gertrude Bell*, 274.

122 Martin Bunton, "Cornwallis, Sir Kinahan (1883–1959)," *Oxford Dictionary of National Biography* (www.oxforddnb.com/view/article/32574).

123 T. E. Lawrence, *Seven Pillars of Wisdom*, 58.

124 Gertrude Bell to Hugh Bell, July 16, 1922 (www.gerty.ncl.ac.uk).

125 Gertrude Bell to J. M. Wilson, quoted in Goodman, *Gertrude Bell*, 114.

126 Quoted in Kerry Ellis, "Queen of the Sands," *History Today*, Jan. 2004, 36.

127 Quoted in Howell, *Daughter of the Desert*, 447–48.

128 *Everybody's Weekly*, Oct. 1, 1927, quoted in Howell, *Daughter of the Desert*, 416.

129 Jack Fairweather, "First Lady of Iraq Makes a Comeback," *Daily Telegraph*, Sept. 25, 2004.

130 S. J. B. Philby, "Gertrude Lowthian Bell 1868–1926," typescript of an obituary written ca. 1947, Philby Papers, MEA, St. Anthony's.

131 Kedourie, *The Chatham House Version and Other Middle-Eastern Studies*, 262.

132 Ibid., 250.

133 Lugard Papers, MSS Lugard, Box 127, File 3, Rhodes House.

134 William Yale, *The Near East*, 325–27.

135 Arnold Wilson to Lugard, Oct. 2, 1931, MSS Lugard, Box 127, File 3.

136 Gilbert Murray to Lugard, May 1, 1931, MSS Lugard, Box 127, File 3.

137 A. D. MacDonald, *Euphrates Exile*, 118–23.

138 Marguerite Harrison, "Gertrude Bell: A Desert Power," *New York Times*, July 18, 1926.

139 Quoted in Liora Lukitz, *A Quest in the Middle East*, 3.

Chapter Six: The Frenzy of Renown

1 For the grim reckoning of casualties, see Niall Ferguson, *The Pity of War*, 282–317. The eight empires were British, French, Russian, German, Austro-Hungarian, Ottoman, Belgian, and Portuguese.

2 Lawrence's *The Odyssey of Homer* (Oxford, 1932) was originally published "as newly translated by T. E. Shaw," as Lawrence then called himself.

3 Lawrence's *Crusader Castles*, chronicling his 1,100-mile walk through Syria and Palestine to inspect sixty-seven castles, appeared first in a 1936 limited edition of a thousand copies, reprinted in 1992 by Immel Publishing Ltd. (London) with a preface by Michael Haag. Spotted, and purchased, by the authors in Palmyra.

4 Bibliographic details can be found in Stephen E. Tabachnick, ed., *The T. E. Lawrence Puzzle*; see "Collecting T. E. Lawrence Materials" by Philip O'Brien, 293–321. See also Malcolm Brown, *Lawrence of Arabia: The Life, The Legend*, 187–210.

5 Details all from Lowell Thomas's contribution to A. W. Lawrence, ed., *T. E. Lawrence, by His Friends*, 177–88.

6 Ibid., 180, 185–86.

7 Hugh Trevor-Roper, "A Humbug Exalted," *The New York Times Book Review*, Nov. 6, 1977, 1, reviewing *T. E. Lawrence*, a 1977 biography by Desmond Stewart.

8 Brown, *Lawrence of Arabia*, 135.

9 B. H. Liddell Hart, *Colonel Lawrence of Arabia*, 380–81.

10 T. E. Lawrence, "Guerrilla Warfare," reprinted in *Treasury of the Encyclopedia Britannica*, 480

11 Ibid., 479–80.

12 Stanley and Rodelle Weintraub, *Evolution of a Revolt*, 108, 110–11.

13 In fact, as few Americans realize, these rules were first codified during the Civil War at Lincoln's order by Francis Lieber, a Prussian-born legal scholar who as a teenager fought in the Waterloo campaigns and later with irregulars in the Greek War of Independence.

14 T. E. Lawrence, *Seven Pillars of Wisdom*, 43.

15 On the contested matter as to whether Lawrence told Faisal of Sykes-Picot, see Jeremy Wilson, *Lawrence of Arabia*, 362–64.

16 Lawrence, *Seven Pillars of Wisdom*, 192, 555; the 1916 memo is cited in Philip Knightley and Colin Simpson, *The Secret Lives of Lawrence of Arabia*, 58–59.

17 Kathryn Tidrick, *Heart-Beguiling Araby*, 170.

18 The full text is at Elie Kedourie, *In the Anglo-Arab Labyrinth*, 19.

19 Text in full at Margaret FitzHerbert, *The Man Who Was Greenmantle*, 143–44.

20 Bruce Westrate, *The Arab Bureau*, 47.

21 Ibid.

22 T. E. Lawrence to E. T. Leeds, Nov. 1915, in *The Letters of T. E. Lawrence*, ed. Malcolm Brown, 62.

23 Elizabeth Monroe, *Britain's Moment in the Middle East, 1914–1956*, 35.

24 The Herbert quote is in FitzHerbert, *The Man Who Was Greenmantle*, 144. The

full text of Lawrence's May 1916 report on the mission is in Wilson, *Lawrence of Arabia*, 949–59.

25 Lawrence, *The Seven Pillars of Wisdom*, cited in Malcolm Brown and Julia Cave, *A Touch of Genius: The Life of T. E. Lawrence*, 65.

26 Lawrence, *Seven Pillars of Wisdom*, 65–67, 77–78.

27 Ibid., 91, 97.

28 Westrate, *The Arab Bureau*, 192–93.

29 David Fromkin, *A Peace to End All Peace*, 312.

30 Quoted in James Lunt, *Glubb Pasha: A Biography*, 62.

31 Lawrence, *Seven Pillars of Wisdom*, 58.

32 Quoted in "The Capture of Damascus" in Elie Kedourie, *The Chatham House Version and Other Middle-Eastern Studies*, 34–35.

33 John E. Mack, *A Prince of Our Disorder*, 172.

34 Sir Alec Seath Kirkbride, *An Awakening: The Arab Campaign, 1917–1918*, 92; cited in John Keay, *Sowing the Wind: The Seeds of Conflict in the Middle East*, 95.

35 Sir Alec Seath Kirkbride, *A Crackle of Thorns*, 9.

36 Ibid.

37 Milton Viorst, *Storm from the East*, 43–44.

38 Albert Hourani, "The Myth of T. E. Lawrence," in William Roger Louis, ed., *Adventures with Britannia*, 16.

39 Ibid., 9.

40 FitzHerbert, *The Man Who Was Greenmantle*, 144.

41 Stanley Weintraub and Rodelle Weintraub, *Lawrence of Arabia: The Literary Impulse*, passim.

42 Jeremy Wilson, *Lawrence of Arabia: The Authorized Biography of T. E. Lawrence*, 681–707.

43 Ibid., 706.

44 Ibid., 210.

45 All details from Raleigh Trevelyn's introduction to *Revolt in the Desert*, as republished in London by the Folio Society, 1–9.

46 Wilson, *Lawrence of Arabia*, 830–31.

47 Ibid., 834.

48 Knightley and Simpson, *Secret Lives*, 266.

49 Lawrence to Marsh, June 10, 1927, letter 311 in *The Letters of T. E. Lawrence*, ed. David Garnett, 521–22. See also Rhea Talley Stewart, *Fire in Afghanistan, 1914–1929: Faith, Hope, and the British Empire*, 457–59.

50 Wilson, *Lawrence of Arabia*, 845.

51 Lawrence, *Seven Pillars of Wisdom*, 21.

52 Lawrence to Charlotte Shaw, March 26, 1824, in *The Letters of T. E. Lawrence*, ed. Malcolm Brown, 261–62.

53 Henry Williamson's encomium is in A. W. Lawrence, ed., *T. E. Lawrence, by His Friends*, 401–08. On Maugham, see Lawrence James, *The Golden Warrior: The Life and Legend of Lawrence of Arabia*, 219–20.

54 James, *Golden Warrior*, 221.

55 Lawrence to George Brough, April 5, 1934, in *Letters*, ed. Brown, 485.

56   Quoted in Wilson, *Lawrence of Arabia*, 923.
57   Miles Malleson, *Filming T. E. Lawrence: Korda's Lost Epics*, 2.
58   Wilson, *Lawrence of Arabia*, 921.
59   Ibid., 935.
60   Malleson, *Filming T. E. Lawrence*, 11.
61   Ibid., 5–27.
62   Michael Korda, *Charmed Lives: A Family Romance*, 340.
63   Joel C. Hodson, *Lawrence of Arabia in American Culture*, 110–18.
64   Ibid., and "Introduction to an Irish Individualist," *New York Times*, Sept. 30, 1962.
65   Hodson, *Lawrence of Arabia in American Culture*, 118.
66   Pauline Kael, *5001 Nights at the Movies*, 321–22.
67   Steven Charles Caton, *Lawrence of Arabia: A Film's Anthropology*, 199.
68   Lawrence to Ernest Thurtle, April 26, 1929, in David Garnett, ed., *The Letters of T. E. Lawrence*, 653.

Chapter Seven: The Apostate

1   All details taken H. St. J. B. Philby, *Arabian Oil Ventures*, 71–134; K. S. Twitchell and Edward J. Jurji, *Saudi Arabia: with an Account of the Development of Its Natural Resources*, 148–70; and Anthony Cave Brown, *Treason in the Blood: H. St. John Philby, Kim Philby, and the Spy Case of the Century*, 111–44.
2   See Daniel Yergin, *The Prize: The Epic Quest for Oil, Money, and Power*, 291–92; Twitchell and Jurji, *Saudi Arabia*, 151; and Brown, *Treason in the Blood*, 154. The male-gendered coinage was a gratuitous precaution, since Austrian talers adorned by Maria Theresa remained standard currency everywhere in the Arab world for more than half a century after her dynasty vanished.
3   Quote about Ryan in Anthony Cave Brown, *Oil, God, and Gold*, 40.
4   Philby, *Arabian Oil Ventures*, 87–88.
5   Ibid., 125–26.
6   "Letter from Jiddah," dated July 1924, in Sir Reader Bullard, *Two Kings in Arabia*, 48–49.
7   Philby, *Arabian Days*, 27.
8   Ibid., 29.
9   Elizabeth Monroe, *Philby of Arabia*, 13; the schoolmate was W. N. Ewer. See also Philby, *Arabian Days*, 29.
10   Philby, *Arabian Days*, 51.
11   All quoted in Robert Irwin, *For Lust of Knowing: The Orientalists and Their Enemies*, 205–06.
12   Quoted in Irwin, *For Lust of Knowing*, 204.
13   Monroe, *Philby of Arabia*, 18. See also Irwin, *For Lust of Knowing*, 204.
14   Philby, *Arabian Days*, 32.
15   Ibid., 40.
16   Brown, *Treason in the Blood*, 12; Monroe, *Philby of Arabia*, 19–20.
17   Brown, *Treason in the Blood*, 20–21.
18   Ibid., 20.

19   Philby, *Arabian Days*, 131.

20   Ibid., 134–35.

21   Ibid., 144.

22   Quoted in Charles Allen, *God's Terrorists: The Wahhabi Cult and the Hidden Roots of Modern Jihad*, 237–39.

23   Philby, *Arabian Days*, 181.

24   Saïd K. Aburish, *House of Saud*, 24.

25   Quoted in Michael B. Oren, *Power, Faith, and Fantasy: America in the Middle East, 1776 to the Present*, 412.

26   Allen, *God's Terrorists*, 245.

27   H. V. F. Winstone, *Captain Shakespear*, epigraph.

28   Philby, *Arabian Days*, 157.

29   Bell, article on Ibn Saud, Shakespear, and Sheikhs, *Arab Bulletin*, no. 38.

30   Monroe, *Philby of Arabia*, 60–61.

31   Philby, *Arabian Days*, 154.

32   Ibid., 160–61.

33   Ibid., 164.

34   Ibid., 166–67.

35   Ibid. 204.

36   Monroe, *Philby of Arabia*, 100–01.

37   Philby, *Arabian Days*, 206–07.

38   H. V. F. Winstone, *Gertrude Bell*, 368.

39   David Hogarth, "Wahhabism and the British Interest," paper read Jan. 29, 1925, British Institute of International Affairs.

40   Bullard, *Two Kings in Arabia*, 76.

41   Monroe, *Philby of Arabia*, 130.

42   D. van der Meulen, *The Wells of Ibn Sa'ud*, 65.

43   Brown, *Treason in the Blood*, 90.

44   Meulen, *Wells of Ibn Sa'ud*, 18.

45   Monroe, *Philby of Arabia*, 151–55.

46   Ibid., ix.

47   Mary C. Wilson, *King Abdullah, Britain, and the Making of Jordan*, 82.

48   Monroe, *Philby of Arabia*, 287.

49   Quoted in Rachel Bronson, *Thicker than Oil: America's Uneasy Partnership with Saudi Arabia*, 15–16.

50   Anthony Sampson, *The Seven Sisters*, 65.

51   Philby, *Arabian Days*, 291.

52   Bronson, *Thicker than Oil*, 19.

53   Quoted in Robert Baer, *Sleeping with the Devil*, 79–80.

54   William A. Eddy, *FDR Meets Ibn Saud*, in U.S. Government Printing Office, *Foreign Relations of the United States*, 42.

55   Date cited in Anthony Cave Brown, *Oil, God, and Gold*, 139–41.

56   Niall Ferguson, "Hatred of America Unites the World," *Sunday Telegraph* (London), Feb. 25, 2007.

57   Bronson, *Thicker than Oil*, 233.

Chapter Eight:"A Splendid Little Army"

The epigraph to this chapter is from John Glubb, Rhymes on the Report of the Anglo-American Commission, undated but ca. 1946–47, St. Antony's Middle East Archives, Glubb Papers, Transjordan, quoted in Benny Morris, *The Road to Jerusalem*, 73.

1 Quoted in James L. Gelvin, *The Israel-Palestine Conflict*, 88.
2 Ronald Storrs, *Orientations*, 122–23.
3 Elizabeth Monroe, *Philby of Arabia*, 104.
4 "The Sherifs," by T. E. Lawrence, Oct. 27, 1916, FO 882/5, 40–41, quoted in Mary Wilson, *King Abdullah, Britain, and the Making of Jordan*, 29–30.
5 Martin Gilbert, *Winston S. Churchill: The Stricken World*, 553, quoted in Fromkin, *A Peace to End All Peace*, 505–06.
6 Gertrude Bell to Hugh Bell, Jan. 19, 1922 (www.gerty.ncl.ac.uk).
7 Philby Diary, Nov. 29, 1921, quoted in Wilson, *King Abdullah*, 68.
8 Philby to Gertrude Bell, Feb. 17, 1922, Box 17, Philby Papers, Middle East Centre, St. Antony's College, Oxford.
9 Ibid.
10 Ibid.
11 Wilson, *King Abdullah*, 44, 48.
12 Alec Seath Kirkbride, *A Crackle of Thorns*, 26–27.
13 Glubb, *Solider with the Arabs*, 5.
14 James Morris, *Farewell the Trumpets*, 250.
15 James Lunt, "Glubb, Sir John Bagot (1897–1986)," rev., *Oxford Dictionary of National Biography*, Oxford University Press, 2004 (online at www.oxforddnb.com/view/article/40128).
16 Jafna L. Cox, "A Splendid Training Ground: The Importance to the Royal Air Force of its Role in Iraq, 1919–32," *The Journal of Imperial and Commonwealth History*, vol. XIII, no. 2, Jan. 1985, 163, 165, 178, fn. 21.
17 Gertrude Bell to Hugh Bell, letters, July 23, 1924 (www.gerty.ncl.ac.uk).
18 Field Marshal Sir Henry Wilson to Henry Rawlinson, July 12, 1921, quoted in Omissi, *Air Power and Colonial Control*, 18.
19 Quoted in Vincent Orange, "Trenchard, Hugh Montague, first Viscount Trenchard (1873–1956)," *Oxford Dictionary of National Biography*.
20 Air Staff Memorandum No. 16, 1924, quoted in Michael A. Longoria, *A Historical View of Air Policing Doctrine: Lessons from the British Experience between the Wars, 1919–39*.
21 Sir John Bagot Glubb, *The Changing Scenes of Life: An Autobiography*, 60.
22 S. S. O. Diwaniya to Air Headquarters, B/D/2/1 of April 29, 1924, Air 23/446, quoted in Sluglett, *Britain in Iraq*, 267.
23 Letter from Sir J. M. Salmond, AIR/505/B/23, 41, quoted in Toby Dodge, *Inventing Iraq*, 152.
24 Glubb to Air Headquarters, D. 495 of Nov. 18, 1923, quoted in Peter Sluglett, *Britain in Iraq, 1914–1932*, 265.
25 Glubb, *Changing Scenes of Life*, 65.
26 Report on Operations against the Bani Huchaim, Air Officer Commanding,

Baghdad to S/S for Air, Dec. 12, 1923, Air 5/344, quoted in Sluglett, *Britain in Iraq*, 266.

27 Gertrude Bell to Hugh Bell, Dec. 11, 1923 (www.gerty.ncl.ac.uk).

28 Churchill to Cox, Private and Unnumbered Telegram, June 7, 1921, CO 730/2/27278, quoted in Sluglett, *Britain in Iraq*, 264.

29 Secretariat of the High Commissioner to Air HQ, Baghdad, May 26, 1923, CO 730/40, 748, quoted in Dodge, *Inventing Iraq*, 144.

30 J. B. Glubb, "Air and Ground Forces in Punitive Expeditions," Royal United Service Institution Journal, 71, no. 483 (Aug. 1926), 782, quoted in Longoria, *A Historical View of Air Policing Doctrine*, 35.

31 Gertrude Bell to Hugh Bell, Baghdad, July 2, 1924 (www.gerty.ncl.ac.uk).

32 G. A. Moore, Special Service Officer, Hillah, Jan. 1924 PRO, Air Ministry Files (AIR) 23/445, I/2106, part 8, 50, quoted in Dodge, *Inventing Iraq*, 132.

33 HC Debs 161 (March 20, 1923), 2460, quoted in Cox, "A Splendid Training Ground," 173.

34 Figures quoted in David E. Omissi, *Air Power and Colonial Control: The Royal Air Force, 1919–1939*, 35. For the Amery quote see Leopold Amery, PRO, Colonial Office 730/82, Iraq 1925, vol. 2, 12, quoted in Dodge, *Inventing Iraq*, 131.

35 Robert Fisk, *The Great War for Civilisation*, 146.

36 Quoted in John Keay, *Sowing the Wind*, 266.

37 Gertrude Bell, March 16, 1922 (www.gerty.ncl.ac.uk).

38 Glubb to James Lunt, quoted in Lunt, *Glubb Pasha*, 49.

39 Saïd K. Aburish, *House of Saud*, 24.

40 James Lunt, "Peake, Frederick Gerard (1886–1970)," *Oxford Dictionary of National Biography*, Oxford University Press, 2004; online ed., May 2005 (http://0-www.oxforddnb.com.library.nysoclib.org:80/view/article/35429).

41 Sir John Bagot Glubb, *The Story of the Arab Legion*, 168.

42 Kirkbride, *A Crackle of Thorns*, 62.

43 J. B. Glubb, Monthly Report, July 1933, quoted in Lunt, *Glubb Pasha*, 86.

44 Ibid.

45 Quoted in Elie Kedouie, *Arabic Political Memoirs and Other Studies*, 280.

46 Quoted in Geoffrey Warner, *Iraq and Syria, 1941*, 14.

47 Figures from Elie Kedourie, *The Chatham House Version and Other Middle-Eastern Studies*, 272.

48 Freya Stark, *Dust in the Lion's Paw; Autobiography, 1939–1946*, 77.

49 Ibid.

50 Cornwallis to F.O., April 11, 1941, quoted in Kedourie, *Arabic Political Memoirs*, 292.

51 Winston Churchill, *The Grand Alliance*, 256.

52 Churchill to Wavell, May 4, 1941, in ibid., 257.

53 Wavell to Churchill, May 8, 1941, in ibid., 260.

54 John Connell, *Auchinleck: A Biography of Field-Marshal Sir Claude Auchinleck*, 222–23 quoted in Warner, *Iraq and Syria, 1941*, 111.

55 Glubb, *Story of the Arab Legion*, 257.

56 Quoted in Warner, *Iraq and Syria, 1941*, 112–13.

57 Sir John Bagot Glubb, *A Soldier with the Arabs*, 312.

58 See David M. Castlewitz, "A British Officer Turned a Desert Police Force into an Elite Army of Professionals for a Newborn Arab Nation," in *Military History*, April 1998, vol. 15, issue 1. See also Somerset de Chair, *The Golden Carpet*, 21; Kirkbride, *A Crackle of Thorns*, 132; and Douglas Porch, "The Other 'Gulf War'—The British Invasion of Iraq in 1941."

59 De Chair, *Golden Carpet*, 18, 211–12.

60 Ibid., 173.

61 "Commander of Trans-Jordan's Arab Legion Killed, Rashid Beg Declares," *New York Times*, May 20, 1941.

62 Quoted in Kedourie, *Arabic Political Memoirs*, 295.

63 De Chair, *Golden Carpet*, 118.

64 Freya Stark, *East Is West*, 160.

65 Ibid., 298.

66 Figure from De Chair, *Golden Carpet*, 122. Other figures—official 130 and the Chief of Police's 2000—are quoted in Keay, *Sowing the Wind*, 275. For other accounts see Edwin Black, *Banking on Baghdad*, 331–38 and Kedourie, *Arabic Political Memoirs*, 283–312.

67 Glubb, *Story of the Arab Legion*, 303.

68 Quoted in Trevor Royle, *Glubb Pasha*, 262.

69 Stark, *Dust in the Lion's Paw*, 76.

70 De Chair, *Golden Carpet*, 32–33.

71 Glubb, *Story of the Arab Legion*, 302.

72 Quoted in De Chair, *Golden Carpet*, 7.

73 Keay, *Dust in the Lion's Paw*, 276. "From a Tikrit Boy to Butcher of Baghdad," *The Observer*, Dec. 31, 2006.

74 *New York Times*, May 26, 1946, 1.

75 "Annual Report on Transjordan for 1947," Kirkbride to Bevin, Jan. 13, 1948, FP 371.68844/E 2010. Quoted in Satloff, *From Abdullah to Hussein*, 5.

76 Quoted in William Roger Louis, *Ends of British Imperialism*, 425.

77 Golda Meir, *My Life*, 188, quoted in Keay, *Dust in the Lion's Paw*, 361.

78 Abdullah's efforts to obtain the largest part of the Palestinian pie is expertly detailed in Avi Shlaim's *Collusion Across the Jordan*. Shlaim maintains that during a key clandestine meeting between Abdullah and the Jewish Agency delegation led by Golda Meyerson (Meir), they arranged to divide Palestine between them with the Jordanians occupying the West Bank. For a dissenting view, see Efraim Karsh, "The Collusion that Never Was: King Abdallah, the Jewish Agency and the Partition of Palestine," *Journal of Contemporary History*, vol. 34 (4), 569–85.

79 Glubb, *A Soldier with the Arabs*, 66.

80 Abdullah Al-Tall, *The Palestine Tragedy* (Arabic), 35–39, quoted in Shlaim, *Collusion Across the Jordan*, 224.

81 Ibid., 6.

82 Kirkbride, *From the Wings*, 131.

83 Wilson, *King Abdullah*, 209.

84 Wilson, *King Abdullah*, 211–12.

85 House of Commons, July 12, 1951, quoted in Wilson, *King Abdullah*, 210.

86 James Lunt, *Hussein of Jordan*, 8.

87 Quoted in Royle, *Glubb Pasha*, 412.

88 *New York Times*, March 3, 1956.

89 Anthony Nutting, *Nasser*, 122.

90 Glubb, *A Soldier with the Arabs*, 357.

91 BBC Broadcast, March 2, 1956 (http://news.bbc.co.uk/onthisday/hi/dates/stories/march/2/newsid_2514000/2514379.stm).

92 Royle, *Glubb Pasha*, 412.

93 Anthony Nutting, *No End of a Lesson*, 47.

94 James Morris, *The Hashemite Kings*, 178.

95 Information from Glubb's *Dictionary of National Biography*, entry by James Lunt. See www.oxforddnb.com/view/article/40128 and Lunt, *Glubb Pasha*, 90.

96 Monroe, *Philby of Arabia*, 282, 283.

97 Quoted in Royle, *Glubb Pasha*, 497–98.

98 See Betty S. Anderson, "Writing the Nation: Textbooks of the Hashemite Kingdom of Jordan," *Comparative Studies of South Asia, Africa and the Middle East*, vol. 28, no. 1, 1–2 (2001).

Chapter Nine: A Very British Coup

The epigraph to this chapter is quoted in Gordon Waterfield, *Professional Diplomat: Sir Percy Loraine of Kirkharle*, 326.

1 V. Sackville-West, *Passenger to Teheran*, 129. Other details are from "An Onlooker, I, Reza, Place this Crown upon my Head," *Atlantic Monthly*, Oct. 1926, 548–53.

2 Cyrus Ghani, *Iran and the Rise of Reza Shah*, 394, fn. 32.

3 Gertrude Bell to Hugh Bell, April 21, 1926, Gertrude Bell Project, University of Newcastle (www.gerty.ncl.ac.uk).

4 Violet Stuart-Wortley, *Life Without Theory, an Autobiography*, 95, quoted in Gordon Waterfield, *Professional Diplomat*, 128–29.

5 Quoted in Ghani, *Iran and the Rise of Reza Shah*, 386.

6 Antony Wynn, *Persia in the Great Game*, 318.

7 R. W. Cottam, *Nationalism in Iran* (1964 ed.), 217.

8 G. N. Curzon, *Persia and the Persian Question*, vol. 1, 3–4 .

9 Ibid., vol. II, 236, 389, 451, quoted in Denis Wright, *The English Amongst the Persians during the Qajar Period, 1787–1921*, 74.

10 Ibid., vol. 1, 480, quoted in Wright, *The English Amongst the Persians*, 102.

11 Wright, *The English Amongst the Persians*, 103.

12 Curzon, *Persia and the Persian Question*, vol. 1, 171. Quoted in Firuz Kazemzadeh, *Russia and Britain in Persia, 1864–1914*, 208.

13 Curzon, *Persia and the Persian Question*, 172–73.

14 Wynn, *Persia in the Great Game*, 125ff.

15 Ibid.

16 Quoted in Kazemzadeh, *Russia and Britain in Persia*, 495.

17 Quoted in David Gilmour, *Curzon*, 377.

18 *The Letters and Friendships of Sir Cecil Spring Rice*, vol. 2, 105.

19 Rouhollah K. Ramazani, *The Foreign Policy of Iran*, 94.

20 Ibid.

21 Quoted in Ghani, *Iran and the Rise of Reza Shah*, 9.

22 W. Morgan Shuster, *The Strangling of Persia*, 334.

23 Wright, *The English Amongst the Persians*, 30.

24 Kazemzadeh, *Russia and Britain in Persia*, 502.

25 Harold Nicolson, "Curzon," in *The Dictionary of National Biography, Twentieth Century, 1922–1930*, 225.

26 Curzon, *Persia and the Persian Question*, vol. 2, 605.

27 Kazemzadeh, *Russia and Britain in Persia*, 357–58.

28 Wright, *The English Amongst the Persians*, 85–86.

29 Waterfield, *Professional Diplomat*, 77.

30 Daniel Yergin, *The Prize: The Epic Quest for Oil, Money, and Power*, 149.

31 Curzon, *The Times*, Nov. 22, 1918, quoted in Stephen Kinzer, *All the Shah's Men*, 50.

32 Harold Nicolson, *Curzon: The Last Phase, 1919–1925*, 129.

33 Curzon, memorandum Aug. 9, 1919, quoted in Richard H. Ullman, *Anglo-Soviet Relations*, vol. 3, 351–52.

34 Cabinet Documents 27/24, quoted in Ghani, *Iran and the Rise of Reza Shah*, 43.

35 FO 371/3873, Norman to Curzon, June 18, 1920, quoted in Ghani, *Iran and the Rise of Reza Shah*, 73.

36 Wright, *The English Amongst the Persians*, 31.

37 Gertrude Bell to her parents, June 5, 1921 (www.gerty.ncl.ac.uk).

38 Gertrude Bell to her parents, Oct. 10, 1920 (www.gerty.ncl.ac.uk). Actually, Ironsides claimed to be fluent in fifteen languages.

39 John C. Cairns, "Ironside, (William) Edmund, first Baron Ironside (1880–1959)," in *Oxford Dictionary of National Biography*, online ed., ed. Lawrence Goldman, http://0-www.oxforddnb.com.library.nysoclib.org:80/view/article/34113 (accessed Oct. 20, 2007).

40 FO 371/4906, War Office to GOC Mesopotamia, Oct. 10, 1920, quoted in Ghani, *Iran and the Rise of Reza Shah*, 107–08.

41 Ironside MS diary, Dec. 14, 1920, quoted in Ullman, *Anglo-Soviet Relations*, 327.

42 Ironside MS diary, Jan. 14, 1921, quoted in Wright, *The English Amongst the Persians*, 181.

43 Curzon to Norman, telegram 521, Oct. 29, 1920; British Documents, vol. XIII, no. 573, quoted in Ullman, *Anglo-Soviet Relations*, 383.

44 V. Sackville-West, *Passenger to Teheran*, 127–28.

45 Ironside MS diary, Jan. 14, 1921, quoted in Ullman, *Anglo-Soviet Relations*, 386.

46 Ibid., 387.

47 See Ghani, *Iran and the Rise of Reza Shah*, 167.

48 Ullman, *Anglo-Soviet Relations*, 385.

49 Ironside MS diary, Feb. 23, 1921, quoted in ibid., 388.

50 Gertrude Bell to Hugh Bell, May 29, 1921.

51 Nicolson, *Curzon*, 147.

52 Curzon to Norman, Feb. 28, 1921; Churchill, minute, March 2, 1921, reacting to an intercepted cable from Caldwell to Secretary of State Hughes: FO 371/6401, quoted in Michael Zirinsky, "Britain and the Rise of Reza Shah, 1921–26," *International Journal of Middle East Studies*, vol. 24 (1992), 646.

53 Loraine to Curzon, despatch no. 551, Sept. 4, 1922, quoted in Zirinsky, "Britain and the Rise of Reza Shah," 650.

54 Gertrude Bell to Percy Loraine, March 25, 1922, quoted in Waterfield, *Professional Diplomat*, 65.

55 Percy Loraine to Gertrude Bell, Dec. 1, 1922, quoted in ibid., 72.

56 Zirinsky, "Britain and the Rise of Reza Shah," 654; Ghani, *Iran and the Rise of Reza Shah*, 335.

57 Eyre Crowe to Loraine, Oct. 6, 1923, quoted in Waterfield, *Professional Diplomat*, 77.

58 Gertrude Bell to Florence Bell, June 10, 1925 (www.gerty.ncl.ac.uk).

59 Gertrude Bell to Hugh Bell, Jan. 15, 1925 (www.gerty.ncl.ac.uk).

60 Loraine, Tehran Oct. 10, 12, Mallet, F.O. Oct. 22, 1925, FO 371/10840, quoted in Zirinsky, "Britain and the Rise of Reza Shah," 656.

61 Mallet, FO Nov. 2, 1925, FO 371/10840, quoted in Zirinsky, "Britain and the Rise of Reza Shah," 656.

62 Havard to Loraine, July 13, 1929, quoted in Waterfield, *Professional Diplomat*, 138.

63 Yergin, *The Prize*, 271.

64 Mohammed Reza Pahlavi, *Answer to History*, 66.

65 Sir Winston Churchill, *The Second World War*, vol. III, *The Grand Alliance*, 477. Quoted in Manucher Farmanfarmaian, *Blood and Oil*, 139.

66 Mohammed Reza Pahlavi, *Answer to History*, 67–68.

67 Denis Wright, "Sir Percy Sykes and Persia," *Central Asian Survey* vol. 12, no. 2 (1993), 217–31.

Chapter Ten: The Quiet American

1 Roosevelt, *Countercoup*, 110.

2 Donald Wilber, *CIA Clandestine Service History*, "Overthrow of Premier Mossadeq of Iran, November 1952–August 1953," March 1954, Summary, iii–iv (online at www.gwu.edu/~nsarchiv/NSAEBB/NSAEBB28/index.html).

3 Roosevelt, *Countercoup*, 18.

4 Ibid.

5 Vincent Sheean, *The New Persia*, 85.

6 Lord Curzon to Cornelius van H. Engert in a private meeting, Euston Hotel, Nov. 4, 1919, summarized in a letter to Ambassador John W. Davis. At the time, Engert was assistant to Admiral Bristol in Constantinople. Engert papers, Box 1/Folder 7, Georgetown University.

7 FO 371/6417, Minute by Curzon, Nov. 12, 1921, quoted in Cyrus Ghani, *Iran and the Rise of Reza Shah*, 236.

8   Ibid., 276.
9   Quoted in James A. Bill, *The Eagle and the Lion*, 19.
10 Quoted in ibid., 28.
11 Quoted in William Roger Louis, *The British Empire in the Middle East, 1945–1951*, 683–84.
12 Stephen Dorril, *MI6: Fifty Years of Special Operations*, 560.
13 Dean Acheson, *Present at the Creation*, 503.
14 Daniel Yergin, *The Prize*, 458.
15 *The Observer*, May 20, 1951, quoted in Mark J. Gasiorowski and Malcolm Byrne, eds., *Mohammed Mosaddeq and the 1953 Coup in Iran*, 135.
16 FO 371/Persia 1951/91459, quoted in Ervand Abrahamian, "The 1953 Coup in Iran," *Science and Society*, vol. 65, no. 2 (2001), 194.
17 Henry Longhurst, *Adventure in Oil: The Story of British Petroleum*, 143–44.
18 Declassified Documents/1975/White House/Doc. 780, quoted in Abrahamian, "The 1953 Coup in Iran," 187.
19 *Time Magazine*, Jan. 4, 1952.
20 Moustafa Elm, *Oil, Power, and Principle: Iran's Oil Nationalization and Its Aftermath*, 120.
21 Ibid., 121.
22 Acheson, *Present at the Creation*, 504.
23 William Roger Louis, "Britain and the Overthrow of Mosaddeq," in Gasiorowski and Byrne, *Mohammed Mosaddeq and the 1953 Coup in Iran*, 132.
24 Bill, *The Eagle and the Lion*, 88–89.
25 Vernon A. Walters, *Silent Missions*, 247.
26 C. M. Woodhouse, *Something Ventured*, 117.
27 Ibid., 107.
28 Quoted in Dorril, *MI6*, 584.
29 Ibid., 121.
30 Cable from British ambassador, Washington to FO, May 21, 1953, PRO FO 371/104659, quoted in William Shawcross, *The Shah's Last Ride*, 65–66.
31 Churchill message to Shah: PRO, London FO 371/104659.80648, quoted in ibid., 66.
32 Woodhouse, *Something Ventured*, 125.
33 Wilber, *CIA Clandestine Service History*, summary, x.
34 Fitzroy Maclean, *Eastern Approaches*, 274.
35 Wilber, *Overthrow*, appendix A, 3.
36 Ibid., 4.
37 Ibid., 18, or check appendix B, 10.
38 Ibid., 3.
39 Roosevelt, *Countercoup*, 168.
40 "Relentless pressure," "adventurer": Wilber, *CIA Clandestine Service History*, section V, 30, 33; "wimp": Evan Thomas, *The Very Best Men: Four Who Dared*, 109.
41 Roosevelt, *Countercoup*, 168.
42 *Saturday Evening Post*, Nov. 6, 1954, quoted in Woodhouse, *Something Ventured*, 129.

43 Quoted in Shawcross, *The Shah's Last Ride*, 70.

44 Roosevelt, *Countercoup*, 201.

45 *The New York Times*, Aug. 20, 1953, quoted in Abrahamian, "The 1953 Coup in Iran," 210.

46 Roosevelt, *Countercoup*, 207.

47 Wilber, *CIA Clandestine Service History*, section IX, 81, quoted in "Britain and the Overthrow of Mosaddeq," 177.

48 Quoted in Stephen E. Ambrose, *Eisenhower*, vol. 2, 129.

49 Donald Wilber, *Adventures in the Middle East*, 189.

50 Minute by Eden, May 4, 1952, FO 371/98690, quoted in Gasiorowski and Byrne, *Mohammed Mosaddeq*, 134.

51 Yergin, *The Prize*, 477.

52 Sattareh Farman-Farmaian and Dona Munker, *Daughter of Persia*, 196–97.

53 *Newsweek*, Oct. 25, 1971.

54 Foreign Office documents from the Public Record Office quoted in *The Observer*, Sept. 9, 2001.

55 *Time Magazine*, Oct. 25, 1971.

56 Shawcross, *The Shah's Last Ride*, 46–47.

57 *The Observer*, Sept. 9, 2001.

58 Lesley Blanch, *Farah, Shahbanou of Iran, Queen of Persia*, 134.

59 Roy Mottahedeh, *The Mantle of the Prophet*, 245.

60 Mohammed Reza Pahlavi, *Answer to History*, 172.

61 Roosevelt, *Countercoup*, 210.

62 Northrup information from Roosevelt's obituary in *The Washington Post*, June 10, 2000.

63 Sallie Pisani, *The CIA and the Marshall Plan*, 125.

64 Maxine Cheshire, "The 'Coup' Untold, and Howar's Exodus," *The Washington Post*, Feb. 1, 1980.

65 Paul T. Sayers, "Roosevelt, Kermit," *American National Biography Online*, July 2001 (www.anb.org/articles/07/07–00750.html).

66 Wilber, *Adventures*, 150.

67 History Channel, *Anatomy of a Coup: The CIA in Iran*, Catalogue No. AAE–43021.

68 Figures from Bill, *The Eagle and the Lion*, 93. Bill states that western consumers paid very low prices for oil, $1.85 between 1954 and 1960, and $1.80 between 1960 and 1971.

69 Abrahamian, "The 1953 Coup in Iran," 184.

70 Abbas Amanat, "The Persian Complex," *New York Times*, May 25, 2006.

Chapter Eleven: The Apprentice Sorcerer

1 Saïd K. Aburish, *The St. George Hotel Bar*, 4–5.

2 Ibid., 9.

3 Harrison E. Salisbury, *Without Fear or Favor*, 521.

4 Wilbur Crane Eveland, *Ropes of Sand: America's Failure in the Middle East*, 144–45.

5 Salisbury, *Without Fear or Favor*, 505.

6 Quoted in Larry J. Kolb, *America at Night*, 2.

7 Eveland, *Ropes of Sand*, 96.

8 Miles Copeland obituary in *The Times*, Jan. 16, 1991.

9 Larry J. Kolb, *Overworld*, 177–79.

10 See *The Times*, Jan. 16, 1991; *The Washington Post*, Jan. 19, 1991; *The New York Times*, Jan. 19, 1991; *The Manchester Guardian Weekly*, Jan. 27, 1991. See also *The Independent*, Jan. 17, 1991, which opts for seventy-four. Copeland's memoir, *The Game Player*, gives no birthdate.

11 Miles Copeland, *The Game Player*, 9–10.

12 Ibid., 11.

13 Ibid., 12.

14 Quoted in David Wise and Thomas B. Ross, *The Invisible Government*, 4.

15 Copeland, *The Game Player*, 83.

16 Ibid., 86.

17 Ibid., 86–87.

18 Ibid., 91–94.

19 Miles Copeland, *The Game of Nations*, 52–53.

20 Patrick Seale, *The Struggle for Syria*, 58–59.

21 Anthony Nutting, *Nasser*, 209.

22 Joyce Laverty Miller, "The Syrian Revolt of 1925," *International Journal of Middle Eastern Studies*, vol. VIII (1977), 545–63.

23 Ibid.

24 On this little-known sect, see John S. Guest, *Survival Among the Kurds: A History of the Yezidis*.

25 Copeland, *The Game Player*.

26 Robert Fisk, *The Great War for Civilisation*, 814.

27 Copeland, *The Game Player*, 142. Regarding Wisner, see Evan Thomas, *The Very Best Men: Four Who Dared*, 320–21.

28 Nutting, *Nasser*, 66.

29 Copeland, *The Game of Nations*, 92.

30 Dean Acheson, *Present at the Creation*, 600.

31 Ibid.

32 Memorandum by Makins, Jan. 25, 1954, CAB 129/06, cited in William Roger Louis, *Ends of British Imperialism*, 591.

33 Quoted and confirmed by Hugh Thomas, *Suez* (New York: 1966), 13.

34 Quoted in Donald Neff, *Warriors at Suez*, 67.

35 See Louis, *Ends of British Imperialism*, 647–49.

36 See Leo McKinstry, "Roseberry, the Other Waiting Scot," *The Spectator*, June 2, 2007, 22.

37 James Morris, *Farewell the Trumpets*, 524–25.

38 Nutting, *Nasser*, 101.

39 Ibid., 135–39.

40 Nutting, *Nasser*, 143–45; John Keay, *Sowing the Wind*, 432–33.

41 Hugh Thomas, *The Suez Affair*, 31.

42　See Brian Urquhart, *A Life in Peace and War*, 134–35.

43　Chester L. Cooper, *The Lion's Last Roar: Suez, 1956*, 70–71.

44　Copeland, *The Game of Nations*, 174–77.

45　Copeland, *The Game Player*, 168.

46　Ibid., 168–69.

47　Ibid.

48　Ibid.

49　Copeland, *The Game of Nations*, 226.

50　See Irene L. Gendzier, *Notes from the Minefield: United States Intervention in Lebanon and the Middle East, 1945–1958*, 295.

51　Philip Khuri Hitti, *Lebanon in History*, 489–90.

52　Ibid.

53　Eveland, *Ropes of Sand*, 342.

54　Sacheverell Sitwell, *Arabesques and Honeycomb*, 6.

55　Copeland, *The Game Player*, 211–12.

56　Ibid.

57　Details from Anthony Cave Brown, *Treason in the Blood*, 508–09.

58　Phillip Knightley, "Turning the Philby Case on Its Head," *New York Review of Books*, April 26, 2007.

59　Andrew Rathmell, *Secret War in the Middle East: The Covert Struggle for Syria, 1949–1961*, 42.

Chapter Twelve: The Man Who Knew Too Much

1　Bob Woodward, *Plan of Attack*, 21.

2　Charles Krauthammer, "The Unipolar Moment," *Foreign Affairs*, vol. 70, no. 1 (1990/91).

3　Robert Kagan, *Of Paradise and Power*, 4.

4　James Mann, *Rise of the Vulcans*, 293.

5　George Packer, *The Assassins' Gate*, 115.

6　Mann, *Rise of the Vulcans*, 187–88.

7　H. Norman Schwarzkopf, *It Doesn't Take a Hero*, 368.

8　Mann, *Rise of the Vulcans*, 192.

9　George H. W. Bush and Brent Scowcroft, *A World Transformed*, 489.

10　Colin Powell, *My American Journey*, 516.

11　Zbigniew Brzezinski, *Second Chance: Three Presidents and the Crisis of American Superpower*, 146–49.

12　Thorstein Veblen, *The Portable Veblen*, 467.

13　Ibid.

14　See Shelemyahu Zacks, "Biographical Memoirs: Jacob Wolfowitz (March 19, 1910–July 16, 1981)," *National Academy of Sciences*, online at www.nap.edu/readingroom/books/biomems/jwolfowitz.html.

15　William Keller, "The Sunshine Warrior," *New York Times Sunday Magazine*, Sept. 22, 2002, passim.

16　Ibid.

17 On the Great Books, see the classic essay by Dwight Macdonald, "The Book of the Millennium Club," in his *Against the American Grain*.

18 Rebecca West, preface to *The Selected Poems of Carl Sandburg*, 15.

19 Mann, *Rise of the Vulcans*, 29–30.

20 For a detailed chronicle of this debate, see Gregg Herken, *Counsels of War*.

21 Paul Wolfowitz, "Nuclear Proliferation in the Middle East," doctoral dissertation, University of Chicago, 1972; cited by Mann, *Rise of the Vulcans*, 30–31.

22 Hans J. Morgenthau, *Politics Among Nations: The Struggle for Power and Peace*, 540–44.

23 Ibid., 540–41.

24 Quoted in Mann, *Rise of the Vulcans*, 26.

25 John Gray, *Black Mass*, 130.

26 Earl Shorris, *The Politics of Heaven: America in Fearful Times*, 178.

27 Ibid., 189.

28 Norman Podhoretz, *The Present Danger*, passim.

29 Quoted in Seymour M. Hersh, *Chain of Command: The Road from 9/11 to Abu Ghraib*, 219–20.

30 See John Cassidy, "The Next Crusade," *The New Yorker*, April 8, 2007.

31 Keller, "The Sunshine Warrior."

32 George P. Schultz, *Turmoil and Triumph*, 183.

33 Peter J. Boyer, "The Believer," *The New Yorker*, Nov. 1, 2004.

34 Ibid.

35 Dexter Filkins, "Where Plan A Left Ahmad Chalabi," *New York Times Magazine*, Nov. 5, 2006.

36 Ibid.

37 Ibid.

38 Ahmad Chalabi, "Iraq: The Past as Prologue?" *Foreign Affairs*, Summer 1991, 20–29.

39 All quotes are from the Department of Defense transcript of Wolfowitz's May 9, 2003, interview with Sam Tannenhaus, online at www.defenselink .miltranscripts/2003/tr20030509-depsecdef0223.html.

40 Filkins, "Where Plan A Left Ahmad Chalabi."

41 Nicholas Lemann, "The Next World Order," *The New Yorker*, April 1, 2002.

42 Quoted in Filkins, "Where Plan A Left Ahmad Chalabi."

43 Larry Jay Diamond, *Squandered Victory*, 31.

44 Ali A. Allawi, *The Occupation of Iraq: Winning the War, Losing the Peace*, 130–31.

45 Paul Bremer, *My Year in Iraq*, 171.

Epilogue: Echoes in a Long Corridor

1 Arthur M. Schlesinger, Jr., *The Cycles of American History*, 141.

2 Tenney Frank, *Roman Imperialism*, 8, 146.

3 Edward N. Luttwak, *The Grand Strategy of the Roman Empire*, 30–31.

4 All quotes from Kathryn Tidrick, *Empire and the English Character*, 228–29.

5 Wilfrid Scawen Blunt, *My Diaries*, vol. 2, 292.

6 Karl E. Meyer and Shareen Blair Brysac, *Tournament of Shadows*, 10.
 7 Ryszard Kapuściński, *The Shadow of the Sun*, 139.
 8 Steve Coll, *Ghost Wars*, 569.
 9 Robert D. Kaplan, *Soldiers of God*, 169.
10 Gershom Gorenberg, *The Accidental Empire*, 271–72.

Bibliography

Archives Consulted

St. Antony's College, Oxford, Middle East Centre Archive
ARAMCO, Gertrude Bell, Sir Reader Bullard, Cairo Conference, Sir Kinahan Cornwallis, Sir Percy Cox, Charles Crane, Lord Cromer, Lt. Col. H. R. Dickson, Lt. General Sir John Glubb, David Hogarth, T. E. Lawrence, Col. Gerard Leachman, Sir Percy Loraine, Elizabeth Monroe, Stewart Perowne, H. S. J. Philby, Sir Herbert Samuel, Sir Ronald Storrs, Sir Mark Sykes, Sir Percy Sykes, and Gordon Waterfield papers

Bodleian Library, Oxford, MSS Division
T. E. Lawrence, Lord Milner, Leo Amery, Mary Sykes, Sir Percy Loraine, and Sir Patrick Reilly papers

Bodleian Library of Commonwealth and African Studies at Rhodes House, Oxford
Papers of Frederick Dealtry Lugard, Baron Lugard of Abinger: 1871–1969, Flora Shaw, Lady Lugard, Marjorie Perham, Cecil Rhodes, and material relating to the Jameson Raid

British Library, Asia, Pacific & Africa Collections (formerly known as the Oriental and India Office Collections [OIOC])
Papers by or relating to Gertrude Bell, Sir Arnold Wilson, Sir Francis Younghusband, Sir Arthur Hirtzel, Lord Curzon, Policy toward Ibn Saud, the Arab Revolt, and the reports of Sir Percy Sykes

Georgetown University
Cornelius van H. Engert, Richard Crane, and William Mulligan papers

Royal Geographical Society
Gertrude Bell, H. S. J. Philby, Arnold T. Wilson, and T. E. Lawrence papers

United States National Archives
Area papers

Robinson Library Special Collections, University of Newcastle upon Tyne
Gertrude Bell papers online at www.gerty.ncl.ac.uk

Works Consulted

Abrahamian, Ervand. *Iran between Two Revolutions*. Princeton: Princeton University Press, 1982.

Aburish, Saïd K. *A Brutal Friendship: The West and the Arab Elite*. London: Victor Gollancz, 1997.

———. *The Rise, Corruption and Coming Fall of the House of Saud*. London: Bloomsbury, 1994.

———. *The St. George Hotel Bar*. London: Bloomsbury, 1989.

Acheson, Dean. *Present at the Creation: My Years in the State Department*. New York: W. W. Norton & Company, 1969.

Adelson, Roger. *London and the Invention of the Middle East: Money, Power, and War, 1902–1922*. New Haven: Yale University Press, 1995.

———. *Mark Sykes: Portrait of an Amateur*. London: Cape, 1975.

Aldington, Richard. *Lawrence of Arabia: A Biographical Enquiry*. London: Collins, 1955.

Allawi, Ali A. *The Occupation of Iraq: Winning the War, Losing the Peace*. New Haven: Yale University Press, 2007.

Allen, Charles. *God's Terrorists: The Wahhabi Cult and the Hidden Roots of Modern Jihad*. London: Little, Brown and Company, 2006.

Ambrose, Stephen E. *Eisenhower*. New York: Simon & Schuster, 1983.

Amery, L. S. *The Leo Amery Diaries*, Vol. 1: *1896–1929*. Ed. John Barnes and David Nicholson. London: Hutchinson, 1980.

Anderson, Benedict, and R. O'Gorman. *Imagined Communities: Reflections on the Origin and Spread of Nationalism*. London: Verso, 1991.

Antonius, George. *The Arab Awakening: The Story of the Arab National Movement*. New York: G. P. Putnam's Sons, 1946.

Armstrong, Karen. *Muhammad: A Biography of the Prophet*. San Francisco: HarperSanFrancisco, 1992.

Ayerst, David. *Guardian: Biography of a Newspaper*. London: Collins, 1971.

Baer, Robert. *Sleeping with the Devil: How Washington Sold Our Soul for Saudi Crude*. New York: Crown, 2003.

Baram, Daphna. *Disenchantment: The Guardian and Israel*. London: Guardian Books, 2004.

Baring, Maurice. *The Puppet Show of Memory*. Boston: Little, Brown and Company, 1922.

Barr, James. *Setting the Desert on Fire: T. E. Lawrence and Britain's Secret War in Arabia, 1916–1918*. New York: W. W. Norton & Company, 2008.

Bell, Enid Hestor Chataway Moberly. *Flora Shaw (Lady Lugard, D.B.E.)*. London: Constable, 1947.

Bell, Gertrude. *The Arab of Mesopotamia*. Basra: Government Press, 1918.

———. *The Arab War: Confidential Information for General Headquarters from Gertrude*

Bell, being Despatches from the Secret "Arab Bulletin." London: The Golden Cockerel Press, 1940.

———. *The Desert and the Sown.* Boston: Beacon Press, 1987.

———. *The Letters of Gertrude Bell.* Harmondsworth, Middlesex, U.K.: Penguin. 1987.

———. *Review of the Civil Administration of Mesopotamia.* London: H.M.S.O., 1920.

———. *Selected Letters of Gertrude Bell.* Ed. Lady Richmond. London: Pelican, 1953.

Bill, James A. *The Eagle and the Lion: The Tragedy of American-Iranian Relations.* New Haven: Yale University Press, 1988.

Black, Edwin. *Banking on Baghdad: Inside Iraq's 7,000-Year History of War, Profit and Conflict.* Hoboken, N.J.: John Wiley & Sons, Inc., 2004.

Blanch, Lesley. *Farah, Shahbanou of Iran, Queen of Persia.* London: Collins, 1978.

Blunt, Wilfrid Scawen. *My Diaries: Being a Personal Narrative of Events, 1888–1914.* 2 vols. New York: A. A. Knopf, 1921.

———. *Secret History of the English Occupation of Egypt: Being a Personal Narrative of Events.* New York: A. A. Knopf, 1922.

Brands, H. W. *Inside the Cold War: Loy Henderson and the Rise of the American Empire 1918–1961.* New York: Oxford University Press, 1991.

Bremer, L. Paul, and Malcolm McConnell. *My Year in Iraq: The Struggle to Build a Future of Hope.* New York: Simon & Schuster, 2006.

Bronson, Rachel. *Thicker than Oil: America's Uneasy Partnership with Saudi Arabia.* New York: Oxford University Press, 2006.

Brown, Anthony Cave. *Oil, God, and Gold.* New York: Houghton Mifflin Company, 1999.

———. *Treason in the Blood: H. St. John Philby, Kim Philby, and the Spy Case of the Century.* London: Robert Hale, 1995.

Brown, Malcolm. *Lawrence of Arabia: The Life, the Legend.* London: Thames & Hudson, 2005.

———, and Julia Cave. *A Touch of Genius: The Life of T. E. Lawrence.* New York: Paragon House, 1989.

Brzezinski, Zbigniew. *Second Chance: Three Presidents and the Crisis of American Superpower.* New York: Basic Books, 2007.

Bullard, Sir Reader William. *Britain and the Middle East from Earliest Times to 1963.* London: Hutchinson, 1964.

———. *The Camels Must Go: An Autobiography.* London: Faber and Faber, 1961.

———. *Letters from Tehran: A British Ambassador in World War II, Persia.* New York: I. B. Tauris, 1991.

———. *Two Kings in Arabia: Letters from Jeddah, 1923–5 and 1936–9.* Reading, U.K.: Ithaca Press, 1993.

Burgoyne, Elizabeth. *Gertrude Bell, from Her Personal Papers.* 2 vols. London: E. Benn, 1958–61.

Busch, Briton Cooper. *Britain and the Persian Gulf, 1894–1914.* Berkeley: University of California Press, 1967.

———. *Britain, India, and the Arabs, 1914–1921.* Berkeley: University of California Press, 1971.

Bush, George H. W. and Brent Scowcroft. *A World Transformed.* New York: Knopf, 1998.

Cannadine, David. *Ornamentalism.* London, New York: Oxford University Press, 2001.

Catherwood, Christopher. *Churchill's Folly: How Winston Churchill Created Modern Iraq*. New York: Carroll & Graf, 2004.

Caton, Steven Charles. *Lawrence of Arabia: A Film's Anthropology*. Berkeley: University of California Press, 1999.

Chaudhuri, Nupur, and Margaret Strobel, eds. *Western Women and Imperialism: Complicity and Resistance*. Bloomington: Indiana University Press, 1992.

Chirol, Sir Valentine. *Fifty Years in a Changing World*. London: J. Cape, 1927.

Churchill, Sir Winston. *Closing the Ring*. Boston: Houghton Mifflin, 1951.

———. *The Gathering Storm*. Boston: Houghton Mifflin, 1948.

———. *The Grand Alliance*. Boston: Houghton Mifflin, 1950.

———. *Great Contemporaries*. New York: Putnam, 1937.

Churchill, Randolph S., and Martin Gilbert. *Winston S. Churchill*, Vol. 4: *1916–1922*. Boston: Houghton Mifflin, 1966.

Coll, Steve. *Ghost Wars: The Secret History of the CIA, Afghanistan, and bin Laden, from the Soviet Invasion to September 10, 2001*. New York: Penguin, 2004.

Connell, John. *Auchinleck: A Biography of Field-Marshal Sir Claude Auchinleck*. 2nd ed. London: Cassell, 1959.

Cooper, Chester L. *The Lion's Last Roar: Suez, 1956*. New York: Harper & Row, 1978.

Copeland, Miles. *The Game of Nations: The Amorality of Power Politics*. New York: Simon & Schuster, 1970.

———. *The Game Player: Confessions of the CIA's Original Political Operative*. London: Aurum Press, 1989.

———. *Without Cloak or Dagger: The Truth about the New Espionage*. New York: Simon & Schuster, 1974.

Cottam, Richard W. *Nationalism in Iran: Updated through 1978*. Pittsburgh: University of Pittsburgh Press, 1979.

Cromer, Earl Evelyn Baring. *Ancient and Modern Imperialism*. London: J. Murray, 1909.

———. *Modern Egypt*. 2 vols. New York: Macmillan, 1908.

Curzon, George Nathaniel Curzon, Marquis of. *Persia and the Persian Question*. London: Longmans, Green, 1892.

Darwin, John. *Britain and Decolonisation: The Retreat from Empire in the Post-War World*. New York: St. Martin's Press, 1988.

———. *Britain, Egypt and the Middle East: Imperial Policy in the Aftermath of War, 1918–1922*. London: Macmillan Press, 1981.

———. *The End of the British Empire: The Historical Debate*. Cambridge, Mass.: B. Blackwell, 1991.

de Chair, Somerset. *The Golden Carpet*. New York: Harcourt, Brace and Company, 1945.

de Gaury, Gerald. *Three Kings in Baghdad, 1921–1958*. London: Hutchinson, 1961.

Diamond, Larry Jay. *Squandered Victory: The American Occupation and the Bungled Effort to Bring Democracy to Iraq*. New York: Times Books, 2005.

Dodge, Toby. *Inventing Iraq: The Failure of Nation Building and a History Denied*. New York: Columbia University Press, 2003.

Dorril, Stephen. *MI6: Fifty Years of Special Operations*. London: Fourth Estate, 2000.

Dos Passos, John. *Orient Express*. New York: Harper & Brothers, 1927.

Dugdale, Blanche. *Arthur James Balfour*. London: Hutchinson, 1939.

Elm, Moustafa. *Oil, Power, and Principle: Iran's Oil Nationalization and Its Aftermath.* Syracuse, N.Y.: Syracuse University Press, 1992.

Elon, Amos. *Jerusalem: City of Mirrors.* Rev. ed. London: Flamingo, 1996.

Encyclopaedia Britannica. 11th ed. Vol. VII. Cambridge, UK, 1910.

Eveland, Wilbur Crane, *Ropes of Sand: America's Failure in the Middle East.* New York: W. W. Norton & Company, 1980.

Farmanfarmaian, Manucher, and Roxane Farmanfarmaian. *Blood and Oil: Memoirs of a Persian Prince.* New York: Random House, 1997.

Farman-Farmaian, Sattareh, and Dona Munker. *Daughter of Persia: A Woman's Journey from Her Father's Harem through the Islamic Revolution.* New York: Crown, 1992.

Farouk-Sluglett, Marion, and Peter Sluglett. *Iraq since 1958: From Revolution to Dictatorship.* Rev. ed. New York: I. B. Tauris, 2001.

Farwell, Byron. *Prisoners of the Mahdi: The Story of the Mahdist Revolt which frustrated Queen Victoria's designs on the Sudan, humbled Egypt, and led to the fall of Khartoum, the death of Gordon, and Kitchener's victory at Omdurman fourteen years later.* New York: W. W. Norton & Company, 1989.

Ferguson, Niall. *The Pity of War.* New York: Basic Books, 1999.

Fisk, Robert. *The Great War for Civilisation: The Conquest of the Middle East.* New York: Alfred A. Knopf, 2005.

FitzHerbert, Margaret. *The Man Who Was Greenmantle: A Biography of Aubrey Herbert.* London: John Murray, 1983.

Flint, John E. *Sir George Goldie and the Making of Nigeria.* London: Oxford University Press, 1960.

Frank, Tenney. *Roman Imperialism.* New York: Cooper Square Publishers, Inc., 1972.

French, Patrick. *Younghusband: The Last Great Imperial Adventurer.* London: HarperCollins, 1994.

Fromkin, David. *A Peace to End All Peace: Creating the Modern Middle East, 1914–1922.* New York: Holt, 1989.

Garnett, David, ed. *The Letters of T. E. Lawrence.* New York: Doubleday, Doran & Co., Inc., 1939.

Garvin, J. L. *The Life of Joseph Chamberlain.* 6 vols. London: Macmillan; New York: St. Martin's Press, 1932–1969.

Gasiorowski, Mark J., and Malcolm Byrne, ed. *Mohammad Mosaddeq and the 1953 Coup in Iran.* Syracuse, N.Y.: Syracuse University Press, 2004.

Gelvin, James L. *The Israel-Palestine Conflict: One Hundred Years of War.* New York: Cambridge University Press, 2005.

Gendzier, Irene L. *Notes from the Minefield: United States Intervention in Lebanon and the Middle East, 1945–1958.* New York: Columbia University Press, 1997.

Ghani, Cyrus. *Iran and the Rise of Reza Shah: From Qajar Collapse to Pahlavi Rule.* New York: I. B. Tauris, 1998.

Gibbon, Edward. *The History of the Decline and Fall of the Roman Empire.* Vol. I. London: The Folio Society, 1983.

Gilbert, Martin. *The Roots of Appeasement.* New York: New American Library, 1967.

Giles, Frank. *A Prince of Journalists: The Life and Times of Henri Stefan Opper De Blowitz.* London: Faber and Faber, 1962.

Gilmour, David. *Curzon.* London: John Murray, 1994.

———. *The Long Recessional: The Imperial Life of Rudyard Kipling.* New York: Farrar, Straus and Giroux, 2002.

Glubb, Sir John Bagot. *Britain and the Arabs: A Study of Fifty Years, 1908 to 1958.* London: Hodder and Stoughton, 1959.

———. *The Changing Scenes of Life: An Autobiography.* New York: Quartet Books, 1983.

———. *A Soldier with the Arabs.* London: Hodder and Stoughton, 1957.

———. *The Story of the Arab Legion.* London: Hodder and Stoughton, 1948.

———. *War in the Desert: an R.A.F. Frontier Campaign.* New York: W. W. Norton & Company, 1960.

Goodman, Susan. *Gertrude Bell.* Dover, N.H.: Berg, 1985.

Gordon, Charles George. *General Gordon's Khartoum Journal.* Ed. Lord Elton. London: Wm. Kimber, 1961.

Gorenberg, Gershom. *The Accidental Empire: Israel and the Birth of the Settlements, 1967–1977.* New York: Times Books, 2006.

Graves, Philip. *The Life of Sir Percy Cox.* London: Hutchinson & Co., Ltd., 1941.

Graves, Robert. *Lawrence and the Arabian Adventure.* Garden City, N.Y.: Doubleday, Doran & Co., 1928.

Gray, John. *Black Mass: Apocalyptic Religion and the Death of Utopia.* New York: Farrar, Straus and Giroux, 2007.

Great Britain. Parliament. House of Commons. *Select Committee on British South Africa, Second Report, together with the Proceedings of the Committee and Minutes of Evidence.* Vol. IX. London: Eyre and Spottiswoode, 1897.

Guest, John S. *Survival Among the Kurds: A History of the Yezidis.* New York: Kegan Paul International, 1993.

Haldane, Lt.-General Sir Aylmer L. *The Insurrection in Mesopotamia, 1920.* Edinburgh and London: Wm. Blackwood and Sons, 1922.

Hamilton, Jill. *God, Guns and Israel: Britain, the First World War and the Jews in the Holy Land.* Stroud: Sutton, 2004.

Harrison, Thomas Skelton. *The Homely Diary of a Diplomat in the East, 1897–1899.* New York: Houghton Mifflin, 1917.

Herbert, Aubrey. *Mons, Anzac and Kut.* London: E. Arnold, 1919.

Herken, Gregg. *Counsels of War.* New York: Knopf, 1985.

Hersh, Seymour M. *Chain of Command: The Road from 9/11 to Abu Ghraib.* New York: HarperCollins, 2004.

Hitti, Philip Khuri. *Lebanon in History, from the Earliest Times to the Present.* London: Macmillan, 1957.

Hobsbawm, Eric, and Terence Ranger, eds. *The Invention of Tradition.* New York: Cambridge University Press, 1983.

Hobson, J. A. *Imperialism: A Study.* New York: Gordon Press, 1975.

Hodson, Joel C. *Lawrence of Arabia in American Culture: The Making of a Transatlantic Legend.* Westport, Conn.: Greenwood Press, 1995.

Hogarth, David George. *The Penetration of Arabia: A Record of the Development of Western Knowledge Concerning the Arabian Peninsula.* London: Alston Rivers, 1905.

Hopwood, Derek. *Egypt, Politics and Society, 1945–1981.* Boston: Allen & Unwin, 1982.

———. *Syria 1945–1986: Politics and Society.* Boston: Unwin Hyman, 1988.

Hourani, Albert Habib. *The Emergence of the Modern Middle East*. Berkeley: University of California Press, 1981.

Howarth, David Armine. *The Desert King: Ibn Saud and His Arabia*. New York: McGraw-Hill, 1964.

Howell, Georgina. *Gertrude Bell: Queen of the Desert, Shaper of Nations*. New York: Farrar, Straus and Giroux, 2007.

Hyam, Ronald. *Britain's Imperial Century, 1815–1914: A Study of Empire and Expansion*. Lanham, MD: Barnes & Noble Books, 1993.

Irwin, Robert. *For Lust of Knowing: The Orientalists and Their Enemies*. London: Penguin Books, 2007.

James, Lawrence. *The Golden Warrior: The Life and Legend of Lawrence of Arabia*. New York: Paragon House, 1993.

The Jameson Raid: A Centennial Retrospective. Houghton, South Africa: Brenthurst Press, 1996.

Jenkins, Roy. *Gladstone*. London: Macmillan, 1995.

Kael, Pauline. *5001 Nights at the Movies: A Guide from A to Z*. New York: Holt, Rinehart and Winston, 1982.

Kagan, Robert. *Of Paradise and Power: America and Europe in the New World Order.* New York: Knopf, 2003.

Kaplan, Robert D. *The Arabists: The Romance of an American Elite*. New York: Free Press, 1993.

———. *Soldiers of God: With the Mujahidin in Afghanistan*. Boston: Houghton, Mifflin, 1990.

Kapuściński, Ryszard. *The Shadow of the Sun: My African Life*. New York: Vintage, 2002.

Karsh, Efraim, and Inari Karsh. *Empires of the Sand: The Struggle for Mastery in the Middle East, 1789–1923*. Cambridge, Mass.: Harvard University Press, 1999.

Katouzian, Homa. *Musaddiq and the Struggle for Power in Iran*. New York: I. B. Tauris, 1990.

———. *State and Society in Iran: The Eclipse of the Qajars and the Emergence of the Pahlavis*. New York: I. B. Tauris, 2000.

Kazemzadeh, Firuz. *Russia and Britain in Persia, 1864–1914: A Study in Imperialism*. New Haven: Yale University Press, 1968.

Keay, John. *Sowing the Wind: The Seeds of Conflict in the Middle East*. New York: W. W. Norton & Company, 2003.

Kedourie, Elie. *Arabic Political Memoirs and Other Studies*. London: Cass, 1974.

———. *The Chatham House Version and Other Middle-Eastern Studies*. Chicago: Ivan R. Dee, 2004.

———. *England and the Middle East: The Destruction of the Ottoman Empire, 1914–1921*. Boulder: Westview Press, 1987.

———. *In the Anglo-Arab Labyrinth: The McMahon-Husayn Correspondence and Its Interpretations, 1914–1939*. London: Frank Cass, 2000.

———. *Islam in the Modern World, and Other Studies*. London: Mansell, 1980.

Kennedy, Paul M. *The Rise and Fall of the Great Powers: Economic Change and Military Conflict from 1500 to 2000*. New York: Random House, 1987.

Kerr, Malcolm H. *The Arab Cold War, 1958–1964: A Study of Ideology in Politics*. New York: Oxford University Press, 1965.

Khalidi, Rashid. *British Policy towards Syria & Palestine, 1906–1914: A Study of the Antecedents of the Hussein-the McMahon Correspondence, the Sykes-Picot Agreement, and the Balfour Declaration.* London: Published for the Middle East Centre, St. Antony's College, Oxford, by Ithaca Press, 1980.

———. *The Iron Cage: The Story of the Palestinian Struggle for Statehood.* Boston: Beacon Press, 2006.

———. *Resurrecting Empire: Western Footprints and America's Perilous Path in the Middle East.* Boston: Beacon Press, 2004.

———, ed. *The Origins of Arab Nationalism.* New York: Columbia University Press, 1991.

Khoury, Philip S. *Syria and the French Mandate: The Politics of Arab Nationalism, 1920–1945.* Princeton: Princeton University Press, 1987.

Kinzer, Stephen. *All the Shah's Men: An American Coup and the Roots of Middle East Terror.* Hoboken, N.J.: John Wiley & Sons, 2003.

Kirkbride, Sir Alec Seath. *A Crackle of Thorns: Experiences in the Middle East.* London: J. Murray, 1956.

———. *From the Wings: Amman Memoirs, 1947–1951.* London: F. Cass, 1976.

Kirk-Greene, Anthony. *Britain's Imperial Administrators, 1858–1966.* New York: St. Martin's Press, 2000.

———. *On Crown Service: A History of HM Colonial and Overseas Civil Services, 1837–1997.* New York: I. B. Tauris, 1999.

Klieman, Aaron S. *Foundations of British Policy in the Arab World: The Cairo Conference of 1921.* Baltimore: Johns Hopkins Press, 1970.

Knightley, Phillip, and Colin Simpson. *The Secret Lives of Lawrence of Arabia.* New York: McGraw-Hill, 1970.

Kolb, Larry J. *America at Night: The True Story of Two Rogue CIA Operatives, Homeland Security Failures, Dirty Money, and a Plot to Steal the 2004 U.S. Presidential Election.* New York: Riverhead Books, 2007.

———. *Overworld: The Life and Times of a Reluctant Spy.* New York: Riverhead, 2004.

Korda, Michael. *Charmed Lives: A Family Romance.* New York: Random House, 1979.

Kroeger, Brooke. *Nellie Bly: Daredevil, Reporter, Feminist.* New York: Times Books, 1994.

Lacey, Robert. *The Kingdom.* New York: Harcourt Brace Jovanovich, 1981.

Landes, David S. *Bankers and Pashas; International Finance and Economic Imperialism in Egypt.* Cambridge: Harvard University Press, 1958.

Lawrence, A. W., ed. *T. E. Lawrence, by His Friends.* Garden City, New York: Doubleday, Doran & Company, Inc., 1937.

Lawrence, T. E. *Crusader Castles.* 2nd rev. ed. London: Immel Publishing Ltd., 1992.

———. *Evolution of a Revolt: Early Post-war Writings of T. E. Lawrence.* Ed. Stanley Weintraub and Rodelle Weintraub. University Park, Pa.: Pennsylvania State University Press, 1968.

———. *The Letters of T. E. Lawrence.* Sel. and ed. Malcolm Brown. London: J. M. Dent, 1988.

———. *Revolt in the Desert.* London: Folio Society, 1986.

———. *The Seven Pillars of Wisdom: A Triumph.* New York: Doubleday, Doran & Company, Inc., 1936.

Leslie, Shane. *Mark Sykes: His Life and Letters*. New York: Cassell, 1923.

Liddell Hart, Sir Basil Henry. *Colonel Lawrence of Arabia: The Man Behind the Legend*. New York: Halcyon House, 1937.

Longford, Elizabeth Harman Pakenham. *Jameson's Raid*. London: Weidenfeld and Nicolson, 1960.

Longhurst, Henry. *Adventure in Oil: The Story of British Petroleum*. London: Sidgwick and Jackson, 1959.

Longoria, Michael A. *A Historical View of Air Policing Doctrine: Lessons from the British Experience between the Wars, 1919–39*. Maxwell Air Force Base, Ala.: Air University Press, 1992. Online at http://aupress.maxwell.af.mil/SAAS_Theses/SAASS_Out/Longoria/longoria.pdf.

Louis, William Roger. *The British Empire in the Middle East, 1945–1951: Arab Nationalism, the United States, and Postwar Imperialism*. New York: Oxford University Press, 1985.

———. *Ends of British Imperialism: The Scramble for Empire, Suez and Decolonization: Collected Essays*. New York: I. B. Tauris, 2006.

———. *Imperialism at Bay: The United States and the Decolonization of the British Empire, 1941–1945*. New York: Oxford University Press, 1978.

———, ed. *Adventures with Britannia: Personalities, Politics and Culture in Britain*. Austin, Tex.: Harry Ransom Humanities Research Center, University of Texas, 1995.

———, and James A. Bill, eds. *Musaddiq, Iranian Nationalism, and Oil*. Austin: University of Texas Press, 1988.

———, and Judith M. Brown. *The Oxford History of the British Empire*, Vol. 4: *The Twentieth Century*. New York: Oxford University Press, 1998.

———, and Robert A. Fernea, eds. *The Iraqi Revolution of 1958: The Old Social Classes Revisited*. New York: I. B. Tauris, 1991.

———, and Roger Owen. *A Revolutionary Year: The Middle East in 1958*. New York: I. B. Tauris, 2002.

Lowry, Donal, ed. *The South African War Reappraised*. Manchester, Eng.: Manchester University Press, 2000.

Lugard, Baron Frederick. *The Dual Mandate in British Tropical Africa*. London: F. Cass, 1965.

———. *Instructions to Political and Other Officers, on Subjects Chiefly Political and Administrative*. London: Waterlow, 1906.

Lukitz, Liora. *A Quest in the Middle East: Gertrude Bell and the Making of Modern Iraq*. New York: I. B. Tauris, 2006.

Lunt, James. *Glubb Pasha, a Biography: Lieutenant-General Sir John Bagot Glubb, Commander of the Arab Legion, 1939–1956*. London: Harvill Press, 1984.

———. *Hussein of Jordan: A Political Biography*. London: Macmillan, 1989.

Luttwak, Edward N. *The Grand Strategy of the Roman Empire from the First Century A.D. to the Third*. Baltimore: Johns Hopkins University Press, 1976.

MacDonald, A. D. *Euphrates Exile*. London: G. Bell, 1936.

Macdonald, Dwight. *Against the American Grain*. New York: Random House, 1962.

Mack, John E. *A Prince of Our Disorder: The Life of T. E. Lawrence*. Boston: Little, Brown, 1976.

MacMillan, Margaret. *Paris 1919: Six Months that Changed the World*. New York: Random House, 2002.

Magnus, Sir Philip Montefiore. *Gladstone: A Biography*. New York: Dutton, 1960.
———. *Kitchener: Portrait of an Imperialist*. London: J. Murray, 1958.
Malleson, Miles. *Filming T. E. Lawrence: Korda's Lost Epics*. New York: I. B. Tauris Publishers, 1997.
Mann, James. *Rise of the Vulcans: The History of Bush's War Cabinet*. New York: Viking, 2004.
Mansfield, Peter. *The British in Egypt*. London: Weidenfeld and Nicolson, 1971.
———. *A History of the Middle East*. 2nd ed. New York: Penguin Putnam, 2003.
Marlowe, John. *Late Victorian: The Life of Sir Arnold Talbot Wilson*. London: Cresset Press, 1967.
Marr, Phebe. *The Modern History of Iraq*. 2nd ed. Boulder, Colo.: Westview Press, 2004.
Marsh, Peter T. *Joseph Chamberlain: Entrepreneur in Politics*. New Haven: Yale University Press, 1994.
Mason, Alpheus Thomas. *Brandeis: A Free Man's Life*. New York: Viking, 1946.
Mason, Philip. *A Matter of Honour*. New York: Holt, Rinehart and Winston, 1974.
Matthew, H. C. G., and Brian Harrison, eds. *The Oxford Dictionary of National Biography*. New York: Oxford University Press, 2004; online ed., 2006.
Meir, Golda. *My Life*. New York: Putnam, 1975.
Menezes, S. L. *Fidelity & Honour: The Indian Army from the Seventeenth to the Twenty-First Century*. New Delhi, India: Viking, Penguin Books India, 1993.
Meulen, D. van der. *The Wells of Ibn Saʻud*. London: Murray, 1957.
Meyer, Karl E. *The Dust of Empire: The Race for Mastery in the Asian Heartland*. New York: PublicAffairs, 2003.
———. and Shareen Blair Brysac. *Tournament of Shadows: The Great Game and the Race for Empire in Central Asia*. Washington, D.C.: Counterpoint, 1999.
Milner, Viscount Alfred. *England in Egypt*. 11th ed. London: E. Arnold, 1904.
Monroe, Elizabeth. *Britain's Moment in the Middle East, 1914–1956*. Baltimore: Johns Hopkins University Press, 1963.
———. *Philby of Arabia*. Reading, Eng.: Ithaca Press, 1998.
Moorehead, Alan. *Gallipoli*. New York: Harper, 1956.
———. *The White Nile*. Rev. ed. London: Hamilton, 1971.
Morgenthau, Hans J. *Politics Among Nations: The Struggle for Power and Peace*. 4th ed. New York: Knopf, 1967.
Morley, John. *The Life of William Ewart Gladstone*, Vol. III: *1880–1898*. New York: Macmillan, 1903.
Morris, Benny. *Israel's Border Wars, 1949–1956: Arab Infiltration, Israeli Retaliation, and the Countdown to the Suez War*. New York: Clarendon Press, 1997.
———. *The Road to Jerusalem: Glubb Pasha, Palestine and the Jews*. New York: I. B. Tauris, 2002.
Morris, James (Jan). *Farewell the Trumpets: An Imperial Retreat*. Boston: Faber and Faber, 1978.
———. *The Hashemite Kings*. New York: Pantheon, 1959.
———. *Islam Inflamed: A Middle East Picture*. New York: Pantheon, 1957.
———. *Pax Britannica: The Climax of an Empire*. London: Faber, 1968.
Mousa, Suleiman. *T. E. Lawrence: An Arab View*. New York: Oxford University Press, 1966.

Neff, Donald. *Warriors at Suez: Eisenhower Takes America into the Middle East.* New York: Simon & Schuster, 1981.

Nicolson, Harold. *Curzon: The Last Phase, 1919–1925.* Boston, New York: Houghton Mifflin, 1934.

———. *Peacemaking, 1919.* London: Constable, 1934.

Nutting, Anthony. *I Saw for Myself: The Aftermath of Suez.* London: Hollis & Carter, 1958.

———. *Nasser.* New York: E. P. Dutton, 1972.

———. *No End of a Lesson: The Story of Suez.* New York: Clarkson N. Potter, Inc., 1967.

Omissi, David E. *Air Power and Colonial Control: The Royal Air Force, 1919–1939.* New York: Manchester University Press, 1990.

Oren, Michael B. *Power, Faith, and Fantasy: America in the Middle East, 1776 to the Present.* New York: W. W. Norton & Company, 2007.

Owen, Roger. *Lord Cromer: Victorian Imperialist, Edwardian Proconsul.* Oxford, New York: Oxford University Press, 2004.

———. *The Middle East in the World Economy, 1800–1914.* New York: I. B. Tauris, 1993.

Packer, George. *The Assassins' Gate.* New York: Farrar, Straus and Giroux, 2005.

Pahlavi, Mohammed Reza, Shah of Iran. *Answer to History.* New York: Stein and Day, 1980.

Pakenham, Thomas. *The Scramble for Africa, 1876–1912.* New York: Random House, 1991.

Pappé, Ilan. *The Making of the Arab-Israeli Conflict, 1947–51.* New York: I. B. Tauris, 1994.

Perham, Dame Margery Freda. *Lugard.* Vol. 1: *The Years of Adventure, 1858–1898*; Vol. 2: *The Years of Authority, 1898–1945.* London: Collins, 1956–60.

Philby, H. St. J. B. *Arabia.* London: E. Benn, 1930.

———. *Arabian Days, an Autobiography.* London: R. Hale, 1948.

———. *Arabian Jubilee.* New York: Day, 1953.

———. *Arabian Oil Ventures.* Washington: Middle East Institute, 1964.

Pisani, Sallie. *The CIA and the Marshall Plan.* Lawrence: Kansas University Press, 1992.

Podhoretz, Norman. *The Present Danger.* New York: Simon & Schuster, 1980.

Powell, Colin, with Joseph E. Persico. *My American Journey.* New York: Random House, 1995.

Ramazani, Rouhollah K. *The Foreign Policy of Iran: A Developing Nation in World Affairs, 1500–1941.* Charlottesville: University Press of Virginia, 1966.

Rathmell, Andrew. *Secret War in the Middle East: The Covert Struggle for Syria, 1949–1961.* London: Tauris Academic Studies, 1995.

Robinson, Ronald Edward, and John Gallagher, with Alice Denny. *Africa and the Victorians; the Climax of Imperialism in the Dark Continent.* New York: St. Martins Press, 1961.

Rodenbeck, Max. *Cairo: The City Victorious.* New York: Knopf, 1999.

Roosevelt, Kermit. *Countercoup, the Struggle for the Control of Iran.* New York: McGraw-Hill, 1979.

Rotberg, Robert I., and Miles F. Shore. *The Founder: Cecil Rhodes and the Pursuit of Power.* New York: Oxford University Press, 1988.

Royle, Trevor. *Glubb Pasha*. London: Abacus, 1993.

Sackville-West, V. *Passenger to Teheran*. New York: Moyer Bell, 1990.

Said, Edward W. *Culture and Imperialism*. New York: Knopf, 1994.

———. *Orientalism*. New York: Pantheon, 1978.

Salisbury, Harrison E., *Without Fear or Favor: The* New York Times *and Its Times*. New York: Times Books, 1980.

Sampson, Anthony. *The Seven Sisters: The Great Oil Companies and the World They Shaped*. New York: Viking Press, 1975.

Sandburg, Carl. *Selected Poems of Carl Sandburg*. Ed. Rebecca West. New York: Harcourt, Brace, 1926.

Satloff, Robert B. *From Abdullah to Hussein: Jordan in Transition*. New York: Oxford University Press, 1994.

Schlesinger, Arthur M., Jr. *The Cycles of American History*. Boston: Houghton Mifflin, 1986.

Schwarzkopf, H. Norman, with Peter Petre. *It Doesn't Take a Hero: General H. Norman Schwarzkopf, the Autobiography*. New York: Bantam Press, 1992.

Seale, Patrick, *The Struggle for Syria: A Study of Post-war Arab Politics, 1945–1958*. New York: Oxford University Press, 1965.

Shaw, Flora Louisa (Lady Lugard). *A Tropical Dependency: An Outline of the Ancient History of the Western Sudan with an account of the Modern Settlement of Northern Nigeria*. Baltimore: Black Classic Press, 1997.

Shawcross, William. *The Shah's Last Ride: The Fate of an Ally*. New York: Simon & Schuster, 1988.

Sheean, Vincent. *The New Persia*. New York: The Century Co., 1927.

———. *Personal History*. Garden City, N.Y.: Doubleday, Doran & Company, 1935.

Shlaim, Avi. *Collusion Across the Jordan: King Abdullah, the Zionist Movement, and the Partition of Palestine*. New York: Columbia University Press, 1988.

———. *The Politics of Partition: King Abdullah, the Zionists, and Palestine, 1921–1951*. New York: Columbia University Press, 1990.

Shorris, Earl. *The Politics of Heaven: America in Fearful Times*. New York: W. W. Norton & Company, 2007.

Shuster, W. Morgan. *The Strangling of Persia; a Story of the European Diplomacy and Oriental Intrigue that Resulted in the Denationalization of Twelve Million Mohammedans, a Personal Narrative*. New York: The Century Co., 1912.

Silvester, Christopher, ed. *The Norton Book of Interviews: An Anthology from 1859 to the Present Day*. New York: W. W. Norton & Company, 1996.

Sitwell, Sacheverell. *Arabesque and Honeycomb*. London: R. Hale, 1957.

Sluglett, Peter. *Britain in Iraq, 1914–1932*. London: Ithaca Press, 1976.

Spring Rice, Cecil Arthur. *The Letters and Friendships of Sir Cecil Spring Rice: A Record*. Rpt. Westport, Conn.: Greenwood Press, 1971.

Stark, Freya. *Baghdad Sketches*. London: J. Murray, 1937.

———. *Dust in the Lion's Paw; Autobiography, 1939–1946*. New York: Harcourt, Brace & World, 1962.

———. *East Is West*. London: John Murray, 1945.

———. *Letters of Freya Stark*, Vol. 4: *Bridge of the* Levant, *1940–43*. Salisbury, Eng.: Compton Russell, 1974–82.

Stein, Leonard. *The Balfour Declaration*. New York: Simon & Schuster, 1961.

Stewart, Rhea Talley. *Fire in Afghanistan, 1914–1929: Faith, Hope, and the British Empire*. Garden City, N.Y.: Doubleday, 1973.

Storrs, Sir Ronald. *Orientations*. London: Nicholson & Watson, 1945.

Strachey, Lytton. *Eminent Victorians: Cardinal Manning, Florence Nightingale, Dr. Arnold, General Gordon*. New York: G. P. Putnam's Sons, 1918.

Sykes, Christopher. *Two Studies in Virtue*. London: Collins, 1953.

Sykes, Christopher Simon. *The Big House: The Story of a Country House and Its Family*. London: HarperCollins, 2004.

Tabachnick, Stephen Ely, ed. *The T. E. Lawrence Puzzle*. Athens, Ga.: University of Georgia Press, 1984.

Taylor, A. J. P. *English History: 1914–1945*. Oxford: Oxford University Press, 1965.

———. *The Struggle for Mastery in Europe, 1848–1918*. New York: Oxford University Press, 1971.

Tenney, Frank. *Roman Imperialism*. New York: Macmillan, 1914.

Thomas, Evan. *The Very Best Men: Four Who Dared: The Early Years of the CIA*. New York: Simon & Schuster, 1995.

Thomas, Hugh. *The Suez Affair*. London: Weidenfeld & Nicolson, 1967.

Thornton, A. P. *The Imperial Idea and its Enemies: A Study in British Power*. New York: St. Martin's Press, 1959.

Tidrick, Kathryn. *Empire and the English Character*. London: Tauris, 1990.

———. *Heart-Beguiling Araby*. New York: Cambridge University Press, 1981.

Times (London, England). *The History of the* Times, Vol. 3: *The Twentieth Century Test, 1884–1912*. New York: Macmillan, 1947.

Tripp, Charles. *A History of Iraq*. Cambridge, Eng.: Cambridge University Press, 2000.

Trollope, Anthony. *An Autobiography*. London: Oxford University Press, 1950.

Trollope, Joanna. *Britannia's Daughters: Women of the British Empire*. London: Hutchinson, 1983.

Tuchman, Barbara Wertheim. *Bible and Sword: England and Palestine from the Bronze Age to Balfour*. New York: New York University Press, 1956.

Twain, Mark. *Innocents Abroad*. Hartford, Conn.: American Publishing Company, 1872.

Twitchell, K. S., and Edward J. Jurji. *Saudi Arabia: with an Account of the Development of Its Natural Resources*. Princeton: Princeton University Press, 1947.

Ullman, Richard H. *Anglo-Soviet Relations, 1917–1921*, vol. 3: *The Anglo-Soviet Accord*. Princeton: Princeton University Press, 1961.

Urquhart, Brian. *A Life in Peace and War*. New York: Harper & Row, 1987.

U.S. Government Printing Office. *Foreign Relations of the United States, 1945*. Vol. VIII.

van der Poel, Jean. *The Jameson Raid*. New York: Oxford University Press, 1951.

Veblen, Thorstein. *The Portable Veblen*. Ed. Max Lerner. New York: Viking Press, 1948.

Viorst, Milton. *Storm from the East: The Struggle between the Arab World and the Christian West*. New York: Modern Library, 2006.

Wallach, Janet. *Desert Queen: The Extraordinary Life of Gertrude Bell, Adventurer, Adviser to Kings, Ally of Lawrence of Arabia*. New York: Nan A. Talese/Doubleday, 1996.

Waller, John H. *Gordon of Khartoum: The Saga of a Victorian Hero.* New York: Atheneum, 1988.

Walters, Vernon A. *Silent Missions.* Garden City, N.Y.: Doubleday, 1978.

Warner, Geoffrey. *Iraq and Syria, 1941.* London: Davis-Poynter, 1979.

Waterfield, Gordon. *Professional Diplomat: Sir Percy Loraine of Kirkharle, Bt., 1880–1961.* London: Murray, 1973.

Weintraub, Stanley, and Rodelle Weintraub, *Lawrence of Arabia: The Literary Impulse.* Baton Rouge, La.: Louisiana State University Press, 1975.

Weizmann, Chaim. *Trial and Error: The Autobiography of Chaim Weizmann.* New York: Harper, 1949.

Westrate, Bruce. *The Arab Bureau: British Policy in the Middle East 1916–1920.* University Park, Pa.: Pennsylvania State University Press, 1992.

Wilber, Donald. *Adventures in the Middle East.* Princeton: The Darwin Press, Inc.,1986.

———. *CIA Clandestine Service History, "Overthrow of Premier Mossadeq of Iran, November 1952–August 1953" March 1954.* Online at www.gwu.edu/~nsarchiv/NSAEBB/NSAEBB28/index.html.

Wilcox, Ron. *Battles on the Tigris: The Mesopotamian Campaign of the First World War.* Barnsley, U.K.: Pen & Sword Books Ltd., 2006.

Williams, Francis. *Dangerous Estate: The Anatomy of Newspapers.* London: Longmans, Green, 1957.

Wilson, A. N. *After the Victorians: The Decline of Britain in the World.* New York: Farrar, Straus and Giroux, 2005.

Wilson, Sir Arnold Talbot. *Loyalties; Mesopotamia, 1914–1917; A Personal and Historical Record.* London: Oxford University Press, 1930.

———. *Mesopotamia, 1917–1920: A Clash of Loyalties: A Personal and Historical Record.* London: Oxford University Press, 1931.

———. *SW. Persia: A Political Officer's Diary.* London: Oxford University Press, 1941.

Wilson, Jeremy. *Lawrence of Arabia: The Authorized Biography of T. E. Lawrence.* New York: Atheneum, 1989.

Wilson, Mary C. *King Abdullah, Britain, and the Making of Jordan.* New York: Cambridge University Press, 1987.

Winstone, H. V. F. *Captain Shakespear: A Portrait.* New ed. New York: Quartet Books, 1978.

———. *Gertrude Bell.* London: Barzan, 2004.

———. *The Illicit Adventure: The Story of Political and Military Intelligence in the Middle East from 1898 to 1926.* London: J. Cape, 1982.

———. *Leachman: "OC Desert": The Life of Lieutenant-Colonel Gerard Leachman D.S.O.* New York: Quartet Books, 1982.

Wise, David, and Thomas B. Ross. *The Invisible Government.* New York: Random House, 1964.

Woodhouse, C. M. *Something Ventured.* New York: Granada, 1982.

Woodward, Bob. *Bush at War.* New York: Simon & Schuster, 2002.

———. *Plan of Attack.* New York: Simon & Schuster, 2004.

———. *State of Denial.* New York: Simon & Schuster, 2006.

Wright, Denis. *The English Amongst the Persians during the Qajar Period 1787–1921.* London: Heinemann, 1977.

Wrigley, Chris, ed. *Warfare, Diplomacy and Politics: Essays in Honour of A. J. P. Taylor.* London: H. Hamilton, 1986.

Wyman, David S. *The Abandonment of the Jews: America and the Holocaust, 1941–1945.* New York: Pantheon Books, 1984.

Wynn, Antony. *Persia in the Great Game: Sir Percy Sykes, Explorer, Consul, Soldier, Spy.* London: John Murray, 2003.

Yale, William. *The Near East: A Modern History.* Rev. ed. Ann Arbor: University of Michigan Press, 1968.

Yapp, Malcolm E. *The Making of the Modern Near East, 1792–1923.* New York: Longman, 1987.

———. *The Near East since the First World War.* New York: Longman, 1991.

Yergin, Daniel. *The Prize: The Epic Quest for Oil, Money, and Power.* New York: Simon & Schuster, 1991.

Zetland, Lawrence John Lumley Dundas, Marquis of, 1876–1961. *Lord Cromer; Being the authorized life of Evelyn Baring, first earl of Cromer by the Marquess of Zetland.* London: Hodder and Stoughton, 1932.

———. *The Life of Lord Curzon, Being the Authorized Biography of George Nathaniel, Marquess Curzon of Kedleston, K.G.* 3 vols. London: E. Benn, Ltd., 1928.

Ziegler, Philip. *Omdurman.* New York: Knopf, 1974.

———. *The Sixth Great Power: Barings 1762–1929.* London: Collins, 1988.

Academic Journals

Abdoul-Enen, Youssef. "The First World War Mesopotamian Campaigns: Military Lessons on Iraqi Ground Warfare." *Strategic Insights,* Vol. IV, Issue 6 (June 2005), online at www.ccc.nps.navy.mil/si/2005/Jun/aboul-eneinJun05.pdf.

Abrahamian, Ervand. "The 1953 Coup in Iran." *Science & Society,* vol. 65, no. 2 (2001), 182–215.

Anderson, Betty S. "Writing the Nation: Textbooks of the Hashemite Kingdom of Jordan." *Comparative Studies of South Asia, Africa and the Middle East,* vol. 21, no. 1–2 (2001), 5–14.

Auchterlonie, Paul. "From the Eastern Question to the Death of General Gordon: Representations of the Middle East in the Victorian Periodical Press, 1876–1885." *British Journal of Middle Eastern Studies,* vol. 28, no. 1 (2001), 5–24.

Baylen, Joseph O. "W. T. Stead's History of the Mystery and the Jameson Raid." *The Journal of British Studies,* vol. 4, no. 1 (1964), 104–32.

Cannon, Byron David. "Nubar Pasha, Evelyn Baring and a Suppressed Article in the Drummond-Wolff Convention." *International Journal of Middle East Studies,* vol. 5, no. 4 (1974), 468–83.

Castlewitz, David M. "Glubb Pasha and the Arab Legion." *Military History Magazine,* April 1998, 16–20.

Chamberlain, M. E. "Lord Cromer's 'Ancient and Modern Imperialism': A Proconsular View of Empire." *The Journal of British Studies,* vol. 12, no. 1 (1972), 61–85.

Cox, Jafana L. "A Splendid Training Ground: The Importance to the Royal Air Force of its Role in Iraq, 1919–1932." *The Journal of Imperial and Commonwealth History,* vol. 13, no. 2 (1985), 157–84.

De Luca, Anthony R. " 'Der Grossmufti' in Berlin: The Politics of Collaboration." *International Journal of Middle East Studies,* vol. 10, no. 1 (1979), 125–38.

Drus, Ethel. "The Question of Imperial Complicity in the Jameson Raid." *The English Historical Review*, vol. 68, no. 269, 582–93.

Ellis, Kerry. "Queen of the Sands." *History Today*, January 2004, 30–37.

Galbraith, John S., and Afaf Lutfi al-Sayyid-Marsot. "The British Occupation of Egypt: Another View." *International Journal of Middle East Studies*, vol. 9, no. 4 (1978), 471–88.

Gasiorowski, Mark J. "The 1953 Coup d'Etat in Iran." *International Journal of Middle East Studies*, vol. 19, no. 3 (1987), 261–86.

Lord Hailey. "Some Problems Dealt with in an African Survey." *International Affairs*, March/April 1939.

Harlow, Vincent, and Fred H. Hamilton. "Sir Frederic Hamilton's Narrative of Events Relative to the Jameson Raid." *The English Historical Review*, vol. 72, no. 283 (1957), 279–305.

Heller, Mark. "Politics and the Military in Iraq and Jordan, 1920–1958: The British Influence." *Armed Forces and Society*, vol. 4, no. 1 (1977), 75–97.

Hopkins, A. G. "The Victorians and Africa: A Reconsideration of the Occupation of Egypt, 1882." *The Journal of African History*, vol. 27, no. 2 (1986), 363–91.

Jeffrey, Keith. " 'An English Barrack in the Oriental Seas'? India in the Aftermath of the First World War." *Modern Asian Studies*, vol. 15, no. 3 (1981), 369–86.

Johnson, Maxwell Orme. "The Arab Bureau and the Arab Revolt: Yanbu' to Aqaba." *Military Affairs*, vol. 46, no. 4 (1982), 194–201.

Karsh, Efraim. "The Collusion That Never Was: King Abdullah, the Jewish Agency and the Partition of Palestine." *Journal of Contemporary History*, vol. 34 (October 1999), 569–85.

Katouzian, Homa. "The Campaign against the Anglo-Iranian Agreement of 1919." *British Journal of Middle Eastern Studies*, vol. 25, no. 1 (1998), 5–46.

Kedourie, Elie. "Sir Mark Sykes and Palestine, 1915–16." *Middle Eastern Studies*, vol. 6, no. 3 (1970), 340–45.

Krauthammer, Charles. "The Unipolar Moment." *Foreign Affairs*, vol. 70, no. 1 (1990/91), 23ff.

Mejcher, Helmut. "British Middle East Policy 1917–21: The Inter-Departmental Level." *Journal of Contemporary History*, vol. 8, no. 4 (1973), 81–101.

Miller, Joyce Laverty. "The Syrian Revolt of 1925." *International Journal of Middle East Studies*, vol. 8, no. 4 (1977), 545–63.

Monroe, Elizabeth. "Gertrude Bell (1868–1926)." *Bulletin (British Society for Middle Eastern Studies)*, vol. 7, no. 1 (1980), 3–23.

Nwabughogu, Anthony I. "The Role of Propaganda in the Development of Indirect Rule in Nigeria, 1890–1929," *The International Journal of African Historical Studies*, vol. 14, no. 1 (1981).

O'Connor, Damian. "The Suez Crisis, 1876–82." *Royal United Services Institute for Defence and Security Studies*, vol. 151, no. 3 (2006).

Paris, Timothy. "British Middle East Policy-Making after the First World War: The Lawrentian and Wilsonian Schools." *The Historical Journal*, vol. 41, no. 3 (1998), 773–93.

Porch, Douglas. "The Other 'Gulf War'—the British Invasion of Iraq in 1941." *Strategic Insights* (Center for Contemporary Conflict), online at www.ccc.nps.navy .mil/rsepResources/si/dec02/middleEast.asp.

Porter, A. N. "Sir Alfred Milner and the Press, 1897–1899." *The Historical Journal*, vol. 16, no. 2 (1973), 323–39.

Reguer, Sara. "Persian Oil and the First Lord: A Chapter in the Career of Winston Churchill." *Military Affairs*, vol. 46, no. 3 (1982), 134–38.

Satia, Priya. "The Defense of Inhumanity: Air Control and the British Idea of Arabia." *The American Historical Review*, vol. 111, no. 3 (2006), 16–51.

Shlaim, Avi. "Britain and the Arab-Israeli War of 1948." *Journal of Palestine Studies*, vol. 16, no. 4 (1987), 50–76.

Simon, Reeva Spector. "The View from Baghdad." *Columbia International Affairs*, online at www.ciaonet.org/book/sir01/sir01_02.pdf.

Vinogradov, Amal. "The 1920 Revolt in Iraq Reconsidered: The Role of Tribes in National Politics." *International Journal of Middle East Studies*, vol. 3, no. 2 (1972), 123–39.

Walker, Eric A. "The Jameson Raid." *Cambridge Historical Journal*, vol. 6, no. 3 (1940), 283–306.

Wright, Denis. "Sir Percy Sykes and Persia." *Central Asian Survey*, vol. 12, no. 2 (1993).

Yaphe, Judith S. "The View from Basra: Southern Iraq's Reaction to War and Occupation, 1915–1925." *Columbia International Affairs*, online at www.ciaonet.org/book/sir01/sir01_01.pdf.

Zahrani, Mostafa T. "The Coup that Changed the Middle East." *World Policy Journal*, vol. 19, no. 2 (2002), 93–99. Available online at www.worldpolicy.org/journal/articles/wpj02-2/Zahrani.pdf.

Zirinsky, Michael P. "Imperial Power and Dictatorship: Britain and the Rise of Reza Shah, 1921–26." *International Journal of Middle East Studies*, vol. 24, no. 4 (1992), 639–63.

Index

Page numbers in *italics* refer to illustrations.